COMPLETE ESSAYS

D H LAWRENCE

BLACKTHORN PRESS

Blackthorn Press, Blackthorn House
Middleton Rd, Pickering YO18 8AL
United Kingdom

ISBN 978 1 906259 13 6

2009

www.blackthornpress.com

CONTENTS

* *A Chapel and a Hay-Hut Among the Mountains* and *Christs in the Tyrol*
are published in *The Complete Short Stories* by the Blackthorn Press.

Late Essays and Articles   1930

IN FORTIFIED GERMANY

I. THE ENGLISH AND THE GERMANS

"Have you," I asked the waiter in the hotel, "any other papers besides German ones?"

He turned round to me swiftly, with the flicker of a smile of triumph.

"No," he said, "only German; Germans to the front, you know."

"Why?" I asked.

"You don't know the saying—from the Chinese war?"

I regretted I neither knew the saying, nor understood its reference to the papers. The waiter smiled. He is very German.

In Metz the Germans *are* German, and the French are French; and I think I am the only Englishman. In Metz there seem to be four soldiers to every civilian. In my hotel seven officers are lodged. Wherever I go to dinner or supper there are officers or soldiers present. I am tired of German soldiers.

They are not like English soldiers. These latter, as a friend of mine said, "feel their bodies." Having no independent spiritual life of their own, they seem to have cultivated a fine flame of physical life. All their soul is in their bodies. As we watch our soldiers go flaunting down the street we feel the pride of the human creature. With the German soldiers it is not so. There marched past me this morning a squad of men with stumpy helmets and trousers bagging over their boots, short, thick men, and they looked for all the world like a division of bears shuffling by. I suppose they are only recruits. But none of the soldiers look, as we should say, military, none of them look martial.

Yet they stare at me aggressively. I am told I look a foreigner in every fibre. I feel it. All the boyish eyes of the private soldiers stare at me from their broad faces, as if to say: "What are *you* doing here?" There is not about them that coldness and indifference one feels in an Englishman's glance. Just as boys, all young things, are "touchy," ready to imagine a slight, are cocky, ready to defend their own manliness, so the German soldiers are "touchy" and "cocky." They impress me remarkably with a feeling of their youngness, an uncouth youngness. They are far more like awkward boys than men.

I am disappointed. I thought they would be warmer than the Englishmen, more generous, more polite. They are warmer, but still less generous in spirit, and not more polite. I am really disappointed.

The English have tempered themselves with morality till they are stiff and brittle and unworkable. These men are free of any such excess of moral temper. But that is not because they have lived further than we have. They are fussy; they make as much trouble over a trifle as if it were their whole soul's value; honour consists in the observance of certain rather trifling conventions.

Indeed, the Germans are not as old a nation as we are, as is evident in almost every face. They are not as old in experience. They are more uncouth. And it goes without saying they are not so sad. I, who am accustomed to the miners of the Midlands, feel inclined to wonder at these Germans, so fat and untroubled. They are on the whole much better-looking than our colliers, but I can't find anywhere among them the fine faces of men that are to be seen in the streets at home. It is the lack of wonder that spoils the German. Wonder is the sense of the vastness and terror and consolation of life: life infinitely great beyond our own consciousness. I know dozens of working men in England in whose faces can be seen that selfsame deep sense of wonder, which, unfortunately, owing to the split that exists in the English nature between the senses and the soul, is usually sad almost to despair. I know the colliers of the Midlands best. And I say, look at the best faces among those men, and see if there is not evident a certain desolation. In England we deny ourselves so much that there is scarcely any active living going on among the best people. We are in life, but we do not live. Thence the despair which looks out of so many English eyes. "*Is* there any value in living?" they have asked, and their own souls have been forced to answer "No." The great creed in the English heart to-day is, "Let us forgo the things we want, for we can do without them." It is not money, not position, nor security our souls want; and these are almost the only things the nation lives for. We want freedom to love, freedom to worship the things our deepest nature approves of. And nowadays it is easier not to live than to live. It is easier to suffer than to insist. It is easier to submit than to conquer.

"After all," the Englishman asks of his own soul, "after all, what does it matter, all this fuss about life?" The average Englishman cares vitally for nothing whatsoever, except for his own security in daily life; that is, he hangs on to life by the sheer strength of his instinct of self-preservation. All the rest, the joy, the progressive activity, is missing. As he takes off his clothes for the night, he puts off his show of living, and for a moment or two before he sleeps knows that he calmly and stoically despairs.

That is the danger for England. It is our own souls we need to reinforce, not our fleet, to make us safe from any German attack. In Germany there seem very few signs of the mania for self-starvation which is so remarkable in England. These men are healthy and lusty. Each one believes in his right to an individual life, in his right to satisfy his individual desires. He is going to have his own way where he can.

Therefore he is effective. The Englishman, older, says, "The Universe is tremendous: I am the smallest atom of one kind of life; there is practically the whole great universe other than I am, and there is the speck of dust that is myself. What do I matter?" So he is ineffective.

If the German, like a lusty, stupid youth, says "I want to give England a licking," he will put his heart and soul into it. The Englishman, defending himself, will be rather bitter at being bothered, like a man who despises dogs when he is attacked by a dog. Why should the more brutal nation in the end always conquer the highly civilised nation? Only because the civilised nation is cynical, despises its own civilisation, and asks to be destroyed. We English are civilised in our very souls, and it makes us beautiful, somewhat noble in ourselves. But we do nothing. What is the good of being noble and of doing nothing! We are like the last members of a noble house of England. Our souls are too civilised to breed.

But why? Why, because we *can* forgo life, why, therefore, should we do so? I know a certain woman wants to love me, I know I want to love her. I can do without loving her, she can do without loving me—just as I can deny myself of something I need. But love is life, both to her and to me. Is it better to live or to forgo life? The English answer is always "to forgo life." But that is a cynicism. A more brutal man will say to me, "It's licence you want, not love nor life." I shall answer, "You are speaking for yourself," and it is he will be ashamed. It is not licence. There is plenty of licence everywhere, for whosoever wants it. There are plenty of well-shaped women in England or in Germany who would love me enough in a licentious fashion. But I don't want them. They are *not* life to me: they would brutalise me. This woman mates my soul. Yet if I love her I shall be no longer respectable, whereas if I loved the other women I should lose no caste. This feeling is stronger in England, I believe, than anywhere else, the insistence on formal respectability. It is most deadly in England, because our souls are refined, civilised, and therefore the brutal way of life is closed to us. Respectability shuts the other door. Hence the atrophy of the souls of many of the best English people, particularly the women. That is why there is a German scare—which seems to me might not be altogether a bogy; because of this strange, perverted will to destroy ourselves, which is common everywhere in England, and which seems comparatively rare here in Germany.

For the German officers are not very much different from the men. See them on Sunday, after service, doing the church parade in the cathedral square, each with his smart lady. The most elegant are slim as wasps, in their frock-tunics of light blue; but these are mostly young. There are three streams of paraders in the cathedral square. The innermost is of the elect. There the officers are perfect dandies; they gaze with perfect vanity through their rimless pince-nez—at nothing. Their ladies have the highest ostrich feathers, of the wildest colours. The second stream is of the second best; the military uniform is still elegant, not barbaric like ours. The ladies are dressed loudly, in slightly worse taste than the first; they are almost frantically dressed. In the last stream there are mostly women. Several are in deep mourning. Two girls of about twenty are armoured in crape, and each has a great length of crape hanging from the back of her hat, something like the worst phase of widow's weeds. This proclaims her sorrow. And so on. It is *not* a civilised nation. Our soldiery is a class apart—barbarous, pagan, curious, and lovable. But in the German soldier the worst national characteristics seem most pronounced—lack of intuition, clumsy sentimentality, affectation; a certain clumsiness of soul, a certain arrogance of stupidity, a certain stupid cleverness.

Nevertheless, the German nation has a warmth and generosity of living, like a full fire roaring, that makes us look very pale. They have none of our wavering, uncertain look about them.

And why we should weaken ourselves, make our wills less strong than those of this people, I do not know. Why we should will to starve ourselves, while these folk—of course masses of English folk are identically the same as the Germans—take their fill, I cannot conceive. Why should the best people leave all the living to the others? Why should so many of our *best* women die of atrophy? Why should our workmen be indifferent, inferior, perhaps, to the German workmen, when they are really superior in soul? If the civilised among us start to live our individual lives intelligently, we are stronger than the whole less-intelligent force. But we do not believe in living; we only believe in going without life, and thus showing our superiority of self-restraint.

II. HOW A SPY IS ARRESTED

We went over the bridges under the cathedral, past the old French houses on the quay, to the road lined with trees and dwellings where so many soldiers live.

3

Soldiers on horseback were riding by: soldiers on foot were fetching and carrying: soldiers in their shirt sleeves were busy about the houses. In one barracks they were singing together in their jolly, careless fashion. The Germans have not yet lost the faculty for enjoying themselves simply and happily together.

Anita and I were discussing life very seriously: at least, she was discussing life seriously, and I was burning with a hundred wraths, as soldier after soldier turned and stared at her, and officers, riding by, moved their heads round woodenly upon their very high collars, to take stock.

"She looks so damnably nice," I said in my heart.

She was wearing a dress of red crape, of a coral colour, that suited her fair hair. And, deep in her sad philosophising, she was unconscious of the swarms of men; which made her the more interesting, I suppose. I love the splendid indifference in her bearing.

We crossed the road to avoid the men, and came to a green place arched with trees. The sunlight fell bright in dapplings among the cold shadow on the grass. Two little paths converged from the highway, leading under the trees. It looked mysterious and inviting, so still and green, as if fauns might be near the road.

"Let us go this way," said Anita suddenly.

We went only some two hundred yards from the road where the trains were running, when we saw on our right a clear place all bright with sunshine.

"There!" said Anita. "Let us sit down, I am tired."

A dozen paces from the path, we lay down. It was a quiet spot, sunny, a grassy bank with water below, and trees. The bank was square, the water curved curiously; I thought, vaguely, it must be some system of draining, towards the Mosel. Anita lay down on the grass, red like a fallen poppy. She rested on her elbows, watching a little beetle labouring over the long, warm grass-stalks.

"You nice little Käfer!" she said tenderly, to the beetle. "Stop here and amuse me, with your little legs."

I also lay face down beside her.

"Look at my sister," she continued to me. "She is a Doctor of Political Economy—quite a leading light, she was. And what did she say to me:—'after all, it is nothing to a woman *by itself* this learning and writing and factory inspecting. It becomes in the end one big dissatisfaction, one big want.' "

"It's like breaking a wild deer into the shafts," I said.

"How?" she asked.

"A deer jumps over the road, four feet together, then stands and looks at me shoulder-deep out of the green corn, its ears lifted. Then something flashes in my heart. I know something. Because I've seen that hind, and she looked at me, I could mend my bicycle better."

"Yes," said Anita doubtfully.

"If we are to *do* anything, our women must keep in direct line with original life, and supply us. But a hind between the shafts! It only makes me want to die."

"To set it free," said Anita.

"Good God, yes!" I said. "But I am only good for *one* woman."

We lay together in the still sunshine. I was twisting Anita's ring, an old square emerald, full of green life.

"But," said Anita, "we keep in direct line with life; we look at our men for them to *see* us, and they *don* 't—and it sends us cracked. The thing doesn't go on, from us to the men; the life, or whatever it is."

"You should get hold of the right men."

"How?—the men are afraid of us. They aren't *big* enough for us."

"They are your children."

At this interesting point of the discussion, Anita started, and looked round.

"Oh!" she exclaimed.

I looked over my shoulder. A young fellow in uniform was standing behind us, looking at us from under the ledge of his helmet. He had evidently been listening to, without understanding, our most interesting conversation, which had been carried on in English.

"What are you doing here?" he asked in German.

"Nothing," said Anita. "Why?"

"It is forbidden to come here," he said, with quiet, authoritative tones, almost threatening.

'Verboten!' One is not in Germany five minutes, without seeing or hearing this word: only it is usually, 'Strengstens verboten.'

"Why!" asked Anita, indignant at the interruption.

He did not answer for a moment, then, with quiet insolence:

"Because these are the fortifications."

"Get up," he said to me.

I would not understand.

"He asks you to get up," said Anita to me in English.

I rose and bowed to her. The young policeman looked at me. His anger began to mount. He had dark hazel eyes, rather beautiful, rather furious, rather stupid; the flush was coming under his swarthy skin; he had a petulant mouth, with the soft growth of a young black moustache.

"The Herr is not German?" he asked of Anita.

"No, an Englishman."

"I must arrest any foreigner who comes here," said the man.

"Aber—how absurd!" cried Anita.

The young policeman's eyes opened with wrath.

"We are twenty paces from the path," she cried.

"Yes!" he answered, with his menacing gravity.

"And I believe you have no right to do this," said Anita.

Instantly the revengeful anger hardened on his face.

"Are you also English?" he asked, beginning to bully her. I was furious.

"No, I am German. My father is the Graf zu —. The gentleman is his friend, and is staying with us."

The young, officious fool looked at her with a sneer.

"You are English," he said.

My blood boiled. Anita's eyes flashed.

"Do I speak like a foreigner!" she said. "Do you *know* the Herrn Graf—?"

"Yes—!" he said, "and where do you live?"

"Kronprinz-Strasse," she answered, too indignant to think.

"There is no such Street."

"Yes!" she cried. "In Montigny."

5

He shook his head, smiling victoriously, and drew out paper and pencil.

"Kronprinz-Ludwig Strasse," I said. "Number 4."

He looked at me. I met his eyes and shrugged my shoulders. His hand trembled with rage.

"Kronprinz Ludwig Strasse—Number 4," I repeated, and mechanically, he copied it down.

"And your name?" he asked, in calm fury. His official authority was being flouted.

"How ridiculous!" cried Anita. "Would they in England insult a stranger so, and twenty paces from the road? What right have you? There is no notice."

"There *is* a notice," he answered, in his rage. "And I must enter all this. What is your name?"

I left it to Anita to tell him. He copied down many particulars.

"But really!" said Anita, forgetting her anger in amusement. "Really! You don't think the Herr Englishman looks dangerous, do you?"

He glanced at me, still in deep anger and suspicion and resentment. All this was *very* serious to him.

"Have you any papers?" he asked.

I would not understand, so Anita repeated. I had just one letter, stamped and addressed to my innocent old aunt in Lübeck. He looked at the cover as if it were something from a museum. I kept my eye on him all the while, rather amused at his babyish game of authority. He handed me my letter back.

"And I don't know a fortress from a factory," I said in English, laughing, to Anita. "If only the poor creature knew the depths of my ignorance."

She also began to laugh. The young policeman bridled with indignation. One felt the vast, stupid mechanism of German officialdom behind him.

"Come away," he said rudely.

We went side by side, Anita and I, laughing but angry with the youth. It was only a minute's walk to the tramway, down the simple path. We stood on the high-road. Still he looked at me suspiciously, as if he would like to put me in a cage quickly.

"Now," said Anita, "where is the notice! There is none. Why have *you* been overstepping your rights with us!"

"Yes, there *is* a notice—there!" he cried, blazing. On an obscure board, in the trees, it said 'Way for military purposes only.'

"And even so," said Anita, "it gives you no right to behave in the way you have done, interfering with honorable people— "

"Moreover, it is forbidden to lie on the grass," he said in wrath.

"That is why they never turn their cows out!" I jested to Anita. Some passers-by collected—some soldiers came up. She, magnificent in her scorn, seemed twice as big as the soldier. He was in a rage. He would have liked to strike her.

"Any foreigner found there I should arrest," he repeated, sticking to the letter of the law—"it is my duty, and—"

I could see he would soon be fulfilling his duty. I lit a cigarette.

"Leave him, Anita," I said, "Leave him."

At the sound of the English he hated me.

"Refer to the Herr Graf zu —," said Anita.

"Yes, we *will* refer to the Herr Graf," replied the man, shutting his lips, putting his note book away, and glaring after us.

"What a fool I am!" said Anita. "I ought to know these German officials—every tiny scrap of a fellow thinks himself as important as the Kaiser."

We went to a friend of Anita's, an officer in the cavalry. He received Anita with great respect, kissing her hands. At home, lacking his sword belt and hat, he was not so impressive. Buttoned up in his pale-blue tunic, with its high pinkish collar, he sat deferentially listening to Anita, who was sitting on the sofa laughing and smoking a cigarette. He also took it seriously, though he politely said, it was nothing.

And even the Graf zu —, Anita's father, looked worried for a moment, then, after that moment, grew indignant. None of them laughed. These fussy little things seem important to them, instead of comic.

Presently came word to my hotel that still everything was not certain concerning me. It was considered, in official quarters, that I was an English officer. That finished me off. I forgave them everything, stood in front of my long mirror, turning this way and that. An English officer! It was *such* a compliment to my figure, as to feel like a sarcasm.

I looked down at the soldiers drilling in the barracks square, and sighed. Then I packed my bags.

III FRENCH SONS OF GERMANY

In Metz I prefer the Frenchmen to the Germans. I am more at my ease with them. It is a question of temperament.

From the Cathedral down to the river is all French. The Cathedral seems very German. It is nothing but nave: a tremendous lofty nave, and nothing else; a great jump at heaven, in the conception; a rather pathetic fall to earth, in execution. Still, the splendid conception is there.

So I go down from the Cathedral to the French quarter. It is full of smells, perhaps, but it is purely itself. A Frenchman has the same soul, whether he is eating his dinner or kissing his baby. A German has no soul when he is eating his dinner, and is beautiful when he kisses his baby. So I prefer the Frenchman, who hasn't the tiresome split between his animal nature and his spiritual, in whom the two are fused.

The barber drinks. He has wild hair and bloodshot eyes. Still, I dare trust my throat and chin to him. I address him in German. He dances before me, answering, in mad French, that he speaks no German. Instantly I love him in spite of all.

"You are a foreigner here?" I remark.

He cannot lather me, he is so wildly excited. "No, he was born in Metz, his father was born in Metz, his grandfather was born in Metz. For all he knows, Adam was born in Metz. But no Leroy has ever spoken German; no, not a syllable. It would split his tongue—he could not, you see, Sir, he could not; his construction would not allow of it." With all of which I agree heartily; whereupon he looks lovingly upon me and continues to lather.

"His wife was a Frenchwoman, born in Paris. I must see his wife." He calls her by some name I do not know, and she appears—fat and tidy.

"You are a subject of France?" my barber demands furiously.

"Certainly," she begins. "I was born in Paris—" As they both talk at once, I can't make out what they say. But they are happy, they continue. At last, with a final flourish of the razor, I am shaved. The barber is very tipsy.

"Monsieur is from Brittany?" he asks me tenderly.

Alas! I am from England.

"But, why?" cries Madame; "you have not an English face; no, never. And a German face—Pah! impossible."

In spite of all I look incurably English. Nevertheless, I start a story about a great-grandfather who was refugeed in England after the revolution. They embrace me, they love me. And I love them.

"Sir," I say, "will you give me a morsel of soap? No, not shaving soap."

"This is French soap, this is German," he says. The French is in a beautiful flowery wrapper, alas! much faded.

"And what is the difference?" I ask.

"The French, of course, is *better*. The German is five pfennigs—one sou, Monsieur—the cheaper."

Of course, I take the French soap. The barber grandly gives my twenty-pfennig tip to the lathering boy, who has just entered, and he bows me to the door. I am in the street, breathless.

A German officer, in a flowing cloak of bluey-grey—like ink and milk—looks at me coldly and inquisitively. I look at him with a "Go to the devil" sort of look, and pass along. I wonder to myself if my dislike of these German officers is racial, or owing to present national feeling, or if it is a temperamental aversion. I decide on the last. A German soldier spills something out of a parcel on to the road and looks round like a frightened boy. I want to shelter him.

I pass along, look at the ridiculous imitation-mediæval church that is built on the islet—or peninsula—in the middle of the river, on the spot that has been called for ages "The Place of Love." I wonder how the Protestant conscience of this ugly church remains easy upon such foundation. I think of the famous "three K's" that are allotted to German women, "Kinder, Kuchen, Kirche, and pity the poor wretches.

Over the river, all is barracks—barracks, and soldiers on foot, and soldiers on horseback. Everywhere these short, baggy German soldiers, with their fair skins and rather stupid blue eyes! I hurry to get away from them. To the right is a steep hill, once, I suppose, the scarp of the river.

At last I found a path, and turned for a little peace to the hillside and the vineyards. The vines are all new young slips, climbing up their sticks. The whole hillside bristles with sticks, like an angry hedgehog. Across lies Montigny; to the right, Metz itself, with its cathedral like a brown rat humped up. I prefer my hillside. In this Mosel valley there is such luxuriance of vegetation. Lilac bushes are only heaps of purple flowers. Some roses are out. Here on the wild hillside there are lovely vetches of all sorts, and white poppies and red; and then the vine shoots, with their tips of most living, sensitive pink and red, just like blood under the skin.

I am happy on the hillside. It is a warm, grey day. The Mosel winds below. The vine sticks bristle against the sky. The little church of the village is in front. I

8

climb the hill, past a Madonna shrine that stands out by the naked path. The faded blue "Lady" is stuck with dying white lilac, She looks rather ugly, but I do not mind. Odd men, and women, are working in the vineyards. They are very swarthy, and they have very small-bladed spades, which glisten in the sun.

At last I come to the cemetery under the church. As I marvel at the bead-work wreaths, with ridiculous little naked china figures of infants floating in the middle, I hear voices, and looking up, see two German soldiers on the natural platform, or terrace, beside the church. Along the vineyard path are squares of yellow and black and white, like notice boards. The two soldiers, in their peculiar caps, almost similar to our round sailors' hats, or blue cooks' caps, are laughing. They watch the squares, then me.

When I go up to the church and round to the terrace, they are gone. The terrace is a natural platform, a fine playground, very dark with great horsechestnuts in flower, and walled up many feet from the hillside, overlooking the far valley of the Mosel. As I sit on a bench, the hens come pecking round me. It is perfectly still and lovely, the only sound being from the boys' school.

Somewhere towards eleven o'clock two more soldiers came. One led his horse, the other was evidently not mounted. They came to the wall, or parapet, to look down the valley at the fort. Meanwhile, to my great joy, the mare belonging to the mounted soldier cocked up her tail and cantered away under the horsechestnuts, down the village. Her owner went racing, shouting after her, making the peculiar *hu-hu!* these Germans use to their horses. She would have been lost had not two men rushed out of the houses, and, shouting in French, stopped her. The soldier jerked her head angrily, and led her back. He was a short, bear-like little German, she was a wicked and delicate mare. He kept her bridle as he returned. Meanwhile, his companion, his hands clasped on his knees, shouted with laughter.

Presently, another, rather taller, rather more manly soldier appeared. He had a sprig of lilac between his teeth. The foot-soldier recounted the escapade with the mare, whereupon the newcomer roared with laughter, and suddenly knocked the horse under the jaw. She reared in terror. He got hold of her by the bridle, teasing her. At last her owner pacified her. Then the newcomer would insist on sticking a piece of lilac in her harness, against her ear. It frightened her, she reared, and she panted, but he would not desist. He teased her, bullied her, coaxed her, took her unawares; she was in torment as he pawed at her head to stick in the flower, she would not allow him. At last, however, he succeeded. She, much discomfited, wore lilac against her ear.

Then the children came out of school—boys, in their quaint pinafores. It is strange how pleasant, how quaint, and manly these little children are; the tiny boys of six seemed more really manly than the soldiers of twenty-one, more alert to the real things. They cried to each other in their keen, naïf way, discussing the action at the fortress, of which I could make out nothing.

And one of the soldiers asked them, "How old are you, Johnny?" Human nature is very much alike. The boys used French in their play, but they answered the soldiers in German.

As I was going up the hill there came on a heavy shower. I sheltered as much as I could under an apple-tree thick with pink blossom; then I hurried down to the village. "Café—Restauration" was written on one house. I wandered into the living-room beyond the courtyard.

9

"Where does one drink?" I asked the busy, hard-worked-looking woman. She answered me in French, as she took me in. At once, though she was a drudge, her fine spirit of politeness made me comfortable.

"This is not France?" I asked of her.

"Oh, no—but always the people have been French," and she looked at me quickly from her black eyes. I made my voice tender as I answered her.

Presently I said: "Give me some cigarettes, please."

"French or German?" she asked.

"What's the difference?" I inquired.

"The French, of course, are better,"

"Then French," I said, laughing, though I do not really love the black, strong French cigarettes.

"Sit and talk to me a minute," I said to her. "It is so nice not to speak German."

"Ah, Monsieur!" she cried, and she loved me. She could not sit, no. She could only stay a minute. Then she sent her man.

I heard her in the other room bid him come. He was shy—he would not. "Ssh!" I heard her go as she pushed him through the door.

He was very swarthy, burned dark with the sun. His eyes were black and very bright. He was a man of about forty-five. I could not persuade him to sit down or to drink with me; he would accept only a cigarette. Then, laughing, he lighted me my cigarette. He was a gentleman, and he had white teeth.

The village, he told me, was Scy: a French name, but a German village.

"And you are a German subject?" I asked.

He bowed to me. He said he had just come in from the vines, and must go back immediately. Last year they had had a bad disease, so that all the plants I had seen were new. I hoped he would get rich with them. He smiled with a peculiar sad grace.

"Not rich, Monsieur, but not a failure this time."

He had a daughter, Angèle: "In Paris—in *France*."

He bowed and looked at me meaningly. I said I was glad. I said:

"I do not like Metz: too many soldiers. I do not like German soldiers."

"They are scarcely polite," he said quietly.

"You find it?" I asked.

He bowed his acquiescence.

It is a strange thing that these two Frenchmen were the only two men—not acquaintances—whom I felt friendly towards me in the whole of Metz.

HAIL IN THE RHINELAND

We were determined to take a long walk this afternoon, in spite of the barometer, which persisted in retreating towards "storm." The morning was warm and mildly sunny. The blossom was still falling from the fruit-trees down the village street, and drifting in pink and white all along the road. The barber was sure it would be fine. But then he'd have sworn to anything I wanted, he liked me so much since I admired, in very bad German, his moustache.

"I may trim your moustache?" he asked.

"You can do what you like with it," I said.

As he was clipping it quite level with my lip he asked:

"You like a short moustache?"

"Ah," I answered, "I could never have anything so beautiful and upstanding as yours."

Whereupon immediately he got excited, and vowed my moustache should stand on end even as Kaiserly as did his own."

"Never," I vowed.

Then he brought me a bottle of mixture, and a gauze bandage, which I was to bind under my nose, and there I should be, in a few weeks, with an upstanding moustache sufficient as a guarantee for any man. But I was modest; I refused even to try.

"No," I said, "I will remember yours." He pitied me, and vowed it would be fine for the afternoon.

I told Johanna so, and she took her parasol. It was really sunny, very hot and pretty, the afternoon. Besides, Johanna's is the only parasol I have seen in Waldbröl, and I am the only Englishman any woman for miles around could boast. So we set off.

We were walking to Nümbrecht, some five or six miles away. Johanna moved with great dignity, and I held the parasol. Every man, even the workmen on the fields, bowed low to us, and every woman looked at us yearningly. And to every woman, and to every man, Johanna gave a bright "Good-day."

"They like it so much," she said. And I believed her.

There was a scent of apple-blossom quite strong on the air. The cottages, set at random and painted white, with their many timbers painted black, have a make-belief, joyful, childish look.

Everywhere the broom was out, great dishevelled blossoms of ruddy gold sticking over the besom strands. The fields were full of dandelion pappus, floating misty bubbles crowded thick, hiding the green grass with their globes. I showed Johanna how to tell the time. "One!" I puffed; "two-three-four-five-six! Six o'clock, my dear."

"Six o'clock what? " she asked.

"Anything you like," I said.

"At six o'clock there will be a storm. The barometer is never wrong," she persisted.

I was disgusted with her. The beech-wood through which we were walking was a vivid flame of green. The sun was warm.

"Johanna," I said. "Seven ladies in England would walk out with me, although they *knew* that at six o'clock a thunder-shower would ruin their blue dresses. Besides, there are two holes in your mittens, and black mittens show so badly."

She quickly hid her arms in the folds of her skirts. "Your English girls have queer taste, to walk out seven at a time with you."

We were arguing the point with some ferocity when, descending a hill in the wood, we came suddenly upon a bullock-wagon. The cows stood like blocks in the harness, though their faces were black with flies. Johanna was very indignant. An old man was on the long, railed wagon, which was piled with last year's brown oak-leaves. A boy was straightening the load, and waiting at the end of the wagon ready to help, a young, strong man, evidently his father, who was struggling uphill with an enormous sack-cloth bundle—enormous, full of dead leaves. The new leaves of the oaks overhead were golden brown, and crinkled with young vigour. The cows stood solid and patient, shutting their eyes, weary of the plague of flies. Johanna flew to their rescue, fanning them with a beech-twig.

"Ah, poor little ones!" she cried. Then, to the old man, in tones of indignation: "These flies will eat up your oxen."

"Yes—their wicked little mouths," he agreed.

"Cannot you prevent them?" she asked.

"They are everywhere," he answered, and he smacked a fly on his hand.

"But you can do something," she persisted.

"You could write a card and stick it between their horns, 'Settling of flies strictly forbidden here,'" I said.

"'Streng verboten,' " he repeated as he laughed.

Johanna looked daggers at me.

"Thank you, young fellow," she said sarcastically. I stuck leafy branches in the head-harness of the cattle. The old man thanked me with much gratitude.

"It is hot weather!" I remarked.

"It will be a thunderstorm, I believe," he answered.

"At six o'clock?" cried Johanna.

But I was along the path.

We went gaily through the woods and open places, and had nearly come to Nümbrecht, when we met a very old man, coming very slowly up the hill with a splendid young bull, of buff-colour and white, which, in its majestic and leisurely way, was dragging a harrow that rode on sledges.

"Fine weather," I remarked, forgetting.

"Jawohl!" he answered. "But there will be a thunderstorm."

"And I knew it," said Johanna.

But we were at Nümbrecht. Johanna drank her mineral water and raspberry juice. It was ten minutes to six.

"It is getting dark," remarked Johanna.

"There is no railway here?" I asked.

"Not for six miles," she replied pointedly.

The landlord was a very handsome man.

"It is getting dark," said Johanna to him.

"There will be a thunderstorm, Madame," he replied with beautiful grace. "Madame is walking?"

"From Waldbröl," she replied. By this time she was statuesque. The landlord went to the door. Girls were leading home the cows.

"It is coming," he said, and immediately there was a rumbling of thunder.

Johanna went to the door.

"An enormous black cloud. The sky is black," she announced. I followed to her side. It was so.

"The barber—" I said.

"Must you live by the word of the barber?" said Johanna.

The landlord retired indoors. He was a very handsome man, but the hair was positively shaved from his head. And I knew Johanna liked the style.

I fled to Stollwerck's chocolate machine, and spent a few anxious moments extracting burnt almonds. The landlord reappeared.

"There is an omnibus goes to Waldbröl for the station and the post.

It passes the door in ten minutes," he said gracefully. No English landlord could have equalled him. I thanked him with all my heart.

The omnibus was an old brown cab—a growler. Its only occupant was a brown-paper parcel for Frau—.

"You don't mind riding?" I said tenderly to Johanna.

"I had rather we were at home. I am terribly afraid of thunderstorms," she answered.

We drove on. A young man in black stopped the omnibus. He bowed to us, then mounted the box with the driver.

"It is Thienes, the Bretzel baker," she said. Bretzel is a loopy, twisty little cake like Kringel.

I do not know why, but after this Johanna and I sat side by side in tense silence. I felt very queerly.

"There, the rain!" she suddenly cried.

"Never mind," I pleaded.

"Oh, I like riding in here," she said.

My heart beat, and I put my hand over hers. She pretended not to notice, which made my heart beat more. I don't know how it would have ended. Suddenly there was such a rattle outside, and something pounding on me. Johanna cried out. It was a great hail-storm—the air was a moving white storm—enormous balls of ice, big as marbles, then bigger, like balls of white carbon that housewives use against moths, came striking in. I put up the window. It was immediately cracked, so I put it down again. A hailstone as big as a pigeon-egg struck me on the knee, hurt me, and bounced against Johanna's arm. She cried out with pain. The horses stood still and would not move. There was a roar of hail. All round, on the road balls of ice were bouncing viciously up again. We could not see six yards out of the carriage.

Suddenly the door opened, and Thienes, excusing himself, appeared. I dragged him in. He was a fresh young man, with naïve, wide eyes. And his best suit of lustrous black was shining now with wet.

"Had you no cover?" we said.

He showed his split umbrella, and burst into a torrent of speech. The hail drummed bruisingly outside.

"It had come like horse-chestnuts of ice," he said.

The fury of the storm lasted for five minutes, all of which time the horses stood stock still. The hailstones shot like great white bullets into the carriage. Johanna clung to me in fear. There was a solid sheet of falling ice outside.

At last the horses moved on. I sat eating large balls of ice and realising myself. When at last the fall ceased Thienes *would* get out on to the box again. I liked him; I wanted him to stay. But he would not.

The country was a sight. All over the road, and fallen thick in the ruts, were balls of ice, pure white, as big as very large marbles, and some as big as bantam-eggs. The ditches looked as if stones and stones' weight of loaf sugar had been emptied into them—white balls and cubes of ice everywhere. Then the sun came out, and under the brilliant green birches a thick white mist, only a foot high, sucked at the fall of ice. It was very cold. I shuddered.

"I was only flirting with Johanna," I said to myself "But, by Jove, I was nearly dished."

The carriage crunched over the hail. All the road was thick with twigs, as green as spring. It made me think of the roads strewed for the entry to Jerusalem. Here it was cherry boughs and twigs and tiny fruits, a thick carpet; next, brilliant green beech; next, pine-brushes, very beautiful, with their creamy pollen cones, making the road into a green bed; then fir twigs, with pretty emerald new shoots like stars, and dark sprigs over the hailstones. Then we passed two small dead birds, fearfully beaten. Johanna began to cry. But we were near a tiny, lonely inn, where the carriage stopped. I said I *must* give Thienes a Schnapps, and I jumped out. The old lady was sweeping away a thick fall of ice-stones from the doorway.

When I next got into the carriage, I suppose I smelled of Schnapps, and was not lovable. Johanna stared out of the window, away from me. The lovely dandelion bubbles were gone, there was a thicket of stripped stalks, all broken. The corn was broken down, the road was matted with fruit twigs. Over the Rhine-land was a grey, desolate mist, very cold.

At the next stopping place, where the driver had to deliver a parcel, a young man passed with a very gaudily apparelled horse, great red trappings. He was a striking young fellow. Johanna watched him. She was not *really* in earnest with me. We might have both made ourselves unhappy for life, but for this storm. A middle-aged man, very brown and sinewy with work, came to the door. He was rugged, and I liked him. He showed me his hand. The back was bruised, and swollen, and already going discoloured. It made me wince. But he laughed rather winsomely, even as if he were glad.

"A hail-stone!" he said, proudly.

We watched the acres of ice-balls slowly pass by, in silence. Neither of us spoke. At last we came to the tiny station, at home. There was the station-master, and, of all people, the barber.

"I can remember fifty-five years," said the station-master, "but nothing like this."

"Not round, but squares, two inches across, of ice," added the barber, with gusto.

"At the shop they have sold out of tiles, so many smashed," said the station-master.

"And in the green-house roofs, at the Asylum, not a shred of glass," sang the barber.

"The windows at the station smashed—"

"And a man"—I missed the name—"hurt quite badly by—" rattled the barber.

"But," I interrupted, "you said it would be fine."

"And," added Johanna, "we went on the strength of it." It is queer, how sarcastic she can be, without *saying* anything really meaningful.

We were four dumb people. But I had a narrow escape, and Johanna had a narrow escape, and we both know it, and thank the terrific hail-storm, though at present *she* is angry—vanity, I suppose.

14

STUDY OF THOMAS HARDY AND OTHER ESSAYS

STUDY OF THOMAS HARDY

CHAPTER I

Of Poppies and Phoenixes and the Beginning of the Argument

1

Man has made such a mighty struggle to feel at home on the face of the earth, without even yet succeeding. Ever since he first discovered himself exposed naked betwixt sky and land, belonging to neither, he has gone on fighting for more food, more clothing, more shelter; and though he has roofed-in the world with houses and though the ground has heaved up massive abundance and excess of nutriment to his hand, still he cannot be appeased, satisfied. He goes on and on. In his anxiety he has evolved nations and tremendous governments to protect his person and his property; his strenuous purpose, unremitting, has brought to pass the whole frantic turmoil of modern industry, that he may have enough, enough to eat and wear, that he may be safe. Even his religion has for the systole of its heart-beat, propitiation of the Unknown God who controls death and the sources of nourishment.

But for the diastole of the heart-beat, there is something more, something else, thank heaven, than this unappeased rage of self-preservation. Even the passion to be rich is not merely the greedy wish to be secure within triple walls of brass, along with a huge barn of plenty. And the history of mankind is not altogether the history of an effort at self-preservation which has at length become over-blown and extravagant.

Working in contradiction to the will of self-preservation, from the very first man wasted himself begetting children, colouring himself and dancing and howling and sticking feathers in his hair, in scratching pictures on, the walls of his cave, and making graven images of his unutterable feelings. So he went on wildly and with gorgeousness taking no thought for the morrow, but, at evening, considering the ruddy lily.

In his sleep, however, it must have come to him early that the lily is a wise and housewifely flower, considerate of herself, laying up secretly her little storehouse and barn, well under the ground, well tucked with supplies. And this providence on the part of the lily, man laid to heart. He went out anxiously at dawn to kill the largest mammoth, so that he should have a huge hill of meat, that he could never eat his way through.

And the old man at the door of the cave, afraid of the coming winter with its scant supplies, watching the young man go forth, told impressive tales to the children of the ant and the grasshopper; and praised the thrift and husbandry of that little red squirrel, and drew a moral from the gaudy, fleeting poppy.

"Don't, my dear children," continued the ancient palaeolithic man as he sat at the door of his cave, "don't behave like that reckless, shameless scarlet flower. Ah, my dears, you little know the amount of labour, the careful architecture, all the chemistry, the weaving and the casting of energy, the business of day after day and night after night, yon gaudy wreck has squandered. Pfff!—and it is gone, and the place thereof shall know it no more. Now, my dear children, don't be like that."

Nevertheless, the old man watched the last poppy coming out, the red flame licking into sight; watched the blaze at the top clinging around a little tender dust, and he wept, thinking of his youth. Till the red flag fell before him, lay in rags on the earth. Then he did not know whether to pay homage to the void, or to preach.

So he compromised, and made a story about a phoenix. "Yes, my dears, in the waste desert, I know the green and graceful tree where the phoenix has her nest. And there I have seen the eternal phoenix escape away into flame, leaving life behind in her ashes. Suddenly she went up in to red flame, and was gone, leaving life to rise from her ashes."

"And did it?"

"Oh, yes, it rose up."

"What did it do then?"

"It grew up, and burst into flame again."

And the flame was all the story and all triumph. The old man knew this. It was this he praised, in his innermost heart, the red outburst at the top of the poppy that had no fear of winter. Even the latent seeds were secondary, within the fire. No red; and there was just a herb, without name or sign of poppy. But he had seen the flower in all its evanescence and its being.

When his educated grandson told him that the red was there to bring the bees and the flies, he knew well enough that more bees and flies and wasps would come to a sticky smear round his grandson's mouth, than to yards of poppy-red.

Therefore his grandson began to talk about the excess which always accompanies reproduction. And the old man died during this talk, and was put away. But his soul was uneasy, and came back from the shades to have the last word, muttering inaudibly in the cave door, "If there is always excess accompanying reproduction, how can you call it excess? When your mother makes a pie, and has too much paste, then that is excess. So she carves a paste rose with her surplus, and sticks it on the top of the pie. That is the flowering of the excess. And children, if they are young enough, clap their hands at this blossom of pastry. And if the pie bloom not too often with the rose of excess, they eat the paste blossom-shaped lump with reverence. But soon they become sophisticated, and know that the rose is no rose, but only excess, surplus, a counterfeit, a lump, unedifying and unattractive, and they say, 'No, thank you, mother; no rose.'

"Wherefore, if you mean to tell me that the red of my shed poppy was no more than the rose of the paste on the pie, you are a fool. You mean to say that young blood had more stuff than he knew what to do with. He knocked his structure of leaves and stalks together, hammered the poppy-knob safe on top, sieved and bolted the essential seeds, shut them up tight, and then said 'Ah!' And whilst he was dusting his hands, he saw a lot of poppy-stuff to spare. 'Must do something with it—must do something with it—mustn't be wasted!' So he just rolled it out into red flakes, and dabbed it round the knobby seed-box, and said, 'There, the simple creature will take it in, and I've got rid of it.'

"My dear child, that is the history of the poppy and of the excess which accompanied his reproduction, is it? That's all you can say of him, when he makes his red splash in the world?—that he had a bit left over from his pie with the five-

and-twenty blackbirds in, so he put a red frill round? My child, it is good you are young, for you are a fool."

So the shade of the ancient man passed back again, to foregather with all the shades. And it shook its head as it went, muttering, "Conceit, conceit of self-preservation and of race-preservation, conceit!" But he had seen the heart of his grandson, with the wasteful red peeping out, like a poppy-bud. So he chuckled.

2

Why, when we are away for our holidays, do we exclaim with rapture, "What a splendid field of poppies!"—or "Isn't the poppy sweet, a red dot among the camomile flowers!"—only to go back on it all, and when the troubles come in, and we walk forth in heaviness, taking ourselves seriously, later on, to cry, in a harsh and bitter voice: "Ah, the gaudy treason of those red weeds in the corn!"— or when children come up with nosegays, "Nasty red flowers, poison, darling, make baby go to sleep," or when we see the scarlet flutter in the wind: "Vanity and flaunting vanity," and with gusto watch the red bits disappear into nothingness, saying: "It is well such scarlet vanity is cast to nought."

Why are we so rarely away on our holidays? Why do we persist in taking ourselves seriously, in counting our money and our goods and our virtues? We are down in the end. We rot and crumble away. And that without ever bursting the bud, the tight economical bud of caution and thrift and self-preservation.

The phoenix grows up to maturity and fulness of wisdom, it attains to fatness and wealth and all things desirable, only to burst into flame and expire in ash. And the flame and the ash are the be-all and the end-all, and the fatness and wisdom and wealth are but the fuel spent. It is a wasteful ordering of things, indeed, to be sure: but so it is, and what must be must be.

But we are very cunning. If we cannot carry our goods and our fatness, at least our goodness can be stored up like coin. And if we are not sure of the credit of the bank, we form ourselves into an unlimited liability company to run the future. We must have an obvious eternal deposit in which to bank our effort. And because the red of the poppy and the fire of the phoenix are contributed to no store, but are spent with the day and disappear, we talk of vanity and foolish mortality.

The phoenix goes gadding off into flame and leaves the future behind, unprovided for, in its ashes. There is no prodigal poppy left to return home in repentance, after the red is squandered in a day. Vanity, and vanity, and pathetic transience of mortality. All that is left us to call eternal is the tick-tack of birth and death, monotonous as time. The vain blaze flapped away into space and is gone, and what is left but the tick-tack of time, of birth and death?

But I will chase that flamy phoenix that gadded off into nothingness. Whoop and halloo and away we go into nothingness, in hot pursuit. Say, where are the flowers of yester-year? *Où sont les neiges de l'antan?* Where's Hippolyta, where's Thaïs, each one loveliest among women? Who knows? Where are the snows of yester-year?

That is all very well, but they must be somewhere. They may not be in any bank or deposit, but they are not lost for ever. The virtue of them is still blowing about in nothingness and in somethingness. I cannot walk up and say, "How do you do, Dido?" as Aeneas did in the shades. But Dido—Dido!—the robin cocks a scornful tail and goes off, disgusted with the noise. You might as well look for your own soul as to look for Dido. "Didon dina dit-on du dos d'un dodu dindon," comes rapidly into my mind, and a few frayed scraps of Virgil, and a vision of fair, round, half-globe breasts and blue eyes with tears in them; and a tightness comes into my heart: all forces rushing into me through my consciousness. But what of Dido my unconsciousness has, I could not tell you. Something, I am sure, and something that has come to me without my knowledge, something that flew away in the flames long ago, something that flew away from that pillar of fire, which was her body, day after day whilst she lived, flocking into nothingness to make a difference there. The reckoning of her money and her mortal assets may be discoverable in print. But what she is in the roomy space of somethingness, called nothingness, is all that matters to me.

She is something, I declare, even if she were utterly forgotten. How could any new thing be born unless it had a new nothingness to breathe? A new creature breathing old air, or even renewed air: it is terrible to think of. A new creature must have new air, absolutely brand-new air to breathe. Otherwise there is no new creature, and birth and death are a tick-tack.

What was Dido was new, absolutely new. It had never been before, and in Dido it *was.* In its own degree, the prickly sow-thistle I have just pulled up *is,* for the first time in all time. It is itself, a new thing. And most vividly it is itself in its yellow little disc of a flower: most vividly. In its flower it is. In its flower it issues something to the world that never was issued before. Its like has been before, its exact equivalent never. And this richness of new being is richest in the flowering yellow disc of my plant.

What then of this excess that accompanies reproduction? The excess is the thing itself at its maximum of being. If it had stopped short of this excess, it would not have been at all. If this excess were missing, darkness would cover the face of the earth. In this excess, the plant is transfigured into flower, it achieves at last itself. The aim, the culmination of all is the red of the poppy, this flame of the phoenix, this extravagant being of Dido, even her so-called waste.

But no, we dare not. We dare not fulfil the last part of our programme. We linger into inactivity at the vegetable, self-preserving stage. As if we preserved ourselves merely for the sake of remaining as we are. Yet there we remain, like the regulation cabbage, hide-bound, a bunch of leaves that may not go any farther for fear of losing a market value. A cabbage seen straddling up into weakly fiery flower is a piteous, almost an indecent sight to us. Better be a weed, and noxious. So we remain tight shut, a bunch of leaves, full of greenness and substance.

But the rising flower thrusts and pushes at the heart of us, strives and wrestles, while the static will holds us immovable. And neither will relent. But the flower, if it cannot beat its way through into being, will thrash destruction about itself. So the bound-up cabbage is beaten rotten at the heart.

Yet we call the poppy "vanity" and we write it down a weed. It is humiliating to think that, when we are taking ourselves seriously, we are considering our own self-preservation, or the greater scheme for the preservation of mankind. What is it that really matters? For the poppy, that the poppy disclose its red: for the cabbage, that it run up into weakly fiery flower: for Dido, that she be Dido, that she become herself, and die as fate will have it. Seed and fruit and produce, these are only a minor aim: children and good works are a minor aim.

Work, in its ordinary meaning, and all effort for the public good, these are labour of self-preservation, they are only means to the end. The final aim is the flower, the fluttering, singing nucleus which is a bird in spring, the magical spurt of being which is a hare all explosive with fulness of self, in the moonlight; the real passage of a man down the road, no sham, no shadow, no counterfeit, whose eyes shine blue with his own reality, as he moves amongst things free as they are, a being; the flitting under the lamp of a woman incontrovertible, distinct from everything and from everybody, as one who is herself, of whom Christ said, "to them that have shall be given."

The final aim of every living thing, creature, or being is the full achievement of itself. This accomplished, it will produce what it will produce, it will bear the fruit of its nature. Not the fruit, however, but the flower is the culmination and climax, the degree to be striven for. Not the work I shall produce, but the real Me I shall achieve, that is the consideration; of the complete Me will come the complete fruit of me, the work, the children.

And I know that the common wild poppy has achieved so far its complete poppy-self, unquestionable. It has uncovered its red. Its light, its self, has risen and shone out, has run on the winds for a moment. It is splendid. The world is a world because of the poppy's red. Otherwise it would be a lump of clay. And I am I as well, since the disclosure. What it is, I breathe it and snuff it up, it is about me and upon me and of me. And I can tell that I do not know it all yet. There is more to disclose. What more, I do not know. I tremble at the inchoate infinity of life when I think of that which the poppy has to reveal, and has not as yet had time to bring forth. I make a jest of it. I say to the flower, "Come, you've played that red card long enough. Let's see what else you have got up your sleeve." But I am premature and impertinent. My impertinence makes me ashamed. He has not played his red card long enough to have outsatisfied me.

Yet we must always hold that life is the great struggle for self-preservation; that this struggle for the means of life is the essence and whole of life. As if it would be anything so futile, so ingestive. Yet we ding-dong at it, always hammering out the same phrase, about the struggle for existence, the right to work, the right to the vote, the right to this and the right to that, all in the struggle for existence, as if any external power could give us the right to ourselves. That we have within ourselves. And if we have it not, then the remainder that we do possess will be taken away from us. "To them that have shall be given, and from them that have not shall be taken away even that which they have."

CHAPTER II

Still introductory: About Women's Suffrage, and Laws, and the War, and the Poor, with Some Fanciful Moralizing

It is so sad that the earnest people of today serve at the old, second-rate altar of self-preservation. The woman-suffragists, who are certainly the bravest, and, in the old sense, most heroic party amongst us, even they are content to fight the old battles on the old ground, to light an old system of self-preservation to obtain a more advanced system of preservation. The vote is only a means, they admit. A means to what? A means to making better laws, laws which shall protect the unprotected girl from a vicious male, which shall protect the sweated woman-labourer from the unscrupulous greed of the capitalist, which shall protect the interest of women in the State. And surely this is worthy and admirable.

Yet it is like protecting the well-being of a cabbage in the cabbage-patch while the cabbage is rotting at the heart for lack of power to run out into blossom. Could you make any law in any land, empowering the poppy to flower? You might make a law refusing it liberty to bloom. But that is another thing. Could any law put into being something which did not before exist? It could not. Law can only modify the conditions, for better or worse, of that which already exists.

But law is a very, very clumsy and mechanical instrument, and we people are very, very delicate and subtle beings. Therefore I only ask that the law shall leave me alone as much as possible. I insist that no law shall have immediate power over me, either for my good or for my ill. And I would wish that many laws be unmade, and no more laws made. Let there be a parliament of men and women for the careful and gradual unmaking of laws.

If it were for this purpose that women wanted the vote, I should be glad, and the opposition would be vital and intense, instead of just flippantly or exasperatedly static. Because then the woman's movement would be a living human movement. But even so, the claiming of a vote for the purpose of unmaking the laws would be rather like taking a malady in order to achieve a cure.

The women, however, want the vote in order to make more laws. That is the most lamentable and pathetic fact. They will take this clumsy machinery to make right the body politic. And, pray, what is the sickness of the body politic? Is it that some men are sex-mad or sex-degraded, and that some, or many, employers are money-degraded? And if so, will you, by making laws for putting in prison the sex-degraded, and putting out of power the money-degraded, thereby make whole and clean the State? Wherever you put them, will not the degradation exist, and continue? And is the State, then, merely an instrument for weeding the public of destructive members? And is this, then, the crying necessity for more thorough weeding?

Whence does the degradation or perversion arise? Is there any great sickness in the body politic? Then where and what is it? Am I, or your suffragist woman, or your voting man, sex-whole and money-healthy, are we sound human beings? Have we achieved to true individuality and to a sufficient completeness in ourselves? Because, if not—then, physician, heal thyself.

That is no taunt, but the finest and most damning criticism ever passed: "Physician, heal thyself." No amount of pity can blind us to the inexorable reality of the challenge.

Where is the source of all money-sickness, and the origin of all the sex-perversion? That is the question to answer. And no cause shall come to life unless it contain an answer to this question. Laws, and all State machinery, these only regulate the sick, separate the sick and the whole, clumsily, oh, so clumsily that it is worse than futile. Who is there who searches out the origin of the sickness, with a hope to quench the malady at its source?

It lies in the heart of man, and not in the conditions—that is obvious, yet always forgotten. It is not a malaria which blows in through the window and attacks us when we are healthy. We are each one of us a swamp, we are like the hide-bound cabbage going rotten at the heart. And for the same reason that, instead of producing our flower, instead of continuing our activity, satisfying our true desire, climbing and clambering till, like the poppy, we lean on the sill of all the unknown, and run our flag out there in the colour and shine of being, having surpassed that which has been before, we hang back, we dare not even peep forth, but, safely shut up in bud, safely and darkly and snugly enclosed, like the regulation cabbage, we remain secure till our hearts go rotten, saying all the while how safe we are.

No wonder there is a war. No wonder there is a great waste and squandering of life. Anything, anything to prove that we are not altogether sealed in our own self-preservation as dying chrysalides. Better the light be blown out, wilfully, recklessly, in the wildest wind, than remain secure under the bushel, saved from every draught.

So we go to war to show that we can throw our lives away. Indeed, they have become of so little value to us. We cannot live, we cannot *be*. Then let us tip-cat with death, let us rush throwing our lives away. Then at any rate we shall have a sensation—and "perhaps", after all, the value of life is in death.

What does the law matter? What does money, power, or public approval matter? All that matters is that each human being shall *be* in his own fulness. If something obstruct us we break it or put it aside, as the shoots of the trees break even through the London pavements. That is, if life is strong enough in us. If not, we are glad to fight with death. Does not the war show us how little, under all our carefulness, we count human life and human suffering, how little we value ourselves at bottom, how we hate our own security. We have many hospitals and many laws and charities for the poor. And at the same time we send ourselves to be killed and torn and tortured, we spread grief and desolation, and then, only then, we are somewhat satisfied. For have we not proved that we can transcend our own self-preservation, that we do not care so much for ourselves after all. Indeed, we almost hate ourselves.

Indeed, well may we talk about a just and righteous war not against Germany, but against ourselves, and our own self-love and caution. It is no war for the freedom of man from militarism or the Prussian yoke: it is a war for freedom of the bonds of our own cowardice and sluggish greed of security and well-being: it is a fight to regain ourselves out of the grip of our own caution.

Tell me no more we care about human life and suffering. We are, every one of us, revelling at this moment in the squandering of human life as if it were something we needed. And it is shameful. And all because that, to *live*, we are afraid to be ourselves. We can only die.

Let there be an end of all this welter of pity, which is only self-pity reflected on to some obvious surface. And let there be an end of this German hatred. We ought to be grateful to Germany that she still has the power to burst the bound hide of the cabbage. Where do I meet a man or a woman who does not draw deep and thorough satisfaction from this war? Because of pure shame that we should have seemed such poltroons, living safe and atrophied, not daring to take one step to life. And this is the only good that can result from the "world disaster": that we realise once more that self-preservation is not the final goal of life; that we realise that we can still squander life and property and inflict suffering wholesale. That will free us, perhaps, from the bushel we cower under, from the paucity of our lives, from the cowardice that will not let us *be*, which will only let us exist in security, unflowering, unreal, fat, under the cosy jam-pot of the State, under the shelter of the social frame.

And we must be prepared to fight, after the war, a renewed rage of activity for greater self-preservation, a renewed outcry for a stronger bushel to shelter our light. We must also undertake the incubus of crippled souls that will come home, and of crippled souls that will be left behind: men in whom the violence of war shall have shaken the life-flow and broken or perverted the course, women who will cease to live henceforth, yet will remain existing in the land, fixed at some lower point of fear or brutality.

Yet if we are left maimed and halt, if you die or I die, it will not matter, so long as there is alive in the land some new sense of what is and what is not, some new courage to let go the securities, and to *be,* to risk ourselves in a forward venture of life, as we are willing to risk ourselves in a rush of death.

Nothing will matter so long as life shall sprout up again strong after this winter of cowardice and well-being, sprout into the unknown. Let us only have had enough of pity: pity, that stands before the glass and weeps for ever over the sight of its own tears. This is what we have made of Christ's commandment: Thou shalt love thy neighbour as thyself" —a mirror for the tears of self-pity. How do we love our neighbour? By taking to heart his poverty, his small wage, and the attendant evils thereof. And is that how we love our neighbour as *ourselves*? Do I then think of myself as a moneyed thing enjoying advantages, or a non-moneyed thing suffering from disadvantages? Evidently I do. Then why the tears? They must rise from the inborn knowledge that neither money or non-money, advantages or disadvantages, matter supremely: what matters is the light under the bushel, the flower fighting under the safeguard of the leaves. I am weeping over my denied self. And I am very sorry for myself, held in the grip of some stronger force. Where can I find an image of myself?—ah, in the poor, in my poor neighbour labouring in the grip of an unjust system of capitalism. Let me look at him, let my heart be wrung, let me give myself to his service. Poor fellow, poor image, he is so badly off. Alas and alas, I do love my neighbour as myself: I am as anxious about his pecuniary welfare as I am about my own. I am so sorry for him, the poor X. He is a man like me. So I lie to myself and to him. For I do not care about him and his poverty: I care about my own unsatisfied soul. But I side-track to him, my poor neighbour, to vent on him my self-pity.

It is as if a poppy, when he is grown taller than his neighbours, but has not come to flower, should look down and because he can get no further, say: "Alas for those poor dwindlers down there: they don't get half as much rain as I do." He grows no more, and his non-growing makes him sad, and he tries to crouch down so as not to be any taller than his neighbour, thinking his sorrow is for his neighbour, and his neighbour struggles weakly into flower, after his fight for the sunshine. But the rich poppy crouches gazing down, nor even once lifts up his head to blossom. He is so afraid of giving himself forth, he cannot move on to expose his new nakedness, up there to confront the horrific space of the void, he is afraid of giving himself away to the unknown. He stays within his shell.

Which is the parable of the rich poppy. The *truth* about him is, he grows as fast as he can, though he devours no man's substance, because he has neither storehouse nor barn to devour them with, and neither a poppy nor a man can devour much through his own mouth. He grows as fast as he can, and from his innermost self he shuttles the red fire out, bit by bit, a little further, till he has brought it together and up to bud. There he hangs his head, hesitates, halts, reflects a moment, shrinking from the great climax when he lets off his fire. He ought to perceive now his neighbours, and to stand arrested, crying "Alas those poor dwindlers." But his fire breaks out of him, and he lifts his head, slowly, subtly, tense in an ecstasy of fear overwhelmed by joy, submits to the issuing of his flame and his fire, and there it hangs at the brink of the void, scarlet and radiant for a little while, imminent on the unknown, a signal, an out-post, an advance-guard, a forlorn, splendid flag, quivering from the brink of the unfathomed void, into which it flutters silently, satisfied, whilst a little ash, a little dusty seed remains behind on the solid ledge of the earth.

And the day is richer for a poppy, the flame of another phoenix is filled in to the universe, something is, which was not.

That is the whole point: something is which was not. And I wish it were true of us. I wish we were all like kindled bonfires on the edge of space, marking out the advance-posts. What is the aim of self-preservation, but to carry us right out to the firing line, where what *is* is in contact with what is not. If many lives be lost by the way, it cannot be helped, nor if much suffering be entailed. I do not go out to war in the intention of avoiding all danger or discomfort: I go to fight for myself. Every step I move forward into being brings a newer, juster proportion into the world, gives me less need of storehouse and barn, allows me to leave all, and to take what I want by the way, sure that it will always be there; allows me in the end to fly the flag of myself, at the extreme tip of life.

He who would save his life must lose it. But why should he go on and waste it? Certainly let him cast it upon the waters? Whence and how and whither it will return is no matter, in terms of values. But like a poppy that has come to bud, when he reaches the shore, when he has traversed his known and come to the beach to meet the unknown, he must strip himself naked and plunge in, and pass out: if he dare. And the rest of his life he will be a stirring at the unknown, cast out upon the waters. But if he dare not plunge in, if he dare not take off his clothes and give himself naked to the flood, then let him prowl in rotten safety weeping for pity of those he imagines worse off than himself. He dare not weep aloud for his own cowardice. And weep he must. So he will find him objects of pity.

CHAPTER III

Containing Six Novels and the Real Tragedy.

This is supposed to be a book about the people in Thomas Hardy's novels. But if one wrote everything they give rise to it would fill the Judgement Book.

One thing about them is that none of the heroes and heroines care very much for money, or immediate self-preservation, and all of them are struggling hard to come into being. What exactly the struggle into being consists in, is the question. But most obviously, from the Wessex novels, the first and chiefest factor is the struggle into love and the struggle with love: by love meaning the love of a man for a woman and a woman for a man. The via media to being, for man or woman, is love, and love alone. Having achieved and accomplished love, then the man passes into the unknown. He has become himself, his tale is told. Of anything that is complete there is no more tale to tell. The tale is about becoming complete, or about the failure to become complete.

It is urged against Thomas Hardy's characters that they do unreasonable things—quite, quite unreasonable things. They are always going off unexpectedly and doing something that nobody would do. That is quite true, and the charge is amusing. These people of Wessex are always bursting suddenly out of bud and taking a wild flight into flower, always shooting something out of a tight convention, a tight, hide-bound cabbage state into something quite madly personal. It would be amusing to count the number of special marriage licences taken out in Hardy's books. Nowhere, except perhaps in Jude, is there the slightest development of personal action in the characters: it is all explosive. Jude, however, does see more or less what he is doing, and acts from choice. He is more consecutive. The rest explode out of the convention. They are people each with a real, vital, potential self, even the apparently wishy-washy heroines of the earlier books, and this self suddenly bursts the shell of manner and convention and commonplace opinion, and acts independently, absurdly, without mental knowledge or acquiescence.

And from such an outburst the tragedy usually develops. For there does exist, after all, the great self-preservation system, and in it we must all live: How to live in it after bursting out of it was the problem these Wessex people found themselves faced with. And they never solved the problem, none of them except the comically-, insufficiently-, treated Ethelberta.

This because they must subscribe to the system in themselves. From the more immediate claims of self-preservation, they could free themselves: from money, from ambition for social success. None of the heroes or heroines of Hardy cared much for these things. But there is the greater idea of self-preservation, which is formulated in the State, in the whole modelling of the Community. And from this idea, the heroes and heroines of Wessex, like the heroes and heroines of almost anywhere else, could not free themselves. In the long run, the State, the Community, the established form of life remained, remained intact and impregnable, the individual, trying to break forth from it, died of fear, of exhaustion, or of exposure to attacks from all sides, like men who have left the walled city to live outside in the precarious open.

This is the tragedy of Hardy, always the same: the tragedy of those who, more or less pioneers, have died in the wilderness whither they had escaped for free action, after having left the walled security, and the comparative imprisonment, of the established convention. This is the theme of novel after novel: remain quite within the convention, and you are good, safe, and happy in the long run, though you never have the vivid pang of sympathy on your side: or, on the other hand, be passionate, individual, wilful, you will find the security of the convention a walled prison, you will escape, and you will die, either of your own lack of strength to bear the isolation and the exposure, or by direct revenge from the community, or from both. This is the tragedy, and only this: it is nothing more metaphysical than the division of a man against himself in such a way: first, that he is a member of the community, and must, upon his honour, in no way move to disintegrate the community either in its moral or its practical form; second, that the convention of the community is a prison to his natural, individual desire, a desire that compels him, whether he feel justified or not, to break the bounds of the community, lands him outside the pale, there to stand alone, and say: "I was right, my desire was real and inevitable; if I was to be myself I must fulfil it, convention or no convention", or else, there to stand alone, doubting, and saying: "Was I right, was I wrong? If I was wrong, oh, let me die"—in which case he courts death.

The growth and the development of this tragedy, the deeper and deeper realisation of this division and this problem, the coming towards some conclusion, is the one theme of the Wessex novels.

And therefore the books must be taken chronologically, to reveal the development and to advance towards the conclusion.

1   *Desperate Remedies.*

Springrove, the dull hero, fast within the convention, dare not tell Cytherea that he is already engaged, and thus prepares the complication. Manston, represented as fleshly passionate, breaks the convention and commits murder, which is very extreme, under compulsion of his desire for Cytherea. He is aided by the darkly passionate, lawless Miss Aldclyffe. He and Miss Aldclyffe meet death and Cytherea and Springrove are united to happiness and success.

2.   *Under the Greenwood Tree.*

After a brief excursion from the beaten track in the pursuit of social ambition and satisfaction of the imagination, figured by the Clergyman, Fancy, the little school-mistress, returns to Dick, renounces imagination, and settles down to steady, solid, physically satisfactory married life, and all is as it should be. But Fancy will carry in her heart all her life many unopened buds that will die unflowered; and Dick will probably have a bad time of it.

3.   *A Pair of Blue Eyes.*

Elfride breaks down in her attempt to jump the first little hedge of convention, when she comes back after running away with Stephen. She cannot stand even a little alone. Knight, his conventional idea backed up by selfish instinct cannot endure Elfride when he thinks she is not virgin, though now she loves him beyond bounds. She submits to him, and owns the conventional idea entirely right, even whilst she is innocent. An aristocrat walks off with her whilst the two men hesitate, and she, poor innocent victim of passion not vital enough to overthrow the most banal conventional ideas, lies in a bright coffin, while the three confirmed lovers mourn, and say how great the tragedy is.

4.   *Far from the Madding Crowd.*

The unruly Bathsheba, though almost pledged to Farmer Boldwood, a ravingly passionate, middle-aged bachelor pretendant, who has suddenly started in mad pursuit of some unreal conception of woman, personified in Bathsheba, lightly runs off and marries Sergeant Troy, an illegitimate aristocrat, unscrupulous and yet sensitive in taking his pleasures. She loves Troy, he does not love her. All the time she is loved faithfully and persistently by the good Gabriel, who is like a dog that watches the bone and bides the time. Sergeant Troy treats Bathsheba badly, never loves her, though he is the only man in the book who knows anything about her. Her pride helps her to recover. Troy is killed by Boldwood, exit the unscrupulous, but discriminative, almost cynical young soldier and the mad, middle-aged pursuer of the Fata Morgana, enter the good steady Gabriel, who marries Bathsheba because he will make her a good husband, and the flower of imaginative fine love is dead for her with Troy's scorn of her.

5.   *The Hand of Ethelberta.*

Ethelberta, a woman of character and of brilliant parts, sets out in pursuit of social success, finds that Julian, the only man she is inclined to love, is too small for her, hands him over to the good little Picotee, and she herself, sacrificing almost cynically what is called her heart, marries the old scoundrelly Lord Mountclere, runs him and his estates and governs well, a sound strong pillar of established society, now she has nipped off the bud of her heart. Moral, it is easier for a butler's daughter to marry a Lord than to find a husband with her love, if she be an exceptional woman.

The Hand of Ethelberta is the one almost cynical comedy. It marks the zenith of a certain feeling in the Wessex novels, the zenith of the feeling that the best thing to do is to kick out the craving for "Love", and substitute common-sense, leaving sentiment to the minor characters.

This novel is a shrug of the shoulders and a last taunt to hope, it is the end of the happy endings, except where sanity and a little cynicism again appear in *The Trumpet-Major,* to bless where they despise. It is the hard resistant, ironical announcement of personal failure, resistant and half grinning. It gives way to violent, angry passions and real tragedy, real killing of beloved people, self-killing. Till now, only Elfride among the beloved has been killed, the good men have always come out on top.

6.   *The Return of the Native.*

This is the first tragic and important novel. Eustacia, dark, wild, passionate, quite conscious of her desires and inheriting no tradition which would make her ashamed of them, since she is of a novelistic Italian birth, loves first the unstable Wildeve, who does not satisfy her, then casts him aside for the newly returned Clym, whom she marries. What does she want? She does not know, but it is evidently some form of self-realisation; she wants to be herself, to attain herself. But she does not know how, by what means, so romantic imagination says Paris and the beau monde. As if that would stay her unsatisfaction.

Clym has found out the vanity of Paris and the beau monde. What then does he want? He does not know, his imagination tells him he wants to serve the moral system of the community, since the material system is despicable. He wants to teach little Egdon boys in school. There is as much vanity in this, easily, as in Eustacia's Paris. For what is the moral system but the ratified form of the material system? What is Clym's altruism but a deep very subtle cowardice, that makes him shirk his own being whilst apparently acting nobly; which makes him choose to improve mankind rather than to struggle at the quick of himself into being. He is not able to undertake his own soul, so he will take a commission for society to enlighten the souls of others. It is a subtle equivocation. Thus both Eustacia and he side-track from themselves, and each leaves the other unconvinced, unsatisfied, unrealised. Eustacia because she moves outside the convention, must die, Clym because he identified himself with the community, is transferred from Paris to preaching. He had never become an integral man, because when faced with the demand to produce himself, he remained under cover of the community and excused by his altruism.

His remorse over his mother is adulterated with sentiment, it is exaggerated by the push of tradition behind it. Even in this he does not ring true. He is always according to pattern, producing his feelings more or less on demand, according to the accepted standard. Practically never is he able to act or even feel in his original self: he is always according to the convention. His punishment is his final loss of all his original self: he is left preaching, out of sheer emptiness.

Thomasin and Venn have nothing in them turbulent enough to push them to the bounds of the convention. There is always room for them inside. They are genuine people, and they get the prize within the walls.

Wildeve, shifty and unhappy, attracted always from outside and never driven from within, can neither stand with or without the established system. He cares nothing for it, because he is unstable, has no positive being. He is an eternal assumption.

The other victim, Clym's mother, is the crashing down of one of the old, rigid pillars of the system. The pressure on her is too great. She is weakened from the inside also, for her nature is non-conventional, it cannot own the bounds.

So, in this book, all the exceptional people, those with strong feelings and unusual characters, are reduced, only those remain who are steady and genuine, if commonplace. Let a man will for himself, and he is destroyed. He must will according to the established system.

The real sense of tragedy is got from the setting. What is the great, tragic power in the book?—it is Egdon Heath. And who are the real spirits of the Heath?—first Eustacia, then Clym's mother, then Wildeve. The natives have little or nothing in common with the place.

What is the real stuff of tragedy in the book? It is the Heath. It is the primitive, primal earth, where the instinctive life heaves up. There, in the deep, rude stirring of the instincts, there was the reality that worked the tragedy. Close to the body of things, there can be heard the stir that makes us and destroys us. The earth heaved with raw instinct, Egdon whose dark soil was strong and crude and organic as the body of a beast. Out of the body of this crude earth are born Eustacia, Wildeve, Mistress Yeobright, Clym, and all the others. They are one year's accidental crop. What matter if some are drowned or dead, and others preaching or married: what matter, any more than the withering heath, the reddening berries, the seedy furze and the dead fern of one autumn of Egdon. The Heath persists. Its body is strong and fecund, it will bear many more crops beside this. Here is the sombre, latent power that will go on producing, no matter what happen to the product. Here is the deep, black source from whence all these little contents of lives are drawn. And the contents of the small lives are spilled and wasted. There is savage satisfaction in it: for so much more remains to come, such a black, powerful fecundity is working there that what does it matter!

Three people die and are taken back into the Heath, they mingle their strong earth again with its powerful soil, having been broken off at their stem. It is very good. Not Egdon is futile, sending forth life on the powerful heave of passion. It cannot be futile, for it is eternal. What is futile is the purpose of man.

Man has a purpose which he has divorced from the passionate purpose that issued him out of the earth, into being. The Heath threw forth its shaggy heather and furze and fern, clean into being. It threw forth Eustacia and Wildeve and Mistress Yeobright and Clym, but to what purpose? Eustacia thought she wanted the hats and bonnets of Paris. Perhaps she was right. The heavy, strong soil of Egdon, breeding original native beings, is under Paris as well as under Wessex, and Eustacia sought herself in the gay city. She thought life there, in Paris, would be tropical, and all her energy and passion out of Egdon would there come into handsome flower. And if

Paris real had been Paris as she imagined it, no doubt she was right, and her instinct was soundly expressed. But Paris real was not Eustacia's imagined Paris. Where was her imagined Paris, the place where her powerful nature could come to blossom? Beside some strong-passioned, unconfined man, her mate.

Which mate Clym might have been. He was born out of passionate Egdon to live as a passionate being whose strong feelings moved him ever further into being. But quite early his life became narrowed down to a small purpose: he must of necessity go into business, and submit his whole being, body and soul as well as mind, to the business and to the greater system it represented. His feelings, that should have produced the man, were suppressed and contained, he worked according to a system imposed from without. The dark struggle of Egdon, a struggle into being as the furze struggles into flower, went on in him, but could not burst the enclosure of the idea, the system which contained him. Impotent to *be,* he must transform himself, and live in an abstraction, in a generalisation, he must identify himself with the system. He must live as Man or Humanity, or as the Community, or as Society, or as Civilisation. "An inner strenuousness was preying on his outer symmetry, and they rated his look as singular———His countenance was overlaid with legible meanings. Without being thought-worn, he yet had certain marks derived from a perception of his surroundings, such as are not unfrequently found on men at the end of the four or five years of endeavour which follow the close of placid pupilage. He already showed that thought is a disease of flesh, and indirectly bore evidence that ideal physical beauty is incompatible with emotional development and a full recognition of the coil of things. Mental luminousness must be fed with the oil of life, even if there is already a physical need for it; and the pitiful sight of two demands on one supply was just showing itself here."

But did the face of Clym show that thought is a disease of flesh, or merely that in his case a dis-ease, an un-ease of flesh produced thought. One does not catch thought like a fever: one produces it. If it be in any way a disease of flesh, it is rather the rash that indicates the disease, than the disease itself The "inner strenuousness" of Clym's nature was not fighting against his physical symmetry, but against the limits imposed on his physical movement. By nature, as a passionate, violent product of Egdon, he should have loved and suffered in flesh and in soul from love, long before this age. He should have lived and moved and had his being, whereas he had only his business, and afterwards his inactivity. His years of pupilage were past, "he was one of whom something original was expected", yet he continued in pupilage. For he produced nothing original in being or in act, and certainly no original thought. None of his ideas were original. Even he himself was not original. He was over-taught, had become an echo. His life had been arrested, and his activity turned into repetition. Far from being emotionally developed, he was emotionally undeveloped, almost entirely. Only his mental faculties were developed. And his emotions were obliged to work according to the label he put upon them: a ready-made label.

Yet he remained for all that an original, the force of life was in him, however much he frustrated and suppressed its natural movement. "As is usual with bright natures, the deity that lies ignominiously chained within an ephemeral human carcase shone out of him like a ray." But was the deity chained within his ephemeral human carcase, or within his limited human consciousness? Was it his blood, which rose dark and potent out of Egdon, which hampered and confined the deity, or was it his mind, that house built of extraneous knowledge and guarded by his will, which formed the prison.

He came back to Egdon—what for? To re-unite himself with the strong, free flow of life that rose out of Egdon as from a source? No—"to preach to the Egdon eremites that they might rise to a serene comprehensiveness without going through the process of enriching themselves." As if the Egdon eremites had not already far more serene comprehensiveness than ever he had himself, rooted as they were in the soil of all things, and living from the root. What did it matter how they enriched themselves, so long as they kept this strong, deep root in the primal soil, so long as their instincts moved out to action and to expression. The system was big enough for them, and had not power over their instincts. They should have taught him rather than he them.

And Egdon made him marry Eustacia. Here was action and life, here was a move into being on his part. But as soon as he got her, she became an idea to him, she had to fit in his system of ideas. According to his way of living, he knew her already, she was labelled and classed and fixed down. He had got into this way of living, and he could not get out of it. He had identified himself with the system, and he could not extricate himself. He did not know that Eustacia had her being beyond him. He did not know that she existed untouched by his system and his mind, where no system had sway and where no consciousness had risen to the surface. He did not know that she was Egdon, the powerful, eternal origin seething with production. He thought he knew. Egdon to him was the tract of common land, producing familiar rough herbage, and having some few unenlightened inhabitants. So he skated over heaven and hell, and having made a map of the surface, thought he knew all. But underneath and among his mapped world, the eternal powerful fecundity worked on heedless of him and his arrogance. His preaching, his superficiality made no difference. 'What did it matter if he had calculated a moral chart from the surface of life? Could that affect life, any more than a chart of the heavens affects the stars, affects the whole stellar universe which exists beyond our knowledge? Could the sound of his words affect the working of the body of Egdon, where in the unfathomable womb was begot and conceived all that would ever come forth. Did not his own heart beat far removed and immune from his thinking and talking. Had he been able to put even his own heart's mysterious resonance upon his map, from which he charted the course of lives in his moral system? And how much more completely, then, had he left out in utter ignorance, the dark, powerful source whence all things rise into being, whence they will always continue to rise, to struggle forward to further being. A little of the static surface he could see, and map out. Then he thought his map was the thing itself. How blind he was, how utterly blind to the tremendous movement carrying and producing the surface. He did not know that the greater part of every life is underground, like roots in the dark in contact with the beyond. He preached thinking lives could be moved like hen-houses from here to there. His blindness indeed brought on the calamity. But what matter if Eustacia or Wildeve or Mrs Yeobright died: what matter if he himself became a mere rattle of repetitive words—what did it matter? It was regrettable, no more. Egdon, the primal impulsive body would go on producing all that was to be produced, eternally, though the will of man should destroy the blossom yet in bud, over and over again. At last he must learn what it is to be at one, in his mind and will, with the primal impulses that rise in him. Till then let him perish or preach.

29

The great reality on which the little tragedies enact themselves cannot be detracted from. The will and words which militate against it are the only vanity.

This is a constant revelation in Hardy's novels: that there exists a great background, vital and vivid, which matters more than the people who move upon it. Against the background of dark, passionate Egdon, of the leafy, sappy passion and sentiment of the woodlands, of the unfathomed stars, is drawn the lesser scheme of lives: *The Return of the Native, The Woodlanders,* or *Two on a Tower.* Upon the vast, incomprehensible pattern of some primal morality greater than ever the human mind can grasp, is drawn the little, pathetic pattern of man's moral life and struggle, pathetic almost ridiculous. The little fold of law and order, the little walled city within which man has to defend himself from the waste enormity of nature becomes always too small, and the pioneers venturing out with the code of the walled city upon them, die confined in the bonds of that code, free and yet unfree, preaching the walled city and looking to the waste.

This is the wonder of Hardy's novels, and gives them their beauty. The vast, unexplored morality of life itself, what we call the immorality of nature, surrounds us in its eternal incomprehensibility, and in its midst goes on the little human morality play, with its queer frame of morality and its mechanised movement; seriously, portentously, till some one of the protagonists chance to look out of the charmed circle, weary of the stage, to look into the wilderness raging round. Then he is lost, his little drama falls to pieces, or becomes mere repetition, but the stupendous theatre outside goes on enacting its own incomprehensible drama, untouched. There is this quality in almost all Hardy's work, and this is the magnificent irony it all contains, the challenge, the contempt. Not the deliberate ironies, little tales of widows or widowers, contain the irony of human life as we live it in our self-aggrandised gravity, but the big novels, *The Return of the Native,* and the others.

And this is the quality Hardy shares with the great writers, Shakespeare or Sophocles or Tolstoi, this setting behind the small action of his protagonists the terrific action of unfathomed nature, setting a smaller system of morality, the one grasped and formulated by the human consciousness within the vast, uncomprehended and incomprehensible morality of nature or of life itself, surpassing human consciousness. The difference is, that whereas in Shakespeare or Sophocles the greater, uncomprehended morality, or fate, is actively transgressed and gives active punishment, in Hardy and Tolstoi the lesser, human morality, the mechanical system is actively transgressed, and holds, and punishes the protagonist, whilst the greater morality is only passively, negatively transgressed, it is represented merely as being present in background, in scenery, not taking any active part, having no direct connection with the protagonist. Oedipus, Hamlet, Macbeth set themselves up against, or find themselves set up against the unfathomed moral forces of nature, and out of this unfathomed force comes their death. Whereas Anna Karenin, Eustacia, Tess, Sue and Jude find themselves up against the established system of human government and morality, they cannot detach themselves, and are brought down. Their real tragedy is that they are unfaithful to the greater unwritten morality, which would have bidden Anna Karenin be patient and wait until she, by virtue of greater right, could take what she needed from society; would have bidden Vronsky detach himself from the system, become an individual, creating a new colony of morality with Anna; would have bidden Eustacia fight Clym for his own soul, and Tess take and claim her Angel, since she had the greater light; would have bidden Jude and Sue endure for very honour's sake, since one must bide by the best that one has known, and not succumb to the lesser good.

Had Oedipus, Hamlet, Macbeth been weaker, less full of real, potent life, they would have made no tragedy: they would have compromised and contrived some arrangement of their affairs, sheltering in the human morality from the great stress and attack of the unknown morality. But, being as they are, men to the fullest capacity, when they themselves daggers drawn with the very forces of life itself, they can only fight till they themselves are killed, since the morality of life, the greater morality, is eternally unalterable and invincible. It can be dodged for some time, but not opposed. On the other hand, Anna, Eustacia, Tess or Sue—what was there in their position that was necessarily tragic? Necessarily painful it was, but they were not at war with God, only with Society. Yet they were all cowed by the mere judgement of man upon them, and all the while by their own souls they were right. And the judgement of man killed them, not the judgement of their own souls, or the judgement of eternal God.

Which is the weakness of modern tragedy, where transgression against the social code is made to bring destruction, as though the social code worked our irrevocable fate. Like Clym, the map appears to us more real than the land. Short sighted almost to blindness, we pore over the chart, map out journeys and confirm them: and we cannot see life itself giving us the lie the whole time.

CHAPTER IV.

An Attack on Work and the Money Appetite and on the State.

There is always excess, the biologists say, a brimming over. For they have made the measure, and the supply must be made to fit. They have charted the course, and if at the end of it there is a jump beyond the bounds into nothingness: well, there is always excess, for they have charted the journey aright.

There is always excess, a brimming over. At spring-time a bird brims over with blue and yellow, a glow worm brims over with a drop of green moonshine, a lark flies up like heady wine, with song, an errand boy whistles down the road, and scents brim over the measure of the flower. Then we say, it is spring.

When is a glow worm a glow worm? When she's got a light on her tail. What is she when she hasn't got a light on her tail? Then she's a mere worm, an insect.

When is a man a man? When he is alight with life. Call it excess? If it is missing, there is no man, only a creature, a clod, undistinguished.

With man, it is always spring—or it may be; with him every day is a blossoming day, if he will. He is a plant eternally in flower, he is an animal eternally in rut, he is a bird eternally in song. He has his excess constantly on his hands, almost every day. It is not with him a case of seasons, spring and autumn and winter. And happy man if his excess come out in blue and gold and singing, if it be not like the paste rose on the pie, a burden, at last a very sickness.

The wild creatures are like fountains whose sources gather their waters until spring-time, when they leap their highest. But man is a fountain that is always playing, leaping, ebbing, sinking, and springing up. It is not for him to gather his waters till spring-time, when his fountain, rising higher, can at last flow out flower-wise in mid-air, teeming awhile with excess, before it falls spent again.

His rhythm is not so simple. A pleasant little stream of life is a bud at autumn and winter, fluttering in flocks over the stubble, the fallow, rustling along. Till spring, when many waters rush in to the sources, and each bird is a fountain playing.

Man, fortunate or unfortunate, is rarely like an autumn bird, to enjoy his pleasant stream of life flowing at ease. Some men are like that, fortunate and delightful. But those men or women will not read this book. Why should they?

The sources of man's life are overfull, they receive more than they give out. And why? Because a man is a well-head built over a strong, perennial spring and enclosing it in, a well-head whence the water may be drawn at will, and under which the water may be held back indefinitely. Sometimes, and in certain ways, according to certain rules, the source may bubble and spring out, but only at certain times, always under control. And the fountain cannot always bide for the permission, the suppressed waters strain at the well-head, and hence so much sadness without cause. Weltschmerz and other unlocalised pains where the source presses for utterance.

And how is it given utterance? In sheer play of being free? That cannot be. It shall be given utterance in work, the conscious mind has unanimously decreed. And the decree is held holy. My life is to be utilised for work, first and foremost,— and this in spite of Mary of Bethany.

Only, or very largely in the work I do, must I live, must my life take movement. And why do I work? To eat,—is the original answer. When I have earned enough to eat, what then? Work for more, to provide for the future. And when I have provided for the future? Work for more to provide for the poor. And when I have worked to provide for the poor, what then? Keep on working, the poor are never provided for, the poor have ye always with you.

That is the best that man has been able to do.

But what a ghastly programme! I do not want to work.—You must,— comes the answer. But nobody wants to work, originally.—Yet everybody works, because he must,—it is repeated. And what when he is not working?—Let him rest and amuse himself, and get ready for tomorrow morning.

Oh my God, work is the great body of life, and sleep and amusement, like two wings, beat only to carry it along. Is this then all?

And Carlyle gets up and says, it is all, and mankind goes on in grim, serious approval, more than acquiescent, approving, thinking itself religiously right.

But let us pull the tail out of the mouth of this serpent. Eternity is not a process of eternal self-inglutination. We must work to eat, and eat to work—that is how it is given out. But the real problem is quite different. "We must work to eat, and eat to—what?" Don't say "work", it is so unoriginal.

In Nottingham, we boys began learning German by learning proverbs. "Man muss essen um zu leben, aber man muss nicht leben um zu essen", was the first. "One must eat to live, but one must not live to eat": a good German proverb according to the lesson book. Starting a step further back, it might be written "one must work to eat, but one must not eat to work". Surely that is just, because the second proverb says "one must eat to live".

"One must work to eat, and eat to live", is the result.

Take this vague and almost uninterpretable word "living". To how great a degree are "to work" and "to live" synonymous? That is the question to answer, when the highest flight that our thought can take, for the sake of living, is to say that we must return to the mediaeval system of handicrafts, and that each man must become a labouring artist, producing a complete article.

Work is, simply, the activity necessary for the production of a sufficient supply of food and shelter: nothing more holy than that. It is the producing of the means of self-preservation. Therefore it is obvious that it is not the be-all and the end-all of existence. We work to provide means of subsistence, and when we have made provision, we proceed to live. But all work is only the making provision for that which is to follow.

It may be argued that work has a fuller meaning, that man lives most intensely when he works. That may be, for some few men, for some few artists whose lives are otherwise empty. But for the mass, for the 99.9 per cent of mankind, work is a form of non-living, of non-existence, of submergence.

It is necessary to produce food and clothing. Then, under necessity the thing must be done as quickly as possible. Is not the highest recommendation for a labourer the fact that he is quick? And how does any man become quick, save through finding the shortest way to his end, and by repeating one set of actions? A man who can repeat certain movements accurately, is an expert, if his movements are those which produce the required result.

And these movements are the calculative or scientific movements of a machine. When a man is working perfectly, he is the perfect machine. Aware of certain forces, he moves accurately along the line of their resultant. The perfect machine does the same.

All work is like this, the approximation to a perfect mechanism, more or less intricate and adjustable. The doctor, the teacher, the lawyer, just as much as the farm-labourer or the mechanic, when working most perfectly is working with the utmost of mechanical, scientific precision, along a line calculated from known fact, calculated instantaneously.

In this work, man has a certain definite, keen satisfaction. When he is utterly impersonal, when he is merely the node where certain mechanical forces meet to find their resultant, then a man is something perfect, the perfect instrument, the perfect machine.

It is a state which, in his own line, every man strives and longs for. It is a state which satisfies his moral craving, almost the deepest craving within him. It is a state when he lies in line with the great force of gravity, partakes perfectly of its subtlest movement and motion, even to psychic vibration.

But it is a state which every man hopes for release from. The dream of every man, is that in the end he shall have to work no more. The joy of every man, is when he is released from his labour, having done his share for the time being.

What does he want to be released from, and what does he want to be released unto? A man is not a machine: when he has finished work, he is not motionless, inert. He begins a new activity. And what?

It seems to me as if a man, in his normal state, were like a palpitating leading-shoot of life, where the unknown, all unresolved, beats and pulses, containing the quick of all experience, as yet unrevealed, not singled out. But when he thinks, when he moves, he is retracing some proved experience. He is as the leading-shoot which, for the moment, remembers only that which is behind, the fixed wood, the cells conducting towards their undifferentiated tissue of life. He moves as it were in the trunk of the tree, in the channels long since built, where the sap must flow as in a canal. He takes knowledge of all this past experience upon which the new tip rides quivering, he becomes again the old life, which has built itself out in the fixed tissue, he lies in line with the old movement, unconscious of where it breaks, at the growing plasm, into something new, unknown. He is happy, all is known, all is finite, all is established, and knowledge can be perfect, here in the trunk of the tree, which life built up and climbed beyond.

Such is a man at work, safe within the proven, deposited experience, thrilling as he traverses the fixed channels and courses of life, he is only matter of some of the open ways which life laid down for its own passage, he has only made himself one with what has been, traveling the old, fixed courses, through which life still passes, but which are not in themselves living.

And in the end, this is always a prison to him, this proven, deposited experience which he must explore, this past of life. For is he not in himself a growing tip, is not his own body a quivering plasm of what will be, and has never yet been. Is not his own soul a fighting line, where what is and what will be separates itself off from what has been. Is not this his purest joy of movement, the indistinguishable, complex movement of being. And is not this his deepest desire, to be himself, to be this quivering bud of growing tissue which he is. He may find knowledge by retracing the old courses, he may satisfy his moral sense by working within the known, certain of what he is doing. But for real, utter satisfaction, he must give himself up to complete quivering uncertainty, to sentient non-knowledge.

And this is why man is always crying out for freedom, to be free. He wants to be free to be himself. For this reason, he has always made a heaven where no work need be done, where to *be* is all, where to *be* comprises all that has been done, in perfect knowledge, and where that which will be done is so swift as to be a sleep, a Nirvana, an absorption.

So there is this deepest craving of all, to be free from the necessity to work. It is obvious in all mankind. "Must I become one with the old, habitual movements?" says man. "I must, to satisfy myself that the new is new and the old is old, that all is one like a tree, though I am no more than the tiniest cell in the tree." So he becomes one with the old, habitual movement: he is the perfect machine, the perfect instrument: he works. But, satisfied for the time being of that which has been and remains now finite, he wearies for his own, limitless being, for the unresolved, quivering, infinitely complex and indefinite movement of new living, he wants to be free.

And ever, as his knowledge of what is past becomes greater, he wants more and more liberty to be himself. There is the necessity for self-preservation, the necessity to submerge himself in the utter mechanical movement. But why so much: why repeat so often the mechanical movement? Let me not have so much of this work to do, let me not be consumed overmuch in my own self-preservation, let me not be imprisoned in this proven, finite experience all my days.

This has been the cry of humanity since the world began. This is the glamour of kings, the glamour of men who had opportunity to *be,* who were not under compulsion to do, to serve. This is why kings were chosen heroes, because they were the beings, the producers of new life, not servants of necessity, repeating old experience.

And humanity has laboured to make work shorter, so we may all be kings. True, we have the necessity to work, more or less, according as we are near the growing tip or further away. Some men are far from the growing tip. They have little for growth in them, only the power for repeating old movement. They will always find their own level. But let those that have life live.

So there has been produced machinery, to take the place of the human machine. And the inventor of the labour saving machine has been hailed as a public benefactor, and we have rejoiced over his discovery. Now there is a railing against the machine, as if it were an evil thing. And the thinkers talk about the return to the mediaeval system of handicrafts. Which is absurd.

As I look round this room, at the bed, at the counterpane, at the books and chairs and the little bottles, and think that machines made them, I am glad. I am very glad of the bedstead, of the white enamelled iron with brass rail. As it stands, I rejoice over its essential simplicity. I would not wish it different. Its lines are straight and parallel, or at right angles, giving a sense of static motionlessness. Only that which is necessary is there, whittled down to the minimum. There is nothing to hurt me or to hinder me; my wish for something to serve my purpose is perfectly fulfilled.

Which is what a machine can do. It can provide me with the perfect mechanical instrument, a thing mathematically and scientifically correct. Which is what I want. I like the books, on the whole, I can scarcely imagine them more convenient to me, I like the common green-glass smelling salts, and the machine turned feet of the common chest of drawers. I hate the machine carving on a chair, and the stamped pattern on a rug. But I have no business to ask a machine to make beautiful things for me. I can ask it for perfect accommodating utensils or articles of use, and I shall get them.

Wherefore I do honour to the machine and to its inventor. It will produce what we want, and save us the necessity of much labour. Which is what it was invented for.

But to what pitiable misuse is it put! Do we use the machine to produce goods for our need, or is it used as a muck-rake for raking together heaps of money? Why, when man, in his godly effort has produced a means to freedom, do we make it a means to more slavery?

Why?—because the heart of man is crude and greedy. Why is a labourer willing to work ten hours a day for a mere pittance? Because he is serving a system for the enrichment of the individual, a system to which he subscribes, because he might himself be that individual, and, since his one ideal is to be rich, he owes his allegiance to the system established for the raking of riches into heaps, a system that satisfies his imagination. Why try to alter the present industrial system on behalf of the working man, when his imagination is satisfied only by such a system?

The poor man and the rich, they are the head and tail of the same penny. Stand them naked side by side, and which is better than the other? The rich man, probably, for he is likely to be the sadder and the wiser.

The universal ideal, the one conscious ideal of the poor people, is riches. The only hope lies in those people who, in fact or imagination, have experienced wealth, and have appetites accordingly.

It is not true, that, before we can get over our absorbing passion to be rich, we must each one of us know wealth. There are sufficient people with sound imagination and normal appetite to put away the whole money tyranny of England today.

There is no evil in money. If there were a million pounds under my bed, and I did not know of it, it would make no difference to me. If there were a million pounds under my bed, and I did know of it, it would make a difference perhaps, to the form of my life, but to the living me, and to my individual purpose, it could make no difference, since I depend neither on riches nor on poverty for my being.

Neither poverty nor riches obsesses me. I would not be like a begging friar to forswear all owning and having For I would .not admit myself so weak, that either I must abstain totally from wealth or succumb to the passion for possessions.

Have I not a normal money appetite, as I have a normal appetite for food? Do I want to kill a hundred bison, to satisfy the imaginative need of my stomach, as the Red Indian did? Then why should I want a thousand pounds, when ten are enough? "Thy eyes are bigger than thy belly," says the mother of the child who takes more than he can eat. "Your pocket is bigger than your breeches," one could say to a man greedy to get rich.

It is only greediness. But it is very wearisome. There are plenty of people who are not greedy, who have normal money appetites. They need a certain amount, and they know they need it. It is no honour to be a pauper. It is only decent that every man should have enough and a little to spare, and every self-respecting man will see he gets it. But why can't we really grow up, and become adult with regard to money as with regard to food. Why can't we know when we have enough, as we know when we have had enough to eat?

We could, of course, if we had any real sense of values. It is all very well to leave, as Christianity tries to leave the dinner to be devoured by the glutton, whilst the Christian draws off in disgust, and fasts. But we each have our place at the board, as we well know, and it is indecent to withdraw before the glutton, leaving the earth to be devoured.

Can we not stay at the board? We must eat to live. And living is not simply not-dying. It is the only real thing, it is the aim and end of all life. Work is only a means to subsistence. The work done, the living earned, how then to go on to enjoy it, to fulfil it, that is the question. How shall a man live? What do we mean by living?

Let every man answer for himself. We only know, we want the freedom to live, the freedom of leisure and means. But there are ample means, there is half an eternity of pure leisure for mankind to take if he would, if he did not think, at the back of his mind, that riches are the means of freedom. Riches would be the means of freedom, if there were no poor, if there were equal riches everywhere. Till then, riches and poverty alike are bonds and prisons, for every man must live in the ring of his own defences, to defend his property. And this ring is the surest of prisons.

So cannot we see, rich and poor alike, how we have circumscribed, hampered, imprisoned ourselves within the limits of our poor-and-rich system, till our life is utterly pot-bound. It is not that some of us want more money and some of us less. It is that our money is like walls between us, we are immured in gold, and we die of starvation or etiolation.

A plant has strength to burst its pot. The shoots of London trees have force to burst through the London pavements. Is there not life enough in us to break out of this system? Let every man take his own, and go his own way, regardless of system and State, when his hour comes. Which is greater, the State or myself? Myself, unquestionably, since the State is only an arrangement made for my convenience. If it is not convenient for me, I must depart from it. There is no need to break laws. The only need is to be a law unto oneself.

And if sufficient people came out of the walled defences, and pitched in the open, then very soon the walled city would be a mere dependent on the free tents of the wilderness. Why should we care about bursting the city walls? We can walk through the gates into the open world. These states and nations with their ideals, their armaments of aggression and defence, what are they to me? They must fight out their own fates. As for me, I would say to every decent man whose heart is straining at the enclosure, "Come away from the crowd and the community, come away and be separate in your own soul, and live. Your business is to produce your own real life, no matter what the nations do. The nations are made up of individual men, each man will know at length that he must single himself out, nor remain any longer embedded in the matrix of his nation, or community, or class. Our time has come, let us draw apart. Let the physician heal himself."

And outside what will it matter save that a man is a man, is himself? If he must work, let him work a few hours a day, a very few, whether it be at wheeling bricks, or shovelling coal into a furnace or tending a machine. Let him do his work, according to his kind, for some three or four hours a day. That will produce supplies in ample sufficiency. Then let him have twenty hours for being himself, for producing himself.

CHAPTER V.

Work and the Angel and the Unbegotten Hero.

It is an inherent passion, this will to work, it is a craving to produce, to create, to be as God. Man turns his back on the unknown, on that which is yet to be, he turns his face towards that which has been, and he sees, he re-discovers, he becomes again that which has been before. But this time he is conscious, he knows what he is doing. He can at will reproduce the movement life made in its initial passage, the movement life still makes, and will continue to make, as a habit, the movement already made so unthinkably often that rather than a movement it has become a state, a condition of all life; it has become matter, or the force of gravity, or cohesion, or heat, or light. These old, old habits of life man rejoices to rediscover in all their detail.

Long, long ago life first rolled itself into seed, and fell to earth, and covered itself up with soil, slowly. And long, long ago man discovered the process, joyfully, and, in this wise as God, repeated it. He found out how soil is shifted. Proud as a needy God, he dug the ground, and threw the little, silent fragments of life under the dust. And was he not doing what life itself had initiated, was he not, in this particular, even greater than life, more definite?

Still further back, in an unthinkable period long before chaos, life formed the habit we call gravitation. This was almost before any differentiation, before all those later, lesser habits, which we call matter or such a thing as centrifugal force, were formed. It was a habit of the great mass of life, not of any part in particular. Therefore it took man's consciousness much longer to apprehend, and even now we have only some indications of it, from various parts. But we rejoice in that which we know. Long long ago, one surface of matter learned to roll on a rolling motion across another surface, as the tide rolls up the land. And long ago man saw this motion, and learned a secret, and made the wheel, and rejoiced.

So, facing both ways, like Janus, face forward, in the quivering, glimmering fringe of the unresolved, facing the unknown, and looking backward over the vast rolling tract of life which follows and repeats the initial movement, man is given up to his dual business, of being, in blindness and wonder and pure godliness, the living stuff of life itself, unrevealed; and of knowing, with unwearying labour and unceasing success, the manner of that which has been, which is revealed.

And work is the repetition of some one of those re-discovered movements, the enacting of some part imitated from life, the attaining of a similar result as life attained. And this, even if it be only shovelling coal on to a fire, or hammering nails into a shoe-sole, or making accounts in ledgers, is what work is and in this lies the initial satisfaction of labour. The motive of labour, that of obtaining wages, is only the overcoming of inertia. It is not the real driving force. When necessity alone compels man, from moment to moment, to work, then man rebels and dies. The driving force is the pleasure in doing something, the living will to work.

And man must always struggle against the *necessity* to work, though the necessity to work is one of the inevitable conditions of man's existence. And no man can continue in any place of work, out of sheer necessity, devoid of any essential pleasure in that work.

It seems as if the great aim and purpose in human life were to bring all life into the human consciousness. And this is the final meaning of work: the extension of human consciousness. The lesser meaning of work is the achieving of self-preservation. From this lesser, immediate necessity man always struggles to be free. From the other, greater necessity, of extending the human consciousness, man does not struggle to be free.

And to the immediate necessity for self-preservation man must concede, but always having in mind the other, greater necessity, to which he would hasten.

But the bringing of life into human consciousness is not an aim in itself, it is only a necessary condition of the progress of life itself. Man is himself the vivid body of life, rolling glimmering against the void. In his fullest living he does not know what he does, his mind, his consciousness, unacquaint, hovers behind, full of extraneous gleams and glances, and altogether devoid of knowledge. Altogether devoid of knowledge and conscious motive is he when he is heaving into uncreated space, when he is actually living, becoming himself. And yet, that he may go on, may proceed with his living, it is necessary that his mind, his consciousness, should extend behind him. The mind itself is one of life's later developed habits. *To know* is a force, like any other force. Knowledge is only one of the conditions of this force, as combustion is one of the conditions of heat. *To will* is only a manifestation of the same force, as expansion may be a manifestation of heat. And this *knowing* is a now inevitable habit of life's developed late, it is a force active in the immediate rear of life, and the greater its activity, the greater the forward, unknown movement ahead of it.

It seems as though one of the conditions of life is, that life shall continually and progressively differentiate itself, almost as though this differentiation were a Purpose. Life starts crude and unspecified, a great Mass. And it proceeds to evolve out of that mass ever more distinct and definite particular forms, an ever-multiplying number of separate species and orders, as if it were working always to the production of the infinite number of perfect individuals, the individual so thorough that he should have nothing in common with any other individual. It is as if all coagulation must be loosened, as if the elements must work themselves free and pure from the compound.

Man's consciousness, that is, his mind, his knowing, is his grosser manifestation of individuality. With his consciousness he can perceive and know that which is not himself. The further he goes, the more extended his consciousness, the more he realises the things that are not himself. Everything he perceives, everything he knows, everything he feels, is something extraneous to him, is not himself, and his perception of it is like a cell wall, or more, a real space separating him. I see a flower, because it is not me. I know a melody, because it is not me. I feel cold, because it is not me. I feel joy when I kiss, because it is not me, the kiss, but rather one of the bounds or limits where I end. But the kiss is a closer division of me from the mass, than a sense of cold or heat. It whittles me the more keenly naked from the gross.

And the more that I am driven from admixture, the more I am singled out into utter individuality, the more this intrinsic me rejoices. For I am as yet a gross impurity, I partake of everything. I am still rudimentary, part of a great, unquickened lump.

In the origin life must have been uniform, a great unmoved, utterly homogeneous infinity, a great not-being, at once a positive and negative infinity: the whole universe, the whole infinity, one motionless homogeneity, a something, a nothing. And yet it can never have been utterly homogeneous: mathematically, yes; actually, no. There must always have been some reaction, infinitesimally faint, stirring somehow through the vast, homogeneous inertia.

And since the beginning, the reaction has become extended and intensified, what was one great mass of individual constituency has stirred and resolved itself into many smaller, characteristic parts, what was an utter, infinite neutrality has become evolved into still rudimentary, but positive, orders and species. So on and on till we get to naked jelly, and from naked jelly to enclosed and separated jelly, from homogeneous tissue to organic tissue, on and on, from invertebrates to mammals, from mammals to man, from man to tribesman, from tribesman to me: and on and on, till, in the future, wonderful, distinct individuals, like angels, move about, each one being himself, perfect as a complete melody or a pure colour.

How one craves that his life should be more individual, that I and you and my neighbour should each be distinct in clarity from each other, perfectly distinct from the general mass. Then it would be a melody if I walked down the road, if I stood with my neighbour it would be a pure harmony.

Could I then, being my perfect self, be selfish? A selfish person is an impure person, one who wants that which is not himself. Selfishness implies admixture, grossness, unclarity of being. How can I, a pure person incapable of being anything but myself, detract from my neighbour? That which is mine is singled out to me from the mass, and to each man is left his own. And what can any man want for, except that which is his own, if he be himself? If he have that which is not his own, it is a burden, he is not himself. And how can I help my neighbour, except by being utterly myself? That gives him into himself: which is the greatest gift a man can receive.

And necessarily accompanying this more perfect being of myself is the more extended knowledge of that which is not myself. That is, the finer, more distinct the individual, the more finely and distinctly is he aware of all other individuality. It needs a delicate, pure soul to distinguish between the souls of others, it needs a thing which is purely itself to see other things in their purity, or their impurity.

Yet in life, so often, one feels that a man who is, by nature, intrinsically an individual, is by practice and knowledge an impurity, almost a nonentity. To each individuality belongs, by nature, its own knowledge. It would seem as if each soul, detaching itself from the mass, the matrix, should achieve its own knowledge. Yet this is not so. Many a soul which we feel should have detached itself and become distinct, remains embedded, and struggles with knowledge that does not pertain to it. It reached a point of distinctness and a degree of personal knowledge, and then became confused, lost itself.

And then, it sought for its whole being in work. By re-enacting some old movement of life's, a struggling soul seeks to detach itself, to become pure. By gathering all the knowledge possible, it seems to receive the stimulus which shall help it to continue to distinguish itself.

"Ye must be born again," it is said to us. Once we are born, detached from the flesh and blood of our parents, issued separate, as distinct creatures. And later on, the incomplete germ which is a young soul must be fertilised, the parent womb which encloses the incomplete individuality must conceive, and we must be brought forth to ourselves, distinct. This is at the age of twenty or thirty.

And we, who imagine we live by knowledge, imagine that the impetus for our second birth must come from knowledge, that the germ, the sperm impulse, can come out of some utterance only. So, when I am young, at eighteen, twenty, twenty-three, when the anguish of desire comes upon me, as I lie in the womb of my times, to receive the quickening, the impetus, I send forth all my calls and call hither and thither, asking for the Word, the Word which is the spermatozoon which shall come and fertilise me and set me free. And it may be the word, the idea exists which shall bring me forth, give me birth. But it may also be that the word, the idea, has never yet been uttered.

Shall I then be able, with all the knowledge in the world, to produce my being, if the knowledge be not extant? I shall not.

And yet we believe that only the Uttered Word can come into us and give us the impetus to our second birth. Give us a religion, give us something to believe in, cries the unsatisfied soul embedded in the womb of our times. Speak the quickening word, it cries, that will deliver us into our own being.

So it searches out the Spoken Word, and finds it, or finds it not. Possibly it is not yet uttered. But all that will be uttered lies potent in life. The fools do not know this. They think the fruit of knowledge is found only in shops. They will go anywhere to find it, save to the Tree. For the Tree is so obvious, and seems so played out.

Therefore the unsatisfied soul remains unsatisfied, and chooses Work, maybe Good Works, for its incomplete action. It thinks that in work it has being, in knowledge it has gained its distinct self.

Whereas all amount of clumsy distinguishing ourselves from some other things will not make us thus become ourselves, and all amount of repeating even the most complex motions of life will not produce one new motion.

We start the wrong way round: thinking by learning what we are not, to know what we as individuals are: whereas the whole of the human consciousness contains, as we know, not a tithe of what *is,* and therefore it is hopeless to proceed by a method of elimination; and thinking, by discovering the motion life has made, to be able therefrom to produce the motion it will make: whereas we know that, in life, the new motion is not the resultant of the old, but something quite new, quite other, according to our perception.

So we struggle mechanically, unformed, unbegotten, unborn, repeating some old process of life, unable to become ourselves, unable to produce anything new.

Looking over the Hardy novels, it is interesting to see which of the heroes one would call a distinct individuality, more or less achieved, which an unaccomplished potential individuality, and which an impure, unindividualised life embedded in the matrix, either achieving its own lower degree of distinction, or not achieving it.

In *Desperate Remedies* there are scarcely any people at all, particularly when the plot is working. The tiresome part about Hardy is that, so often, he will neither write a morality-play nor a novel. The people of the first book, as far as the plot is concerned, are not people: they are the heroine, faultless and white; the hero, with a small spot on his whiteness; the villainess, red and black, but more red than black; the villain, black and red; the Murderer, aided by the Adulteress, obtains power over the Virgin, who, rescued at the last moment by the Virgin Knight, evades the evil clutch. Then the Murderer, overtaken by vengeance, is put to death, whilst Divine Justice descends upon the Adulteress. Then the Virgin unites with the Virgin Knight, and receives Divine Blessing.

That is a morality-play, and if the morality were vigorous and original, all well and good. But, between whiles, we see that the Virgin is being played by a nice, rather ordinary girl.

In *A Laodicean*, there is all the way through a "predilection d'artiste" for the aristocrat, and all the way through a moral condemnation of him, a substituting the middle or lower class personage with bourgeois virtues into his place. This was the root of Hardy's pessimism. Not until he comes to Tess and Jude does he ever sympathise with the aristocrat—unless it be in *The Mayor of Casterbridge*, and then he sympathises only to slay. He always presents them the same, as having some vital weakness, some radical ineffectuality. From first to last it is the same.

Miss Aldclyffe and Manston, Elfride and the sickly lord she married, Troy and Farmer Boldwood, Eustacia Vye and Wildeve, de Stancy in *A Laodicean*, Lady Constantine in *Two on a Tower*, the Mayor of Casterbridge and Lucetta, Mrs Charmond and Dr Fitzpiers in *The Woodlanders*, Tess and Alec d'Urberville, and Jude, they are all in the same spirit. There is the dark, passionate, arrogant lady,

Miss Aldclyffe, Eustacia, Lucetta, Mrs Charmond, all of them essentially aristocratic, or at least, wealthy. There is the fair, passionate, submissive lady, always of blue blood: Elfride, Lady Constantine, Tess. There is the dark, passionate, arrogant man: Manston, Farmer Boldwood, de Stancy, the Mayor of Casterbridge, Dr Fitzpiers, Alec d'Urberville, and, though different, Jude. There is also the blond, passionate, yielding man: Sergeant Troy, Wildeve, and, in spirit, Jude.

These are all, in their way, the aristocrat-characters of Hardy. They must every one die, every single one.

Why has Hardy this *prédilection d'artiste* for the aristocrat, and why, at the same time, this moral antagonism to him?

It is fairly obvious in *A Laodicean,* a book where, the spirit being small, the complaint is narrow. The heroine, the daughter of a famous railway engineer, lives in the castle of the old de Stancys. She sighs, wishing she were of the de Stancy line: the tombs and portraits have a spell over her. "But," says the hero to her, "have you forgotten your father's line of ancestry: Archimedes, Newcomen, Watt, Telford, Stephenson?"—"But I have a predilection d'artiste for ancestors of the other sort," sighs Paula. And the hero despairs of impressing her with the list of his architect ancestors: Pheidias, Ictinus and Callicrates, Chersiphron, Vitruvius, Wilars of Cambray, William of Wykeham. He deplores her marked preference for an "animal pedigree".

But what is this "animal pedigree"? If a family pedigree of her ancestors, working men and burghers, had been kept, Paula would not have gloried in it, animal though it were. Hers was a prédilection d'artiste.

And this because the aristocrat alone has occupied a position where he could afford to *be,* to be himself, to create himself, to live as himself. That is his eternal fascination. This is why the preference for him is a prédilection d'artiste. The preference for the architect line would be a prédilection de savant, the preference for the engineer pedigree would be a prédilection d'economiste.

The prédilection d'artiste—Hardy has it strongly, and it is rooted deeply in every imaginative human being. The glory of mankind has been to produce lives, to produce vivid, independent, individual men, not buildings or engineering works or even art, nor even the public good. The glory of mankind is not in a host of secure, comfortable, law abiding citizens, but in the few or more fine, clear lives, beings, individuals, distinct, detached, single as may be from the public.

And these the artist of all time has chosen. Why then, must the aristocrat always be condemned to death, in Hardy? Has the community come to consciousness in him, as in the French Revolutionaries, determined to destroy all that is not the average? Certainly in the Wessex novels, all but the average people die. But why? Is there the germ of death in these more single, distinguished people, or has the artist himself a bourgeois taint, a jealous vindictiveness that will now take revenge, now that the community, the average, has gained power over the aristocrat, the exception?

It is evident that both is true. Starting with the bourgeois morality, Hardy makes every exceptional person a villain, all exceptional or strong individual traits he holds up as weaknesses or wicked faults. So in *Desperate Remedies, Under the Greenwood Tree, Far from the Madding Crowd, The Hand of Ethelberta, The Return of the Native,* (but in *The Trumpet-Major* there is an ironical dig in the ribs to this civic, communal morality), *A Laodicean, Two on a Tower, The Mayor of*

Casterbridge, and *Tess,* in steadily weakening degree. The blackest villain is Manston, the next, perhaps, Troy, the next Eustacia and Wildeve, always becoming less villainous and more human. The first show of real sympathy, nearly conquering the bourgeois or communal morality is for Eustacia whilst the dark villain is becoming merely a weak, pitiable person in Dr Fitzpiers, duly condemned, Alec d'Urberville is not unlikeable, and Jude is a complete tragic hero, at once the old Virgin Knight and Dark Villain. The condemnation gradually shifts over from the dark villain to the blond bourgeois virgin hero, from Alec d'Urberville to Angel Clare, till in Jude they are united and loved, though the preponderance is of dark villain, now dark, beloved, passionate hero. The condemnation shifts over at last from the dark villainess to the white virgin, the bourgeois in soul: from Arabella to Sue. Infinitely more subtle and sad is the condemnation at the end, but there it is: the virgin knight is hated with intensity, yet still loved; the white virgin, the beloved, is the arch-sinner against life at last, and the last note of hatred is against her.

It is a complete and devastating shift over, it is a complete volte-face of moralities. Black does not become white, but it takes white's place as good; white remains white, but it is found bad. The old, communal morality is like a leprosy, a white sickness: the old, anti-social individualist morality is alone on the side of life and health.

But yet, the aristocrat must die, all the way through: even Jude. *Was* the germ of death in him at the start? Or was he merely at outs with his times, the times of the Average in triumph? Would Manston, Troy, Farmer Boldwood, Eustacia, de Stancy, Henchard, Alec d'Urberville, Jude, have been real heroes in heroic times, without tragedy. It seems as if Manston, Boldwood, Eustacia, Henchard, Alec d'Urberville, and almost Jude, might have been. In an heroic age they might have lived and more or less triumphed. But Troy, Wildeve, de Stancy, Fitzpiers, and Jude have something fatal in them. There is a rottenness at the core of them. The failure, the misfortune, or the tragedy, whichever it may be, was inherent in them: as it was in Elfride, Lady Constantine, Marty South in *The Woodlanders,* and Tess. They have all passionate natures, and in them all failure is inherent.

So that we have, of men, the noble Lord in *A Pair of Blue Eyes,* Sergeant Troy, Wildeve, de Stancy, Fitzpiers, and Jude, all passionate, aristocratic males, doomed by their very being, to tragedy, or to misfortune in the end.

Of the same class among women are: Elfride, Lady Constantine, Marty South, and Tess, all aristocratic, passionate, yet necessarily unfortunate females.

We have also, of men, Manston, Farmer Boldwood, Henchard, Alec d'Urberville, and perhaps Jude, all passionate, aristocratic males, who fell before the weight of the average, the lawful crowd, but who, in more primitive times, would have formed romantic rather than tragic figures.

Of women in the same class are Miss Aldclyffe, Eustacia, Lucetta, Mrs Charmond.

The third class, of bourgeois or average hero, whose purpose is to live and have his being in the community, contains the successful hero of *Desperate Remedies,* the unsuccessful but not very much injured two heroes of *A Pair of Blue Eyes,* the successful Gabriel Oak, the unsuccessful, left-preaching Clym, the unsuccessful but not very much injured astronomer of *Two on a Tower,* the successful Scotchman of Casterbridge, the unsuccessful and expired Giles

Winterborne of *The Woodlanders,* the arch-type, Angel Clare, and perhaps a little of Jude.

The companion women to these men are, the heroine of *Desperate Remedies,* Bathsheba, Thomasin, Paula, Henchard's daughter, Grace in *The Woodlanders,* and Sue.

This, then, is the moral conclusion drawn from the novels:

1.   The physical individualist is in the end an inferior thing which must fall before the community: Manston, Henchard etc.

2.   The physical and spiritual individualist is a fine thing which must fall because of its own isolation, because it is a sport, not in the true line of life: Jude, Tess, Lady Constantine.

3.   The physical individualist and spiritual bourgeois or communist is a thing, finally, of ugly, undeveloped, non-distinguished or perverted physical instinct, and must fall physically: Sue, Angel Clare, Clym, Knight. It remains, however, fitted into the community.

4.   The undistinguished, bourgeois or average being with average or civic virtues usually succeeds in the end. If he fails, he is left practically uninjured. If he expire during probation, he has flowers on his grave.

By individualist is meant, not a selfish or greedy person anxious to satisfy appetites, but a man of distinct being, who must act in his own particular way to fulfil his own individual nature. He is a man who, being beyond the average, chooses to rule his own life to his own completion, and as such is an aristocrat.

The artist always has a predilection for him. But Hardy, like Tolstoi, is forced in the issue always to stand with the community in condemnation of the aristocrat. He cannot help himself, but must stand with the average against the exception, he must, in his ultimate judgement represent the interests of humanity, or the community as a whole, and rule out the individual interest.

To do this, however, he must go against himself. His private sympathy is always with the individual, against the community: as is the case with every artist. Therefore he will create a more or less blameless individual and, making him seek his own fulfilment, his highest aim, will show him destroyed by the community, or by that in himself which represents the community, or by some close embodiment of the civic idea. Hence the pessimism. To do this, however, he must select his individual with a definite weakness, a certain coldness of temper, inelastic, a certain inevitable and inconquerable adhesion to the community.

This is obvious in Troy, Clym, Tess, and Jude. They have naturally distinct individuality, but, as it were, a weak life-flow, so that they cannot break away from the old adhesion, they cannot separate themselves from the mass which bore them, they cannot detach themselves from the common. Therefore they are pathetic rather than tragic figures. They have not the necessary strength: the question of their unfortunate end is begged in the beginning.

Whereas Oedipus or Agamemnon or Clytemnestra or Orestes, or Macbeth or Hamlet or Lear, these, are destroyed by their own conflicting passions. Out of greed for adventure, a desire to be off, Agamemnon sacrifices Iphigenia: moreover he has his love-affairs outside Troy: and this brings on him death from the mother of his daughter, and from his pledged wife. Which is the working of the natural law. Hamlet, a later Orestes, is commanded by the Erinyes of his father to kill his mother and his uncle: but his maternal filial feeling tears him. It is almost the same tragedy as Orestes, without any Goddess or God to grant peace.

In these plays, conventional morality is transcended. The action is between the great, single, individual forces in the nature of Man, not between the dictates of the community and the original passion. The Commandment says: "Thou shalt not kill. But doubtless Macbeth had killed many a man who was in his way. Certainly Hamlet suffered no qualms about killing the old man behind the curtain. Why should he. But when Macbeth killed Duncan, he divided himself in twain, into two hostile parts. It was all in his own soul and blood: it was   nothing   outside himself: as it was, really, with Clym, Troy, Tess, Jude. Troy would probably have been faithful to his little unfortunate person, had she been a lady, and had he not felt himself cut off from society in his very being, whilst all the time he cleaved to it. Tess allowed herself to be condemned, and asked for punishment from Angel Clare. Why?—She had done nothing particularly, or at least irrevocably unnatural, were her life young and strong. But she sided with the community's condemnation of her. And almost the bitterest, most pathetic, deepest part of Jude's misfortune was his failure to obtain admission to Oxford, his failure to gain his place and standing in the world's knowledge, in the world's work.

There is a lack of sternness, there is a hesitating betwixt life and public opinion, which diminishes the Wessex novels from the rank of pure tragedy. It is not so much the eternal, immutable laws of being which are transgressed, it is not that vital life-forces are set in conflict with each other, bringing almost inevitable tragedy—yet not necessarily death, as we see in the most splendid Aeschylus. It is, in Wessex, that the individual succumbs to what is in its shallowest, public opinion, in its deepest, the human compact by which we live together, to form a community.

CHAPTER VI.

The Axle and the Wheel of Eternity.

It is agreed, then, that we will do a little work—two or three hours a day—labouring for the community, to produce the ample necessities of life. Then we will be free.

Free for what? The terror of the ordinary man is lest leisure should come upon him. His eternal, divine instinct is to free himself from the labour of providing what we call the necessities of life, in the common sense. And his personal horror is of finding himself with nothing to do.

What does a flower do? It provides itself with the necessities of life, it propagates itself in its seeds, and it has its fling all in one. Out from the crest and summit comes the fiery self, the flower, gorgeously.

This is the fall into the future, like a waterfall that tumbles over the edge of the known world into the unknown. The little, individualized river of life issues out of its source, its little seed, its well-head, flows on and on, making its course as it goes, establishing a bed of green tissue and stalks, flows on and draws near the edge where all things disappear. Then the stream divides. Part hangs back, recovers itself, and lies quiescent, in seed. The rest flows over, the red dips into the unknown, and is gone.

The same with man. He has to build his own tissue and form, serving the community for the means wherewithal, and then he comes to the climax. And at the climax, simultaneously, he begins to roll to the edge of the unknown, and in the same moment, lays down his seed for security's sake. That is the secret of love: it contains the lesser motions in the greater. In love, a man, a woman, flows on, to the very furthest edge of known feeling, being, and out beyond the furthest edge: and taking the superb and supreme risk, deposits a security of life in the womb.

Am I here to deposit security, continuance of life in the flesh? Or is that only a minor function in me? Is it not merely a preservative measure, procreation. It is the same for me as for any man or woman. That she bear children is not a woman's significance. But that she bear herself, that is her supreme and risky fate: that she drive on to the edge of the unknown, and beyond. She may leave children behind, for security. It is arranged so.

It is so arranged that the very act which carries us out into the unknown, shall probably deposit seed for security to be left behind. But the act, called the sexual act, is not for the depositing of seed. It is for leaping off into the unknown, as from a cliff's edge, like Sappho into the sea.

It is so plain in my plant, my poppy. Out of the living river, a fine silver stream detaches itself, and flows through a green bed which it makes for itself. It flows on and on, till it reaches the crest beyond which is ethereal space. Then, in tiny, concentrated pools, a little hangs back, in reservoirs that shall later seal themselves up as quick but silent sources. But the whole, almost the whole, splashes splendidly over, is seen in red just as it dips into darkness and disappears.

So with a man in the act of love. A little of him, a very little, flows into the tiny quick pool to start another source. But the whole spills over in waste to the beyond.

And only at high flood should the little hollows fill to make a new source. Only when the whole rises to pour in a great wave over the edge of all that has been, should the little seed-wells run full. In the woman lie the reservoirs. And when there comes the flood-tide, then the dual stream of woman and man, as the whole two waves meet and break to foam, bursting into the unknown, these wells and fountain heads are filled.

Thus man and woman pass beyond this Has-been and this is when the two waves meet in flood and heave over and out of Time, leaving their dole to Time deposited. It is for this man needs liberty, and to prepare him for this he must use his leisure.

Always so that the wave of his being shall meet the other wave, that the two shall make flood which shall flow beyond the face of the earth, must a man live. Always the dual wave. Where does my poppy spill over in red, but there where the two streams have flowed and clashed together, where the pollen stream clashes into the pistil stream, where the male clashes into the female, and the two heave out in utterance. There, in the seethe of male and female, seeds are filled as the flood rises to pour out in a red fall. There, only there where the male seethes against the female, comes the transcendent flame and the filling of seeds.

In plants where the male stream and the female stream flow separately, as in dogs-mercury or in the oak-tree, where is the flame? It is not. But in my poppy, where at the summit the two streams, which till now have run deviously, scattered down many ways, at length flow concentrated together, and the pure male stream meets the pure female stream in a heave and an overflowing, there there is the flower indeed.

And this is happiness: that my poppy gather his material and build his tissue till he has led the stream of life in him on and on to the end, to the whirlpool at the summit, where the male seethes and whirls in incredible speed upon the pivot of the female, where the two are one, as axle and wheel are one, and the motion travels out to infinity. There, where he is a complete full stream, travelling with and upon the other complete female stream, the twain make a flood over the face of all the earth, which shall pass away from the earth.

And since I am a man with a body of flesh, I shall contain the need to make sure this continuing of life in this body of flesh, I shall contain the need for the woman of flesh in whom to beget my children.

But this is an incorporate need: it is really no separate or distinct need. The clear, full inevitable need in me is that I, the male, meet the female stream which shall carry mine so that the two run to fullest flood, to furthest motion. It is no primary need of the begetting of children. It is the arriving at my highest mark of activity, of being; it is her arrival at her intensest self.

Why do we consider the male stream, and the female stream, as being only in the flesh: it is something other than physical. The physical, what we call in its narrowest meaning, the sex, is only a definite indication of the great male and female duality and unity. It is that part which is settled into an almost mechanised system of detaining some of the life which otherwise sweeps on and is lost in the full adventure.

There is female apart from Woman, as we know, and male apart from Man. There is male and female in my poppy plant, and this is neither man nor woman. It is part of the great twin river, eternally each branch resistant to the other, eternally running each to meet the other.

It may be said that male and female are terms relative only to physical sex. But this is the consistent indication of the greater meaning. Do we for a moment believe that a man is a man and a woman a woman, merely according to, and for the purpose of, the begetting of children? If there were organic reproduction of children, would there be no distinction between man and woman? Should we all be asexual?

We know that our view is partial. Man is man, and woman is woman, whether no children be born any more for ever. As long as time lasts, man is man. In eternity, where infinite motion becomes rest, the two may be one. But until eternity man is man. Until eternity, there shall be this separateness, this interaction of man upon woman, male upon female, this suffering, this delight, this imperfection. In eternity, maybe, the action may be perfect. In infinity, the spinning of the wheel upon the hub may be a frictionless whole, complete, an unbroken sleep that is infinite, motion that is utter rest, a duality that is sheerly one.

But except in infinity, everything of life is male or female, distinct. But the consciousness, that is of both: and the flower, that is of both. Every impulse that stirs in life, every single impulse, is either male or female, distinct, except the being of the complete flower, of the completed consciousness, which is two in one, fused. These are infinite and eternal. The consciousness, what we call the truth, is eternal, beyond change or motion, beyond time or limit.

But that which is not conscious, which is Time, and Life, that is our field.

CHAPTER VII.

Of Being and Not-Being

In life, then, no new thing has ever arisen, or can arise, save out of the impulse of the male upon the female, the female upon the male. The interaction of the male and female spirit begot the wheel, the plough, and the first utterance that was made on the face of the earth.

As in my flower, the pistil, female, is the centre and swivel, the stamens, male, are close clasping the hub, and the blossom is the great motion outwards into the unknown, so in a man's life, the female is the swivel and centre on which he turns closely, producing his movement. And the female to a man is the obvious form, a woman. And normally, the centre, the turning pivot of a man's life is his sex life, the centre and swivel of his being in the sexual act. Upon this turns the whole rest of his life, from this emanates every motion he betrays. And that this should be so, every man makes his effort. The supreme effort each man makes, for himself, is the effort to clasp as a hub the woman who shall be the axle, compelling him to true motion, without aberration. The supreme desire of every man is for mating with a woman, such that the sexual act be the closest, most concentrated motion in his life, closest upon the axle, the prime movement of himself, of which all the rest of his motion is a continuance in the same kind. And the vital desire of every woman is that she shall be clasped as axle to the hub of the man, that his motion shall portray her motionlessness, convey her static being into movement, complete and radiating out into infinity, starting from her stable eternality, and reaching eternity again, after having covered the whole of time.

This is complete movement: man upon woman, woman within man. This is the desire, the achieving of which, frictionless, is impossible, yet for which every man will try, with greater or less intensity, achieving more or less success.

This is the desire of every man, that his movement, the manner of his walk, and the supremest effort of his mind, shall be the pulsation outwards from stimulus received in the sex, in the sexual act, that the woman of his body shall be the begetter of his whole life, that she, in her female spirit, shall beget in him his idea, his motion, himself. When a man shall look at the work of his hands, that has succeeded, and shall know that it was begotten in him by the woman of his body, then he shall know what fundamental happiness is. Just as when a woman shall look at her child, that was begotten in her by the man of her spirit, she shall know what it is to be happy, fundamentally. But when a woman looks at her children that were begotten in her by a strange man, not the man of her spirit, she must know what it is to be happy with anguish, and to love with pain. So with a man who looks at his work which was not begotten in him by the woman of his body. He rejoices, trembles, and suffers an agony like death which contains resurrection.

For while, ideally, the soul of the woman possesses the soul of the man, procreates it and makes it big with new idea, motion, in the sexual act, yet, most commonly, it is not so. Usually, sex is only functional, a matter of relief or sensation, equivalent to eating or drinking or passing of excrement.

Then, if a man must produce work, he must produce it to some other than the woman of his body: as, in the same case, if a woman produce children, it must be to some other than the man of her desire.

In this case, a man must seek elsewhere than in woman for the female to possess his soul, to fertilise him and make him big with increase. And the female exists in much more than his woman. And the finding of it for himself gives a man his vision of God.

And since no man and no woman can get a perfect mate, nor obtain complete satisfaction at all times, each man according to his need must have a God, an idea, that shall compel him to the movement of his own being. And then, when he lies with his woman, the man may concurrently be with God, and so get increase of his soul. Or he may have communion with his God apart and averse from the woman.

Every man seeks in woman, for that which is stable, eternal. And if, under his motion, this break down in her, in the particular woman, so that she be no axle for his hub, but be driven away from herself, then he must seek elsewhere for his stability, for the centre to himself.

Then either he must seek another woman, or he must seek to make conscious his desire to find a symbol, to create and define in his consciousness the object of his desire, so that he may have it at will, for his own complete satisfaction.

In doing this latter, he seeks with his desire the female elsewhere than in the particular woman. Since everything that is, is either male or female or both, whether it be clouds or sunshine or hills or trees or a fallen feather from a bird, therefore in other things and in such things man seeks for his complement. And he must at last always call God the unutterable and the inexpressible, the unknowable, because it is his unrealised complement.

But all Gods have some attributes in common. They are the unexpressed Absolute: eternal, infinite, unchanging. Eternal, Infinite, Unchanging: the High God of all Humanity is this.

Yet man, the male, is essentially a thing of movement and time and change. Until he is stirred into thought, he is complete in movement and change. But once he thinks, he must have the Absolute, the Eternal, Infinite, Unchanging.

And man is stirred into thought by dissatisfaction, or unsatisfaction, as heat is born of friction. Consciousness is the same effort in male and female to obtain perfect frictionless interaction, perfect as Nirvana. It is the reflex both of male and female from defect in their dual motion. Being reflex from the dual motion, consciousness contains the two in one, and is therefore in itself Absolute.

And desire is the admitting of deficiency. And the embodiment of the object of desire reveals the original defect or the defaulture. So that the attributes of God will reveal that which man lacked and yearned for in his living. And these attributes are always, in their essence, Eternality, Infinity, Immutability.

And these are the qualities man feels in a woman, as a principle. Let a man walk alone on the face of the earth, and he feels himself like a loose speck blown at random. Let him have a woman to whom he belongs, and he will feel as though he had a wall to back up against, even though the woman be mentally a fool. No man can endure the sense of space, of chaos, on four sides of him. It drives him mad. He must be able to put his back to the wall. And this wall is his woman.

From her he has a sense of stability. She supplies him with the feeling of Immutability, Permanence, Eternality. He himself is a raging activity, change potent within change. He dare not even conceive of himself save when his is sure of the woman permanent beneath him, beside him. He dare not leap into the unknown save from the sure stability of the unyielding female. Like a wheel, if he turn without an axle, his motion is wandering neutrality.

So always the fear of a ma is that he shall find no axle for his motion, that no woman can centralise his activity. And always, the fear of a woman is that she can find no hub for her stability, no man to convey into motion her full stability. Either the particular woman breaks down before the stress of the man, becomes erratic herself, no stay, no centre, or else the man is insufficiently active to carry out the static principle of his female, of his woman.

So life consists in the dual form of the Will-to-Motion and the Will-to-Inertia, and everything we see and know and are is the resultant of these two Wills. But the One Will, of which they are dual forms, that is as yet unthinkable.

And according as the Will-to-Motion predominates in a race, or the Will-to-Inertia, so must that race's conception of the One Will enlarge the attributes which are lacking or deficient in the race.

Since there is never to he found a perfect balance or accord of the two Wills, but always one triumphs over the other, in life, according to our knowledge, so must the human effort be always to recover balance, to symbolise and so to possess that which is missing. Which is the religious effort of Man.

There seems to be a fundamental, insuperable division, difference, between man's artistic effort and his religious effort. The two efforts are mixed with each other, as they are revealed, but all the while they remain two, not one, all the while they are separate, single, never compounded.

The religious effort is to conceive, to symbolise that which the human soul, or the soul of the race, lacks, that which it is not, and which it requires, yearns for. It is the portrayal of that complement to the race-life which is known only as a desire: it is the symbolising of a great desire, the statement of the desire in terms which have no meaning apart from the desire.

Whereas the artistic effort is the effort of utterance, the supreme effort of expressing knowledge, that which has been for once, that which was enacted, where the two wills met and interacted and left their result, complete for the moment. The artistic effort is the portraying of a moment of union between the two wills, according to knowledge. The religious effort is the portrayal or symbolising of the eternal union of the two wills, according to aspiration. But in this eternal union, the features of one or the other Will are always salient.

The dual Will we call the Will-to-Motion and the Will-to-Inertia. These cause the whole of life, from the ebb and flow of a wave, to the stable equilibrium of the whole universe, from birth and being and knowledge to death and decay and forgetfulness. And the Will-to-Motion we call the male will or spirit, the Will-to-Inertia the female. This will to inertia is not negative, and the other positive. Rather, according to some conception, is Motion negative and Inertia, the static, geometric idea, positive. That is according to the point of view.

According to the race-conception of God, we can see whether in that race the male or the female element triumphs, becomes predominant.

But is must first be seen that the division into male and female is arbitrary, for the purpose of thought. The rapid motion of the rim of a wheel is the same as the perfect rest at the centre of the wheel. How can one divide them? Motion and rest are the same, when seen completely. Motion is only true of things outside oneself. When I am in a moving train, strictly, the land moves under me, I and the train are still. If I were both land and train, if I were small enough, there would be no motion. And if I were very very small, every fibre of the train would be in motion for me, the point of rest would be infinitely reduced.

How can one say, there is motion and rest? If all things move together in one infinite motion, that is rest. Rest and motion are only two degrees of motion, or two degrees of rest. Infinite motion and infinite rest are the same thing. It is obvious. Since, if motion were infinite, there would be no standing ground from which to regard it as motion. And the same with rest.

It is easier to conceive that there is no such thing as rest. For a thing to us at rest is only a thing travelling at our own rate of motion: or, from another point of view, it is a thing moving at the lowest rate of motion we can recognise. But this table on which I write, which I call at rest, I know is really in motion.

So there is no such thing as rest. There is only infinite motion. But infinite motion must contain every degree of rest. So that motion and rest are the same thing. Rest is the lowest speed of motion which I recognise under normal conditions.

So how can one speak of a Will-to-Motion or a Will-to-Inertia when there is no such thing as rest or motion. And yet starting from any given degree of motion, and travelling forward in ever-increasing degree, one comes to a state of speed which covers the whole of space instantaneously, and is therefore rest, utter rest. And starting from the same speed and reducing the motion infinitely, one reaches the same condition of utter rest. And the direction or method of approach to this infinite rest is different to our conception. And only travelling upon the slower, does the swifter reach the infinite rest of speed. And only by travelling upon the swifter does the slower reach the infinite rest of inertia: which is the same as the infinite rest of speed, the two things having united to surpass our comprehension.

So we may speak of Male and Female, of the Will-to-Motion and of the Will-to-Inertia. And so, looking at a race, we can say whether the Will-to-Inertia or the Will-to-Motion has gained the ascendancy, and in which direction this race tends to disappear.

For it is as if life were a double cycle, of men and of women, facing opposite ways, travelling opposite ways, revolving upon each other, man reaching forward with outstretched hand, woman reaching forward with outstretched hand, and neither able to move till their hands have grasped each other, when they draw towards each other from opposite directions, draw nearer and nearer, each travelling in his separate cycle, till the two are abreast, and side by side, until they pass on again, away from each other, travelling their opposite ways to the same infinite goal.

Each travelling to the same goal of infinity, but entering it from the opposite ends of space. And man, remembering what lies behind him, how the hands met and grasped and tore apart, utters his tragic art. Then moreover, facing the other way into the unknown, conscious of the tug of the goal at his heart, he hails the woman coming from the place whither he is travelling, searches in her for signs, and makes his God from the suggestion he receives, as she advances.

Then she draws near, and he is full of delight. She is so close, that they touch, and then there is a joyful utterance of religious art. They are torn apart, and he gives the cry of tragedy, and goes on remembering, till the dance slows down and breaks, and there is only a crowd.

It is as if this cycle dance where the female makes the chain with the male became ever wider, ever more extended, and the further they get from the source, from the infinity, the more distinct and individual do the dancers become. At first they are only figures. In the Jewish cycle, David, with his hand stretched forth, cannot recognise the woman, the female. He can only recognise some likeness of himself. For both he and she have not danced very far from the source and origin where they were both one. Though she is in the gross utterly other than he, yet she is not very distinct from him. And he hails her Father, Almighty, God, Beloved, Strength, hails her in his own image. And with hand outstretched, fearful and passionate, he reaches to her. But it is Solomon who touches her hand, with rapture and joy, and cries out his gladness in the Song of Songs. Who is the Shulamite, but God come close, for a moment into physical contact? The Song may be a drama: it is still religious art. It is the development of the Psalms. It is utterly different from the Book of Job, which is remembrance.

Always the threefold utterance: the declaring of the God seen approaching, the rapture of contact, the anguished joy of remembrance, when the meeting has passed into separation. Such is religion, religious art, and tragic art.

But the chain is not broken by the letting-go of hands. It is broken by the overbearing of one cycle by the other. David, when he lay with a woman, lay also with God. Solomon, when he lay with a woman, knew God and possessed him and was possessed by him. For in Solomon and in the Woman, the male clasped hands with the female.

But in the terrible moment, when they should break free again, the male in the Jew was too weak, the female overbore him. He remained in the grip of the female. The force of inertia overpowered him, and he remained remembering. But very true had been David's vision, and very real Solomon's contact. So that the living thing was conserved, kept always alive and powerful, but restrained, restricted, partial.

For centuries, the Jew knew God as David had perceived him, as Solomon had known him. It was the God of the body, the rudimentary God of physical laws and physical functions. The Jew lived on in physical contact with God. Each of his physical functions he shared with God, he kept his body always like the body of a bride ready to serve the bridegroom. He had become the servant of his God, the female, passive. The female in him predominated, held him passive; set utter bounds to his movement, to his roving, kept his mind as a slave to guard intact the state of sensation wherein he found himself. Which persisted century after century, the secret, scrupulous voluptuousness of the Jew, become almost self-voluptuousness, engaged in the consciousness of his own physique, or in the extracted existence of his own physique. His own physique included the woman, naturally, since the man's body included the woman's, the woman's the man's. His religion had become a physical morality, deep and fundamental, but entirely of one sort. Its living element was this scrupulous physical voluptuousness, wonderful and satisfying in a large measure.

Its conscious element was a resistance to the male or active principle. Being female, occupied in self-feeling, in realisation of the ego, in submission to sensation, the Jewish temper was antagonistic to the active male principle, which would deny the ego and refuse sensation, seeking ever to make transformation, desiring to be an instrument of change, to register relationships. So this race recognised only male sins: it conceived only sins of commission, sins of change, of transformation. In the whole of the ten commandments, it is the female who speaks. It is natural to the male to make the male God a God of benevolence and mercy, susceptible to pity. Such is the male conception of God. It was the female spirit which conceived the saying: "For I, the Lord thy God, am a jealous God, visiting the iniquities of the fathers upon the children unto the third and fourth generation of them that hate me, and showing mercy unto thousands of them that love me."

It was a female conception. For is not man the child of woman. Does she not see in him her body, even more vividly than in her own. Man is more her body to her, even than her own body. For the whole of flesh is hers. Woman knows that she is the fountain of all flesh. And her pride is that the body of man is of her issue. She can see the man as the One Being, for she knows he is of her issue.

It were a male conception to see God with a manifold Being, even though he be One God. For man is ever keenly aware of the multiplicity of things, and their diversity. But woman issuing from the other end of infinity, coming forth as the flesh, manifest in sensation, is obsessed by the one-ness of things, the One Being, undifferentiated. Man, on the other hand, coming forth as the desire to single out one thing from another, to reduce each thing to its intrinsic self by process of elimination, cannot but be possessed by the infinite diversity and contrariety in life, by a passionate sense of isolation, and a poignant yearning to be at one.

That is the fundamental of female conception: that there is but One Being: this Being necessarily female. Whereas man conceives a manifold Being, the supreme of which is male. And owing to the complete Monism of the female, which is essentially static, self-sufficient, the expression of God has been left always to the male, so that the supreme God is forever He.

Nevertheless, in the God of the Ancient Jew, the female has triumphed. That which was born of Woman, that is indeed the God of the Old Testament. So utterly is he born of Woman, that he scarcely needs to consider Woman: she is there unuttered.

And the Jewish race continued in this Monism, stable, circumscribed, utterly unadventurous, utterly self-preservative, yet very deeply living, until the present century.

But Christ rose from the suppressed male spirit of Judea, and uttered a new commandment: thou shalt love thy neighbour as thyself. He repudiated woman: "Who is my mother?" He lived the male life utterly apart from woman.

"Thou shalt love thy neighbour as thyself"—that is the great utterance against Monism, and the compromise with Monism. It does not say "Thou shalt love thy neighbour because he is thyself", as the ancient Jew would have said. It commands "Thou shalt recognise thy neighbour's distinction from thyself, and allow his separate being, because he also is of God, even though he be almost a contradiction to thyself."

Such is the cry of anguish of Christianity: that man is separate from his brother, separate, maybe even, in his measure, inimical to him. This the Jew had to learn. The old Jewish creed of identity, that Eve was identical with Adam, and all men children of one single parent, and therefore, in the absolute, identical, this must be destroyed.

Cunning and according to female suggestion is the story of the Creation: that Eve was born from the single body of Adam, without intervention of sex, both issuing from one flesh, as a child at birth seems to issue from one flesh of its mother. And the birth of Jesus is the retaliation of this: a child is born, not to the flesh, but to the spirit: and you, woman, shall conceive, not to the body but to the Word. "In the beginning was the Word," says the New Testament.

The great assertion of the Male, was the New Testament, and, in its beauty, the Union of Male and Female. Christ was born of Woman, begotten by the Holy Spirit. This was why Christ should be called the Son of Man. For he was born of Woman. He was born to the Spirit, the Word, the Man, the Male.

And the assertion entailed the sacrifice of the Son of Woman. The body of Christ must be destroyed, that of him which was Woman must be put to death, to testify that he was Spirit, that he was Male, that he was Man, without any womanly part.

So the other great camp was made. In the creation, Man was driven forth from Paradise to labour for his body and for the woman. All was lost for the knowledge of the flesh. Out of the innocence and Nirvana of Paradise came, with the Fall, the consciousness of the flesh, the body of man and woman came into very being.

This was the first great movement of Man: the movement into the conscious possession of a body. And this consciousness of the body came through woman. And this knowledge, this possession, this enjoyment, was jealously guarded. In spite of all criticism and attack, Job remained true to this knowledge, to the utter belief in his body, in the God of his body. Though the Woman herself turned tempter, he remained true to it.

The senses, sensation, sensuousness, these things which are incontrovertibly Me, these are my God, these belong to God, said Job. And he persisted and he was right. They issue from God on the female side.

But Christ came with his contradiction: that which is Not-Me, that is God. All is God, except that which I know immediately as Myself. First I must lose Myself, then I find God. You must be born again.

Unto what must man be born again? Unto knowledge of his own separate existence, as in Woman he is conscious of his own incorporate existence. Man must be born unto knowledge of his own distinct identity, as in woman he was born to knowledge of his identification with the Whole. Man must be born to the knowledge, that in the whole being he is nothing, as he was born to know that in the whole being he was all. He must be born to the knowledge that other things exist beside himself, and utterly apart from all, and before he can exist himself as a separate identity, he must allow and recognise their distinct existence. Whereas previously, on the more female Jewish side, it had been said: "All that exists, is as Me. We are all one family, out of one God, having one being."

With Christ ended the Monism of the Jew. God, the One God, became a Trinity, three-fold. He was the Father, the All-containing; he was the Son, the Word, the Changer, the Separator, and he was the Spirit, the Comforter, the Reconciliator between the Two.

And according to its conditions, Christianity has, since Christ, worshipped the Father or the Son, the one more than the other. Out of an over-female race came the male utterance of Christ. Throughout Europe, the suppressed, inadequate male desire, both in men and women, stretched to the idea of Christ, as a woman should stretch her hands out to a man. But Greece, in whom the female was overriden and neglected, became silent. So through the Middle Ages went on in Europe this fight against the body, against the senses, against this continual triumph of the senses. The worship of Europe, predominantly female, all through the mediaeval period was to the male, to the incorporeal Christ, as a bridegroom, whilst the art produced was the collective, stupendous emotional gesture of the Cathedrals, where a blind, collective impulse rose into concrete form. It was the profound, sensuous desire and gratitude which produced an art of architecture, whose essence is in utter stability, of movement resolved and centralised, of absolute movement, that has no relationship with any other form, that admits the existence of no other form, but is conclusive, propounding in its sum, the One Being of All.

There was, however, in the Cathedrals, already the denial of the Monism which the Whole uttered. All the little figures, the gargoyles, the imps, the human faces, whilst subordinated within the Great Conclusion of the Whole, still, from their obscurity, jeered their mockery of the Absolute, and declared for multiplicity, polygeny. But all mediaeval art has the static, architectural, absolute quality, in the main, even whilst in detail it is differentiated and distinct. Such is Dürer, for example.' When his art succeeds, it conveys the sense of Absolute Movement, movement proper only to the given form, and not relative to other movements. It portrays the Object, with its Movement contained and not the movement which contains in one of its moments, the Object.

It is only when the Greek stimulus is received, with its addition of male influence, its addition of relative movement, its revelation of movement driving the object, the highest revelation which had yet been made, that Mediaeval art became complete Renaissance Art, that there was the Union and fusion of the male and female spirits, creating a perfect expression for the time being.

During the mediaeval times, the God had been Christ on the Cross, the Body Crucified, the flesh destroyed, the Virgin, Chastity combating Desire. Such had been the God of the Aspiration. But the God of Knowledge, of that which they acknowledged as themselves, had been the Father, the God of the Ancient Jew.

But now, with the Renaissance, the God of Aspiration became in accord with the God of Knowledge, and there was a great outburst of joy, and the theme was not Christ Crucified, but Christ born of Woman, the Infant Saviour and the Virgin; or of the Annunciation, the Spirit embracing the flesh in pure embrace.

This was the perfect union of male and female, in this the hands met and clasped and never was such a manifestation of Joy. This Joy reached its highest utterance perhaps in Botticelli, as in his "Nativity of the Saviour" in our National Gallery. Still there is the architectural composition, but what an outburst of movement from the source of motion. The Infant Christ is a centre, a radiating spark of movement, the Virgin is bowed in Absolute Movement, the earthly father, Joseph, is folded up, like a clod or a boulder, obliterated, whilst the Angels fly round in ecstasy, embracing and linking hands.

The bodily father is almost obliterated. As balance to the Virgin Mother, he is there, presented, but silenced, only the movement of his loin conveyed. He is not the male. The male is the radiant infant, over which the mother leans. They two are the ecstatic centre, the complete origin, the force is both centrifugal and centripetal.

This is the joyous utterance of the Renaissance, to which we listen forever. Perhaps there is a melancholy in Botticelli, a pain of Woman mated to the

Spirit, a nakedness of the Aphrodite issued exposed to the clear elements, to the fleshlessness of the male. But still it is joy transparent over pain. It is the utterance of complete, perfect religious art, unwilling perhaps, when the true male and the female meet. In the Song of Solomon, the female was preponderant, the male was impure, not single. But here the heart is satisfied for the moment, there is a moment of perfect being.

And it seems to be so in other religions: the most perfect moment centres round the mother and the male child, whilst the physical male is deified separately, as a bull, perhaps.

After Botticelli came Correggio. In him the development from gesture to articulate expression was continued, unconsciously, the movement from the symbolic to the representation went on in him, from the object to the animate creature. The Virgin and Child are no longer symbolic, in Correggio: they no longer belong to religious art, but are distinctly secular. The effort is to render the living person, the individual perceived, and not the great aspiration, or an idea. Art now passes from the naive, intuitive stage, to the state of knowledge. The female impulse, to feel and to live in feeling, is now embraced by the male impulse—to know, and almost carried off by knowledge. But not yet. Still Correggio is unconscious, in his art, he is in that state of elation which represents the marriage of male and female, with the pride of the male perhaps predominant. In the "Madonna with the Basket" of the National Gallery, the Madonna is most thoroughly a wife, the child is most triumphantly a man's child. The Father is the origin. He is seen labouring in the distance, the true support of this mother and child. There is no Virgin worship, none of the mystery of woman. The artist has reached to a sufficiency of knowledge. He knows his woman. What he is now concerned with, is not her great female mystery, but her individual character. The picture has become almost lyrical—it is the woman as known by the man, it is the woman as he has experienced her. But still she is also unknown, also she is the mystery. But Correggio's chief business is to portray the woman of his own experience and knowledge, rather than the woman of his aspiration and fear. The artist is now concerned with his own experience, rather than with his own desire. The female is now more or less within the power and reach of the male. But still she is there, to centralise and control his movement, still the two react and are not resolved. But for the man, the woman is henceforth part of a stream of movement, she is herself a stream of movement, carried along with himself. He sees everything as motion, retarded perhaps by the flesh, or by the stable being of this life in the body. But still man is held and pivoted by the object, even if he tend to wear down the pivot to a nothingness.

Thus Correggio leads on to the whole of modern art, where the male still wrestles with the female, in unconscious struggle, but where he gains ever gradually over her, reducing her to nothing. Ever there is more and more vibration, movement, and less and less stability, centralisation. Ever man is more and more occupied with his own experience, with his own overpowering of resistance, ever less and less aware of any resistance in the object, less and less aware of any stability, less and less aware of anything unknown, more and more preoccupied with that which he knows, till his knowledge tends to become an abstraction, because it is limited by no unknown.

It is the contradiction of Dürer, as the Parthenon Frieze was the contradiction of Babylon and Egypt. To Dürer woman did not exist, even as to a child at the breast, woman does not exist separately. She is the overwhelming condition of life. She was to Dürer that which possessed him, and not that which he possessed. Her being overpowered his, he could only see in her terms, in terms of stability and of stable, incontrovertible being. He is overpowered by the vast assurance   at whose breasts he is suckled, and as if astounded, he grasps at the unknown. He knows that he rests within some great stability, and marvelling at his own power for movement, touches the objects of this stability, becomes familiar with them. It is a question of the starting point. Dürer starts with a sense of that which he does not know and would discover, Correggio with the sense of that which he has known, and would re-create.

And in the Renaissance, after Botticelli, the motion begins to divide in these two directions. The hands no longer clasp in perfect union, but one clasp overbears the other. Botticelli develops to Correggio and to Andrea del Sarto, develops forward to Rembrandt, and Rembrandt to the Impressionists, to the male extreme of motion. But Botticelli on the other hand becomes Raphael, Raphael and Michael Angelo.

In Raphael we see the stable, architectural developing out further, and becoming the geometric: the denial or refusal of all movement. In the "Madonna degli Ansidei" the child is drooping motionless, the mother stereotyped, the picture geometric, static, abstract. When there is any union of male and female, there is no goal of abstraction: the abstract is used in place, as a means of a real union. The goal of the male impulse is the announcement of motion, endless motion, endless diversity, endless change. The goal of the female impulse is the announcement of infinite oneness, of infinite stability. When the two are working in combination, as they must in life, there is, as it were, a dual motion, centrifugal for the male, fleeing abroad, away from the centre, outward to infinite vibration, and centripetal for the female, fleeing in to the eternal centre of rest. A combination of the two movements produces a sum of motion and stability at once, satisfying. But in life there tends always to be more of one than the other. The Cathedrals, Fra Angelico, frighten us or bore us with their final annunciation of centrality and stability. We want to escape. The influence is too female for us.

In Botticelli, the architecture remains, but there is the wonderful movement outwards, the joyous if still clumsy, escape from the centre. His religious pictures tend to be stereotyped, resigned. The Primavera herself is static, melancholy, a stability become almost a negation. It is as if the female, instead of being the great, unknown Positive, towards which all must flow, became the great Negative, the centre which denied all motion. And the Aphrodite stands there not as a force, to draw all things unto her, but as the naked, almost unwilling pivot, as the keystone which endured all thrust and remained static. But still there is the joy, the great motion around her, sky and sea, all the elements and living, joyful forces.

Raphael, however, seeks and finds nothing there. He goes to the centre to ask: "What is this mystery we are all pivoted upon?" To Fra Angelico it was the unknown Omnipotent. It was a goal, to which man travelled inevitably. It was the desired, the end of the long horizontal journey. But to Raphael it was the negation. Still he is a seeker, an aspirant, still his art is religious art. But the Virgin, the essential female, was to him a negation, a neutrality. Such must have been his vivid experience. But still he seeks her. Still he desires the stability, the positive keystone which grasps the arch together, not the negative keystone neutralising the thrust, itself a neutrality. And reacting upon his own desire, the male reacting upon itself, he creates the Abstraction, the geometric conception of life. The fundament of all, is the geometry of all. Which is Plato's conception. And the desire is to formulate the complete geometry.

So Raphael, knowing that his desire reaches out beyond the range of possible experience, sensible that he will not find satisfaction in any one woman, sensible that the female impulse does not, or cannot unite in him with the male impulse sufficiently to create a stability, an eternal moment of truth for him, of realisation, closes his eyes and his mind upon experience, and abstracting himself, reacting upon himself, produces the geometric conception of the fundamental truth, departs from religion, from any God-idea, and becomes philosophic.

Raphael is the real end of the Renaissance in Italy; almost he is the real end of Italy, as Plato was the real end of Greece. When the God-idea passes into the philosophic or geometric-idea, then there is a sign that the male impulse has thrown the female impulse, and has recoiled upon itself, has become abstract, asexual.

Michael Angelo, however, too physically passionate, containing too much of the female in his body ever to reach the geometric abstraction, unable to abstract himself, and at the same time, like Raphael, unable to find any woman, who in her being should resist him and reserve still some unknown from him, strives to obtain his own physical satisfaction in his art. he is obsessed by the desire of the body. And he must react upon himself to produce his own bodily satisfaction, aware that he can never obtain it through woman. He must seek the moment, the consummation, the keystone, the pivot, in his own flesh. For his own body is both male and female.

Raphael and Michael Angelo are men of different nature placed in the same position and resolving the same question in their several ways. Socrates and Plato are a parallel pair, and, in another degree, Tolstoi and Turgenev, and perhaps, St. Paul and St. John the Evangelist, and perhaps, Shakespeare and Shelley.

The body it is which attaches us directly to the female. Sex, as we call it, is only the point where the dual stream begins to divide, where it is nearly together, almost one. An infant is of no very determinate sex: that is, it is of both. Only at adolescence is there a real differentiation, the one is singled out to predominate. In what we call happy natures, in the lazy, contented, people, there is a fairly equable balance of sex. There is sufficient of the female in the body of such a man as to leave him fairly free. He does not suffer the torture of desire of a more male being. It is obvious even from the physique of such a man, that in him there is a proper proportion between male and female, so that he can be easy, balanced, and without excess. The Greek sculptors of the "best" period, Phidias and Myron, then Sophocles, Alcibiades, then Horace, must have been fairly well-balanced men, not passionate to any excess, tending to voluptuousness rather than to passion. So also Victor Hugo and Schiller and Tennyson. The real voluptuary is a man who is female as well as male, and who lives according to the female side of his nature, like Lord Byron.   5

The pure male is himself almost an abstraction, almost bodyless, like Shelley or Edmund Spenser. But, as we know humanity, this condition comes of an omission of some vital part. In the ordinary sense, Shelley never lived. He transcended life. But we do not want to transcend life, since we are of life.

Why should Shelley say of the skylark:

"Hail to thee, blithe spirit, bird thou never wert—"

Why should he insist on the bodylessness of beauty, when we cannot know of any save embodied beauty. Who would wish that the skylark were not a bird, but a spirit? If the whistling skylark were a spirit, then we should all wish to be spirits. Which were impious and flippant.

I can think of no being in the world so transcendently male as Shelley. He is phenomenal. The rest of us have bodies which contain the male and the female. If we were so singled out as Shelley, we should not belong to life, as he did not belong to life. But it were impious to wish to be like the angels. So long as mankind exists it must exist in the body, and so long must each body pertain both to the male and the female.

In the degree of pure maleness below Shelley are Plato and Raphael and Wordsworth, then Goethe and Milton and Dante, then Michael Angelo, then Shakespeare, then Tolstoi, then St. Paul.

A man who is well balanced between male and female, in his own nature, is as a rule, happy, easy to mate, easy to satisfy, and content to exist. It is only a disproportion, or a dissatisfaction, which makes the man struggle into articulation. And the articulation is of two sorts, the cry of desire or the cry of realisation, the cry of satisfaction, the effort to prolong the sense of satisfaction, to prolong the moment of consummation.

A bird in spring sings with the dawn, ringing out, out from the moment of consummation in wider and wider circles. Dürer, Fra Angelico, Botticelli all sing of the moment of consummations some of them still marvelling and lost in the wonder at the other being, Botticelli poignant with distinct memory. Raphael too sings of the moment of consummation. But he was not lost in the moment, only sufficiently lost to know what it was. In the moment, he was not completely consummated. He must strive to complete his satisfaction from himself. So, whilst making his great acknowledgement to the Woman, he must add to her to make her whole, he must give her his completion. So he rings her round with pure geometry, till she becomes herself almost part of the geometric figure, an abstraction. The picture becomes a great ellipse crossed by a dark column. This is the "Madonna degli Ansidei". The Madonna herself is almost insignificant. She and the child are contained within the shaft thrust across the ellipse.

This column must always stand for the male aspiration, the arch or ellipse for the female completeness containing this aspiration. And the whole picture is a geometric symbol of the consummation of life.

What we call the Truth is, in actual experience, that momentary state in living when the union between the male and the female is consummated. This consummation may be also physical, between the male body and the female body. But it may be only spiritual, between the male and female spirit.

And the symbol by which Raphael expresses this moment of consummation is by a dark, strong shaft or column leaping up into, and almost transgressing a faint, radiant, inclusive ellipse.

To express the same moment Botticelli uses no symbol, but builds up a complicated system of circles, of movements wheeling in their horizontal plane about their fixed centres, the whole builded up dome-shape, and then the dome surpassed by another singing cycle in the open air above.

This is Botticelli always: different cycles of joy, different moments of embrace, different forms of dancing round, all contained in one picture, without solution. He has not solved it yet.

And Raphael, in reaching the pure symbolic solution, has surpassed art and become almost mathematics. Since the business of art is never to solve, but only to declare.

There is no such thing as solution. Nietzsche talks about the Ewige Wiederkehr. It is like Botticelli singing cycles. But each cycle is different. There is no real recurrence.

And to single out one cycle, one moment, and to exclude from this moment all context, and to make this moment timeless, is what Raphael does, and what Plato does. So that their absolute Truth, their geometric Truth, is only true in timelessness.

Michael Angelo, on the other hand, seeks for no absolute Truth. His desire is to realise in his body, in his feeling, the moment-consummation which is for Man the perfect truth-experience. But he knows of no embrace. For him, personally, woman does not exist. For Botticelli she existed as the Virgin-Mother, and as the Primavera, and as Aphrodite. She existed as the pure origin of life on the female side, as the bringer of light and delight, and as the passionately Desired of every man, as the Known and Unknown in one. To Raphael she existed either as a minor part of his experience, having nothing to do with his aspiration, or else his aspiration merely used her as a statement included within the Great Abstraction.

To Michael Angelo the female scarcely existed outside his own physique. There he knew of her and knew the desire of her. But Raphael, in his passion to be self-complete, roused his desire for consummation to a white-hot pitch, so that he became incandescent, re-acting on himself, consuming his own flesh and his own bodily life, to reach the pitch of perfect abstraction, the resisting body holding back the raging stream of outward force, till the two formed a stable incandescence, a luminous geometric conception of permanence and inviolability. Meanwhile his body burned away, overpowered, in this state of incandescence.

Michael Angelo's will was different. The body in him, that which knew of the female and therefore was the female, was stronger and more insistent. His desire for consummation was desire for the satisfying moment when the male and female spirits touch in closest embrace, vivifying each other, not one destroying the other, but still are two. He knew that for Man, consummation is a temporal state. The pure male spirit must ever conceive of timelessness, the pure female—of the moment. And Michael Angelo, more mixed than Raphael, must always rage within the limits of time and of temporal form. So he re-acted upon himself, sought the female in himself, aggrandised it, and so reached a wonderful momentary stability, of flesh exaggerated till it became tenuous, but filled and balanced by the outward-pressing force. And he reached his consummation in that way, reached the perfect moment, when he realised and revealed his figures in all their marvellous equilibrium. The Jewish tradition with its great physical God, source of male and female, attracted him. By turning towards the female goal, of utter stability and permanence in Time, he arrived at his consummation. But only by re-acting on

60

himself, by withdrawing his own mobility. Thus he made his great figures, the Moses, static and looming, announcing, like the Jewish God, the magnificence and eternality of the physical law; the David, young, but with too much body for a young figure, the physique exaggerated, the clear, outward-leaping, essential spirit of the young man smothered over, the real maleness cloaked, so that the statue is almost a falsity. Then the Slaves, heaving in body, fastened in bondage, that refuses them movement; the motionless Madonna, no Virgin, but Woman in the flesh, not the pure female conception, but the spouse of man, the mother of bodily children. The men are not male, nor the women female, to any degree.

The Adam can scarcely stir into life. That large body of almost transparent, tenuous texture is not established enough for motion. It is not that it is too ponderous: it is too unsubstantial, unreal. It is not motion, life, he craves, but body. Give him but a firm, concentrated physique. That is the cry of all Michael Angelo's pictures.

But, powerful male as he was, he satisfies his desire by insisting upon and exaggerating the body in him, he reaches the point of consummation in the most marvellous equilibrium which his figures show. To attain this equilibrium he must exaggerate and exaggerate and exaggerate the flesh, make it ever more tenuous, keeping **it** really in true ratio. And then comes the moment, the perfect stable poise, the perfect balance between object and movement, the perfect combination of male and female in one figure.

It is wonderful, and peaceful, this equilibrium, once reached. But it is reached through anguish and self-battle and self-repression, therefore it is sad. Always, Michael Angelo's pictures are full of the effects of self-repression, as Raphael's pictures are full of joy, of self-acceptance and self-proclamation. Michael Angelo fought and arrested the mobile male in him, Raphael was proud in the male he was, and gave himself utter liberty, at the female expense.

And it seems as though Italy had ever since the Renaissance been possessed by the Raphaelesque conception of the ultimate geometric basis of life, the geometric essentiality of all things. There is in the Italian, at the very bottom of all, the fundamental, geometric conception of absolute static combination. There is the shaft enclosed in the ellipse, as a permanent symbol. There exists no shaft, no ellipse separately, but only the whole complete thing; there is neither male nor female, but an absolute interlocking of the two in one, an absolute combination, so that each is gone in the complete identity. There is only the geometric abstraction of the moment of consummation, a moment made timeless. And this conception of a long, clinched, timeless embrace, this overwhelming conception of timeless consummation, of which there is no beginning nor end, from which there is no escape, has arrested the Italian race for three centuries. It is the source of its indifference and its fatalism and its positive abandon, and of its utter incapacity to be sceptical, in the Russian sense.

This conception contains also, naturally, as part of the same idea, Aphrodite-worship and Phallic-worship. But these are subordinate, and belong to a sort of initiatory period. The real conception, for the individual, is Marriage, inviolable marriage, which always was and always has been, no matter what apparent aberrations there may or may not be. And the manifestation of divinity is the child. In marriage, in utter, interlocked marriage, man and woman cease to be two beings and become one, one and one only, not two in one as with us, but absolute One, a geometric absolute, timeless, the Absolute, the Divine. And the child, as issue of this divine and timeless state, is hailed with love and joy.

But the Italian is now beginning to withdraw from his clinched and timeless embrace, from his geometric abstraction, into the northern conception of himself and the woman as two separate identities, which meet, combine, but always must withdraw again.

So that the Futurist Boccioni now makes his sculpture "Development of a Bottle through Space", try to express the withdrawal, and at the same lime he must adhere to the conception of this same interlocked state of marriage between centripetal and centrifugal forces, the geometric abstraction of the bottle. But he can neither do one thing nor the other. He wants to re-state the real abstraction. And at the same time he has an unsatisfied desire to satisfy. He must insist on the centrifugal force, and so destroy at once his abstraction. He must insist on the male spirit of motion outwards, because, during three static centuries, there has necessarily come to pass a preponderance of the female in the race, so that the Italian is rather more female than male, now, as is the whole Latin race rather voluptuous than passionate, too much aware of their utter lockedness male with female, and too hopeless, as males, to act, to be passionate. So that when I look at Boccioni's sculpture, and see him trying to state the timeless, abstract being of a bottle, the pure geometric abstraction of the bottle, I am fascinated. But then, when I see him driven by his desire for the male complement into portraying motion, simple motion, trying to give expression to the bottle in terms of mechanics, I am confused. It is for science to explain the bottle in terms of force and motion. Geometry, pure mathematics, is very near to art, and the vivid attempt to render the bottle as a pure geometric abstraction, might give rise to a work of art, because of the resistance of the medium, the stone. But a representation in stone of the lines of force which create that state of rest called a bottle, that is a model in mechanics.

And the two representations require two different states of mind in the appreciator, so that the result is almost nothingness, mere confusion. And the portraying of a state of mind is impossible. There can only be made scientific diagrams of states of mind. A state of mind is a resultant between an attack and a resistance. And how can one produce a resultant without first causing the collision of the originating forces?

The attitude of the Futurists is the scientific attitude, as the attitude of Italy is mainly scientific. It is the forgetting of the old, perfect Abstraction, it is the departure of the male from the female, it is the act of withdrawal: the denying of consummation and the starting afresh, the learning of the alphabet.

CHAPTER VIII.

"The Light of the World.

The climax that was reached in Italy with Raphael has never been reached in like manner in England. There has never been, in England, the great embrace, the surprising consummation, which Botticelli recorded and which Raphael fixed in a perfect Abstraction.

Correggio, Andrea del Sarto, both men of less force than those other supreme three, continued the direct line of development, turning no curve. They still found women whom they could not exhaust: in them, the male still reacted upon the incontrovertible female. But ever there was a tendency to greater movement, to a closer characterisation, a tendency to individualise the human being, and to represent him as being embedded in some common, divine matrix.

Till after the Renaissance, supreme God had always been God the Father. The Church moved and had its being in Almighty God, Christ was only the distant, incandescent gleam towards which humanity aspired, but which it did not know.

Raphael and Michael Angelo were both servants of the Father, of the Eternal Law, of the Prime Being. Raphael, faced with the question of Not-Being, when it was forced upon him that he would never accomplish his own being in the flesh, that he would never know completeness, the momentary consummation, in the body, accomplished the Geometric Abstraction, which is the abstraction from the Law, which is the Father.

There was, Christ's great assertion of Not-Being, of Non-Consummation, of life after death, to reckon with. It was after the Renaissance, Christianity began to exist. It had not existed before.

In God the Father we are all one body, one flesh. But in Christ we abjure the flesh, there is no flesh. A man must lose his life to save it. All the natural desires of the body, these a man must be able to deny, before he can live. And then, when he lives, he shall live in the knowledge that he is himself, so that he can always say: "I am I."

In the Father we are one flesh, in Christ we are crucified, and rise again, and are One with Him in Spirit. It is the difference between Law and Love. Each man shall live according to the Law, which changeth not, says the old religion. Each man shall live according to Love, which shall save us from death and from the Law, says the new religion.

But what is Love? What is the deepest desire Man has yet known? It is always for this consummation, this momentary contact or union of male with female, of spirit with spirit and flesh with flesh, when each is complete in itself and rejoices in its own being, when each is in himself or in herself complete and single and essential. And love is the great aspiration towards this complete consummation and this joy; it is the aspiration of each man that all men, that all life, shall know it and rejoice. Since, until all men shall know it, no man shall fully know it. Since, by the Law, we are all one flesh. So that Love is only a closer vision of the Law, a more comprehensive interpretation: "Think not I come to destroy the Law, or the prophets: I come not to destroy, but to fulfil! For verily I say unto you, till heaven and earth pass, one jot or one tittle shall in no wise pass from the Law, till all be fulfilled.

In Christ, I must save my soul through love, I must lose my life, and thereby find it. The Law bids me preserve my life to the Glory of God. But Love bids me lose my life to the Glory of God, In Christ, when I shall have overcome every desire I know in myself so that I adhere to nothing, but am loosed and set free and single, then, being without fear, and having nothing that I can lose, I shall know what I am, I, transcendent, intrinsic, eternal.

The Christian commandment "Thou shalt love thy neighbour as thyself" is a more indirect and moving, a more emotional form of the Greek commandment

"Know thyself." This is what Christianity says, indirectly: "Know thyself, and each man shall thereby know himself."

Now in the Law, no man shall know himself, save in the Law. And the Law is the immediate law of the body. And the necessity of each man to know himself, to achieve his own consummation, shall be satisfied and fulfilled in the body. God, Almighty God, is the father, and in fatherhood man draws nearest to him. In the act of love, in the act of begetting, Man is with God and of God. Such is the Law. And there shall be no other God devised. That is the great obstructive commandment.

This is the old religious leap down, absolutely, even if not in direct statement. It is the Law. But through Christ it was at last declared that in the physical act of love, in the begetting of children, man does not necessarily know himself, nor become Godlike, nor satisfy his deep, innate desire to *BE*. The physical act of love may be a complete disappointment, a nothing, and fatherhood may be the least significant attribute to a man. And physical love may fail utterly, may prove a sterility, a nothingness. Is a man then duped, and is his deepest desire a joke played on him?

There is a law, beyond the known law, there is a new Commandment. There is love. A man shall find his consummation in the crucifixion of the body and the resurrection of the spirit.

Christ, the Bridegroom, or the Bride, as may be, awaits the desiring soul that shall seek Him, and in Him shall all men find their consummation, after their new birth. It is the New Law, the Old Law is revoked.

"This is my body, take, and eat," says Christ, in the communion, the ritual representing the Consummation. "Come unto me all ye that labour and are heavy laden, and I will give you rest.

For each man, there is the bride, for each woman the bridegroom, for all, the Mystic Marriage. It is the New Law. In the mystic embrace of Christ each man shall find fulfilment and relief, each man shall become himself, a male individual, tried, proved, completed, and satisfied. In the mystic embrace of Christ each man shall say "I am myself, and Christ is Christ." Each woman shall be proud and satisfied, saying "It is enough." So, by the New Law, man shall satisfy this his deepest desire. "In the body ye must die, even as I died, on the cross," says Christ, "that ye may have everlasting life." But this is a real contradiction of the Old Law, which says "In the life of the body we are one with the Father." The Old Law bids us live: it is the old, original commandment, that we shall live in the Law, and not die. So that the new Christian preaching of Christ Crucified is indeed against the Law. "And when ye are dead in the body, ye shall be one with the spirit, ye shall know the Bride, and be consummate in Her Embrace, in the Spirit," continues the Christian Commandment.

It is a larger interpretation of the Law, but also, it is a breach of the Law. For by the Law, Man shall in no wise injure or deny or desecrate his living body of flesh, which is of the Father. Therefore, though Christ gave the Holy Ghost, the Comforter; though he bowed before the Father, though he said, that no man should be forgiven the denial of the Holy Spirit, the Reconciler between the Father and the Son; yet did the Son deny the Father, must he deny the Father?

"Ye are My Spirit, in the Spirit ye know Me, and in marriage of the Spirit I am fulfilled of you," said the Son.

And it is the Unforgivable Sin to declare that these two are contradictions one of the other, though contradictions they are. Between them is linked the Holy Spirit, as a reconciliation, and whoso shall speak hurtfully against the Holy Spirit shall find no forgiveness.

So Christ, up in arms against the Father, exculpated himself and bowed to the Father. Yet man must insist either on one or on the other, either he must adhere to the Son or to the Father. And since the Renaissance, disappointed in the flesh, the northern races have sought the consummation through Love; and they have denied the Father.

The greatest and deepest human desire, for consummation, for Self-Knowledge, has sought a different satisfaction. In Love, in the act of love, that which is mixed in me becomes pure, that which is female in me is given to the female, that which is male in her draws into me, I am complete, I am pure male, she is pure female, we rejoice in contact perfect and naked and clear, singled out unto ourselves, and given the surpassing freedom. No longer we see through a glass, darkly. For she is she and I am I, and, clasped together with her, I know how perfectly she is not me, how perfectly I am not her, how utterly we are two, the light and the darkness, and how infinitely and eternally not-to-be-comprehended by either of us, is the surpassing One we make. Yet of this One, this incomprehensible, we have an inkling that satisfies us.

And through Christ Jesus, I know that I shall find my Bride, when I have overcome the impurity of the flesh. When the flesh in me is put   away, I shall embrace the Bride, and I shall know as I am known.

But why the Schism? Why shall the Father say "Thou shalt have no other God before me"? Why is the Lord Our God a jealous God? Why, when the body fails me, must I still adhere to the Law, and give It praise as the perfect Abstraction, like Raphael, announce It as the Absolute? Why must I be imprisoned within the flesh, like Michael Angelo, till I must stop the voice of my crying out, and be satisfied with a little where I wanted completeness?

And why, on the other hand, must I lose my life to save it? Why must I die, before I can be born again? Can I not be born again, save out of my own ashes, save in resurrection from the dead? Why must I deny the Father, to love the Son? Why are they not One God to me, as we always protest they are?

It is time that the schism ended, that man ceased to oppose the Father to the Son, the Son to the Father. It is time that the Protestant Church, the Church of the Son, should be one again with the Roman Catholic Church, the Church of the Father. It is time that man shall cease, first to live in the flesh, with joy, and then, unsatisfied, to renounce and to mortify the flesh, declaring that the Spirit alone exists, that Christ he is God.

If a man find incomplete satisfaction in the body, why therefore shall he renounce the body and say, it is of the devil? And why, at the start, shall a man say, "The body, that is all, and the consummation, that is complete in the flesh, for me."

Must it always be, that a man set out with a worship of passion and a blindness to love, and that he end with a stern commandment to love and a renunciation of passion?

Does not a youth now know that he desires the body as the via media, that consummation is consummation of body and spirit, both?

How can a man say "I am this body", when he will desire beyond the body tomorrow? And how can a man say "I am this spirit", when his own mouth gives lie to the words it forms?

Why is a race, like the Italian race, fundamentally melancholy, save that it has circumscribed its consummation within the body? And the Jewish race for the same reason has become now almost hollow with a pit of emptiness and misery in their eyes.

And why is the English race neutral, indifferent, like a thing that eschews life, save that it has said so insistently: "I am this spirit. This body, it is not me, it is unworthy." The body at last begins to wilt and become corrupt. But before it submits, half the life of the English race must be a lie. The life of the body, denied by the professed adherence to the spirit, must be something disowned, corrupt, ugly.

Why should the worship of the Son entail the denial of the Father? Since the Renaissance, northern humanity has sought for consummation in the spirit, it has sought for the female apart from woman. "I am I, and the Spirit is the Spirit, in the Spirit I am myself", and this has been the utterance of our art since Raphael.

There has been the ever-developing dissolution of form, the dissolving of the solid body within the spirit. He began to break the clear outline of the object, to seek for further marriage, not only between body and body, not the perfect, stable union of body with body, not the utter completeness and accomplishment of architectural form, with its recurrent cycles, but the marriage between body and spirit, or between spirit and spirit.

It is no longer the Catholic exultation "God is God"; but the Christian annunciation "Light is come into the world. No longer has a man only to obey, but he has to die and be born again, he has to close his eyes upon his own immediate desires, and in the darkness receive the perfect light. He has to know himself in the spirit, he has to follow Christ to the Cross, and rise again in the light of life.

And, in this light of life, he will see his Bride, he will embrace his complement and his fulfilment, and achieve his consummation. "It is the spirit that quickeneth; the flesh profiteth nothing; the words I speak unto you, they are the spirit, and they are the life.

And though in the Gospel, according to John particularly, Jesus constantly asserts that the Father has sent him, and that he is of the Father, yet there is always the spirit of antagonism to the Father.

"And it came to pass, as he spake these things, a certain woman of the company lifted up her voice and said unto him, 'Blessed is the womb that bare thee, and the paps thou hast sucked.'

"But he said, 'Yea, rather, blessed are they that hear the word of God, and keep it.'

And the woman who heard this, knew that she was denied of the honour of her womb, and that the blessing of her breasts was taken away.

Again he said: "And there be those that were born eunuchs; and there be those that were made eunuchs by men, and there be eunuchs which have made themselves eunuchs for the kingdom of heaven's sake. He that is able to receive it, let him receive it." But before the Father a eunuch is blemished, even a childless man is without honour.

So that the spirit of Jesus is antagonistic to the spirit of the Father. And St. John enhances this antagonism. But in St. John, there is the constant insistence on the Oneness of Father and Son, and on the Holy Spirit.

Since the Renaissance there has been the striving for the Light, and the escape from the Flesh, from the Body, the Object. And sometimes there has been the antagonism to the Father, sometimes reconciliation with Him. In painting, the Spirit, the Word, the Love, all that was represented by John, has appeared as light. Light is the constant symbol of Christ in the New Testament. It is light, actual sunlight or the luminous quality of day which has infused more and more into the defined body, fusing away the outline, absolving the concrete reality, making a marriage, an embrace between the two things, light and object.

In Rembrandt there is the first great evidence of this, the new exposition of the commandment "Know thyself." It is more than the "Hail, holy Light!" of Milton. It is the declaration that light is our medium of existence, that where the light falls upon our darkness, there we *are:* that I am but the point where light and darkness meet, and break upon one another.

There is now a new conception of life, an utterly new conception, of duality, of two-fold existence, light and darkness, object and spirit two-fold, and almost inimical.

The old desire, for movement about a centre of rest, for stability, is gone, and in its place rises the desire for pure ambience, pure spirit of change, free from all laws and conditions of being.

Henceforward there are two things, and not one. But there is journeying towards the one thing again. There is no longer the One God who contains us all, and in whom we live and move and have our being, and to whom belongs each one of our movements. I am no longer a child of the Father, brother of all men. I am no longer part of the great body of God, as all men are part of it. I am no longer consummate in the body of God, identified with it and divine in the act of marriage.

The conception has utterly changed. There is the Spirit, and there is Myself. I exist in contact with the Spirit, but I am not the Spirit. I am other, I am Myself. Now I am become a man, I am no more a child of the Father. I am a man. And there are many men. And the Father has lost his importance. We are multiple, manyfold men, we own only one Hope, one Desire, one Bride, one Spirit.

At last man insists upon his own separate Self, insists that he has a distinct, inconquerable being which stands apart even from Spirit, which exists other than the Spirit, and which seeks marriage with the Spirit.

And he must study himself and marvel over himself in the light of the Spirit, he must become lyrical: but he must glorify the Spirit, above all. Since that is the Bride. So Rembrandt paints his own portrait again and again, sees it again and again within the light.

He has no hatred of the flesh. That he was not completed in the flesh, even in the marriage of the body, is inevitable. But he is married in the flesh, and his wife is with him in the body, he loves his body, which she gave him complete, and he loves her body, which is not himself, but which he has known. He has known and rejoiced in the earthly bride, he will adhere to her always. But there is the Spirit beyond her: there is his desire which transcends her, there is the Bride still he craves for and courts. And he knows, this is the Spirit, it is not the body. And he paints it as the light. And he paints himself within the light. For he has a deep desire to know

67

himself in the embrace of the Spirit. For he does not know himself, he is never consummated.

The Old Law, fulfilled in him, he is not appeased, he must transcend the Law. The Woman is embraced, caught up, and carried forward, the male spirit, passing on half satisfied, must seek a new bride, a further consummation. For there is no bride on earth for him.

To Dürer, the whole earth was as a bride, unknown and unaccomplished, offering inexhaustible satisfaction to him. And he sought out the earth endlessly, as a man seeks to know a bride who surpasses him. It was all: the Bride.

But to Rembrandt, the bride was not to be found, he must re-act upon himself, he must seek in himself for his own consummation. There was the Light, the Spirit, the Bridegroom. But when Rembrandt sought the complete Bride, sought for his own consummation, he knew it was not to be found, he knew she did not exist in the concrete. He knew, as Michael Angelo knew, that there was not on the earth a woman to satisfy him, to be his mate. He must seek for the Bride beyond the physical woman, he must seek for the great female principle in an abstraction.

But the abstraction was not the geometric abstraction, created from knowledge, a state of Absolute Remembering, making Absolute of the Consummation which had been, as in Raphael. It was the desired Unknown, the goodly Unknown, the Spirit, the Light. And with this Light Rembrandt must seek even the marriage of the body. Everything he did approximates to the Consummation, but never can realise it. He paints always faith, belief, hope, never Raphael's terrible, dead certainty.

To Dürer, every moment of his existence was occupied. He existed within the embrace of the Bride, which embrace he could never fathom nor exhaust.

Raphael knew and outraged the Bride, but he harked back, obsessed by the consummation which had been.

To Rembrandt, woman was only the first acquaintance with the Bride. Of woman he obtained and expected no complete satisfaction. He knew he must go on, beyond the woman. But though the flesh could not find its consummation, still he did not deny the flesh. He was an artist, and in his art no artist ever could blaspheme the Holy Spirit, the Reconciler. Only a dogmatist could do that. Rembrandt did not deny the flesh, as so many artists try to do. He went on from her to the fuller knowledge of the Bride, in true progression. Which makes the wonderful beauty of Rembrandt.

But, like Michael Angelo, owning the flesh, and, a northern Christian being bent on personal salvation, personal consummation, consummation in the flesh, such as a Christian feels with us when he receives the Sacrament and hears the words "This is my Body, take, and eat", Rembrandt craved to marry the flesh and the Spirit, to achieve consummation in the flesh through marriage with the Spirit.

Which is the great northern confusion. For the flesh is of the flesh, and the Spirit of the Spirit, and they are two, even as the Father and the Son are two, and not One.

Raphael conceived the two as One, thereby revoking Time. Michael Angelo would have created the bridal Flesh, to satisfy himself. Rembrandt would have married his own flesh to the Spirit, taken the consummate Kiss of the Light upon his fleshly face.

Which is a confusion. For the Father cannot know the Son, nor the Son the Father. So in Rembrandt the marriage is always imperfect, the embrace is never close nor consummate, as it is in Botticelli or in Raphael or in Michael Angelo. There is an eternal non-marriage betwixt flesh and spirit. They are two, they are never Two-in-One. So that in Rembrandt, there is never complete marriage betwixt the Light and the Body. They are contiguous, never consummate.

This has been the confusion and the error of the northern countries, but particularly of Germany, this desire to have the spirit mate with the flesh, the flesh with the spirit. Spirit can mate with spirit, and flesh with flesh, and the two matings can take place in one, but they are always Two-in-One. Or the two matings can take place separately, flesh with flesh, or spirit with spirit. But to try to mate flesh with spirit makes confusion.

The bride I mate with my body may or may not be the Bride in whom I find my consummation. It may be that, at times, the great female principle does not abide abundantly in woman: that, at certain periods, woman, in the body, is not the supreme representative of the Bride. It may be the Bride is hidden from Man, as the Light, or as the Darkness, which he can never know in the flesh.

It may be, in the same way, that the great male principle is only weakly evidenced in man during certain periods, that the Bridegroom be hidden away from woman, for a century or centuries, and that she can only find Him as the voice, or the Wind? So I think it was with her during the mediaeval period; that the greatest women of the period knew that the Bridegroom did not exist for them in the body, but as the Christ, the Spirit.

And, in times of the absence of the bridegroom from the body, then woman in the body must either die in the body, or, mating in the body, she must mate with the Bridegroom in the Spirit, in a separate marriage. She cannot mate her body with the Spirit, nor mate her spirit with the Body. That is confusion. Let her mate the man in body, and her spirit with the Spirit, in a separate marriage. But let her not try to mate her spirit with the body of the man, that does not mate her Spirit.

The effort to mate spirit with body, body with spirit, is the crying confusion and pain of our times.

Rembrandt made the first effort. But art has developed to a clarity since then. It reached its climax in our own Turner. He did not seek to mate body with spirit. He mated his body easily, he did not deny it. But what he sought was the mating of the Spirit. Ever, he sought the consummation in the Spirit, and he reached it at last. Ever, he sought the Light, to make the light transfuse the body, till the body was carried away, a mere bloodstain, became a ruddy stain of red sunlight within white sunlight. This was perfect consummation in Turner, when, the body gone, the ruddy light meets the crystal light in a perfect fusion, the utter dawn, the utter golden sunset, the extreme of all life, where all is One, One-Being, a perfect glowing One-ness.

Like Raphael, it becomes an abstraction. But this, in Turner, is the abstraction from the spiritual marriage and consummation, the final transcending of all the Law, the achieving of what is to us almost a nullity. If Turner had ever painted his last picture, it would have been a white, incandescent surface, the same whiteness when he finished as when he began, proceeding from nullity to nullity, through all the range of colour.

Turner is perfect. Such a picture as his "Norham Castle, Sunrise", where only the shadow of life stains the light, is the last word that can be uttered, before the blazing and timeless silence.

He sought, and he found, perfect marriage in the spirit. It was apart from woman. His Bride was the Light. Or he was the bride himself, and the Light—the Bridegroom. Be that as it may, he became one and consummate with the Light, and gave us the consummate revelation.

Corot also, nearer to the Latin tradition of utter consummation in the body, made a wonderful marriage in the spirit between light and darkness, just tinctured with life. But he contained more of the two consummations together, the marriage in the body, represented in geometric form, and the marriage in the spirit, represented by shimmering transfusion and infusion of light through darkness.

But Turner is the crisis in this effort: he achieves pure light, pure and singing. In him the consummation is perfect, the perfect marriage in the spirit.

In the body his marriage was other. He never attempted to mingle the two. The marriage in the body, with the woman, was apart from, completed away from the marriage in the Spirit, with the Bride, the Light.

But I cannot look at a later Turner picture without abstracting myself, without denying that I have limbs, knees and thighs and breast. If I look at the "Norham Castle", and remember my own knees and my own breast, then the picture is a nothing to me. I must not know. And if I look at Raphael's "Madonna degli Ansidei", I am cut off from my future, from aspiration. The gate is shut upon me, I can go no further. The thought of Turner's Sunrise becomes magic and fascinating, it gives the lie to this completed symbol. I know I am the other thing as well.

So that, whenever art or any expression becomes perfect, it becomes a lie. For it is only perfect by reason of abstraction from that context by which and in which it exists as truth.

So Turner is a lie, and Raphael is a lie, and the marriage in the spirit is a lie, and the marriage in the body is a lie, each is a lie without the other. Since each excludes the other in these instances, they are both lies. If they were brought together, and reconciled, then there were a jubilee. But where is the Holy Spirit that shall reconcile Raphael and Turner?

There must be marriage of body in body, and of spirit in spirit, and Two-in-One. And the marriage in the body must not deny the marriage in the spirit, for that is blasphemy against the Holy Ghost; and the marriage in the spirit shall not deny the marriage in the body, for that is blasphemy against the Holy Ghost. But the two must be forever reconciled, even if they must exist on occasions apart one from the other.

For in Botticelli the dual marriage is perfect, or almost perfect, body and spirit reconciled, or almost reconciled, in a perfect dual consummation. And in all art, there is testimony to the wonderful dual marriage, the true consummation. But in Raphael, the marriage in the spirit is left out so much that it is almost denied, so that the picture is almost a lie, almost a blasphemy. And in Turner, the marriage in the body is almost denied in the same way, so that his picture is almost a blasphemy. But neither in Raphael nor in Turner is the denial positive: it is only an over-affirmation of the one at the expense of the other.

But in some men, in some small men, like bishops, the denial of marriage in the body is positive and blasphemous, a sin against the Holy Ghost. And in some men, like Prussian army officers, the denial of marriage in the spirit is an equal blasphemy. But which of the two is a greater sinner, working better for the destruction of his fellow man, that is for the One God to judge.

CHAPTER IX.

A nos Moutons.

1

Most fascinating in all artists is this antinomy between the Law and Love, between the Flesh and the Spirit, between the Father and the Son.

For the moralist it is easy. He can insist on that aspect of the Law or Love, which is in the immediate line of development for his age, and he can sternly and severely exclude or suppress all the rest.

So that all morality is of temporary value, useful to its times. But Art must give a deeper satisfaction. It must give fair play all round.

Yet every work of art adheres to some system of morality. But if it be really a work of art, it must contain the essential criticism on the morality to which it adheres. And hence the antinomy, hence the conflict necessary to every tragic conception.

The degree to which the system of morality, or the metaphysic, of any work of art is submitted to criticism within the work of art makes the lasting value and satisfaction of that work. Aeschylus, having caught the oriental idea of Love, correcting the tremendous Greek conception of the Law with this new idea, produces the intoxicating satisfaction of the Orestean trilogy. The Law, and Love, they are here the Two-in-One in all their magnificence. But Euripides, with his aspiration towards Love, Love the supreme, and his almost hatred of the Law, Law the Triumphant but Base Closer of Doom, is less satisfactory, because of the very fact that he holds Love always Supreme, and yet must endure the chagrin of seeing Love perpetually transgressed and overthrown. So he makes his tragedy: the higher thing eternally pulled down by the lower. And this unfairness in the use of terms, higher and lower, but above all, the unfairness of showing Love always violated and suffering, never supreme and triumphant, makes us disbelieve Euripides in the end. For we have to bring in pity, we must admit that Love is at a fundamental disadvantage before the Law, and cannot therefore ever hold its own. Which is weak philosophy.

If Aeschylus have a metaphysic to his art, this metaphysic is that Love and Law are Two eternally in conflict, and eternally being reconciled. This is the tragic significance of Aeschylus.

But the metaphysic of Euripides is that the Law and Love are two eternally in conflict, and unequally matched, so that Love must always be borne down. In Love a man shall only suffer. There is also a Reconciliation, otherwise Euripides were not so great. But there is always the unfair matching, this disposition insisted on, which at last leaves one cold and unbelieving.

The moments of pure satisfaction come in the choruses, in the pure lyrics, when Love is put into true relations with the Law, apart from knowledge, transcending knowledge, transcending the metaphysic, where the aspiration to Love meets the acknowledgement of the Law in a consummate marriage, for the moment.

Where Euripides adheres to his metaphysic, he is unsatisfactory. Where he transcends his metaphysic, he gives that supreme equilibrium wherein we know satisfaction.

The adherence to a metaphysic does not necessarily give artistic form. Indeed the overstrong adherence to a metaphysic usually destroys any possibility of artistic form. Artistic form is a revelation of the two principles of Love and the Law in a state of conflict and yet reconciled: pure motion struggling against and yet reconciled with the Spirit: active force meeting and overcoming and yet not overcoming inertia. It is the conjunction of the two which makes form. And since the two must always meet under fresh conditions, form must always be different. Each work of art has its own form, which has no relation to any other form. When a young painter studies an old master, he studies, not the form, that is an abstraction, which does not exist: he studies maybe the method of the old great artist: but he studies chiefly to understand how the old great artist suffered in himself the conflict of Love and Law, and brought them to a reconciliation. Apart from artistic method, it is not Art that the young man is studying, but the State of Soul of the great old artist, so that he, the young artist, may understand his own soul and gain a reconciliation between the aspiration and the resistant.

It is most wonderful in poetry, this sense of conflict contained within a reconciliation:

> "Hail to thee, blithe spirit,
> Bird thou never wert
> That from heaven, or near it,
> Pourest forth thy heart
> In profusest strains of unpremeditated lay."

Shelley wishes to say, the skylark is a pure, untrammelled spirit, a pure motion. But the very "Bird thou never wert", admits that the skylark *is* in very fact a bird, a concrete, momentary thing. If the line ran, "Bird thou never art", that would spoil it all. Shelley wishes to say, the song is poured out of heaven: but "or near it", he admits. There is the perfect relation between heaven and earth. And the last line is the tumbling sound of a lark's singing, the real Two-in-One.

The very adherence to rhyme and regular rhythm is a concession to the Law, a concession to the body, to the being and requirements of the body. They are an admission of the living, positive inertia which is the other half of life, other than the pure will-to-motion. In this consummation, they are the resistance and response of the Bride in the arms of the Bridegroom. And according as the Bride and Bridegroom come closer together, so is the response and resistance more fine, indistinguishable, so much the more, in this act of consummation, is the movement that of Two-in-One, indistinguishable each from the other, and not the movement of two brought together clumsily.

So that in Swinburne, where almost all is concession to the body, so that the poetry becomes almost a sensation and not an experience or a consummation, justifying Spinoza's "Amor est titillatio, concomitante idea causae externae"," we find continual adherence to the body, to the Rose, to the Flesh, the physical in everything, in the Sea, in the marshes; there is an overbalance in the favour of

Supreme Law; Love is not Love, but passion, part of the Law; there is no Love, there is only Supreme Law. And the poet sings the Supreme Law to gain rebalance in himself, for he hovers always on the edge of death, of Not-Being, he is always out of reach of the Law, bodiless, in the faintness of Love that has triumphed and denied the Law, in the dread of an overdeveloped, oversensitive soul which exists always on the point of dissolution from the body.

But he is not divided against himself. It is the novelists and dramatists who have the hardest task in reconciling their metaphysic, their theory of being and knowing, with their living sense of being. Because a novel is a microcosm, and because man in viewing the universe must view it in the light of a theory, therefore every novel must have the background or the structural skeleton of some theory of being, some metaphysic. But the metaphysic must always subserve the artistic purpose beyond the artist's conscious aim. Otherwise the novel becomes a treatise.

And the danger is, that a man shall make himself a metaphysic to excuse or cover his own faults or failure. Indeed, a sense of fault or failure is the usual cause of a man's making himself a metaphysic, to justify himself.

Then, having made himself a metaphysic of self-justification, or a metaphysic of self-denial, the novelist proceeds to apply the world to this, instead of applying this to the world.

Tolstoi is a flagrant example of this. Probably because of profligacy in his youth, because he had disgusted himself in his own flesh, by excess or by prostitution, therefore Tolstoi, in his metaphysic, renounced the flesh altogether, later on, when he had tried and had failed to achieve complete marriage in the flesh. But above all things, Tolstoi was a child of the Law, he belonged to the Father. He had a marvellous sensuous understanding, and very little clarity of mind.

So that, in his metaphysic, he had to deny himself, his own being, in order to escape his own disgust of what he had done to himself, and to escape admission of his own failure.

Which made all the later part of his life a crying falsity and shame. Reading the reminiscences of Tolstoi, one can only feel shame at the way Tolstoi denied all that was great in him, with vehement cowardice.

He degraded himself infinitely, he perjured himself far more than did Peter when he denied Christ. For Peter repented. But Tolstoi denied the Father, and propagated a great system of his recusancy, elaborating his own weakness, blaspheming his own strength. "What difficulty is there in writing about how an officer fell in love with a married woman?" he used to say of his Anna Karenin, "there's no difficulty in it, and, above all, no good in it."

Because he was mouthpiece to the Father, in uttering the law of passion, he said there was no difficulty in it, because it came naturally to him. Christ might just as easily have said, there was no difficulty in the Parable of the Sower, and no good in it either, because it flowed out of him without effort.

And Thomas Hardy's metaphysic is something like Tolstoi's. "There is no reconciliation between Love and the Law," says Hardy. "The spirit of Love must always succumb before the blind, stupid, but overwhelming power of the Law."

Already as early as *The Return of the Native,* he has come to this theory, in order to explain his own sense of failure. But before that time, from the very start, he has had an overweening theoretic antagonism to the Law. "That which is physical, of the body, is weak, despicable, bad," he said at the very start. He represented his fleshly heroes as villains, but very weak and maundering villains. At its worst, the Law is a weak, craven sensuality: at its best, it is a passive inertia. It is the gap in the armour, it is the hole in the foundation.

Such a metaphysic is almost silly. If it were not that the man is much stronger in feeling than in thought, the Wessex novels would be sheer rubbish, as they are already in parts. The *Well-Beloved* is sheer rubbish, fatuity, as is a good deal of the *Dynasts* conception.

But it is not as a metaphysician that one must consider Hardy. He makes a poor show there. For nothing in his work is so pitiable as his clumsy efforts to push events into line with his theory of being, and to make calamity fall on those who represent the principle of Love. He does it exceedingly badly, and owing to this effort his form is execrable in the extreme.

His feeling, his instinct, his sensuous understanding is, however, apart from his metaphysic, very great and deep, deeper than that perhaps of any other English novelist. Putting aside his metaphysic, which must always obtrude when he thinks of people, and turning to the earth, to landscape, then he is true to himself.

Always he must start from the earth, from the great source of the Law, and his people move in his landscape almost insignificantly, somewhat like tame animals wandering in the wild. The earth is the manifestation of the Father, of the Creator, Who made us in the Law. God still speaks aloud in His Works, as to Job, so to Hardy, surpassing human conception and the human law. "Dost thou know the balancings of the clouds, the wondrous works of him which is perfect in knowledge?—How thy garments are warm, when he quieteth the earth by the south wind?—Hast thou with him spread out the sky, which is strong?—"

This is the true attitude of Hardy—"with God is terrible majesty". The theory of knowledge, the metaphysic of the man, is much smaller than the man himself. So with Tolstoi.

"Knowest thou the time when the wild goats of the rock bring forth? Or canst thou mark when the hinds do calve?—Canst thou number the months that they fulfil? Or knowest thou the time when they bring forth?—They bow themselves, they bring forth their young ones, they cast out their sorrows.—Their young ones are good in liking, they grow up with corn; they go forth, and return not unto them."

There is a good deal of this in Hardy. But in Hardy there is more than the conceipt of *Job,* protesting his integrity. Job says in the end: "Therefore have I uttered that I understood not; things too wonderful for me, which I knew not.

"I have heard of thee by hearing of the ear; but now mine eye seeth thee.

"Wherefore I abhor myself, and repent in dust and ashes."

But Jude ends where Job began, cursing the day and the services of his birth, and in so much cursing the act of the Lord, "who made him in the womb."

It is the same cry all through Hardy, this curse upon the birth in the flesh, and this unconscious adherence to the flesh. The instincts, the bodily passions are strong and sudden in all Hardy's men. They are too strong and sudden. They fling Jude into the arms of Arabella, years after he has known Sue, and against his own will.

For every man comprises male and female in his being, the male always struggling for predominance. A woman likewise consists in male, and female, with female predominant.

And a man who is strongly male tends to deny, to refute the female in him. A real "man" takes no heed for his body, which is the more female part of him. He considers himself only as an instrument, to be used in the service of some idea.

The true female, on the other hand, will eternally hold her body superior to any idea, will hold full life in the body to be the real happiness. The male exists in doing, the female in being. The male lives in the satisfaction of some purpose achieved, the female in the satisfaction of some purpose contained.

In Aeschylus, in the "Eumenides", there is Apollo, Loxias, the Sun God, Love, the prophet, the male: there are the Erinyes, daughters of primeval Mother Night, representing here the female risen in retribution for some crime against the flesh; and there is Pallas, unbegotten daughter of Zeus, who is as the Holy Spirit in the Christian religion, the spirit of wisdom.

Orestes is bidden by the male god, Apollo, to avenge the murder of his father, Agamemnon, by his mother: that is, the male, murdered by the female, must he avenged by the male. But Orestes is child of his mother. He is in himself female. So that in himself the conscience, the madness, the violated part of his own self, his own body, drives him to the Furies. On the male side, he is right; on the female, wrong. But peace is given at last by Pallas, the Arbitrator, the Spirit of wisdom.

And although Aeschylus in his consciousness makes the Furies hideous, and Apollo supreme, yet, in his own self and in very fact, he makes the Furies wonderful and noble, with their tremendous hymns, and makes Apollo a trivial, sixth-form braggard and ranter. Clytemnestra also, wherever she appears, is wonderful and noble. Her sin is the sin of pride: she was the first to be injured. Agamemnon is a feeble thing beside her.

So Aeschylus adheres still to the Law, to Right, to the Creator who created man in His Own Image, and in his Law. What he has learned of Love, he does not yet quite believe.

Hardy has the same belief in the Law, but in conceipt of his own understanding, which cannot understand the Law, he says that the Law is nothing, a blind confusion.

And in conceipt of understanding, he deprecates and destroys both women and men who would represent the old primeval Law, the great Law of the Womb, the primeval Female principle. The Female shall not exist. Where it appears, it is a criminal tendency, to be stamped out.

This in Manston, Troy, Boldwood, Eustacia, Wildeve, Henchard, Tess, Jude, everybody. The women approved of are not Female in any real sense. They are passive subjects to the male, the re-echo from the male. As in the Christian religion, the Virgin worship is no real Female worship, but worship of the Female as she is passive and subjected to the male. Hence the sadness of Botticelli's Virgins.

Thus Tess sets out, not as any positive thing, containing all purpose, but as the acquiescent complement to the male. The female in her has become inert. Then Alec d'Urberville comes along, and possesses her. From the man who takes her, Tess expects her own consummation, the singling out of herself, the addition of the male complement. She is of an old line, and has the aristocratic quality of respect for the other being. She does not see the other person as an extension of herself, existing in a universe of which she is the centre and pivot. She knows that other people are outside her. Therein she is an aristocrat. And out of this attitude to the other person came her passivity. It is not the same as the passive quality in the other little heroines, such as the girl in *The Woodlanders,* who is passive because she is small.

Tess is passive out of self-acceptance, a true aristocratic quality, amounting almost to self-indifference. She knows she is herself incontrovertibly, and she knows that other people are not herself. This is a very rare quality, even in a woman. And in a civilisation so unequal, it is almost a weakness.

Tess never tries to alter or to change anybody, neither to alter nor to change nor to divert. What another person decides, that is his decision. She respects utterly the other's right to be. She is herself always.

But the others do not respect her right to be. Alec d'Urvervillc sees her as the embodied fulfilment of his own desire: something, that is, belonging to him. She cannot, in his conception, exist apart from him nor have any being apart from his being. For she is the embodiment of his desire.

This is very natural and common in men, this attitude to the world. But in Alec d'Urberville it applies only to the woman of his desire. He cares only for her. Such a man adheres to the female like a parasite.

It is a male quality to resolve a purpose to its fulfilment. It is the male quality, to seek the motive power in the female, and to convey this to a fulfilment: to receive some impulse into his senses, and to transmit it into expression.

Alec d'Urberville does not do this. He is male enough, in his way: but only physically male. He is constitutionally an enemy of the principle of self-subordination, which principle is inherent in every man. It is this principle which makes a man, a true male, see his job through, at no matter what cost. A man is strictly only himself when he is fulfilling some purpose he has conceived: so that the principle is not of self-subordination, but of continuity, of development. Only when insisted on, as in Christianity, does it become self-sacrifice. And this resistance to self-sacrifice on Alec d'Urberville's part does not make him an individualist, an egoist, but rather a non-individual, an incomplete, almost a fragmentary thing.

There seems to be in d'Urberville an inherent antagonism to any progression in himself. Yet he seeks with all his power for the source of stimulus in woman. He takes the deep impulse from the female. In this he is exceptional. No ordinary man could really have betrayed Tess. Even if she had had an illegitimate child to another man, to Angel Clare, for example, it would not have shattered her as did her connection with Alec d'Urberville. For Alec d'Urberville could reach some of the real sources of the female in a woman, and draw from them. Troy could also do this. And, as a woman instinctively knows, such men are rare. Therefore they have a power over a woman. They draw from the depth of her being.

And what they draw, they betray. With a natural male, what he draws from the source of the female, the impulse he receives from the source he transmits through his own being into utterance, motion, action, expression. But Troy and Alec d'Urberville, what they received they knew only as gratification in the senses, some perverse will prevented them from submitting to it, from becoming instrumental to it.

Which was why Tess was shattered by Alec d'Urberville, and why she murdered him in the end. The murder is badly done, altogether the book is botched, owing to the way of thinking in the author, owing to the weak yet obstinate theory of being. Nevertheless, the murder is true, the whole book is true, in its conception.

Angel Glare has the very opposite qualities to those of Alec d'Urberville. To the latter, the female in himself is the only part of himself he will acknowledge: the body, the senses, that which he shares with the female, which the female shares with him. To Angel Clare, the female in himself is detestable, the body, the senses, that which he will share with a woman, is held degraded. What he wants really is to receive the female impulse other than through the body. But his thinking has made him criticise Christianity, his deeper instinct has forbidden him to deny his body any further, a deadlock in his own being, which denies him any purpose, so that he must take to labour out of sheer impotence to resolve himself, drives him unwillingly to woman. But he must see her only as the Female Principle, he cannot bear to see her as the Woman in the Body. Her he thinks degraded. To marry her, to have a physical marriage with her, he must overcome all his ascetic revulsion, he must, in his own mind, put off his own divinity, his pure maleness, his singleness, his pure completeness, and descend to the heated welter of the flesh. It is objectionable to him. Yet his body, his life, is too strong for him.

Who is he, that he shall be pure male, and deny the existence of the female? This is the question the Creator asks of him. Is then the male the exclusive whole of life?—is he even the higher or supreme part of life? Angel Clare thinks so: as Christ thought.

Yet it is not so, as even Angel Clare must find out. Life, that is Two-in-One, Male and Female. Nor is either part greater than the other.

It is not Angel Clare's fault that he cannot come to Tess when he finds that she has, in his words, been defiled. It is the result of generations of ultra-Christian training, which had left in him an inherent aversion to the female, and to all in himself which pertained to the female. What he, in his Christian sense, conceived of as Woman, was only the servant and attendant and administering spirit to the male. He had no idea that there was such a thing as positive Woman, as the Female, another great living Principle counterbalancing his own male principle. He conceived of the world as consisting of the One, the Male Principle.

Which conception was already gendered in Botticelli, whence the melancholy of the Virgin. Which conception reached its fullest in Turner's pictures, which were utterly bodiless: and also in the great scientists or thinkers of the last generation, even Darwin and Spencer and Huxley. For these last conceived of evolution, of one spirit or principle starting at the far end of time, and lonelily traversing Time. But there is not one principle, there are two, travelling always to meet, each step of each one lessening the distance between the two of them. And Space, which so frightened Herbert Spencer, is as a Bride to us. And the cry of Man does not ring out into the Void. It rings out to Woman, whom we know not.

This Tess knew, unconsciously. An aristocrat she was, developed through generations to the belief in her own self-establishment. She could help, but she could not be helped. She could give, but she could not receive. She could attend to the wants of the other person, but no other person, save another aristocrat,—and there is scarcely such a thing as another aristocrat,—could attend to her wants, her deepest wants.

So it is the aristocrat alone, who has any real and vital sense of the "neighbour", of the other person; who has the habit of submerging himself, putting himself entirely away before the other person: because he expects to receive nothing from the other person. So that now, he has lost much of his initiative force, and exists almost isolated, detached, and without the surging ego of the ordinary man, because he has controlled his nature according to the other man, to exclude him.

And Tess, despising herself in the flesh, despising the deep Female she was, because Alec d'Urberville had betrayed her very sources, loved Angel Clare, who also despised and hated the flesh. She did not hate d'Urberville. What a man did, he did, and if he did it to her, it was her look-out. She did not conceive of him as having any human duty towards her.

The same with Angel Clare as with Alec d'Urberville. She was very grateful to him for saving her from her despair of contamination, and from her bewildered isolation. But when he accused her, she could not plead or answer. For she had no right to his goodness. She stood alone.

The female was strong in her. She was herself. But she was out of place, utterly out of her elements and her times. Hence her utter bewilderment. This is the reason why she was so overcome. She was outwearied from the start, in her spirit. For it is only by receiving from all our fellows, that we are kept fresh and vital. Tess was herself, female, intrinsically a woman.

The female in her was indomitable, unchangeable, she was utterly constant to herself. But she was, by long breeding, intact from mankind. Though Alec d'Urberville was of no kin to her, yet, in the book, he has always a quality of kinship. It was as if only a kinsman, an aristocrat, could approach her. And this to her undoing. Angel Clare would never have reached her. She would have abandoned herself to him, but he would never have reached her. It needed a physical aristocrat. She would have lived with her husband, Clare, in a state of abandon to him, like a coma. Alec d'Urberville forced her to realise him, and to realise herself. He came close to her, as Clare could never have done. So she murdered him. For she was herself.

And just as the aristocratic principle had isolated Tess, it had isolated Alec d'Urberville. For though Hardy consciously made the young betrayer a plebeian and an impostor, unconsciously, with the supreme justice of the artist, he made him the same as de Stancy, a true aristocrat, or as Fitzpiers, or Troy. He did not give him the tiredness, the touch of exhaustion necessary, in Hardy's mind, to an aristocrat. But he gave him the intrinsic qualities.

With the men as with the women of old descent: they have nothing to do with mankind in general, they are exceedingly personal. For many generations they have been accustomed to regard their own desires as their own supreme laws. They have not been bound by the conventional morality: this they have transcended, being a code unto themselves. The other person has been always present to their imagination, in the spectacular sense. He has always existed to them. But he has always existed as something other than themselves.

Hence the inevitable isolation, detachment of the aristocrat. His one aim, during centuries, has been to keep himself detached. At last he finds himself, by his very nature, cut off.

Then either he must go his own way, or he must struggle towards re-union with the mass of mankind. Either he must be an incomplete individualist, like de Stancy, or like the famous Russian nobles, he must become a wild humanitarian and reformer.

For as all the governing power has gradually been taken from the nobleman, and as, by tradition, by inherent inclination, he does not occupy himself with profession other than government, how shall he use that power which is in him and which comes in to him.

He is, by virtue of breed and long training, a perfect instrument. He knows, as every pure-bred thing knows, that his root and source is in his female. He seeks the motive power in the woman. And, having taken it, has nothing to do with it, can find, in this democratic plebeian age, no means by which to transfer it into action, expression, utterance. So there is a continual gnawing of unsatisfaction, a constant seeking of another woman, still another woman. For each time the impulse comes fresh, everything seems all right.

It may be, also, that in the aristocrat a certain weariness makes him purposeless, vicious, like a form of death. But that is not necessary. One feels that in Manston, and Troy, and Fitzpiers, and Alec d'Urberville there is good stuff gone wrong. Just as in Angel Clare, there is good stuff gone wrong in the other direction.

There can never be one extreme of wrong, without the other extreme. If there had never been the extravagant Puritan idea, that the Female Principle was to be denied, cast out by man from his soul, that only the Male Principle, of Abstraction, of Good, of Public Good, of the Community, embodied in "thou shalt love thy neighbour as thyself", really existed, there would never have been produced the extreme cavalier type, which says that only the Female Principle endures in man, that all the Abstraction, the Good, the Public Elevation, the Community, was a grovelling cowardice, and that man lived by enjoyment, through his senses, enjoyment which ended in his senses. Or perhaps better, if the extreme Cavalier type had never been produced, we should not have had the Puritan, the extreme correction.

The one extreme produces the other. It is inevitable for Angel Clare and for Alec d'Urberville mutually to destroy the woman they both loved. Each does her the extreme of wrong, so she is destroyed. The book is handled with very uncertain skill, botched and bungled. But it contains the elements of the greatest tragedy: Alec d'Urberville, who has killed the male in himself, as Clytemnestra symbolically for Orestes, killed Agamemnon; Angel Clare, who has killed the female in himself, as Orestes killed Clytemnestra: and Tess, the Woman, the Life, destroyed by a mechanical fate, in the communal law.

There is no reconciliation. Tess, Angel Clare, Alec d'Urberville, they are all as good as dead. For Angel Clare, though still apparently alive, is in reality no more than a mouth, a piece of paper, like Clym left preaching.

There is no reconciliation, only death. And so Hardy really states his case, which is not his consciously stated metaphysic, by any means, but a statement how man has gone wrong, and brought death on himself: how man has violated the Law, how he has supererogated himself, gone so far in his male conceit as to supersede the Creator, and win death as a reward. Indeed the works of supererogation of our male assiduity help us to a better salvation.

2

Jude is only Tess turned round about. Instead of the heroine containing the two principles, male and female, at strife within her one being, it is Jude who contains them both, whilst the two women with him take the place of the two men to Tess.

Arabella is Alec d'Urberville, Sue is Angel Clare. These represent the same pair of principles.

But first, let it be said again that Hardy is a bad artist. Because he must condemn Alec d'Urberville, according to his own personal creed, therefore he shows him a vulgar intriguer of coarse lasses, and as ridiculous convert to evangelism. But Alec d'Urberville, by the artist's account, is neither of these. It is, in actual life, a rare man who seeks and seeks among women for one of such character and intrinsic female being as Tess. The ordinary sensualist avoids such characters. They implicate him too deeply. An ordinary sensualist would have been much too common, much too afraid, to turn to Tess. In a way, d'Urberville was her mate. And his subsequent passion for her is in its way noble enough. But whatever his passion, as a male, he must be a betrayer, even if he had been the most faithful husband on earth. He betrayed the female in a woman, by taking her, and by responding with no male impulse from himself. He roused her, but never satisfied her. He could never satisfy her. It was like a soul-disease in him: he was, in the strict, though not the technical sense, impotent. But he must have wanted, later on, not to be so. But he could not help himself. He was spiritually impotent in love.

Arabella was the same. She, like d'Urberville, was converted by an evangelical preacher. It is significant in both of them. They were not just shallow, as Hardy would have made them out.

He is, however, more contemptuous in his personal attitude to the woman than to the man. He insists that she is a pig-killer's daughter; he insists that she drag Jude into pig-killing: he lays stress on her false tail of hair. That is not the point at all. This is only Hardy's bad art. He himself, as an artist, manages in the whole picture of Arabella almost to make insignificant in her these pig-sticking false hair crudities. But he must have his personal revenge on her, for her coarseness, which offends him, because he is something of an Angel Clare.

The pig-sticking and so-forth are not so important in the real picture. As for the false tail of hair, few women dared have been so open and natural about it. Few women, indeed, dared have made Jude marry them. It may have been a case for Arabella of "fools rush in". But she was not such a fool. And her motives are explained in the book. Life is not in the actual, such a simple affair of getting a fellow and getting married. It is, even for Arabella, an affair on which she places her all. No barmaid marries anybody, the first man she can lay her hands on. She cannot. It must be a personal thing to her. And no ordinary woman would want Jude. Moreover, no ordinary woman could have laid her hands on Jude.

It is an absurd fallacy this, that a small man wants a woman bigger and finer than he is himself. A man is as big as his real desires. Let a man, seeing with his eyes a woman of force and being, want her for his own, then that man is intrinsically an equal of that woman. And the same with a woman.

A coarse, shallow woman does not want to marry a sensitive, deep-feeling man. She feels no desire for him, she is not drawn to him, but repelled, knowing he will contemn her. She wants a man to correspond to herself: that is, if she is a young woman looking for a mate, as Arabella was.

What an old, jaded, yet still unsatisfied woman or man wants, is another matter. Yet not even one of these will take a young creature of real character, superior in force. Instinct and fear prevent it.

Arabella was, under all her disguise of pig-fat and false hair, and vulgar speech, in character somewhere an aristocrat. She was, like Eustacia, amazingly lawless, even splendidly so. She believed in herself and she was not altered by any outside opinion of herself. Her fault was pride. She thought herself the centre of life, that all which existed, belonged to her in so far as she wanted it.

In this she was something like Job. His attitude was "I am strong and rich, and also, I am a good man." He gave out of his own sense of bounty, and felt no indebtedness. Arabella was almost the same. She felt also strong and abundant, arrogant in her hold on life. She needed a complement: and the nearest thing to her satisfaction was Jude. For as she, intrinsically, was a strong female, by far overpowering her Annies and her friends, so was he a strong male.

The difference between them was not so much a difference of quality, or degree, as a difference of form. Jude, like Tess, wanted full consummation. Arabella, like Alec d'Urberville, had that in her which resisted full consummation, wanted only to enjoy herself in contact with the male. She would have no transmission.

There are two attitudes to love. A man in love with a woman says either: "I, the man, the male, am the supreme, I am the one, and the woman is administered unto me, and this is her highest function, to be administered unto me." This was the conscious attitude of the Greeks. But their unconscious attitude was the reverse: they were in truth afraid of the female principle, their vaunt was empty, they went in deep, inner dread of her. So did the Jews, so do the Italians. But after the Renaissance, there was a change. Then began conscious Woman-reverence, and a lack of instinctive reverence, rather only an instinctive pity. It is according to the balance between the Male and Female Principles.

The other attitude of a man in love, besides this of "she is administered unto my maleness", is: "she is the unknown, the undiscovered, into which I plunge to discovery, losing myself".

And what we call real love has always this latter attitude.

The first attitude which belongs to passion, makes a man feel proud, splendid. It is a powerful stimulant to him, the female administered to him. He feels full of blood, he walks the earth like a Lord. And it is to this state Nietzsche aspires in his "Wille zur Macht" It is this the passionate nations crave.

And under all this, there is, naturally, the sense of fear, transition, and the sadness of mortality. For, the female being herself an independent force, may she not withdraw, and leave a man empty, like ash, as one sees a Jew or an Italian so often.

This first attitude, too, of male pride receiving the female administration may, and often does, contain the corresponding intense fear and reverence of the female, as of the unknown. So that, starting from the male assertion, there came in the old days the full consummation; as of often there comes the full consummation now.

But not always. The man may retain all the while of possession the sense of himself, the primary male, receiving gratification. This constant reaction upon himself at length dulls his senses and his sensibility, and makes him mechanical, automatic. He grows gradually incapable of receiving any gratification from the female, and becomes a roué, only automatically alive, and frantic with the knowledge thereof.

It is unfortunately the tendency of the Parisian—or has been—to take this attitude to love, and to intercourse. The woman knows herself all the while as the primary female receiving administration of the male. So she becomes hard and external, and inwardly jaded, fired out. It is the tendency of English women to take this attitude also. And it is this attitude of love, more than anything else, which devitalises a race, and makes it barren.

It is an attitude natural enough to start with. Every young man must think that it is the highest honour he can do to a woman, to receive from her her female administration to his male being, whilst he meanwhile gives her the gratification of himself. But intimacy usually corrects this, love, or use, or marriage: a married man ceases to think of himself as the primary male: hence often his dulness. Unfortunately, he also fails in the many cases to realise the gladness of a man in contact with the unknown in the female, which gives him a sense of richness and oneness with all life, as if, by being part of life, he were infinitely rich. Which is different from the sense of power, of dominating life. The Wille zur Macht is a spurious feeling.

For a man who dares to look upon, and to venture within the unknown of the female, losing himself, like a man who gives himself to the sea, or a man who enters a primeval, virgin forest, feels, when he returns, the utmost gladness of singing. This is certainly the gladness of a male bird in his singing, the amazing joy of return from the adventure into the unknown, rich with addition to his soul, rich with the knowledge of the utterly illimitable depth and breadth of the unknown; the ever yielding extent of the unacquired, the unattained; the inexhaustible riches lain under unknown skies over unknown seas, all the magnificence that *is,* and yet which is unknown to any of us. And the knowledge of the reality with which it awaits me, the male, the knowledge of the calling and struggling of all the unknown, illimitable Female towards me, unembraced as yet, towards those men who will endlessly follow me, who will endlessly struggle after me, beyond me, further into this calling, unrealised vastness, nearer to the outstretched, eager, advancing unknown in the woman.

It is for this sense of All the magnificence that is unknown to me, of All that which stretches forth arms and breast to the Inexhaustible Embrace of all the ages, towards me, whose arms are outstretched, for this moment's embrace which gives me the inkling of the Inexhaustible Embrace, that every man must and does yearn. And whether he be a roué, and vicious, or young and virgin, this is the bottom of every man's desire, for the embrace, for the advancing into the unknown, for the landing on the shore of the undiscovered half of the world, where the wealth of the female lies before us.

What is true of men is so of women. If we turn our faces west towards nightfall and the unknown within the dark embrace of a wife, they turn their faces east, towards the sunrise and the brilliant, bewildering, active embrace of a husband. And as we are dazed with the unknown in her, so is she dazed with the unknown in us. It is so. And we throw up our joy to heaven like towers and spires and fountains and leaping flowers, so glad we are.

But always, we are divided within ourselves. Is it not that I am wonderful. Is it not a gratification for me when a stranger shall land on my shores and enjoy what he finds there. Shall I not also enjoy it? Shall I not enjoy the strange motion of the stranger, like a pleasant sensation of silk and warmth against me, stirring unknown fibres? Shall I not take this enjoyment without venturing out in dangerous waters, losing myself, perhaps destroying myself seeking the unknown. Shall I not stay at home, and by feeling the swift, soft airs blow out of the unknown upon my body, shall I not have rich pleasure of myself.

And, because they were afraid of the unknown, and because they wanted to retain the full-veined gratification of self-pleasure, men have kept their women tightly in bondage. But when the men were no longer afraid of the unknown, when they deemed it exhausted, they said, "There are no women, there are only daughters of men"—as we say now, as the Greeks tried to say. Hence the "Virgin" conception of woman, the passionless, passive conception, progressing from Fielding's "Amelia" to Dickens' "Agnes", and on to Hardy's Sue.

Whereas Arabella in *Jude the Obscure* has what one might call the selfish instinct for love, Jude himself has the other, the unselfish. She sees in him a male who can gratify her. She takes him, and is gratified by him. Which makes a man of him. He becomes a grown, independent man in the arms of Arabella, conscious of having met, and satisfied, the female demand in him. This makes a man of any youth. He is proven unto himself as a male being, initiated into the freedom of life.

But Arabella refused his purpose. She refused to combine with him in one purpose. Just like Alec d'Urberville, she had from the outset an antagonism to the submission to any change in herself, to any development. She had the will to remain where she was, static, and to receive and exhaust all impulse she received from the male, in her senses. Whereas in a normal woman, impulse received from the male drives her on to a sense of joy and wonder and glad freedom in touch with the unknown of which she is made aware, so that she exists on the edge of the unknown half in rapture. Which is the state the writers wish to portray in "Amelia", and "Agnes", but particularly in the former; which Reynolds wishes to portray in his pictures of women.

To all this Arabella was antagonistic. It seems like a perversion in her, as if she played havoc with the stuff she was made of, as Alec d'Urberville did. Nevertheless she remained always unswervable female, she never truckled to the male idea, but was self-responsible, without fear. It is easier to imagine such a woman, out of one's desires, than to find her in real life. For, where a half criminal type, a reckless daredevil type resembling her may be found on the outskirts of society, yet these are not Arabella. Which criminal type, or reckless, low woman, would want to marry Jude? Arabella wanted Jude. And it is evident she was not too coarse for him, since she made no show of refinement from the first. The female in her, reckless and unconstrained, was strong enough to draw him after her, as her male, right to the end. Which other woman could have done this? At least let acknowledgement be made to her great female force of character. Her coarseness seems to me exaggerated to make the moralist's case good against her.

Jude could never hate her. She did a great deal for the true making of him, for making him a grown man. She gave him to himself.

And there was danger at the outset that he should never become a man, but that he should remain incorporeal, smothered out under his idea of learning. He was somewhat in Angel Clare's position. Not that generations of particular training had made him almost rigid and paralysed to the female: but that his whole passion was concentrated away from woman to re-inforce in him the male impulse towards extending the consciousness. His family was a difficult family to marry. And this

83

because, that whilst the men were physically vital, with a passion towards the female from which no moral training had restrained them, like a plant tied to a stick and diverted, they had at the same time, an inherent complete contempt of the female, valuing only that which was male. So that they were strongly divided against themselves, with no external hold, such as a moral system, to grip to.

It would have been possible for Jude, monkish, passionate, mediaeval, belonging to woman yet striving away from her, refusing to know her, to have gone on denying one side of his nature, adhering to his idea of learning, till he had stultified the physical impulse of his being and perverted it entirely. Arabella brought him to himself, gave him himself, made him free, sound as a physical male.

That she would not, or could not, combine her life with him for the fulfilment of a purpose was their misfortune. But at any rate, his purpose of becoming an Oxford Don, was a cut and dried purpose which had no connection with his living body, and for which probably no woman could have united with him.

No doubt Arabella hated his books, and hated his whole attitude to study. What had he, a passionate, emotional nature, to do with learning for learning's sake, with mere academics. Any woman must know it was ridiculous. But he persisted with the tenacity of all pervertedness. And she, in this something of an aristocrat, like Tess, feeling that she had not right to him, no right to receive anything from him, except his sex, in which she felt she gave and did not receive, for she conceived of herself as the primary female, as that which, in taking the male, conferred on him his greatest boon, she left him alone. Her attitude was, that he would find all he desired in coming to her. She was occupied with herself. It was not that she wanted *him*. She wanted to have the sensation of herself in contact with him. His being she refused. She allowed only her own being.

Therefore she scarcely troubled him, when he earned little money and took no notice of her. He did not refuse to take notice of her because he hated her, or was deceived by her, or disappointed in her. He was not. He refused to consider her seriously because he adhered with all his pertinacity to the idea of study, from which he excluded her.

Which she saw and knew, and allowed. She would not force him to notice her, or to consider her seriously. She would compel him to nothing. She had had a certain satisfaction of him, which would be no more if she stayed for ever. For she was non-developing. When she knew him in her senses she knew the end of him, as far as she was concerned. That was all.

So she just went her way. He did not blame her. He scarcely missed her. He returned to his books.

Really, he had lost nothing by his marriage with Arabella: neither innocence nor belief nor hope. He had indeed gained his manhood. She left him the stronger and completer.

And now he would concentrate all on his male idea, of arresting himself, of becoming himself a non-developing quality, an academic mechanism. That was his obsession. That was his craving: to have nothing to do with his own life. This was the same as Tess when she turned to Angel Clare. She wanted life merely in the secondary, outside form, in the consciousness.

It was another form of the disease, or decay of old family, which possessed Alec d'Urberville; a different form, but closely related. D'Urberville wanted to arrest all his activity in his senses, Jude Fawley wanted to arrest all his activity in his mind. Each of them wanted to become an impersonal force working automatically. Each of them wanted to deny, or escape the responsibility and trouble of living as a complete person, a full individual.

And neither was able to bring it off. Jude's real desire was, not to live in the body. He wanted to exist only in his mentality, he was as if bored, or blasé, in the body, just like Tess. This seems to be the result of coming of an old family, that had been long conscious, long self-conscious, specialised, separate, exhausted.

This drove him to Sue. She was his kinswoman, as d'Urberville was kinsman to Tess. She was like himself in her being and her desire; like Jude, she wanted to live partially, in the consciousness, in the mind only. She wanted no experience in the senses, she wished only to know.

She belonged with Tess, to the old woman-type of witch or prophetess, which adhered to the male principle, and destroyed the female. But in the true prophetess, in Cassandra, for example, the denial of the female cost a strong and almost maddening effort. But in Sue, it was done before she was born.

She was born with the vital female atrophied in her: she was almost male. Her *will* was male. It was wrong for Jude to take her physically, it was a violation of her. She was not the Virgin type, but the witch type, which has no sex. Why should she be forced into intercourse that was not natural to her?

It was not natural for her to have children. It is inevitable that her children die. It is not natural for Tess nor for Angel Clare to have children, nor for Arabella nor for Alec d'Urberville. Because none of these wished to give of themselves to the lover, none of them wished to mate: they only wanted their own experience. For Jude alone it was natural to have children, and this in spite of himself.

Sue wished to identify herself utterly with the male principle. That which was female in her she wanted to consume within the male force, to consume it in the fire of understanding, of giving utterance. Whereas an ordinary woman knows that she *contains* all understanding, that she is the unutterable which man must for ever continue to try to utter, Sue felt that all must be uttered, must be given to the male, that in truth, only Male existed, that everything was the Word, and the Word was everything.

Sue is the production of the long selection by man of the woman in whom the female is subordinated to the male principle. A long line of Amelias and Agneses, those women who submitted to the man-idea, flattered the man, and bored him, the Gretchens and the Turgenev heroines, those who have betrayed the female and who therefore only seem to exist to be betrayed by their men, these have produced at length a Sue, the pure thing. And as soon as she is produced she is execrated.

What Cassandra and Aspasia became to the Greeks, Sue has become to the northern civilisation. But the Greeks never pitied Woman. They did not show her that highest impertinence—not even Euripides.

But Sue is scarcely a woman at all, though she is feminine enough. Cassandra submitted to Apollo, and gave him the Word of affiance, brought forth prophecy to him, not children. She received the embrace of the spirit, He breathed His Grace upon her: and she conceived and brought forth a prophecy. It was still a marriage. Not the marriage of the Virgin with the Spirit, but the marriage of the female spirit with the male spirit, bodiless.

85

With Sue, however, the marriage was no marriage, but a submission, a service, a slavery. Her female spirit did not wed with the male spirit: she could not prophesy. Her spirit submitted to the male spirit, owned the priority of the male spirit, wished to become the male spirit. That which was female in her, resistant, gave her only her critical faculty. When she sought out the physical quality in the Greeks, that was her effort to make even the unknowable physique a part of knowledge, to contain the body within the mind.

One of the supremest products of our civilisation is Sue, and a product that well frightens us. It is quite natural, that with all her mental alertness, she married Phillotson without ever considering the physical quality of marriage. Deep instinct made her avoid the consideration. And the duality of her nature made her extremely liable to self-destruction. The suppressed, atrophied female in her, like a potent fury, was always there, suggesting her to make the fatal mistake. She contained always the rarest, most deadly anarchy in her own being.

It needed that she should have some place in society where the clarity of her mental being, which was in itself a form of death, could shine out without attracting any desire for her body. She needed a refinement on Angel Clare. For she herself was a more specialised, more highly civilised product on the female side, than Angel Clare on the male. Yet the atrophied female in her would still want the bodily male.

She attracted to herself Jude. His experience with Arabella had for the time being diverted his attention altogether from the female. His attitude was that of service to the pure male spirit. But the physical male in him, that which knew and belonged to the female, was potent, and roused the female in Sue as much as she wanted it rousing, so much that it was a stimulant to her, making her mind the brighter.

It was a cruelly difficult position. She must, by the constitution of her nature, remain quite physically intact, for the female was atrophied in her, to the enlargement of the male activity. Yet she wanted some quickening for this atrophied female. She wanted even kisses. That the new rousing might give her a sense of life. But she could only *live* in the mind.

Then, where could she find a man who would be able to feed her with his male vitality, through kisses, proximity, without demanding the female return. For she was such that she could only receive quickening from a strong male, for she was herself no small thing. Could she then find a man, a strong, passionate male, who would devote himself entirely to the production of the mind in her, to the production of male activity, or of female activity critical to the male.

She could only receive the highest stimulus, which she must inevitably seek, from a man who put her in constant jeopardy. Her essentiality rested upon her remaining intact. Any suggestion of the physical was utter confusion to her. Her principle was the ultra-Christian principle—of living entirely according to the Spirit, to the One, male spirit, which knows, and utters, and shines, but exists beyond feeling, beyond joy or sorrow, or pain, exists only in Knowing. In tune with this, she was herself. Let her, however, be turned under the influence of the other dark, silent, strong principle, of the female, and she would break like a fine instrument under discord.

Yet, to live at all in tune with the male spirit, she must receive the male stimulus from a man. Otherwise she was as an instrument without a player. She must feel the hands of a man upon her, she must be infused with his male vitality, or she was not alive.

Here then was her difficulty: to find a man whose vitality could infuse her and make her live, and who would not, at the same time, demand of her a return, the return of the female impulse into him. What man could receive this drainage, receiving nothing back again. He must either die, or revolt.

One man had died. She knew it well enough. She knew her own fatality. She knew she drained the vital, male stimulus out of a man, producing in him only knowledge of the mind, only mental clarity: which man must always strive to attain, but which is not life in him, rather the product of life.

Just as Alec d'Urberville, on the other hand, drained the female vitality out of a woman, and gave her only sensation, only experience in the senses, a sense of herself, nothing to the soul or spirit, thereby exhausting her.

Now Jude, after Arabella, and following his own idée fixe, hunted this mental clarity, this knowing, above all. What he contained in himself, of male and female impulse, he wanted to bring forth, to draw into his mind, to resolve into understanding, as a plant resolves that which it contains into flower.

This Sue could do for him. By creating a vacuum, she could cause the vivid flow which clarified him. By rousing him, by drawing from him his turgid vitality, made thick and heavy and physical with Arabella, she could bring into consciousness that which he contained. For he was heavy and full of unrealised life, clogged with untransmuted knowledge, with accretion of his senses. His whole life had been till now an indrawing, ingestion. Arabella had been a vital experience for him, received into his blood. And how was he to bring out all this fulness into knowledge, or utterance. For all the time, he was being roused to new physical desire, new life-experience, new sense-enrichening, and he could not perform his male function of transmitting this into expression, or action. The particular form his flowering should take, he could not find. So he hunted and studied, to find the call, the appeal which should call out of him that which was in him.

And great was his transport when the appeal came from Sue. She wanted, at first, only his words. That of him which could come to her through speech, through his consciousness, her mind, like a bottomless gulf, cried out for. She wanted satisfaction through the mind, and cried out for him to satisfy her through the mind.

Great then was his joy at giving himself out to her. He gave, for it was more blessed then to give than to receive. He gave, and she received some satisfaction. But where she was not satisfied, there he must try still to satisfy her. He struggled to bring it all forth. She was as himself asking himself what he was. And he strove to answer, in a transport.

And he answered in a great measure. He singled himself out from the old matrix of the accepted idea, he produced an individual flower of his own.

It was for this he loved Sue. She did for him quickly what he would have done for himself slowly, through study. By patient, diligent study, he would have used up the surplus of that turgid energy in him, and would, by long contact with old truth, have arrived at the form of truth which was in him. What he indeed wanted to get from study, was not a store of learning, nor the vanity of education, a sort of superiority of educational wealth, though this also gave him pleasure. He wanted, through familiarity with the true thinkers and poets, particularly with the classic and theological thinkers, because of their comparative sensuousness, to find conscious expression for that which he held in his blood. And to do this, it was necessary for him to resolve and to reduce his blood, to overcome the female sensuousness in himself, to transmute his sensuous being into another state, a state of clarity, of consciousness. Slowly, laboriously, struggling with the Greek and the Latin, he would have burned down his thick blood as fuel, and have come to the true light of himself.

This Sue did for him. In marriage, each party fulfils a dual function with regard to the other: exhaustive and enriching. The female at the same time exhausts and invigorates the male, the male at the same time exhausts and invigorates the female. The exhaustion and invigoration are both temporary and relative. The male, making the effort to penetrate into the female, exhausts himself and invigorates her. But that which, at the end, he discovers and carries off from her, some seed of being, enrichens him and exhausts her. Arabella, in taking Jude, accepted very little from him. She absorbed very little of his strength and virility into herself. For she only wanted to be aware of herself in contact with him, she did not want him to penetrate into her very being, till he moved her to her very depths, till she loosened to him some of her very self, for his enrichening. She was intrinsically impotent, as was Alec d'Urberville.

So that in her, Jude went very little further in Knowledge, or in Self-Knowledge. He took only the first step: of knowing himself sexually, as a sexual male. That is only the first, the first, necessary, but rudimentary step.

When he came to Sue, he found her physically impotent, but spiritually potent. That was what he wanted. Of Knowledge in the blood he had a rich enough store: more than he knew what to do with. He wished for the further step, of reduction, of essentialising into Knowledge. Which Sue gave to him.

So that his experience with Arabella plus his first experience of trembling intimacy and incandescent realisation with Sue made one complete marriage: that is, the two women added together made One Bride.

When Jude had exhausted his surplus self, in spiritual intimacy with Sue, when he had gained through her all the wonderful understanding she could evoke in him, when he was clarified to himself, then his marriage with Sue was over. Jude's marriage with Sue was over before he knew her physically. She had, physically, nothing to give him.

Which in her deepest instinct, she knew. She made no mistake in marrying Phillotson. She acted according to the pure logic of her nature. Phillotson was a man who wanted no marriage whatsoever with the female. Sexually, he wanted her as an instrument through which he obtained relief, and some gratification: but really, relief. Spiritually, he wanted her as a thing to be wondered over and delighted in, but quite separately from himself He knew quite well he could never marry her. He was a human being as near to mechanical functioning as a human being can be. The whole process of digestion, masticating, swallowing, digesting, excretion, is a sort of super-mechanical process. And Phillotson was like this. He was an organ, a function-fulfilling organ, he had no separate existence. He could not create a single new movement or thought or expression. Everything he did was a repetition of what had been. All his study was a study of what had been. It was a mechanical functional process. He was a true, if small, form of the "Savant". He could understand only the functional laws of living, but these he understood honestly. He was true to himself, he was not overcome by any cant or sentimentalising. So that in this he was splendid. But it is a cruel thing for a complete, or a spiritual individuality to be submitted to a functional organism.

The Widow Edlin said that there are some men no woman of any feeling could touch, and Phillotson was one of them. If the Widow knew this, why was Sue's instinct so short.

But Mrs Edlin was a full human being, creating life in a new form through her personality. She must have known Sue's deficiency. It was natural for Sue to read and to turn again to:

"Thou hast conquered, O pale Galilean:
The world has grown grey from thy breath."

In her, the pale Galilean had indeed triumphed. Her body was as insentient as hoar-frost. She knew well enough that she was not alive in the ordinary human sense. She did not, like an ordinary woman, receive all she knew through her senses, her instincts, but through her consciousness. The pale Galilean had a pure disciple in her: in her He was fulfilled. For the senses, the body, did not exist to her, she existed as a consciousness. And this so much so, that she was almost an Apostate.

She turned to look at Venus and Apollo. As if she could know either Venus or Apollo, save as ideas. Nor Venus nor Aphrodite had anything to do with her, but only Pallas and Christ.

She was unhappy every moment of her life, poor Sue, with the knowledge of her own non-existence within life. She felt all the time the ghastly sickness of dissolution upon her, she was as a void unto herself.

So she married Phillotson, the only man she could, in reality, marry. To him she could be a wife: she could give him the sexual relief he wanted of her, and supply him with the transcendence which was a pleasure to him; it was hers to seal him with the seal which made an honourable human being of him. For he felt, deep within himself, something a reptile feels. And she was his guarantee, his crown.

Why does a snake horrify us, or even a newt? Why was Phillotson like a newt? What is it, in our life or in our feeling, to which a newt corresponds? Is it that life has the two sides, of growth and of decay, symbolised most acutely in our bodies by the semen and the excreta? Is it that the newt, the reptile, belong to the putrescent activity of life, the bird, the fish to the growth activity? Is it that the newt and the reptile are suggested to us through those sensations connected with excretion? And was Phillotson more or less connected with the decay activity of life? Was it his function to reorganise the life-excreta of the ages? At any rate, one can honour him, for he was true to himself.

Sue married Phillotson according to her true instinct. But, being almost pure Christian, in the sense of having no physical life, she had turned to the Greeks, and with her mind was an Aphrodite-worshipper. In craving for the highest form of that which she lacked, she worshipped Aphrodite. There are two sets of Aphrodite-worshippers: daughters of Aphrodite and the almost neutral daughters of Mary of Bethany. Sue was, oh, cruelly far from being a daughter of Aphrodite. She was the furthest alien from Aphrodite. She might excuse herself through her Venus Urania—but it was hopeless.

Therefore, when she left Phillotson, in whose marriage she consummated her own crucifixion, to go to Jude, she was deserting the God of her being for the God of her hopeless want. How much could she become a living, physical woman? But she would get away from Phillotson.

She went to Jude to continue the spiritual marriage, bodiless. That was all very well, if he had been satisfied. If he had been satisfied, they might have lived in this spiritual intimacy, without physical contact, for the rest of their lives, so strong was her true instinct for herself.

He, however, was not satisfied. He reached the point where he was clarified, where he had reduced from his blood into his consciousness all that was uncompounded before. He had become himself as far as he could, he had fulfilled himself All that he had gathered in his youth, all that he had gathered from Arabella, was assimilated now, fused and transformed into one clear Jude.

Now he wants that which is necessary for him if he is to go on. He wants, at its lowest, the physical, sexual relief. For continually balked sexual desire, or necessity, makes a man unable to live freely, scotches him, stultifies him. And where a man is roused to the fullest pitch, as Jude was roused by Sue, then the principal connection becomes a necessity, if only for relief. Anything else is a violation.

Sue ran away to escape physical connection with Phillotson, only to find herself in the arms of Jude. But Jude wanted of her more than Phillotson wanted. This was what terrified her to the bottom of her nature. Whereas Phillotson always only wanted sexual relief of her, Jude wanted the consummation of marriage. He wanted that deepest experience, that penetrating far into the unknown and undiscovered which lies in the body and blood of man and woman, during life. He wanted to receive from her the quickening, the primitive seed and impulse which should start him to a new birth. And for this he must go back deep into the primal, unshown, unknown life of the blood, the thick, source-stream of life in her.

And she was terrified lest he should find her out, that it was wanting in her. This was her deepest dread, to see him inevitably disappointed in her. She could not bear to be put into the balance, wherein she knew she would be found wanting.

For she knew in herself that she was cut off from the source and origin of life. For her, the way back was lost irrevocably. And when Jude came to her, wanting to retrace with her the course right back to the springs and the welling-out, she was more afraid than of death. For she could not. She was like a flower broken off from the tree, that lives a while in water, and even puts forth. So Sue lived sustained and nourished by the rarefied life of books and art, and by the inflow from the man. But, owing to centuries and centuries of weaning away from the body of life, centuries of insisting upon the supremacy and bodilessness of Love, centuries of striving to escape the conditions of being and of striving to attain the condition of Knowledge, centuries of pure Christianity, she had gone too far. She had climbed and climbed and climbed to be near the stars. And now at last, on the topmost pinnacle, exposed to all the horrors and the magnificence of space, she could not go back. Her strength had fallen from her. Up at that great height, with scarcely any foothold, but only space, space all round her, rising up to her from beneath, she was like a thing suspended, supported almost at the point of extinction by the density of the medium. Her body was lost to her, fallen away, gone. She existed there as a point of consciousness, no more, like one swooned at a great height, held up at the tip of a fine pinnacle, that drove upwards into nothingness.

Jude rose to that height with her. But he did not die as she died. Beneath him the foothold was more, he did not swoon. There came a time when he wanted to go back, down to earth. But she was fastened like Andromeda.

Perhaps, if Jude had not known Arabella, Sue might have persuaded him that he too was bodiless, only a point of consciousness.   But she was too late, another had been before her, and given her the lie.

Arabella was never so jealous of Sue as Sue of Arabella. How shall the saint that tips the pinnacle, Saint Simeon Stylites thrust on the highest needle that pricks the heavens, be envied by the man who   walks the horizontal earth? But Sue was cruelly anguished with jealousy of Arabella. It was only this, this knowledge that Jude wanted Arabella, which made Sue give him access to her own body.

When she did that, she died. The Sue that had been till then, the glimmering, pale, star-like Sue, died and was revoked on the night when Arabella called at their house at Aldbrickham and Jude went out in his slippers to look for her, and did not find her, but came back to Sue, who in her anguish gave him then the access to her body. Till that day, Sue had been, in her will and in her very self, true to one motion, to Love, to Knowledge, to the Light, to the upward motion. Phillotson had not altered this. When she had suffered him, she had said: "He does not touch me, I am beyond him."

But now she must give her body to Jude. At that moment her light began to go out, all she had lived for and by began to turn into a falseness, Sue began to nullify herself.

She could never become physical. She could never return down to earth. But there, lying bound at the pinnacle-tip, she had to pretend she was lying on the horizontal earth, prostrate with a man.

It was a profanation and a pollution, worse than the pollution of Cassandra or of the Vestals. Sue had her own form: to break this form was to destroy her. Her destruction began only when she said to Jude "I give in."

As for Jude, he dragged his body after his consciousness. His instinct could never have made him actually desire physical connection with Sue. He was roused by an appeal made through his consciousness. This appeal automatically roused his senses. His consciousness desired Sue. So his senses were forced to follow his consciousness.

But he must have felt, in knowing her, the "frisson" of sacrilege, something like the Frenchman who lay with a corpse. Her body, the body of a Vestal, was swooned into that state of bloodless ecstasy wherein it was dead to the senses. Or it was the body of an insane woman, whose senses are directed from the disordered mind, whose mind is not subjected to the senses.

But Jude was physically undeveloped. Altogether he was mediaeval. His senses were vigorous but not delicate. He never realised what it meant to *him,* his taking Sue. He thought he was satisfied.

But if it was death to her, or profanation, or pollution, or breaking, it was unnatural to him, blasphemy. How could he, a living, loving man, warm and productive, take with his body the moonlit cold body of a woman who did not live to him, and did not want him. It was monstrous, and it sent him mad.

91

She knew it was wrong, she knew it should never be. But what else could she do? Jude loved her now with his will. To have left him to Arabella would have been to destroy him. To have shared him with Arabella would have been possible to Sue, but impossible to him, for he had the strong, purist idea, that a man's body should follow and be subordinate to his spirit, his senses should be subordinate to and subsequent to his mind. Which idea is utterly false.

So Jude and Sue are damned, partly by their very being, but chiefly by their incapacity to accept the conditions of their own and each other's being. If Jude could have known that he did not want Sue, physically, and then have made his choice, they might not have wasted their lives. But he could not know.

If he could have known, after a while, after he had taken her many times, that it was wrong, still they might have made a life. He must have known that, after taking Sue, he was depressed as she was depressed. He must have known worse than that. He must have felt the devastating sense of the unlivingness of life, things must have ceased to exist for him, when he rose from taking Sue, and he must have felt that he walked in a ghastly blank, confronted just by space, void.

But he would acknowledge nothing of what he felt. He must feel according to his idea and his will. Nevertheless, they were too truthful ever to marry. A man as real and personal as Jude cannot, from his deeper religious sense, marry a woman unless indeed he can marry her, unless with her he can find or approach the real consummation of marriage. And Sue and Jude could not lie to themselves, in their last and deepest feelings. They knew it was no marriage: they knew it was wrong, all along: they knew they were sinning against life, in forcing a physical marriage between themselves.

How many people, man and woman, live together, in England, and have children, and are never, never asked whether they have been through the marriage ceremony together! Why then should Jude and Sue have been brought to task? Only because of their own uneasy sense of wrong, of sin, which they communicated to other people. And this wrong or sin was not against the community, but against their own being, against life. Which is why they were, the pair of them, instinctively disliked.

They never knew of happiness, actual, sure-footed happiness, not for a moment. That was incompatible with Sue's nature. But what they knew was a very delightful but poignant and unhealthy condition of lightnened conciousness. They reacted on each other to stimulate the conciousness. So that, when they went to the flower-show, her sense of the roses, and Jude's sense of the roses, would be most, most poignant. There is always this pathos, this poignancy, this trembling on the verge of pain and tears, in their happiness.

"Happy?" he murmured. She nodded.

The roses, how the roses glowed for them! The flowers had more being than either he or she. But as their ecstasy over things sank a little, they felt, the pair of them, as if they themselves were wanting in real body, as if they were too unsubstantial, too thin and evanescent in substance, as if the other solid people might jostle right through them, two wandering shades as they were.

This they felt themselves. Hence their uncertainty in contact with other people, hence their abnormal sensitiveness. But they had their own form of happiness nevertheless, this trembling on the verge of ecstasy, when, the senses strongly roused to the service of the consciousness, the things they contemplated took flaming being, became flaming symbols of their own emotions to them.

So that the real marriage of Jude and Sue was in the roses. Then, in the third state, in the spirit, their two beings met upon the roses and in the roses were symbolized in consummation. The rose is the symbol of marriage-consummation in its beauty. To them, it is more than a symbol, it is a fact, a flaming experience.

They went home trembling glad. And then horror when, because of Jude's unsatisfaction, he must take Sue sexually. The flaming experience becomes a falsity, or an ignis fatuus leading them on.

They exhausted their lives, he in the consciousness, she in the body. She was glad to have children, to prove she was a woman. But in her it was a perversity to wish to prove she was a woman. She was no woman. And her children, the proof thereof, vanished like hoar-frost from her.

It was not the stone-masonry that exhausted him and weakened him and made him ill. It was this continuous feeding of his consciousness from his senses, this continuous state of incandescence of the consciousness, when his body, his vital tissue, the very protoplasm in him, was being slowly consumed away. For he had no life in the body. Every time he went to Sue, physically, his inner experience must have been a shock back from life and from this form of outgoing, like that of a man who lies with a corpse. He had no life in the senses: he had no inflow from the source to make up for the enormous wastage. So he gradually became exhausted, burned more and more away, till he was frail as an ember.

And she, her body also suffered. But it was in the mind that she had had her being, and it was in the mind she paid her price. She tried and tried to receive and to satisfy Jude physically. She bore him children, she gave herself' to the life of the body.

But as she was formed she was formed, and there was no altering it. She needed all the life that belonged to her, and more, for the supplying of her mind. Since such a mind as hers is found only, healthily, in a person of powerful vitality. For the mind, in a common person, is created out of the surplus vitality, or out of the remainder after all the sensuous life has been fulfilled.

Sue needed all the life that belonged to her, for her mind, It was her form. To disturb that arrangement was to make her into somebody else, not herself Therefore, when she became a physical wife and a mother, she forswore her own being. She abjured her own mind, she denied it, took her faith, her belief, her very living away from it.

It is most probable she lived chiefly in her children. They were her guarantee as a physical woman, the being to which she now laid claim. She had forsaken the ideal of an independent mind.

She would love her children with anguish, afraid always for their safety, never certain of their stable existence, never assured of their real reality. When they were out of her sight, she would be uneasy, uneasy almost as if they did not exist. There would be a gnawing at her till they came back. She would not be satisfied till she had them crushed on her breast. And even then, she would not be sure, she would not be sure. She could not be sure, in life, of anything. She could only be sure, in the old days, of what she saw with her mind. Of that she was absolutely sure.

Meanwhile Jude became exhausted in vitality, bewildered, aimless, lost, pathetically unproductive.

Again one can see what instinct, what feeling it was which made Arabella's boy bring about the death of the children and of himself. He, sensitive, so bodiless, so self-less as to be a sort of automaton, is very badly suggested, exaggerated, but one can see what is meant. And he feels, as any child will feel, as many children feel today, that they are really anachronisms, accidents, fatal accidents, unreal, false notes in their mothers' lives, that, according to her, they have no being: that, if they have being, then she has not. So he takes away all the children.

And then Sue ceases to be: she strikes the line through her own existence, cancels herself There exists no more Sue Fawley. She cancels herself She wishes to cease to exist, as a person, she wishes to be absorbed away, so that she is no longer self-responsible.

For she denied and forsook and broke her own real form, her own independent, cool-lighted mind-life. And now her children are not only dead, but self-slain, these pledges of the physical life for which she abandoned the other.

She has a passion to expiate, to expiate, to expiate. Her children should never have been born: her instinct always knew this. Now their dead bodies drive her mad with a sense of blasphemy. And she blasphemed the Holy Spirit which told her she is guilty of their birth and their death, of the horrible nullity, nothing, which they are. She is even guilty of their little, palpitating sufferings and joys of mortal life, now made nothing. She cannot bear it—who could? And she wants to expiate, doubly expiate. Her mind which she set up in her conceit, and then forswore, she must stamp it out of existence, as one stamps out fire. She would never again think or decide for herself. The world, the past, should have written every decision for her. The last act of her intellect was the utter renunciation of her mind and the embracing of utter orthodoxy, where every belief, every thought, every decision was made ready for her, so that she did not exist self-responsible. And then her loathed body, which had committed the crime of bearing dead children, which had come to life only to spread nihilism like a pestilence, that too should be scourged out of existence. She chose the bitterest penalty in going back to Phillotson.

There was no more Sue. Body, soul, and spirit, she annihilated herself. All that remained of her was the will by which she annihilated herself. That remained fixed, a locked centre of self-hatred, life-hatred so utter that it had no hope of death. It knew that life is life, and there is no death for life.

Jude was too exhausted himself to save her. He says of her she was not worth a man's love. But that was not the point. It was not a question of her worth. It was a question of her being. If he had said she was not capable of receiving a man's love as he wished to bestow it, he might have spoken nearer the truth. But she practically told him this. She made it plain to him what she wanted, what she could take. But he overrode her. She tried hard to abide by her own form. But he forced her. He had no case against her, unless that she made the great appeal for him, that he should flow to her, whilst at the same time she could not take him completely, body and spirit both.

She asked for what he could not give—what perhaps man can give: passionate love without physical desire. She had blame for him: she had no love for him. Self-love triumphed in her when she first knew him. She almost deliberately asked for more, far more, than she intended to give. Self-hatred triumphed in the end. So it had to be.

As for Jude, he had been dying slowly, but much quicker than she, since the first night she took him. It was best to get it done quickly in the end.

And this tragedy is the result of overdevelopment of one principle of human life at the expense of the other; an overbalancing; a laying of all the stress on the Male, the Love, the Spirit, the Mind, the Consciousness, a denying, a blaspheming against the Female, the Law, the Soul, the Senses, the Feelings. But she is developed to the very extreme, she scarcely lives in the body at all. Being of the feminine gender, she is yet no woman at all, nor male, she is almost neuter. He is nearer the balance, nearer the centre, nearer the wholeness. But the whole human effort, towards pure life in the spirit, towards becoming pure Sue, drags him along, he identifies himself with this effort, destroys himself and her in his adherence to this identification.

But why, in casting off one or another form of religion, has man ceased to be religious altogether? Why will he not recognise Sue and Jude, as Cassandra was recognised long ago, and Achilles, and the Vestals, and the nuns, and the monks. Why must being be denied altogether.

Sue had a being, special and beautiful. Why must not Jude recognise it in all its speciality? Why must man be so utterly irreverent, that he approaches each being as if it were no-being? Why must it be assumed that Sue is an "ordinary" woman—as if such a thing existed. Why must she feel ashamed if she is special? And why must Jude, owing to the conception he is brought up in, force her to act as if she were his "ordinary" abstraction, a woman.

She was not a woman. She was Sue Bridehead, something very particular. Why was there no place for her? Cassandra had the temple   of Apollo. Why are we so foul, that we have no reverence for that which we are and for that which is amongst us. If we had reverence for our life, our life would take at once religious form. But as it is, in our filthy irreverence, it remains a disgusting slough, where each one of us goes so thoroughly disguised in dirt that we are all alike and indistinguishable.

If we had reverence for what we are, our life would take real form, and Sue would have a place, as Cassandra had a place, she would have a place which does not yet exist, because we are all so vulgar, we have nothing.

CHAPTER X.

It seems as if the history of humanity were divided into two epochs: the Epoch of the Law and the Epoch of Love. It seems as though humanity, during the time of its activity on earth, has made two great efforts: the effort to appreciate the Law and the effort to overcome the Law in Love. And in both efforts it has succeeded. It has reached and proved the Two Complementary Absolutes, the Absolute of the Father, of the Law, of Nature, and the Absolute of the Son, of Love, of Knowledge. What remains is to reconcile the two.

In the beginning, Man said "What am I, and whence is this world around me, and why is it as it is?" Then he proceeded to explore and to personify and to deify the Natural Law, which he called Father. And having reached the point where he conceived of the Natural Law in its purity, he had finished his journey, and was arrested.

But he found that he could not remain at rest. He must still go on. Then there was to discover by what principle he must proceed further than the Law. And he received an inkling of Love. All over the world the same, the second great epoch started with the incipient conception of Love, and continued until the principle of Love was conceived in all its purity. Then man was again at an end, in a cul de sac.

The Law it is by which we exist. It was the Father, the Law-Maker, who said "Let there be light":' it was He who breathed life into the handful of dust and made man. "Thus have I made man, in mine own image. I have ordered his outgoing and his incoming, and have cast the line whereby he shall walk." So said the Father. And man went out and came in according to the ordering of the Lord, he walked by the line of the Lord and did not deviate. Till the path was worn barren, and man knew all the way, and the end seemed to have drawn nigh.

Then he said "I will leave the path. I will go out as the Lord hath not ordained, and come in when my hour is fulfilled. For it is written, a man shall eat and drink with the Lord: but I will neither eat nor drink, I will go hungry, yet I will not die. It is written, a man shall take himself a wife and beget him seed unto the glory of God. But I will not take me a wife, nor beget seed, but I will know no woman. Yet will I not die. And it is written, a man shall save his body from harm, and preserve his flesh from hurt, for he is made in the image and likeness of the Father. But I will deliver up my body to hurt, and give my flesh unto the dust, yet will I not die, but live. For man does not live by bread alone, nor by the common law of the Father. Beyond this common law, I am I. When my body is destroyed and my bones have perished, then I am I. Yea, not until my body is consumed and my bones have mingled with the dust, not until then am I whole, not until then do I live. But I die in Christ, and rise again. And when I am risen again, I live in the spirit. Neither hunger nor cold can lay hold on me, nor desire lay hands on me. When I am risen again, then I shall *know.* Then I shall live in the ineffable bliss of knowledge. When the sun goes forth in the morning, I shall know the glory of God, who passes the sun from His left hand to His right, in the peace of His Understanding. As the night comes in her divers shadows, I know the peace that passeth all understanding. For God knoweth. Neither does he Will nor Command nor desire nor act, but exists perfect in the peace of knowledge."

If a man must live still and act in the body, then let his action be to the recognising of the life in other bodies. Each man is to himself the Natural Law. He can only conceive of the Natural Law as he knows it in himself. The hardest thing for any man to do is for him to recognise and to know that the natural law of his neighbour is other than, and maybe even hostile to, his own natural law, and yet is true. This hard lesson Christ tried to instil in the doctrine of the other cheek. Orestes could not conceive that it was the natural law of Clytemnestra's nature, that she should murder Agamemnon for sacrificing her daughter, and for leaving herself abandoned in the pride of her womanhood, unmated because he wanted the pleasure of war, and for his unfaithfulness to her with other women. Clytemnestra could not understand that Orestes should want to kill her for fulfilling the law of her own nature. The law of the mother's nature was other than the law of the son's nature. This they could neither of them see, hence the killing. This Christianity would teach them: to recognise and to admit the law of the other person, outside and different from the law of one's own being. It is the hardest lesson of love. And the lesson of love learnt, there must be learned the next lesson, of reconciliation between different, maybe hostile things. That is the final lesson. Christianity ends in submission, in recognising and submitting to the law of the other person: "Thou shalt love thy enemy."

Therefore, since by the law man must act or move, let his motion be the utterance of the God of Peace, of the perfect, unutterable Peace of Knowledge.

And man has striven this way, to utter the Universal Peace of God. And striving on, he has passed beyond the limits of utterance, and has reached once more the silence of the beginning.

After Sue, after Dostoievsky's *Idiot,* after Turner's latest pictures, after the symbolist poetry of Mallarmé and the others, after the music of Debussy, there is no further possible utterance of the peace that passeth all understanding, the peace of God which is Perfect Knowledge. There is only silence beyond this.

Just as after Plato, after Dante, after Raphael, there was no further utterance of the Absoluteness of the Law, of the Immutability of the Divine Conception.

So that, as the great pause came over Greece, and over Italy after the Renaissance, when the Law had been uttered in its absoluteness, so there comes over us now, over England and Russia and France, the pause of finality, now we have seen the purity of Knowledge, the great, white, uninterrupted Light, infinite and eternal.

But that is not the end. The two great conceptions, of Law and of Knowledge or Love, are not diverse and accidental, but complementary. They are, in a way, contradictions each of the other. But they are complementary. They are the Fixed Absolute, the Geometric Absolute, and they are the radiant Absolute, the Unthinkable Absolute of pure, free motion. They are the perfect Stability, and they are the perfect Mobility. They are the fixed condition of our being, and they are the transcendent condition of knowledge in us. They are our Soul, and our Spirit. They are our Feelings, and our Mind. They are our Body and our Brain. They are Two-in-One.

And everything that has ever been produced, has been produced by the combined activity of the two, in humanity, by the combined activity of soul and spirit. When the two are acting together, then Life is produced, then Life, or Utterance, Something, is *created.* And nothing is or can be created save by combined effort of the two principles, Law and Love.

All through the mediaeval times, Law and Love were striving together to give the perfect expression to the Law, to arrive at the perfect conception of the Law. All through the rise of the Greek nation, to its culmination, the Law and Love were working in that nation to attain the perfect expression of the Law. They were driven by the Unknown Desire, the Holy Spirit, the Unknown and Unexpressed. But the Holy Spirit is the Reconciler, and the Originator. Him we do not know.

The greatest of all Utterance of the Law, has given expression to the Law as it is in relation to Love, both ruled by the Holy Spirit. Such is the Book of Job, such Aeschylus, in the Trilogy, such, more or less, is Dante, such is Botticelli. Those who gave expression to the Law after these, suppressed the contact, and achieved an abstraction—Plato, Raphael.

The greatest utterance of Love has given expression to Love as it is in relation to the Law: so Rembrandt, Shakespeare, Shelley, Wordsworth, Goethe,

Tolstoi. But beyond these, there has been Turner, who suppressed the context of the Law. Also there have been Dostoievsky, Hardy, Flaubert. These have shown Love in conflict with the Law, and only Death the resultant, no Reconciliation. So that humanity does not continue for long to accept the conclusions of these writers, nor even of Euripides, and Shakespeare always. These great tragic writers endure by reason of the truth of the conflict they describe, because of its completeness, Law, Love, and Reconciliation all active. But with regard to their conclusions, they leave the soul finally unsatisfied, unbelieving.

Now the aim of man remains to recognise and seek out the Holy Spirit, the Reconciler, the Originator, He who drives the twin principles of Law and of Love across the ages.

Now it remains for us to know the Law and to know the Love, and further to seek out the Reconciliation. It is time for us to build our temples to the Holy Spirit, and to raise our altars to the Holy Ghost, the Supreme, Who is beyond us but is with us.

We know of the Law, and we know of Love, and to that little we know of each of these we have given our full expression. But have not completed one perfect utterance, not one. Small as is the circle of our knowledge, we are not able to cast it complete. In Aeschylus' "Eumenides", Apollo is foolish, Athena mechanical. In Shakespeare's "Hamlet", the conclusion is all foolish. If we had conceived each party in his proper force, if Apollo had been equally potent with the Furies, and no Pallas had appeared to settle the question merely by dropping a pebble, how would Aeschylus have solved his riddle. He could not work out the solution he knew must come, so he forced it.

And so it has always been, always: either a wrong conclusion, or one forced by the artist, as if he put his thumb in the scale to equalise a balance which he could not make level. Now it remains for us to seek the true balance, to give each party, Apollo and the Furies, Love and the Law, his due, and so to seek the Reconciler.

Now the principle of the Law is found strongest in Woman, and the principle of Love in Man. In every creature, the mobility, the law of change, is found exemplified in the male, the stability, the conservatism is found in the female. In woman, man finds his root and establishment. In man, woman finds her exfoliation and florescence. The woman grows downwards, like a root, towards the centre and the darkness and the origin. The man grows upwards, like the stalk, towards discovery and light and utterance. '

Man and Woman are, roughly, the embodiment of Love and the Law: they are the two complementary parts. In the body they are most alike, in genitals they are almost one. Starting from the connection, almost unification, of the genitals, and travelling towards the feelings and the mind, there becomes ever a greater difference and a finer distinction between the two, male and female, till at last, at the other closing in the circle, in pure utterance, the two are really one again, so that any pure utterance is a perfect unity, the two as one, united by the Holy Spirit.

We start from one side or the other, from the female side or the male, but what we want is always the perfect union of the two. That is the Law of the Holy Spirit, the law of Consummate Marriage. That every living thing seeks, individually and collectively. Every man starts with his deepest desire, a desire for consummation of marriage between himself and the female, a desire for completeness, that completeness of being which will give completeness of satisfaction and completeness of utterance. No man can as yet find perfect consummation of marriage between himself and the Bride, be the bride either Woman or an Idea, but he can approximate to it, and every generation can get a little nearer.

But it needs that a man shall first know in reverence and submit to the Natural Law of his own individual being: that he shall also know that he is but contained within the great Natural Law, that he is but a Child of God, and not God himself: that he shall then poignantly and personally recognise that the law of another man's nature is different from the law of his own nature, that it may be even hostile to him, and yet is part of the great Law of God, to be admitted: this is the Christian action of "loving thy neighbour", and of dying to be born again: lastly, that a man shall know that between his law and the law of his neighbour, there is an affinity, that all is contained in one, through the Holy Spirit.

It needs that a man shall know the natural law of his own being, then that he shall seek out the law of the female, with which to join himself as complement. He must know that he is half, and the woman is the other half: that they are two, but that they are two-in-one.

He must with reverence submit to the law of himself: and he must with suffering and joy know and submit to the law of the woman: and he must know that they two together are one within the Great Law, reconciled within the Great Peace. Out of this final knowledge shall come his supreme art. There shall be the art which recognises and utters his own law; there shall be the art which recognises his own and also the law of the woman, his neighbour, utters the glad embrace and the struggle between them, and the submission of one; there shall be the art which knows the struggle between the two conflicting laws, and knows the final reconciliation, where both are equal, two-in-one, complete. This is the supreme art, which yet remains to be done. Some men have attempted it, and left us the results of efforts. But it remains to be fully done.

But when the two clasp hands, a moment, male and female, clasp hands and are one, the poppy, the gay poppy flies into flower again; and when the two fling their arms about each other, the moonlight runs and clashes against the shadow, and when the two toss back their hair, all the larks break out singing, and when they kiss on the mouth, a lovely human utterance is heard again—and so it is.

ART AND THE INDIVIDUAL

A Paper for Socialists

This paragraph from a Socialist Member of Parliament is fairly well known: "The present aim of socialists is to find work for the unemployed, food for the hungry, and clothes for the naked. After that it will make the conquest of the intellectual and artistic world." We who are readers of the "New Age," also remember the critic's comment: "Men, women and children want food and raiment now; we also need our Beauty—in our streets, in our crafts, in our paintings. Let that obsessed socialist go mend his ways; too many think as he does. In the meantime we starve, and our cities starve, for beauty—while politicians prate of the large sums of money diverted to philanthropy." If the only duty of Socialism is to fight the battle of the hungry and naked, then is it for the Ironsides of Snowden to wage war; we, who are not hungry and thirsty for material things, and who have not the tough spirit or the single purpose of a political fighter, we will stay at home, and in wicked sloth forget the din that rages round the platform, such time as in our own fields the lark is high. Have we not been seized, we who love the lotus buds, and thrust into some horrid meeting where voices jangled like weapons?; was it not hideous?; did we not determine to martyr ourselves also for the cause, to clap on the motion and with a double-edged sword go smite the lofty from their seats?; and the next day, when the sunflowers began to colour the morning mists, did we not recant? We, who had rather sing the melodies of Schubert than the Marseillaise, and who love the lyrics and the Sensitive Plant far better than Queen Mab, do we not also dread that fierce socialist friend of ours who scans us with pitying regret, since he knows we are limbs dead, hopelessly dead?; and do we not hate a Civil War?; and do we not detest utterly the thought of the Commonwealth and the Rule by Zealots.

Ours is not, moreover, a weak, selfish cowering that shrinks from the brunt. We are as right as are those who yell for Rights down a trumpet; we believe we are more right, for we are more silent. But we are teachers, and we call upon those unanswerable oracles, the authorities on Education, to defend us; we are victors. Listen! "The ultimate goal of Education is to produce an individual of high moral character." Socialists bow assent, and we mutter "a bit more verbiage." What on earth is a "high moral character"?—Well, since everybody knows, there is no need to explain. We will just remark that a moral person must be well cultivated; must be able to reckon on the great influences which move men, and to estimate the results of such; must, also, have a good sense of proportion, a quality strangely lacking in most highly moral persons. Sense of proportion precludes a well-balanced soul—or mind, if you like. You Ironsides, where is your balance? Have you not plumped down one scale with the great weight of human miseries? You say a state of balance is inert and ineffectual, well, perhaps I have sunk down on the side Beauty, and so we make a social equipoise, which is delightful, is it not? But my muttons, my muttons! —We must have a balance somewhere, admit it,—either in the individual soul or in the social. Well then, all the great forces that influence human action must be directed to the present life we live with as little confusion as possible. And the great forces! Will you accept the great Interests, classified by Herbart, whom we revere, as Six, but to which we will humbly add a seventh, since the moderns have decreed it so? Here is the table:

	1. Knowledge	1. Empirical
	(Intellectual)	2. Speculative
		3. Aesthetic
Interests		
Arise from	2. Sympathy	1. Sympathetic
	(Emotional)	2. Social
		3. Religious
	3. (Action)	

Here is the explanation:

I 1. Empirical: —   Interest in concrete individual things and instances.
   2. Specualtive: —   Interest in deeper connections and causes of phenomena
etc. —   these interests become philosophic and scientific studies.
   3. Aesthetic: —   Interest aroused neither by phenomena or causes as such,
but by the approval which their harmony and adaptability to an end win from me.
(this is Herbart, not me)

II 1. Sympathetic: —   personal sympathy

   2. Social:—   growing comprehension of the incorporation of the
individual in the great social body whose interests are large beyond his personal
feelings. (Socialists —enlarge)
   3. Religious:—   when this extended sympathy is directed to the history
                             (origin) and destiny of mankind, when it   reverentially
                             recognises the vast scope of the laws of nature, and
                             discovers something of intelligible and consistent
                             purpose working through the whole natural world and
                             human consciousness, religious   interest is developed.
                             Then the sense of a man's own importance, and that of
                             his day, is merged in some wonder and reverence—a
                             fruitful condition.
III   Lastly comes the wonderful interest in action—doing something. Cricketers
and tennis-players need no enlargement.

May I offer you an example. You are sitting by a sunlit lakelet, and a swan steers
proudly up to you. "Look," you cry "there's a swan. Come on, come on! I wish I
had something to throw him. Doesn't he arch his wings! And there's his mate
coming peeping in every bend!" (Empirical). "I wonder why he puts his wings up
like that? The other one is quite slim. Is she the female? And he does it to attract
her? He really seems to be showing off to us." (Speculative). "But aren't they
handsome! She is like a slim boat gliding through the water, and he's a haughty
vessel. Look how their long necks are supple—they wave like shadows under the
water when they're looking for food. Isn't there strength in those great hard curves
of his wing; they say he could break your leg; I guess he needs strong wings,
though. Oh, tell him to go into the water again; what hideous black legs against that
plumage; and the way he balances, and his ridiculous gait. Get into the water, you
poor fool, you are absurd on shore!" (This is aesthetic interest, appreciation of
adaptability of swans to water, and harmony between them and their surroundings. I
don't say that there is not another feeling mingled with this.)
       Example number 2. Evening primroses and the tobacco plant we grow in
our gardens are exceedingly beautiful by night. Their pure white or sulphur yellow
flowers unfold so magically when the sun goes down, and gleam so exquisitely in
the moonlight; those clumps of red phlox are black, and their scent is coarse; but the
primroses are painted specially for moonlight, and their scent is like the serenade,
prepared for night time when the moth will come to minister to the wakeful flowers,
and will take back their sweet love-honey and their pollen kisses; for evening
primroses have tubes so deep that only the moth with his long whip of a tongue can
sip up the nectar, so these night preparations are for the satisfying lover. Moreover,

flowers and insects have developed thus side by side; if the nicotiana and the evening primrose have deepened their tubes and waited till evening to unfold to hide their treasures from crawling flies and to ensure cross-pollination, the moth for his part has developed his tongue to touch the deeps of his beloved. Unconsciously, I think, we appreciate some of the harmony of this mutual adaptability, and that is how aesthetics come to be allied to religion, for they are a recognition, one of those recognitions which move unknown, having no revealing cloak of words and word ideas, of the great underlying purpose which is made visible in this instance, and which it is, perhaps, the artist's duty to seek. This universal Purpose is the germ of the God-Idea. It may be that as the plant develops from the germ, it is twisted and clipped into some fantastic Jehovah-shape, but—:

Remark how the scale of Interests rises. The Aesthetic and the Religious are the highest in their two groups. Remark again that you are conscious of the activity of the Interests Empiric, Speculative, Sympathetic, Social, and Religious; but which of us has done other than let his aesthetic interest lead him into a blundering "like and dislike" for which he can give no reason? You like a thing, and there's an end of it; no matter how many overlaying material influences thwart your poor aesthetic soul, and pervert its action, you never question your likings; if some superior artistic person has a slight contempt for the objects of your taste, it is like his impudence; even if you weary of a thing you once loved, and paste over the picture you framed with your own hands with gusto a lustre ago, you regret your inconstancy of soul, and fear you have fallen away from the old enthusiastic appreciation. You ought to rejoice, and say "the soul of an artist is developing in me," just as you would when you found that Rider Haggard was not a prince of entertainers, but even that distant voice of Sir Thos. More could beat him.

Consider "Aesthetic Interest" and its definition more closely. It is not satisfactory to us as it stands; it is too intellectual. Beauty comes under the shelter of Aesthetics, and our appreciation of Beauty is very often not appreciation, but a strong mingled emotion. Indeed the whole aim of Art seems to be to rouse a certain emotion; this emotion may have some expression in words or thoughts, or it may not; and as for thought, it depends entirely on language, and so is limited, and leaves untouched even the majority of our feelings. There have always been two schools of aesthetic thought. The first is the intellectual and mystic:

I. Art—"Beauty is the expression of the perfect and divine Idea," —considering the Idea in the Platonic sense as of some pure unborn soul or idea forever struggling to find perfect expression through matter, just as one of the Erewhonian Unborns might pester two unfortunate humans to give him an existence during which he might perfect some art—say that of making impeccable soup. The Hegelian school propounds that "Beauty is the shining of the Idea through matter"; the making of beautiful things, according to Goethe, is the "weaving for God the garment we see him by."

The opposing emotional and material school is divided:

II.   1. "Art is an activity arising even in the animal kingdom, and springing from sexual desire and propensity to play—and it is accompanied by pleasurable excitement"—Darwin. In this class come Schiller, Spencer and others as well as Darwin. They explain the dandy, who decks himself as he wins toward maturity, and flirts from a propensity to play. Pray, ladies in short skins, recognise the dandy as a natural and admirable object, as you did the swan.

2. "Art is the external manifestation by lines, color, words, sounds, movements, of emotions felt by man."

3. "Art is the production of some permanent object or passing action fitted to convey pleasurable impressions quite apart from personal advantage"—which is, I think, the definition of Grant Allen.

The first school bases its Beauty on Herbart's "Adaptation"—perfect adaptation shows clearly the fundamental idea and purpose.

Harmony is the name we give to a certain emotional state roused by certain blended components. So Herbart proceeded somewhat towards the second school in his definition, if not very far.

Now let us take a few exceptions and try to prove the rules of our schoolmen. Consider the writings of Poe, De Maupassant, Ibsen, Maxim Gorky; consider the Laocoon, some of the French Realistic paintings, even the "Outcasts" of Luke Fildes, or Watts' "Mammon," if this last be Art. These show no divine idea; these are no garments of God; nor are they activities arising from sense of play or sex; nor do they convey pleasure, in the ordinary sense of the word. Their sole object is to set vibrating in the second person the emotion which moved the producer; and this seems to be the mission of Art. It must be, as Tolstoi says, the second great means of communication between men, and, he insists, the language of Art must be intelligible. But since "being intelligible" means "able to be thought of," and since thought takes place in language more or less precise, Art has no very great value, since the same effect, or somewhat the same, might have been obtained without recourse to any other form than simple prose. True, as Tolstoi says, if a lad tells a tale to his sister which brings tears to her eyes, then he is an artist; and Carlyle's Heroes were artists, for they could not speak but in song, for a vigorous emotion moulded all their speech. But when the lad told the tale, the words were only as the simple melody running clear through the piece; the art was more likely to be in the tones, the gestures; and the value of song is its music, and its power to call up new pictures; and the value, the beauty of the tale or the song lies in the emotion which follows the music of the tones, the harmony of looks and gesture, the quivering feelings for which there are no words, and the pictures which were never on the retina, and never will be. True, some words are themselves artistic, some few rare words such as *wonder;* it is a beautiful, wonderful word; French has no equivalent; see how much gathers round it; and how will you express it? Then words like laughter, chatter, and flash are expressive. But words can rarely describe, call up in another, the feeling that was mother and father to them. They have to "pair like lovers, and chime in the ear"; they must "progress in cosmic fellowship" —they must, in short, have form, style.

> "Words were nothing if words could say all: ever behind our singing is the silence out of which it broke.
> So too, behind this little book with its words of franchise, my enfranchisement remains untold.
> The trees swing in the gale and make music in it; but in the Earth abiding they keep silence.
> So for you, beloved, abiding in your love, my heart keeps silence while I sing."

It is Art which opens to us the silences, the primordial silences which hold the secret of things, the great purposes, which are themselves silent; there are no words to speak of them with, and no thoughts to think of them in, so we struggle to touch them through art; and the eager, unsatisfied world seeks to put them all into a religious phrase.

Tolstoi defeated his own ends, then, when he demanded that art should be intelligible. It seems to be human fate to strive to know to the uttermost, and men in general cannot bear to touch the Mystery nakedly, without a garment of words. The deepest secrets of all are hidden in human experience, in human feeling, and the human heart is never satisfied till it can command the secret, dress the unutterable experience in the livery of an idea, and prison it with fetters of words. The music of some of the great Germans is too vague, confusing, unintelligible; the poetry of Verlaine, Maeterlinck, and Baudelaire; the pictures of George Clausen and others are too sketchy; we cannot feel the outline; it is as if we were in a mist. People complain continually, along with Tolstoi, in such terms. They should know that they are purposely led to the edge of the great darkness, where no word-lights twinkle. They had rather listen to a great din of a battle-piece and exclaim "There, the trumpet sounds charge!, hark, you can tell it's horses galloping!—do you hear the rumble of cannon? —isn't it fine!" The true battle-piece would call up the fury and fear in the hearts of a mass of soldiers, the pain and the primeval lust, without tin-pan clash-of-swords imitation. So Chopin's Funeral March seems far superior to the March in Saul; it has no drum thumping and artifice and extravagance.

Having discussed at some length what Art may do, we can more easily proclaim what it may not do. It may not call up harmful emotions; if it does it is bad art. Conclusion, French novels are bad art, Marie Corelli is not. I leave it to you to continue making syllogisms on the limitations of Art.

Everyone sets out, in his own opinion, ready equipped to pass judgment on things of beauty and taste. Unfortunately, his opinion is peculiarly his own; he is condemned for bad taste. "It is a matter of opinion," he says. It is not. If a thing is in bad taste it is so absolutely, just as a sum in mathematics is either wrong or right. If the obnoxious thing appears good to the owner, it is because he has a number of harmful influences perverting his judgment, or because he is so woefully undeveloped that there is no appeal to him save through the primary colours, or because a shallow emotion evokes a similar one in him.

Example: That popular picture, "Wedded," by Lord Leighton. The emotion conveyed is weak and shallow. A bare-legged, leopard-skin-clad, black haired lad kisses the fingers of a girl in a manner impossible unless he were standing on a little balcony specially erected by an artist for public exhibition. Contrast the passion in Maurice Greiffenhagen's "Idyll." But Leighton's picture is beautiful—the technique—. The delight of form in art is said to be largely physical. The movement of the eye is grateful and pleasing along certain curves, certain combinations such as the rhythmic folds of drapery in Leighton's pictures. Exactly, but the form, the artistic form is purely sensuous, it is beautiful, but not so highly profitable. Look at Watts' "Mammon"; it is hideous and hateful; it does not help us one jot to have a ghastly idol with beastly eyes set up in warning to us not to worship it; the emotion of the artist did not find satisfactory expression. So we condemn one artist because, although he has a sumptuous manner, his feeling is shallow and unprofitable, and another because in the violence of his feeling he outrages art and offends us. The third group that displeases us is that of the English sentimentalists, who wallow in emotion:—little girls about to be mown down by the hand of Time, he who cuts off the fairest flowers—all this written by somebody who thought it a good subject. Sentimentality is by far the most grievous disease that an artist can contract; it renders Art despicable. Let us condemn it severely, if we can.

The triumph of Art? "The chief triumph of Art" says Hume, "is to insensibly refine the temper, and to point out to us those dispositions which we should endeavour to attain by constant bent of mind and by repeated habit" —"By constant bent of mind and repeated habit"— that is, by carefully educating yourself. You are not a born judge of Beauty—you must learn, by studying the best examples, and by searching your own soul carefully. Then, when your temper is refined, you will undergo a thousand experiences to which you were before dead; you will never find time long, or an hour dreary; a life- long holiday would not be long enough to make you wish you had something to do, for a new charm will be always inviting your soul, and you can remain in delightful possession of yourself, needing no-one to cheer you and fill in the blanks.

RACHEL ANNAND TAYLOR

Mrs Rachel Annand Taylor is not ripe yet to be gathered as fruit for lectures and papers. She is young, not more than thirty; she has been married and her husband has left her: she lives in Chelsea, visits Professor Gilbert Murray in Oxford, and says strange, ironic things of many literary people, in a plaintive, peculiar fashion. This, then, is raw green fruit to offer you, to be received with suspicion, to be tasted charily and spat out without much revolving and tasting. It is impossible to appreciate the verse of a green fresh poet. He must be sun-dried by time and sunshine of favourable criticism, like muscatels and prunes: you must remove the crude sap of living: then the flavour of his eternal poetry comes out unobscured and unpolluted by what is temporal in him. Is it not so?

Mrs Taylor is, however, personally, all that could be desired of a poetess: in appearance, purely Rossettian: slim, svelte; big, beautiful bushes of reddish hair hanging over her eyes, which peer from the warm shadow; delicate colouring, scarlet, small, shut mouth; a dark, plain dress with a big boss of a brooch on her bosom, a curious, carven witch's brooch; then long white languorous hands of the correct subtle radiance. All that a poetess should be.

She is a Scotch-woman. Brought up lonelily as a child, she lived on the bible, on the Arabian Nights, and later, on Malory's King Arthur. Her up-bringing was not Calvinistic. Left to herself, she developed as a choice romanticist. She lived apart from life, and still she cherishes a yew-darkened garden in her soul where she can remain withdrawn, sublimating experience into odours.

This is her value, then: that to a world almost satisfied with the excitement of Realism's Reign of Terror, she hangs out the flags of Romance, and sounds the music of citherns and violes. She is mediaeval; she is as pagan and as romantic as the old minstrels. She belongs to the company of Aucassin and Nicolette, and to no other.

The first volume of poems was published in 1904. Listen to the titles of the poems:

Romances—	The Bride, A Song of Gold, The Queen, The Daughter of Herodias, Arthurian Songs, The Knights at Ringstead.
Devotional—	Flagellants, An Early Christian, Rosa Mundi, An Art-lover to Christ.
Chant D'Amour—	Love's Fool to His Lady, Saint Mary of the Flowers', The Immortal Hour.
Reveries—	The Hostel of Sleep.

I will read you four of the love songs. Against the first, in the book Mrs Taylor gave me, I found a dried lily of the valley, that the authoress had evidently overlooked. She would have dropped it in the fire, being an ironical romanticist. However, here is the poem, stained yellow with a lily: it is called "Desire." (p. 73)

That is the first of the love songs. The second is called "Surrender" (p. 80)— the third, which is retrospective, is "Unrealised"

and the fourth is "Renunciation."

There is the story of Mrs Taylor's married life, that those who run may read.

Needless to say, the poetess' heart was broken.

"There is nothing more tormenting" I said to her, "than to be loved overmuch."

"Yes, one thing more tormenting" she replied.

"And what's that?" I asked her. "To love," she said, very quietly.

However, it is rather useful to a poetess or poet to have a broken heart. Then the rare fine liquor from the fragile vial is spilled in little splashes of verse most interesting to the reader, most consoling to the writer. A broken heart does give colour to life.

Mrs Taylor, in her second volume, "Rose and Vine" published last year, makes the splashes of verse from her spilled treasure of love. But they are not crude startling bloody drops. They are vermeil and gold and beryl green. Mrs Taylor takes the "pageant of her bleeding heart," first marches it ironically by the brutal daylight, then lovingly she draws it away into her magic, obscure place apart, where she breathes spells upon it, filters upon it delicate lights, tricks it with dreams and fancy, and then re-issues the pageant.

"Rose and Vine" is much superior to the "Poems" of 1904. It is gorgeous, sumptuous. All the full, luscious buds of promise are full blown here, till heavy, crimson petals seem to brush one's hips in passing, and in front, white blooms seem leaning to meet one's breasts. There is a great deal of sensuous colour, but it is all abstract, impersonal in feeling, not the least sensual. One tires of it in the same way that one tires of some of Strauss's music—"Electra," for instance. It is emotionally insufficient, though splendid in craftmanship.

Mrs Taylor is, indeed, an exquisite craftsman of verse. Moreover, in her metres and rhythms she is orthodox. She allows herself none of the modern looseness but retains the same stanza form to the end of a lyric. I should like more time to criticise the form of this verse.

However, to turn to "Rose and Vine". There is not much recognisable biography here. Most of the verses are transformed from the experience beyond recognition. A really new note is the note of motherhood. I often wonder why, when a woman artist comes, she never reveals the meaning of maternity, but either paints horses or Venuses or sweet children, as we see them in the Tate Gallery, or deals with courtship and affairs, like Charlotte Brontë and George Eliot. Mrs Taylor has a touch of the mother note. I read you "Four Crimson Violers."

And now "Song of Fruition (For an October Mother)".— What my mother would have said to that, when she had me an autumn baby, I don't know.

A fine piece of thoughtful writing is "Music of Resurrection," which, significantly, opens the "Rose and Vine" volume.

That was last year. This year, came the "Hours of Fiammetta"—a sonnet sequence. There are 61 sonnets in the Shakespeare form, and, besides these, a Prologue of Dreaming Women, an Epilogue of Dreaming Women, and an Introduction. In the Introduction Mrs Taylor says there are two traditions of women—the Madonna, and the Dreaming Woman. The latter is always, the former never, the artist.—Which explains, I suppose, why women-artists do not sing maternity. Mrs Taylor represents the Dreaming Woman of Today, and she is almost unique in her position, when all the women who are not exclusively mothers are suffragists or reformers. Unfortunately, Mrs Taylor has begun to dream of her past life and of herself very absorbedly, and to tell her dreams in symbols which are not always illuminating. She is esoteric. Her symbols do not show what they stand for of themselves: they are cousins of that Celtic and French form of symbolism which says "Let x = the winds of passion and y = the yearning of the soul for love:

Now the dim, white petalled y
Draws dimly over the pallid atmosphere
The scalded kisses of x."

Mrs Taylor has begun the same dodge.

"Since from the subtle silk of agony
Our lamentable veils of flesh are spun."

Subtle silk of agony may claim to sound well, but to me it is meaningless.

But I read you the "Prologue of the Dreaming Women," which surely is haunting.

How dare a woman, a woman, sister of Suffragists and lady doctors, how dare she breathe such a thing.

But Mrs Taylor is bolder still. Listen to the "Epilogue of the Dreaming Women."

It is, I think, a very significant poem, to think over, and to think of again when one reads "Mrs Bull."

But these are not Fiammetta. They are her creed. Her idiosyncrasies are in the sonnets, which, upon close acquaintance, are as interesting, more interesting far to trace, than a psychological novel. I read you only one, number XVIII.

Some of these sonnets are very fine: they stand apart in an age of "Open road" and Empire thumping verse.

You talk about the future of the baby, little cherub, when he's in his cradle cooing: and it's a romantic, glamorous subject. You also talk, with the parson, about the future of the wicked old grandfather who is at last lying on his death-bed. And there again you have a subject for much vague emotion, chiefly of fear this time.

How do we feel about the novel? Do we bounce with joy thinking of the wonderful novelistic days ahead? Or do we grimly shake our heads and hope the wicked creature will be spared a little longer?

Is the novel on his death-bed, old sinner? Or is he just toddling round his cradle, sweet little thing?

Let us have another look at him, before we decide.

There he is, the monster with many faces, many branches to him like a tree: the modern novel. And he is almost dual like a Siamese twin. On the one hand, the pale-faced, high-browed, earnest novel which you have to take seriously: on the other, that smirking, rather plausible hussy, the popular novel.

Let us just for the moment feel the pulses of *Ulysses* and of Miss Dorothy Richardson and Monsieur Marcel Proust, on the earnest side of Briareus; on the other, the throb of *The Sheik* and Mr Zane Grey, and, if you will, Mr Robert Chambers and the rest.

Is *Ulysses* in his cradle? Oh dear, what a grey face! And *Pointed Roofs,* are they a gay little toy for nice little girls? And M. Proust?

Alas, you can hear the death-rattle in their throats. They can hear it themselves. They are listening to it with acute interest, trying to discover whether the intervals are minor thirds or major fourths. Which is rather infantile, really.

So there you have the "serious" novel, dying in a very long-drawn-out fourteen-volume death-agony, and absorbedly, childishly interested in the phenomenon. "Did I feel a twinge in my little toe, or didn't I?" asks every character in Mr Joyce or Miss Richardson or Monsieur Proust. "Is the odour of my perspiration a blend of frankincense and orange pekoe and boot-blacking, or is it myrrh and bacon-fat and Shetland tweed?"

The audience round the death-bed gapes for the answer. And when, in a sepulchral tone, the answer comes at length, after hundreds of pages: "It is none of these, it is abysmal chloro-coryambasis," the audience quivers all over, and murmurs: "That's just how I feel myself."

Which is the dismal, long-drawn-out comedy of the death-bed of the serious novel. It is self-consciousness picked into such fine bits that the bits are most of them invisible, and you have to go by smell. Through thousands and thousands of pages Mr Joyce and Miss Richardson tear themselves to pieces, strip their smallest emotions to the finest threads, till you feel you are sewed inside a wool mattress that is being slowly shaken up, and you are turning to wool along with the rest of the woollyness.

It's awful. And it's childish. It really is childish, after a certain age, to be absorbedly self-conscious. One has to be self-conscious at seventeen: still a little self-conscious at twenty-seven; but if we are going it strong at thirty-seven, then it is a sign of arrested development, nothing else. And if it is still continuing at forty-seven, it is obvious senile precocity.

And there's the serious novel: senile precocious. Absorbedly, childishly concerned with *What I am.* "I am this, I am that, I am the other. My reactions are such, and such, and such. And oh Lord, if I liked to watch myself closely enough, if I liked to analyse my feelings, minutely, as I unbutton my pants, instead of saying crudely I unbuttoned them, then I could go on to a million pages, instead of a thousand. In fact, the more I come to think of it, it is gross, it is uncivilised bluntly to say: I unbuttoned my pants. After all, the absorbing adventure of it! Which button did I begin with?—?" etc. etc.

The people in the serious novels so absorbedly concerned with themselves and what they feel and don't feel, and how they react to every mortal trouser-button; and their audience as frenziedly absorbed in the application of the author's discoveries to their own reactions; "that's me! that's exactly it! I'm just *finding* myself in this book!"—why, this is more than death-bed, it is almost *post mortem* behaviour.

Some convulsion or cataclysm will have to get the serious novel out of its self-consciousness. The last great war made it worse. What's to be done?

Because, poor thing, it is really young yet. The novel has never become fully adult. It has never quite grown to years of discretion. It has always youthfully hoped for the best, and felt rather sorry for itself on the last page. Which is just childish.

The childishness has become very long-drawn-out. So very many adolescents who drag their adolescence on into their forties and their fifties and their sixties.

There needs some sort of a surgical operation, somewhere.

Then the popular novels—the *Sheiks* and *Babbitts* and Zane Greys. They are just as self-conscious, only they do have more illusions about themselves. The heroines do think they are lovelier, and more fascinating, and purer. The heroes do see themselves more heroic, braver, more chivalrous, more fetching. The mass of the populace "find themselves" in the popular novels.

But nowadays it's a funny sort of self they find. A Sheik with a whip up his sleeve, and a heroine with weals on some part of her anatomy: but adored in the end, adored, the whip out of sight, but the weals still faintly visible on the unmentionable part of her anatomy.

It's a funny sort of self they discover in the popular novels. And the essential moral, of *If Winter Comes* for example, is so shaky. "The gooder you are, the worse it is for you, poor you, oh poor you. Don't you be so blimey good, it's not good enough." Or *Babbitt*: "Go on, you make your pile, and then pretend you're too good for it. Put it over the rest of the dirty grabbers that way. They're only pleased with themselves when they've made their pile. You go one better."

Always the same sort of baking-powder gas to make you rise: the soda counteracting the cream of tartar, and the tartar counteracted by the soda. Sheik heroines with whipped posteriors, wildly adored. Babbitts with solid fortunes, weeping from self-pity. Winter-Comes heroes as good as pie, hauled off to gaol. *Moral:* Don't be too good because you'll go to gaol for it. *Moral:* Don't feel sorry for yourself till you've made your pile and don't need to feel sorry for yourself. *Moral:* Don't let him adore you till he's whipped you into it. Then you'll be partners in mild crime as well as in holy matrimony!

Which again is childish. Adolescence which *can't* grow up. Got into the self-conscious rut and going crazy, quite crazy in it. Carrying on their adolescence into middle age and old age, like the loony Cleopatra in *Dombey and Son,* murmuring "Rose-coloured curtains—" with her dying breath, old hag.

The Future of the Novel. Poor old novel, it's in a rather dirty, messy tight corner. And it's either got to get over the wall, or knock a hole through it.

In other words, it's got to grow up. Put away childish things like: "Do I love the girl or don't I?"—"Am I pure and sweet or aren't I?"—"Do I unbutton my pants from the left or from the right?"—"Did my mother ruin my life by refusing to drink the cocoa which my bride had boiled for her?" These questions, and their answers, don't really interest me any more, though the world still goes sawing them over. I simply don't care whether I love the girl or not, whether I'm pure or impure, according to government standards, whether I unbutton my pants with my left hand or my right, or what my mother feels about me. I don't give a damn for any of these things any more: though I used to.

In short, the purely emotional and self-analytical stunts are played out in me. I'm finished. I'm deaf to the whole band. I'm blind to the whole blooming circus.

But I'm neither blasé nor cynical, for all that. I'm just interested in something else.

Supposing a bomb were put under this whole scheme of things, what would we be after? What feelings do we want to carry through, into the next epoch? What feelings will carry us through? What is the underlying impulse in us that will provide the motive-power for a new state of things, when this democratic-industrial-lovey-dovey-darling-take-me-to-mammy state of things is bust?

What next? That's what interests me. *What now!* is no fun any more.

If you like to look in the past for *What-next?* books, you can find the little early novels by Saint Matthew, Saint Mark, Saint Luke and Saint John, called the Gospels. But these are novels with a clue for the future, a new impulse, a new motive, a new inspiration. They don't care about how it *is* just now, or how it *was* in the past: indifferent entirely to *Main Street* and *Winter Coming* and *Sheiks* and *Scarlet Pimpernels.* What they want is to put a new impulse into the world.

And they are little novels, in the highest sense. You can't deny it.

Plato's Dialogues, too, are queer little novels.

It seems to me it was the greatest pity in the world, when philosophy and fiction got split. They used to be one, right from the days of myth. Then they went and parted, like a nagging married couple, with Aristotle and Thomas Aquinas and that beastly Kant. So the novel went sloppy, and philosophy went abstract-dry. The two should come together again, in the novel. And we get modern kind of gospels, and modern myths, and a new way of understanding.

You've got to find a new impulse for new things, in mankind. And it's really fatal to find it through abstraction. Even in the Gospels there is rather too much sermon. Blessed are X, Y, and Z. —I don't care about X, Y, and Z. Let me see Tom, Dick, and Harry, each *in propria persona,* being blessed. Let me see if Tom is blessed when he's being meek, or whether he's more blessed when he's being haughty. Those X's in the Beatitudes won't do. X may be all right when he's poor in spirit, but Jack is detestable in the same shoes.

No no, philosophy, and religion, they've both gone too far on the algebraical tack; let X stand for sheep and Y for goats: then X — Y = Heaven and X + Y = Earth and Y — X = Hell.

Thank you! But what coloured shirt does X have on?

And novels have gone too far on the emotional tack. In novels people always sit down and suffer their feelings, or sit down and enjoy 'em. They never say: "Let's get up and change 'em."

No, it's only the novels like the four Gospels, or the picaresque Acts of the Apostles, or Augustine's Confessions, or Religio Medici that really try to make a great change in feeling, to get on into something really new. And these do stumble a bit among X's, Y's, and Z's.

The novel has got a future. Its future is to take the place of gospels, philosophies, and the present-day novel as we know it. It's got to have the courage to tackle new propositions without using abstractions; it's got to present us with new, really new feelings, a whole new line of emotion, which will get us out of the old emotional rut. Instead of snivelling about what is and has been, or inventing new sensations in the old line, it's got to break a way through, like a hole in a wall. And the public will scream and say it is sacrilege: because, of course, when you've been jammed for a long time in a tight corner, you get really used to its stuffiness and its tightness, till you find it absolutely stinkingly cosy; and then, of course you're horrified when you see a new glaring hole in what was your cosy wall. You're horrified. You back away from the cold stream of fresh air as if it was killing you.

But gradually first one and then another of the sheep filters through the gap, and finds a new world outside.

A BRITISHER HAS A WORD WITH AN EDITOR

In October's POETRY, the Editor tells what a real tea-party she had in Britain, among the poets: not a Bostonian one, either.

But she, alas, has to throw the dregs of her tea-cup in the faces of her hosts. She wonders whether British poets will have anything very essential to say, as long as the King remains, and the "oligarchic social system" continues. The poor King, casting a damper on poetry! And this about oligarchies is good, from an American.

"In England I found no such evidence of athletic sincerity in artistic experiment, of vitality and variety and—yes!—(YES!!) beauty, in artistic achievement, as I get from the poets of our own land."

YANKEE DOODLE, KEEP IT UP.

As for that "worthless dude" George IV, what poet could possibly have flourished under his contemptible régime? Harriet, look in the history book, and see.

Oh what might not Milton have been, if he'd written under Calvin Coolidge!

111

It is part of the common clap-trap, that "art is immoral." Behold everywhere artists running to put on jazz underwear, to demoralise themselves; or at least, to débourgeoiser themselves.

For the bourgeois is supposed to be the fount of morality. Myself, I have found artists far more morally finicky.

Anyhow, what has a water-pitcher and six insecure apples on a crumpled tablecloth got to do with bourgeois morality? Yet I notice that most people, who have not learnt the trick of being arty, feel a real moral repugnance for a Cézanne still-life. They think it is not *right*.

For them, it isn't.

Yet how can they feel, as they do, that it is subtly *immoral?*

The very same design, if it was humanised, and the tablecloth was a draped nude and the water-pitcher a nude semi-draped, weeping over the draped one, would instantly become highly moral. Why?

Perhaps from painting better than from any other art we can realise the subtlety of the distinction between what is dumbly *felt* to be moral, and what is felt to be immoral. The moral instinct of the man in the street.

But instinct is largely habit. The moral instinct of the man in the street is largely an emotional defence of an old habit.

Yet what can there be, in a Cézanne still-life, to rouse the aggressive moral instinct of the man in the street? What ancient habit in man do these six apples and a water-pitcher succeed in hindering?

A water-pitcher that isn't so very much like a water-pitcher, apples that aren't very appley, and a tablecloth that's not particularly much of a tablecloth. I could do better myself!

Probably! But then, why not dismiss the picture as a poor attempt? Whence this anger, this hostility? The derisive resentment?

Six apples, a pitcher, and a tablecloth can't suggest improper *behaviour.* They don't—not even to a Freudian. If they did, the man in the street would feel much more at home with them.

Where, then, does the immorality come in? Because come in it does.

Because of a very curious habit that civilised man has been forming down the whole course of civilisation, and in which he is now hard-boiled. The slowly-formed habit of seeing just as the photographic camera sees.

You may say, the object reflected on the retina is *always* photographic. It may be. I doubt it. But whatever the image on the retina may be, it is rarely, even now, the photographic image of the object which is actually *taken in* by the man who sees the object. He does not, even now, see for himself. He sees what the kodak has taught him to see. And man, try as he may, is not a kodak.

When a child sees a man, what does the child *take in,* as an impression? Two eyes, a nose, a mouth of teeth, two straight legs, two straight arms: a sort of hieroglyph, which the human child has used through all the ages, to represent man. At least, the old hieroglyph was still in use when I was a child.

Is this what the child actually *sees?*

If you mean by seeing, consciously registering, then this is what the child actually sees. The photographic image may be there all right, upon the retina. But there the child leaves it: outside the door, as it were.

Through many ages, mankind has been striving to register the image on the retina *as it is:* no more glyphs and hieroglyphs. We'll have the real objective reality.

And we have succeeded. As soon as we succeed, the kodak is invented, to prove our success. Could lies come out of a black box, into which nothing but light had entered? Impossible! It takes life to tell a lie.

Colour also, which primitive man cannot really *see,* is now seen by us, and fitted to the spectrum.

Eureka! We have seen it, with our own eyes.

When we see a red cow, we see a red cow. We are quite sure of it, because the unimpeachable kodak sees exactly the same.

But supposing we had all of us been born blind, and had to get our image of a red cow by touching her, and smelling her, hearing her moo, and "feeling" her. Whatever should we think of her? Whatever sort of image should we have of her, in our dark minds? Something very different, surely!

As vision developed towards the kodak, man's idea of himself developed towards the snapshot. Primitive man simply didn't know *what* he was: he was always half in the dark. But we have learned to see, and each of us has a complete kodak-idea of himself.

You take a snap of your sweetheart, in the field among the buttercups, smiling tenderly at the red cow with a calf, and dauntlessly offering a cabbage-leaf.

Awfully nice, and absolutely "real." There is your sweetheart, complete in herself, enjoying a sort of absolute objective reality: complete, perfect, all her surroundings contributing to her, incontestable. She is really "a picture."

This is the habit we have formed: of visualising *everything*. Each man to himself is a picture. That is, he is a complete little objective reality, complete in himself, existing by himself, absolutely, in the middle of the picture. All the rest is just setting, background. To every man, to every woman, the universe is just a setting to the absolute little picture of himself, herself.

This has been the development of the conscious ego in man, through several thousand years: since Greece first broke the spell of "darkness." Man has learnt to *see* himself. So now, he *is* what he sees. He makes himself in his own image.

Previously, even in Egypt, men had not learned to *see straight*. They fumbled in the dark, and didn't quite know where they were, or what they were. Like men in a dark room, they only felt their own existence surging in the darkness of other existences.

We, however, have learned to see ourselves for what we are, as the sun sees us. The kodak bears witness. We see as the All-seeing Eye sees, with the universal vision. And we *are* what is seen: each man to himself an identity, an isolated absolute, corresponding with a universe of isolated absolutes. A picture! A kodak snap, in a universal film of snaps.

We have achieved universal vision. Even God could not see *differently* from what we see: only more extensively, like a telescope, or more intensively, like a microscope. But the same vision. A vision of images which are real, and each one limited to itself.

113

We behave as if we had got to the bottom of the sack, and seen the Platonic Idea with our own eyes, in all its photographically-developed perfection, lying in the bottom of the sack of the universe. Our own ego!

The identifying of ourselves with the visual image of ourselves has become an instinct; the habit is already old. The picture of me, the me that is *seen,* is me.

As soon as we are supremely satisfied about it, somebody starts to upset us. Comes Cézanne with his pitcher and his apples, which not only are not life-like, but are a living lie. The kodak will prove it.

The kodak will take all sorts of snaps, misty, atmospheric, sun-dazed, dancing—all quite different. Yet the image is *the* image. There is only more or less sun, more or less vapor, more or less light and shade.

The All-seeing Eye sees with every degree of intensity and in every possible kind of mood; Giotto, Titian, El Greco, Turner, all so different, yet all the true image in the All-seeing Eye.

This Cézanne still-life, however, is *contrary* to the All-seeing Eye. Apples, to the eye of God, could not look like that, nor could a tablecloth, nor could a pitcher. So, it is *wrong.*

Because man, since he grew out of a personal God, has taken over to himself all the attributes of the Personal godhead. It is the all-seeing human eye which is now the Eternal Eye.

And if apples don't *look* like that, in any light or circumstance, or under any mood, then they shouldn't be painted like that.

Oh là-là-là! The apples *are* just like that, to me! cries Cézanne. They *are* like that, no matter what they look like.

Apples are always apples! says Vox Populi, Vox Dei. Sometimes they're a sin, sometimes they're a knock on the head, sometimes they're a bellyache, sometimes they're part of a pie, sometimes they're sauce for the goose— And you can't see a bellyache, neither can you see a sin, neither can you see a knock on the head. So paint the apple in these aspects, and you get—probably, or approximately—a Cézanne still-life.

What an apple looks like to an urchin, to a thrush, to a browsing cow, to Sir Isaac Newton, to a caterpillar, to a hornet, to a mackerel who finds one bobbing on the sea, I leave you to conjecture. But the All-seeing must have mackerel's eyes, as well as man's.

And this is the immorality in Cézanne: he begins to see more than the All-seeing Eye of humanity can possibly see, kodak-wise. If you can see in the apple a bellyache and a knock on the head, and paint these in the image, among the prettyness, then it is the death of the kodak and the movies, and must be immoral.

It's all very well talking about decoration and illustration, significant form, or tactile values, or plastique, or movement or space-composition or colour-mass relations, afterwards. You might as well force your guest to eat the menu card, at the end of the dinner.

What art has got to do, and will go on doing, is to reveal things in their different relationships. That is to say, you've got to see in the apple the bellyache, Sir Isaac's knock on the cranium, the vast moist wall through which the insect bores to lay her eggs in the middle, and the untasted unknown quality which Eve saw hanging on a tree. Add to this the glaucous glimpse that the mackerel gets as he comes to the surface, and Fantin Latour's apples are no more to you than enamelled rissoles.

The true artist doesn't substitute immorality for morality. On the contrary, he *always* substitutes a finer morality for a grosser. And as soon as you see a finer morality, the grosser becomes relatively immoral.

The universe is like Father Ocean, a stream of all things slowly moving. We move, and the rock of ages moves. And since we move and move forever, in no discernible direction, there is no centre to the movement, as far as we can see. To us, the centre shifts at every moment. Even the pole-star ceases to sit on the pole. Allons! there is no road before us!

There is nothing to do, but to maintain a true relationship to the things we move with and amongst and against. The apple, like the moon, has still an unseen side. The movement of Ocean will turn it round to us, or us to it.

There is nothing man can do, but maintain himself in true relationship to his contiguous universe. An ancient Rameses can sit in stone absolute, absolved from visual contact, deep in the silent ocean of sensual contact. Michael Angelo's Adam can open his eyes for the first time, and see the old man in the skies, objectively. Turner can tumble into the open mouth of the objective universe of light, till we see nothing but his disappearing heels. As the stream carries him, each in his own relatedness, each one differently, so a man must go through life.

Each thing, living or unliving, streams in its own odd, intertwining flux, and nothing, not even man nor the God of man, nor anything that man has thought or felt or known, is fixed or abiding. All moves. And nothing is true, or good, or right, except in its own living relatedness to its own circumambient universe; to the things that are in the stream with it.

Design, in art, is a recognition of the relation between various things, various elements in the creative flux. You can't *invent* a design. You recognise it, in the fourth dimension. That is, with your blood and your bones, even more than with your eyes.

Egypt had a wonderful relation to a vast living universe, only dimly visual in its reality. The dim eye-vision and the powerful blood-feeling of the negro African, even today, gives us strange images, which our eyes can hardly see, but which we know are surpassing. The big, silent statue of Rameses is like a drop of water, hanging through the centuries in dark suspense, and never static. The African fetish-statues have no movement, visually represented. Yet one little motionless wooden figure stirs more than all the Parthenon frieze. It sits in the place where no kodak can snap it.

As for us, we have our kodak-vision, all in bits that group or jig. Like the movies, that jerk but never move. An endless shifting and rattling together of isolated images, "snaps," miles of them, all of them jigging, but each one utterly incapable of movement or change, in itself. A kaleidoscope of inert images, mechanically shaken.

And this is our vaunted "consciousness," made up, really, of inert visual images and little else: like the cinematograph.

Let Cézanne's apples go rolling off the table for ever. They live by their own laws, in their own ambiente, and not by the law of the kodak—or of man. They are *casually* related to man. But to those apples, man is by no means the absolute.

A new relationship between ourselves and the universe means a new morality. Taste the unsteady apples of Cézanne, and the nailed-down apples of Fantin Latour are apples of Sodom. If the *status quo* were paradise, it would indeed be a sin to taste the new apples. But since the *status quo* is much more prison than paradise, we can go ahead.

MORALITY AND THE NOVEL

The business of art is to reveal the relation between man and his circumambient universe, at the living moment. As mankind is always struggling in the toils of old relationships, art is always ahead of the "times," which themselves are always far in the rear of the living moment.

When Van Gogh paints sunflowers, he reveals, or achieves, the vivid relation between himself, as man, and the sunflower, as sunflower, at that quick moment of time. His painting does not represent the sunflower itself. We shall never know what the sunflower itself is. And the camera will *visualise* the sunflower far more perfectly than Van Gogh can.

The vision on the canvas is a third thing, utterly intangible and inexplicable, the offspring of the sunflower itself and Van Gogh himself. The vision on the canvas is forever incommensurable with the canvas, or the paint, or Van Gogh as a human organism, or the sunflower as a botanical organism. You cannot weigh nor measure nor even describe the vision on the canvas. It exists, to tell the truth, only in the much-debated fourth dimension. In dimensional space it has no existence.

It is a revelation of the perfected relation, at a certain moment, between a man and a sunflower. It is neither man-in-the-mirror nor flower-in-the-mirror, neither is it above or below or across anything. It is in-between everything, in the fourth dimension.

And this perfected relation between man and his circumambient universe is life itself, for mankind. It has the fourth-dimensional quality of eternity and perfection. Yet it is momentaneous.

Man and the sunflower both pass away from the moment, in the process of forming a new relationship. The relation between all things changes from day to day, in a subtle stealth of change. Hence art, which reveals or attains to another perfect relationship, will be forever new.

At the same time, that which exists in the non-dimensional space of pure relationship, is deathless, lifeless, and eternal. That is, it gives us the *feeling* of being beyond life or death. We say an Assyrian lion or an Egyptian hawk's-head "lives." What we really mean is that it is beyond life, and therefore beyond death. It gives us that feeling. And there is something inside us which must also be beyond life and beyond death, since that "feeling" which we get from an Assyrian lion or an Egyptian hawk's-head is so infinitely precious to us. As the evening star, that spark of pure relation between night and day, has been precious to man since time began.

If we think about it, we find that our life *consists in* this achieving of a pure relationship between ourselves and the living universe about us. This is how I "save my soul," by accomplishing a pure relationship between me and another person, me and other people, me and a nation, me and a race of men, me and the animals, me and the trees or flowers, me and the earth, me and the skies and sun and stars, me and the moon; an infinity of pure relations, big and little, like the stars of the sky: that makes our eternity, for each one of us. Me and the timber I am sawing, the lines of force I follow, me and the dough I knead for bread, me and the very motion with which I write, me and the bit of gold I have got. This, if we knew it, is our life and our eternity: the subtle, perfected relation between me and my whole circumambient universe.

And morality is that delicate, forever trembling and changing *balance* between me and my circumambient universe, which precedes and accompanies a true relatedness.

Now here we see the beauty and the great value of the novel. Philosophy, religion, science, they are all of them busy nailing things down, to get a stable equilibrium. Religion, with its nailed down One God, who says *Thou shalt, Thou shan't,* and hammers home every time; philosophy, with its fixed ideas; science, with its "laws": they all of them, all the time, want to nail us on to some tree or other.

But the novel, no. The novel is the highest complex of subtle inter-relatedness that man has discovered. Everything is true in its own time, place, circumstance, and untrue outside of its own place, time, circumstance. If you try to nail anything down, in the novel, either it kills the novel, or the novel gets up and walks away with the nail.

Morality in the novel is the trembling instability of the balance. When the novelist puts his thumb in the scale, to pull down the balance to his own predilection, that is immorality.

The modern novel tends to become more and more immoral, as the novelist tends to press his thumb heavier and heavier in the pan: either on the side of love, pure love: or on the side of licentious "freedom."

The novel is not, as a rule, immoral because the novelist has any dominant *idea,* or *purpose.* The immorality lies in the novelist's helpless, unconscious predilection. Love is a great emotion. But if you set out to write a novel, and you yourself are in the throes of the great predilection for love, love as the supreme, the only emotion worth living for, then you will write an immoral novel.

Because *no* emotion is supreme, or exclusively worth living for. *All* emotions go to the achieving of a living relationship between a human being and the other human being or creature or thing he becomes purely related to.

All emotions, including love and hate, and rage and tenderness, go to the adjusting of the oscillating, unestablished balance between two people who amount to anything. If the novelist puts his thumb in the pan, for love, tenderness, sweetness, peace, then he commits an immoral act: he *prevents* the possibility of a pure relationship, a pure relatedness, the only thing that matters: and he makes inevitable the horrible reaction, when he lets his thumb go, towards hate and brutality, cruelty and destruction.

Life is so made, that opposites sway about a trembling centre of balance. The sins of the fathers are visited on the children. If the fathers drag down the balance on the side of love, peace, and production, then in the third or fourth generation the balance will swing back violently to hate, rage, and destruction. We must balance as we go.

And of all the art forms, the novel most of all demands the trembling and oscillating of the balance. The "sweet" novel is more falsified, and therefore more immoral than the blood and thunder novel.

The same with the smart and smudgily cynical novel, which says it doesn't matter what you do, because one thing is as good as another, anyhow, and prostitution is just as much "life" as anything else.

This misses the point entirely. A thing isn't life, just because somebody does it. This the artist ought to know, perfectly well. The ordinary bank-clerk buying himself a new straw hat isn't "life" at all: it is just existence, quite all right, like everyday dinners: but not "life."

By life, we mean something that gleams, that has the fourth dimensional quality. If the bank-clerk feels really piquant about his hat, if he establishes a lively relation with it, and goes out of the shop with the new straw on his head, a changed man, be-aureoled, then that is life.

The same with the prostitute. If a man establishes a living relation to her, if only for one moment, then it is life. But if he doesn't: if it is just money and function, then it is no life, but sordidness, and a betrayal of living.

If a novel reveals true and vivid relationships, it is a moral work, no matter what the relationships may consist in. If the novelist *honours* the relationship in itself, it will be a great novel.

But there are so many relationships which are not real. When the man in *Crime and Punishment* murders the old woman for sixpence, although it is *actual* enough, it is never quite real. The balance between the murderer and the old woman is gone entirely, it is only a mess. It is actuality, but it is not "life," in the living sense.

The popular novel, on the other hand, dishes up a rechauffé of old relationships: *If Winter Comes*. And old relationships dished up are likewise immoral. Even a magnificent painter like Raphael does nothing more than dress up in gorgeous new dresses relationships which have already been experienced. And this gives a gluttonous kind of pleasure to the mass: a voluptuousness, a wallowing. For centuries, men say of their voluptuously ideal woman: "She is a Raphael Madonna." And women are only just learning to take it as an insult.

A new relation, a new relatedness hurts somewhat in the attaining: and will always hurt. So life will always hurt. Because real voluptuousness lies in re-acting old relationships, and at the best, getting an alcoholic sort of pleasure out of it, slightly depraving.

Each time we strive to a new relation, with anyone or anything, it is bound to hurt somewhat. Because it means the struggle with and the displacing of old connections, and this is never pleasant. And moreover, between living things at least, an adjustment means also a fight; for each party, inevitably, must "seek its own" in the other, and be denied. When, in the two parties, each of them seeks his own, her own, absolutely, then it is a fight to the death. And this is true of the thing called "passion." On the other hand, when, of the two parties, one yields utterly to the other, this is called sacrifice, and it also means death. So The Constant Nymph died of her eighteen-months of constancy.

It isn't the nature of nymphs to be constant. She should have been constant in her nymph-hood. And it is unmanly to accept sacrifices. He should have abided by his own manhood.

There is, however, the third thing, which is neither sacrifice nor fight to the death: when each seeks only the true relatedness to the other. Each must be true to himself, herself, his own manhood, her own womanhood, and let the relationship work out of itself. This means courage above all things: and then discipline. Courage to accept the life-thrust from within oneself, and from the other person. Discipline, not to exceed oneself any more than one can help. Courage, when one has exceeded oneself, to accept the fact and not whine about it.

Obviously, to read a really new novel will *always* hurt, to some extent. There will always be resistance. The same with new pictures, new music. You may judge of their reality by the fact that they do arouse a certain resistance, and compel, at length, a certain acquiescence.

The great relationship, for humanity, will always be the relation between man and woman. The relation between man and man, woman and woman, parent and child, will always be subsidiary.

And the relation between man and woman will change forever, and will forever be the new central clue to human life. It is the *relation itself* which is the quick and the central clue to life, not the man, nor the woman, nor the children that result from the relationship, as a contingency.

It is no use thinking you can put a stamp on the relation between man and woman, to keep it in the *status quo.* You can't. You might as well try to put a stamp on the rainbow of the rain.

As for the bond of love, better put it off when it galls. It is an absurdity, to say that men and women *must love.* Men and women will be forever subtly and changingly related to one another, no need to yoke them with any "bond" at all. The only morality is to have man true to his manhood, woman to her womanhood, and let the relationship form of itself, in all honour. For it is, to each, *life itself.*

If we are going to be moral, let us refrain from driving pegs through anything, either through each other or through the third thing, the relationship, which is forever the Ghost of both of us. Every sacrificial crucifixion needs five pegs, four short ones and a long one, each one an abomination. But when you try to nail down the relationship itself, and write over it *Love* instead of *This is the King of the Jews,* then you can go on putting in nails forever. Even Jesus called it the Holy Ghost, to show you that you can't lay salt on its tail.

The novel is a perfect medium for revealing to us the changing rainbow of our living relationships. The novel can help us to live, as nothing else can: no didactic Scripture, anyhow. If the novelist keeps his thumb out of the pan.

But when the novelist *has* his thumb in the pan, the novel becomes an unparalleled perverter of men and women. To be compared only, perhaps, to that great mischief of sentimental hymns like *Lead Kindly Light!* which have helped to rot the marrow in the bones of the present generation.

THE NOVEL

Somebody says the novel is doomed. Somebody else says it is the green bay tree getting greener. Everybody says something, so why shouldn't I!

Mr Santayana sees the modern novel expiring because it is getting so thin;—which means, Mr Santayana is bored.

I am rather bored myself. It becomes harder and harder to read the *whole* of any modern novel. One reads a bit, and knows the rest; or else one doesn't want to know any more.

This is sad. But again, I don't think it's the novel's fault. Rather the novelists'.

You can put anything you like in a novel. So why do people *always* go on putting the same thing? Why is the *vol au vent* always chicken! Chicken *vol au vents* may be the rage. But who sickens first shouts first for something else.

The novel is a great discovery: far greater than Galileo's telescope or somebody else's wireless. The novel is the highest form of human expression so far attained. Why? Because it is so incapable of the absolute.

In a novel, everything is relative to everything else, if that novel is art at all. There may be didactic bits, but they aren't the novel. And the author may have a didactic "purpose" up his sleeve. Indeed most great novelists have, as Tolstoi had his Christian-socialism, and Hardy his pessimism, and Flaubert his intellectual desperation. But even a didactic purpose so wicked as Tolstoi's or Flaubert's cannot put to death the novel.

You can tell me, Flaubert had a "philosophy," not a "purpose." But what is a novelist's philosophy but a purpose on a rather higher level? And since every novelist who amounts to anything has a philosophy—even Balzac—any novel of importance has a purpose. If only the "purpose" be large enough, and not at outs with the passional inspiration.

Vronsky sinned, did he? But also the sinning was a consummation devoutly to be wished. The novel makes that obvious: in spite of old Leo Tolstoi. And the would-be-pious Prince in *Resurrection* is a muff, with his piety that nobody wants or believes in.

There you have the greatness of the novel itself. It won't *let* you tell didactic lies, and put them over. Nobody in the world is anything but delighted when Vronsky gets Anna Karenin. Then what about the sin?—Why, when you look at it, all the tragedy comes from Vronsky's and Anna's fear of *society*. The monster was social, not phallic at all. They couldn't live in the pride of their sincere passion, and spit in Mother Grundy's eye. And that, that cowardice, was the real "sin." The novel makes it obvious, and knocks all old Leo's teeth out. "As an officer, I am still useful. But as a man, I am a ruin," says Vronsky—or words to that effect. Well what a skunk, collapsing as a man and a male, and remaining merely as a social instrument; an "officer," God love us!—merely because people at the opera turn their backs on him!"—As if people's backs weren't preferable to their faces, anyhow!

And old Leo tries to make out, it was all because of the phallic sin. Old liar! Because where would any of Leo's books be, without the phallic splendour? And then to blame the column of blood, which really gave him all his life riches! The Judas! Cringe to a mingy, bloodless Society, and try to dress up that dirty old Mother Grundy in a new bonnet and face-powder of Christian-Socialism. Brothers indeed! Sons of a castrated Father!

The novel itself gives Vronsky a kick in the behind, and knocks old Leo's teeth out, and leaves us to learn.

It is such a bore that nearly all great novelists have a didactic purpose, otherwise a philosophy, directly opposite to their passional inspiration. In their passional inspiration, they are all phallic worshippers. From Balzac to Hardy, it is so. Nay, from Apuleius to E. M. Forster. Yet all of them, when it comes to their philosophy, or what they think-they-are, they are all crucified Jesuses. What a bore! And what a burden for the novel to carry!

But the novel has carried it. Several thousands of thousands of lamentable crucifixions of self-heroes and self-heroines. Even the silly duplicity of *Resurrection,* and the wickeder duplicity of *Salammbô,* with that flayed phallic Matho, tortured upon the Cross of a gilt Princess."

You can't fool the novel. Even with man crucified upon a woman: his "dear cross." The novel will show you how dear she was: dear at any price. And it will leave you with a bad taste of disgust against these heroes who *turn* their women into a "dear cross," and *ask* for their own crucifixion.

You can fool pretty nearly every other medium. You can make a poem pietistic, and still it will be a poem. You can write *Hamlet* in drama: if you wrote him in a novel, he'd be half comic, or a trifle suspicious: a suspicious character, like Dostoevsky's Idiot. Somehow, you sweep the ground a bit too clear in the poem or the drama, and you let the human Word fly a bit too freely. Now in a novel there's always a tom-cat, a black tom-cat that pounces on the white dove of the Word, if the dove doesn't watch it; and there is a banana-skin to trip on; and you know there is a water-closet on the premises. All these things help to keep the balance.

If, in Plato's Dialogues, somebody had suddenly stood on his head and given smooth Plato a kick in the wind, and set the whole school in an uproar, then Plato would have been put into a much truer relation to the universe. Or if, in the midst of the Timaeus, Plato had only paused to say: "And now, my dear Cleon— (or whoever it was)—I have a belly-ache, and must retreat to the privy: this too is part of the Eternal Idea of man," then we never need have fallen so low as Freud.

And if, when Jesus told the rich man to take all he had and give it to the poor, the rich man had replied: *"All right, old sport! You are poor, aren't you? Come on, I'll give you a fortune. Come on!"*—Then a great deal of snivelling and mistakenness would have been spared us all, and we might never have produced a Marx and a Lenin. If only Jesus had *accepted* the fortune!

Yes, it's a pity of pities that Matthew, Mark, Luke, and John didn't write straight novels. They did write novels; but a bit crooked. The Evangels are wonderful novels, by authors "with a purpose." Pity there's so much Sermon-on-the-Mounting.

"Matthew, Mark, Luke, and John
Went to bed with their breeches on!" —

as every child knows. Ah, if only they'd taken them off!

Greater novels, to my mind, are the books of the Old Testament, Genesis, Exodus, Samuel, Kings, by authors whose purpose was so big, it didn't quarrel with their passional inspiration. The purpose and the inspiration were almost one. Why, in the name of everything bad, the two ever should have got separated, is a mystery! But in the modern novel they are hopelessly divorced. When there *is* any inspiration there: to be divorced from.

This, then, is what is the matter with the modern novel. The modern novelist is possessed, hag-ridden, by such a stale old "purpose," or idea-of-himself, that his inspiration succumbs. Of course he denies having any didactic purpose at all: because a purpose is supposed to be like catarrh, something to be ashamed of. But he's got it.—They've all got it: the same snivelling purpose.

They're all little Jesuses in their own eyes, and their "purpose" is to prove it. Oh *Lord!—Lord Jim! Sylvestre Bonnard! If Winter Comes! Main Street! Ulysses! Pan! —They* are all pathetic or sympathetic or antipathetic little Jesuses *accomplis* or *manqués.* And there is a heroine who is always "pure," usually, nowadays, on the muck-heap! Like the Green Hatted Woman. She is all the time at the feet of Jesus, though her behaviour there may be misleading. Heaven knows what the Saviour really makes of it: whether she's a Green Hat or a Constant Nymph (eighteen months of constancy, and her heart failed), or any of the rest of 'em. They are all, heroes and heroines, novelists and she-novelists, little Jesuses or Jesusesses. They may be wallowing in the mire: but then didn't Jesus harrow Hell! *A la bonne heure!*

Oh, they are all novelists with an idea of themselves! Which is a "purpose," with a vengeance! For what a weary, false, sickening idea it is nowadays! The novel gives them away. They can't fool the novel.

Now really, it's time we left off insulting the novel any further. If your purpose is to prove your own Jesus qualifications, and the thin stream of your inspiration is "sin," then dry up, for the interest is dead. *Life as it is!* What's the good of pretending that the lives of a set of tuppenny Green Hats and Constant Nymphs is Life-as-it-is, when the novel itself proves that all it amounts to is life as it is isn't life, but a sort of everlasting and intricate and boring habit: of Jesus peccant and Jesusa peccante.

These wearisome sickening little personal novels! After all, they aren't novels at all. In every great novel, who is the hero all the time? Not any of the characters, but some unnamed and nameless flame behind them all. Just as God is the pivotal interest in the books of the Old Testament. But just a trifle too intimate, too *frère et cochon,* there. In the great novel, the felt but unknown flame stands behind all the characters, and in their words and gestures there is a flicker of the presence. If you are too *personal, too* human, the flicker fades out, leaving you with something awfully lifelike, and as lifeless as most people are.

We have to choose between the quick and the dead. The quick is God-flame, in everything. And the dead is dead. In this room where I write, there is a little table that is dead: it doesn't even weakly exist. And there is a ridiculous little iron stove, which for some unknown reason is quick. And there is an iron wardrobe trunk, which for some still more mysterious reason is quick. And there are several books, whose mere corpus is dead, utterly dead and non-existent. And there is a sleeping cat, very quick. And a glass lamp, that, alas, is dead.

What makes the difference? *Quien sabe!* But difference there is. And I *know* it.

And the sum and source of all quickness, we will call God. And the sum and total of all deadness we may call human.

And if one tries to find out, wherein the quickness of the quick lies, it is in a certain weird relationship between that which is quick and—I don't know; perhaps all the rest of things. It seems to consist in an odd sort of fluid, changing, grotesque or beautiful relatedness. That silly iron stove somehow *belongs.* Whereas this thin-shanked table doesn't belong. It is a mere disconnected lump, like a cut-off finger.

And now we see the great, great merits of the novel. It can't exist without being "quick." The ordinary unquick novel, even if it be a best seller, disappears into absolute nothingness, the dead burying their dead with surprising speed. For even the dead like to be tickled. But the next minute, they've forgotten both the tickling and the tickler.

Secondly, the novel contains no didactive absolute. All that is quick, and all that is said and done by the quick, is, in some way, godly. So that Vronsky's taking Anna Karenin we must count godly, since it is quick. And that Prince in *Resurrection,* following the convict girl, we must Count dead. The convict train is quick and alive. But that would-be-expiatory Prince is as dead as lumber.

The novel itself lays down these laws for us, and we spend our time evading them. The man in the novel must be "quick." And this means one thing, among a host of unknown meaning: it means he must have a quick relatedness to all the other things in the novel: snow, bed-bugs, sunshine, the phallus, trains, silk-hats, cats, sorrow, people, food, diphtheria, fuchsias, stars, ideas, God, tooth-paste, lightning, and toilet-paper. He must be in quick relation to all these things. What he says and does must be relative to them all.

And this is why Pierre, for example, in *War and Peace,* is more dull and less quick than Prince André. Pierre is quite nicely related to ideas, tooth-paste, God, people, food, trains, silk-hats, sorrow, diphtheria, stars. But his relation to snow and sunshine, cats, lightning and the phallus, fuchsias and toilet-paper, is sluggish and mussy. He's not quick enough.

The really quick, Tolstoi loved to kill them off or muss them over. Like a true Bolshevist. One can't help feeling Natasha is rather mussy and unfresh, married to that Pierre.

Pierre was what we call, "so human." Which means, "so limited." Men clotting together into social masses in order to limit their individual liabilities: this is humanity. And this is Pierre. And this is Tolstoi, the philosopher with a very nauseating Christian-brotherhood idea of himself. Why limit man to a Christian-brotherhood? I myself, I could belong to the sweetest Christian-brotherhood one day, and ride after Attila with a raw beefsteak for my saddle-cloth, to see the red cock crow in flame over all Christendom, next day.

And that is man! That, really, was Tolstoi. That, even, was Lenin, God in the machine of Christian-brotherhood, that hashes men up into social sausage-meat.

Damn all absolutes. Oh damn, damn, damn all absolutes! I tell you, no absolute is going to make the lion lie down with the lamb: unless, like the limerick, the lamb is inside.

"They returned from the ride
With lamb Leo inside
And a smile on the face of the tiger!
Sing fol-di-lol-lol!
Fol-di-lol-lol!
Fol-di-lol-ol-di-lol-olly!"

For man, there is neither absolute nor absolution. Such things should be left to monsters like the right-angled triangle, which does only exist in the ideal consciousness. A man can't have a square on his hypotenuse, let him try as he may.

Ay! Ay! Ay!—Man handing out absolutes to man, as if we were all books of geometry with axioms, postulates and definitions in front. God with a pair of compasses! Moses with a set-square! Man a geometric bifurcation, not even a radish!

Holy Moses!

"Honour thy father and thy mother!"—That's awfully cute! But supposing they are not honourable? How then, Moses?

Voice of thunder from *Sinai:—"Pretend to honour them!"*

"Love thy neighbour as thyself."

Alas, my neighbour happens to be mean and detestable.

Voice of the lambent Dove, cooing: *"Put it over him, that you love him."*

Talk about the cunning of serpents! I never saw even a serpent kissing his instinctive enemy.

Pfui! I wouldn't blacken my mouth, kissing my neighbour, who, I repeat, to me is mean and detestable.

Dove, go home!

The Goat and Compasses, indeed!

Everything is relative. Every Commandment that ever issued out of the mouth of God or man, is strictly relative: adhering to the particular time, place and circumstance.

And this is the beauty of the novel; everything is true in its own relationship, and no further.

For the relatedness and interrelatedness of all things flows and changes and trembles like a stream, and like a fish in the stream the characters in the novel swim and drift and float and turn belly-up when they're dead.

So, if a character in a novel wants two wives—or three—or thirty: well, that is true of that man, at that time, in that circumstance. It may be true of other men, elsewhere and elsewhen. But to infer that all men at all times want two, three, or thirty wives; or that the novelist himself is advocating furious polygamy; is just imbecility.

It has been just as imbecile to infer that, because Dante worshipped a remote Beatrice, every man, all men, should go worshipping remote Beatrices.

And that wouldn't have been so bad, if Dante had put the thing in its true light. Why do we slur over the actual fact that Dante had a cosy bifurcated wife in his bed, and a family of lusty little Dantinos? Petrarch, with his Laura in the distance," had *twelve* little legitimate Petrarchs of his own, between his knees. Yet all we hear is *Laura! Laura! Beatrice! Beatrice! Distance! Distance!*

What bunk! Why didn't Dante and Petrarch chant in chorus:

"Oh be my spiritual concubine
Beatrice!
Laura!
My old girl's got several babies that are mine,
But *thou* be my spiritual concubine,
Beatrice!
Laura!

Then there would have been an honest relation between all the bunch. Nobody grudges the gents their spiritual concubines. But keeping a wife and family—twelve children—up one's sleeve, has always been recognised as a dirty trick.

Which reveals how *immoral* the absolute is! Invariably keeping some vital fact dark! Dishonorable!

Here we come upon the third essential quality of the novel. Unlike the essay, the poem, the drama, the book of philosophy, or the scientific treatise: all of which may beg the question, when they don't downright filch it; the novel inherently is and must be:

1.	Quick.
2.	Interrelated in all its parts, vitally, organically.
3.	Honourable.

I call Dante's *Commedia* slightly dishonourable, with never a mention of the cosy bifurcated wife, and the kids. And *War and Peace* I call downright dishonourable, with that fat, diluted Pierre for a hero, stuck up as preferable and desirable, when everybody knows that he *wasn't* attractive, even to Tolstoi.

Of course Tolstoi, being a great creative artist, was true to his characters. But being a man with a philosophy, he wasn't true to his *own character.*

Character is a curious thing. It is the flame of a man, which burns brighter or dimmer, bluer or yellower or redder, rising or sinking or flaring according to the draughts of circumstance and the changing air of life, changing itself continually, yet remaining one single, separate flame, flickering in a strange world: unless it be blown out at last by too much adversity.

If Tolstoi had looked into the flame of his own belly, he would have seen that he didn't really like the fat, fuzzy Pierre, who was a poor tool, after all. But Tolstoi was a personality even more than a character. And a personality is a self-conscious *I am:* being all that is left in us of a once-almighty Personal God. So being a personality and an almighty *I am,* Leo proceeded deliberately to lionise that Pierre, who was a domestic sort of house-dog.

Doesn't anybody call that dishonourable on Leo's part? He might just as well have been true to *himself!* But no! His self-conscious personality was superior to his own belly and knees, so he thought he'd improve on himself, by creeping inside the skin of a lamb: the doddering old lion that he was! Leo! León!

Secretly, Leo worshipped the human male, man as a column of rapacious and living blood. He could hardly meet three lusty, roisterous young guardsmen in the street, without crying with envy: and ten minutes later, fulminating on them black oblivion and annihilation, utmost moral thunder-bolts.

How boring, in a great man! And how boring, in a great nation like Russia, to let its old-Adam manhood be so improved upon by these reformers, who all feel themselves short of something, and therefore live by spite, that at last there's nothing left but a lot of shells of men, improving themselves steadily emptier and emptier, till they rattle with words and formulae, as if they'd swallowed the whole encyclopædia of socialism.

But wait! There is life in the Russians. Something new and strange will emerge out of their weird transmogrification into Bolshevists.

When the lion swallows the lamb, fluff and all, he usually gets a pain, and there's a rumpus. But when the lion tries to force himself down the throat of the huge and popular lamb—a nasty old sheep, really—then it's a phenomenon. Old Leo did it: wedged himself bit by bit down the throat of wooly Russia. And now out of the mouth of the bolshevist lambkin still waves an angry, mistaken, tufted leonine tail, like an agitated exclamation mark.

Meanwhile it's a deadlock.

But what a dishonourable thing for that claw-biting little Leo to do! And in his novels you see him at it. So that the papery lips of *Resurrection* whisper: *"Alas! I would have been a novel. But Leo spoiled me."* Count Tolstoi had that last weakness of a great man: he wanted the absolute: the absolute of love, if you like to call it that. Talk about the "last infirmity of noble minds"! It's a perfect epidemic of senility. He wanted to *be* absolute: a universal brother. Leo was too tight for Tolstoi. He wanted to puff, and puff, and puff, till he became Universal Brotherhood itself, the great gooseberry of our globe.

Then pop went Leo! And from the bits sprang up bolshevists.

It's all bunk. No man can be absolute. No man can be absolutely good or absolutely right, nor absolutely lovable, nor absolutely beloved nor absolutely loving. Even Jesus, the paragon, was only relatively good and relatively right. Judas could take him by the nose.

No god, that men can conceive of, could possibly be absolute or absolutely right. All the gods that men ever discovered are still God: and they contradict one another and fly down one another's throats, marvellously. Yet they are *all* God: the incalculable Pan.

It is rather nice, to know what a lot of gods there are, and have been, and will be, and that they are all of them God all the while. Each of them utters an absolute: which, in the ears of all the rest of them, falls flat. This makes even eternity lively.

But man, poor man, bobbing like a cork in the stream of time, must hitch himself to some absolute star of righteousness overhead. So he throws out his line, and hooks on. Only to find, after a while, that his star is slowly falling: till it drops into the stream of time with a fizzle, and there's *another* absolute star gone out.

Then we scan the heavens afresh.

As for the babe of love, we're simply tired of changing its napkins. Put the brat down, and let it learn to run about, and manage its own little breeches.

But it's nice to think that all the gods are God all the while. And if a god only genuinely feels to you like God, then it *is* God. But if it doesn't feel quite, quite altogether like God to you, then wait awhile, and you'll hear him fizzle.

The novel knows all this, irrevocably. "My dear," it kindly says, "one God is relative to another god, until he gets into a machine; and then it's a case for the traffic cop!"

"But what am I to do!" cries the despairing novelist. "From Amon and Ra to Mrs Eddy, from Ashtaroth and Jupiter to Annie Besant, I don't know where I am."

"Oh yes you do, my dear!" replies the novel. "You are where you are, so you needn't hitch yourself on to the skins either of Ashtaroth or Eddy.

If you meet them, say *how-do-you-do!* to them quite courteously. But don't hook on, or I shall turn you down."

126

Refrain from hooking on! says the novel.

But be honourable among the host! he adds.

Honour! Why, the gods are like the rainbow, all colours and shades. Since light itself is invisible, a manifestation has got to be pink or black or blue or white or yellow or vermilion, or "tinted."

You may be a theosophist, and then you will cry: *Avaunt! Thou dark-red aura! Away!!!—Oh come! Thou pale-blue or thou primrose aura, come!*

This you may cry if you are a theosophist. And if you put a theosophist in a novel, he or she may cry *avaunt!* to the heart's content.

But a theosophist cannot be a novelist, as a trumpet cannot be a regimental band. A theosophist, or a Christian, or a Holy Roller, may be *contained* in a novelist. But a novelist may not put up a fence. The wind bloweth where it listeth, and auras will be red when they want to.

As a matter of fact, only the Holy Ghost knows truly what righteousness is. And heaven only knows what the Holy Ghost is! But it sounds all right. So the Holy Ghost hovers among the flames, from the red to the blue and the black to the yellow, putting brand to brand and flame to flame, as the wind changes, and life travels in flame from the unseen to the unseen, men will never know how or why. Only travel it must, and not die down in nasty fumes.

And the honour, which the novel demands of you, is only that you shall be true to the flame that leaps in you. When that Prince in *Resurrection* so cruelly betrayed and abandoned the girl, at the beginning of her life, he betrayed and wetted on the flame of his own manhood. When, later, he bullied her with his repentant benevolence, he again betrayed and slobbered upon the flame of his waning manhood, till in the end his manhood is extinct, and he's just a lump of half-alive elderly meat.

It's the oldest Pan-mystery. God is the flame-life in all the universe. Multifarious, multifarious flames, all colours and beauties and pains and sombrenesses. Whichever flame flames in your manhood, that is you, for the time being. It is your manhood, don't make water on it, says the novel. A man's manhood is to honour the flames in him, and to know that none of them is absolute. Even a flame is only relative.

But see old Leo Tolstoi wetting on the flame. As if even his wet were absolute!

Sex is flame, too, the novel announces. Flame burning against every absolute, even against the phallic. For sex is so much more than phallic, and so much deeper than functional desire. The flame of sex singes your absolute, and cruelly scorches your ego. What, will you assert your ego in the universe? Wait till the flames of sex leap at you like striped tigers.

> 'They returned from the ride
> With the lady inside,
> And a smile on the face of the tiger."

You will play with sex, will you! You will tickle yourself with sex as with an ice-cold drink from a soda-fountain! You will pet your best girl, will you, and spoon with her, and titillate yourself and her, and do as you like with your sex?

127

Wait! Only wait till the flame you have dribbled on flies back at you, later! Only wait!

Sex is a life-flame, a dark one, reserved and mostly invisible. It is a deep reserve in a man, one of the core-flames of his manhood.

What, would you play with it? Would you make it cheap and nasty!

Buy a king-cobra, and try playing with that.

Sex is even a majestic reserve in the sun.

Oh, give me the novel! Let me hear what the novel says.

As for the novelist, he is usually a dribbling liar.

WHY THE NOVEL MATTERS

We have curious ideas of ourselves. We think of ourselves as a body with a spirit in it, or a body with a soul in it, or a body with a mind in it. *Mens sana in corpore sano.* The years drink up the wine, and at last throw the bottle away: the body, of course, being the bottle.

It is a funny sort of superstition. Why should I look at my hand, as it so cleverly writes these words, and decide that it is a mere nothing compared to the mind that directs it? Is there really any huge difference between my hand and my brain?—or my mind? My hand is alive, it flickers with a life of its own. It meets all the strange universe, in touch, and learns a vast number of things, and knows a vast number of things. My hand, as it writes these words, slips gaily along, jumps like a grasshopper to dot an i, feels the table rather cold, gets a little bored if I write too long, has its own rudiments of thought, and is just as much *me* as is my brain, my mind, or my soul. Why should I imagine that there is a *me* which is more *me* than my hand is? Since my hand is absolutely alive, me alive.

Whereas, of course, as far as I am concerned, my pen isn't alive at all. My pen *isn't* me alive. Me alive ends at my finger-tips.

Whatever is me alive is me. Every tiny bit of my hands is alive, every little freckle and hair and fold of skin. And whatever is me alive is me. Only my finger-nails, those ten little weapons between me and an inanimate universe, they cross the mysterious Rubicon between me alive and things like my pen, which are not alive, in my own sense.

So, seeing my hand is all alive, and me alive, wherein is it just a bottle, or a jug, or a tin can, or a vessel of clay, or any of the rest of that nonsense? True, if I cut it it will bleed, like a can of cherries. But then the skin that is cut, and the veins that bleed, and the bones that should never be seen, they are all just as alive as the blood that flows. So the tin can business, or vessel of clay, is just bunk.

And that's what you learn, when you're a novelist. And that's what you are very liable *not* to know, if you're a parson, or a philosopher, or a scientist, or a stupid person. If you're a parson, you talk about souls in heaven. If you're a novelist, you know that paradise is in the palm of your hand, and on the end of your nose: because both are alive; and alive, and man-alive, which is more than you can say, for certain, of paradise. Paradise is after life, and I for one am not keen on anything that is *after* life.—If you are a philosopher, you talk about infinity, and the pure spirit which knows all things. But if you pick up a novel, you realise immediately that infinity is just a handle to this self-same jug of a body of mine;

while as for knowing, if I put my finger in the fire, I know that fire burns, with a knowledge so emphatic and vital, it leaves Nirvana merely a conjecture. Oh yes, my body, me alive, *knows,* and knows intensely. And as for the sum of all knowledge, it can't be anything more than an accumulation of all the things I know in the body, and you, dear reader, know in the body.

These damned philosophers, they talk as if they suddenly went off in steam, and were then much more important than they are when they're in their shirts. It is nonsense. Every man, philosopher included, ends in his own finger-tips. That's the end of his man alive. As for the words and thoughts and sighs and aspirations that fly from him, they are so many tremulations in the ether, and not alive at all. But if the tremulations reach another man alive, he may receive them into his life, and his life may take on a new colour, like a chameleon creeping from a brown rock on to a green leaf. All very well and good. It still doesn't alter the fact that the so-called spirit, the message or teaching of the philosopher or the saint, isn't alive at all, but just a tremulation upon the ether, like a radio message. All this spirit stuff is just tremulations upon the ether. If you, as man alive, quiver from the tremulation of the ether into new life, that is because you are man alive, and you take sustenance and stimulation into your alive man in a myriad ways. But to say that the message, or the spirit which is communicated to you, is more important than your living body, is nonsense. You might as well say that the potato at dinner was more important.

Nothing is important but life. And for myself, I can absolutely see life nowhere but in the living. Life with a capital L is only man alive. Even a cabbage in the rain is cabbage alive. All things that are alive are amazing. And all things that are dead are subsidiary to the living. Better a live dog than a dead lion. But better a live lion than a live dog. *C'est la vie.*

It seems impossible to get a saint, or a philosopher, or a scientist, to stick to this simple truth. They are all, in a sense, renegades. The saint wishes to offer himself up as spiritual food for the multitude. Even Francis of Assisi turns himself into a sort of angel cake, of which anyone may take a slice. But an angel cake is rather less than man alive. And poor St. Francis might well apologise to his body, when he was dying. "Oh pardon me, my body, the wrong I did you through the years!"—It was no wafer, for others to eat. The philosopher on the other hand, because he can think, decides that nothing but thoughts matter. It is as if a rabbit, because he can make little pills, should decide that nothing but little pills matter. As for the scientist he has absolutely no use for me so long as I am man alive. To the scientist I am dead. He puts under the microscope a bit of dead me, and calls it me. He takes me to pieces, and says first one piece, and then another piece, is me. My heart, my liver, my stomach have all been scientifically me, according to the scientist; and nowadays I am either a brain, or nerves, or glands, or something more up-to-date in the tissue line.

Now I absolutely flatly deny that I am a soul, or a body, or a mind, or an intelligence, or a brain, or a nervous system, or a bunch of glands, or any of the rest of these bits of me. The whole is greater than the part. And therefore I, who am man alive, am greater than my soul, or spirit, or body, or mind, or consciousness, or anything else that is merely a part of me. I am a man, and alive. I am man alive, and as long as I can, I intend to go on being man alive.

For this reason I am a novelist. And being a novelist, I consider myself superior to the saint, the scientist, the philosopher and the poet, who are all great masters of different bits of man-alive, but never get the whole hog.

The novel is the one bright book of life. Books are not life. They are only tremulations on the ether. But the novel as a tremulation *can* make the whole man-alive tremble. Which is more than poetry, philosophy, science or any other book-tremulation can do. —The novel is the book of life. In this sense, the Bible is a great confused novel. You may say, it is about God. But it is really about man-alive. Adam, Eve, Sarai, Abraham, Isaac, Jacob, Samuel, David, Bathsheba, Ruth, Esther, Solomon, Job, Isaiah, Jesus, Mark, Judas, Paul, Peter; what is it but man-alive, from start to finish? Man-alive, not mere bits. Even the Lord is another man-alive, in a burning bush, throwing the tablets of stone at Moses' head.

I do hope you begin to get my idea, why the novel is supremely important, as a tremulation on the ether. Plato makes the perfect ideal being tremble in me. But that's only a bit of me. Perfection is only a bit, in the strange make-up of man-alive. The Sermon on the Mount makes the selfless spirit of me quiver. But that too is only a bit of me. The Ten Commandments sets the old Adam shivering in me, warning me that I am a thief and a murderer, unless I watch it. But even the old Adam is only a bit of me.

I very much like all these bits of me to be set trembling with life and the wisdom of life. But I do ask that the whole of me shall tremble in its wholeness, some time or other.

And this, of course, must happen in my living.

But as far as it can happen from a communication, it can only happen when a whole novel communicates itself to me. The Bible—but *all* the Bible—and Homer, and Shakespeare: these are the supreme old novels. These are all things to all men. Which means that in their wholeness they affect the whole man alive, which is the man himself, beyond any part of him. They set the whole tree trembling with a new access of life, they do not just stimulate growth in one direction.

I don't want to grow in any one direction any more. And if I can help it, I don't want to stimulate anybody else into some particular direction. A particular direction ends in a cul de sac. We're in a cul de sac at present.

I don't believe in any dazzling revelation, or in any supreme Word. "The grass withereth, the flower fadeth, but the Word of the Lord shall stand for ever." — That's the kind of stuff we've drugged ourselves with. As a matter of fact, the grass withereth, but comes up all the greener for that reason, after the rains. The flower fadeth, and therefore the bud opens. But the Word of the Lord, being man-uttered and a mere vibration on the ether, becomes staler and staler, more and more boring, till at last we turn a deaf ear and it ceases to exist, far more finally than any withered grass. It is grass that renews its youth like the eagle, not any Word.

We should ask for no absolutes, or absolute. Once and for all and forever, let us have done with the ugly imperialism of any absolute. There is no absolute good, there is nothing absolutely right. All things flow and change, and even change is not absolute. The whole is a strange assembly of apparently incongruous parts, slipping past one another.

Me, man alive, I am a very curious assembly of incongruous parts. My yea! of today is oddly different from my yea! of yesterday. My tears of tomorrow will have nothing to do with my tears of a year ago. If the one I love remains unchanged and unchanging, I shall cease to love her. It is only because she changes and startles me into change and defies my inertia, and is herself staggered in her inertia by my changing, that I can continue to love her. If she stayed put, I might as well love the pepper pot.

In all this change, I maintain a certain integrity. But woe betide me if I try to put my finger on it. If I say of myself: I am this, I am that!—then, if I stick to it, I turn into a stupid fixed thing like a lamp post. I shall never know wherein lies my integrity, my individuality, my me. I *can* never know it. It is useless to talk about my ego. That only means that I have made up an *idea* of myself, and that I am trying to cut myself out to pattern. Which is no good. You can cut your cloth to fit your coat, but you can't clip bits off your living body, to trim it down to your idea. True, you can put yourself into ideal corsets. But even in ideal corsets, fashions change.

Let us learn from the novel. In the novel, the characters can do nothing but *live*. If they keep on being good, according to pattern, or bad, according to pattern, or even volatile, according to pattern, they cease to live, and the novel falls dead. A character in a novel has got to live, or it is nothing.

We, likewise, in life have got to live, or we are nothing.

What we mean by living is, of course, just as indescribable as what we mean by *being*. Men get ideas into their heads, of what they mean by Life, and they proceed to cut life out to pattern. Sometimes they go into the desert to seek God, sometimes they go into the desert to seek cash, sometimes it is wine, woman, and song, and again it is water, political reform, and votes. You never know what it will be next: from killing your neighbour with hideous bombs and gas that tears the lungs, to supporting a Foundlings Home and preaching infinite Love, and being co-respondent in a divorce.

In all this wild welter, we need some sort of guide. It's no good inventing Thou Shalt Nots!

What then? Turn truly, honourably to the novel, and see wherein you are man alive, and wherein you are dead man in life. You may love a woman as man alive, and you may be making love to a woman as sheer dead man in life. You may eat your dinner as man alive, or as a mere masticating corpse. As man alive you may have a shot at your enemy. But as a ghastly simulacrum of life you may be firing bombs into men who are neither your enemies nor your friends, but just things you are dead to. Which is criminal, when the things happen to be live.

To be alive, to be man alive, to be whole man alive: that is the point. And at its best, the novel, and the novel supremely can help you. It can help you not to be dead man in life. So much of a man walks about dead and a carcase in the Street and house, today: so much of women is merely dead. Like a pianoforte with half the notes mute.

But in the novel you can see, plainly, when the man goes dead, the woman goes inert. You can develop an instinct for life, if you will, instead of a theory of right and wrong, good and bad.

In life, there is right and wrong, good and bad, all the time. But what is right in one case is wrong in another. And in the novel you see one man becoming a corpse, because of his so-called goodness, another going dead because of his so-called wickedness. Right and wrong is an instinct: but an instinct of the whole consciousness in a man, bodily, mental, spiritual at once. And only in the novel are *all* things given full play; or at least, they may be given full play, when we realise

131

that life itself, and not inert safety, is the reason for living. For out of the full play of all things emerges the only thing that is anything, the wholeness of a man, the wholeness of a woman, man alive, and live woman.

THE NOVEL AND THE FEELINGS

We think we are so civilised, so highly educated and civilised. It is farcical. Because, of course, all our civilisation consists in harping on one string. Or at most, on two or three strings. Harp, harp, harp, twingle-twingle-twang! That's our civilisation, always on one note.

The note itself is all right. It's the exclusiveness of it that is awful. Always the same note, always the same note!—"Ah, how can you run after other women, when your wife is so delightful, a lovely plump partridge?"—Then the husband laid his hand on his waistcoat, and a frightened look came over his face. "Nothing but partridge?" he exclaimed.

Toujours perdrix! It was up to that wife to be a goose and a cow, an oyster and an inedible vixen, at intervals.

Wherein are we educated? Come now, in what are we educated? In politics, in geography, in history, in machinery, in soft drinks and in hard, in social economy and social extravagance: ugh, a frightful universality of knowings.

But it's all France without Paris, *Hamlet* without the Prince, and bricks without straw. For we know nothing, or next to nothing, about ourselves. After hundreds of thousands of years we have learned how to wash our faces and bob our hair, and that is about all we *have* learned, *individually.* Collectively, of course, as a species, we have combed the round earth with a tooth-comb, and pulled down the stars almost within grasp. And then what? Here sit I, a two-legged individual with a risky temper, knowing all about—take a pinch of salt—Tierra del Fuego and Relativity and the composition of celluloid, the appearance of the anthrax bacillus and solar eclipses, and the latest fashion in shoes; and it don't do me *no* good! as the charlady said of near beer. It doesn't leave me feeling no less lonesome inside! as the old Englishwoman said, long ago, of tea without rum.

Our knowledge, like the prohibition beer, is always near. But it never gets there. It leaves us feeling just as lonesome inside.

We are hopelessly uneducated in ourselves. We pretend that when we know a smattering of the Patagonian idiom we have in-so-far educated ourselves. What nonsense! The leather of my boots is just as effectual in turning me into a bull, or a young steer. Alas! we wear our education just as externally as we wear our boots, and to far less profit. It is all external education, anyhow.

What am I, when I am at home? I'm supposed to be a sensible human being. Yet I carry a whole waste-paper basket of ideas at the top of my head, and in some other part of my anatomy, the dark continent of my self, I have a whole stormy chaos of "feelings." And with these self-same feelings I simply don't get a chance. Some of them roar like lions, some twist like snakes, some bleat like snow-white lambs, some warble like linnets, some are absolutely dumb, but swift as slippery fishes, some are oysters that open on occasion: and lo! here am I, adding another scrap of paper to the ideal accumulation in the waste-paper basket, hoping to settle the matter that way.

The lion springs on me! I wave an idea at him. The serpent casts a terrifying glance at me, and I hand him a Moody and Sankey hymn-book. Matters go from bad to worse.

The wild creatures are coming forth from the darkest Africa inside us. In the night you can hear them bellowing. If you're a big game hunter, like Billy Sunday, you may shoulder your elephant gun. But since the forest is inside all of us, and in every forest there's a whole assortment of big game and dangerous creatures, it's one against a thousand. We've managed to keep clear of the darkest Africa inside us, for a long time. We've been so busy finding the North Pole and converting the Patagonians, loving our neighbour and devising new means of exterminating him, listening in and shutting out.

But now, my dear, dear reader, Nemesis is blowing his nose. And muffled roarings are heard out of darkest Africa, with stifled shrieks.

I say feelings, not emotions. Emotions are things we more or less recognise. We see love, like a woolly lamb, or like a decorative decadent panther in Paris clothes: according as it is sacred or profane. We see hate, like a dog chained to a kennel. We see fear, like a shivering monkey. We see anger, like a bull with a ring through his nose, and greed, like a pig. Our emotions are our domesticated animals, noble like the horse, timid like the rabbit, but all completely at our service. The rabbit goes into the pot, and the horse into the shafts. For we are creatures of circumstance, and must fill our bellies and our pockets.

Convenience! Convenience! There are convenient emotions, and inconvenient ones. The inconvenient ones we chain up, or put a ring through their nose. The convenient ones are our pets. Love is our pet favourite.

And that's as far as our education goes, in the direction of feelings. We have no language for the feelings, because our feelings do not even exist for us.

Yet what is a man? Is he really just a little engine that you stoke with potatoes and beef-steak? Does all the strange flow of life in him come out of meat and potatoes, and turn into the so-called physical energy?

Educated! We are not even *born,* as far as our feelings are concerned. You can eat till you're bloated, and "get ahead" till you're a by-word, and still, inside you, will be the darkest Africa whence come roars and shrieks.

Man is not a little engine of cause and effect. We must put that out of our minds for ever. The *cause* in man is something we shall never fathom. But there it is, a strange dark continent that we do not explore, because we do not even allow that it exists. Yet all the time, it is within us: the *cause* of us, and of our days.

And our feelings are the first manifestations within the aboriginal jungle of us. Till now, in sheer terror of ourselves, we have turned our backs on the jungle, fenced it in with an enormous entanglement of barbed wire, and declared it did not exist.

But alas! We ourselves only exist because of the life that bounds and leaps into our limbs and our consciousness, from out of the original dark forest within us. We may wish to exclude this inbounding, in-leaping life. We may wish to be as our domesticated animals are, tame. But let us remember that even our cats and dogs have, in each generation, to be tamed. They are not now a tame species. Take away the control, and they will cease to be tame. They will not tame *themselves.*

Man is the only creature who has deliberately tried to tame himself. He has succeeded. But alas, it is a process you cannot set a limit to. Tameness, like alcohol,

133

destroys its own creator. Tameness is an effect of control. But the tamed thing loses the power of control, in itself. It must be controlled from without. Man has pretty well tamed himself, and he calls his tameness civilisation. True civilisation would be something very different. But man is now tame. Tameness means the loss of the peculiar power of command. The tame are always commanded by the untame. Man has tamed himself, and so has lost his power for command, the power to give himself direction. He has no choice in himself. He is tamed, like a tame horse waiting for the rein.

Supposing all horses were suddenly rendered masterless, what would they do? They would run wild. But supposing they were left still shut up in their fields, paddocks, corrals, stables, what would they do? They would go insane.

And that is precisely man's predicament. He is tamed. There are no untamed to give the command and the direction. Yet he is shut up within all his barb-wire fences. He can only go insane, degenerate.

What is the alternative? It is nonsense to pretend we can un-tame ourselves in five minutes. That, too, is a slow and strange process, that has to be undertaken seriously. It is nonsense to pretend we can break the fences and dash out into the wilds. There are no wilds left, comparatively, and man is a dog that returns to his vomit.

Yet, unless we proceed to connect ourselves up with our own primeval sources, we shall degenerate. And degenerating, we shall break up into a strange orgy of feelings. They will be decomposition feelings, like the colours of autumn. And they will precede whole storms of death, like leaves in a wind.

There is no help for it. Man cannot tame himself and then stay tame. The moment he tries to stay tame he begins to degenerate, and gets the second sort of wildness, the wildness of destruction, which may be autumnal-beautiful for a while, like yellow leaves. Yet yellow leaves can only fall and rot.

Man tames himself in order to learn to untame himself again. To be civilised, we must not deny and blank out our feelings. Tameness is not civilisation. It is only burning down the brush and ploughing the land. Our civilisation has hardly realised yet the necessity for ploughing the soul. Later, we sow wild seed. But so far, we've only been burning off and rooting out the old wild brush. Our civilisation, as far as our own souls go, has been a destructive process, up to now. The landscape of our souls is a charred wilderness of burnt-off stumps, with a green bit of water here, and a tin shanty with a little iron stove.

Now we have to sow wild seed again. We have to cultivate our feelings. It is no good trying to be popular, to let a whole rank tangle of liberated, degenerate feelings spring up. It will give us no satisfaction.

And it is no use doing as the psychoanalysts have done. The psychoanalysts show the greatest fear of all, of the innermost primeval place in man, where God is, if He is anywhere. The old Jewish horror of the true Adam, the mysterious "natural man," rises to a shriek in psychoanalysis. Like the idiot who foams and bites his wrists till they bleed. So great is the Freudian hatred of the oldest, old Adam, from whom God is not yet separated off, that the psychoanalyst sees this Adam as nothing but a monster of perversity, a bunch of engendering adders, horribly clotted.

This vision is the perverted vision of the degenerate tame: tamed through thousands of shameful years. The old Adam is the forever untamed: he who is of the tame hated, with a horror of fearful hate: but who is held in innermost respect by the fearless.

In the oldest of the old Adam, was God: behind the dark wall of his breast, under the seal of the navel. Then man had a revulsion against himself, and God was separated off, lodged in the outermost space.

Now we have to return. Now again the old Adam must lift up his face and his breast, and untame himself. Not in viciousness nor in wantonness, but having God within the walls of himself. In the very darkest continent of the body, there is God. And from Him issues the first dark rays of our feeling, wordless, and utterly previous to words; the innermost rays, the first messengers, the primeval, honourable beasts of our being, whose voice echoes wordless and forever wordless down the darkest avenues of the soul, but full of potent speech. Our own inner meaning.

Now we have to educate ourselves, not by laying down laws and inscribing tablets of stone, but by listening. Not listening-in to noises from Chicago or Timbuctoo. But listening-in to the voices of the honourable beasts that call in the dark paths of the veins of our body, from the God in the heart. Listening inwards, inwards, not for words nor for inspiration, but to the lowing of the innermost beasts, the feelings, that roam in the forest of the blood, from the feet of God within the red, dark heart.

And how? How? How shall we even begin to educate ourselves in the feelings?

Not by laying down laws, or commandments, or axioms and postulates. Not even by making assertions that such and such is blessed. Not by words at all.

If we can't hear the cries far down in our own forests of dark veins, we can look in the real novels, and there listen in. Not listen to the didactic statements of the author, but to the low, calling cries of the characters, as they wander in the dark woods of their destiny.

JOHN GALSWORTHY

Literary Criticism can be no more than a reasoned account of the feeling produced upon the critic by the book he is criticising. Criticism can never be a science: it is, in the first place, much too personal, and in the second, it is concerned with values that science ignores. The touch-stone is emotion, not reason. We judge a work of art by its effect on our sincere and vital emotion, and nothing else. All the critical twiddle-twaddle about style, and form, all this pseudo-scientific classifying and analysing of books in an imitation-botanical fashion, is mere impertinence, and mostly dull jargon.

A critic must be able to *feel* the impact of a work of art in all its complexity and its force. To do so, he must be a man of force and complexity himself, which few critics are. A man with a paltry, impudent nature will never write anything but paltry, impudent criticism. And a man who is *emotionally* educated is rare as a phœnix. The more scholastically educated a man is, generally, the more he is an emotional boor.

More than this, even an artistically and emotionally educated man must be a man of good faith. He must have the courage to admit what he feels, as well as the flexibility to *know* what he feels. So Sainte Beuve remains, to me, a great critic. And a man like Macaulay, brilliant as he is, is unsatisfactory, because he is not honest. He is emotionally very alive, but he juggles his feelings. He prefers a fine effect to the sincere statement of his aesthetic and emotional reaction. He is quite intellectually capable of giving us a true account of what he feels. But not morally. A critic must be emotionally alive in every fibre, intellectually capable and skilful in essential logic, and then morally very honest.

Then it seems to me, a good critic should give his reader a few standards to go by, He can change the standards for every new critical attempt, so long as he keeps good faith. But it is just as well to say: This, and this, is the standard we judge by.

Sainte Beuve, on the whole, set up the standard of the "good man." He sincerely believed that the great man was essentially the good man, in the widest range of human sympathy. This remained his universal standard. Pater's standard was the lonely philosopher of pure thought and pure aesthetic truth. Macaulay's standard was tainted by a political or democratic bias: he must be on the side of the weak. Gibbon tried a purely moral standard, individual morality.

Reading Galsworthy again—or most of him, for all is too much—one feels oneself in need of a standard, some conception of a real man and a real woman, by which to judge all these Forsytes and their contemporaries. One cannot judge them by the standard of the good man, nor of the man of pure thought, nor of the treasured humble nor the moral individual. One would like to judge them by the standard of the human being, but what, after all, is that? This is the trouble with the Forsytes. They are human enough, since anything in humanity is human, just as anything in nature is natural. Yet not one of them seems to be a really vivid human being. They are social beings.—And what do we mean by that?

It remains to define, just for the purposes of this criticism, what we mean by a social being as distinct from a human being. The necessity arises from the sense of dissatisfaction which these Forsytes give us. Why can't we admit them as human beings? Why can't we have them in the same category as Sairey Gamp, for example, who is satirically conceived, or of Jane Austen's people, who are social enough? We can accept Mrs Gamp or Jane Austen's characters or even George Meredith's Egoist as human beings, in the same category as ourselves. Whence arises this repulsion from the Forsytes, this refusal, this emotional refusal, to have them identified with our common humanity? Why do we feel so instinctively that they are inferiors?

It is because they seem to us to have lost caste, as human beings, and to have sunk to the level of the social being, that peculiar creature that takes the place, in our civilisation, of the slave in the old civilisations. The human individual is a queer animal, always changing. But the fatal change, today, is the collapse from the psychology of the free human individual into the psychology of the social being: just as the fatal change in the past was a collapse from the free-man's psyche to the psyche of the slave. The free moral and the slave moral: the human moral and the social moral: these are the abiding antitheses.

While a man remains a man, a true human individual, there is at the core of him a certain innocence or naïveté which defies all analysis, and which you cannot bargain with, you can only deal with it, in good faith, from your own corresponding innocence or naïveté. This does not mean that the human being is nothing but naïve or innocent. He is Mr Worldly Wiseman also, to his own degree. But in his essential core he is naïve, and money does not touch him. Money, of course, with every man living, goes a long way. With the alive human being it may go as far as his penultimate feeling. But in the last, naked him it does not enter.

With the social being, it goes right through the centre, and is the controlling principle, no matter how much he may pretend, nor how much bluff he may put up. He may give away all he has to the poor, and still reveal himself as a social being swayed finally and helplessly by the money-sway, and by the social moral, which is inhuman.

It seems to me, that when the human being becomes too much divided between his subjective and objective consciousness, at last something splits in him, and he becomes a social being. When he becomes too much aware of objective reality, and of his own isolation in the face of a universe of objective reality, the core of his identity splits, his nucleus collapses, his innocence or his naïveté perishes, and he becomes only a subjective-objective reality, a divided thing hinged together but not strictly individual.

While a man remains a man, before he falls and becomes a social individual, he innocently feels himself altogether within the great continuum of the universe. He is not divided nor cut off. Men may be against him, the tide of affairs may be rising to sweep him away. But he is one with the living continuum of the universe. From this he cannot be swept away. Hamlet and Lear feel it, as does Œdipus or Phaedra. It is the last and deepest feeling that is in a man, while he remains a man. It is there the same as in a deist like Voltaire or a scientist like Darwin: it is there, imperishable, in every great man: in Napoleon the same, till material things piled too much on him, and he lost it, and was doomed. It is the essential innocence and naïveté of the human being, the sense of being at one with the great universe-continuum of space-time-life, which is vivid in a great man, and a pure nuclear spark in every man who is still free.

But if man loses his mysterious naïve assurance, which is his innocence; if he gives *too* much importance to the external objective reality, and so collapses in his natural innocent pride; then he becomes obsessed with the idea of objective or material assurance; he wants to *insure* himself, and perhaps everybody else: universal insurance. The impulse rests on fear. Once the individual loses his naïve at-oneness with the living universe, he falls into a state of fear, and tries to insure himself with wealth. If he is an altruist, he wants to insure everybody, and feels it is the tragedy of tragedies if this can't be done. But the whole necessity for thus materially insuring oneself with wealth, money, arises from the state of fear into which a man falls who has lost his at-oneness with the living universe, lost his peculiar nuclear innocence, and fallen into fragmentariness. Money, material salvation is the only salvation. What is salvation is God. Hence money is God. The social being may rebel even against this god, as do many of Galsworthy's characters. But that does not give them back their innocence. They are only anti-materialists instead of positive materialists. And the anti-materialist is a social being just the same as the materialist: neither more nor less. He is castrated just the same, made a neuter by having lost his innocence, the bright little individual spark of his at-oneness.

When one reads Mr Galsworthy's books, it seems as if there were not on earth one single human individual. They are all these social beings, positive and negative. There is not a free soul among them: not even Mrs Pendyce, or June

Forsyte. If money does not actively determine their being, it does negatively. Money, or property: which is the same thing. Mrs Pendyce, lovable as she is, is utterly circumscribed by property. Ultimately, she is not lovable at all, she is part of the fraud: she is prostituted to property. And there is nobody else. Old Jolyon is merely a sentimental materialist.—Only for one moment do we see a man: and that is the road-sweeper in *Fraternity,* after he comes out of prison, and covers his face. But even *his* manhood has to be explained away by a wound in the head: an abnormality.

Now it looks as if Mr Galsworthy set out to make that very point: to show that the Forsytes were not full human individuals, but social beings, fallen to a lower level of life. They have lost that bit of free manhood and free womanhood which makes men and women. *The Man of Property* has the elements of a very great novel, a very great satire. It sets out to reveal the social being in all his strength and inferiority. But the author has not the courage to carry it through. The greatness of the book rests in its new and sincere and amazingly profound satire. It is the ultimate satire on modern humanity, and done from the inside, with really consummate skill and sincere creative passion, something quite new. It seems to be a real effort to show up the social being in all his weirdness. And then it fizzles out.

Then, in the love-affair of Irene and Bosinney, and in the sentimentalising of old Jolyon Forsyte, the thing is fatally blemished. Galsworthy had not quite enough of the superb courage of his satire. He faltered, and gave in to the Forsytes. It is a thousand pities. He might have been the surgeon the modern soul needs so badly to cut away the proud flesh of our Forsytes from the living body of men who are fully alive. Instead, he put down the knife and laid on a soft sentimental poultice, and helped to make the corruption worse.

Satire exists for the very purpose of killing the social being, of showing him what an inferior he is, and, with all his parade of social honesty, how subtly and corruptly debased. Dishonest to life, dishonest to the living universe on which he is parasitic as a louse. By ridiculing the social being, the satirist helps the true individual, the real human being, to rise to his feet again and go on with the battle. For it is always a battle, and always will be.

Not that the majority are necessarily social beings. But the majority is only *conscious* socially: humanly, mankind is helpless and unconscious, unaware even of the thing most precious to any human being, that core of manhood or womanhood, naïve, innocent at-oneness with the living universe-continuum, which alone makes a man individual, and as an individual, essentially happy, even if he be driven mad like Lear. Lear was *essentially* happy, even in his greatest misery. A happiness from which Goneril and Regan were excluded as lice and bugs are excluded from happiness; being social beings, and as such, parasites, fallen from true freedom and independence.

But the tragedy today is that men are only materially and socially conscious. They are unconscious of their own manhood, and so they let it be destroyed. Out of free men we produce social beings by the thousand, every week.

The Forsytes are all parasites, and Mr Galsworthy set out, in a really magnificent attempt, to let us see it. They are parasites upon the thought, the feelings, the whole body of life of really living individuals who have gone before them and who exist alongside with them. All they can do, having no individual life of their own, is out of fear to rake together property, and to feed upon the life that has been given by living men to mankind. They have no life, and so they live forever, in perpetual fear of death, accumulating property to ward off death. They can keep up conventions: but they cannot carry on a tradition. There is a tremendous difference between the two things. To carry on a tradition, you must add something to the tradition. But to keep up a convention needs only the monotonous persistency of a parasite, the endless endurance of the craven, those who fear life because they are not alive, and who cannot die because they cannot live. The social beings.

As far as I can see, there is nothing but Forsyte in Galsworthy's books: Forsyte positive, or Forsyte negative: Forsyte successful, or Forsyte *manqué.* That is, every single character is determined by money: either the getting it, or the having it, or the wanting it, or the utter lacking it. Getting it are the Forsytes as such: having it are the Pendyces and patricians and Hilarys and Biancas and all that lot: wanting it are the Irenes and Bosinneys and young Jolyons; and utterly lacking it are all the charwomen and squalid poor who form the background: the shadows of the "having" ones, as old Mr Stone says. This is the whole Galsworthy gamut, all absolutely determined by money, and not an individual soul among them. They are all fallen, all social beings, a castrated lot.

Perhaps the overwhelming numerousness of the Forsytes frightened Mr Galsworthy from utterly damning them. Or perhaps it was something else, something more serious in him. Perhaps it was his utter failure to see what you were when you *weren't* a Forsyte. What was there *besides* Forsytes in all the wide human world? Mr Galsworthy looked, and found nothing. Strictly and truly, after his frightened search, he had found nothing. But he came back with Irene and Bosinney, and offered us that. Here! he seems to say. Here is the anti-Forsyte! Here! Here you have it! Love! Pa-assion! PASSION.

We look at this love, this PASSION, and we see nothing but a doggish amorousness and a sort of anti-Forsytism. They are the *anti* half of the show. Runaway dogs of these Forsytes, running in the back garden and furtively and ignominiously copulating —this is the effect, on me, of Mr Galsworthy's grand love affairs, Dark Flowers or Bosinneys or Apple Trees, or George Pendyce—whatever they be. About every one of them, something ignominious and doggish, like dogs copulating in the street, and looking round to see if the Forsytes are watching.

Alas! this is the Forsyte trying to be freely sensual. He can't do it; he's lost it. He can only be doggishly messy. Bosinney is not only a Forsyte, but an anti-Forsyte, with a vast grudge against property. And the thing a man has a vast grudge against is the man's determinant. Bosinney is a property-hound, but he has run away from the kennels, or been born outside the kennels, so he is a rebel. So he goes sniffing round the property-bitches, to get even with the successful property-hounds that way.—One cannot help preferring Soames Forsyte, in a choice of evils.

Just as one prefers June or any of the old aunts, to Irene. Irene seems to me a sneaking, creeping, spiteful sort of bitch, an anti-Forsyte, absolutely living off the Forsytes—yes, to the very end; absolutely living off their money, and trying to do them dirt. She is like Bosinney, a property-mongrel doing dirt in the property kennels. But she is a real property-prostitute, like the little model in *Fraternity.* Only she is *anti!* It is a type recurring again and again in Galsworthy: the parasite upon the parasites. "Big fleas have little fleas etc." And Bosinney and Irene, as well as the vagabond in *The Island Pharisees,* are among the little fleas. And as a tramp loves his own vermin, so the Forsytes and the Hilarys love these, their own particular body-parasites, their *antis.*

It is when he comes to sex, that Mr Galsworthy collapses finally. He becomes nastily sentimental. He wants to make sex important, and he only makes it repulsive. Sentimentalism is the working off on yourself of feelings you haven't really got. We all *want* to have certain feelings: feelings of love, of passionate sex, of kindliness, and so forth. Very few people really feel love, or sex passion, or kindliness, or anything else that goes at all deep. So the mass just fake these feelings inside themselves. Faked feelings! The world is all gummy with them. They are better than real feelings, because you can spit them out when you rush your teeth; and then tomorrow you can fake them afresh.

Shelton, in *The Island Pharisees,* is the first of Mr Galsworthy's lovers, and he might as well be the last. He is almost comical. All we know of his passion for Antonia is that he feels, at the beginning, a "hunger" for her: as if she were a beefsteak. And towards the end he once kisses her, and expects her, no doubt, to fall instantly at his feet, overwhelmed. He never, for a second, feels a moment of gentle sympathy with her. She is class-bound, but she doesn't seem to have been inhuman. The inhuman one was the lover. He can gloat over her in the distance, as if she were a dish of pig's trotters, *pieds truffés:* she can be an angelic *vision* to him, a little way off. But when the poor thing has to be just a rather ordinary middle-class girl to him, quite near, he hates her with a comical, rancorous hate. It is most queer. He is helplessly *anti.* He hates her for even existing as a woman of her own class, for even having her own existence. Apparently, she should just be a floating female sex-organ, hovering round to satisfy his little "hungers," and then *basta.* Anything of the real meaning of sex, which involves the whole of a human being, never occurs to him. It is a function, and the female is a sort of sexual appliance: no more.

And so we have it again and again, on this low and bastard level, all the human correspondence lacking. The sexual level is extraordinarily low, like dogs. The Galsworthy heroes are all weirdly in love with themselves, when we know them better; afflicted with chronic narcissism. They know just three types of women: the Pendyce mother, prostitute to property; the Irene, the essential *anti* prostitute, the floating, flaunting female organ; and the social woman, the mere lady. All three are loved and hated in turn, by the recurrent heroes. But it is all on the debased level of property, positive or *anti.* It is all a doggy form of prostitution. Be quick and have done.

One of the funniest stories is *The Apple Tree.* The young man finds, at a lonely Devon farm, a little Welsh farm-girl who, being a Celt and not a Saxon, at once falls for the Galsworthian hero. This young gentleman, in the throes of narcissistic love for his marvellous self, falls for the maid because she has fallen so utterly and abjectly for him. She doesn't call him "My King," not being Wellsian. She only says: "I can't live away from you. Do what you like with me. Only let me come with you!" The proper prostitutional announcement!

For this, of course, a narcissistic young gentleman just down from Oxford falls at once. Ensues a grand pa-assion. He goes to buy her a proper frock to be carried away in: meets a college friend with a young lady sister: has jam for tea and stays the night: and the grand pa-assion has died a natural death by the time he spreads the marmalade on his bread. He has returned to his own class, and nothing else exists. He marries the young lady. True to his class. But to fill the cup of his vanity, the maid drowns herself. It is funny that maids only seem to do it for these narcissistic young gentlemen who, looking in the pool for their own image, desire the added satisfaction of seeing the face of drowned Ophelia there as well; saving them the necessity of taking the narcissus plunge in person. We have gone one better than the myth. Narcissus in Mr Galsworthy doesn't drown himself. He asks Ophelia, or Megan, kindly to drown herself instead. And, in this fiction, she actually does. And he feels so *wonderful* about it!!

Mr Galsworthy's treatment of passion is really rather shameful. The whole thing is doggy to a degree. The man has a temporary "hunger"; he is "on the heat" as they say of dogs. The heat passes. It's done. Trot away, if you're not tangled. Trot off, looking shamefacedly over your shoulder. People have been watching! Damn them! But never mind, it'll blow over. Thank God the bitch is trotting in the other direction. She'll soon have another trail of dogs after her. That'll wipe out my traces. Good for that! Next time, I'll get properly married, and do my doggishness in my own house.

With the fall of the individual, sex falls into a dog's heat. Oh, if only Mr Galsworthy had had the strength to satirise this too, instead of pouring a sauce of sentimental savouriness over it. Of course, if he had done so, he would never have been a popular writer. But he would have been a great one.

However, he chose to sentimentalise and glorify the most doggy sort of sex. Setting out to satirise the Forsyte, he glorifies the *anti,* who is one worse. While the individual remains real and unfallen, sex remains a vital and supremely important thing. But once you have the fall into social beings, sex becomes disgusting, like dogs on the heat. Dogs are social beings, with no true canine individuality. Wolves and foxes don't copulate on the pavement. Their sex is wild, and in act, utterly private. Howls you may hear. But you will never see anything.—But the dog is tame. And he makes excrement and he copulates on the pavement, as if to spite you. He is the Forsyte *anti.*

The same with human beings. Once they become tame, they become, in a measure, exhibitionists, as if to spite everything. They have no real feelings of their own. Unless somebody "catches them at it," they don't really feel they've felt anything at all. And this is how the mob is today. It is Forsyte *anti.* It is the social being spiting society.

Oh, if only Mr Galsworthy had satirised *this* side of Forsytism, the anti-Forsyte posturing of the "rebel," the narcissus and the exhibitionist, the dogs copulating on the pavement! Instead of that, he glorified it, to the eternal shame of English literature.

The satire, which in *The Man of Property* really had a certain noble touch, soon fizzles out, and we get that series of Galsworthian "rebels" who are like all the rest of the modern middle-class rebels, not in rebellion at all. They are merely social beings behaving in an anti-social manner. They worship their own class, but they pretend to go one better, and sneer at it. They are Forsyte *antis,* feeling snobbish about snobbery. Nevertheless, they want to attract attention and make money. That's why they are *anti.* It is the vicious circle of Forsytism. Money means more to them than it does to a Soames Forsyte, so they pretend to go one better, and despise it, but they will do anything, anything to have it: things which Soames Forsyte would not have done.

If there is one thing more repulsive than the social being positive, it is the social being negative, the mere *anti.* In the great debacle of decency, this gentleman is the most indecent. In a subtle way, Bosinney and Irene are more dishonest and more indecent than Soames and Winifred. But they are *anti,* so they are glorified. It is pretty sickening.

The introduction to *The Island Pharisees* explains the whole show.—"Each man born into the world is born to go a journey, and for the most part he is born on the high road—As soon as he can toddle, he moves, by the queer instinct we call the love of life, along this road:—his fathers went this way before him, they made this road for him to tread, and, when they bred him, passed into his fibre the love of doing things as they themselves had done them. So he walks on and on.—Suddenly one day, without intending to, he notices a path or opening in the hedge, leading to right or left, and he stands looking at the undiscovered. After that, he stops at all the openings in the hedge; one day, with a beating heart, he tries one. And this is where the fun begins."—Nine out of ten get back to the broad road again, and side-track no more. They snuggle down comfortably in the next inn, and think where they might have been.—"But the poor silly tenth is faring on. Nine times out of ten he goes down in a bog; the undiscovered has engulfed him."—But the tenth time, he gets across, and a new road is opened to mankind.— It is a class-bound consciousness, or at least a hopeless social consciousness which sees life as a high-road between two hedges. And the only way out is gaps in the hedge, and excursions into naughtiness! These little *anti* excursions. From which the wayfarer slinks back to solid comfort, nine times out of ten: an odd one goes down in a bog: and a very rare one finds a way across and opens out a new road. In Mr Galsworthy's novels we see the nine, the ninety-nine, the nine hundred and ninety-nine slinking back to solid comfort; we see an odd Bosinney go under a bus, because he hadn't guts enough to do something else, the poor *anti;* but that rare figure sidetracking into the unknown we do *not* see.

Because as a matter of fact, the whole figure is faulty at that point. If life is a great high-way, then it must forge on ahead into the unknown. Sidetracking gets nowhere. That is mere *anti.* The tip of the road is always unfinished, in the wilderness. If it comes to a precipice and a canyon—well, then there is need for some exploring.

But we see Mr Galsworthy, after *The Country House,* very safe on the old high-way, very secure in comfort, wealth, and renown. He at least has gone down in no bog, nor lost himself striking new paths. The hedges nowadays are ragged with gaps, anybody who likes strays out on the little trips of "unconvention." But the Forsyte road has not moved on at all. It has only become dishevelled and sordid with excursionists doing the *anti* tricks and being "unconventional," and leaving tin cans behind.   5

In the three early novels, *The Island Pharisees, The Man of Property, Fraternity,* it looked as if Mr Galsworthy might break through the blind end of the high-way, with the dynamite of satire, and help us out on to a new lap. But the sex ingredient of his dynamite was damp and muzzy, the explosions gradually fizzled off in sentimentality, and we are left in a worse state than before.

The later novels are purely commercial, and, if it had not been for the early novels, of no importance. They are popular, they sell well, and there's the end of them. They contain the explosive powder of the first books, in minute quantities, fizzling as silly squibs. When you arrive at *To Let,* and the end, at least the *promised* end of the Forsytes, what have you? Just money! Money, money, money, and a certain snobbish silliness, and many more *anti* tricks and poses. Nothing else. The story is feeble, the characters have no blood and bones, the emotions are faked, faked, faked. It is one great fake. Not necessarily of Mr Galsworthy's. The characters fake their own emotions. But that doesn't help us. And if you look closely at the characters, the meanness and low-level vulgarity are very distasteful. You have all the Forsyte meanness, with none of the energy. Jolyon and Irene are meaner and more treacherous to their son than the older Forsytes were to theirs. The young ones are of a limited, mechanical vulgar egoism far surpassing that of Swithin or James, their ancestors. There is in it all a vulgar sense of being rich, and therefore we do as we like: an utter incapacity for anything like *true* feeling, especially in the women, Fleur, Irene, Annette, June: a glib crassness, a youthful spontaneity which is just impertinence and lack of feeling; and all the time, a creeping, "having" sort of vulgarity of money and self-will, money and self-will:— so that we wonder, sometimes, if Mr Galsworthy is not treating his public in real bad faith, and being cynical and rancorous under his rainbow sentimentalism.

Fleur he destroys in one word: she is "having." It is perfectly true. We don't blame the young Jon for clearing out.—Irene he destroys in a phrase out of Fleur's mouth to June: "Didn't she spoil your life too?"—And it is precisely what she did. Sneaking and mean, Irene prevented June from getting her lover. Sneaking and mean, she prevents Fleur. She is the bitch in the manger. She is the sneaking anti. Irene, the most beautiful woman on earth!—And Mr Galsworthy, with the cynicism of a successful old sentimentalist, turns it off by making June say: "Nobody can spoil a life, my dear. That's nonsense. Things happen, but we bob up."

This is the final philosophy of it all. "Things happen, but we bob up." Very well, then write the book in that key, the keynote of a frank old cynic. There's no point in sentimentalising it and being a sneaking old cynic. Why pour out masses of feelings that pretend to be genuine, and then turn it all off with: "things happen, but we bob up."

It is quite true, things happen, and we bob up. If we are vulgar sentimentalists, we bob up just the same, so nothing has happened, and nothing can happen. All is vulgarity. But it pays. There is money in it.

Vulgarity pays, and cheap cynicism smothered in sentimentalism pays better than anything else. Because nothing *can* happen to the degraded social being. So let's pretend it does, and then bob up!

It is time somebody began to spit out the jam of sentimentalism, at least, which smothers the "bobbing-up" philosophy. It is time we turned a straight light on this horde of rats, these younger Forsyte sentimentalists whose name is legion. It is sentimentalism which is stifling us. Let the social beings keep on bobbing up while ever they can. But it is time an effort was made to turn a hose-pipe on the sentimentalism they ooze over everything. The world is one sticky mess, in which the little Forsytes indeed may keep on bobbing still, but in which an honest feeling can't breathe.

But if the sticky mess gets much deeper, even the little Forsytes won't be able to bob up any more. They'll be smothered in their own slime, along with everything else. Which is a comfort.

CERTAIN AMERICANS AND AN ENGLISHMAN

I arrive in New Mexico at a moment of crisis. I suppose every man always does, here. The crisis is a thing called the Bursum Bill, and it affects the Pueblo Indians. I wouldn't know a thing about it, if I needn't. But it's Bursum Bursum Bursum!! the Bill! the Bill! the Bill! Twitchell, Twitchell, Twitchell!! O Mr. Secretary Fall, Fall, Fall! O Mr. Secretary Fall! you bad man, you good man, you Fall, you Rise, you Fall!!! The Joy Survey, Oh Joy, No Joy, Once Joy, now Woe! Woe! Whoa! Whoa Bursum! Woa Bill! Whoa-a-a!—like a Lindsay Boom-Boom bellowing it goes on in my unwonted ears, till I have to take heed. And then I solemnly sit down in a chair and read the Bill, the Bill, the Printed Bursum Bill, Section one—two—three—four—five—six— seven, whereas and wherefore and heretobefore, right to the damned and distant end. Then I start the Insomuch—as of Mr. Francis Wilson's Brief concerning the Bill. Then I read Mr. C's passionate article against, and Mrs. H's hatchet-stroke summary against, and Mr. M's sharp-knife jugglery *for* the Bill. After which I feel I'm getting mixed up, and Bear Ye One Another's Bursum. Then Lamb-like, ram-like, I feel I'll do a bit of butting too, on a stage where every known animal butts.

But first I toddle to a corner and, like a dog when music is going on in the room, put my paws exasperatedly over my ears, and my nose to the ground, and groan softly. So doing I try to hypnotise myself back into my old natural world, outside the circus-tent, where horses don't buck and prance so much, and where not every lady is leaping through the hoop and crashing through the paper confines of the universe at every hand's turn.

Try to extricate my lamb-like soul into its fleecy isolation, and then adjust myself. Adjust myself to that much-talked-of actor in the Wild West show, the Red Indian.

Don't imagine, indulgent reader, that I'm talking at you or down to you; or trying to put something over on you. No, no, imagine me lamb-like and bewildered muttering softly to myself, between soft groans, trying to make head-or-tail of myself in my present situation. And then you'll get the spirit of these effusions.

The Indian is not an American citizen. He is apparently in the position of a defenceless nation protected by a benevolent Congress. He is an American subject, but a member of a dominated, defenceless nation which Congress undertakes to protect and cherish. The Indian Bureau is supposed to do the cherishing.

Around about the pueblos live Mexican and American settlers who are American citizens, who do pay taxes and who do vote. They have cattle ranches, sheep ranches, little farms, and so on, and are most of them in debt.

These are the first two items: the dark spots of the protected pueblos; the hungry, unscrupulous frontier population squatting, rather scattered and rather impoverished, around.

There is plenty of land: sage brush desert. All depends on water. The pueblos, of course, are pitched upon the waters. The beautiful Taos Valley culminates in Taos Pueblo. The ranches and farms straggle round and try to encroach on this watered place. Six miles away is a deserted Mexican village, waterless.

Already you have a situation.

Now, when the United States took over New Mexico in 1848, Congress decided to abide by all the conditions established by Spain and old Mexico in this State. Congress also, apparently, decreed that to each pueblo belonged the four square leagues of land surrounding the pueblo; whether in accordance with ancient Spanish grant or not, isn't for me to say. Anyhow, there it is. Taos Pueblo owning four square leagues, which is thirty-six square miles of land immediately surrounding the pueblo; measuring a league in each direction from the centre of the pueblo. There are 800 Indians in the pueblo. But much of the land is dry desert or stony hill. True, some of the desert might be irrigated—if the water were there to irrigate it with, or if the Indians would make the effort.

At the same time Congress will abide by all the old Spanish or Mexican grants, titles, and so forth, which were in existence at the time of the taking over of this territory.

Immediately a problem. Because the Indian four square leagues has been much of it for centuries occupied by Spanish or Mexican or white settlers. There they sit. Taos Plaza, that is the white village of Taos, stands itself entirely within the four square leagues decreed to Taos   Pueblo. There are Spanish grants from governors; there are Mexican grants; and there are forged grants, forged deeds. Well, then, a terrible problem. For Taos Plaza has probably been standing for at least 200 years. Almost as old as New York.

Terrible problem! Why hasn't the place run with blood? Because the Indian never measured any leagues, but tilled his land around the pueblo itself. Much of the space intervening between the pueblo and the plaza is just sage desert. And this definite uncontested Indian land— uncontested for the moment, that is, so long as there is no Bursum bill—lies between plaza and pueblo as a sort of frontier. Nobody cut anybody's throat, because the occasion didn't arrive. Many squatters squat within the bounds of these four square leagues, but they are beyond a no-man's land still of sage desert, away from the heart where the pueblo rises, among the cotton-wood trees, and tills its land around the waters.

Thus the situation.

Then the highbrows come and say: "Poor Indian, dear Indian! why, all America ought to belong to him! Why look you now at the injustice that has been done to him! Not only has all America been snatched from him, but even his four square leagues are invaded by vile white men, greedy white men, hateful white men!"

So sing the highbrow palefaces. Till the Indian gradually begins to get his tail up.

Luckily for us he is few; unluckily for himself. Because if the tiny prairie dog yaps too hard at the western American airedale, alas for prairie dogs!

Now things begin to stir. It is time this business of grants and titles was settled. Old Spanish grants to Spaniards versus these four square leagues. Taos Plaza versus Taos Pueblo. Spanish grants, Mexican titles, forged deeds suddenly fluttering into life in a breath of hot wind of contest, Four square leagues flying away on the wings of old Spanish grants, which Congress is bound to validify, and the Indian perching on his big toe end, trying to poise on four square inches. Or, vice versa, an appeal to Congress, and Congress is sovereign majesty, and the Indians can come and take their brooms and sweep old José or old Fernandez or old

Maria, with all Taos village, pell-mell over the border of the four square leagues, into limbo.

Not that the Indian is likely to take Congress by the ear and do it. The Indian is afflicted with the lovable malady of laissez-faire. But then you never know what some of those white highbrows will be up to, these palefaces who love the dear Indian, the poor Indian, and who would like to see all America restored to him, let alone four square leagues, which is thirty-six square miles.

Now I believe the lands of some of the pueblos, sadly, very sadly enough, have been eaten right up by encroachments. But let me not be very sad. Taos isn't sad. Let me stay by Taos.

It will be obvious to everybody that a move had to be made about these leagues and these grants. And New Mexico made the move. Senator Bursum is the black knight who has hopped on to the four leagues. His famous Bursum bill has passed the Senate and comes before the House, presumably this month (December).

And here is the Bursum bill: an absolute checkmate to Pueblo, highbrow and all. It is the frontiersman biting off as much as he can chew.

"A bill to ascertain and settle land claims of persons not Indian, within Pueblo Indian land, land grants, and reservations in the State of New Mexico."

A court called the District Court of the United States for the District of New Mexico shall assume jurisdiction over all crimes, offenses, &c., committed within the areas of pueblo grants, by any person, Indian or non-Indian, so long as the Indians are occupying that land or claim that land.

(So this nice New Mexico court, which knows just what it wants for itself, takes a first modest step.)

2. This court shall have exclusive original jurisdiction in all suits of a civil nature, in all suits involving any right or title to any land within the said pueblo reservations, also in all suits involving property of Indians, also in all suits involving any question of internal government of any of the said pueblos. (Which means that the old, autonomous tribal body of the pueblo is placed at the mercy of this distant district court.)

4. All persons or corporations who have had possession of lands within the pueblo grants since prior to the Guadalupe Hidalgo Treaty of 1848 shall be entitled to a decree in their favour for all lands so possessed. In proof, secondary evidence shall he admissible and competent.

5. All persons who have held possession of lands within the pueblo grants for more than ten years previous to July, 1910, without colour of title shall be entitled to a decree in their favour for all lands so possessed. But in return to the Indians, the Secretary of the Interior shall have some other bit of adjacent land allotted to the Pueblo if any such land be available. (None of the available land is any good.) Otherwise the Pueblo shall be compensated in cash, as the Secretary thinks fit.

6. Pueblos shall have the right to the use of just as much water as they use at this minute (even though this amount be sadly insufficient to irrigate the present fields). But if any dam or reservoir be made, damming up the pueblo supplies, then all the surplus water and the control thereof shall be adjudicated according to the laws of the State of New Mexico.

7. All proceedings under this act shall be without cost to parties.

8. All suits under this act must be brought within five years.

9. The "Joy Surveys" (which were made to give evidence as to how Indian lands had been wrongly invaded) shall be accepted as prima facie evidence.

12. That any person or persons making any claim whatsoever to any lands within pueblo grants, whether they squatted on it only yesterday, may, with approval of the court, purchase the land at the court's valuation, and the money paid shall be held by the Secretary of the Interior on behalf of the Indians. (Which means that if I want a chunk of pueblo land I put a fence around it and pay the Secretary of the Interior a sum which the court will, if it likes me, kindly make as small as possible, and the Indian sits staring at the Charybdis of me and the Scylla of Mr. Secretary Fall and holding out his hand for a bit of charity bread.)

It is obvious this means the scattering of the Pueblos. The squatters and Mexicans interested—and where land grabbing is the game, every neighbour is interested—openly declare that the pueblos will be finished in ten years. That is, five years for the claims to be all made and five for their final enforcement. And then the Indians will have merged. They will be scattered day labourers through the States and the nucleus will be broken.

The great desire to turn them into white men will be fulfilled as far as it can be fulfilled. They will all be wage earners, and that's enough. For the rest, lost, mutilated intelligences.

As it is, the Pueblos are slowly disbanding; there are the Indian schools, a doom in themselves. The young men all speak American. They go as hired labourers. And man is like a dog—he believes in the hand that feeds him. He belongs where he is fed.

The end of the Pueblos. But at least let them die a natural death. To me the Bursum bill is amusing in its bare-facedness—a cool joke. It startles any English mind a little to realize that it may become law.

Let the Pueblos die a natural death. The Bursum bill plays the Wild West scalping trick a little too brazenly. Surely the great Federal Government is capable of instituting an efficient Indian Commission to inquire fairly and settle fairly. Or a small Indian office that knows what it's about. For Heaven's sake keep these Indians out of the clutches of politics.

Because, finally, in some curious way, the pueblos still lie here at the core of American life. In some curious way, it is the Indians still who are American. This great welter of whites is not yet a nation, not yet a people. The Indians keep burning an eternal fire, the sacred fire of the old dark religion. To the vast white America, either in our generation or in the time of our children or grandchildren, will come some fearful convulsion. Some terrible convulsion will take place among the millions of this country, sooner or later. When the pueblos are gone. But oh, let us have the grace and dignity to shelter these ancient centres of life, so that, if die they must, they die a natural death. And at the same time, let us try to adjust ourselves again to the Indian outlook, to take up an old dark thread from their vision, and see again as they see, without forgetting we are ourselves.

For it is a new era we have now got to cross into. And our own electric light won't show us over the gulf. We have to feel our way by the dark thread of the old vision. Before it lapses, let us take it up.

Before the pueblos disappear, let there be just one moment of reconciliation between the white spirit and the dark.

And whether there be this moment of reconciliation or not, let us prevent Jack Grab and Juan Arrapar from putting their foot on the pueblos.

Besides, if the Bursum bill passes, what a lively shooting match will go on between all the jacks and the juans who claim the bits of land in question, ten claimants to every inch!

And then, again, what business is it of mine, foreigner and newcomer?

INDIANS AND AN ENGLISHMAN

Supposing one fell on to the moon, and found them talking English, it would be something the same as falling out of the open world plump down here in the middle of America. "Here" means New Mexico, the South West, wild and woolly and artistic and sage-brush desert.

It is all rather like comic opera played with solemn intensity. All the wildness and woollyness and westernity and motor-cars and art and sage and savage are so mixed up, so incongruous, that it is a farce, and everybody knows it. But they refuse to play it as farce. The wild and woolly section insists on being heavily dramatic, bold and bad on purpose; the art insists on being real American and artistic; motor-cars insist on being thrilled, moved to the marrow; high-brows insist on being ecstatic, Mexicans insist on being Mexicans, squeezing the last black drop of macabre joy out of life, and Indians wind themselves in white cotton sheets like Hamlet's father's ghost, with a lurking smile.

And here am I, a lone lorn Englishman, tumbled out of the known world of the British Empire on to this stage: for it persists in seeming like a stage to me, and not like the proper world.

Whatever makes a proper world, I don't know. But surely two elements are necessary: a common purpose and a common sympathy. I can't see any common purpose. The Indians and Mexicans don't even seem very keen on dollars. That full moon of a silver dollar doesn't strike me as overwhelmingly hypnotic out here. As for a common sympathy or understanding, that's beyond imagining. West is wild and woolly and bad on purpose, commerce is a little self-conscious about its own pioneering importance — Pioneers, Oh Pioneers! — high-brow is bent on getting to the bottom of everything and saving the lost soul down there in the depths, Mexican is bent on being Mexican and not yet Gringo, and the Indian is all the things that all the others aren't. And so everybody smirks at everybody else, and says tacitly: "Go on, you do your little stunt, and I'll do mine," and they're like the various troupes in a circus, all performing at once, with nobody for Master of Ceremonies.

It seems to me, in this country, everything is taken so damn seriously that nothing remains serious. Nothing is so farcical as insistent drama. Everybody is lurkingly conscious of this. Each section or troupe is quite willing to admit that all the other sections are buffoon stunts. But it itself is the real thing, solemnly bad in its badness, good in its goodness, wild in its wildness, woolly in its woollyness, arty in its artiness, deep in its depths, in a word, earnest.

In such a masquerade of earnestness, a bewildered straggler out of the far-flung British Empire, myself! Don't let me for a moment pretend to *know* anything. I know less than nothing. I simply gasp like a bumpkin in a circus ring, with the horse-lady leaping over my head, the Apache war-whooping in my ear, the Mexican staggering under crosses and bumping me as he goes by, the artist whirling colours across my dazzled vision, the high-brows solemnly declaiming at me from all the cross-roads. If, dear reader, you, being the audience who has paid to come in, feel that you must take up an attitude to me, let it be one of amused pity.

One has to take sides. First, one must be either pro-Mexican or pro-Indian; then, either art or intellect: then, republican or democrat: and so on. But as for me, poor lost lamb, if I bleat at all in the circus-ring, it will be my own shorn lonely bleat of a lamb who's lost his mother.

The first Indians I really saw were the Apaches in the Apache Reservation of this state. We drove in a motor-car, across desert and mesa, down canyons and up divides and along arroyos and so forth, two days, till at afternoon our two Indian men ran the car aside from the trail and sat under the pine-tree to comb their long black hair and roll it into the two roll-plaits that hang in front of their shoulders, and put on all their silver-and-turquoise jewellery and their best blankets: because we were nearly there. On the trail were horsemen passing, and wagons with Ute Indians and Navajos.

"Da donde viene, Usted?"

We came at dusk from the high shallows and saw on a low crest the points of Indian tents, the tepees, and smoke, and silhouettes of tethered horses and blanketted figures moving. In the shadow a rider was following a flock of white goats that flowed like water. The car ran to the top of the crest, and there was a hollow basin with a lake in the distance, pale in the dying light. And this shallow upland basin, dotted with Indian tents, and the fires flickering in front, and crouching blanketted figures, and horsemen crossing the dusk from tent to tent, horsemen in big steeple hats sitting glued on their ponies, and bells tinkling, and dogs yapping, and tilted wagons trailing in on the trail below, and a smell of woodsmoke and of cooking, and wagons coming in from far off, and tents pricking on the ridge of the round *vallum*, and horsemen dipping down and emerging again, and more red sparks of fires glittering, and crouching bundles of women's figures squatting at a fire before a little tent made of boughs, and little girls in full petticoats hovering, and wild barefoot boys throwing bones at thin-tailed dogs, and tents away in the distance, in the growing dark, on the slopes, and the trail crossing the floor of the hollows in the low dusk.

There you had it all, as in the hollow of your hand. And to my heart, born in England and kindled with Fenimore Cooper, it wasn't the wild and woolly west, it was the nomad nations gathering still in the continent of hemlock trees and prairies. The Apaches came and talked to us, in their steeple black hats, and plaits wrapped with beaver fur, and their silver and beads and turquoise. Some talked strong American, and some talked only Spanish. And they had strange lines in their faces.

The two kivas, the rings of cut aspen trees stuck in the ground like the walls of a big hut of living trees, were on the plain, at either end of the race-track. And as the sun went down, the drums began to beat, the drums with their strong-weak, strong-weak pulse that beat on the plasm of one's tissue. The car slid down to the south kiva.

Two elderly men held the drum, and danced the pit-pat, pit-pat, quick beat on flat feet, like birds that move from the feet only, and sang with wide mouths, Hie! Hie! Hie! Hy-a! Hy-a! Hy-a! Hie! Hie! Hie!Ay-away-away!! Strange dark faces with wide, shouting mouths and rows of small, close-set teeth, and strange lines on the faces, part ecstasy, part mockery, part humorous, part devilish, and the strange, calling, summoning sound in a wild song-shout, to the thud-thud of the drum. Answer of the same from the other kiva, as of a challenge accepted. And from the gathering darkness around, men drifting slowly in, each carrying an aspen-twig, each joining to cluster close in two rows upon the drum, holding each his aspen twig inwards, their faces all together, mouths all open in the song-shout, and all of them all the time going on the two feet, pàt-pat, pàt-pat, pàt-pat, to the thud-thud of the drum and the strange, plangent yell of the chant, edging inch by inch, pàt-pat, pàt-pat, pàt-pat, sideways in a cluster along the track, towards the distant cluster of the challengers from the other kiva, who were sing-shouting and edging onwards, sideways in the dusk, their faces all together, their leaves all inwards, towards the drum, and their feet going pàt-pat, pàt-pat, on the dust, with their buttocks stuck out a little, faces all inwards shouting open-mouthed to the drum, and half laughing, half mocking, half devilment, half fun. *Hie! Hie! Hie! Hie-away-awaya!* The strange yell, song, shout rising so lonely in the dusk, as if pine-trees could suddenly, shaggily sing. Almost a pre-animal sound, full of triumph in life, and devilment against other life, and mockery, and humorousness, and the pàt-pat, pàt-pat of the rhythm. Sometimes more youths coming up, and as they draw near laughing they give the war-whoop, like a turkey giving a startled shriek and then gobble-gobbling with laughter—Ugh!—the shriek half laughter, then the gobble-gobble-gobble like a great demoniac chuckle. The chuckle in the war whoop.—.They produce the gobble from the deeps of the stomach, and say it makes them feel good.

Listening, an acute sadness, and a nostalgia, unbearable yearning for something, and a sickness of the soul came over me. The gobble-gobble chuckle in the whoop surprised me in my very tissues. Then I got used to it, and could hear in it the humanness, the playfulness, and then, beyond that, the mockery and the diabolical, pre-human, pine-tree fun of cutting dusky throats and letting the blood spurt out unconfined. Gobble-agobble-agobble, the unconfined loose blood, gobble-agobble, the dead, mutilated lump, gobble-agobble-agobble, the fun, the greatest man-fun. The war-whoop!

So I felt. I may have been all wrong, and other folk may feel much more natural and reasonable things. But so I felt. And the sadness and the nostalgia of the song-calling, and the resinous continent of pine-trees and turkeys, the feet of birds treading a dance, far-off, when man was dusky and not individualised.

I am no ethnologist. The point is, what is the feeling that passes from an Indian to me, when we meet. We are both men, but how do we feel together? I shall never forget that first evening when I first came into contact with Red Men, away in the Apache country. It was not what I had thought it would be. It was something of a shock. Again something in my soul broke down, letting in a bitterer dark, a pungent awakening to the lost past, old darkness, new terror, new root-griefs, old root-richnesses.

The Apaches have a cult of water-hatred; they never wash flesh or rag. So never in my life have I smelt such an unbearable sulphur-human smell as comes from them when they cluster: a smell that takes the breath from the nostrils.

We drove the car away half a mile or more, back from the Apache hollow, to a lonely ridge, where we pitched camp under pine trees. Our two Indians made the fire, dragged in wood, then wrapped themselves in their best blankets and went off to the tepees of their friends. The night was cold and starry.

After supper I wrapped myself in a red serape up to the nose, and went down alone to the Apache encampment. It is good, on a chilly night in a strange country, to be wrapped almost to the eyes in a good Navajo blanket. Then you feel warm inside yourself, and as good as invisible, and the dark air thick with enemies. So I stumbled on, startling the hobbled horses that jerked aside from me. Reaching the rim-crest one saw many fires burning in red spots round the slopes of the hollow, and against the fires, many crouching figures. Dogs barked, a baby cried from a bough shelter, there was a queer low crackle of voices. So I stumbled alone over the ditches and past the tents, down to the kiva. Just near was a shelter with a big fire in front, and a man, an Indian, selling drinks, no doubt Budweiser beer and grape juice, non-intoxicants. Cowboys in chaps and big hats were drinking too, and one screechy, ungentle cow-girl in khaki. So I went on in the dark up the opposite slope. The dark Indians passing in the night peered at me. The air was full of a sort of sportiveness, playfulness, that had a jeering, malevolent vibration in it, to my fancy. As if this play were another kind of harmless-harmful warfare, overbearing. Just the antithesis of what I understand by jolliness: ridicule. Comic sort of bullying. No jolly, free laughter. Yet a great deal of laughter. But with a sort of gibe in it.

This, of course, may just be the limitation of my European fancy. But that was my feeling. One felt a stress of will, of human wills, in the dark air, gibing even in the comic laughter. And a sort of unconscious animosity.

Again a sound of a drum down below, so again I stumbled down to the kiva. A bunch of young men were clustered—seven or eight round a drum, and standing with their faces together loudly and mockingly singing the song yells, some of them treading the pat-pat, some not bothering. Just behind was the blazing fire and the open shelter of the drink tent, with Indians in tall black hats and long plaits in front of their shoulders, and bead-braided waistcoats, and hands in their pockets; some swathed in sheets, some in brilliant blankets, and all grinning, laughing. The cowboys with big spurs still there, horses' bridles trailing, and cow-girl screeching her laugh. One felt an inevitable silent gibing, animosity in each group, one for the other. At the same time, an absolute avoidance of any evidence of this.

The young men round the drum died out and started again. As they died out, the strange uplifted voice in the kiva was heard. It seemed to me the outside drumming and singing served to cover the voice within the kiva.

The kiva of young green trees was just near, two paces only. On the ground outside, boughs and twigs were strewn round to prevent anyone's coming close to the enclosure. Within was the firelight. And one could see through the green of the leaf-screen, men round a fire inside there, and one old man, the same old man always facing the open entrance, the fire between him and it. Other Indians sat in a circle, of which he was the key. The old man had his dark face lifted, his head bare, his two plaits falling on his shoulders. His close-shutting Indian lips were drawn open, his eyes were as if half veiled, as he went on and on, on and on, in a distinct, plangent, recitative voice, male and yet strangely far off and plaintive, reciting, reciting, reciting like a somnambulist, telling, no doubt, the history of the tribe interwoven with the gods. Other Apaches sat round the fire. Those nearest the old teller were stationary, though one chewed gum all the time and one ate bread cake and others lit cigarettes. Those nearer the entrance rose after a time, restless. At first some strolled in, stood a minute, then strolled out, desultory. But as the night went on, the ring round the fire inside the wall of green young trees was complete, all squatting on the ground, the old man with the lifted face and parted lips and half-unseeing eyes going on and on, across the fire. Some men stood lounging with the half-self-conscious ease of the Indian behind the seated men. They lit cigarettes. Some drifted out. Another filtered in. I stood wrapped in my blanket in the cold night, at some little distance from the entrance, looking on.

A big young Indian came and pushed his face under my hat to see who or what I was.

"Buenos!"

"Buenos!"

"Que quiere?"

"No hablo espagnol."

"Oh only English, eh?—You can't come in here."

"I don't want to."

"This Indian Church."

"Is it?"

"I don't let people come, only Apache, only Indian."

"You keep watch?"

"I keep watch, yes; Indian church, eh?"

"And the old man preaches?"

"Yes, he preaches."

After which I stood quite still and uncommunicative. He waited for a further development. There was none. So, after giving me another look, he went to talk to other Indians, sotto voce, by the door.

The circle was complete, groups stood behind the squatting ring, some men were huddled in blankets, some sitting just in trousers and shirt, in the warmth near the fire, some wrapped close in white cotton sheets. The firelight shone on the dark, unconcerned faces of the listeners, as they chewed gum, or ate bread, or smoked a cigarette. Some had big silver ear-rings swinging, and necklaces of turquoise. Some had waistcoats all bead braids. Some wore store shirts and store trousers, like Americans. From time to time one man pushed another piece of wood on the fire.

They seemed to be paying no attention, it all had a very perfunctory appearance. But they kept silent, and the voice of the old reciter went on blindly, from his lifted, bronze mask of a face with its wide-opened lips. They furl back their teeth as they speak, and they use a sort of resonant tenor voice, that has a plangent half-sad, twanging sound, vibrating deep from the chest. The old man went on and on, for hours, in that urgent, far-off voice. His hair was grey, and parted, and his two round plaits hung in front of his shoulders on his shirt. From his ears dangled pieces of blue turquoise, tied with string. An old green blanket was wrapped round above his waist, and his feet in old moccasins were crossed before the fire. There was a deep pathos, for me, in the old, mask-like, virile figure, with its metallic courage of persistence, old memory, and its twanging male voice. So far, so great a memory. So dauntless a persistence in the piece of living red earth seated on the naked earth, before the fire; this old, bronze-resonant man with his eyes as if glazed in old memory, and his voice issuing in endless plangent monotony from the wide, unfurled mouth.

And the young men, who chewed chewing gum and listened without listening. The voice no doubt registered on their under-consciousness, as they looked around, and lit a cigarette, and spat sometimes aside. With their day-consciousness they hardly attended.

As for me, standing outside, beyond the open entrance, I was no enemy of theirs; far from it. The voice out of the far-off time was not for my ears. Its language was unknown to me. And I did not wish to know. It was enough to hear the sound issuing plangent from the bristling pine-tree darkness of the far past, to see the bronze mask of the face lifted, the white, small, close-packed teeth showing all the time. It was not for me, and I knew it. Nor had I any curiosity to understand. The soul is as old as the oldest day, and has its own hushed echoes, its own far-off tribal understandings sunk and incorporated. We do not need to live the past over again. Our darkest tissues are twisted in this old tribal experience, our warmest blood came out of the old tribal fire. And they vibrate still in answer, our blood, our tissue. But me, the conscious me, I have gone a long road since then. And as I look back, like memory terrible as blood-shed, the dark faces round the fire in the night, and one blood beating in me and them. But I don't want to go back to them, ah never. I never want to deny them, or break with them. But there is no going back. Always onward, still further. The great devious onward-flowing stream of conscious human blood. From them to me, and from me on.

I don't want to live again the tribal mysteries my blood has lived long since. I don't want to know as I have known, in the tribal exclusiveness. But every drop of me trembles still alive to the old sound, every thread in my body quivers to the frenzy of the old mystery. I know my derivation. I was born of no virgin, of no Holy Ghost. Ah no, these old men telling the tribal tale were my fathers. I have a dark-faced, bronze-voiced father far back in the resinous ages. My mother was no virgin. She lay in her hour with this dusky-lipped tribe-father. And I have not forgotten him. But he, like many an old father with a changeling son, he would like to deny me. But I stand on the far edge of their fire light and am neither denied nor accepted. My way is my own, old red father; I can't cluster at the drum any more.

Just near, the young men were still standing clustered on the drum and singing and treading unevenly, holding the tom-tom drum in their midst and clustering on it as on some nucleus. And all the time the thud-thud of the drum, the half-hearted rhythm, the halfhearted bird-tread of the dance, the half-hearted wild song. And all the time the horse-play and the jokes and the laughter.

The night was getting late, and the cowboys had ridden off, white men had lapsed out. A new sound came into the voices, a new savagery in the air. The dark eyes of the Apache loungers by the drink-booth seemed to grow bigger, with a sort of dark glare, like the glare of a night animal. The individual, that lonely phenomenon evolved through struggle of ages, was lapsing right out again, the one bloodstream was swimming before their eyes. They looked at me strangely, as if they could not see me, but sensed my presence like an irritant in the night, as a mountain lion might feel the rankling of a thorn in his flesh without knowing where or what it was. And I, I stood in my isolate individuality, and let them look. They didn't want me there, so at last I went slowly away, out of the hollow and over the rim, and across the darkness to find my own lonely camp, where I imagined the American woman who was camp-companion had gone to bed tired. The camp was over the brow of a *[manuscript ends here]*

The Indians say Taos is the heart of the world. Their world, maybe. Some places seem temporary on the face of the earth: San Francisco for example. Some places seem final. They have a true nodality. I never felt that so powerfully as, years ago, in London. The intense powerful nodality of that great heart of the world. And during the war that heart, for me, broke. So it is. Places can lose their living nodality. Rome, to me, has lost hers. In Venice one feels the magic of the glamorous old node that once united East and West, but it is the beauty of an afterlife.

Taos pueblo still retains its old nodality. Not like a great city. But, in its way, like one of the monasteries of Europe. You cannot come upon the ruins of the old great monasteries of England, beside their waters, in some lovely valley, now remote, without feeling that here is one of the choice spots of the earth, where the spirit dwelt. To me it is so important to remember that when Rome collapsed, when the great Roman Empire fell into smoking ruins, and bears roamed in the streets of Lyons, and wolves howled in the deserted streets of Rome, and Europe really was a dark ruin, then, it was not in castles or manors or cottages that life remained vivid. Then those whose souls were still alive withdrew together and gradually built monasteries, and these monasteries and convents, little communities of quiet labour and courage, isolated, helpless, and yet never overcome in a world flooded with devastation, these alone kept the human spirit from disintegration, from going quite dark, in the Dark Ages. These men made the Church, which again made Europe, inspiring the martial faith of the Middle Ages

Taos pueblo affects me rather like one of the old monasteries. When you get there you feel something final. There is an arrival. The nodality still holds good.

But this is the pueblo. And from the north side to the south side, from the south side to the north side, the perpetual silent wandering intentness of a full-skirted, black-shawled, long-fringed woman in her wide white deerskin boots, the running of children, the silent sauntering of dark-faced men, bare-headed, the two plaits in front of their thin shoulders, and a white sheet like a sash swathed round their loins. They must have something to swathe themselves in.

And if it were sunset, the men swathing themselves in their sheets like shrouds, leaving only the black place of the eyes visible. And women, darker than ever, with shawls over their heads, busy at the ovens. And cattle being driven to sheds. And men and boys trotting in from the fields, on ponies. And as the night is dark, on one of the roofs, or more often on the bridge, the inevitable drum-drum-drum of the tom-tom, and young men in the dark lifting their voices to the song, like wolves or coyotes crying in music.

There it is then, the pueblo, as it has been since heaven knows when. And the slow dark weaving of the Indian life going on still, though perhaps more waveringly. And oneself, sitting there on a pony, a far-off stranger with gulfs of time between me and this. And yet, the old nodality of the pueblo still holding, like a dark ganglion spinning invisible threads of consciousness. A sense of dryness, almost of weariness, about the pueblo. And a sense of the inalterable. It brings a sick sort of feeling over me, always, to get into the Indian vibration. Like breathing chlorine.

The next day in the morning we went to help erect the great stripped may-pole. It was the straight, smoothed yellow trunk of a big tree. Of course one of the white boys took the bossing of the show. But the Indians were none too ready to obey, and their own fat dark-faced boss gave counter-orders. It was the old, amusing contradiction between the white and the dark races. As for me, I just gave a hand steadying the pole as it went up, outsider at both ends of the game.

An American girl came with a camera, and got a snap of us all struggling in the morning light with the great yellow trunk. One of the Indians went to her abruptly, in his quiet, insidious way.

"You give me that kodak. You ain't allowed take no snaps here. You pay fine—one dollar." She was frightened, but she clung to her camera.

"You're not going to take my kodak from me," she said.

"I'm going to take that film out. And you pay one dollar, fine, see." The girl relinquished the camera, the Indian took out the film.

"Now you pay me one dollar, or I don't give you back this kodak."

Rather sullenly, she took out her purse and gave the two silver half-dollars. The Indian returned the camera, pocketed the money, and turned aside with a sort of triumph. Done it over one specimen of the white race.

There were not very many Indians helping to put up the pole.

"I never see so few boys helping put up the pole," said Tony Romero to me.

"Where are they all?" I asked. He shrugged his shoulders.

Dr. West, a woman doctor from New York who has settled in one of the villages, was with us. Mass was being said inside the church, and she would have liked to go in. She is well enough known too. But two Indians were at the church-door, and one put his elbow in front of her.

"You Catholic?"

"No, I'm not."

"Then you can't come in."

The same almost jeering triumph in giving the white man—or the white woman—a kick. It is the same the whole world over, between dark-skin and white. Dr. West, of course, thinks everything Indian wonderful. But she wasn't used to being rebuffed, and she didn't like it. But she found excuses.

"Of course," she said, "they're quite right to exclude the white people, if the white people can't behave themselves. It seems there were some Americans, boys and girls, in the church yesterday, insulting the images of the saints, shrieking, laughing, and saying they looked like monkeys. So now no white people are allowed inside the church." I listened and said nothing. I had heard the same story at Buddhist temples in Ceylon. For my own part, I have long since passed the stage when I want to crowd up and stare at anybody's spectacle, white man's or dark man's.

I stood on one of the first roofs of the north pueblo. The iron bell of the church began to bang-bang-bang. The sun was down beyond the far-off, thin clear line of the western mesa, the light had ceased glowing on the piñon-dotted foot-hills beyond the south pueblo. The square beneath was thick with people. And the Indians began to come out of church.

Two Indian women brought a little dressed-up Madonna to her platform in the green starting-bower. Then the men slowly gathered round the drum. The bell clanged. The tom-tom beat. The men slowly uplifted their voices. The wild music resounded strangely against the banging of that iron bell, the silence of the many faces, as the group of Indians in their sheets and their best blankets, and in their ear-rings and brilliant scarlet trousers, or emerald trousers, or purple trousers, trimmed with beads, trod the slow bird-dance sideways, in feet of beaded moccasins, or yellow doeskin moccasins, singing all the time like drumming coyotes, slowly down and across the bridge to the south side, and up the incline to the south kiva. One or two Apaches in their beaded waist-coats and big black hats were among the singers, distinguishable by their thick build also. An old Navajo chief was among the encouragers.

As dusk fell, the singers came back under a certain house by the south kiva, and as they passed under the platform they broke and dispersed, it was over. They seemed as if they were grinning subtly as they went: grinning at being there in all that white crowd of inquisitives. It must have been a sort of ordeal, to sing and tread the slow dance between that solid wall of silent, impassive white faces. But the Indians seemed to take no notice. And the crowd only silently, impassively watched. Watched with that strange, static American quality of *laisser faire* and of indomitable curiosity.

AU REVOIR, U. S. A.

"Say au revoir
But not goodbye
This parting brings
A bitter sigh….

It really does, when you find yourself in an unkempt Pullman trailing through endless deserts, south of El Paso, fed on doubtful scraps at enormous charge and at the will of a rather shoddy smallpox-marked Mexican Pullman-boy who knows there's been a revolution and that his end is up. Then you remember the neat and nice nigger who looked after you as far as El Paso, before you crossed the Rio Grande into desert and chaos, and you sigh, if you have time before a curse chokes you.

Yet, U. S. A., you do put a strain on the nerves. Mexico puts a strain on the temper. Choose which you prefer. Mine's the latter. I'd rather be in a temper than be pulled taut. Which is what the U. S. A. did to me. Tight as a fiddle string, tense over the bridge of the solar plexus. Any how the solar plexus goes a bit loose and has a bit of play down here.

I still don't know why the U. S. A. pulls one so tight and makes one feel like a chicken that is being drawn. The people on the whole are quite as amenable as people anywhere else. They don't pick your pocket, or even your personality. They're not unfriendly. It's not the people. Something in the air tightens one's nerves like fiddle strings, screws them up, squeak-squeak!. . . till one's nerves will give out nothing but a shrill fine shriek of overwroughtness. Why, in the name of heaven? Nobody knows. It's just the spirit of place.

You cross the Rio Grande, and change from tension into exasperation. You feel like hitting the impudent Pullman waiter with a beer-bottle. In the U. S. A. you don't even think of such a thing.

Of course, one might get used to a state of tension. And then one would pine for the United States. Meanwhile one merely snarls back at the dragons of San Juan Teotihuacán.

It's a queer continent—as much as I've seen of it. It's a fanged continent. It's got a rattle-snake coiled in its heart, has this democracy of the New World. It's a dangerous animal, once it lifts its head again. Meanwhile, the dove still nests in the coils of the rattlesnake, the stone coiled rattlesnake of Aztec eternity. The dove lays her eggs on his flat head.

The old people had a marvellous feeling for snakes and fangs, down here in Mexico. And after all, Mexico is only the sort of solar plexus of North America. The great paleface overlay hasn't gone into the soil half an inch. The Spanish churches and palaces stagger, the most ricketty things imaginable, always just on the point of falling down. And the peon still grins his Indian grin behind the Cross. And there's quite a lively light in his eyes, much more so than in the eyes of the Northern Indian. He knows his gods.

These old civilisations down here, they never got any higher than Quetzalcoatl. And he's just a sort of feathered snake. Who needed the smoke of a little heart's-blood now and then, even he.

"Only the ugly is aesthetic now," said the young Mexican artist. Personally, he seems as gentle and self-effacing as the nicest of lambs. Yet his caricatures are hideous, hideous without mirth or whimsicality. Blood-hideous. Grim, earnest hideousness.

Like the Aztec things, the Aztec carvings. They all twist and bite. That's all they do. Twist and writhe and bite, or crouch in lumps. And coiled rattle-snakes, many, like dark heaps of excrement. And out at San Juan Teotihuacán where are the great pyramids of a vanished, pre-Aztec people, as we are told—and the so-called Temple of Quetzalcoatl—there, behold you, huge gnashing heads jut out jagged from the wall-face of the low pyramid, and a huge snake stretches along the base, and one grasps at a carved fish, that swims in old stone and for once seems harmless. Actually a harmless fish!

But look out! The great stone heads snarl at you from the wall, trying to bite you:—and one great dark green blob of an obsidian eye, you never saw anything so blindly malevolent: and then white fangs. Great white fangs, smooth today, the white fangs, with tiny cracks in them. Enamelled. These bygone pyramid-building Americans, who were a dead-and-gone mystery even to the Aztecs, when the Spaniards arrived, they applied their highest art to the enamelling of the great fangs of these venomous stone heads, and there is the enamel today, white and smooth. You can stroke the great fang with your finger and see. And the blob of an obsidian eye looks down at you.

It's a queer continent. The anthropologists may make what prettiness they like out of myths. But come here, and you'll see that the gods bit. There is none of the phallic pre-occupation of the old Mediterranean. Here they hadn't got even as far as hotblooded sex. Fangs, and cold serpent folds, and bird-snakes with fierce cold blood and claws. I admit that I feel bewildered. There is always something a bit amiably comic about Chinese dragons and contortions. There's nothing amiably comic in these ancient monsters. They're dead in earnest about biting and writhing, snake-blooded birds.

And the Spanish white superimposition, with rococo church-towers among pepper-trees and column cactuses, seems so ricketty and temporary, the pyramids seem so indigenous, rising like hills out of the earth itself. The one goes down with a clatter, the other remains.

And this is what seems to me the difference between Mexico and the United States. And this is why, it seems to me, Mexico exasperates, whereas the U. S. A. puts an unbearable tension on one. Because here in Mexico the fangs are still obvious. Everybody knows the gods are going to bite within the next five minutes. While in the United States, the gods have had their teeth pulled, and their claws cut, and their tails docked, till they seem real mild lambs. Yet all the time, inside, it's the same old dragon's blood. The same old aboriginal American dragon's blood.

And that discrepancy of course is a strain on the human psyche.

DEAR OLD HORSE, A LONDON LETTER

Yesterday came the Horse, capering a trifle woodenly, and today a fall of snow. Enough bright white snow on the ground to make a bit of daylight. I've been here exactly a month, in London, and day has never broken all the time. A dull, heavy, mortified half-light that seems to take the place of day in London in winter. I can't stand it.

However, with a bit of snow-brightness in the air, and a bit of a rather wooden neigh from the Horse in my ears, I prick up and write you a London Letter.

Dear old Azure Horse, Turquoise Horse, Hobby Horse, Trojan Horse with a few scared heroes in your belly; Horse, laughing your Horse Laugh, you do actually ramp in with a bit of horse sense. I'm all for horse sense, O Horsie! Come down to it, and it's the Centaur. Good old Horse, be patted, and be persuaded to grin and to be a Centaur getting your own back.

Even if you're only a hobby Horse, with a wooden head and a Spoodle on your broom-stick flanks, you're welcome just now. Very welcome. Here's an apple. Be tempted, like Adam, and take it. And for the sake of all horses, be braver than Adam, who only bit a bite out and dropped the main. Eat up the whole gaudy apple, O Horse. Let's have the centaur back.

Dear old Horse, you'd never be azure or turquoise here in London. Oh, London is awful: so dark, so damp, so yellow-grey, so mouldering piecemeal. With crowds of people going about in a mouldering, damp, half-visible sort of way, as if they were all mouldering bits of rag that had fallen from an old garment. Horse, Horse, be as hobby as you like, but let me get on your back and ride away again to New Mexico. I don't care how frozen it is, how grey the desert, how cold the air, in Taos, in Lobo, in Santa Fe. It isn't choky, it is bright day at daytime, and bright dark night at night. And one isn't wrapped like a mummy in winding-sheet after winding-sheet of yellow, damp, unclean, cloved, ancient, breathed-to-death so-called air. Oh Horse, Horse, Horse, when you kick your heels you shatter an enclosure every time. And over here the Horse is dead: he'll kick his heels no more. I don't know whether it's the Pale Galilean who has triumphed, or a paleness paler than the pallor even of

Jesus. But a yellow and jaundiced paleness has triumphed over here, the Turquoise Horse has been long dead, and churned into sausages. I find it unbearable.

Let the horse laugh. I'm all for a horse that laughs. Though I don't care for him when he merely sniggers.

I'm all for a horse, it's not even the Houyhnhnms. They aren't blue enough for me. It's a turquoise centaur who laughs, who laughs longest and who laughs last. I believe in him. I believe he's there, over the desert in the south-west. I believe if you'll cajole him with a bit of proper corn, he'll come down to Santa Fe and bite your noses off and then laugh at you again.

Two-legged man is no good. If he's going to stand steady, he must stand on four feet. Like the Centaur. When Jesus was born, the spirits wailed round the Mediterranean: Pan is dead. Great Pan is dead. And at the Renaissance the centaur gave a final groan, and expired. At least, I seem to remember him lamenting and about to expire, in the Uffizi.

It would be a terrible thing if the Horse in us died forever: as he seems to have died in Europe. How awful it would be, if at this present moment I sat in the yellow mummy-swathings of London atmosphere—the snow is melting—inside the dreadful mummy-sarcophagus of Europe, and didn't know that the blue horse was still kicking his heels and making a few sparks fly, across the tops of the Rockies. It would be a truly sad case for me.

As it is, I say to myself: Bah! In Lobo, in Taos, in Santa Fe the Turquoise Horse is waving snow out of his tail, and trotting gaily to the blue mountains of the far distance. And in Mexico his mane is bright yellow on his blue body, so streaming with sun, and he's lashing out again like the devil, till his hoofs are red. Good old Horse!

But talking seriously, Man must be centaur. This two-legged forked radish is going flabby.

The Centaur's Lament! Not at all. The laugh of the Turquoise Man Horse. Let the forked radish do the lamenting.

In modern symbolism, the Horse is supposed to stand for the passions. Passions be blowed. What does the Centaur stand for, Chiron or any other of that quondam four-footed gentry. Sense! Horse Sense. Sound, powerful, four-footed Sense, that's what the Horse stands for. Horse sense, I tell you. That's the Centaur. That's the blue horse of the ancient Mediterranean, before the pale Galilean or the extra pale German or Nordic gentleman conquered. First of all, Sense, Good Sense, Sound Sense, Horse Sense. And then, a laugh, a loud, sensible Horse Laugh. After that these same passions, glossy and dangerous in the flanks. And after these again, hoofs, irresistible, splintering hoofs, that can kick the walls of the world down.

Horse-sense, Horse-laughter, Horse-passion, Horse-hoofs: ask the Indians if it is not so.

Tell me the Horse is dead? Tell me the Centaur has died out? It may easily be so, in Europe here, since the Renaissance. But in the wide blue skies of the southwest, and far-away south over Mexico: over the grey deserts and the red deserts beneath the Rockies and the Sierra Madre; down the canyons and across the mesas and along the depths of the barrancas goes the Turquoise Horse, uneasy, bethinking himself, and just on the point of bursting into a loud laugh, after all, laughing longest and laughing last.

Ask the Indians, if there isn't a little blue foal born every year, in the pueblos, out of the old dark earth-coloured mottled mare. Tell me the centaur can't beget centaurs?—Ask the Indian, ask the Navajo, ask the Mexican under his big hat.

It's no good. I've got to ride on a laughing horse. The forked radish has ceased to perambulate. I've got to ride a laughing horse. And I whistle for him, call him, spread corn for him, and hold out an apple to him here in England. No go! No answer! The poor devil's dead and churned into Cambridge sausages. Flabby flaccid forked radishes, sausages, pairs of sausages in dead skins: these seem to drift about in the soup of the London air.

There's no answer. There's no blue cave to stable the Turquoise Horse, here. There's no dark earth-coloured mare to bear his foals. There's no far-away blue distance for him to roam across. He's dead.

And yet I've got to ride, centaur, on a blue stallion.

So, thanks be to the oldest of Gods, comes a wooden little Laughing Horse sliding down from the blue air of the Rockies, riding on his hobby stick like a rocket, summoning me to mount and away.

Hurray! Hup-a-la! Up we go! Like a witch on a broom-stick, riding West.

PARIS LETTER

I promised to write a letter to you from Paris. Probably I should have forgotten, but I saw a little picture—or sculpture—in the Tuileries, of Hercules slaying the Centaur, and that reminded me. I had so much rather the Centaur had slain Hercules, and men had never developed souls. Seems to me they're the greatest ailment humanity ever had. However, they've got it.

Paris is still monumental and handsome. Along the river where its splendours are, there's no denying its man-made beauty. The poor, pale little Seine runs rapidly north to the sea, the sky is pale, pale jade overhead, greenish and Parisian, the trees of black wire stand in rows, and flourish their black wire brushes against a low sky of jade-pale cobwebs, and the huge dark-grey palaces rear up their masses of stone and slope off towards the sky still with a massive, satisfying suggestion of pyramids. There is something noble and man-made about it all.

My wife says she wishes that grandeur still squared its shoulders on the earth. She wishes she could sit sumptuously in the river windows of the Tuileries, and see a royal spouse—who wouldn't be me—cross the bridge at the head of a tossing, silk and silver cavalcade. She wishes she had a bevy of ladies-in-waiting around her, as a peacock has its tail, as she crossed the weary expanses of pavement in the Champs Elysées.

Well, she can have it. At least, she can't. The world has lost its faculty for splendour, and Paris is like an old, weary peacock that sports a bunch of dirty twigs at its rump, where it used to have a tail. Democracy has collapsed into more and more democracy, and men, particularly Frenchmen, have collapsed into little, rather insignificant, rather wistful, rather nice and helplessly commonplace little fellows who rouse one's mother-instinct and make one feel they should be tucked away in bed and left to sleep, like Rip Van Winkle, till the rest of the storms rolled by.

It's a queer thing to sit in the Tuileries on a Sunday afternoon and watch the crowd drag through the galleries. Instead of a gay and wicked court, the weary,

weary crowd, that looks as if it had nothing at heart to keep it going. As if the human creature had been dwindling and dwindling through the processes of democracy, amid the ponderous ridicule of the aristocratic setting, till soon he will dwindle right away.

Oh, those galleries. Oh, those pictures and those statues of nude, nude women: nude, nude, insistently and hopelessly nude. At last the eyes fall in absolute weariness, the moment they catch sight of a bit of pink-and-white painting, or a pair of white marble fesses. It becomes an inquisition; like being *forced* to go on eating pink marzipan icing. And yet there is a fat and very undistinguished bourgeois with a little beard and a fat and hopelessly petit bourgeoise wife and awful little girl, standing in front of a huge heap of twisting marble, while he, with a goose-grease unctuous simper, strokes the marble hip of the huge marble female, and points out its niceness *to his wife.* She is not in the least jealous. She knows, no doubt, that her own hip and the marble hip are the only ones he will stroke without paying various prices, one of which, and the last he could pay, would be the price of the spunk.

It seems to me the French are just worn out. And not nearly so much with the late great war as with the pink nudities of women. The men are just worn out, making offerings on the shrine of Aphrodite in elastic garters. And the women are worn out, keeping the men up to it. The rest is all nervous exasperation.

And the table. One shouldn't forget that other, four-legged mistress of man, more unwitherable than Cleopatra. The table. The good kindly tables of Paris, with Coquilles Saint Martin, and escargots and oysters and Chateaubriands and the good red wine. If they can afford it, the men sit and eat themselves pink. And no wonder. But the Aphrodite in a hard black hat opposite, when she has eaten herself also pink, is going to insist on further delights, to which somebody has got to play up. Weariness isn't the word for it.

May the Lord deliver us from our own enjoyments, we gasp at last—And he won't. We actually have to deliver ourselves.

One goes out again from the restaurant comfortably fed and soothed with food and drink, to find the pale-jade sky of Paris crumbling in a wet dust of rain; motor-cars skidding till they turn clean around, and are facing south when they were going north: a boy on a bicycle coming smack, and picking himself up with his bicycle pump between his legs: and the men still fishing, as if it were a Sisyphus penalty, with long sticks fishing for invisible fishes in the Seine: and the huge buildings of the Louvre and the Tuileries standing ponderously, with their Parisian suggestion of pyramids.

And no, in the old style of grandeur I never want to be grand. That sort of regality, that builds itself up in piles of stone and masonry, and prides itself on living inside the monstrous heaps, once they're built is not for me. My wife asks why she can't live in the Petit Palais, while she's in Paris. Well, even if she might, she'd live alone.

I don't believe any more in democracy. But I can't believe in the old sort of aristocracy, either, nor can I wish it back, splendid as it was. What I believe in is the old Homeric aristocracy, when the grandeur was inside the man, and he lived in a simple wooden house. Then, the men that were grand inside themselves, like Ulysses, were the chieftains and the aristocrats by instinct and by choice. At least we'll hope so. And the Red Indians only knew the aristocrat by instinct. The leader was leader in his own being, not because he was somebody's son or had so much money.

It's got to be so again. They say it won't work. I say, why not? If men could once recognise the natural aristocrat when they set eyes on him, they can still. They can still choose him if they would.

But this business of dynasties is a weariness. House of Valois, House of Tudor! Who would want to be a House, or a bit of a House! Let a man be a man, and damn the House business. I'm absolutely a democrat as far as that goes.

But that men are all brothers and all equal is a greater lie than the other. Some men are always aristocrats. But it doesn't go by birth. A always contains B, but B is not contained in C.

Democracy, however, says that there is no such thing as an aristocrat. All men have two legs and one nose, ergo, they are all alike. Nosily and leggily, maybe. But otherwise, very different.

Democracy says that B is not contained in C, and neither is it contained in A. B, that is, the aristocrat, does not exist.

Now this is palpably a greater lie than the old dynastic lie. Aristocracy truly does not go by birth. But it still goes. And the tradition of aristocracy will help it a lot.

The aristocrats tried to fortify themselves inside these palaces and these splendours. Regal Paris built up the external evidences of her regality. But the two-limbed man inside these vast shells died, poor worm, of over-encumbrance.

The natural aristocrat has got to fortify himself inside his own will, according to his own strength. The moment he builds himself external evidences, like palaces, he builds himself in, and commits his own doom. The moment he depends on his jewels, he has lost his virtue.

It always seems to me that the next civilisation won't want to raise these ponderous, massive, deadly buildings that refuse to crumble away with their epoch and weigh men helplessly down. Neither palaces nor cathedrals nor any other hugenesses. Material simplicity is after all the highest sign of civilisation. Here in Paris one knows it finally. The ponderous and depressing museum that is regal Paris. And living humanity like poor worms struggling inside the shell of history, all of them inside the museum. The dead life and the living life, all one museum.

Monuments, museums, permanencies and ponderosities are all anathema. But brave men are forever born, and nothing else is worth having.

LETTER FROM GERMANY

We are going back to Paris tomorrow, so this is the last moment to write a letter from Germany. Only from the fringe of Germany too.

It's a miserable journey from Paris to Nancy, through that Marne country, where the country still seems to have had the soul blasted out of it, though the dreary fields are ploughed and level, and the pale wire trees stand up. But it is all void and null. And in the villages, the smashed houses in the street rows, like rotten teeth between good teeth.

You come to Strasburg, and the people still talk Alsatian German, as ever, in spite of French shop signs. The place feels dead. And full of cotton goods, white goods, from Mülhausen, from the factories that once were German. Such cheap white cotton goods, in a glut.

The cathedral-front rearing up high and flat and fanciful, a sort of darkness in the dark, with round rose windows and long, long prisms of stone. Queer, that men should have ever wanted to put stone upon fanciful stone to such a height, without having it fall down. The gothic! I was always glad when my card castles fell. But these goths and alemans seemed to have a craze for peaky height.

The Rhine is still the Rhine, the great divider. You feel it as you cross. The flat, frozen, watery places. Then the cold and curving river. Then the other side, seeming so cold, so empty, so frozen, so forsaken. The train stands and steams fiercely. Then it draws through the flat Rhine plain, past frozen pools of flood-water, and frozen fields, in the emptiness of this bit of occupied territory.

Immediately you are over the Rhine, the spirit of place has changed. There is no more attempt at the bluff of geniality. The marshy places are frozen. The fields are vacant. There seems nobody in the world.

It is as if the life had retreated eastwards. As if the Germanic life were slowly ebbing away from contact with western Europe, ebbing to the deserts of the east. And there stand the heavy, ponderous round hills of the Black Forest, black with an inky blackness of Germanic trees, and patched with a whiteness of snow. They are like a series of huge, involved black mounds, obstructing the vision eastwards. You look at them from the Rhine plain, and know that you stand on an actual border, up against something.

The moment you are in Germany, you know. It feels empty, and somehow, menacing. So must the Roman soldiers have watched those black, massive round hills: with a certain fear, and with the knowledge that they were at their own limit. A fear of the invisible natives. A fear of the invisible life lurking among the woods. A fear of their own opposite.

So it is with the French: this almost mystic fear. But one should not insult even one's fears.

Germany, this bit of Germany, is very different from what it was two and a half years ago, when I was here. Then it was still open to Europe. Then it still looked to western Europe for a re-union, for a sort of reconciliation. Now that is over. The inevitable, mysterious barrier has fallen again, and the great leaning of the Germanic spirit is once more eastwards; towards Russia, towards Tartary. The strange vortex of Tartary has become the positive centre again, the positivity of western Europe is broken. The positivity of our civilisation has broken. The influences that come, come invisibly out of Tartary. So that all Germany reads *Men Beasts and Gods*, with a kind of fascination. Returning again to the fascination of the destructive East, that produced Attila.

So it is at night. Baden Baden is a little quiet place, all its guests gone. No more Turgenevs or Dostoevskys or Grand Dukes or King Edwards coming to drink the waters. All the outward effect of a world-famous watering place. But empty now, a mere Black Forest village with the wagon-loads of timber going through, to the French.

The Rentenmark, the new Gold Mark of Germany, is abominably dear. Prices are high in England, but English money buys less in Baden than it buys in London, by a long chalk. And there is no work— consequently no money. Nobody buys anything, except absolute necessities. The shop keepers are in despair. And there is less and less work.

Everybody gives up the telephone—can't afford it. The tram-cars don't run, except about three times a day to the station. Up to the Annaberg, the suburb, the lines are rusty, no trams ever go. The people can't afford the ten Pfennigs for the fare. Ten pfennigs is an important sum now: one penny. It is really a hundred Milliards of Marks.

Money becomes insane, and people with it.

At night the place is almost dark, economising light. Economy, economy, economy—that too becomes an insanity. Luckily the government keeps bread fairly cheap.

But at night you feel strange things stirring in the darkness, strange feelings stirring out of this still-unconquered Black Forest. You stiffen your backbone and you listen to the night. There is a sense of danger. It is not the people. They don't seem dangerous. Out of the very air comes a sense of danger, a queer, *bristling* feeling of uncanny danger.

Something has happened. Something has happened which has not yet eventuated. The old spell of the old world has broken, and the old, bristling, savage spirit has set in. The war did not break the old peace-and-production hope of the world, though it gave it a severe wrench. Yet the old peace-and-production hope still governs, at least the consciousness. Even in Germany it has not quite gone.

But it feels as if, virtually, it were gone. The last two years have done it. The hope in peace-and-production is broken. The old flow, the old adherence is ruptured. And a still older flow has set in. Back, back to the savage polarity of Tartary, and away from the polarity of civilised Christian Europe. This, it seems to me, has already happened. And it is a happening of far more profound import than any actual event. It is the father of the next phase of events.

And the feeling never relaxes. As you travel up the Rhine valley, still the same latent sense of danger, of silence, of suspension. Not that the people are actually planning or plotting or preparing. I don't believe it for a minute. But something has happened to the human soul, beyond all help. The human soul recoiling now from unison, and making itself strong elsewhere. The ancient spirit of pre-historic Germany coming back, at the end of history.

The same in Heidelberg. Heidelberg full, full, full of people. Students the same, youths with rucksacks the same, boys and maidens in gangs, come down from the hills. The same, and not the same. These queer gangs of Young Socialists, youths and girls, with their non-materialistic professions, their half mystical assertions, they strike one as strange. Something primitive, like loose roving gangs of broken, scattered tribes, so they affect one. And the swarms of people somehow produce an impression of silence, of secrecy, of stealth. It is as if everything and everybody recoiled away from the old unison, as barbarians lurking in a wood recoil out of sight. The old habits remain. But the bulk of the people have no money. And the whole stream of feeling is reversed.

So, you stand in the woods above the town and see the Neckar flowing green and swift and slippery out of the gulf of Germany, to the Rhine. And the sun sets slow and scarlet into the haze of the Rhine valley. And the old, pinkish stone of the ruined castle across looks sultry, the marshalry is in shadow below, the peaked roofs of old, tight Heidelberg compressed in its river gateway glimmer and glimmer out. There is a blue haze.

And it all looks as if the years were wheeling swiftly backwards, no more onwards. Like a spring that is broken, and whirls swiftly back, so time seems to be whirling with mysterious swiftness to a sort of death. Whirling to the ghost of the old Middle Ages of Germany, then to the Roman days, then to the days of the silent forest and the dangerous, lurking barbarian.

Something about the Germanic races is unalterable. White skinned, elemental, and dangerous. Our civilisation has come from the fusion of the dark-eyes with the blue. The meeting and mixing and mingling of the two races has been the joy of our ages. And the Celt has been there, alien, but necessary as some chemical reagent to the fusion. So the civilisation of Europe rose up. So these Cathedrals and these thoughts.

But now the Celt is the disintegrating agent. And the Latin and southern races are falling out of association with the northern races, the northern Germanic impulse is recoiling towards Tartary, the destructive vortex of Tartary.

It is a fate, nobody now can alter it. It is a fate. The very blood changes. Within the last three years, the very constituency of the blood has changed, in European veins. But particularly in Germanic veins.

At the same time, we have brought it about ourselves—by a Ruhr occupation, by an English nullity, and by a German false will. We have done it ourselves. But apparently it was not to be helped.

Quos vult perdere Deus, dementat prius.

PAN IN AMERICA

At the beginning of the Christian era, voices were heard off the coasts of Greece, out to sea, on the Mediterranean, wailing: "Pan is dead! Great Pan is dead!"

The father of fauns and nymphs, satyrs and dryads and naiads was dead, with only the voices in the air to lament him. Humanity hardly noticed.

But who was he, really? Down the long lanes and overgrown ridings of history we catch odd glimpses of a lurking rustic god with a goat's white lightning in his eyes. A sort of fugitive, hidden among leaves, and laughing with the uncanny derision of one who feels himself defeated by something lesser than himself.

An outlaw, even in the early days of the gods. A sort of Ishmael among the bushes.

Yet always his lingering title: The Great God Pan. As if he was, or had been, the greatest.

Lurking among the leafy recesses, he was almost more demon than god. To be feared, not loved or approached. A man who should see Pan by daylight fell dead, as if blasted by lightning.

Yet you might dimly see him in the night, a dark body within the darkness. And then, it was a vision filling the limbs and the trunk of a man with power, as with new, strong-mounting sap. The Pan power! You went on your way in the darkness secretly and subtly elated with blind energy, and you could cast a spell, by your mere presence, on women and men. But particularly on women.

165

In the woods and the remote places ran the children of Pan, all the nymphs and fauns of the forest and the spring and the river and the rocks. These, too, it was dangerous to see by day. The man who looked up to see the white arms of a nymph flash as she darted behind the thick wild laurels, away from him, followed helplessly. He was a nympholept. Fascinated by the swift limbs and the wild, fresh sides of the nymph, he followed forever, forever, in the endless monotony of his desire. Unless came some wise being who could absolve him from the spell.

But the nymphs, running among the trees and curling to sleep under the bushes, made the myrtles blossom more gaily, and the spring bubble up with greater urge, and the birds splash with a strength of life. And the lithe flanks of the faun gave life to the oak groves, the vast trees hummed with energy. And the wheat sprouted like green rain returning out of the ground, in the little fields, and the vine hung its black drops in abundance, urging a secret.

Gradually, men moved into cities. And they loved the display of people better than the display of a tree. They liked the glory they got of overpowering one another in war. And above all, they loved the vainglory of their own words, the pomp of argument and the vanity of ideas.

So Pan became old and grey-bearded and goat-legged, and his passion was degraded with the lust of senility. His power to blast and to brighten dwindled. His nymphs became coarse and vulgar.

Till at last, the old Pan died, and was turned into the devil of the Christians. The old god Pan became the Christian devil, with the cloven hoofs and the horns, the tail, and the laugh of derision. Old Nick, the Old Gentleman who is responsible for all our wickednesses, but especially our sensual excesses, this is all that is left of the great god Pan.

It is strange. It is a most strange ending for a god with such a name. Pan! All! That which is everything, has goats' feet and a tail! With a black face!

This really is curious.

Yet this was all that remained of Pan, except that he acquired brimstone and hell-fire, for many, many centuries. The nymphs turned into the nasty-smelling witches of a Walpurgis night, and the fauns that danced became sorcerers riding the air, or fairies no bigger than your thumb.

But Pan keeps on being re-born, in all kinds of strange shapes. There he was, at the Renaissance. And in the eighteenth century he had quite a vogue. He gave rise to an "ism"; and there were many Pantheists, Wordsworth one of the first. They worshipped Nature in her sweet-and-pure aspect, her Lucy Gray aspect.

"Oft have I heard of Lucy Gray," the school child began to recite, on examination day.

"So have I," interrupted the bored inspector. Lucy Gray, alas, was the form that William Wordsworth thought fit to give to the Great God Pan.

And then he crossed over to the young United States: I mean Pan did. Suddenly he gets a new name. He becomes the Oversoul, the Allness of everything. To this new Lucifer Gray of a Pan, Whitman sings the famous *Song of Myself* "I am All, and All is Me." That is: "I am Pan and Pan is me."

The old goat-legged gentleman from Greece thoughtfully strokes his beard, and answers:

"All A is B, but all B is not A."

Aristotle did not live for nothing. All Walt is Pan, but all Pan is not Walt. This, even to Whitman, is incontrovertible. So the new American pantheism collapses.

Then the poets dress up a few fauns and nymphs, to let them run riskily— oh, would there were any risk!—in their private "grounds." But alas, these tame guinea pigs soon became boring. Change the game.

We still *pretend* to believe that there is One mysterious Something-or-other back of Everything, ordaining all things for the ultimate good of humanity. It wasn't back of the Germans in 1914, of course, and whether it's back of the bolshevist is still a grave question. But still, it's back of *us,* so that's all right.

Alas, poor Pan! Is this what you've come to. Legless, hornless, faceless, even smileless, you are less than everything or anything, except a lie.

And yet here, in America, the oldest of all old Pan is still alive.

When Pan was greatest, he was not even Pan. He was nameless and unconceived, mentally. Just as a small baby new from the womb may say Mama! Dada! Whereas in the womb it said nothing, so humanity, in the womb of Pan, said nought. But when humanity was born into a separate idea of itself, it said *Pan*!

In the days before man got too-much separated off from the universe, he *was* Pan, along with all the rest.

As a tree still is. A strong-willed, powerful thing-in-itself, reaching up and reaching down. With a powerful will of its own it thrusts green hands and huge limbs at the light above, and sends huge legs and gripping toes down, down between the earth and rocks, to the earth's middle.

Here, on this little ranch under the Rocky Mountains, a big pine tree rises like a guardian spirit in front of the cabin where we live. Long, long ago the Indians blazed it. And the lightning, or the storm has cut off its crest. Yet its column is always there, alive and changeless, alive and changing. The tree has its own aura of life. And in winter the snow slips off it, and in June it sprinkles down its little catkin-like pollen-tips, and it hisses in the wind, and it makes a silence within a silence. It is a great tree, under which the house is built. And the tree is still within the allness of Pan. At night, when the lamplight shines out of the window, the great trunk dimly shows, in the near darkness, like an Egyptian column, supporting some powerful mystery in the over-branching darkness. By day, it is just a tree.

It is just a tree. The chipmunks skeeter a little way up it, the little black-and-white birds, tree-creepers, walk quick as mice on its rough perpendicular, tapping: the blue jays throng in its branches, high up, at dawn, and in the afternoon you hear the faintest rustle of many little wild doves alighting in its upper remoteness. It is a tree, which is still Pan.

And we live beneath it, without noticing. Yet sometimes, when one suddenly looks far up and sees those wild doves there, or when one glances quickly at the inhuman-human hammering of a woodpecker, one realises that the tree is asserting itself as much as I am. It gives out life, as I give out life. Our two lives meet and cross one another, unknowingly: the tree's life penetrates my life, and my life, the tree's. We cannot live near one another, as we do, without affecting one another.

The tree gathers up earth-power from the dark bowels of the earth, and a roaming sky-glitter from above. And all unto itself, which is a tree, woody, enormous, slow but unyielding with life, bristling with acquisitive energy, obscurely radiating some of its great strength.

It vibrates its presence into my soul, and I am with Pan. I think no man could live near a pine-tree and remain quite suave and supple and compliant. Something fierce and bristling is communicated. The piney sweetness is rousing and defiant, like turpentine, the noise of the needles is keen with aeons of sharpness. In the volleys of wind from the western desert, the tree hisses and resists. It does not lean eastward at all. It resists with a vast force of resistance, from within itself, and its column is a ribbed, magnificent assertion.

I have become conscious of the tree, and of its interpenetration into my life. Long ago, the Indians must have been even more acutely conscious of it, when they blazed it to leave their mark on it.

I am conscious that it helps to change me, vitally. I am even conscious that shivers of energy cross my living plasm, from the tree, and I become a degree more like unto the tree, more bristling and turpentiney, in Pan. And the tree gets a certain shade and alertness of my life, within itself.

Of course, if I like to cut myself off, and say it is all bunk, a tree is merely so much lumber not yet sawn, then in a great measure I shall *be* cut off So much depends on one's attitude. One can shut many, many doors of receptivity in one's self: or one can open many doors that are shut.

I prefer to open my doors to the coming of the tree. Its raw earth-power and its raw sky-power, its resinous erectness and resistance, its sharpness of hissing needles and relentlessness of roots, all that goes to the primitive savageness of a pine-tree, goes also to the strength of a man.

Give me of your power, then, oh tree! And I will give you of mine.

And this is what men must have said, more naively, less sophisticatedly, in the days when all was Pan. It is what, in a way, the aboriginal Indians still say, and still *mean,* intensely: especially when they dance the sacred dance, with the tree: or with the spruce twigs tied above their elbows.

Give me your power, oh tree, to help me in my life. And I will give you my power even symbolized in a rag torn from my clothing.

This is the oldest Pan.

Or again, I say: "Oh you, you big tree, standing so strong and swallowing juice from the earth's inner body, warmth from the sky, beware of me. Beware of me, because I am strongest. I am going to cut you down and take your life and make you into beams for my house, and into a fire. Prepare to deliver up your life to me."

Is this any less true than when the lumberman glances at a pine-tree, sees if it will cut good lumber, dabs a mark or a number upon it, and goes his way absolutely without further thought or feeling? Is he truer to life? Is it truer to life, to insulate oneself entirely from the influence of the tree's life, and to walk about in an inanimate forest of standing lumber, marketable in St. Louis, Mo? Or is it truer to life to know, with a pantheistic sensuality, that the tree has its own life, its own assertive existence, its own living relatedness to me: that my life is added to or militated against, by the tree's life.

Which is really truer?

Which is truer, to live among the living, or to run on wheels?

And who can sit with the Indians around a big camp-fire of logs, in the mountains at night, when a man rises and turns his breast and his curiously-smiling bronze face away from the blaze, and stands voluptuously warming his thighs and buttocks and loins, his back to the fire, faintly smiling the inscrutable Pan-smile into the dark trees surrounding, without hearing him say, in the Pan-voice: "Aha! Tree! Aha! Tree! Who has triumphed now? I drank the heat of your blood into my face and breast, and now I am drinking it into my loins and buttocks and legs, Oh tree! I am drinking your heat right through me, Oh tree! Fire is life, and I take your life for mine. I am drinking it up, Oh tree, even into my buttocks. Aha! Tree! I am warm! I am strong! I am happy, Tree, in this cold night in the mountains!"

And the old man, glancing up and seeing the flames flapping in flamy rags at the dark smoke, in the upper fire-hurry towards the stars and the dark spaces between the stars, sits stonily and inscrutable; yet one knows that he is saying: "Go back, Oh fire! Go back like honey! Go back, honey of life, to where you came from, before you were hidden in the tree. The trees climb into the sky and steal the honey of the sun, like bears stealing from a hollow tree-trunk. But when the tree falls and is put on to the fire, the honey flames and goes straight back to where it came from. And the smell of burning pine is as the smell of honey."

So the old man says, with his lightless Indian eyes. But he is careful never to utter one word of the mystery. Speech is the death of Pan, who can but laugh and sound the reed-flute.

Is it better, I ask you, to cross the room and turn on the heat at the radiator, glancing at the thermometer and saying: "We're just a bit below the level, in here"? Then to go back to the newspaper!

What can a man do with his life but live it? And what does life consist in, save a vivid relatedness between the man and the living universe that surrounds him. Yet man insulates himself more and more into mechanism, and repudiates everything but the machine and the contrivance of which he himself is master, God in the machine.

Morning comes, and white ash lies in the fire-hollow, and the old man looks at it broodingly.

"The fire is gone," he says in the Pan silence, that is so full of unutterable things. "Look! there is no more tree! We drank his warmth, and he is gone. He is way, way off in the sky, his smoke is in the blueness, with the sweet smell of a pine-wood fire, and his yellow flame is in the sun. It is morning, with the ashes of night. There is no more tree. Tree is gone. But perhaps there is fire among the ashes. I shall blow it, and it will be alive. There is always fire, between the tree that goes and the tree that stays.—One day I shall go—"

So they cook their meat, and rise, and go in silence.

There is a big rock towering up above the trees, a cliff. And silently a man glances at it. You hear him say, without speech:

"Oh you big rock! If a man fall down from you, he dies. Don't let me fall down from you. Oh you big pale rock, you are so still, you know lots of things. You know a lot. Help me then, with your stillness. I go to find deer. Help me find deer."

And the man slips aside, and secretly lays a twig, or a pebble, some little object in a niche of the rock, as a pact between him and the rock.

The rock will give him some of its radiant-cold stillness and enduring presence, and he makes a symbolic return, of gratitude.

Is it foolish? Would it have been better to invent a gun, to shoot his game from a great distance, so that he need not approach it with any of that living stealth and preparedness with which one live thing approaches another. Is it better to have a machine in one's hands, and so avoid the life-contact: the trouble! the pains! Is it better to see the rock as a mere nothing, not worth noticing because it has no value, and you can't eat it as you can a deer?

But the old hunter steals on, in the stillness of the eternal Pan, which is so full of soundless sounds. And in his soul he is saying "Deer! Oh you thin-legged deer! I am coming! Where are you, with your feet like little stones bounding down a hill? I know you Yes, I know you. But you don't know me. You don't know where I am, and you don't know me, anyhow. But I know you. I am thinking of you. I shall get you. I've got to get you. I got to, so it will be.—I shall get you, and shoot an arrow right in you."

In this state of abstraction, and subtle, hunter's communion with the quarry—a weird psychic connection between hunter and hunted—the man creeps into the mountains.

And even a white man who is a born hunter, must fall into this state. Gun or no gun! He projects his deepest, most primitive hunter's consciousness abroad, and finds his game, not by accident, nor even chiefly by looking for signs, but primarily, by a psychic attraction, a sort of telepathy: the hunter's telepathy. Then when he finds his quarry, he aims with a pure, spell-bound volition. If there is no flaw in his abstracted huntsman's *will,* he cannot miss. Arrow or bullet, it flies like a movement of pure will, straight to the spot. And the deer, once she has let her quivering alertness be overmastered or stilled by the hunter's subtle, hypnotic, *following* spell, she cannot escape.

This is Pan, the Pan-mystery, the Pan-power. What can men who sit at home in their studies, and drink hot milk and have lambs-wool slippers on their feet, and write anthropology, what *can* they possibly know about men, the men of Pan?

Among the creatures of Pan, there is an eternal struggle for life, between lives. Man, defenceless, rapacious man, has needed the qualities of every living thing, at one time or other. The hard, silent abidingness of a rock, the surging resistance of a tree, the still evasion of a puma, the dogged earth-knowledge of the bear, the light alertness of the deer, the sky-prowling vision of the eagle: turn by turn man has needed the power of every living thing. Tree, stone, or hill, river, or little stream, or water-fall, or salmon in the fall—man can be master, and complete in himself, only by assuming the living powers of each of them, as the occasion requires.

He used to make himself master by a great effort of will, and sensitive, intuitive cunning, and immense labour of body.

Then he discovered the "idea." He found that all things were related by certain *laws.* The moment man learned to abstract, he began to make engines that would do the work of his body. So, instead of concentrating upon his quarry, or upon the living things which made his universe, he concentrated upon the engines or instruments which should intervene between him and the living universe, and give him mastery.

This was the death of the great Pan. The idea and the engine came between man and all things, like a death. The old connection, the old Allness, was severed, and can never be ideally restored. Great Pan is dead.

Yet what do we live for, except to live? Man has lived to conquer the phenomenal universe. To a great extent, he has succeeded. With all the mechanisms of the human world, man is to a great extent master of all life, and of most phenomena.

And what then? Once you have conquered a thing, you have lost it. Its real relation to you collapses.

A conquered world is no good to man. He sits stupefied with boredom upon his conquest.

We need the universe to live again, so that we can live with it. A conquered universe, a dead Pan, leaves us nothing to live with.

You have to abandon the conquest, before Pan will live again. You have to live to live, not to conquer. What's the good of conquering even the North Pole, if after the conquest you've nothing left but an inert fact? Better leave it a mystery.

It was better to be a hunter in the woods of Pan, than it is to be a clerk in a city store. The hunter hungered, laboured, suffered tortures of fatigue. But at least he lived in a ceaseless living relation to his surrounding universe.

At evening, when the deer was killed, he went home to the tents, and threw down the deer-meat on the swept place before the tent of his women. And the women came out to greet him softly, with a sort of reverence, as he stood before the meat, the life-stuff. He came back spent, yet full of power, bringing the life-stuff. And the children looked with black eyes at the meat, and at that wonder-being, the man, the bringer of meat.

Perhaps the children of the store-clerk look at their father with a *tiny* bit of the same mystery. And perhaps the clerk feels a fragment of the old glorification, when he hands his wife the paper dollars.

But about the tents the women move silently. Then when the cooking-fire dies low, the man crouches in silence and toasts meat on a stick, while the dogs lurk round like shadows, and the children watch avidly. The man eats as the sun goes down. And as the glitter departs, he says: "Lo, the sun is going, and I stay. All goes, but still I stay. Power of deer-meat is in my belly, power of sun is in my body. I am tired, but it is with power.—There the small moon gives her first sharp sign. So! So! I watch her. I will give her something, she is very sharp and bright, and I do not know her power. Lo! I will give the woman something for this moon, which troubles me above the sunset, and has power. Lo! how very curved and sharp she is! Lo! how she troubles me!"

Thus, always aware, always watchful, subtly poising himself in the world of Pan, among the powers of the living universe, he sustains his life and is sustained. There is no boredom, because *everything is* alive and active, and danger is inherent in all movement. The contact between all things is keen and wary: for wariness is also a sort of reverence, or respect. And nothing, in the world of Pan, may be taken for granted.

So when the fire is extinguished, and the moon sinks, the man says to the woman: Oh woman, be very soft, be very soft and deep towards me, with the deep silence. Oh woman, do not speak and stir and wound me with the sharp horns of yourself. Let me come into the deep, soft places, the dark soft places deep as between the stars. Oh, let me lose there the weariness of the day: let me come in the power of the night.—Oh, do not speak to me, nor break the deep night of my silence and my power. Be softer than dust, and darker than any flower. Oh woman, wonderful is the craft of your softness, the distance of your dark depths. Oh open silently the deep that has no end, and do not turn the horns of the moon~ against me—

This is the might of Pan, and the power of Pan.

And still, in America, among the Indians, the oldest Pan is alive. But here also, dying fast.

It is useless to glorify the savage. For he will kill Pan with his own hands, for the sake of a motor-car. And a bored savage, for whom Pan is dead, is the stupefied image of all boredom.

And we cannot return to the primitive life, to live in teepees and hunt with bows and arrows.

Yet live we must. And once life has been conquered, it is pretty difficult to live. What are we going to do, with a conquered universe?

The Pan relationship, which the world of man once had with all the world, was better than anything man has now. The savage, today, if you give him the chance, will become more mechanical and unliving than any civilised man. But civilised man, having conquered the universe, may as well leave off bossing it. Because when all is said and done, life itself consists in a live relatedness between man and his universe;—sun, moon, stars, earth, trees, flowers, birds, animals, men, everything—and not in a "conquest" of anything by anything. Even the conquest of the air makes the world smaller, tighter, and more airless.

And whether we are a store-clerk or a bus-conductor, we can still choose between the living universe of Pan, and the mechanical conquered universe of modern humanity. The machine has no windows. But even the most mechanised human being has only got his windows nailed up, or bricked in.

SEE MEXICO AFTER, BY LUIS Q.

My home's in Mexico.
That's where you want to go.
Life's one long *cine* show. . .

As a matter of fact I am a hard-worked, lean individual poked in the corner of a would-be important building in Mexico D. F.

That's that.

I am—married, so this is not a matrimonial ad. But I, as I said, am lean, pale, hard-worked, with indiscriminate fair hair and, I hope, nice blue eyes. Anyhow they aren't black. And I am young. And I am Mexican: oh don't doubt it for a second. Mejicano soy. La-la-la-la! I'll jabber your head off in Spanish. But where is my gun and red sash!

Ay-de-mi! That's how one sighs in Spanish. I am sighing because I am Mexican, for who would be a Mexican? Where would he be if he was one?—I am an official—without doubt important, since every four-farthing sparrow etc.—And being an important official, I am always having to receive people. Receive. Deceive. Believe. Rather, they're not usually people. They're almost always commissions.

"Please to meet you, Mister," the say. "Not American, are you?"

I seize my chin in trepidation. "Good God! Am I?" There is a Monroe doctrine, and there is a continent, or two continents. Am I American?—by any chance?

"Pardon me one moment!" I say, with true Mexican courtesy.

And I dash upstairs to the top floor—the fourth—no elevators— to my little corner office that looks out over the flat roofs and bubbly church-domes and streaks of wire of Mexico D. F., I rush to the window, I look out, and ah!—Yes! *Qué tal? Amigo*! How lucky you're there! Say, boy, will you tell me whether you're American or not? Because if you are, I am.

This interesting announcement is addressed to my old friend Popo, who is lounging his heavy shoulders under the sky, smoking a cigarette end, a la Mexicaine. Further, since I'm paid to give information, Popo is the imperturbable volcano, known at length as Popocatepetl, with the accent on the tay, so I beg you not to put it on the cat, who is usually loitering in the vicinity of Mexico D. F.

No, I shan't tell you what the D. F. is: or *who* it is. Take it for yourself if you like. I never come pulling the tail of your D. C. —Washington.

Popo gives another puff to his eternal cigarette, and replies, as every Mexican should:

"Quien sabe?"

"Who knows?—Ask me another, boy!"

Ca! —as a matter of fact, we don't say *Caramba*! very much. But I'll say it to please. I say it. I tear my hair. I dash downstairs to the Committee, or rather Commission, which is waiting with bated breath (mint) to know whether I'm American or not. I smile ingratiatingly. "Do pardon me for the interruption, gentlemen. (One of them is usually a lady, but she's best interpreted by *gentlemen.*) You ask me, am I American?—Quien sabe?"

"Then you're *not.*"

"Am I not, gentlemen? Ay-de-mi!"

"Ever been in America?"

Good God! Again? Ah, my chin, let me seize thee!

Once more I flee upstairs and poke myself out of that window; and say *Oiga*! *Viejo*!—*Oiga*! is a very important word. And I am in the Bureau of Information.

"*Oiga! Viejo*! Are you in America?"

"Quien sabe!" He bumps the other white shoulder at me. Snow!

"Oh gentlemen!" I pant. "Quien sabe!"

"Then you haven't."

"But I've been to New York."

"Why didn't you say so!"

"Have I then been to America?"

"Hey! Who's running this Information Bureau?"

"I am. Let me run it."

So I dart upstairs again, and address myself to Popo.

"Popo! I have been to America, via New York, and you haven't."

Down I dart, to my Commission. On the way I remember how everything—I mean the loud walls—in New York, said SEE AMERICA FIRST.— Thank God! I say to myself, wiping my wet face before entering to the Commission: On American evidence, I've seen him, her, or it. But whether en todo or en parte, Quién sabe!

I open the door, and I give a supercilious sniff. Such are my American manners.

173

I am just smelling my Commission.—As usual! I say to myself, snobbishly: *Oil*!

There are all sorts and sizes of commissions, every sort and size and condition of commission. But oil predominates. Usually, I can smell oil down the telephone.

There are others.—Railway Commissions, Mines Commissions, American Women's Christian Missions, American Bankers' Missions, American Bootleggers Missions, American Episcopalian, Presbyterian, Mormon, and Jewish Missions, American Tramps Missions—

I, however, in my little office, am Mohammet. If you would like to see Mexico summed up into one unique figure, see me, a la Mohammet, in my little office, saying: Let these mountains come to *me*.

And they come. They come in whole ranges, in sierras, in Cordilleras. I smell oil, and I see the backbone of America walking up the stair-case (no elevators). I hear the sound of footsteps, and behold the entire Sierra Madre marching me-wards. Ask me if leave Mohammet with cold feet! Oh, I am *muy Mejicano*, I am!

I feel I am still SEEING AMERICA FIRST, and they are seeing Mexico after. I feel myself getting starrier and stripeyer every day, I see such a lot of America first.

But what happens to them, when they see Mexico after?

Quien sabe!

I am always murmuring: You see, Mexico and America are not in the same boat.

I want to add: They're not even floating on the same ocean. I doubt if they're gyrating in the same cosmos.

But superlatives are not well-mannered.

Still, it is hard on a young man like me to be merely Mexican, when my father, merely by moving up the map a little while he was still strong and lusty, might have left me hundred-per-cent-plus American. I'm sure I should have been plus.

It is hard on me, I say. As it is hard on Popo. He might have been Mount Brown or Mount Abraham. How can any mountain, when you come to think of it, be Popocatepetl?—and *tay*-petl at that!

There there! let me soothe myself.

In fact, I am always a little sorry for the Americans who come seeing Mexico after.—"I am left such a long way behind!" as the burro said when he fell down an abandoned mine.

Still, the Commissioners and missioners often stay quite brisk. They really do wonders. They put up chimneys and they make all sorts of wheels go round. The Mexicans are simply enraptured. But after a while, being nothing but naughty boys and greasers, they are pining to put their spokes in those wheels. Mischief, I tell you. *Brummm!* go the spokes! And the wheels pause to wonder, while the bits fly. That's fun!

Other gentlemen who are very sharp-eyed, seeing Mexico after, are the political see-ers. America is too hot for them, as a rule, so they move into cool, cool Mexico. They are some boys, they are! At least, so they tell me. And they belong to weird things that only exist as initials, such I. W. W.'s and A. F. L.'s and P. J. P,'s.—Give me a job, say these gentlemen, and I'll take the rest.

Why certainly, what could be more accommodating! Whereupon instantly, these gentlemen acquire the gift of Spanish, with an almost Pentecostal suddenness; they pat you on the shoulder and tell you sulphureous Mexican stories which certainly you would never have heard but for them. Oh hot stuff! Hot dog! They even cry aloud *Perro caliente*! —and the walls of the city quake.

Moreover they proceed to organise our Labour, after having so firmly insisted that we haven't any. But we produce some, for their sakes. And they proceed to organize it: without music. And in throes of self-esteem they cry: Ah, Mexico's the place. America can't touch it! God bless Mexico!

Whereupon all the Mexicans present burst into tears.

You want no darn Gringoes and gringo capital down here! they say.

We cross ourselves rapidly! Absit omen.

But alas, these thrilling gentlemen always leave us. They return with luggage, having come without, to AMERICA.

Well, adios! eh, boy? Come up there one day. Show you something.

Tears, the train moves out.

No, I am Mexican. I might as well be Jonah in the whale's belly, so perfectly, so mysteriously am I nowhere.

But they come. They come as tourists, for example, looking round the whale's interior.

"My wife's a college graduate," says the he-man.

She looks it. And she may thank her lucky stars—Rudolph Valentino is the first-magnitude—she will go on looking it all her days.

Ah, the first time she felt Rudolfino's Italianino-Argentino-swoon-between-o kisses! On the screen, of course.—Ah, that first time!

On the back porch, afterwards: Bill, I'm so tired of clean, hygienic kisses.

Poor Bill spits away his still-good, five-cents, mint-covered Wrigley's chewing-gum gag, and with it, the last straw he had to cling to.

Now, aged thirty-five, and never quite a Valentino, he's brought her to see Mexico after—she'd seen Ramon Novarro's face, with the skin-you-love-to-touch. On the screen, of course.

Bill has brought her south. She has crossed the border with Bill. Ah, her eyes at the Pullman window! Where is the skin I would love to touch? they cry. And a dirty Indian pushes his black face and glaring eyes towards her, offering to sell her enchiladas.

It is no use *my* being sorry for her. Bill is better-looking than I am. So she re-falls in love with Bill, the dark-eyed flour-faced creatures make such eyes at him, down here. Call them women! Down-trodden things!

The escaped husband is another one. He drinks, swears, looks at all the women meaningly over a red nose, and lives with a prostitute. Hot *dog*!

Then the young lady collecting information! Golly! Quite nice-looking too. And the things she does! One would think the invisible unicorn that protects virgins was ramping round her every moment. But it's not that. Not even the toughest bandit, not even Pancho Villa, could carry off all that information, though she as good as typed out her temptation to him.

175

Then the home-town aristocrats, of Little Bull, Arizona, or of Old Hat, Illinois. They are just looking round for something: seeing Mexico after: and very rarely finding it. It really is extraordinary the things there are in Little Bull and in Old Hat, that there aren't in Mexico. Cold slaw, for example! Why, in Little Bull—!

San Juan Teotihuacán! Hey, boy, why don't you get the parson to sprinkle him with a new tag. Never stand a name like that for half a day, in Little Bull, Illinois. Or was it Arizona?

Such a pity, to have to see Mexico after you've seen America first: or at least, Little Bull, which is probably more so.

The ends won't meet. America isn't just a civilisation, it is CIVILISATION. So what is Mexico? Beside Little Bull, what is Mexico?

Of course Mexico went in for civilisation long, long, long ago. But it got left.

The snake crawled on, leaving his tail behind him. The snake crawled, lap by lap, all round the globe, till it got back to America. And by that time he was some snake, was civilisation. But where was his tail? He'd forgotten it?

Hey, boy! What's that?

Mexico!

Mexico!—the snake didn't know his own tail. *Mexico*! Garn! That's nothing. It's mere nothing, but the darn silly emptiness where I'm not. Not yet.

So he opens his mouth, and Mexico, his old tail, shivers.

But before civilisation swallows its own tail, that tail will buzz. For civilisation's a rattler: anyhow Mexico is.

NEW MEXICO

Superficially, the world has become small and known. Poor little globe of earth, the tourist trots around you as easily as they trot round the Bois or round Central Park. There is no mystery left, we've been there, we've seen it, we know all about it. We've done the globe, and the globe is done.

This is quite true, superficially. On the superficies, horizontally, we've been everywhere, and done everything, we know all about it. Yet the more we know, superficially, the less we penetrate, vertically. It's all very well skimming across the surface of the ocean, and saying you know all about the sea. There still remain the terrifying under-deeps, of which we have utterly no experience.

The same is true of land travel. We skim along, we get there, we see it all, we've done it all. And, as a rule, we never once go through the curious film which railroads, ships, motor-cars and hotels stretch over the surface of the whole earth. Pekin is just the same as New York, with a few different things to look at; rather more Chinese about, etc. Poor creatures that we are, we crave for experience, yet we are like flies that crawl on the pure and transparent mucous-paper in which the world, like a bon-bon, is wrapped so carefully that we can never get at it, though we see it there all the time as we move about it, apparently in contact, yet actually as far removed as if it were the moon.

As a matter of fact, our great-grandfathers, who never went anywhere, in actuality had more experience of the world than we have, who have seen everything. When they listened to a lecture with lantern-slides, they really held their breath before the unknown, as they sat in the village school-room. We, howling along in a rickshaw in Ceylon, say to ourselves: It's very much what you'd expect: we really know it all.

We are mistaken. The know-it-all state of mind is just the result of being outside the mucous-paper wrapping of civilisation. Underneath is everything we don't know and are afraid of knowing.

I realised this with shattering force when I went to New Mexico. New Mexico, one of the United States, part of the U.S.A. New Mexico, the picturesque reservation and playground of the Eastern States, very romantic, old Spanish, Red Indian, desert-mesas, pueblos, cow-boys, penitentes, all that film-stuff. Very nice, the great Southwest; put on a sombrero and knot a red kerchief round your neck, to go out in the great free spaces.

That is New Mexico wrapped in the absolutely hygienic and shiny mucous-paper of our trite civilisation. That is the New Mexico known to most of the Americans who know all about it. But break through the shiny sterilised wrapping, and actually touch the country, and you will never be the same again.

I think New Mexico was the greatest experience from the outside world that I have ever had. It certainly changed me for ever. Curious as it may sound, it was New Mexico that liberated me from the present era of civilisation, the great era of material and mechanical development. Months spent in holy Kandy, in Ceylon, the holy of holies of southern Buddhism, had not touched the great psyche of materialism and idealism which dominated me. And years, even, in the exquisite beauty of Sicily, right among the old Greek paganism that still lives there, had not shattered the essential Christianity on which my character was established. Australia was a sort of dream or trance, like being under a spell, the self remaining unchanged, so long as the trance did not last too long. Tahiti, in a mere glimpse, repelled me; and so did California, after a stay of a few weeks. There seemed a strange brutality in the spirit of the western coast, and I felt: Oh, let me get away!

But the moment I saw the brilliant, proud morning shine high up over the deserts of Santa Fe, something stood still in my soul, and I started to attend. There was a certain magnificence in the high-up day, a certain eagle-like royalty, so different from the equally pure, equally pristine and lovely morning of Australia, which is so soft, so utterly pure in its softness, and betrayed by green parrots flying. But in the lovely morning of Australia one went into a dream. In the magnificent fierce morning of New Mexico one sprang awake, a new part of the soul woke up suddenly, and the old world gave way to a new.

There are all kinds of beauty in the world, thank God, though ugliness is homogeneous. How lovely is Sicily, with Calabria across the sea like an opal, and Etna with her snow in a world above and beyond! How lovely is Tuscany, with little red tulips wild among the corn; or bluebells at dusk in England, or mimosa in clouds of pure yellow among the grey-green dun foliage of Australia, under a soft, blue, unbreathed sky! But for a *greatness* of beauty I have never experienced anything like New Mexico. All those mornings when I went with a hoe along the ditch to the canyon, at the ranch, and stood, in the fierce, proud silence of the Rockies, on their foot-hills, to look far over the desert to the blue mountains away in Arizona, blue as chalcedony, with the sage-brush desert sweeping grey-blue in between, dotted with tiny cube-crystals of houses: the vast amphitheatre of lofty, indomitable desert, sweeping round to the ponderous Sangre de Cristo Mountains on the east, and coming up flush at the pine-dotted foot-hills of the Rockies! What splendour! Only the tawny eagle could really sail out into the splendour of it all. Leo Stein once wrote to me: "It is the most aesthetically-satisfying landscape I know."—To me it was much more than that. It had a splendid, silent terror, and a vast, far-and-wide magnificence which made it way beyond mere aesthetic appreciation. Never is the light more pure and overweening than there, arching with a royalty almost cruel over the hollow, uptilted world. For it is curious that the land which has produced modern political democracy at its highest pitch should give one the greatest sense of overweening, terrible proudness and mercilessness: but so beautiful, God! so beautiful! Those that have spent morning after morning alone there pitched among the pines above the great proud world of desert will know, almost unbearably, how beautiful it is, how clear and unquestioned is the might of the day. Just day itself is tremendous there. It is so easy to understand that the Aztecs gave hearts of men to the sun. For the sun is not merely hot or scorching, not at all. It is of a brilliant and unchallengeable purity and haughty serenity which would make one sacrifice the heart to it. Ah, yes, in New Mexico the heart is sacrificed to the sun, and the human being is left stark, heartless, but undauntedly religious.

And that was the second revelation out there. I had looked over all the world for something that would strike me as religious. The simple piety of some English people, the semi-pagan mystery of some Catholics in southern Italy, the intensity of some Bavarian peasants, the semi-ecstasy of Buddhists or Brahmins: all this had seemed religious all right, as far as the parties concerned were involved, but it didn't involve me. I looked on at their religiousness from the outside. For it is still harder to feel religion at will, than to love at will.

I had seen what I felt was a hint of wild religion in the so-called devil dances of a group of naked villagers from the far-remote jungle in Ceylon, dancing at midnight under the torches, glittering wet with sweat on their dark bodies as if they had been gilded, at the celebration of the Pera-hera in Kandy, given to the Prince of Wales. And the utter dark absorption of these naked men, as they danced with their knees wide apart, suddenly affected me with a *sense* of religion, I *felt* religion for a moment. For religion is an experience, an uncontrollable, sensual experience even more so than love: I use sensual to mean an experience deep down in the senses, inexplicable and inscrutable.

But this experience was fleeting, gone in the curious turmoil of the Pera-hera, and I had no permanent feeling of religion till I came to New Mexico and penetrated into the old human race-experience there. It is curious that it should be in America, of all places, that a European should really experience religion, after touching the old Mediterranean and the East. It is curious that one should get a sense of living religion from the Red Indians, having failed to get it from Hindus or Sicilian Catholics or Cinghalese.

Let me make a reservation. I don't stand up to praise the Red Indian as he reveals himself in contact with white civilisation. From that angle, I am forced to admit he may be thoroughly objectionable. Even my small experience knows it. But also I know he *may* be thoroughly nice, even in his dealings with white men. It's a question of individuals, a good deal, on both sides.

But in this article I don't want to deal with the everyday or superficial aspect of New Mexico, outside the mucous-paper wrapping. I *want* to go beneath the surface. And therefore the American Indian in his behaviour as an American citizen doesn't really concern me. What concerns me is what he is, or what he seems to me to be, in his ancient, ancient race-self and religious self.

For the Red Indian seems to me much older than Greeks or Hindus or any Europeans or even Egyptians. The Red Indian, as a civilised and truly religious man, civilised beyond tabu and totem, as he is in the south, is religious in perhaps the oldest sense, and deepest, of the word. That is to say, he is a remnant of the most deeply religious race still living. So it seems to me.

But again let me protect myself The Indian who sells you baskets on Albuquerque station or who slinks around Taos plaza may be an utter waster and an indescribably low dog. Personally, he may be even less religious than a New York sneak-thief He may have broken with his tribe, or his tribe itself may have collapsed finally from its old religious integrity, and ceased, really, to exist. Then he is only fit for rapid absorption into white civilisation, which must make the best of him.

But while a tribe retains its religion and keeps up its religious practices, and while any member of the tribe shares in those practices, then there is a tribal integrity and a living tradition going back far beyond the birth of Christ, beyond the pyramids, beyond Moses. A vast, old religion which once swayed the earth lingers in unbroken practice there in New Mexico, older, perhaps, than anything in the world save Australian aboriginal tabu and totem, and that is not yet religion.

You can feel it, the atmosphere of it, around the pueblo. Not, of course, when the place is crowded with sight-seers and motor-cars. But go to Taos pueblo on some brilliant snowy morning, and see the white figures on the roof: or come riding through at dusk on some windy evening, when the black skirts of the silent women blow around the white wide boots, and you will feel the old, old root of human consciousness still reaching down to depths we know nothing of: and of which, only too often, we are jealous. It seems it will not be long before the pueblos are uprooted.

But never shall I forget watching the dancers, the men with the fox-skin swaying down from their buttocks, file out at San Geronimo, and the women with seed-rattles following. The long, streaming, glistening black hair of the men. Even in ancient Crete long hair was sacred in a man, as it is still in the Indians. Never shall I forget the utter absorption of the dance, so quiet, so steadily, timelessly rhythmic, and silent, with the ceaseless down-tread, always to the earth's centre, the very reverse of the upflow of Dionysiac or Christian ecstasy. Never shall I forget the deep singing of the men at the drum, swelling and sinking, the deepest sound I have heard in all my life, deeper than thunder, deeper than the sound of the Pacific Ocean, deeper than the roar of a deep waterfall: the wonderful deep sound of men calling to the unspeakable depths.

Never shall I forget coming into the little pueblo of San Felipe one sunny morning in spring, unexpectedly, when bloom was on the trees in the perfect little pueblo more old, more utterly peaceful and idyllic than anything in Theocritus, and seeing a little casual dance. Not impressive as a spectacle, only, to me, profoundly moving, because of the truly terrifying religious absorption of it.

Never shall I forget the Christmas dances at Taos, twilight, snow, the darkness coming over the great wintry mountains and the lonely pueblo, then suddenly, again, like dark calling to dark, the deep Indian cluster-singing around the drum, wild and awful, suddenly rousing on the last dusk as the procession starts.

And then the bonfires leaping suddenly in pure spurts of high flame, columns of sudden flame forming an alley for the procession.

Never shall I forget the khiva of birch-trees, away in the Apache country, in Arizona this time, the teepees and flickering fires, the neighing of horses unseen under the huge dark night, and the Apaches all abroad, in their silent moccasined feet: and in the khiva, beyond a little fire, the old man reciting, reciting in the unknown Apache speech, in the strange wild Indian voice that re-echoes away back to before the Flood, reciting apparently the traditions and legends of the tribe, going on and on, while the young men, the *braves* of today, wandered in, listened, and wandered away again, overcome with the power and majesty of that utterly old tribal voice, yet uneasy with their half-adherence to the modern civilisation, the two things in contact. And one of these *braves* shoved his face under my hat, in the night, and stared with his glittering eyes close to mine. He'd have killed me then and there, had he dared. He didn't dare: and I knew it: and he knew it.

Never shall I forget the Indian races, when the young men, even the boys, run naked, smeared with white earth and stuck with bits of eagle fluff for the swiftness of the heavens, and the old men brush them with eagle feathers, to give them power. And they run in the strange hurling fashion of the primitive world, hurled forward, not making speed deliberately. And the race is not for victory. It is not a contest. There is no competition. It is a great cumulative effort. The tribe this day is adding up its male energy and exerting to the utmost: for what? To get power, to get strength: to come, by sheer cumulative, hurling effort of the bodies of men, into contact with the great cosmic source of vitality which gives strength, power, energy to the men who can grasp it, energy for the year of attainment.

It was a vast old religion, greater than anything we know: more darkly and nakedly religious. There is no God, no conception of a god. All is god. But it is not the pantheism we are accustomed to, which expresses itself as "God is everywhere, god is in everything." In the oldest religion, everything was alive, not supernaturally but naturally alive. There were only deeper and deeper streams of life, vibrations of life more and more vast. So rocks were alive, but a mountain had a deeper, vaster life than a rock, and it was much harder for a man to bring his spirit, or his energy, into contact with the life of the mountain, and so draw strength from the mountain, as from a great standing well of life, than it was to come into contact with the rock. And he had to put forth a greater religious effort. For the whole life-effort of man was to get his life into direct contact with the elemental life of the cosmos, mountain-life, cloud-life, thunder-life, air-life, earth-life, sun-life. To come into immediate felt contact, and so derive energy, power, and a dark sort of joy. This effort into sheer, naked contact, *without an intermediary or mediator,* is the real meaning of religion. And at the sacred races the runners hurled themselves in a terrible cumulative effort, through the air, to come at last into naked contact with the very life of the air, which is the life of the clouds, and so of the rain.

It was a vast and pure religion, without idols or images, even mental ones. It is the oldest religion, a cosmic religion the same for all peoples, not broken up into specific gods or saviours or systems. It is the religion which precedes the god-concept, and is therefore greater and deeper than any god-religion.

And it lingers still, for a little while, in New Mexico: but long enough to have been a revelation to me. And the Indian, however objectionable he may be on occasion, has still some of the strange beauty and pathos of the religion that brought him forth and is now shedding him away into oblivion. When Trinidad, the Indian boy, and I planted corn at the ranch, my soul paused to see his brown hands softly moving the earth over the maize in pure ritual. He was back in his old religious self, and the ages stood still. Ten minutes later he was making a fool of himself with the horses. Horses were never part of the Indian's religious life, never would be. He hasn't a tithe of the feeling for them that he has for a bear, for example. So horses don't like Indians.

But there it is: the newest democracy ousting the oldest religion! And once the oldest religion is ousted, one feels the democracy and all its paraphernalia will collapse, and the oldest religion, which comes down to us from man's pre-war days, will start again. The sky-scraper will scatter on the winds like thistledown, and the genuine America, the America of New Mexico, will start on its course again. This is an interregnum.

JUST BACK FROM THE SNAKE DANCE

One wonders what one went for—what all those people went for. The Hopi country is hideous—a clayey pale-grey desert with death-grey mesas, sticking up like broken pieces of ancient, dry, grey bread. And the hell of a bumpy trail, for forty miles. Yet car after car lurched and hobbled and ducked across the dismalness, on Sunday afternoon.

The Hopi country is some forty miles across, and three stale mesas jut up in its desert. The dance was on the last mesa, and on the furthest brim of the last mesa, in Hotevilla. The various Hopi villages are like broken edges of bread crust, utterly grey and arid, on the top of these mesas: and so you pass them: first Walpi: then unseen Chimopova: then Oraibi, on the last mesa: and beyond Oraibi, on the same mesa, but on a still higher level of grey rag-rock, and away at the western brim, is Hotevilla.

The pueblos of little grey houses are largely in ruin, dry, raggy bits of disheartening ruin. One wonders what dire necessity or what Cain-like stubbornness drove the Hopis to these dismal grey heights and extremities! Anyhow once they got there there was evidently no going back. But the pueblos are mostly ruin. And even then, very small.

Hotevilla is a scrap of a place with a plaza no bigger than a fair-sized back yard: and the chief house on the square, a ruin. But into this plaza finally three thousand onlookers piled. A mile from the village was improvised the official camping ground, like a corral with hundreds of black motor cars. Across the death-grey desert, bump and lurch, came strings of more black cars, like a funeral cortège. Till everybody had come—about three thousand bodies.

And all these bodies piled in the little oblong plaza, on the roofs, in the ruined windows, and thick around on the sandy floor, under the old walls: a great crowd. There were Americans of all sorts, wild west and tame west, American women in pants, an extraordinary assortment of female breeches: and at least two women in skirts, relics of the last era. There were Navajo women in full skirts and velvet bodices: there were Hopi women in bright shawls: a negress in a low-cut black blouse and a black sailor hat: various half breeds: and all the men to match. The ruined house had two wide square window holes; in the one was posed an apparently naked young lady with a little black hat on. She laid her naked handsome arm like a white anaconda along the sill, and posed as Queen Semiramis seated and waiting! Behind her, the heads of various Americans to match: perhaps movie people. In the next window hole, a poppy-show of Indian women in coloured shawls and glistening long black fringe above their conventionally demure eyes—Two windows to the west!

And what had they all come to see?—come so far, over so weary a way, to camp uncomfortably? To see a little bit of a snake dance in a plaza no bigger than a back-yard? Eight grey-daubed antelope priests— (so-called)—and a dozen black-daubed snake-priests (so-called). No drums, no pageantry. A hollow muttering. And then one of the snake priests hopping slowly round with the neck of a pale, bird-like snake nipped between his teeth, while six elder priests dusted the six younger, snake-adorned priests with prayer feathers, on the shoulders, hopping behind like a children's game. Like a children's game—Old Roger is dead and is low in his grave! After a few little rounds, the man set his snake on the sand, and away it steered, towards the massed spectators sitting around. And after it came a snake priest with a snake stick, picked it up with a flourish from the shrinking crowd, and handed it to an antelope priest in the background. The six young men renewed their snake as the eagle his youth—sometimes the youngest, a boy of fourteen or so, had a rattle snake ornamentally drooping from his teeth, sometimes a racer, a thin whip snake, sometimes a heavier bull-snake, which wrapped its long end round his knee like a garter—till he calmly undid it. More snakes, till the priests at the back had little armfuls, like armfuls of silk stockings that they were going to hang on the line to dry.

When all the snakes had had their little ride in a man's mouth, and had made their little excursion towards the crowd, they were all gathered, like a real lot of wet silk stockings—say forty—or thirty— and let to wriggle all together for a minute in meal, corn-meal, that the women of the pueblo had laid down on the sand of the plaza. Then hey—presto! —they were snatched up like fallen washing, and the two priests ran away with them westward, down the mesa, to set them free among the rocks, at the snake-shrine (so-called).

And it was over. Navajos began to ride to the sunset, black motor cars began to scuttle with their backs to the light. It was over.

And what had we come to see, all of us? Men with snakes in their mouths, like a circus? Nice clean snakes, all washed and cold-creamed by the priests (so-called). Like wet, pale silk stockings. Snakes with little, naïve, bird-like heads, that bit nobody, but looked more harmless than doves? And funny men with blackened faces and whitened jaws, like a corpse band?

A show? But it was a tiny little show, for all that distance. Just a show! The South west is the great playground of the white American. The desert isn't good for anything else. But it does make a fine national playground. And the Indian, with his long hair and his bits of pottery and blankets and clumsy home-made trinkets, he's a wonderful live toy to play with. More fun than keeping rabbits, and just as harmless. Wonderful, really, hopping round with a snake in his mouth. Lots of fun! Oh, the wild west is lots of fun: the Land of Enchantment. Like being right inside the circus-ring: lots of sand, and painted savages jabbering, and snakes and all that. Come on, boys! Lots of fun!

The great South-west, the natural circus-ground. Come on, boys; we've every bit as much right to it as anybody else. Lots of fun!

As for the hopping Indian with his queer muttering gibberish and his dangling snake—Why, he sure is cute! He says he's dancing to make his corn grow. What price irrigation, Jimmy? He says the snakes are emissaries to his rain god, to tell him to send rain to the corn on the Hopi Reservation, so the Hopis will have lots of corn meal. What price a spell of work on the railway, Jimmy? Get all the corn-meal you want with two dollars a day, anyhow.— But oh, dry up! Let every man have his own religion. And if there wasn't any snake dance we couldn't come to see it. Miss lots of fun. Good old Hopi, he sure is cute with a rattler between his teeth. You sure should see him, boy. If you don't, you miss a lot.

REFLECTIONS ON THE DEATH OF A PORCUPINE
& OTHER ESSAYS

LOVE

Love is the happiness of the world. But happiness is not the whole of fulfilment.

Love is a coming together. But there can be no coming together without an equivalent going asunder. In love, all things unite in a oneness of joy and praise. But they could not unite unless they were previously apart. And having united in a whole circle of unity, they can go no further in love. The motion of love, like a tide, is fulfilled in this instance; there must be an ebb.

So that the coming together depends on the going apart; the systole depends on the diastole; the flow depends upon the ebb. There can never be love universal and unbroken. The sea can never rise to high tide over all the globe at once. The undisputed reign of love can never be.

Because love is strictly a travelling. "It is better to travel than to arrive somebody has said. This is the essence of unbelief. It is a belief in absolute love, when love is by nature relative. It is a belief in the means but not in the end. It is strictly a belief in force, for love is a unifying force.

How shall we believe in force? Force is instrumental and functional; it is neither a beginning nor an end. We travel in order to arrive; we do not travel in order to travel. At least, such travelling is mere futility. We travel in order to arrive.

Sad love is a travelling, a motion, a speed of coming together. Love is the force of creation. But all force, spiritual or physical, has its polarity, its positive and its negative. All things that fall, fall by gravitation to the earth. But has not the earth, in the opposite of gravitation, cast off the moon and held her at bay in our heavens during all the æons of time?

So with love. Love is the hastening gravitation of spirit towards spirit and body towards body, in the joy of creation. But if all be united in one bond of love, then there is no more love. The triumph of love is the end of love. And therefore, for those who are in love with love, to travel is better than to arrive. For in arriving one passes beyond love, or, rather, one encompasses love in a new transcendence. To arrive is the supreme joy after all our travelling.

The bond of love! What worse bondage can we conceive than the bond of love? It is an attempt to wall in the high tide; it is a will to arrest the spring, never to let May dissolve into June, never to let the hawthorn petal fall for the berrying.

This has been our idea of immortality, this infinite of love, love universal and triumphant. And what is this but a prison and a bondage? What is eternity but the endless passage of time? What is infinity but an endless progression through space? Eternity, infinity, our great ideas of rest and arrival, what are they but ideas of endless travelling? Eternity is the endless travelling through time, infinity is the endless travelling through space; no more, however we try to argue it. And immortality, what is it, in our idea, but an endless continuing in the same sort. A continuing, a living for ever, a lasting and enduring for ever—what is this but travelling? An assumption into heaven, a becoming one with God—what is this, likewise, but a projection into the infinite? And how is the infinite an arrival? The infinite is no arrival. When we come to find exactly what we mean by God, by the infinite, by our immortality, it is a meaning of endless continuing in the same line and in the same sort, endless travelling in one direction. This is infinity, endless travelling in one direction. And the God of Love is our idea of the progression *ad infinitum* of the force of love. Infinity is no arrival. It is as much a *cul de sac as* is the bottomless pit. And what is the infinity of love but a *cul de sac* or a bottomless pit?

Love is a progression towards one goal. Therefore it is a progression away from the opposite goal. Love travels heavenwards. What then does love depart from? Hellwards, what is there? Love is at last a positive infinite. What then is the negative infinite? Positive and negative infinite are the same, since there is only one infinite. How then will it matter whether we travel heavenwards, *ad infinitum,* or in the opposite direction, hellwards, to infinity? Since the infinity obtained is the same in either case; the infinite of pure homogeneity, which is nothingness, or everythingness, it does not matter which.

Infinity, the infinite, is no goal. It is a *cul de sac,* or, in another sense, it is the bottomless pit. To fall down the bottomless pit is to travel for ever. And a pleasant-walled *cul de sac* may be a perfect heaven. But to arrive in a sheltered, paradisal *cul de sac* of peace and unblemished happiness, this will not satisfy us. And to fall for ever down the bottomless pit of progression, this will not do either.

Love is not a goal; it is only a travelling. Likewise death is not a goal; it is a travelling asunder into elemental chaos. And from the elemental chaos all is cast forth again into creation. Therefore death is but a *cul de sac,* a melting-pot.

There is a goal, but the goal is neither love nor death. It is a goal neither infinite nor eternal. It is the realm of calm delight, it is the other-kingdom of bliss. We are like a rose, which is a miracle of pure centrality, pure absolved equilibrium. Balanced in perfection in the midst of time and space, the rose is perfect in the realm of perfection, neither temporal nor spatial, but absolved by the quality of perfection pure immanence of absolution.

We are creatures of time and space. But we are like a rose; we accomplish perfection, we arrive in the absolute. We are creatures of time and space. And we are at once creatures of pure transcendence, absolved from time and space, perfected in the realm of the absolute, the other-world of bliss.

And love, love is encompassed and surpassed. Love always has been encompassed and surpassed by the fine lovers. We are like a rose, a perfect arrival.

Love is manifold, it is not of one sort only. There is the love between man and woman, sacred and profane. There is Christian love "thou shalt love thy neighbour as thyself. And there is the love of God. But always love is a joining together.

Only in the conjunction of man and woman has love kept a duality of meaning. Sacred love and profane love, they are opposed and yet are both love. The love between man and woman is the greatest and most complete passion the world will ever see, because it is dual, because it is of two opposing kinds. The love between man and woman is the perfect heart-beat of life, systole, diastole.

Sacred love is selfless, seeking not its own. The lover serves his beloved and seeks perfect communion of oneness with her. But whole love between man and woman is sacred and profane together. Profane love seeks its own. I seek my own in the beloved, I wrestle with her to wrest it from her. We are not clear, we are mixed and mingled. I am in the beloved also, and she is in me. Which should not be, for this is confusion and chaos. Therefore I will gather myself complete and free from the beloved, she shall single herself out in utter contradistinction to me. There is twilight in our souls, neither light nor dark. The light must draw itself together in purity, the dark must stand on the other hand; they must be two complete in opposition, neither one partaking of the other, but each single in its own stead.

We are like a rose. In the pure passion for oneness, in the pure passion for distinctness and separateness, a dual passion of unutterable separation and lovely conjunction of the two, the new configuration takes place, the transcendence, the two in their perfect singleness transported into one surpassing heaven of a rose-blossom.

But the love between a man and a woman, when it is whole, is dual. It is the melting into pure communion, and it is the friction of sheer sensuality, both. In pure communion I become whole in love. And in pure, fierce passion of sensuality I am burned into essentiality, I am driven from the matrix into sheer separate distinction. I become my single self, inviolable and unique, as the gems were perhaps once driven into themselves out of the confusion of earths. The woman and I, we are the confusion of earths. Then in the fire of their extreme sensual love, in the friction of intense, destructive flames, I am destroyed and reduced to essentiality; she is destroyed and reduced to her essential otherness. It is a destructive fire, this profane love. But it is the only fire that will purify us into singleness, fuse us from the chaos into our own unique gem-like separateness of being.

All whole love between man and woman is thus dual, a love which is the motion of melting, fusing together into oneness, and a love which is the intense, frictional, and sensual gratification of being burnt down, burnt apart into separate clarity of being, unthinkable otherness and separateness. But not all love between man and woman is whole. It may be all gentle, the merging into oneness, like St. Francis and St. Clare, or Mary of Bethany and Jesus. There may be no separateness discovered, no singleness won, no unique otherness admitted. This is a half love, what is called sacred love. And this is the love which knows the purest happiness. On the other hand, the love may be all a lovely battle of sensual gratification, the beautiful but deadly counterposing of male against female, as Tristan and Isolde. These are the lovers that top the summit of pride, they go with the grandest banners, they are the gem-like beings, he pure male singled and separated out in superb jewel-like isolation of arrogant manhood, she purely woman, a lily balanced in rocking pride of beauty and perfume of womanhood. This is the profane love, that ends in flamboyant and lacerating tragedy when the two which are so singled out are torn finally apart by death. But if profane love ends in piercing tragedy, none the less the sacred love ends in a poignant yearning and exquisite submissive grief. St. Francis dies and leaves St. Clare to her pure sorrow.

There must be two in one, always two in one—the sweet love of communion and the fierce, proud love of sensual fulfilment, both together in one love. And then we are like a rose. We surpass even love, love is encompassed and surpassed. We are two who have a pure conjunction. We are two, isolated like gems in our unthinkable otherness. But the rose contains and transcends us, we are one rose, beyond.

The Christian love, the brotherly love, this is always sacred. I love my neighbour as myself. What then? I am enlarged, I surpass myself, I become whole in mankind. In the whole of perfect humanity I am whole. I am the microcosm, the epitome of the great macrocosm. I speak of the perfectibility of man. Man can be made perfect in love, he can become a creature of love alone, Then humanity shall be one whole of love. This is the perfect future for those who love their neighbours as themselves.

But, alas! however much I may be the microcosm, the exemplar of brotherly love, there is in me this necessity to separate and distinguish myself into gem-like singleness, distinct and apart from all the rest, proud as a lion, isolated as a star. This is a necessity within me. And as this necessity is unfulfilled, it becomes stronger and stronger until it becomes dominant.

Then I shall hate the self that I am, powerfully and profoundly shall I hate this microcosm that I have become, this epitome of mankind. I shall hate myself with madness the more I persist in adhering to my achieved self of brotherly love. Still I shall persist in representing a whole loving humanity, until the unfulfilled passion for singleness drives me into action. Then shall I hate my neighbour as I hate myself. And then, woe betide my neighbour and me! Whom the gods wish to destroy they first make mad. And this is how we become mad, by being impelled into activity by the subconscious reaction against the self we maintain, without ever ceasing to maintain this detested self. We are bewildered, dazed. In the name of brotherly love we rush into stupendous blind activities of brotherly hate. We are made mad by the split, the duality in ourselves. The gods wish to destroy us because we serve them too well. Which is the end of brotherly love, *liberté, fraternité, égalité.* How can there be liberty when I am not free to be other than fraternal and equal? I must be free to be separate and unequal in the finest sense if I am to be free. *Fraternité* and *égalité,* these are tyranny of tyrannies.

There must be brotherly love, a wholeness of humanity. But there must also be pure, separate individuality, separate and proud as a lion or a hawk. There must be both. In the duality lies fulfilment. Man must act in concert with man, creatively and happily. This is greatest happiness. But man must also act separately and distinctly, apart from every other man, single and self-responsible and proud with unquenchable pride, moving for himself without reference to his neighbour. These two movements are opposite, yet they do not negate each other. We have understanding. And if we understand, then we balance perfectly between the two motions, we are single, isolated individuals, we are a great concordant humanity, both, and then the rose of perfection transcends us, the rose of the world which has never yet blossomed, but which will blossom from us when we begin to understand both sides and to live in both directions, freely and without fear, following the inmost desires of our body and spirit, which arrive in us out of the unknown.

Lastly there is the love of God; we become whole with God. But God as we know Him is either infinite love or infinite pride and power, always one or the other, Christ or Jehovah, always one half excluding the other half. Therefore, God is forever jealous. If we love one God, we must hate this one sooner or later, and choose the other. This is the tragedy of religious experience. But the Holy Spirit, the unknowable, is single and perfect for us.

There is that which we cannot love, because it surpasses either love or hate. There is the unknown and the unknowable which propounds all creation. This we cannot love, we can only accept it as a term of our own limitation and ratification. We can only know that from the unknown profound desires enter in upon us, and that the fulfilling of these desires is the fulfilling of creation. We know that the rose comes to blossom. We know that we are incipient with blossom. It is our business to go as we are impelled, with faith and pure spontaneous morality, knowing that the rose blossoms, and taking that knowledge for sufficient.

LIFE

Midmost between the beginning and the end is Man. He is neither the created nor the creator. But he is the quick of creation. He has on one hand the primal unknown from which all creation issues; on the other hand, the whole created universe, even the world of finite spirits. But between the two man is distinct and other; he is creation itself, that which is perfect.

Man is born unfulfilled from chaos, uncreated, incomplete, a baby, a child, a thing immature and inconclusive. It is for him to become fulfilled, to enter at last the state of perfection, to achieve pure and immitigable being, like a star between day and night, disclosing the other world which has no beginning nor end, the otherworld of utterly completed creation, perfect beyond the creator, and conclusive beyond the thing created, living beyond life itself, and deathly beyond death, partaking of both and transcending both.

When he comes into his own, man has being beyond life and beyond death; he is perfect of both. There he comprehends the singing of birds and the silence of the snake.

Yet man cannot create himself, nor can he achieve the finality of a thing created. All his time he hovers in the no-land, hovering till he can enter the otherworld of perfection; he still does not create himself, nor does he arrive at the static finality of a thing created. Why should he, since he has transcended the state of creativity and the state of being created, both?

Midway between the beginning and the end is man, midway between that which creates and that which is created, midway in an otherworld partaking of both, yet transcending.

All the while man is referred back. He cannot create himself. At no moment can man create himself. He can but submit to the Creator, to the primal unknown out of which issues the all. At every moment we issue like a balanced flame from the primal unknown. We are not self-contained nor self-accomplished. At every moment we derive from the unknown.

This is the first and greatest truth of our being. Upon this elemental truth all our knowledge rests. We issue from the primal unknown. Behold my hands and feet, where I end upon the created Universe! But who can see the quick, the well-head, where I have egress from the primordial creativity? Yet at every moment, like a flame which burns balanced upon a wick, do I burn in pure and transcendent equilibrium upon the wick of my soul, balanced and clipped like a flame corporeal between the fecund darkness of the first unknown and the final darkness of the afterlife, wherein is all that is created and finished.

We are balanced like a flame between the two darknesses, the darkness of the beginning and the darkness of the end. We derive from the unknown, and we result into the unknown. But for us the beginning is not the end, for us the two are not one.

It is our business to burn, pure flame, between the two unknowns. We are to be fulfilled in the world of perfection, which is the world of pure creation. We must come into being in the transcendent otherworld of perfection, consummated in life and death both, two in one.

I turn my face which is blind and yet which knows, like a blind man turning to the sun, I turn my face to the unknown, which is the beginning, and like a blind man who lifts his face to the sun I know the sweetness of the influx from the source of creation into me. Blind, for ever blind, yet knowing, I receive the gift, I know myself the ingress of the creative unknown. Like a seed which unknowing receives the sun and is made whole, I open on to the great invisible warmth of primal creativity and begin to be fulfilled.

This is the law. We shall never know what is the beginning. We shall never know how it comes to pass that we have form and being. But we may always know how through the doorways of the spirit and the body enters the vivid unknown, which is made known in us. Who comes, who is that we hear outside in the night? Who knocks, who knocks again? Who is that that unlatches the painful door?

Then behold, there is something new in our midst. We blink our eyes, we cannot see. We lift the lamp of previous understanding, we illuminate the stranger with the light of our established knowledge. Then at last we accept the newcomer, he is enrolled among us.

So is our life. How do we become new? How is it we change and develop? Whence comes the newness, the further being, into us? What is added unto us, and how does it come to pass?

There is an arrival in us from the unknown, from the primal unknown whence all creation issues. Did we call for this arrival, did we summon the new being, did we command the new creation of ourselves, the new fulfilment? We did not, it is not of us. We are not created of ourselves. But from the unknown, from the great darkness of the outside that which is strange and new arrives on our threshold, enters and takes place in us. Not of ourselves, it is not of ourselves, but of the unknown which is the outside.

This is the first and greatest truth of our being and of our existence. How do we come to pass? We do not come to pass of ourselves. Who can say, of myself I will bring forth newness? Not of myself; but of the unknown which has ingress into me.

And how has the unknown ingress into me? The unknown has ingress into me because, whilst I live, I am never sealed and set apart; I am but a flame conducting unknown to unknown, through the bright transition of creation. I do but conduct the unknown of my beginning to the unknown of my end, through the transfiguration of perfect being. What is the unknown of the beginning, and what is the unknown of the end? That I can never answer, save that in my completeness of being the two unknowns are consummated in a oneness, a rose of perfect explanation.

The unknown of my beginning has ingress into me, through the spirit. My spirit is troubled, it is uneasy. Far off it hears the approach of footsteps through the night. Who is coming? Ah, let the newcomer arrive, let the newcomer arrive. In my spirit I am lonely and inert, I wait for the newcomer. My spirit aches with misery, dread of the newcomer. But also there is the tension of expectancy. I expect a visit, I expect a newcomer. For oh, I am conceited and unrefreshed, I am alone and barren. Yet still is my spirit alert and chuckling with subtle expectancy, awaiting the visit. It will come to pass. The stranger will come.

I listen, in my spirit I listen and listen. Many sounds there are from the unknown. And surely those are footsteps? In haste I open the door. But, alas! there is no one there. I must wait in patience, wait and always wait up for the stranger. Not of myself, it cannot happen of myself. With this in mind I check my impatience, I learn to wait and to watch.

And at last, out of all my desire and weariness, the door opens and this is the stranger. Ah, now! ah, joy! There is the new creation in me! Ah, beautiful! Ah, delight of delights! I am come to pass from the unknown, the unknown is added on to me. The sources of joy and strength are filled in me; I rise up to a new achievement of being, a new fulfilment in creation, a new rose of roses, new heavens on earth.

This is the story of our coming to pass. There is no other way. I must have patience in my soul, to stand and wait. Above all, it must be said in my soul that I wait for the unknown, for I cannot avail anything of myself. I wait upon the unknown, and from the unknown comes my new beginning. Not of myself, not of myself, but of my insuperable faith, my waiting. I am like a small house on the edge of the forest. Out of the unknown darkness of the forest, in the eternal night of the beginning, comes the spirit of creation towards me. But I must keep the light shining in the window, or how will the spirit see my house? If my house is in darkness of sleep or fear, the angel will pass it by. Above all, I must have no fear. I must watch and wait. Like a blind man looking for the sun, I must lift my face to the unknown darkness of space and wait until the sun lights on me. It is a question of creative courage. It is no good if I crouch over a coal-fire. This will never bring me to pass.

Once the new has entered into my spirit, from the beginning, I am glad. No one and nothing can make me sorry any more. For I am potential with a new fulfilment, I am enriched with a new incipient perfection. Now no longer do I hover in the doorway listlessly, seeking for something to make up my life. The quota is made up in me, I can begin. It is conceived in me, the invisible rose of fulfilment, which in the end will shine out of the skies of absolution. So long as it is conceived in me, all labour of travail is joy. If I am in bud with the unseen rose of creation, what is labour to me, and what is pain, but pang after pang of new strange joy. My heart is always glad like a star. My heart is a vivid, quivering star which will fan itself slowly out in flakes and gains creation, a rose of roses taking place.

Where do I pay homage, whereunto do I yield myself? To the unknown, only to the unknown, the Holy Ghost. I wait for the beginning, when the great and all-creative unknown shall take notice of me, shall turn to me and inform me. This is my joy and my delight. And again, I turn to the unknown of the end, the darkness which is final, which will gather me into finality.

Do I fear the strange approach of the creative unknown to my door? I fear it only with pain and with unspeakable joy. And do I fear the invisible dark hand of death plucking me into the darkness, gathering me blossom by blossom from the stem of my life, into the unknown of my afterwards? I fear it only in reverence and with strange satisfaction. For this is my final satisfaction, to be gathered blossom by blossom, all my life long, into the finality of the unknown which is my end.

WHISTLING OF BIRDS

The frost held for many weeks, until the birds were dying rapidly. Everywhere in the fields and under the hedges lay the ragged remains of lapwings, starlings, thrushes, redwings, innumerable ragged, bloody cloaks of birds, whence the flesh was eaten by invisible beasts of prey.

Then, quite suddenly, one morning, the change came. The wind went to the south, came off the sea warm and soothing. In the afternoon there were little gleams of sunshine, and the doves began, without interval, slowly and awkwardly to coo. The doves were cooing, though with a laboured sound, as if they were still winter-stunned. Nevertheless, all the afternoon they continued their noise, in the mild air, before the frost had thawed off the road. At evening the wind blew gently, still gathering a bruising quality of frost from the hard earth. Then, in the yellow-gleamy sunset, wild birds began to whistle faintly in the blackthorn thickets of the stream-bottom.

It was startling and almost frightening, after the heavy silence of frost. How could they sing at once, when the ground was thickly strewn with the torn carcases of birds? Yet out of the evening came the uncertain, silvery sounds that made one's soul start alert, almost with fear. How could the little silver bugles sound the rally so swiftly, in the soft air, when the earth was yet bound? Yet the birds continued their whistling, rather dimly and brokenly, but throwing the threads of silver, germinating noise into the air.

It was almost a pain to realize, so swiftly, the new world. *Le monde est mort. Vive le monde!* But the birds omitted even the first part of the announcement, their cry was only a faint, blind, fecund *"vive!"*

There is another world. The winter is gone. There is a new world of spring. The voice of the turtle is heard in the land. But the flesh shrinks from so sudden a transition. Surely the call is premature, while the clods are still frozen, and the ground is littered with the remains of wings! Yet we have no choice. In the bottoms of impenetrable blackthorn, each evening and morning now, out flickers a whistling of birds.

Where does it come from, the song? After so long a cruelty, how can they make it up so quickly? But it bubbles through them, they are like little well-heads, little fountain-heads whence the spring trickles and bubbles forth. It is not of their own doing. In their throats the new life distils itself into sound. It is the rising of the silvery sap of a new summer, gurgling itself forth.

All the time, whilst the earth lay choked and killed and winter-mortified, the deep undersprings were quiet. They only wait for the ponderous encumbrance of the old order to give way, yield in the thaw, and there they are, a silver realm at once. Under the surge of ruin, unmitigated winter, lies the silver potentiality of all blossom. One day the black tide must spend itself and fade back. Then all-suddenly appears the crocus, hovering triumphant in the rear, and we know the order has changed, there is a new régime, sound of a new *Vive! vive!*

It is no use any more to look at the torn remnants of birds that lie exposed. It is no longer any use remembering the sullen thunder of frost and the intolerable pressure of cold upon us. For whether we will or not, they are gone. The choice is not ours. We may remain wintry and destructive for a little longer, if we wish it, but the winter is gone out of us, and wily-nilly our hearts sing a little at sunset.

Even whilst we stare at the ragged horror of birds scattered broadcast, part-eaten, the soft, uneven cooing of the pigeon ripples from the outhouses, and there is a faint silver whistling in the bushes come twilight. No matter, we stand and stare at the torn and unsightly ruins of life, we watch the weary, mutilated columns of winter retreating under our eyes. Yet in our ears are the silver vivid bugles of a new creation advancing on us from behind, we hear the rolling of the soft and happy drums of the doves.

We may not choose the world. We have hardly any choice for ourselves. We follow with our eyes the bloody and horrid line of march of this extreme winter, as it passes away. But we cannot hold back the spring. We cannot make the birds silent, prevent the bubbling of the wood-pigeons. We cannot stay the fine world of silver-fecund creation from gathering itself and taking place upon us. Whether we will or no, the daphne tree will soon be giving off perfume, the lambs dancing on two feet, the celandines will twinkle all over the ground, there will be new heaven and new earth.

For it is in us, as well as without us. Those who can may follow the columns of winter in their retreat from off the earth. Some of us, we have no choice, the spring is within us, the silver fountain begins to bubble under our breast, there is a gladness in spite of ourselves. And on the instant we accept the gladness! The first day of change, out whistles an unusual, interrupted pæan, a fragment that will augment itself imperceptibly. And this in spite of the extreme bitterness of the suffering, in spite of the myriads of torn dead.

Such a long, long winter, and the frost only broke yesterday. Yet it seems already, we cannot remember it. It is strangely remote, like a far-off darkness. It is as unreal as a dream in the night. This is the morning of reality, when we are ourselves. This is natural and real, the glimmering of a new creation that stirs in us and about us. We know there was winter, long, fearful. We know the earth was strangled and mortified, we know the body of life was torn and scattered broadcast. But what is this retrospective knowledge? It is something extraneous to us, extraneous to this that we are now. And what we are, and what, it seems, we always have been, is this quickening lovely silver plasm of pure creativity. All the mortification and tearing, ah yes, it was upon us, encompassing us. It was like a storm or a mist or a falling from a height. It was entangled upon us, like bats in our hair, driving us mad. But it was never really our innermost self. Within, we were always apart, we were this, this limpid fountain of silver, then quiescent, rising and breaking now into the flowering.

It is strange, the utter incompatibility of death with life. Whilst there is death, life is not to be found. It is all death, one overwhelming flood. And then a new tide rises, and it is all life, a fountain of silvery blissfulness. It is one or the other. We are for life, or we are death, one or the other, but never in our essence both at once.

192

Death takes us, and all is a torn redness, passing into darkness. Life rises, and we are faint fine jets of silver running out to blossom. All is incompatible with all. There is the silvery-speckled, incandescent-lovely thrush, whistling pipingly his first song in the blackthorn thicket. How is he to be connected with the bloody, feathered unsightliness of thrush-remnants just outside the bushes? There is no connection. They are not to be referred the one to the other. Where one is, the other is not. In the kingdom of death the silvery song is not. But where there is life, there is no death. No death whatever, only silvery gladness, perfect, the otherworld.

The blackbird cannot stop his song, neither can the pigeon. It takes place in him, even though all his race was yesterday destroyed. He cannot mourn, or be silent, or adhere to the dead. Of the dead he is not, since life has kept him. The dead must bury their dead. Life has now taken hold on him and tossed him into the new ether of a new firmament, where he bursts into song as if he were combustible.

What is the past, those others, now he is tossed clean into the new across the untranslatable difference?

In his song is heard the first brokenness and uncertainty of the transition. The transit from the grip of death into new being is a death from death, in its sheer metempsychosis a dizzy agony. But only for a second, the moment of trajectory, the passage from one state to the other, from the grip of death to the liberty of newness. In a moment he is in the kingdom of wonder, singing at the centre of a new creation.

The bird did not hang back. He did not cling to his death and his dead. There is no death, and the dead have buried their dead. Tossed into the chasm between two worlds, he lifted his wings in dread, and found himself carried on the impulse.

We are lifted to be cast away into the new beginning. Under our hearts the fountain surges, to toss us forth. Who can thwart the impulse that comes upon us? It comes from the unknown upon us, and it behoves us to pass delicately and exquisitely upon the subtle new wind from heaven, conveyed like birds in unreasoning migration from death to life.

THE REALITY OF PEACE

I

The Transference

Peace is the state of fulfilling the deepest desire of the soul. It is the condition of flying within the greatest impulse that enters us from the unknown. Our life becomes a mechanical round, and it is difficult for us to know or to admit the new creative desires that come upon us. We cling tenaciously to the old states, we resist our own fulfilment with a perseverance that would almost stop the sun in its course. But in the end we are overborne. If we cannot cast off the old habitual life, then we bring it down over our heads in a blind frenzy. Once the temple becomes our prison, we drag at the pillars till the roof falls crashing down on top of us and we are obliterated.

There is a great systole diastole of the universe. It has no why or wherefore, no aim or purpose. At all times it *is,* like the beating of the everlasting heart. What it is, is forever beyond saying. It is unto itself. We only know that the end is the heaven on earth, like the wild rose in blossom.

We are like the blood that travels. We are like the shuttle that flies from never to forever, from forever back to never. We are the subject of the eternal systole diastole. We fly according to the perfect impulse, and we have peace. We resist, and we have the gnawing misery of nullification which we have known previously.

Who can choose beforehand what the world shall be? All law, all knowledge holds good for that which already exists in the created world. But there is no law, no knowledge of the unknown which is to take place. We cannot know, we cannot declare beforehand. We can only come at length to that perfect state of understanding, of acquiescence, when we sleep upon the living drift of the unknown, when we are given to the direction of creation, when we fly like a shuttle that flies from hand to hand in a line across the loom. The pattern is woven of us without our foreknowing, but not without our perfect unison of acquiescence.

What is will, divorced from the impulse of the unknown? What can we achieve by this insulated self-will? Who can take his way into the unknown by will? We are driven. Subtly and beautifully, we are impelled. It is our peace and bliss to follow the rarest prompting. We sleep upon the impulse; we lapse on the strange incoming tide, which rises now where no tide ever rose; we are conveyed to the new ends. And this is peace when we sleep upon the perfect impulse in the spirit. This is peace even whilst we run the gauntlet of destruction. Still we sleep in peace upon the pure impulse.

When we have become very still, when there is an inner silence as complete as death, then, as in the grave, we hear the rare, superfine whispering of the new direction; the intelligence comes. After the pain of being destroyed in all our old securities that we used to call peace, after the pain and death of our destruction in the old life comes the inward suggestion of fulfilment in the new.

This is peace like a river. This is peace like a river to flow upon the tide of the creative direction, towards an end we know nothing of, but which only fills us with bliss of confidence. Our will is a rudder that steers us and keeps us faithfully adjusted to the current. Our will is the strength that throws itself upon the tiller when we are caught by a wrong current. We steer by the delicacy of adjusted understanding, and our will is the strength that serves us in this. Our will is never tired of adjusting the helm according to our pure understanding. Our will is prompt and ready to shove off from any obstruction, to overcome any impediment. We steer with the subtlety of understanding, and the strength of our will sees us through.

But all the while our greatest effort and our supreme aim is to adjust ourselves to the river that carries us, so that we may be carried safely to the end, neither wrecked nor stranded nor clogged in weeds. All the while we are but given to the stream, we are borne upon the surpassing impulse which has our end in view beyond us. None of us know the way. The way is given on the way.

There is a sacrifice demanded—only one, an old sacrifice that was demanded of the first man, and will be demanded of the last. It is demanded of all created life. I must submit my will and my understanding—all I must submit, not to any other will, not to any other understanding, not to anything that is, but to the exquisitest suggestion from the unknown that comes upon me. This I must attend to and submit to. It is not me, it is upon me.

There is no visible security; pure faith is the only security. There is no given way; there will never be any given way. We have no foreknowledge, no security of chart and regulation; there is no pole-star save only pure faith.

We must give up our assurance, our conceit of final knowledge, our vanity of charted right and wrong. We must give these up for ever. We cannot map out the way. We shall never be able to map out the way to the new. All our maps, all our charts, all our right and wrong is only record from the past. But for the new there is a new and forever incalculable element.

We must give ourselves and be given, not to anything that has been, but to the river of peace that bears us. We must abide by the able impulse of creation; we must sleep in faith. It will seem to us we are nowhere. We shall be afraid of anarchy and confusion. But, in fact, there is no anarchy so horrid as the anarchy of fixed law, which is mechanism.

We must be given in faith, like sleep. We must lapse upon a current that carries us like repose, and extinguishes in repose our self-insistence and self-will. It will seem to us we are nothing when we are no longer actuated by the stress of self-will. It will seem we have no progression, nothing progressive happens. Yet if we look, we shall see the banks of the old slipping noiselessly by; we shall see a new world unfolding round us. It is pure adventure, most beautiful.

But first it needs this act of courage: that we yield up our will to the unknown, that we deliver our course to the current of the invisible. With what rigid, cruel insistence we clutch the control of our lives; with what a morbid frenzy we try to force our conclusions; with what madness of ghastly persistence we break ourselves under our own will! We think to work everything out mathematically and mechanically, forgetting that peace far transcends mathematics and mechanics.

There is a far sublimer courage than the courage of the indomitable will. It is not the courage of the man smiling contemptuously in the face of death that will save us all from death. It is the courage which yields itself to the perfectest suggestion from within. When a man yields himself implicitly to the suggestion which transcends him, when he accepts gently and honourably his own creative fate, he is beautiful and beyond aspersion.

In self-assertive courage a man may smile serenely amid the most acute pains of death, like a Red Indian of America. He may perform acts of stupendous heroism. But this is the courage of death. The strength to die bravely is not enough.

Where has there been on earth a finer courage of death and endurance than in the Red Indian of America? And where has there been more complete absence of the courage of life? Has not this super-brave savage maintained himself in the conceit and strength of his own will since time began, as it seems? He has held himself aloof from all pure change; he has kept his will intact and insulated from life till he is an automaton—mad, living only in the acute inward agony of a negated impulse of creation. His living spirit is crushed down from him, confined within bonds of an unbreakable will, as the feet of a Chinese woman are bound up and clinched in torment. He only knows that he lives by the piercing of anguish and the thrill of peril. He needs the sharp sensation of peril; he needs the progression through danger and the interchange of mortal hate; he needs the outward torture to correspond with the inward torment of the restricted spirit. For that which happens at the quick of a man's life will finally have its full expression in his body. And the Red Indian finds relief in the final tortures of death, for these correspond at last with the inward agony of the cramped spirit; he is released at last to the pure and sacred readjustment of death.

He has all the fearful courage of death. He has all the repulsive dignity of a static, indomitable will. He has all the noble, sensational beauty of arrestedness, the splendour of insulated changelessness, the pride of static resistance to every impulse of mobile, delicate life. And what is the end? He is benumbed against all life, therefore he needs torture to penetrate him with vital sensation. He is cut off from growth, therefore he finds his fulfilment in the slow and mortal anguish of destruction. He knows no consummation of peace, but falls at last in the great conclusion of death.

Having all the resultant courage of negation, he has failed in the great crisis of life. He had not the courage to yield himself to the unknown that should make him new and vivid, to yield himself, deliberately, in faith. Does any story of martyrdom affect us like the story of the conversion of Paul? In an age of barrenness, where people glibly talk of epilepsy on the road to Damascus, we shy off from the history, we hold back from realising what is told. We dare not know. We dare to gloat on the crucifixion, but we dare not face the mortal fact of the conversion from the accepted world, to the new world which was not yet conceived, that took place in the soul of St. Paul on the road to Damascus.

It is a passage through a crisis greater than death or martyrdom. It is the passage from the old way of death to the new way of creation. It is a transition out of assurance into peace. It is a change of state from comprehension to faith. It is a submission and allegiance given to the new which approaches us, in place of defiance and self-insistence, insistence on the known, that which lies static and external.

Sappho leaped off into the sea of death? But this is easy. Who dares leap off from the old world into the inception of the new? Who dares give himself to the tide of living peace? Many have gone in the tide of death. Who dares leap into the tide of new life? Who dares to perish from the old static entity, lend himself to the unresolved wonder? Who dares have done with his old self? Who dares have done with himself, and with all the rest of the old-established world; who dares have done with his own righteousness; who dares have done with humanity? It is time to have done with all these, and be given to the unknown which will come to pass.

It is the only way. There is this supreme act of courage demanded from every man who would move in a world of life. Empedocles ostentatiously leaps into the crater of the volcano? But a living man must leap away from himself into the much more awful fires of creation. Empedocles knew well enough where he was going when he leaped into Etna. He was only leaping hastily into death, where he would have to go whether or not. He merely forestalled himself a little. For we must all die. But we need not live. We have always the door of death in front of us, and, howsoever our track winds and travels, it comes to that door at last. We *must* die within an allotted term; there is not the least atom of choice allowed us in this.

But we are not compelled to live. We are only compelled to die. We may refuse to live; we may refuse to pass into the unknown of life; we may deny ourselves to life altogether. So much choice we have. There is so much free will that we are perfectly free to forestall our date of death, and perfectly free to postpone our date of life as long as we like.

We must *choose* life, for life will never compel us. Sometimes we have even no choice; we have no alternative to death. Then, again, life is with us; there is the soft impulse of peace. But this we may deny emphatically and to the end, and it is denied of us. We may reject life completely and finally from ourselves. Unless we submit our will to the flooding of life, there is no life in us.

If a man have no alternative but death, death is his honour and his fulfilment. If he is wintry in discontent and resistance, then winter is his portion and his truth. Why should he be cajoled or bullied into a declaration for life? Let him declare for death with a whole heart. Let every man search in his own soul to find there the quick suggestion, whether his soul be quick for life or quick for death. Then let him act as he finds it. For the greatest of all misery is a lie; and if a man belong to the line of obstinate death, he has at least the satisfaction of pursuing this line simply. But we will not call this peace. There is all the world of difference between the sharp, drug-delicious satisfaction of resignation and self-gratifying humility and the true freedom of peace. Peace is when I accept life; when I accept death I have the hopeless equivalent of peace, which is quiescence and resignation.

Life does not break the self-insistent will. But death does. Death compels us and leaves us without choice. And all compulsion whatsoever is death, and nothing but death.

To life we must cede our will, acquiesce and be at one with it, or we stand alone, we are excluded, we are exempt from living. The service of life is voluntary.

This fact of conversion, which has seemed, in its connection with religion, to smack of unreality, to be, like the miracles, not quite creditable, even if demonstrable, is as a matter of fact essentially natural and our highest credit. We know what it is now to live in a confessed state of death. We know what it is to prosecute death with all our strength of soul and body. We know what it is to be fulfilled with the activity of death. We have given ourselves body and soul, altogether, to the making of all the engines and contrivances and inventions of death. We have wanted to deal death, ever more and more death. We have wanted to compel every man whatsoever to the activity of death. We have wanted to envelop the world in a vast unison of death, to let nothing escape. We have been filled with a frenzy of compulsion; our insistent will has co-ordinated into a monstrous engine of compulsion and death.

So now our fundamental being has come out. True, our banner is ostensible peace. But let us not degrade ourselves with lying. We were filled with the might of death. And this has been gathering in us for a hundred years. Our strength of death passion has accumulated from our fathers; it has grown stronger and stronger from generation to generation. And in us it is confessed.

Therefore, we are in a position to understand the "phenomenon" of conversion. It is very simple. Let every man look into his own heart and see what is fundamental there. Is there a gnawing and unappeasable discontent? Is there a secret desire that there shall be new strife? Is there a prophecy that the worst is yet to come; is there a subtle thrill in the anticipation of a fearful tearing of the body of life at home, here, between the classes of men in England; a great darkness coming over England; the sound of a great rending of destruction? Is there a desire to partake in this rending, either on one side or the other? Is there a longing to see the masses rise up and make an end of the wrong old order? Is there a will to circumvent these masses and subject them to superior wisdom? Shall we govern them for their own good, strongly?

It does not matter on which side the desire stands, it is the desire of death. If we prophesy a triumph of the people over their degenerate rulers, still we prophesy from the inspiration of death. If we cry out in the name of the subjected herds of mankind against iniquitous tyranny, still we are purely deathly. If we talk of the wise controlling the unwise, this is the same death.

For all strife between things old is pure death. The very division of mankind into two halves, the humble and the proud, is death. Unless we pull off the old badges and become ourselves, single and new, we are divided unto death. It helps nothing whether we are on the side of the proud or the humble.

But if, in our heart of hearts, we can find one spark of happiness that is absolved from strife, then we are converted to the new life the moment we accept this spark as the treasure of our being. This is conversion. If there is a quick, new desire to have new heaven and earth, and if we are given triumphantly to this desire, if we know that it will be fulfilled of us, finally and without fail, we are converted. If we will have a new creation on earth, if our souls are chafing to make a beginning, if our fingers are itching to start the new work of building up a new world, a whole new world with a new open sky above us, then we are transported across the unthinkable chasm, from the old dead way to the beginning of all that is to be.

II

The beginning of spring lies in the awakening from winter. For us, to understand is to overcome. We have a winter of death, of destruction, sensationalism of going asunder, the wintry glory of tragical experience to surmount and surpass. Thrusting through these things with the understanding, we come forth in first-flowers of our spring with pale and icy blossoms, like bulb-flowers, the pure understanding of death. When we know the death in ourselves we are merging into the new epoch. For whilst we are in the full flux of death, we can find no bottom of resistance from which to understand. When at last life stands under us we can know what the flood is, in which we are immersed.

That which is understood by man is surpassed by man. When we understand our extreme being in death, we have surpassed into a new being. Many bitter and fearsome things there are for us to know, that we may go beyond them, they have no power over us any more.

Understanding, however, does not belong to every man, is not incumbent on every man. But it is vital that some men understand, that some few go through this final pain and relief of knowledge. For the rest, they have only to know peace when it is given them. But for the few there is the bitter necessity to understand the death that has been, so that we may pass quite clear of it.

The anguish of this knowledge, the knowledge of what we ourselves, we righteous ones, have been and are within the flux of death, is a death in itself. It is the death of our established belief in ourselves, it is the end of our current self-esteem. Those who live in the mind must also perish in the mind. The mindless are spared this.

We are not only creatures of light and virtue. We are also alive in corruption and death. It is necessary to balance the dark against the light if we are ever going to be free. We must know that we, ourselves, are the living stream of seething corruption, this also, all the while, as well as the bright river of life. We must recover our balance to be free. From our bodies comes the issue of corruption as well as the issue of creation. We must have our being in both, our knowledge must consist in both. The veils of the old temple must be rent, for they are but screens to hide from us our own being in corruption.

It is our self-knowledge that must be torn across before we are whole. The man I know myself to be must be destroyed before the true man I am can exist. The old man in me must die and be put away.

Either we can and will understand the other thing that we are, the flux of darkness and lively decomposition, and so become free and whole, or we fight shy of this half of ourselves, as man has always fought shy of it, and gone under the burden of secret shame and self-abhorrence. For the tide of our own corruption is rising higher, and unless we adjust ourselves, unless we come out of our veiled temples, and see and know, and take the tide as it comes, ride upon it and so escape it, we are lost.

Within our bowels flows the slow stream of corruption, to the issue of corruption. This is one direction. Within our veins flows the stream of life, towards the issue of pure creation. This is the other direction. We are of both. We are the watershed from which flow the dark rivers of hell on the one hand, and the shimmering rivers of heaven on the other.

If we are ashamed, instead of covering the shame with a veil, let us accept that thing which makes us ashamed, understand it and be at one with it. If we shrink from some sickening issue of ourselves, of recoiling and rising above ourselves, let us go down into ourselves, enter the hell of corruption and putrescence, and rise not fouled, but fulfilled and free. If there is a loathsome thought or suggestion, let us not despatch it instantly with impertinent righteousness, let us admit it with simplicity, let us accept it, be responsible for it. It is no good casting out devils. They belong to us, we must accept them and be at peace with them. For they are of us. We are angels and we are devils, both, in our own proper person. But we are more even than this. We are whole beings, gifted with understanding. A full, undiminished being is complete beyond the angels and the devils.

This is the condition of freedom: that in the understanding I fear nothing. In the body I fear pain, in love I fear hate, in death I fear life. But in the   understanding I fear neither love nor hate nor death nor pain nor abhorrence. I am brave even against abhorrence; even the abhorrent I will understand and be at peace with. Not by exclusion, but by incorporation and unison. There is no hope in exclusion. For whatsoever limbo we cast our devils into will receive us ourselves at last. W   e shall fall into the cesspool of our own abhorrence.

If there is a serpent of secret and shameful desire in my soul, let me not beat it out of my consciousness with sticks. It will lie beyond, in the marsh of the so-called subconsciousness, where I cannot follow it with my sticks. Let me bring it to the fire to see what it is. For a serpent is a thing created. It has its own *raison d'être.* In its own being it has beauty and reality. Even my horror is a tribute to its reality. And I must admit the genuineness of my horror, accept it, and not exclude it from my understanding.

There is nothing on earth to be ashamed of, nor under the earth, except only the craven veils we hang up to save our appearances. Pull down the veils and understand everything, each man in his own self-responsible soul. Then we are free.

Who made us a judge of the things that be? Who says that the water-lily shall rock on the still pool, but the snake shall not hiss in the festering marshy border? I must humble myself before the abhorred serpent and give him his dues as he lifts his flattened head from the secret grass of my soul. Can I exterminate what is created? Not while the condition of its creation lasts. There is no killing the serpent so long as his principle endures. And his principle moves slowly in my belly; I must disembowel myself to get rid of him. "If thine eye offend thee, pluck it out." But the offence is not in the eye, but in the principle it perceives. And howsoever I may pluck out my eyes, I cannot pluck a principle from the created universe. To this I must submit. And I must adjust myself to that which offends me, I must make my peace with it, and cease, in my delicate understanding, to be offended. Maybe the serpent of my abhorrence nests in my very heart. If so, I can but in honour say to him, "Serpent, serpent, thou art at home." Then I shall know that my heart is a marsh. But maybe my understanding will drain the swampy place, and the serpent will evaporate as his condition evaporates. That is as it is. While there is a marsh, the serpent has his holy ground.

I must make my peace with the serpent of abhorrence that is within me. I must own my most secret shame and my most secret shameful desire. I must say, "Shame, thou art me, I am thee. Let us understand each other and be at peace." Who am I that I should hold myself above my last or worst desire? My desires are me, they are the beginning of me, my stem and branch and root. To assume a better angel is an impertinence. Did I create myself? According to the maximum of my desire is my flower and my blossoming. This is beyond my will for ever. I can only learn to acquiesce.

And there is in me the great desire of creation and the great desire of dissolution. Perhaps these two are pure equivalents. Perhaps the decay of autumn purely balances the putting forth of spring. Certainly the two are necessary each to the other; they are the systole diastole of the physical universe. But the initial force is the force of spring, as is evident. The undoing of autumn can only follow the putting forth of spring. So that creation is primal and original, corruption is only a consequence. Nevertheless, it is the inevitable consequence, as inevitable as that water flows downhill.

There is in me the desire of creation and the desire of dissolution. Shall I deny either? Then neither is fulfilled. If there is no autumn and winter of corruption, there is no spring and summer. All the time I must be dissolved from my old being. The wheat is put together by the pure activity of creation. It is the bread of pure creation I eat in the body. The fire of creation from out of the wheat passes into my blood, and what was put together in the pure grain now comes asunder, the fire mounts up into my blood, the watery mould washes back down my belly to the underearth. These are the two motions wherein we have our life. Is either a shame to me? Is it a pride to me that in my blood the fire flickers out of the wheaten bread I have partaken of, flickers up to further and higher creation? Then how shall it be a shame that from my blood exudes the bitter sweat of corruption on the journey back to dissolution; how shall it be a that in my consciousness appear the heavy marsh-flowers of the flux of putrescence, which have their natural roots in the slow stream of decomposition that flows for ever down my bowels?

There is a natural marsh in my belly, and there the snake is naturally at home. Shall he not crawl into my consciousness? Shall I kill him with sticks the moment he lifts his flattened head on my sight? Shall I kill him, or pluck out the eye which sees him? None the less, he will swarm within the marsh.

Then let the serpent of living corruption take his place among us honourably. Come then, brindled abhorrent one, you have your own being and your own righteousness, yes, and your own desirable beauty. Come then, lie down delicately in the sun of my mind, sleep on the bosom of my understanding; I shall know your living weight and be gratified.

But keep to your own ways and your own being. Come in just proportion, there in the grass beneath the bushes where the birds are. For the Lord is the lord of all things, not of some only. And everything shall in its proportion drink its own draught of life. But I, who have the gift of understanding, I must keep most delicately and transcendingly the balance of creation within myself, because now I am taken over into the peace of creation. Most delicately and justly I must bring forth the blossom of my spring and provide for the serpent of my living corruption. But each in its proportion. If I am over into the stream of death I must fling myself into the business of dissolution, and the serpent must writhe at my right hand, my good familiar. But since it is spring with me, the snake must wreathe his way secretly along the paths that belong to him, and when I see him asleep in the sunshine I shall admire him in his place.

I shall accept all my desires and repudiate none. It will be a sign of bliss in me when I am reconciled with the serpent of my own horror when I am free both from the fascination and the revulsion. For secret fascination is a fearful tyranny. And then my desire of life will encompass my desire of death, and I shall be quite whole, have fulfilment in both. Death will take its place in me, subordinate but not subjected, I shall be fulfilled of corruption within the strength of creation. The serpent will have his own pure place in me, and I shall be free.

For there are ultimately only two desires, the desire of life and the desire of death. Beyond these is pure being, where I am absolved from desire and made perfect. This is when I am like a rose, when I balance for a space in pure adjustment and pure understanding. The timeless quality of *being* is understanding; when I understand fully, flesh and blood and bone, and mind and soul and spirit one rose of unison, then I *am*. Then I am unrelated and perfect. In true understanding I am always perfect and timeless. In my utterance of that which I have understood I am timeless as a jewel.

The rose as it bursts into blossom reveals the absolute world before us. The brindled, slim adder, as she lifts her delicate head attentively in the spring sunshine—for they say she is deaf—suddenly throws open the world of unchanging, pure perfection to our startled breast. In our whole understanding, when sense and spirit and mind are consummated into pure unison, then we are free in the world of the absolute. The lark sings in a heaven of pure understanding, she drops back into a world of duality and change.

And it does not matter whether we understand according to death or according to life; the understanding is a consummating of the two in one, and a transcending into absolution. This is true of tragedy and of psalms of praise and of the Sermon on the Mount. It is true of the serpent and of the dove, of the tiger and the fragile dappled doe. For all things that emerge pure in being from the matrix of chaos are roses of pure understanding; in them death and life are adjusted, darkness is in perfect equilibrium with light. This is the meaning of understanding. This is why the leopard gleams to my eye a blossom of pure significance, whilst a hyæna seems only a clod thrown at me in contumely. The leopard is a piece of understanding uttered in terms of fire, the dove is expressed in gurgling watery sound. But in them both there is that perfect conjunction of sun and dew which makes for absolution and the world beyond worlds. Only the leopard starts from the sun and must for ever quench himself with the living soft fire of the fawn; the dove must fly up to the sun like mist drawn up.

We are all desire and understanding, only these two. And desire is twofold, desire of life and desire of death. All the time we are active in these two great powers, which are for ever contrary and complementary. Except in understanding, and there we are immune and perfect, there the two are one. Yet even understanding is twofold in its appearance. It comes forth as understanding of life or as understanding of death, in strong, glad words like Paul and David, or in pain like Shakespeare.

All active life is either desire of life or desire of death, desire of putting together or desire of putting asunder. We come forth ourselves in terms of fire, like the rose, or in terms of water, like the lily. We wish to say that we are single in our desire for life and creation and putting together. But it is a lie, since we must eat life to live. We must, like the leopard, drink up the lesser life to bring forth our greater. We wish to conquer death. But it is absurd, since only by death do we live, like the leopard. We wish not to die; we wish for life everlasting. But this is mistaken interpretation. What we mean by immortality is this fulfilment of death with life and life with death in us where we are consummated and absolved into heaven, the heaven on earth.

We can never conquer death, that is folly. Death and the great dark flux of undoing, this is the inevitable half. Life feeds death, death feeds life. If life is just one point the stronger in the long run, it is only because death is inevitably the stronger in the short run of each separate existence. They are like the hare and the tortoise.

It is only in understanding that we pass beyond the scope of this duality into perfection, in actual living equipoise of blood and bone and spirit. But our understanding must be dual, it must be death understood and life understood.

We understand death, and in this there is no death. Life has put together all that is put together. Death is the consequent putting asunder. We have been torn to shreds in the hands of death, like Osiris in the myth. But still within us life lay intact like seeds in winter.

That is how we know death, have suffered it and lived. It is now no mystery, finally. Death is understood in us, and thus we transcend it. Henceforward actual death is a fulfilling of our own knowledge.

Nevertheless, we only transcend death by understanding down to the last ebb the great process of death in us. We can never destroy death. We can only transcend it in pure understanding. We can envelop it and contain it. And then we are free.

By standing in the light we see in terms of shadow. We cannot see the light we stand in. So our understanding of death in life is an act of living.

If we live in the mind, we must die in the mind, and in the mind we must understand death. Understanding is not necessarily mental. It is of the senses and the spirit.

But we live also in the mind. And the first great act of living is to encompass death in the understanding. Therefore the first great activity of the living mind is to understand death in the mind. Without this there is no freedom of the mind, there is no life of the mind, since creative life is the attaining a perfect consummation with death. When in my mind there rises the idea of life, then this idea must encompass the idea of death, and this encompassing is the germination of a new epoch of the mind.

III

We long most of all to belong to life. This primal desire, the desire to come into being, the desire to achieve a transcendent state of existence, is all we shall ever know of a *primum mobile.* But it is enough.

And corresponding with this desire for absolute life, immediately consequent is the desire for death. This we will never admit. We cannot admit the desire of death in ourselves even when it is single and dominant. We must still deceive ourselves with the name of life.

This is the root of all confusion, this inability for man to admit, "Now I am single in my desire for destructive death." When it is autumn in the world, the autumn of a human epoch, then the desire for death becomes single and dominant. I want to kill, I want violent sensationalism, I want to break down, I want to put asunder, I want anarchic revolution—it is all the same, the single desire for death.

We long most of all for life and creation. That is the final truth. But not all life belongs to life. Not all life is progressing to a state of transcendent being. For many who are born and live year after year there is no such thing as coming to blossom. Many are saprophyte, living on the dead body of the past. Many are parasite, living on the old and enfeebled body politic; and many, many more are mere impurities. Many, in these days, most human beings, having come into world on the impulse of death, find that the impulse is not enough to carry them into absolution. They reach a maturity of physical life, and then the advance ends. They have not the strength for the further passage into darkness. They are born short, they wash on a slack tide; they will never be flung into the transcendence of the second death. They are spent before they arrive; their life is a slow lapsing out, a slow inward corruption. Their flood is the flood of decomposition and decay; in this they have their being. They are like the large green cabbages that cannot move on into flower. They attain a fatness and magnificence of leaves, then they rot inside. There is not sufficient creative impulse, they lapse into green corpulence. So with the sheep and the pigs of our domestic life. They frisk into life as if they would pass on to pure being. But the tide fails them. They grow fat; their only *raison d'être* is to provide food for a really living organism. They have only the moment of first youth, then they lapse gradually into nullity. It is given us to devour them.

So with very many human lives, especially in what is called the periods of decadence. They have mouths and stomachs, and an obscene *will* of their own. Yes,

203

they have also prolific procreative wombs whence they bring forth increasing insufficiency. But the germ of intrinsic creation they have none, neither have they the courage of true death. They never live. They are like the sheep in the fields that have their noses to the ground, and anticipate only the thrill of increase.

These will never understand, neither life nor death. But they will bleat mechanically about life and righteousness, since this is how they can save their appearances. And in their eyes is the furtive tyranny of nullity. They will understand no word of living death, since death encompasses them. If a man understands the living death, he is a man in the quick of creation.

The quick can encompass death, but the living dead are encompassed. Let the dead bury their dead. Let the living dead attend to the dead dead. What has creation to do with them?

The righteousness of the living dead is an abominable nullity. They, the sheep of the meadow, they eat and eat to swell out their living nullity. They are so many, their power is immense, and the negative power of their nullity bleeds us of life as if they were vampires. Thank God for the tigers and the butchers that will free us from the abominable tyranny of these greedy, negative sheep.

It is very natural that every word about death they will decry as evil. For if death be understood, they are found out. They are multitudes of slow, greedy-mouthed decay.

There are the isolated heroes of passionate and beautiful death, Tristan, Achilles, Napoleon. These are the royal lions and tigers of our life. There are many wonderful initiators into the death for re-birth, like Christ and St. Paul and St. Francis. But there is a ghastly multitude of obscene nullity, flocks of hideous sheep with blind mouths and still blinder crying, and hideous cowards' eye of tyranny for the sake of their own bloated nothingness.

These are the enemy and the abomination. And they are so many we shall with difficulty save ourselves from them. Indeed, the word humanity has come to mean only this obscene flock of blind mouths and blinder bleating, and most hideous cowards' tyranny of negation. Save us, oh, holy death; carry us beyond them, oh, holy life of creation; for how shall we save ourselves against such ubiquitous multitudes of living dead? It needs a faith in that which has created all creation, and will therefore never fall before the blind mouth of nullity.

The sheep, the hideous myrmidons of sheep, all *will* and belly and prolific womb, they have their own absolution. They have the base absolution of the *I*. A vile entity detaches itself and shuts itself off immune from the flame of creation and from the stream of death likewise. They assert a free will. And this free will is a horny, glassy, insentient covering into which they creep, like some tough bugs, and therein remain active and secure from life and death. So they swarm in insulated completeness, obscene like bugs.

We are quite insulated from life. And we think ourselves quite immune from death. But death, beautiful death searches us out, even in our armour of insulated will. Death is within us, while we tighten our will to keep him out. Death, beautiful clean death, washes slowly within us and carries us away. We have never known life, save, perhaps, for a few moments during childhood. Well may heaven lie about us in our infancy, if our maturity is but the bug-like security of a vast and impervious envelope of insentience, the insentience of the human mass. Heaven lies about us in our consummation of manhood, if we are men. If we are men, we attain to heaven in our achieved manhood, our flowering maturity. But if we are like bugs, our first sight of this good earth may well seem heavenly. For we soon learn not to see. A bug, and a sheep, sees only with its fear and its belly. Its eyes look out in a coward's will not-to-see, a self-righteous vision.

It is not the will of the overweening individual we have to fear today, but the consenting together of a vast host of null ones. It is no Napoleon or Nero, but the innumerable myrmidons of nothingness. It is not the leopard or the hot tiger, but the masses of rank sheep. Shall I be pressed to death, shall I be suffocated under the slow and evil weight of countless long-faced sheep? This is a fate of ignominy indeed. Who compels us to-day? The malignant null sheep. Who overwhelms us? The persistent, purblind, bug-like sheep. It is a horrid death to be suffocated under these fat-smelling ones.

There is an egoism far more ghastly than that of the tyrannous individual. It is the egoism of the flock. What if a tiger pull me down? It is a straight death. But what if the flock which counts me part of itself compress me and squeeze me with slow malice to death? It cannot be, it shall not be. I cry to the spirit of life, I cry to the spirit of death to save me. I *must* be saved from the vast and obscene self-conceit which is the ruling force of the world that envelops me.

The tiger is sufficient unto himself, a law unto himself. Even the grisly condor sits isolated on the peak. It is the will of the flock that is the obscenity of obscenities. Timeless and clinched in stone is the naked head of the vulture. Timeless as rock, the great condor sits inaccessible in the heights. It is the last brink of deathly life, just alive, just dying, not quite static. It has locked its unalterable will forever against life and death. It persists in the flux of unclean death. It leans forever motionless on death. The will is fixed, there shall be no yielding to life, no yielding to death. Yet death gradually steals over the huge obscene birds. Gradually the leaves fall from the rotten branch, the feathers leave naked the too-dead neck of the vulture.

But worse than the fixed and obscene will of the isolated individual is the will of the obscene herd. They cringe, the herd; they shrink their buttocks downward like the hyæna. They are one flock. They are a nauseous herd together, keeping up a steady heat in the whole. They have one temperature, one aim, one will, enveloping them into an obscene oneness, like a mass of insects or sheep or carrion-eaters. What do they want? They want to maintain themselves insulated from life and death. Their will has asserted its own absolution. They are the arrogant immitigable beings who have achieved a secure entity. They are *it*. Nothing can be added to them, nor detracted. Enclosed and complete, they have their completion in the whole herd, they have their wholeness in the whole flock, they have their oneness in their multiplicity. Such are the sheep, such is humanity, an obscene whole which is no whole, only a multiplied nullity. But in their multiplicity they are so strong that they can defy both life and death for a time, existing like weak insects, powerful and horrible because of their countless numbers.

It is in vain to appeal to these ghastly myrmidons. They understand neither the language of life nor the language of death. They are fat and prolific and all-powerful, innumerable. They are in truth nauseous slaves of decay. But now, alas! the slaves have got the upper hand. Nevertheless, it only needs that we go forth with whips, like the old chieftain. Swords will not frighten them, they are too many. At all costs the herd of nullity must be subdued. It is the worst coward. It has triumphed, this slave herd, and its tyranny is the tyranny of a pack of jackals. But it can be frightened back to its place. For its cowardice is as great as its arrogance.

Sweet, beautiful death, come to our help. Break in among the herd, make gaps in its insulated completion. Give us a chance, sweet death, to escape from this herd and gather together against it a few living beings. Purify us with death, O death, cleanse from us the rank stench of the mass, make us clean and single. Release us from the intolerable oneness with a negative humanity. Break for us this foul prison where we suffocate in the reek of the flock of the living dead. Smash, beautiful destructive death, smash the complete will of the hosts of man, the will of the self-absorbed bug. Smash the great obscene unison. Death, assert your strength now, for it is time. They have defied you so long. They have even, in their mad arrogance, begun to deal in death as if it also were subjugated. They thought to use death as they have used life this long time, for their own base end of nullification. Swift death was to serve their end of enclosed, arrogant, self-assertion. Death was to help them maintain themselves *in statu quo,* the benevolent and self-righteous bugs of humanity.

Let there be no humanity, let there be a few men. Sweet death, save us from humanity. Death, noble, unstainable death, smash the glassy rind of humanity, as one would smash the brittle hide of the insulated bug. Smash humanity, and make an end of it. Let there emerge a few pure and single men—men who give themselves to the unknown of life and death and are fulfilled. Make an end of our unholy oneness, O death, give us to our single being. Release me from the debased social body, O death, release me at last; let me be by myself, let me be myself. Let me know other men who are single and not contained by any multiple oneness. Let me find a few men who are distinct and at ease in themselves like stars. Let me derive no more from the body of mankind. Let me derive direct from life or direct from death, according to the impulse that is in me.

IV

The Orbit

It is no good thinking of the living dead. The thought of them is as hurtful as their presence. One cannot fight them. One can only know them as the great static evil which stands against life and against death; and then one skirts them round as if they were a great gap in existence. It is most fearful to fall into that gap. But it is necessary to move in strength round about it, on the actual fields of life and death. We must ignore the static nullity of the living dead, and speak of life and speak of death.

There are two ways and two goals, as it has always been. And so it will always be. Some are set upon one road, the road of death and undoing and some are set upon the other road, the road of creation. And the fulfilment of every man is the following his own separate road to its end. No man can cause another man to have the same goal or the same path as himself. All paths lead either to death or to the heaven on earth, ultimately. But the paths are like the degrees of longitude, the lines of longitude drawn on a geographer's globe— all separate.

Every man has his goal, and this there is no altering. Except by asserting the free will. A man may choose nullity. He may choose to absolve himself from his fate either of life or death. He may oppose his self-will, his free will, between life and his own small entity, or between true death and himself. He may insulate and cut himself off from the systole diastole of life and death, either within his own small horny integument of a will, or within the big horny will of the herd of humanity. Humanity is like a mass of beetles: it is one monstrosity of multiple identical units. It is like the much-vaunted ant-swarms, an insulated oneness made out of myriads of null units, one big self-absorbed nullity. Such is humanity when it is self-absorbed.

And so much free will have we: if life comes to us, like a potentiality of transcendence, we *must* yield our ultimate will to the unknown impulse or remain outside, abide alone, like the corn of wheat, outside the river of life; if death comes to us, the desire to act in strength of death, we *must* have the courage of our desire, and ride deathwards like the knights of the Dark Ages, covered with armour of imperviousness and carrying a spear and a shield by which we are known; we must do this, of our own free will and courage accept the mission of death, or else roll up like a wood-louse enfolded upon our own ego, our own entity, our own self-will, roll up tight on our own free will, and remain outside. So much free will there is. That the free will of humanity can provide a great unified hive of immunity from life and death does not make us any more intrinsically alone from life and death. That we are many millions cut off from life and death does not make us any less cut off. That we are contained within the vast nullity of humanity does not make us other than null. That we are a vast colony of wood-lice, fabricating elaborate social communities like the bees or the wasps or the ants, does not make us any less wood-lice curled up upon nothingness, immune in a vast and multiple negation. It only shows us that the most perfect social systems are probably the most complete nullities, that all relentless organisation is in the end pure negation. Who wants to be like an ant? An ant is a little scavenger, a perfect social system of scavengers.

So much free will there is. There is the free will to choose between submitting the will, and so becoming a spark in a great tendency, or withholding the will, curling up within the will, and so remaining outside, exempt from life or death. That death triumphs in the end,   even then, does not alter the fact that we can live exempt in nullity, exerting our free will to negation.

All we can do is to know in singleness of heart *which* is our road, then take it unflinching to the end, having given ourselves over to the road. For the straight road of death has splendour and brave colour; it is emblazoned with passion and adventure, sparkling of running leopards and steel and wounds, languorous with drenched lilies that glisten cold and narcotic from the corrupt mould of self-sacrifice. And the road of life has the buttercups and wild birds' whistling of real spring, magnificent architecture of created dreams. I tread the subtle way of edged hostility, bursting through the glamorous pageant of blood for the undying glory of our gentle Iseult, some delicate dame, some lily unblemished watered by blood. Or I bring forth an exquisite unknown rose from the tree of my veins, a rose of the living spirit, beyond any woman and beyond any man transcendent. To the null, my rose of glistening transcendence is only a quite small cabbage. When the sheep get into the garden they eat the roses indifferently, but the cabbages with gluttonous absorption. To the null, my pageantry of death is so much mountebank performing; or if I tilt my spear under the negative nose, it is monstrous, inhuman criminality, to be crushed out and stifled, to be put down with an unanimous hideous bleating of righteousness.

There are two roads and a no-road. We will not concern ourselves with the no-road. Who wants to go down a road which is no road? The proprietor may sit at the end of his no-road, like a cabbage on its blind gut of a stalk.

There are two roads, the no-road forgotten. There are two roads. There is hot sunshine leaping down and interpenetrating the earth to blossom. And there is red fire rushing upward on its path to return, in the coming asunder. Down comes the fire from the sun to the seed, splash into the water of the tiny reservoir of life. Up spurts the foam and steam of greenness, a tree, a fountain of roses, a cloud of steamy pear-blossom. Back again goes the fire, leaves shrivel and roses fall, back goes the fire to the sun, away goes the dim water.

So and such is all life and death—apart from the slug-like sheep. There is a swift death, and slow. I set a light to the flowery bush, and the balance overtopples into the road of flame; up rushes the bush on wings of fiery death, away goes the dim water in smoke.

The sheep feed upon the moist, fat grass till they are sodden mounds of scarcely kindled grey mould. Quick, the balance! Quick, the golden lion of wrath, pierce them with flame, drink them up to a superb leonine being. It is the quick way of death. Sheep blaze up to the sun in the golden bonfire of the lion; they trickle to darkness in spilled dark blood. The deer is a trembling flower full of shadow and quenched light, fostered in the immunity of the herd. The self-preservation of the herd is round about the shy doe; she will multiply so that the earth is alive with her offspring—if it were not for the tiger. The tiger like a brand of fire leaps upon her to restore the balance. His too-much heat drinks their coolness, he waters his thirst with the moist fawn. And the flame of him goes up to the sun brindled with tongues of smoke; the deer dissipate like dark mists into the air and the earth. He is a crackling bush burning back to the sun, and burning not away. They are the mists of morning stealing forth and distilling themselves over the sweet earth. So the uneasy balance of life adjusts itself here with the aid of violent death.

Shall we be all like lambs, pellucid flickerings of shadow? Yes, but for the quick mottled leopard and the all-vivid spark of the sharp steel knife. Shall we be all tigers, brands seized in the burning? It is impossible. For even the mother-tiger is quenched with insuperable tenderness when the milk is in her udder; she lies still, and her dreams are frail like fawns. All is somehow adjusted in a strange unstable equilibrium.

We are tigers, we are lambs. Yet are we also neither tigers nor lambs, nor immune sluggish sheep. We are beyond all this, this relative life of uneasy balancing. We are roses of pure and lovely being. This we are, ultimately, beyond all dark and light. Yes, we are tigers, we are lambs, both, in our various hour. We are both these, and more. Because we are both these, because we are lambs, frail and exposed, because we are lions furious and devouring, because we are both, and have the courage to be both, in our separate hour, therefore we transcend both, we pass into a beyond, we are roses of perfect consummation.

Immediately we must be both these, both tigers and lambs, according to the hour and the unknown balance; we must be both, in the immediate life, that ultimately we are roses of unfailing glad peace.

Nevertheless, this is the greatest truth: we are neither lions of pride and strength, nor lambs of love and submission. We are roses of perfect being.

It is very great to be a lion of glory, like David or Alexander. But these only exist on the lives they consume, as a fire needs fuel. It is very beautiful to be the lamb of innocence and humility, like St. Francis and St. Clare? But these only shine so star-like because of the darkness of the night on which they have risen, like the lily of light balances herself upon a fountain of unutterable shadow.

Where is there peace, if I take my being from the balance of pure opposition? If all men were Alexanders, what then? And even if all men followed St. Francis or St. Bernard, the race of mankind would be extinct in a generation. Think, if there were no night, we could not bear it; we should have to die. For the half of us is shadow. And if there were no day, we should dissolve in the darkness and be gone, for we are creatures of light.

Therefore, if I assert myself a creature purely of light, it is in opposition to the darkness which is in me. If I vaunt myself a lion of strength, I am merely set over and balanced against the lambs which are gentle and meek. My form and shape in either case depend on the virtue of resistance, my life and my whole being. I am like of the cells in any organism, the pressure from within and the resistance from without keep me as I am. Either I follow the impulse to power, or I follow the impulse of submission. Whichever it is, I am only half, complemented by my opposite. In a world of petty Alexanders, St. Francis is the star. In a world of sheep the wolf is god. Each saint or wolf, shines by virtue of opposition.

Where, then, is there peace? If I am a lamb with Christ, I exist in a state of pure tension of opposition to the lion of wrath. Am I the lion of pride? It is my fate for ever to fall upon the lamb of meekness and love. Is this peace, or freedom? Is the lamb devoured more free than the lion devouring, or the lion than the lamb? Where is there freedom?

Shall I expect the lion to lie down with the lamb? Shall I expect such a thing? I might as well hope for the earth to cast no shadow, or for burning fire to give no heat. It is no good, these are mere words. When the lion lies down with the lamb he is no lion, and the lamb, lying down with him, is no lamb. They are merely a neutralisation, a nothingness. If I mix fire and water, I get quenched ash. And so if I mix the lion and the lamb. They are both quenched into nothingness.

Where, then, is there peace? The lion will never lie down with the lamb; in all reverence let it be spoken. Whilst the lion is lion, he must fall on the lamb, to devour her. This is his lionhood and his peace, in so far as he has any peace. And the peace of the lamb is to be devourable.

Where, then, is there peace? There is no peace of reconciliation. Let that be accepted for ever. Darkness will never be light, neither will the one ever triumph over the other. Whilst there is darkness, there is light; and when there is an end of darkness, there is an end of light. There are lions, and there are lambs; there are lambs, and thus there are lions predicated. If there are no lions feline, we are the devourers, leonine enough. This is our manhood also, that we devour the lambs. Am I in my conceit more than myself? Not more, but less. I lie down with the lamb and eat grass. What then, I am only the neutralisation of a man.

Where, then, is there peace, which we must seek and pursue, since it is the ultimate condition of our nature? It is peace for the lion when he carries the crushed lamb in his jaws. It is peace for the lamb when she quivers light and irresponsible within the strong, supporting apprehension of the lion. Where is the skipping joyfulness of the lamb when the magnificent, strong responsibility of the lion is removed? The lamb need take no thought; the lion is responsible for death in her world.

But let there be no lion, and no exquisite apprehension in the lamb, what does she degenerate into? A clod of stupid weight. Look in the eyes of your sheep, and see there the pitch of tension which holds her against the golden lion of pride. See in the eyes of the sheep the soul of the sheep, giving with coward's jeering malice the lie to the great mystic truth of death. Look at the doe of the fallow deer as she turns back her eyes in apprehension. What does she ask for, what is her helpless passion? Some unutterable thrill in her waits with unbearable acuteness for the leap of the mottled leopard. Not of the conjunction with the hart is she consummated, but of the exquisite laceration of fear, as the leopard springs upon her loins, and his claws strike in, and he dips his mouth in her. This is the white-hot pitch of her helpless desire. She cannot save herself. Her moment of frenzied fulfilment is the moment when she is torn and scattered beneath the paws of the leopard, like a quenched fire scattered into the darkness. Nothing can alter it. This is the extremity of her desire, this desire for the fearful fury of the brand upon her. She is balanced over at the extreme edge of submission, balanced against the bright beam of the leopard like a shadow against him. The two exist by virtue of juxtaposition, in pure polarity. To destroy the one would be to destroy the other; they would vanish together. And to try to reconcile them is only to bring about their nullification.

Where, then, is there peace if the primary law of all the universe is a law of dual attraction and repulsion, a law of polarity? How does the earth pulse round her orbit save in her overwhelming haste towards the sun and her equivalent rejection back from the sun? She swings in these two, the earth of our habitation, making the systole diastole of our diurnal, of our yearly life. She pulses in a diurnal leap of attraction and repulsion, she travels in a great rhythm of approach and repulse.

Where, then, is there peace? There is peace in that perfect consummation when duality and polarity is transcended into absolution. In lovely, perfect peace the earth rests on her orbit. She has found the pure resultant of gravitation. She goes on for ever in pure rest, she rests for ever in perfect motion, consummated into absolution from a complete duality. Fulfilled from two, she is transported into the perfection of her orbit.

And this is peace. The lion is but a lion, the lamb is but a lamb, half and half separate. But we are the two halves together. I am a lion of pride and wrath, I am a lamb with Christ in meekness. They live in one wide landscape of my soul; the roaring and the tremulous bleating of their different voices sound from the distance like pure music.

It is by rage and strength of the lion, and the white, joyous freedom from strength of the lamb, by the equipoise of these two in perfect conjunction, that I pass from the limitation of a relative world into the glad absolution of the rose. It is when I am drawn by centripetal force into communion with the whole, and when I flee in equivalent centrifugal force away into the splendour of beaming isolation, that these two balance and match each other in mid-space, that suddenly, like a miracle, I find the peace of my orbit. Then I travel neither back nor forth, I hover in the unending delight of a rapid, resultant orbit.

When the darkness of which I am an involved seed, and the light which is involved in me as in a seed, when these two draw from the infinite sources towards me, when they meet and embrace in a perfect kiss and a perfect contest of me, when they foam and mount in their ever-intensifying communion in me until they achieve a resultant absolution of oneness, a rose of being blossoming upon the bush of my mortality, then I have peace.

It is not of love that we are fulfilled, but of love in such intimate equipoise with hate that the transcendence takes place. It is not in pride that we are free, but in pride so perfectly matched by meekness that we are liberated as into blossom. There is a transfiguration, a rose with glimmering petals, upon a bush that knew no more than the dusk of green leaves heretofore. There is a new heaven on the earth, there is a new heaven and new earth, the heaven and earth of the perfect rose.

I am not born fulfilled. The end is not before the beginning. I am born uncreated. I am a mixed handful of life as I issue from the womb. Thenceforth I extricate myself into singleness, the slow-developed singleness of manhood. And then I set out to meet the other, the unknown of womanhood. I give myself to the love that makes me join and fuse towards a universal oneness, I give myself to that makes me detach myself, extricate myself vividly from the other in sharp passion; I am given up into universality of fellowship and communion, I am distinguished in keen resistance and isolation, both so utterly, so exquisitely, that I am and I am not at once; suddenly I lapse out of the duality into a sheer beauty of fulfilment, I am a rose of lovely peace.

CLOUDS

My little nephew, three years of age, stood looking up through the window where the snowy ridge rises outside crested with uneasy thin larch-trees. It was morning, and the sun shone, and no one was thinking of him.

"The sky's *moving*," he said, with real surprise, and a little of that childish wonder which seems to suggest mysteries.

"Yes Jacky-boy. Didn't you know?" replied his aunt.

To which he paid no attention, but silently watched outwards for a few more moments.

"Why does it?" he asked.

"The sky always moves when the wind blows," said his aunt.

"Does it!" he ejaculated faintly, politely, not impressed.

Still he watched upwards, with that queer little mocking look coming on his face, which appears when something is beyond him.

"Why does it move when the wind blows?" he asked, a little against his will. For he has a delicate contempt for grown-up answers, does not take them seriously, and almost cynically prefers to leave things unsolved till he can solve them for himself. Yet, grudgingly, and almost with malice prepense, he invariably asks.

"Because the wind blows the clouds along, Jacky-boy."

He watched the travelling sky with a mocking light in his eyes. "Clouds!" he re-echoed.

"Yes," replied his aunt, bending down to him and pointing up through the window. "Don't you see those big ones, how they're going?"

The child politely looked in the direction indicated.

"Yes," he said.

Then he turned away as if neither clouds, sky, nor aunt existed, and began dragging toys out of a corner. Yet occasionally he stands eyeing the sky. His gods are furnaces, steam-rollers, traction-engines, and railways. He cares nothing for animals, rather dislikes the importunity of their existence. I wonder what he feels when he pertly watches the sky. He looks at it as if it were up against him. Perhaps he resents that it doesn't go by machinery, and have a *driver*. For to him a *driver* is the divinity on earth, a driver of an engine, that is, not a driver of horses. A driver of horses is a nonentity.

On the day of Jacky's discovery that the sky was in motion, a horrible east wind was bearing clouds irregularly over the heavens. The north-east wind had blown for a long time, and brought the snow. For days the sky had been like a level invisible doom, distilling small snow-flakes in hosts. Then it broke occasionally, clouds rolled apart, only to coagulate again. At length, one morning there was an opening out. Brilliant sun shone on the snow, and white crisp clouds sailed high in heaven. After a while, darker, heavier clouds must stagger into view, from out of the eastern heavens, riding low in the blue. Then like dark pack-ice advanced the grey, to blot out the light—and snow once more began to crumble downwards. But towards evening, with strange rapidity, just at sundown the sky decided to empty again, clouds disappearing as if dismissed from heaven, and the western light gushing up into a clear, but rather pallid, ice-seared heaven.

The weather was finer after this. Every morning I opened my eyes to see bright blue sky with high, dainty, happy-looking clouds, like a blue and silvery livery of spring. Although instantly I took regard of the direction of these gay silvery page-boy clouds, yet I was always caught in an illusion. The sky looked like spring, like summer, and I expected a yellow-green earth. To my chagrin I saw the clouds flying out of the deadly east. I *knew* what the real case was. And yet, lying looking, I drifted away again to an unconscious expectation of almond blossom and bird-singing.

It was invariably a shock, a great shock to rise and see the slopes all white with snow, and frozen hard. The illusion of spring was so strong, that the intelligence which the clouds conveyed, of deadly easterliness, could not alter the mood. Only the ghastly sight of white hills did this.

On these brighter days some lovely clouds came down. In the morning they surged high and white, riding very lofty in their domed magnificence, and scarcely glancing at the earth, so radiant, so super-celestial. But as the afternoon wore on, they sank lower, and seemed to darken. They lost their great buoyant form, huddled down, and became aggressive. Some came wedge-shaped. One afternoon, behind the ridge of the bank a great golden-grey prow slid along, sharp, slow, sinister, stealing exactly as a great grey battleship slinks past the land. The prow was the naked fore-part of a dreadnought, but behind came heavy, battling grey piles of cloud. They looked smoky and unhealthy. And yet again they caught a transfusion of gold through their bitter ice-smoke. So they wedged and broke along, till sunset, when suddenly they all left the heavens, made a solid wall or rampart in the western sky, behind which the sun went down, throwing back a fusion of pale light, vivid on the edge of the sombre wall, semi-crystal in the ice-bell of the heavens.

Morning after morning the sky was blue and white. Morning after morning, my first thought was, which way are they coming? And morning after morning they came from the east, the days froze with heavy, ugly freezing, the thawing of the powerful sun was slow. Inch by inch the frost fought the sun, where the shadow fell on the cleared spaces of the high-road; nay, at the shadow's sheer edge the frost was indomitable, though the sun flashed up against it. It was a contest.

How we longed for the east wind to change! How we thought of the west, of Cornwall where the winds blow in wild and full of life. A west wind, we thought, is the loveliest gift of the changing sky.

And then, suddenly, we awoke with a start. In the utter darkness the wind raved extraordinarily, and the western windows were lashed with an unprecedented fury by a flail of icy sleet. The house rattled like a kettle-drum, and hummed like a big bass drum reverberating.

"The wind is west," I said, as we listened astonished.

It was so. In the morning I woke to a clear and cloudless sky, of a richer more jewel-like blue than before. I lay entranced, watching for a sign. Still the sky was morning-new and soft as a violet. But the wind roared till the body was vibrated into sheer storm-unison, and one heard it no more.

I had not long to watch the sky. Helter-skelter came a torn fragment, and then a long scarf of wonderful glistening cloud. With astonishing swiftness a fleecy fringe of brightness streamed in front of a darkness. With a crash the storm was on us again. Perfectly horizontal the snow, sleet and rain shot dense past the south window, the western window was muffled in running icy coagulation. Like an incredibly rapid, level stream the dense sleet passed the house. It lasted some minutes, then stopped, leaving the world stupefied. Broken clouds staggered after the retreating darkness. Then the sky was open, the sun blazed, the wind roared.

This treatment played havoc with the snow. On the opposite slopes that front the sun, the dark real earth began to appear out of the whiteness, to my great joy.

Several times in the day, from the western folding of the flat-topped hills we saw a fleecy darkness approaching, a strange grey veil hanging and swinging and expanding in the valley. With the suddenness of a burst of artillery the sleet struck the house and streamed horizontal past us. It was surprising. But by evening the opposite slope looked like some strange arctic tiger, grey, and banded with ribs of arctic white, where deep snow lay in the long folds.

The storms came on after sunrise, and always about sundown. The clearest part of the day was now from eleven o'clock till tea-time. When the great wind abated, it was flying snowstorms that suddenly leapt out of the west. In the intertwining of the valley was a long-fronted mist, waving and volleying slightly, pale, curious. It always surprised me. Yet I had not been looking at it for a minute before the tiny snowflakes came at the window with a high, curvetting leap, the cloud was on us, sweeping past the window in straight lines.

Today is the last day of March. The cold west wind has quieted somewhat, though it is still icy. But the sun has shone nearly all day long. I descended into the valley, where it is soft and warm, and the bright stream runs swiftly, strangely like a stream in the living underworld of shadow. Spring has come beneath the snow. The leaves of the arum are up, green, folded, on the water-levels. The dogs-mercury draws himself out of the earth, bent over like a hoop, his strings of green flowers all ready. Willow catkins are silver and tiny, hazel catkins a doubtful gold. The twigs of some sallow bushes burn upwards with a lovely inward red. But the heavy snow has made sad havoc, particularly with the thorn-trees, tearing them to pieces.

On the opposite slopes, blue-bells are up: and on one warm, level place, where marjoram-stalks and seed-boxes stand in a tiny red-brown forest, the first primroses glinted. Here and there among the grey turf a flower was out, many many buds showed their yellow sparks. There was almost more flower than plant, for the primrose-leaves hardly appeared, they were so tiny and uncertain and tight-keeping.

On a lovely high level I lay down in the sun. A hawk softly left as I came. It was warm. Just in front of me was an old grey fence of stone, and four wild, storm-mutilated pine-trees. Across the valley, on the home sides, the slope is all snow, chequered with black: it is almost like the speckled silver and black belly of a newt. Above this go the lovely clouds.

They are very beautiful in the sun, the March clouds. I see that there are two worlds. Near, white fleecy radiant shapes hasten at intervals. They traverse just behind the snow-slope, that looks so ghastly and transfixed by comparison, with its small tuft of iron trees, naked, wire-stemmed, as in a classic landscape. Swift and light-footed go the fleecy clouds, some like heaps of fleece, some long, some in light, long cones.

But behind these lies another cloud-world. There massive white clouds radiant with distance, seem to stand still, suspended in their own marvellous atmosphere. Some are immense, like magnificent many-budded sky-flowers, round like the flowers we call snow-balls. There are two like great white lions of the snow-fields, running side by side, with snow-heads lowered and watching, snow-manes curled. There is a tower like a great white bud on the point of unfolding. All seem still, changeless, perfected in form, living in skied that move no more, nor change. For in front of them the radiant, fleecy clouds hurry along, obstructing the view. But the static clouds do change. Very slowly they drive together, pile together like great masses of tangible, sun-rounded snow. So they draw slowly to the east, and draw away also, to the transcendent distance.

As I go home, the sky dims. Near sunset, I see a mist in the knot of the valley. Here comes the snow, away it goes driving in myriad white, horizontal, parallel lines past the window. It ceases, and the sun goes down. But in the west is a wall of uneasy cloud, over which glimmers an evening star, in the sky of dark crystal.

The sky is strange in its motions. I do not believe the things scientists tell us, of hot air and cold air and collisions of trade-winds. Or at least, it is very well, as far as it goes. But it does not reveal to me the fountains of the clouds, nor whence they came, nor how they disperse, nor their strange, inscrutable motions. They have their paths and their awful intentions. They seem like foreigners, wondering upon us and going by.

It seems to me they come, they arrive, not as our exhaled vapours, but blossoming from the unfathomable blue. The blue above seems fathomless, it gives birth to the clouds. It is filled with a great travelling. Out of the blue the sun's rays alight on us, having travelled their great distance. The flame of our burning, we see it enter the blue arches as it sets out on its journey to the heart of the sky, back to the sun. So with the invisible waters. They mount up, without asking permission, and pass beyond our ken. We are told the air above is very cold. But invisible waters seem to have a perfect home in the unspeakable cold. They become as the sky itself, the blue dust of their sheer cold infinitude, the rare ice-ether of the upper heavens triumphs in space, till it crosses the unknown boundary and enters the sphere of the sun. Then like an indrawn breath they enter to refresh the heart of the sun.

Anaximander, or Herakleitos, or some very early Greek said that the sun was fed with water, and shed it forth again, and that the dual travelling went on all the time across the firmament: the travelling and the returning of the invisible waters, and the parallel travelling and return of fire. The invisible waters and the fire, in their central clasp of opposition, centripetal burst forth into perfection, the blazing heart of the sun; and all the travelling of our revolving universe arises from the hastening together of the first waters and fire of the cosmos, in the affinity of their opposition, whilst from their haste asunder we receive the sunbeams and the rain.

Be it as it may, if we lie and look at the clouds, we must believe that they alight on the first terraces of our firmament from out of infinite space. They are not mere vapours tossed up like homing pigeons from the restless sea, merely to return again. When vapours rise, they take wing for the long journey; far, far away, to some strange consummation in the sun. And after their fulfilment they return, seeming the same, but unimaginably renewed and different.

Who says it is not so? I am tired of clouds like conjuror's balls flying up and down from the palm of the sea. My clouds come from great distances, arriving from the deeps of the sky.

DEMOCRACY

I

The Average

Democracy!

What about it, in this year of Grace?

Democracy, Democracy!

We live in it and by it and for it. And how does it agree with us? All sorts and conditions of Democracy, the rule of Demos. If Demos is keen on money and property, that's not Democracy's fault.—Democracy, Democracy, Democracy!

Of the ideal brand of Democracy we have heard so much, and seen so little. That's the worst of ideals. They have such a nasty way of materialising.

Whitman gave two laws or principles for the establishment of Democracy. We may epitomise them as (1) the Law of the Average and (2) the Principle of Individualism, or Personalism, or Identity.

The Law of the Average is well known to us. Upon this law rests all the vague dissertation concerning equality and social perfection. Rights of Man, Equality of Man, Social Perfectibility of Man, all these sweet abstractions, once so inspiring, rest upon the fatal little hypothesis of the Average. Since Man writ large is just the Average Man.

What is the Average Man? As we are well aware, there is no such animal. It is a pure abstraction. It is the reduction of the human being to a mathematical unit. Every human being numbers one, one single unit. That is the grand proposition of the Average.

Let us further examine this mysterious One, this unit, this Average, let us examine it corporeally. The average human being: put him on the table, the little divinity, and let us see what his works are like. He is just a little idol: eidolons, eidolons! He has two legs, two eyes, one nose—all exact. He has a stomach and a penis. He is a little organism. He is one very complicated organ, a unit, an identity.

What is he for? If he's an organ, he must have a functional purpose. If he's an organism, he must have a vital purpose. The question is premature. Yet it shall be answered. Since he has a mouth, he is made for eating. Since he has hands, he is made for working. Since he has feet, he is made for walking. Since he has a penis, he is made for reproducing his species. And so on, and so on.

What a loathsome little idol he is, this Average Man, this Unit, this Homunculus. Yet he has his purposes. He is useful to measure by. That's the purpose of all averages. An average is not invented to be an Archetype. What a really comical mistake we have made about him. He is invented to serve as a standard in the business of comparison. He is invented to serve as a standard, just like any other standard, like the metre, or the gramme, or the English pound sterling. That's what he is for—nothing else. He was never intended to be worshipped. What comical fetish-smitten savages we are.

We use a foot-rule to tell us how big our house is. We don't proceed to say that the foot-rule is the sceptre which sways the earth and all the stars. Yet we have said as much of this little standardised invention of ours, the Average Man, the Man-in-the-Street. We have made prime fools of ourselves.

Now let us pull the gilt off the image, and see exactly what it is, and what we want it for. It is a mathematical quantity, like the metre or the foot-rule: a purely arbitrary institution of the human mind. Let us be quite clear about that.

But the human mind has invented the institution for its own purpose. Granted. What are the purposes? Merely for the comparing of one *living* man with another *living* man, in case of necessity: just as money is merely a contrivance for comparing a leg of mutton with a volume of Keats' poems. The money in itself is nothing. It is simply the arbitrary static measure for human desires. We mistake the measure for the thing it measures, and proceed to base our desires on money. It is nonsensical materialism.

Now for the Average Man himself! He is five-feet-six-inches high: and therefore you, John, will take an over-size pair of trousers, reach-me-downs, and you, *François mon cher,* will take an undersize. The Average Man also has a mouth and a stomach, which consume two pounds of bread and six ounces of meat per day: and therefore you, Fritz, exceed the normal consumption of food, while you, dear Emily, consume less than your share. The Average Man also has a penis: and therefore all of you, François, Fritz, John, and Giacomo, you may begin begetting children at the average age, let us say, of twenty-five.

The Average Man is somehow very unsatisfactory. He is not sufficiently worked out. It is astonishing that we have not perfected him before now. But that is because we have mixed the issues. How could we scientifically establish the Average, whilst we had to keep him draped upon a pedestal, as an Ideal? Haul him down at once. He is no Ideal. He is just a Standard, the creature on whom Standard suits and Standard boots are fitted, to whose stomach Standard bread is adjusted, and for whose eyes the Standard lamps are lighted, the Standard Oil Company is busy refining its gallons. He comes under the Government Weights and Measures Act.

Perfect him quickly: the Average, the Normal, the Man-in-the-Street. He is so many inches high, broad, deep, he weighs so many pounds. He must eat so much, and sleep so much, and work so much, and play so much, and love so much, and think so much, and argue so much, and read so many newspapers and have so many children. Somebody, quick, some Professor of Social Economy, draw up a perfect Average, and let us have him before the middle of next week. He is urgently required at the moment.

This is all your Man-in-the-Street amounts to: this tailor's dummy of an average. He is the image and effigy of all your equality. Men are not equal, and never were, and never will be, save by the arbitrary determination of some ridiculous human Ideal. But still, in the normal course of things, all men *do* have two eyes and one nose and a stomach and a penis. In the teeth of all opposition we assert it. In the normal course of things, all men *do* hunger and thirst and sleep and laugh and feel miserable and fall in love and ache for coition and ache to escape from the woman again. And the Average Man just represents what all men need and desire, physically, functionally, materially, and socially. *Materially* need: that's the point. The Average Man is the standard of Material need in the human.

Please keep out all Spiritual and Mystical needs. They have nothing to do with the Average. You cannot Average such things. As far as the stomach goes, it is not really true that one man's meat is another man's poison. No. The law of the Average holds good for the stomach. All young mammals suck milk, without exception. But in the creative or spontaneous or religious self, one man's meat is frequently another man's poison. And therefore you *can't* draw any average. You can't *have* an average; unless you are going to poison everybody.

Now we will settle for ever the Equality of Man, and the Rights of Man. Society means people living together. People *must* live together. And to live together, they must have some Standard, some *Material* Standard. This is where the Average comes in. And this is where Socialism, and Modern Democracy comes in. For Democracy and Socialism rest upon the Equality of Man, which is the Average. And this is sound enough, so long as the Average represents the real basic material needs of mankind—basic material needs—we insist and insist again. For Society, or Democracy, or any Political State or Community exists not for the sake of the individual, nor should ever exist for the sake of the individual, but simply to establish the Average, in order to make living together possible: that is, to make proper facilities for every man's clothing, feeding, housing himself, working, sleeping, mating, playing, according to his necessity as a common unit, an average. Everything beyond that common necessity depends on himself alone.

The proper adjustment of material means of existence: for this the State exists, but for nothing further. The State is a dead ideal. *Nation* is a dead ideal. Democracy and Socialism are dead ideals. They are one and all just *contrivances* for the supplying of the lowest material needs of a people. They are just vast hotels, or hostels, where every guest does some scrap of the business of the day's routine—if it's only lounging gracefully to give the appearance of ease—and for this contribution gets his suitable accommodation.

England, France, Germany, America—these great Nations, they have no vital meaning any more, except as great Food Committees and Housing Committees for a throng of people whose material tastes are somewhat in accord. No doubt they *had* other meanings. No doubt the French individuals of the Seventeenth Century still felt themselves gloriously expressed in stone, in Versailles. But man loses more and more his faculty for collective self-expression. Nay, the great development in collective expression in mankind has been a progress towards the possibility of purely individual expression. The highest Collectivity has for its true goal the purest individualism, pure individual spontaneity. But once more we have mistaken the means for the end: so that presidents, those representatives of the collected masses, instead of being accounted the chief machine-section of society, which they are, are revered as ideal beings. The thing to do is not to raise the idea of a Nation, or even of Internationalism, higher. The need is to take away every scrap of ideal drapery from nationalism and from internationalism, to show it all as a material contrivance for housing and feeding and conveying innumerable people. The housing and feeding, the method of conveyance and the rules of the road may be as different as you please—just as the methods of one great business house, and even of one hotel, are different from those of another. But that is all it is.

Man no longer expresses himself in his form of government, and his President is strictly only his superlative butler. This is the true course of evolution: the great collective activities are at last merely auxiliary to the purely individual activities. Business houses may be magnificent, but there is nothing divine in it all. This is why the Kaiser sounded so foolish. He was really only the head of a very great business concern. His God was the most intolerable part of his stock-in-trade. Genuine business houses may quarrel and compete, but they don't go to war. Why? Because they are not ideal or passional concerns. They are just practical material concerns. It is only Ideal concerns which go to war, and slaughter indiscriminately with a feeling of exalted righteousness. But when a business concern masquerades as an ideal concern, and behaves in this fashion, it is really unbearable.

There are two things to do. Strip off at once all the ideal drapery from nationality, from nations, peoples, states, empires, and *even from Internationalism* and Leagues of Nations. Leagues of Nations should be just flatly and simply committees where representatives of the various business houses, so-called Nations, meet and consult. Consultations, board meetings of the State business men: no more. *Representatives of Peoples*—who can represent me? I am myself I don't intend anybody to represent me.

You, you Cabinet Minister—what are you? You are the arch-grocer, the super-hotel-manager, the foreman over the ships and railways. What else are you? You are the super-tradesman, same paunch, same ingratiating manner, same everything. Governments, what are they? Just board meetings of big business men. Very useful too very thankful we are that somebody *will* look after this business. But Ideal! An Ideal Government! What nonsense. We as well talk of an Ideal Cook's Tourist Agency, or an Ideal Achille Serre Cleaners and Dyers. Even the ideal Ford is only an ideal motor-car, or rather, an ideal *average* cheap car. Ford's employees are not spontaneous, nonchalant human beings, à la Whitman. They are good, well-tested, well-oiled motor-car sections.

Politics—what are they? Just another, extra-large commercial wrangle over buying and selling—nothing else. Very good to have the wrangle. Let us have the buying and selling well done. But *ideal* Politics *ideal! Political Idealists!* What rank gewgaw and nonsense. We have just enough sense not to talk about Ideal Selfridges or Ideal Krupps or Ideal Heidsiecks. Then let us have enough sense to drop the ideal of England or Europe or anywhere else. Let us be men, and women, and keep our house in order. But let us pose no longer as houses, or as England, or as housemaids, or democrats.

Pull the ideal drapery off Governments, States, Nations and Internations. Show them for what they are: big business concerns for manufacturing and retailing Standard goods. Put up a statue of the Average Man, something like those abominable statues of men in woolen underwear, which surmount a shop at the corner of Oxford Street and Tottenham Court Road. Let your statue be grotesque: in fact, borrow those ignominious statues of men in pants and vests: the fat one for Germany, the thin one for England, the middling one for France, the gaunt one for the United States. Point to these statues, which shall guard the entrance to the House of Commons, to the Chamber, to the Senate, to the Reichstag—and let every Prime Minister and President know the quick of his own ignominy. Let every bursting politician see himself in his commercial underwear. Let every senatorial idealist and saviour of mankind be reminded that his office depends on the quality of the hosiery he supplies to the State. Let every fiery and rhetorical Deputy remember that he is only held together by his patent suspenders.

And then, when the people of the world have finally got over the state of giddy idealising of Governments, Nations, Internations, politics, democracies, empires, and so forth, when they really understand that their collective activities are only cook-housemaid to their sheer individual activities, when they at last calmly accept a business concern for what it is, then at last we may actually see free men in the streets.

II

Identity

Let us repeat that Whitman establishes the true Democracy on two bases, the Average, and Individualism, Personalism, or Identity.

The Average is much easier to settle and define than is Individualism or Identity. The Average is the same as the Man-in-the-Street, the unit of Humanity. This unit is in the first place just an abstraction, an invention of the human mind. In the first place, the Man-in-the-Street is no more than an abstract idea. But in the second place, by application to Tom, Dick and Harry, he becomes a substantial, material, functioning unit. This is how the ideal world is created. It is invented exactly as man invents machinery.

First there is an idea; then the idea is substantiated, the inventor fabricates his machine; and then he proceeds to worship his fabrication, and himself as mouthpiece of the Logos. This is how the world, the universe, was invented from the Logos: exactly as man has invented machinery and the whole ideal of humanity. The vital universe was never created from any Logos; but the ideal universe of man was certainly so invented. Man's overweening mind uttered the Word and the Word was God. So that the world exists today as a flesh-and-blood-and-iron substantiation of this uttered Word.

This is all the trouble: that the invented *ideal* world of man is superimposed upon living men and women, and men and women are thus turned into abstracted, functioning mechanical units. This is all the great ideal of Humanity amounts to: an aggregation of ideally-functioning units: never a man or woman possible.

Ideals, all ideals and every ideal, are a trick of the devil. They are a superimposition of the abstracted, automatic, invented universe of the spontaneous creative universe. So much for the Average, the Man-in-the-Street, and the great Ideal of Humanity: all a little trick men have played on us. But quite a useful little trick—so long as we merely use it as one uses the trick of making cakes or pies or bread, just for feeding purposes, and suchlike.

Let us leave the Average, and look at the second basis of Democracy. With the Average we settle the cooking, eating, sleeping, housing, mating and clothing problem. But Whitman insisted on exalting his Democracy, he would not quite leave it on the cooking-eating-mating level. We cook to eat, we eat to sleep, we sleep to build houses, we build houses in order to beget and bear children in safety, we bear children in order to clothe them, we clothe them in order that they may start the old cycle over again, cook and eat and sleep and house and mate and clothe, and so on *ad infinitum.* That is the Average. It is the business of a government to superintend it.

But Whitman insisted on raising Democracy above government, or even above public service or humanity or love of one's neighbour. Heaven knows what his Democracy is—but something as yet unattained. It is something beyond governments and even beyond Ideals. It must be beyond Ideals, because it has never yet been stated. As an idea it doesn't yet exist. Even Whitman, with all his reiteration got no further than *hinting*, and rather bad hints, many of them.

We've heard the Average hint—enough of that. Now for Individualism, Personalism, and Identity. We catch hold of the tail of the hint, and proceed with Identity.

What has Identity got to do with Democracy? It can't have anything to do with politics and governments. It can't much affect one's love for one's neighbour, or for humanity. Yet stay—it can Whitman says there is One Identity in all things. It is only the old dogma. All things emanate from the Supreme Being. All things, being all emanations from the Supreme Being, have One Identity.

Very nice. But we don't like the look of this Supreme Being. It is too much like the Man-in-the-Street. This Supreme Being, this Anima Mundi, this Logos was surely just invented to suit the human needs. It is surely the magnified Average, abstracted from men, and then clapped on to them again, like identity-medals on wretched khaki soldiers. But instead of a magnified average-function-unit, we have here the magnified unit of Consciousness, or Spirit.

Like the Average, this One Identity invention is useful enough, if we use it aright. It is not a matter of provisioning the body, this time, but of provisioning the spirit, the consciousness. We are all one, and therefore every bit partakes of all the rest. That is, the Whole is inherent in every fragment. That is, every human consciousness has the same intrinsic value as every other human consciousness, because each is an essential part of the Great Consciousness? This is the One Identity which identifies us all.

It is very nice, theoretically. And it is a very great stimulus to universal comprehension, it leads us all to want to know everything, it even tempts us all to imagine we do know everything beforehand, and need make no effort. It is the subtlest means of inflating the consciousness. But when you have inflated your consciousness, even to infinity, what then? Do you really become God? When in your understanding you embrace everything, then surely you are divine? But no! With a nasty bump you have to come down and realise that, in spite of your infinite comprehension, you are not really any other than you were before: not a bit more divine or superhuman or enlarged. Your *consciousness* may embrace infinity. That doesn't make *you* infinite. Your *mental consciousness* is not *you*.

This big bump of falling out of the infinite back into your own pair of pants leads you to suspect that the One Identity is not *the* identity. There is another, little sort of identity, which you can't get away from, except by breaking your neck. The One Identity is very like a magnification of the Average. It is what you are when you aren't yourself. It is what you are when you imagine you're something hugely big—the Infinite, for example. And the consciousness is really capable of arriving at the illusion of infinity. But there you are! Your consciousness has to fly back to the old tree, to peck the old apples, and sleep under the leaves. It was all only an excursion. It was wearing a magic cap. You yourself invented the cap, and then puffed up your head to fit it. But a swelled head at last begins to ache, and you realise it's only your own old chump after all. All the extended consciousness that ranges the infinite heavens must sleep under the thatch of your hair at night: and you are only you: and your *spirit* is only a bird in your tree, that flies, and then settles, whistles, and then is silent.

Man is a queer beast. He spends dozens of centuries puffing himself up and drawing himself in, and at last he has to be content to be just his own size, neither infinitely big nor infinitely little. Man is tragic-comical. His insatiable desire to be *everything* has made him clean forget that he might be himself. To be everything—to be everything: the history of mankind is only a history of this insane craving in man. You can magnify yourself into a Jehovah, and a huge Egyptian king-god: or you can reverse the spy-glass, and dwindle yourself away into a speck, lost in the Infinite of Love, as the later great races have done. But still you'll only be chasing the one mad reward, the reward of infinity: which, when you've got it, bursts like a bubble in your hand, and leaves you looking at your own fingers. Well, and what's wrong with your own fingers?

It is a bubble, the One Identity. But chasing it, man gets his education. It is his education process, the chase of the All, the extension of the consciousness. He *learns* everything: except the last lesson of all, which he can't learn till the bubble has burst in his fingers.

The last lesson? Ah, the lesson of his own fingers: himself: the little identity; little, but real. Better, far better, to be oneself, than to be any bursting Infinite, or swollen One-Identity.

It is a radical passion in man, however, the passion to include *everything* in himself, grasp it all. There are two ways of gratifying this passion. The first is Alexander's way, the way of power, power over the material universe. This is what the alchemists and magicians sought. This is what Satan offered Jesus, in the Temptations: power, mystic and actual, over the material world. And power, we know, is a bubble: a platitudinous bubble.

But Jesus chose the other way: not to *have* all, but to *be* all. Not to *grasp* everything into supreme possession; but to *be* everything through supreme acceptance. It is the same thing, at the very last. The king-god and the crucified-god hold the same bubble in their hands: the bubble of the All, the Infinite. The king-god extends the dominion of his own consciousness and will over all things: the crucified identifies his will and consciousness with all things But the submission of love is at last a process of pure materialism, like the supreme extension of power Up to a certain point, both in mastering, which is power, and in submitting, which is love, the soul *learns* and fulfils itself. Beyond a certain point, it merely collapses from its centrality, and lapses into the material sequence of cause and effect. The tyranny of Power is no worse than the tyranny of No-power. Government by the highest is no more fatal than government by the lowest.—Let the Average govern, let him be called super-butler, let us have a faint but tolerant contempt for him. But let us keep our very self integral, greater than any having or knowing, centrally alive and quick.

The last lesson: the myriad, mysterious identities, no one of which can *comprehend* another. They can only exist side by side, as stars do. The lesson of lessons: not in any oneness with the rest of things can we have our pure being: but in clean, fine singleness. Oneness, and collectiveness, these are our lesser states, inferior; our impurity. They are mere states of consciousness and of having: of becoming, as the theosophists say.

It is all very well to talk about a Supreme Being, an Anima Mundi, an Oversoul, an Infinite: but it is all just human invention. Come down to actuality. Where do you see Being?—in individual men and women. Where do you find an *Anima?—in* living individual creatures. Where would you look for a soul?—in a man, in an animal, in a tree or flower. And all the rest, about Supreme Beings and Anima Mundis and Oversouls is just abstraction. Show me the very animal!—You can't. It is merely a trick of the human will, trying to get power over everything, and therefore making the wish father of the thought. The cart foals the horse, and there you are: a Logos, a Supreme Being, a What-not.

But there are two sorts of individual identity. Every factory-made pitcher has its own little identity, resulting from a certain mechanical combination of Matter with Forces. These are the material identities. They sum up to the material Infinite.

The other identity, however, is the identity of the living self. If we look for God, let us look in the bush where he sings. That is, in living creatures. Every living creature is single in itself, a *ne plus ultra* of creative reality, *fons et origo* of creative manifestation. Why go further? Why begin to abstract and generalise and include? There you have it. Every single living creature is a single creative unit, a unique, incommutable self. Primarily, in its own spontaneous reality, it knows no law. It is a law unto itself. Secondarily, in its material reality it submits to all the laws of the material universe. But the primal spontaneous self in any creature has ascendance, truly, over the material laws of the universe, it uses these laws and converts the mystery of creation.

This then is the true identity: the inscrutable, single self, the little unfathonable well-head that bubbles forth into being and doing. We cannot analyse it. We can only know it is there. It is not by any means a Logos. It precedes any knowing. It is the fountain-head of everything: the quick of the self.

222

Not people smelted into a oneness: that is not the new Democracy. But people released into their single, starry identity, each one distinct and incommutable. This will never be an ideal: for of the living self you cannot make an idea, just as you have not been able to turn the individual "soul" into an idea. Both are impossible to idealise. An idea is an abstraction from reality, a generalisation. And you can't generalise the incommutable.

So the Whitman One-Identity, the En-Masse, is a horrible nullification of true identity and being. At the best, our en masse activities can be but servile, serving the free soul. At the worst, they are sheer self-destruction. Let us put them in their place. Let us get over our rage of social activity, public being, universal self-estimation, republicanism, bolshevism, socialism, empire—all these mad manifestations of en masse and One-Identity. They are all self-betrayal. Let our Democracy be in the singleness of the clear, clean self, and let our En Masse be no more than an arrangement for the liberty of this self. Let us drop looking after our neighbour. It only robs him of his chance of looking after himself. Which is robbing him of his freedom, with a vengeance.

III

Personality

"One's-Self I sing, a simple separate person,
Yet utter the word Democratic, the word En-Masse—"

Such are the opening words of *Leaves of Grass.* It is Whitman's whole *motif,* the key to all his Democracy. First and last he sings of "the great pride of man in himself." First and last he is Chanter of Personality. If it is not Personality it is Identity, and if not Identity, it is the Individual: and along with these, Democracy and En-Masse.

In Whitman, at all times, the true and the false are so near, so interchangeable, that we are almost inevitably left with divided feelings. The Average, one of his greatest idols, we flatly refuse to worship. Again, when we come to do real reverence to identity, we never know whether we shall be taking off our hats to that great mystery, the unique individual self, distinct and primal in every separate man, or whether we shall be saluting that old great idol of the past, the Supreme One which swallows up all true identity.

And now for Personality. What meaning does "person" really carry? A *person* is given in the dictionary as *an individual human being.* But surely the words *person* and *individual* suggest very different things. It is not at all the same to have personality, as to have individuality, though you may not be able to define the difference. And the distinction between a person and a human being is perhaps even greater. Some "persons" hardly seem like human beings at all.

The derivation this time helps. *Persona,* in Latin, is a player's mask, or a character in a play: and perhaps the word is cognate with *sonare,* to sound. An *individual* is that which is not divided or not dividable. A *being* we shall not attempt to define, because it is undefinable.

So now, there must be a radical difference between something which was originally a player's mask, or a transmitted sound, and something which means "the undivided." The old meaning lingers in *person,* and is almost obvious in *personality.* A person is a human being *as he appears to others:* and personality is that which is transmitted from the person to his audience: the transmissible effect of a man.

A good actor can assume a personality: he can never assume an individuality. Either he has his own, or none. So that personality is something much more superficial, or at least more volatile than individuality. This volatile quality is the one we must examine.

Let us take a sentence from an American novel. "My ego had played a trick on me, and made me think I wanted babies, when I only wanted the man." This is a perfectly straight and lucid statement. But what is the difference between the authoress's *ego* and her *me.* The ego is obviously a sort of second self, which she carries about with her. It is her stock of accepted consciousness, which she has inherited more or less ready-made from her father and grandfathers. This secondary self is very pernicious, dictating to her issues which are quite false to her true, deeper, spontaneous self, her creative identity: her *me.*

Nothing in the world is more pernicious than the ego or spurious self, the conscious entity with which every individual is saddled. He receives it almost *en bloc* from the preceding generation, and spends the rest of his life trying to drag his spontaneous self from beneath the horrible incubus. And the most fatal part of the incubus, by far, is the dead, leaden weight of handed-on ideals. So that every individual is born with a mill-stone of ideals round his neck, and, whether he knows it or not, either spends his time trying to get his neck free, like a wild animal wrestling with a collar to which a log is fastened; or else he spends his days decorating his mill-stone, his log with fantastic colours.

And a finely or fantastically decorated mill-stone is called a personality. Never trust for one moment any individual who has unmistakeable *personality.* He is sure to be a life-traitor. His personality is only a sort of actor's mask. It is his self-conscious ego, his *ideal* self masquerading and prancing round, *showing off* He may not be aware of it. But that makes no matter. He is a painted bug.

The ideal self: this is personality. The self that is begotten and from the idea, this is the ideal self: a spurious, detestable product. This is man created from his own Logos. This is man born out of his own head. This is the self-conscious ego, the entity of fixed ideas and ideals, prancing and displaying itself like an actor. And this is personality. This is what makes the American authoress gush about babies. And this gush is her peculiar form of personality, which renders her attractive to the American men, who prefer so much to deal with personalities and egos, rather than with real beings: because personalities and egos, after all, are quite reasonable which means they are subject to the laws of cause-and-effect, they are safe and calculable: materialists, units of the material world of force and matter.

Your idealist alone is a perfect materialist. This is no paradox. What is the idea, or the ideal, after all? It is only a fixed, static entity an abstraction, an extraction from the living body of life. Creative life is characterised by spontaneous mutability: it brings forth unknown issues, impossible to preconceive. But an ideal is just a machine which is in process of being built. A man gets the idea for some engine, and proceeds to work it out in steel and copper. In exactly the same way, man gets some ideal of man, and proceeds to work it out in flesh and blood, as a fixed static entity: just as a machine is a static entity, so is the ideal Humanity.

If we want to find the real enemy today, here it is: idealism. If we want to find this enemy incarnate, here he is: a personality. If we want to know the steam which drives this mechanical little incarnation, here it is: love of humanity, the public good.

There have been other ideals than ours, other forms of personality, other sorts of steam. We quite fail to see what sort of personality Rameses II had, or what sort of steam built the pyramids. Still we admire the pyramids: chiefly, I suppose, because they are a very great load on the face of the earth.

Is love of humanity the same as real, warm, individual love? Nonsense. It is the moonshine of our warm day, a hateful reflection. Is personality the same as individual being? We know it is a mere mask. Is idealism the same as creation? Rubbish! Idealism is no more than a plan of a marvellous Human Machine, drawn up by the great Draughtsman-Minds of the past. Give God a pair of compasses, and let the designs be measured and formed. What insufferable nonsense! As if creation proceeded from a pair of compasses. Better say that man is a forked radish, as Carlyle did: it's nearer the mark than this Pair of Compasses business.

You can have life two ways. Either everything is created from the mind, downwards: or else everything proceeds from the creative quick, outwards into foliage and blossom. Either a great Mind floats in space: God, the Anima Mundi, the Oversoul, drawing with a pair of compasses and making everything to scale, even emotions and self-conscious effusions: or else creation proceeds from the forever inscrutable quicks of living beings, men, women, animals, plants. The actual living quick itself is alone the creative reality. Once you abstract from this, once you generalise and postulate Universals, you have departed from the creative reality, and entered the realm of static mechanism, materialism.

Now let us put salt on the tail of that sly old bird of "attractive personallity." It isn't a bird at all. It is a self-conscious, self-important befeathered snail: and salt is good for snails. It is the snail which has eaten off our flowers till none are left. Now let us no longer be taken in by the feathers. Anyhow, put salt on his tail.

No personalities in our Democracy. No ideals either. When still more personalities come round hawking their pretty ideals, we must be ready to upset their apple-cart. I say, a man's self is a law unto itself: not unto *himself* mind you. Itself. When a man talks about *himself* he is talking about his idea of himself: his own ideal self, that fancy little homunculus he has fathered in his brain. When a man is conscious of himself he is trading his own personality.

You can't make an *idea* of the living self: hence it can never become an ideal. Thank heaven for that. There it is, an inscrutable, unfindable, vivid quick, giving us off as a life-issue. It is not *spirit*. Spirit is merely our mental *consciousness,* a finished essence extracted from our life-being, just as alcohol, spirits of wine, is the material, finished essence extracted from the living grape. The living self is not spirit. You cannot postulate it. How can you postulate that which is *there*? The moon might as well try to hold forth in heaven, postulating the sun. Or a child hanging on to his mother's skirt might as well commence in a long diatribe to postulate his mother's existence, in order to prove his own existence. Which is exactly what man has been busily doing for two thousand years. What amazing nonsense!

The quick of the self is *there*. You needn't try to get behind it. As leave try to get behind the sun. You needn't try to idealise it, for by so doing you will only slime about with feathers in your tail, a gorgeous befeathered snail of an ego and a personality. You needn't try to show it off to your neighbour: he'll put salt on your tail if you do. And you needn't go trying to save the living self of your neighbour. It's hands off. Do you think you are such a God-almighty bird of paradise, that you can grow your neighbour's goose-quills for him on your own loving house-sparrow wings? Every bird must grow his own feathers, you are not the almighty dodo, you've got nobody's wings to feather but your own.

IV

Individualism

It is obvious that Whitman's Democracy is not merely a political system, or a system of government—or even a social system. It is an attempt to conceive a new way of life, to establish new values. It is a struggle to liberate human beings from the fixed, arbitrary control of ideals, into free spontaneity.

So, the ideal of Oneness, the unification of all mankind into the homogeneous whole, is done away with. The great *desire* is that each single individual shall be incommutably himself, spontaneous and single, that he shall not in any way be reduced to a term, a unit of any Whole.

We must discriminate between an ideal and a desire. A desire proceeds from within, from the unknown, spontaneous soul or self. But an ideal is superimposed from above, from the mind, it is a fixed arbitrary thing, like a machine control. The great lesson is to learn to break all the fixed ideals, to allow the soul's own deep desires to come direct, spontaneous into consciousness. But it is a lesson which will take many aeons to learn.

Our life, our being depends upon the incalculable issue from the central Mystery, into indefinable *presence*. This sounds in itself an abstraction. But not so. It is rather the perfect absence of abstraction. The central Mystery is no generalised abstraction. It is each man's primal original soul or self, within him. And *presence* is nothing mystic or ghostly. On the contrary. It is the actual man present before us. The fact that an actual man present before us is an inscrutable and incarnate Mystery, untranslateable, this is the fact upon which any great scheme of social life must be based. It is the fact of *otherness*.

Each human self is single, incommutable, and unique. This is its *first* reality. Each self is unique, and therefore incomparable. It is a single well-head of creation, unquestionable: it cannot be compared with another self, another well-head, because, in its prime or creative reality it can never be comprehended by any other self.

The living self has one purpose only: to come into its own fullness of being as a tree comes into full blossom, or a bird into spring beauty, or a tiger into lustre.

But this coming into full, spontaneous being is the most difficult thing of all. Man's nature is balanced between spontaneous creativity and mechanical-material activity. Spontaneous being is subject to no law. But mechanical-material existence is subject to all the laws of the mechanical-physical world. Man has almost half his nature in the material world. His spontaneous nature *just* takes precedence.

The only thing man has to trust to in coming to himself is his desire and his impulse But both desire and impulse tend to fall into mechanical automatism: to fall from spontaneous reality into dead or material reality. All our education should be a guarding against this fall.

The fall is possible in a two-fold manner. Desires tend to automise into functional appetites, and impulses tend to automatise into fixed aspirations or ideals. These are the two great temptations of man. Falling into the first temptation, the whole will pivots on some function, some material activity, which then works the whole being: like an *idée fixe* in the mental consciousness. This automatised, dominant appetite we call a lust: a lust for power, a lust for success, a lust for being loved.—The second great temptation is the inclination to set up some fixed centre, in the mind, and make the whole soul turn upon this centre. This we call idealism. Instead of the will fixing upon some sensational activity, it fixes upon some aspirational activity, and pivots this activity upon an idea or an ideal. The whole soul streams in the energy of aspiration and turns automatically, like a machine, upon the ideal.

These are the two great temptations of the fall of man, the fall from spontaneous, single, pure being, into what we call materialism or automatism or mechanism of the self. All education must tend against this fall: and all our efforts in all our life must be to preserve the soul free and spontaneous. The whole soul of man must *never* be subjected to one motion or emotion, the life-activity must never be degraded into a fixed activity, there must be *no fixed direction.*

There can be no ideal goal for human life. Any ideal goal means mechanisation, materialism, and nullity. There is no pulling open the buds to see what the blossom will be. Leaves must unroll, buds swell and open, and *then* the blossom. And even after that, when the flower dies and the leaves fall, *still* we shall not know. There will be more leaves, more buds, more blossoms: and again, a blossom is an unfolding of the creative unknown. Impossible, utterly impossible to preconceive the unrevealed blossom. You cannot foretell it, from the last blossom. We know the flower of today, but the flower of tomorrow is all beyond us. Only in the material-mechanical world can man foresee, foreknow, calculate, and establish laws.

So, we more or less grasp the first term of the new Democracy. We see something of what a man will be unto himself.

Next, what will a man be unto his neighbour?—Since every individual is, in his first reality, a single, incommutable soul, not to be calculated or defined in terms of any other soul, there can be no establishing of a mathematical ratio. We cannot say that all men are equal. We cannot say A = B. Nor can we say that men are unequal. We may not declare that A = B + C.

Where each thing is unique in itself, there can be no comparison made. One man is neither equal nor unequal to another man. When I stand in the presence of another man, and I am my own pure self, am I aware of the presence of an equal, or of an inferior, or of a superior? I am not. When I stand with another man, who is himself, and when I am truly myself, then I am only aware of a Presence, and of the strange reality of Otherness. There is me, and there is *another being.* That is the first part of the reality. There is no comparing or estimating. There is only this strange recognition of *present otherness*. I may be glad, angry, or sad, because of the presence of the other. But still no comparison enters in. Comparison enters only when one of us departs from his own integral being, and enters the material-mechanical world. Then equality and disquality starts at once.

So, we know the first great purpose of Democracy: that each man shall be spontaneously himself—each man himself, each woman herself, without any question of equality or unequality entering in at all; and that no man shall try to determine the being of any other man, or of any other woman.

But, because of the temptation which awaits every individual, the temptation to fall out of being, into automatism and mechanisation, every individual must be ready at all times to defend his own being against the mechanisation and materialism forced upon him by those people who have fallen or departed from being. It is the long unending fight, the fight for the soul's own freedom, of spontaneous being, against the mechanism and materialism of the fallen.

All the foregoing deals really with the integral, whole nature of man. If men would but *keep* whole, integral, everything could be left at that. There would be no need for laws and governments: agreement would be spontaneous. Even the great concerted social ~activities would be essentially spontaneous.

But in his present state of mechanical degeneration, man is unable to distinguish his own spontaneous integrity from his mechanical lusts and aspirations. Hence there must still be laws and governments. But laws and governments henceforth, we see it clearly and we must never forget it, relate only to the material world: to property, the possession of property and the means of life, and to the material-mechanical nature of man.

In the past, no doubt, there were great ideals to fulfil: ideals of brotherhood, oneness, and equality. Great sections of humanity tended to cohere into particular brotherhoods, expressing their oneness and their equality and their united purpose in a manner peculiar to themselves. For no matter how single an ideal may be, even such a mathematical ideal as equality and oneness, it will find the most diverse and even opposite expressions. So that brotherhood and oneness in Germany never meant the same as brotherhood and oneness in France. Yet each was brotherhood, and each was oneness. Souls, as they work out the same ideal, work it out differently: always differently, until they reach the point where, owing to over-insistence on the ideal, the spontaneous integrity of being finally breaks. And then, when pure mechanisation or materialism sets in, the soul is automatically pivoted, and the most diverse of creatures fall into a common mechanical unison. This we see in America. It is not a homogeneous spontaneous coherence, so much as a disintegrated amorphousness which lends itself to perfect mechanical unison.

Men have reached the point where, in further fulfilling their ideals they break down the living integrity of their being and fall into sheer mechanical materialism. They become automatic units, determined entirely by mechanical law.

This is horribly true of modern democracy—socialism, conservatism, bolshevism, liberalism, republicanism, communism: all alike. The one principle that governs all the *isms* is the same: the principle idealised unit, the possessor of property. Man has his highest fulfilment as a possessor of property: so they all say, really. One half says that the uneducated, being the majority, should possess the property: the other half says that the educated, being the enlightened, should possess the property. There is no more to it. No need to write books about it.

This is the last of the ideals. This is the last phase of the ideal of equality, brotherhood, and oneness. All ideals work down to the sheer materialism which is their intrinsic reality at last.

It doesn't matter, now, who has the property: they have all lost their being over it. Even property, that most substantial of realities, evaporates once man loses his integral nature. It is curious that it is so, but it is undeniable. So that property is now fast evaporating.

Wherein lies the hope. For with it evaporates the last ideal. Sometime, somewhere, man will wake up and realise that property is only there to be used, not to be possessed. He will realise that possession is a kind of illness of the spirit, and a hopeless encumbrance upon the spontaneous self. The little pronouns "my" and "our" will lose all their mystic spell.

The question of property will never be settled, till people cease to care for property. Then it will settle itself. A man only needs so much as will help him to his own fulfilment. Surely the individual who wants a motor-car merely for the sake of having it and riding in it is as hopeless an automaton as the motor-car itself.

When men are no longer obsessed with the desire to possess property, or with the parallel desire, to prevent another man's possessing it, then, and only then shall we be glad to turn it over to the State. Our way of State-ownership is merely a farcical exchange of words, not of ways. We only intend our states to be Unlimited Liability Companies instead of Limited Liability Companies.

The Prime Minister of the future will be no more than a sort of steward, the Minister of Commerce will be the great housekeeper, the Minister of Transport the head coachman: all just chief servants, no more: servants.

When men become their own decent selves again, then we can so easily arrange the material world. The arrangement will come, as it must come, spontaneously, not by previous ordering. Until such time, what is the good of talking about it? All discussion and idealising of the possession of property, whether individual or group or State possession, amounts now to no more than a fatal betrayal of the spontaneous self. All settlement of the property question must arise spontaneously out of the new impulse in man, to free himself from the extraneous load of possession, and walk naked and light. Every attempt at pre-ordaining a new material world only adds another last straw to the load that already has broken so many backs. If we are to keep our backs unbroken, we must deposit all property on the ground, and learn to walk without it. We must stand aside. And when many men stand aside, they stand in a new world, a new world of man has come to pass. This is the Democracy, the new order.

EDUCATION OF THE PEOPLE

I

What is education all about? What is it doing? Does anybody know? It doesn't matter so much for people with money. For them social intercourse is an end in itself; a sort of charming game for which they need a little polish of manner, a trifle of social grace, and a certain amount of accomplishment, mental and otherwise.

Even supposing they look on life as a serious affair, it only means they intend, in some way or other, to devote themselves to the service of the nation. And the service of the nation, though an important matter surely, is by now a somewhat cut-and-dried business.

The point is, the nation which is served. And what is the nation? attempting a high-flown definition, it is the people. And who are the people? Why, they are the proletariat. For according to the modern democratic ideal under which we still march, *ideally,* the upper classes exist only for the purpose of devoting themselves to the good of the people. Everything works back to the people, to the proletariat, strictly. If a man justifies his existence nowadays—and what man doesn't—he proclaims that he is a servant and benefactor of the people, the vast proletariat. From the King downwards, this is so.

And the people, the proletariat. What about them and their education? They are the be-all and the end-all. To them everything is *ideally* devoted (mind, we are only writing now of education as it exists for us as an ideal, or an idea). There is not an idealist, or a man living who does not ostensibly come forward, like the Pope in Holy Week, with a basin and a towel to bathe the feet of the poor. And the poor sit aloft while their feet are laved. And then what? What *are* the poor, actually?

Because, before you can educate the people, you must know what the people are. We know well enough they are the proletariat, the implements of industry. But that, we argue, is in their utilitarian aspect only. They have a higher reality. Their proletarian or laborious nature is their mundane nature. When the Pope washes the feet of the poor men, it is not because the poor men have been shunting trucks on the railway and got their feet hot and dirty. Not at all. He washes their feet as an act of symbolic recognition of the divine nature which is alive in each of these poor men. In this world, we are content to recognise divinity only in those that serve. The whole world screams *Ich Dien.* Heaven knows *what* it serves! And yet, if we go back to the Pope, we shall realise that it is not in the *service*, the *labour* that he recognises the divinity, but in the actual nature of the *servant*, the laborer, the humble individual. He washes the feet of the humble, not the feet of trades-unionistic, strike-menacing truck-shunters.

The man and his job. You've got to make a distinction between the two. If Louis Quatorze was content to be a State, we can't allow (ideally, at least) our dustman Jim Shepherd to regard himself as the apotheosis of dust-bins. When Louis Quatorze said that He was the State, or the State was Him, he belittled himself really. For after all, it is a much rarer and more difficult thing to be oneself, than to be either a State or a dust-bin. At his best, a man is himself; his job, even if it be State-swaying, comes a long way after. For almost anybody could sway a State or swing a dust-tub. But no man can take on another man's self. If you want to be unique, be yourself. And the spark of divinity in each being, however humble, is what the Pope recognises in Holy Week.

The job is not by any means holy: and the man, in some degree, is. No doubt here we shall raise the wind of opposition from labour units and employers' units. But we don't care. We represent the true idealists who even now sit on the Board of Education and foggily but fervently enact their ideals. The job is not at all divine, the laborer in some measure *is.* So let technical education remain apart.

But here comes the first dilemma. Because, however cloistral our elementary schools may be, sheltering the eternal flame of the high ideal of human existence, Jimmy Shepherd, aged twelve, and Nancy Shepherd, aged thirteen, know very well that the eternal flame of the high ideal is all my-eye. It's all toffee, my dear sirs. What you've got to do is to *get a job,* and when you've got your job then you must *make a decent screw.* First and last, this is the state of man. So says little Jimmy Shepherd, and so says his sister Nancy. She's got her thirteen-year-old eye on a laundry, and he's got his twelve-year-old eye on a bottle-factory. Head-master and head-mistress and all the teachers know perfectly well that the high goal of all *their* endeavours is the laundry and the bottle-factory. They try to stunt a bit sometimes about the high ideal of human existence, the dignity of human life or the nobility of labour. But if they *really* want to put the fear of the Lord into Jimmy or Nancy they say "You'll break more bottles than you'll make, my young genius," or else "You'll burn more shirt-fronts than you'll brighten, my girl: and *then* you'll know what you're in for, at the week-end." This mystic week-end is not the sacred Sabbath of Holy Communion. It is *pay-day,* and nothing else.

The high idealists up in Whitehall may preserve some illusion around themselves. But there is absolutely no illusion for the elementary school-teachers. They know what the end will be. And the know that they've got to keep their *own* job, and they've got to struggle for a head-ship. And between the disillusion of their scholars' destiny, on the one hand, and the disillusion of their own mean and humiliating destiny, on the other, they haven't much breath left for the fanning of the high flame of noble human existence.

If ever there is a poor devil on the face of the earth it is the elementary school-teacher. He is invested with a wretched idealist sort of authority over a pack of children, an authority which parents jeer at and despise. For they know the teacher is under *their* thumb. '*I* pay for you, I'll let you know, out of the rates. *I'm* your employer. And therefore you'll treat my child properly, or I'm going up to the Town Hall." All of which Jimmy and Nancy exultingly hear, and the teacher, guardian of the high flame of human divinity, quakes because he knows his job is in danger. He is insulted from above and from below. Comes along an inspector of schools, a university man himself, with no respect for the sordid promiscuity of the elementary school. For elementary schools know no remoteness and dignity of the rostrum. The teacher is on a level with the scholars, or inferior to them. And an elementary school knows no code of honour, no *esprit de corps.* There is the profound cynicism of the laundry and the bottle-factory at the bottom of everything. How should a refined soul from Oxford fail to find it a little sordid and common.

The elementary school-teacher is in a vile and false position. Set up as representative of an ideal which is all toffee, invested in an authority which has absolutely no base except in the teacher's own will, he is sneered at by the idealists above and jeered at by the materialists below, and ends by being a mongrel who is neither a wage-earner nor a professional, neither a head-worker nor a hand-worker, neither living by his brain nor by his physical toil, but a bit of both, and despised for both. He is caught between the upper and nether millstones of idealism and materialism, and every shred of natural pride is ground out of him, so that he has to die or to cultivate some unpleasant *suffisance* which makes him objectionable for ever.

Yet who dare say that the idealists are wrong? And who dare say that the materialists are right? The elementary school is where the two meet, like millstones. And teacher and scholars are ground between the two.

231

It is absolutely fatal for the manhood of the teacher. And it is bitterly detrimental for the scholars. You can hardly keep a boy for ten years in the elementary schools, "educating him" to be himself, "educating him" up to the high ideal of human existence, with the bottle-factory outside the gate all the time, without producing a state of cynicism in the child's soul. Children are wonderfully subtle at dodging a hateful conclusion. If they are going to live, they must keep some illusions.—But alas, they know the shoddiness of their illusions. What boy of fourteen, in an elementary school, but is a subtle cynic about all ideals?

What is wrong then? The system. But when you've said that you've said nothing. The system, after all, is only the outcome of the human psyche, the human desires. We shout and blame the machine. But who on earth makes the machine, if we don't? And any alterations in the system are only modifications in the machine.—The system is *in us,* it is not something external to us. The machine is in us, or it would never come out of us. Well then, there's nothing to blame but ourselves, and there's nothing to change except inside ourselves.

For instance, you may exclude technical training from the elementary schools: you may prolong the school years to the age of sixteen—or to the age of twenty, if you like. And what then? At the gate of the school lies the sphinx who puts this question to every emerging scholar, boy or girl: "How are you going to make your living?" And every boy or girl must answer or die: so the poor things believe.

We call this the system. It isn't really. The trouble lies in us who are so afraid of this particular sphinx. "My dear sphinx, my wants are very small, my needs still smaller. I wonder you trouble yourself about so trivial a matter. I am going to get a job in a bottle-factory where I shall have to spend a certain number of hours a day. But that is the least of my concerns. My dear sphinx, you are a kitten at riddles. If you'd asked me now what I'm going to do with my life, apart from the bottle-factory, you might have frightened me. As it is, really, every smoky tall chimney is an answer to you."

Curious that when the toothless old sphinx croaks "How are you going to get your living?" our knees give way beneath us. What has happened to us, that we are so frightened of that toothless old lion of *want*. Do we really think we might not be able to earn our bread and butter—or bread and margarine, at the worst? Why are we so frightened? Out of fifty million people, about ten thousand can't obtain their bread and butter, without the workhouse or some such aid. But what's the odds? The odds against your earning your living are one in five thousand. There are not so many odds against your dying of typhoid, or being killed in a street-accident. Yet you don't really care a snap about street-accidents or typhoid. Then why are you so afraid of dying of starvation? You'll never die of starvation, So what *are* you afraid of!

The fear of penury is very curious, in our age. In really poor ages men did not fear penury. They didn't care. But we are abjectly terrified of it. Why? It isn't any such awful thing, if you don't care about keeping up appearances.

There is no cure for this craven terror of poverty save in human courage and insouciance. A sphinx has you by your cravenness. Œdipus and all those before him might just have easily answered his sphinx by saying: "Oh my dear Sphinx, that's quite easy. A Borogrove of course. What, don't you know what a Borogove is? My dear Sphinx go to school, go to school. I knew all about Borogoves before I was out of the cradle, and here you are heaven knows how old, propounding silly riddles to which Borogove is the answer, and you admit you've never heard of one. I absolutely refuse to concern myself with *your* solution, if you know nothing of mine." Exit the Sphinx with its tail between its legs.—

And so with the Sphinx of our material existence. She'll never go off with her tail between her legs till we simply jeer at her. "Earn my living, you crazy old bitch? Why I'm going Jimmy-Shepherding. No, not sheep at all. *Jimmishepherding.* You don't understand. Worse luck for you, old bird."

You can set up State Aid and Old Age Pensions and Young Age Pensions till you're black in the face. But if you can't cure people of being frightened for their own existence, you'll educate them in vain. You may as well let a frightened little Jimmy Shepherd go bottle-blowing at the age of four. If he's frightened for his own existence, he'll never do more than keep himself assertively materially alive. And that's the end of it. So he might just as well start young, and avoid those lying years of idealistic education.

So that the first thing to be done, in the education of the people, is to cure them of the fear of not earning their own living. This won't be easy. The fear goes deep, in our nervous age. Men will go through all the agonies of war, and come out more frightened still of not being able to earn their living. It is a mystery. They will face guns and shells and unspeakable horrors, almost with equanimity. After all, that's merely death. It's not life. Life is the thing to be afraid of—and having enough money to live on is the anguished soul-problem It has become an *idée fixe,* the idea of earning, or not earning, a living. And we are all monomaniacs in it.

And yet, the only way to solve the whole problem is to cure mankind, from the inside, of the fear. And this is the business of our reformed education. At present, we are all in the boat because our idealists are just as terrified of not earning their living as are the materialists. Even more.

That's the point! The idealists are more terrified than the materialists about not being able to earn their living. The materialists are brutal about it. They don't have to excuse themselves. They handle the tools and do the graft. But the idealists, those that sit in the Olympus of Whitehall, for example? It is they who tremble. They are earning their living tooth-and-nail, by promulgating up there in the clouds. But the material world cocks its eye on them. It keeps them there as a luxury, as the Greeks kept their Olympic gods. After all, the idealists butter our motives with fair words, and their own parsnips. When we have at last decided that our motives are none the better for the fair-word buttering of idealism, then the idealists will have to eat their Olympic parsnips very dry. Which is what they are afraid of. So they churn fair words, up there, and the proletariat chums margarine and a little butter down below, and so far, there is an exchange. But as the price of butter rises the price of fair words depreciates, till the idealists are in a fair way of doing no trade at all, up on Olympus. Which is what they are afraid of. So they churn phrases like mad, hoping to bring out something that will catch the market.

And there we are. Between the idealists and the materialists our poor "elementary" children have their education shaken into them. Which is a shame. It is a shame to treat children as we treat them in school, to a lot of highfalutin and lies, and to a lot of fear and humiliation. Instead of putting the fear of the Lord into them we put the fear of the job. After which the job rises up and gives us a nasty knock in the eye, we get strikes and Labour menaces, and idealism is in a fair way of being kicked off Olympus altogether. Materialism threatens to sit aloft. And Olympus fawns and cringes, and is terrified because it doesn't know how it will earn its living.

Idealism would be all right if it weren't *frightened.* But it *is* frightened: frightened to death. It is terrified that it won't be able to butter its parsnips. It is terrified that it won't be able to make a living. Curious thing, but rich people are inwardly more terrified of poverty, want, destitution, even than poor people. Even the proletariat is not so agonised with fear of not being able to make a living as are millionaires and dukes. The more the money the more intense the fear.

So there we are, all living in an agony and nightmare of fear of not being able to make a living. But we actually *are* the living. We live, and therefore everything is ours. Whence then the fear?—Just a sort of irrational mob-panic.

Idealism *must* get over its fright. It is most to blame. There it sits in a fog promulgating ideas and ideals, and all the time in a mad panic for fear of losing its job. There it sits decreeing that our children shall be educated pure from the taint of materialism and industrialism, and all the time it is fawning and cringing before industrialism and materialism, and having throes and spasms of agony about its own salary. Certainly even idealists must have a salary. But why are in such agonies of fear lest it be not forthcoming? After all, if they draw a salary, it is because they are *not* frightened. Their salary is the tithe due to their living fearlessly. And so, cadging their screw in panic, they are a swindle. And they cause our children to be educated to the tune of their swindlery.

And then no wonder that our children, the children of the people, look down their nose at ideals. It is no wonder the young workmen sneer at all idealism, all idealists, and at everything higher than wages and short hours. They're having their own back on the lie, and on the liars that educated them in school. They've been educated in the lie, and therefore they also can spout idealism at will. But by their deeds ye shall know them: both parties.

Here's the end then of the first word on Education. Idealism is no good without fearlessness. To follow a high aim, you must be fearless of the consequences. To promulgate a high aim and to be fearful of the consequences—as our idealists today—is much worse than leaving high aims alone altogether. Teach the three R's and leave the children to look out for their own aims. That's the very best thing we can do at the moment, since we are all cowards.

But later, when we've plucked a bit of our courage up, we'll embark on a new course of education, and *vogue la galère.* Those of us that are going to starve, why, we'll take our chance. Who has wits and *guts,* doesn't starve: neither does he care about starving. *Courage, mes amis.*

II

Elementary Education today assumes two responsibilities. It has in its hands the moulding of the nation. And elementary school-teachers are taught that they are to mould the young nation to two ends. They are to strive to produce in the child under their charge:

        1. The perfect citizen
        2. The perfect individual.

Unfortunately the teachers are not enlightened as to what we mean by a perfect citizen and a perfect individual. When they are, during their training, instructed and lectured upon the teaching of history, they are told that the examples of history teach us the virtues of citizenship: and when drawing and painting and literary composition are under discussion, these subjects are supposed to teach the child self-expression.

Citizenship has been an indefinite Fata Morgana to the elementary teacher: but self-expression has been a worse. Before the war we sailed serene under this flag of self-expression. Each child was to *express himself*: why, nobody thought necessary to explain. But infants were to express *themselves,* and nothing but themselves. Here was a pretty task for a teacher: he was to make his pupil *express himself* Which *self* was left vague. A child was to be given a lump of soft clay and told to express himself, presumably in the pious hope that he might model a Tanagra figure or a Donatello plaque, all on his little lonely-o.

Now it is obvious that every boy's first act of self-expression would be to throw the lump of soft clay at something: preferably at the teacher. This impulse is to be suppressed. On what grounds, metaphysically? since the soft clay was given for self-expression. To this just question there is no answer. Self-expression in infants means, presumably, incipient Tanagra figurines and Donatello plaques, incipient Iliads and Macbeths and Odes to the Nightingale a world of infant prodigies, in short. And the responsibility for all this foolery was heaped on the shoulders of that public clown, the elementary school-teacher.

The war, however, brought us to our senses a little, and we ran the flag of citizenship up above the flag of self-expression. This was easier for the teacher. At least now the ideal was *service,* not self-expression. "Work, and learn to serve your country." Service means authority: while self-expression means pure negation of all authority. So that teaching became a somewhat simpler matter under the idea of national service.

However, the war is over, and there is a slump in national service. The public isn't inspired by the ideal of serving its country any more: it has had its whack. And the idealists, who must run to give the public the inspiration it fancies at the moment, are again coming forward with trayfuls of infant prodigies and "self-expression."

Now citizenship and self-expression are all right, as ideals for the education of the people, if only we knew what we meant by the two terms. The interpretation we give them is just ludicrous. Self-sacrifice in time of need: disinterested nobility of heart to enable each one to vote properly at a general election: an understanding of what is meant by income tax and money interest: all vague and fuzzy. Nobody proceeds to enlighten the teacher as to the mysteries of citizenship. Nobody attempts to instruct *him* in the relationship of the individual to the community. Nothing at all. There is a little gas about *esprit de corps* and national interest—but it is all gas.

None of which would matter if we would just leave the ideals *out* of our educational system. If we were content to teach a child to read and write and do his modicum of arithmetic, just as at an earlier stage his mother teaches him to walk and to talk, so that he may toddle his little way upon the face of the earth by himself, it would be all right. It would be a thousand times better, as things stand, to chuck overboard all your drawing and painting and music and modelling and pseudo-science and "graphic" history and "graphic" geography and "self-expression," all the lot. Pitch them overboard, teach the three R's, and then let the child look after himself. Teach the three R's, and then proceed with a certain amount of technical instruction, in preparation for the coming job. For all the rest, for all that concerns the child himself, leave him alone. If he likes to learn, the means of learning are in his hands. Brilliant scholars could be drafted on to secondary schools. If he doesn't like to learn, it is his affair. The quality of learning is not strained. Is not radical *unlearnedness* just as true a form of self-expression, and just as desirable a state, for many natures (even the bulk), as learnedness? Here we talk of free self-expression, and we proceed to force all natures into ideal and aesthetic expression. We talk about individuality, and try to drag up every weed into a rose-bush. If a nettle likes to be a nettle, if it likes to have no flowers to speak of, why, that's the nettle's affair. Why should we force some poor devil of an elementary school-teacher to sting his fingers to bits, trying to graft the obstreperous nettle-stem with rose and vine? We, who sail under the flag of freedom, are bullies such as the world has never known before: idealist bullies: bullying idealism, which will allow nothing except in terms of itself.

Every teacher knows that it is worse than useless trying to educate at least fifty per-cent of his scholars. Worse than useless: it is dangerous: perilously dangerous. What is the result of it? Drag a lad who has no capacity for true learning or understanding through the processes of education, and what do you produce in him, in the end? A profound contempt for education, and for all educated people. It has meant nothing to him but irritation and disgust. And that which a man finds irritating and disgusting he finds odious and contemptible.

And this is the point to which we are bringing the nation, inevitably. Everybody is educated: and what is education? A sort of *unmanliness*. Go down in the hearts of the masses of the people and this is what you'll find: the cynical conviction that every educated man is unmanly, less manly than an uneducated man. Every little Jimmy Shepherd has dabbled his bit in pseudo-science and in the arts, he has seen a test-tube and he has handled plasticine and a camel's-hair brush, he knows that a+a+b = 2a+b. What more is there for him to know? Nothing. Pfui to your learning.

A little learning *is* a dangerous thing: how dangerous, we are likely to be finding out. A man who has not the soul, or the spirit, to learn and to *understand,* he whose whole petty education consists in the acquiring of a few tricks will inevitably, in the end, come to regard all educated or understanding people as tricksters. And once *that* happens, what becomes of your State? It is inevitably at the mercy of your bottle-washing Jimmy Shepherds and his parallel Nancies. For the uninstructible outnumber the instructible by a very large majority. Behold us then in the grimy fist of Jimmy Shepherd, the uninstructible Brobdingnag. Fools we are, we've put ourselves there: so if he pulls all our heads off, serves us right. He is brobdingnagian because he is legion. Whilst we poor instructible mortals are lilliputian in comparison. And the one power we had, the power of commanding reverence or respect in the brobdingnag, a power God-given to us, we ourselves have squandered and degraded. On our own heads be it.

For a sensible system of education, then. Begin at the age of seven—five is too soon—and teach reading, writing, arithmetic as the only necessary mental subjects: reading to include geography, map practice, history, and so on. Three hours a day is enough for these. Another hour a day might be devoted to physical and domestic training. Leave a child alone for the rest: out of sight and out of mind.

At the age of twelve make a division. Teachers, school-masters, school-inspectors and parents will carefully decide what children shall be educated further. These shall be drafted to secondary schools where an extended curriculum includes Latin or French, and some true science. Secondary scholars will remain till the age of sixteen.

The children who will not be drafted to the secondary schools will, at the age of twelve, have their "mental" education reduced to two hours, whilst three hours will be devoted to physical and domestic training: that is, martial exercises and the rudiments of domestic labour, such as boot-mending, plumbing, soldering, painting and paper-hanging, gardening—all those minor trades on which domestic life depends, and in which every working man should have some proficiency. This is to continue for three years.

Then on the completion of the fourteenth year, these scholars will be apprenticed half-time to some trade to which they are judged fitting by a consensus of teachers and parents and the scholars themselves. For two years these half-timers shall spend the morning at their own trade, and some two hours in the afternoon at martial exercises and reading and at what we call domestic training, boot mending etc. At the age of sixteen they enter on their regular labours, as artizans.

The secondary scholars shall for two years, from the age of twelve to the age of fourteen follow the curriculum of the secondary school for four hours a day, but shall put in one hour a day at the workshops and at physical training. At the completion of the fourteenth year a division shall be made among these secondary scholars. Those who are apparently "complete," as far as mental education can make them according to their own nature and capacity, shall be drafted into some apprenticeship for some sort of semi-profession, such as school-teaching, and all forms of clerking. Like the elementary scholars, however, all secondary scholars put in two hours in the afternoon at reading and in the workshops or at physical training: one hour for the mental education, one hour for the physical. At the age of sixteen clerks, school-teachers etc. shall enter their regular work, or the regular training for their work.

The remaining scholars, of the third or highest class shall at the age of sixteen be drafted into colleges. Those that have a scientific bent shall be trained scientifically, those that incline to the liberal arts shall be educated according to their inclination, and those that have gifts in the pure arts or in the technical arts shall find artistic training. But an hour a day shall be devoted to some craft, and to physical training. Every man shall have a craft at which finally he is expert—or two crafts if he choose—even if he be destined for professional activity as a doctor, a lawyer, a priest, a professor, and so on.

The scholars of the third class shall remain in their colleges till the age of twenty, receiving there a general education as in our colleges today, although emphasis is laid on some particular branch of the education. At the age of twenty these scholars shall be drafted for their years of final training—as doctors, lawyers, priests, artists and so on. At the age of twenty-two they shall enter the world.

All education should be State education. All children should start together in the elementary schools. From the age of seven to the age of twelve boys and girls of every class should be educated together in the elementary schools. This will give us a common human basis, a common radical understanding. All children, boys and girls, should receive a training in the respective male and female domestic crafts. Every man should finally be expert at some craft, and should be a trained *free* soldier, no matter what his profession. Every woman also should have her chosen, expert craft, so that each individual is master of some kind of work.

Of course a great deal will depend on teachers and head-masters. The elementary teachers will not be so terribly important, but they will be carefully selected for their power to control and instruct children, not for their power to pass examinations. Head-masters will always be men of the highest education, invested with sound authority. A head-master, once established, will be like a magistrate in a community.

Because one of the most important parts in this system of education will be the judging of the scholars. Teachers, masters inspectors and parents will all of them unite to decide the next move for the child. The child will be consulted—but the last decision will be left to the head-master and the inspector—the final word to the inspector.

Again, no decision will be final. If at any time it shall become apparent that a child is unfit for the group he occupies, then after a proper consultation he shall be removed to his own natural group. Again if a child has no capacity for arithmetic, we shall not persist for five years in drilling arithmetic into him. Some form of useful manual work will be substituted for the arithmetic lesson: and so on.

Such is a brief sketch of a sensible system of education for a civilised people. It may be argued that it puts too much power into the hands of school-masters and school-inspectors. But better there than in the hands of factory-owners and trades unions. The position of masters and inspectors will be discussed later.

Again, it may be argued that there is too much rule and government here. As a matter of fact, we are all limited to our own natures. And the aim above all others in this system is to recognise the true nature in each child, and to give each its natural chance. If we want to be free, we cannot be free to do otherwise than follow our own soul, our own true nature, to its fulfilment. And for this purpose primarily the suggested scheme would exist. Each individual is to be helped wisely, reverently, towards his own natural fulfilment. Children can't choose for themselves. They are not sufficiently conscious. A choice is made, even if nobody makes it. The bungle of circumstances decrees the fate of almost every child today. Which is why most men hate their fates, circumstantial and false as they are.

And then, as to cost: which is always important. Our present system of education is extravagantly expensive, and simply dangerous to our social existence. It turns out a lot of half-informed youth despise the whole business of understanding and wisdom, and who realise that in a world like ours nothing but money matters. Our system of education tacitly grants that nothing but money matters, but puts up a little parasol of human ideals under which human divinity can foolishly masquerade for a few hours during school life, and on Sundays. Coming from under this parasol little Jimmy Shepherd knows that he's quite as divine as anybody else. He's quite as much a little god as anybody else, because he's been told so in school from the age of five till the age of fifteen, so he ought to know.

Nobody's any better than *he* is: he's quite as good as anybody else; and, because he's a poor dustman's son, even more acceptable in the eyes of God. And therefore why hasn't he got as much money? since money is all that he can make any use of. His own human divinity is no more use to him than anybody else's human divinity, and once it comes to fighting for shillings he's absolutely not going to be put off by any toffee about ideals. And there we are with little Jimmy Shepherd, aged fifteen. He's a right dangerous little party, all of our own making: and his name is legion.

Our system of education today threatens our whole social existence tomorrow. We should be wise if by decree we shut up all elementary schools at once, and kept them shut. Failing that, we must look round for a better system, one that will work.

But if we try a new system, we must know what we're about. No good floundering into another muddle. While education was strictly a religious process, it had a true goal. While it existed for governing classes, it had a goal. And *universal elementary* education has had a goal. But a fatal one.

We have assumed that we could educate Jimmy Shepherd and make him a Shelley or an Isaac Newton. At the very least, we were sure we could make him a highly intelligent being. And we're just beginning to find our mistake. We can't make a highly intelligent being out of Jimmy Shepherd. Why should we, if the Lord created him only moderately intelligent? Why do we want always to go one better than the Creator?

So now, having gone a very long way downhill on a very dangerous road, and having got ourselves thoroughly entangled in a vast mob which may at any moment start to bolt down to the precipice Gadarene-wise, why, the best we can do is to try to steer uphill.

We've got first to find which way *is* uphill. We've got to shape our course by some just idea. We shaped it by a faulty idea of equality and the perfectibility of man. Now for the true idea: either that or the precipice edge.

III

It is obvious that the old idea of Equality won't do. It is landing us daily deeper in a mess. And yet no idea which has passionately swayed mankind can be altogether wrong: not even the most fallacious-seeming. Therefore, before we can dispose of the equality ideal, the ideal that all men are essentially equal, we have got to find how far it is true.

In no sense whatever are men actually equal. Physically, some are big and some are small, some weak, some strong; mentally, some are intelligent, some are not, and the degrees of difference are infinite; spiritually, some are rare and fine, some are vulgar; morally, some are repulsive and some attractive. True, all men have noses, mouths, stomachs and so on. But then this is a mere abstraction. Every nose, every stomach is different, actually, from every other nose and stomach. It is according to the individual. Noses and stomachs are not interchangeable. You might perhaps graft the end of one man's nose on the nose of another man. But the grafted gentleman would not thereby have a dual identity. His essential self would remain the same: a little disfigured, perhaps, but not metamorphosed. Whatever tricks you may perform, of grafting one bit of an individual on another, you don't produce a new individual, a new type. You only produce a disfigured, patched-up old individual. It isn't like grafting roses. You couldn't graft bits of Lord Northcliffe on a thousand journalists and produce a thousand Napoleons of the Press. Every journalist would remain himself: a little disfigured or mutilated, maybe.

It is quite sickening to hear scientists rambling on about the interchange of tissue and members from one individual to another. They have at last reached the old alchemistic fantasy of producing the homunculus. They hope to take the hind leg of a pig and by happy grafting produce a marvellous composite individual, a fused erection of living tissue which will at last prove that man can *make* man, that therefore he isn't divine at all, he is a purely human marvel, only so extraordinarily clever and marvellous that the sun will stop still to look at him.

When science begins to generalise from its own performances it is puerile as the alchemists were, at last. The truth about man, before he falls into imbecility, is that each one is just himself. That's the first, the middle truth. Every man has his own identity, which he preserves till he falls into imbecility or worse. Upon this clue of his own identity every man is fashioned. And the clue of a man's own identity is a man's own self or soul, that which is incommutable and incommunicable in him. Every man, while he remains a man and does not lapse into disintegration, becoming a lump of chaos, is truly himself, only himself, no matter how many fantastic attitudes he may assume. True it is, that man goes and gets a host of ideas in his head and proceeds to reconstruct himself according to those ideas. But he never actually succeeds in this business of reconstructing himself out of his own head, until he has gone cracked. And then he may prance on all fours like Nebuchadnezzar, or do as he likes. But whilst he remains sane the buzzing ideas in his head will never allow him to change or metamorphose his own identity: modify, yes; but never change. While a man remains sane he remains himself and nothing but himself, no matter how fantastically he may attitudinise according to some pet idea. For example this of equality. Saint Francis was ready to fall in rapture at the feet of the peasant. But he wasn't ready to take the muck-rake from the peasant's hands and start spreading manure at twopence a day, an insignificant and forgotten nobody, a serf. Not at all. Saint Francis kept his disciples and was a leader of men, in spite of all humility, poverty, and equality. Quite right, because Saint Francis was by nature a leader of men, and what has any creed or theory of equality to do with it? He was born such: it was his own intrinsic being. In his soul he was a leader. Where does equality come in? Why, by his poverty Saint Francis wished to prove his own intrinsic superiority, not his equality.—And if a man is a born leader, what does it matter if he hasn't got twopence or if he has got two million. His own nature is his destiny, not his purse.

All a man can be, at the very best, is himself. At the very worst he can be something a great deal less than himself, a money-grubber, a millionaire, a State, like Louis Quatorze, a self-conscious ascetic, a spiritual prig, a grass-chewing Nebuchadnezzar.

So where does equality come in? Men are palpably unequal in *every* sense except the mathematical sense. Every man counts one: and this is the root of all equality: here, in a pure intellectual abstraction.

The moment you come to compare them, men are unequal, and their inequalities are infinite. But supposing you *don't* compare them. Supposing, when you meet a man, you have the pure decency not to compare him either with yourself or with anything else. Supposing you can meet a man with this same singleness of heart. What then? Is the man your equal, your inferior, your superior? He can't be, if there is no comparison. If there be no comparison, he is the incomparable. He is the incomparable. He is single. He is himself.—When I am single-hearted, I don't compare myself with my neighbour. He is immediate to me, I to him. He is not my equal, because this presumes comparison. He is incomparably himself, I am incomparably myself. We behold each other in our pristine and simple being. And this is the first, the finest, the perfect way of human intercourse.

And on this great first-truth of the pristine incomparable nature of every individual soul is founded, mistakenly, the theory of equality. Every man, when he is incontestably himself, is single, incomparable, beyond compare. But to deduce from this that all men are equal is a sheer false deduction: a simple *non sequitur*. Let every man be himself, purely himself. And then, in the evil hour when you *do* start to compare, you will see the endless inequality between men.

In the perfect human intercourse, a relation establishes itself happily and spontaneously. No two men meet one another direct without a spontaneous equilibrium taking place. Doubtless there is inequality between the two. But there is no *sense* of inequality. The give and take is perfect; without knowing, each is adjusted to the other. It is as the stars fall into their place, great and small. The small are as perfect as the great, because each is itself and in its own place. But the great are none the less the great, the small the small. And the joy of each is that it is so.

The moment I begin to pay direct mental attention to my neighbour, however; the moment I begin to scrutinise him and attempt to set myself over *against* him, the element of comparison enters. Immediately I am aware of the inequalities between us. But even so, it is inequalities and not inequality. There is *never* either any equality or any inequality between me and my neighbour. Each of us is himself, and as such is single, alone in the universe, and not to be compared. Only in our parts are we comparable. And our parts are vastly unequal.

Which finishes Equality for ever, as an ideal. Finishes also Fraternity. For fraternity implies a consanguinity which is almost the same as equality. Men are not equal, neither are they brothers. They are themselves. Each one is himself, and each one is essentially, starrily responsible for himself. Any assumption by one person of responsibility for another person is an interference, and a destructive tyranny. No person is responsible for the *being* of any other person. Each one is starrily single, starrily self-responsible, not to be blurred or confused.

Here then is the new ideal for society: not that all men are equal, but that each man is himself: "one is one and all alone and ever more shall be so." Particularly this is the ideal for a new system of education. Every man shall be himself, shall have every opportunity to come to his own intrinsic fulness of being. There are unfortunately many individuals to whom these words mean nothing: mere verbiage. We must have a proper contempt and defiance of these individuals, though their name be legion.

How are we to obtain that a man shall come to his own fulness of being, that a child shall grow up true to his own essential self. It is no use just letting the child do as it likes. Because the human being, more than any other living thing, is susceptible to falsification. We alone have mental consciousness, speech and thought. And this mental consciousness is our greatest peril.

A child in the bath sees the soap, and wants it, and won't be happy till he gets it. When he gets it he rubs it into his eyes and sucks it, and is in a far more unhappy state. Why? To see the soap and to want it is a natural act on the part of any young animal, a sign of that wonderful naïve curiosity which is so beautiful in young life. But the "he won't be happy till he gets it" quality is alas, purely human. A young animal, if diverted, would forget the piece of soap at once. It is only an accident in his horizon. Or, given the piece of soap, he would sniff it, perhaps turn it over, and then merely abandon it. Beautiful to us is the pure nonchalance of a young animal which *forgets* the piece of soap the moment it has sniffed it and found it no good. Only the intelligent human baby proceeds to fill its mouth, stomach and eyes with acute pain, on account of the piece of soap.—Why? Because the poor little wretch got an idea, an incipient idea into its little head. The rabbit never gets an idea into its head, so it can sniff the soap and turn away. But a human baby, poor, tormented little creature, *can't help* getting an idea into his young head. And then he *can't help* acting on his idea: no matter what the consequences.—And this bit of soap shows us what a bitter responsibility our mental consciousness is to us, and how it leads astray even the infant in his bath. Poor innocent: we like to imagine him a spontaneous, unsophisticated little creature. But what do we mean by sophistication? We mean that a being is at the mercy of some idea which it has got into its head, and which has no true relation to its actual desire or need. Witness the piece of soap. The baby saw the piece of soap, and got an idea into its head that the soap was immeasurably desirable. Acting on this simple idea it nearly killed itself, and filled an hour or so of its young life with horrid misery.

It is only when we grow up that we learn not to be run away with by ideas which we get in our heads and which don't correspond to any true natural desire or need. At least, education and growing-up is supposed to be a process of learning to escape the automatism of ideas, to live direct from the spontaneous, vital centre of oneself.

Anyhow, it is criminal to expect children to "express themselves" and to bring themselves up. They will eat the soap and pour the treacle over their hair and put their fingers in the candle-flame, in the acts of physical self-expression, and in the wildness of spiritual self-expression they will just go to pieces. All because, really, they enough mental intelligence to obliterate their instinctive intelligence and to send them to destruction. A little animal that can crawl will manage to live, if abandoned. Abandon a child of five years and it won't merely die, it will almost certainly maim and kill itself. This mental consciousness we are born with is the most double-edged blessing of all, and grown-ups must spend years and years guarding their children from the disastrous effects of this blessing.

Now let us go back to the maxim that every human being must come to the fulness of himself. It is part of our sentimental and trashy creed today that a little child is most purely himself, and that growing up perverts him away from himself. We assume he starts as a spontaneous little soul, limpid, purely self-expressive, and grows up to be a sad sophisticated machine. Which is all very well, and might easily be so, if the mind of the little innocent didn't start to work so soon and to interfere with all his little spontaneity. Nothing is so subject to small, but fatal automatisation as a child: some little thing it sets its *mind* on, and the game is up. And a child is always setting its little mind on something, usually something which doesn't at all correspond with the true and restless desire of its living soul. And then, which will win, the little mind or the little soul? We all know, to our sorrow. When a child sets its little mind on the soap, its little soul, not to speak of its little eyes and stomach, is thrown to the winds. And yet the desire for the soap is only the misdirection of the eternally-yearning, desirous soul of an infant.

Here we are then. Instead of waiting for the wisdom out of the mouths of babes and sucklings, let us see that we keep the soap-tablet out of the same mouths. We've got to educate our children, and it's no light responsibility. We've got to try to educate them to that point where at last there will be a perfect correspondence between the spontaneous, yearning, impulsive-desirous soul and the automatic mind which runs on little wheels of ideas. And this the hardest job we could possibly set ourselves. For man just doesn't know how to interpret his own soul-promptings, and therefore he sets up a complicated arrangement of ideas and ideals and works himself automatically till he works himself into the grave or the lunatic asylum.

We've got to educate our children. Which means, we've got to decide for them: day after day, year after year, we've got to go on deciding for our children. It's not the slightest use asking little Jimmy "What would you like, dear?"—because little Jimmy doesn't know And if he *thinks* he knows, it's only because, as a rule, he's got some fatal little idea into his head, like the soap-tablet. Yet listen to the egregious British parent solemnly soliciting his young son "What would you like to be, dear? A doctor or a clergyman?"—"An engine-driver," replies Jimmy, and the comedy of babes-and-sucklings continues.

We've got to decide for our children: for years and years we have to make their decisions. And we've got to take the responsibility onto ourselves, as a community. It's no good feeding our young with a sticky ideal education till they are fourteen years old, then pitching them out, pap-fed, into the whirling industrial machine and the warren of back streets. It's no good expecting parents to do anything. Parents don't know how to decide, they go to little Jimmy as if he were the godhead. And even if they did know how to decide, they can do nothing in face of the factory and the trades union and the back streets.

We, the educators, have got to decide for the children: decide the steps of their young fates, seriously and reverently. It is a sacred business, and unless we can act from our deep, believing souls, we'd best not act at all, but leave it to Northcliffe and trades unions.

We must choose, with this end in view. We want quality of life, not quantity. We don't want swarms and swarms of people in back streets. We want distinct individuals, and these are incompatible with swarms and masses. A small, choice population, not a horde of hopeless units.

And every man to be himself, to come to his own fulness of being. Not every man a little wonder of cleverness or high ideals. Every man himself, according to his true nature. And those who are comparatively non-mental can form a vigorous, passionate proletariat of indomitable individuals: and those who will work as clerks to be free and energetic, not humiliated as they are now, but fierce with their own freedom of beings: and the *man* will be always more than his job, the job will be a minor business.

We must have an ideal. So let our ideal be living, spontaneous individuality in every man and woman. Which living, spontaneous individuality, being the hardest thing of all to come at, will need most careful rearing. Educators will take a grave responsibility upon themselves. They will be the priests of life, deep in the wisdom of life. They will be the life-priests of the new era. And the leaders, the inspectors, will be men deeply initiated into the mysteries of life, adepts in the dark mystery of living, fearing nothing but life itself, and subject to nothing but their own reverence for the incalculable life-gesture.

IV

It is obvious that a system of education such as the one we so briefly sketched out in our second chapter will inevitably produce distinct classes of society. The basis is the great class of workers. From this class will rise also the masters of industry, and probably, the leading soldiers. Second comes the clerkly caste, which will include teachers and minor professionals, and which will produce the local government bodies. Thirdly we have the class of the higher professions, legal, medical, scholastic: and this class will produce the chief legislators. Finally, there is the small class of the supreme judges: not merely legal judges, but judges of the destiny of the nation.

These classes will not arise accidentally, through the accident of money, as today. They will not derive through heredity, as the great oriental castes. There will be no automatism. A man will not be chosen to a class, or a caste, because he is exceptionally fitted for a particular job. If a child shows an astonishing aptitude, let us say for designing clocks, and at the same time has a profound natural life-understanding, then he will pass on to the caste of professional masters, or even to that of supreme judges, and his skill in clocks will only be one of his accomplishments, his *private* craft. The whole business of educators will be to estimate, not the particular faculty of the child for some particular job: not at all; nor even a specific intellectual capacity; the whole business will be to estimate the profound life-quality, the very nature of the child, that which makes him ultimately what he is, his soul-strength and his soul-wisdom which cause him to be a natural master of life. Technical capacity is all the time subsidiary. The highest quality is living understanding—not intellectual understanding. Intellectual understanding belongs to the technical activities. But vital understanding belongs to the masters of life. And all the professionals in our new world are not mere technical experts: they are life-directors. They, combine with their soul-power some great technical skill. But the first quality will be the soul-quality, the quality of being, and the power for the directing of life itself.

Hence we shall see that the system is primarily religious, and only secondarily practical. Our supreme judges and our master-professors will be primarily *priests.* Let us not take fright at the word. The true religious faculty is the most powerful and the highest faculty in man, once he exercises it. And by the religious faculty we mean the inward worship of the creative life-mystery: the implicit knowledge that life is unfathomable and unsearchable in its motives, not to be described, having no ascribable goal save the bringing-forth of an ever-changing, ever-unfolding creation: that new creative being and impulse surges up all the time in the deep fountains of the soul, from some great source which the world has known as God; that the business of man is to become so spontaneous that he shall utter at last direct the act and the *state* which arises in him from his deep being: and finally, that the mind with all its great powers is only the servant of the inscrutable, unfathomable soul. The *idea* or the *ideal* is only instrumental in the unfolding of the soul of man, a tool, not a goal. Always simply a tool.

We shall have the courage to refrain from dogma. Dogma is the translation of the religious impulse into an intellectual term. An intellectual term is a finite, fixed, mechanical thing. We must be content forever to live from the undescribed and indescribable impulse. Our God is the Unnamed, the Veiled, and any attempt to give names, or to remove veils, is just a mental impertinence which ends in nothing but futility and impertinencies.

So, the new system will be established upon the living religious faculty in men. In some men this faculty has a more direct expression in consciousness than in other men. Some men are aware of the deep troublings of the creative sources of their own souls, they are aware, they find speech or utterance in act, they come forth in consciousness. In other men the troublings are dumb, they will never come forth in expression, unless they find a mediator, a minister, an interpreter.

And this is how the great castes naturally arrange themselves. Those whose souls are alive and strong but whose voices are unmodulated, and whose thoughts unformed and slow, these constitute the great base of all peoples at all times: and it will always be so. For the creative soul is forever charged with the potency of still unborn speech, still unknown thoughts. It is the everlasting source which surges everlastingly with the massive, subterranean fires of creation, new creative being: and whose fires find issue in pure jets and bubblings of unthinkable newness only here and there, in a few, or comparatively few individuals.

It must always be so. We cannot imagine the deep fires of the earth rushing out everywhere, in a myriad myriad jets. The great volcanoes stand isolate. And at the same time the life-issues concentrate in certain individuals. Why it is so, we don't know. But why should we know? We are after all *only* individuals, we are not the eternal life-mystery itself.

And therefore, there will always be the vast, living masses of mankind, incoherent and almost expressionless by themselves, carried to perfect expression in the great individuals of their race and time. As the leaves of a tree accumulate towards blossom, so will the great bulk of mankind at all time accumulate towards its leaders. We don't want to turn every leaf of an apple-tree into a flower. And so why should we want to turn every individual human being into a unit of complete expression. Why should it be our goal to turn every coal-miner into a Shelley or a Parnell? We can't do either. Coal-miners are consummated in a Parnell, and Parnells are consummated in a Shelley. That is how life takes its way: in rising as a volcano rises to an apex, not in a countless multiplicity of small issues.

Time to recognise again this great truth of human life, and to put it once more into practice. Democracy is gone beyond itself. The true democracy is that in which a people gradually cumulates, from the vast base of the populace upwards through the zones of life and understanding to the summit where the great man, or the most perfect Utterer, is alone. The false democracy is that wherein every issue, even the highest, is dragged down to the lowest issue, the myriad-multiple lowest human issue: today, the wage.

Mankind may have a perverse, self-wounding satisfaction in this reversal of the life-course. But it is a poor, spiteful, ignominious satisfaction.

In its living periods mankind accumulates upwards, through the zones of life-expression and passionate consciousness, upwards to the supreme utterer, or utterers. In its disintegrating periods the reverse is the case. Man accumulates downwards, down to the lowest issue. And the great men of the downward

245

development are the men who symbolise the gradually sinking zones of being, till the final symbol, the great man who represents the wage-reality rises up and is hailed as the supreme. No doubt he is the material, mechanical universal of mankind, a unit of automatised existence.

It is a pity that democracy should be identified with this downward tendency. We who believe that every man's soul is single and incomparable, we thought we were democrats. But evidently democracy is a question of the integral wage, not the integral soul. If everything comes down to the wage, then down it comes. When it is a question of the human soul, the direction must be a cumulation upwards: upwards from the very roots, in the vast Demos, up to the very summit of the supreme judge and utterer, the first of men. There is a first of men: and there is the vast, basic Demos: always, at every age in every continent. The people is an organic whole, rising from the roots, through trunk and branch and leaf, to the perfect blossom. This is the tree of human life. The supreme blossom utters the whole tree, supremely. Roots, stem, branch, these have their own being. But their perfect climax is in the blossom which is beyond them, and which yet is organically one with them.

We see mankind through countless ages trying to express this truth. There is the rising up through degrees of aristocracy up to kings or emperors; there is a rising up through degrees of church dignity, to the pope; there is a rising up through zones of priestly and military elevation, to the Egyptian King-God; there is the strange accumulation of caste.

And what is the fault mankind has had to find with all these great systems? The fact that *somewhere,* the individual soul was discounted, abrogated. And where? Usually at the bottom. The slave, the serf, the vast populace, had no soul. It has been left to our era to put the populace in possession of its own soul. But no populace will ever know, by itself, what to do with its own soul. Left to itself it will never do more than demand a pound a day, and so on. The populace finds its living soul-expression cumulatively through the rising up of the classes above it, towards pure utterance or expression or being. And the populace has its supreme satisfaction in the up-flowing of the sap of life from its vast roots and trunk, up to the perfect blossom. The populace partakes of the flower of life: but it can never *be* the supreme, lofty flower of life: only leaves of grass. And shall we hew down the Tree of Life for the sake of the leaves of grass?

It is time to start afresh. And we need a system. Those who cry out against our present system, blame it for all evils of modern life, call it the Machine which devours us all, and demand the abolition of all systems, these people confuse the issue. They actually desire the disintegration of mankind into amorphousness and oblivion: like the parched dust of Babylon. Well, that is a goal, for those that want it.

As a matter of fact, all life is organic. You can't have the merest speck of rudimentary life, without organic differentiation. And men who are collectively active in organic life-production must be organised. Men who are active purely in material production must be mechanized. There is the duality.

Obviously a system which is established for the purposes of pure material production, as ours today, is in its very nature a mechanism, a social machine. In this system we live and die. But even such a system as the great popes tried to establish was palpably not a machine but an organisation, a social organism. There is nothing at all to be gained from disunion, disintegration, and amorphousness. From mechanical systematisation there is vast material productivity to be gained. But from an organic system of human life we shall produce the real blossoms of life and being.

There must be a system; there *must* be classes of men; there *must* be differentiation: either that, or amorphous nothingness. The true choice is not between system and no-system. The choice is between system and system, mechanical or organic.

We have blamed the great aristocratic systems of the past, because of the automatic principle of heredity upon which they were established. A great man does not necessarily have a son at all great. We have blamed the great ecclesiastical system of the Church of Rome for the autocratic principle of mediation on which it was established; we blame the automatism of caste, and of dogma. And then what? What do we put in place of all these semi-vital principles? The utterly non-vital, completely automatised system of material production. The ghosts of the great dead must turn on us.

What good is our own intelligence to us, if we will not use it in the greatest issues? Nothing will excuse us from the responsibility of living: even death is no excuse. We have to live. So we may as well live fully. We are doomed to live. And therefore it is not the smallest use running into *pis allers* and trying to shirk the responsibility of living. We can't get out of it.

And therefore the only thing to do is to undertake the responsibility with good grace. What responsibility? The responsibility of establishing a new system: a new, organic system, free as far as ever it can be from automatism or mechanism: a system which depends on the profound spontaneous soul of men.

How to begin? Is it any good having revolutions and cataclysms? Who knows. Revolutions and cataclysms may be inevitable. But they are merely hopeless and catastrophic unless there come to life the germ of a new mode. And the new mode must be incipient somewhere. And therefore, let us start with education.

Let us start at once with a new system of education: a system which will cost us no more, nay, less than the dangerous present system. At least we shall produce capable individuals. Let us first of all have compulsory instruction of all teachers, in the new idea. Then let us begin with the schools. Life can go on just the same. It is not a cataclysmic revolution. It is a forming of new buds upon the tree, under the harsh old foliage.

What do we want? We want to produce the new society of the future, gradually, livingly. It will be a slow job, but why not? We cut down the curriculum for the elementary school at once. We abolish all the smatterings. The smatterings of science, drawing, painting and music are only the absolute death-blow to real science and song and artistic capacity. Folk song lives till we have schools: and then it is dead, and the shrill shriek of self-conscious scholars is supposed to take its place.

Away with all smatterings. Away with the imbecile pretence of culture in the elementary schools. Remember the back streets, remember that the souls of the working people are only rendered neurasthenic by your false culture. We want to keep the young populace robust and sufficiently nonchalant. Teach a boy to read, to write, and to do simple sums and you have opened the door of all culture to him, if he wants to go through.

Even if we do no more, let us do so much. Away with all smatterings. Three hours a day of reading, writing and arithmetic, and that's the lot of mental education, until the age of twelve. When we say three hours a day, we mean the three hours of the morning. What it will amount to will be two hours of work: two intervals of absolutely free play, twenty minutes each interval: and twenty for assembly and clearing-up and dismissal.

In the afternoon, actual *martial* exercises, swimming, and games, actual gymnasium *games,* but no Swedish drill. None of that physical-exercise business, that meaningless, vicious self-automatisation: no athleticism. Never let physical movement be didactic, didactically performed from the mind.

Thus doing, we shall reduce the cost of our schools hugely, and we can hope to get sane children, not the smirking, self-conscious, nervous little creatures we do produce. If we dare to have workshops, let us convert some of our schools into genuine worksheds, where boys learn to mend boots and do joinering and carpentry and plumbing such as they will need in their own homes; other schools into kitchens, sculleries, and sewing-rooms, for the girls. But let this be definite technical instruction for practical use, not some nonsense of fancy wood-carving and model churches. And let the craft-instructors be actual craftsmen, not school-teachers. Separate the workshop entirely from the school. Let there be no connection. Avoid all "correlation," it is most vicious. Craftsmanship is a physical-spontaneous intelligence, quite apart from *ideal* intelligence and ruined by the introduction of the deliberate mental act.

And all the time, watch the *being* in each scholar. Let the school-master and the crafts master and the games master all watch the individual lads, to find out the living nature in each child, so that, ultimately, a man's destiny shall be shaped into the natural form of that man's being, not as now, where children are rammed down into ready-made destinies, like so much canned fish.

You can cut down the expenses of the morning school to one-half. Big classes will not matter. The *personal* element, personal supervision is of no moment.

V

State Education has a dual aim.

1. The production of the desirable citizen
2. The development of the individual.

You can obtain one kind of perfect citizen by suppressing individuality and cultivating the public virtues: which has been the invariable tendency of reform, and of social idealism in modern days. A real individual has a spark of danger in him, a menace to society. Quench this spark and you quench the individuality, you obtain a social unit, not an integral man. All modern progress has tended, and still tends, to the production of quenched social units: dangerless beings, ideal creatures!

On the other hand, by the over-development of the individualistic qualifies, you produce a disintegration of all society. This was the Greek danger, as the quenching of the individual in the social unti was the Roman danger.

You must have a harmony and an inter-relation between the two modes. Because, though man is first and foremost an individual being, yet the very accomplishing of his individuality rests upon his fulfilment in social life. If you isolate an individual you deprive him of his life: if you leave him no isolation you deprive him of himself. And there it is! Life consists in the interaction between a man and his fellows, from the individual, integral core in each.

And upon what does human relationship rest? It rests upon our accepted attitude to life, our belief in the life-aims, and in our conception of right and wrong. No matter how we may pretend, for example, to be free from moral dogma, every one of our actions and even our emotions is under the influence of our in-grown moral creed. We cannot act without moral bias. Still more, we are influenced by our conception of the nature of man. We believe that, being men and women, we are therefore such and such and such. Without formulating or putting into any conscious expression what our idea of a man and a woman, a white man and a white woman *is,* we still have a large, potent idea, accumulated in our psyche through course of ages. And according to this *idea* of what we ourselves are, and of what our neighbour is, we take up our attitude to the world, and we model all our behaviour. Lastly, though we express it or not, we believe that life has some great goal, of happiness and peace and harmony, and all our judgments are biassed by this belief.

Here we are, then, born and swaddled in fixed beliefs, no matter how we may deny our beliefs, with lip-denial. There they are, in our very tissue. And they are not to be ousted save by new beliefs.

Such is man: a creature of beliefs and of foregone conclusion. As a matter of fact, we should never put one foot before the other, save for the foregone conclusion that we shall find the earth beneath the outstretched foot. Man travels a long journey through time. And the nature of the ground which he finds beneath his feet, in the darkness of his travels, varies from time to time. Sometimes even he discovers himself upon the brink of a precipice, on the shore of a sea. Remains then to adopt a new conclusion, to take a new direction, to put the feet down differently. When we pass from Arabia Felix to Arabia Petraea, it needs must be with a different tread. Man *must* walk. And to walk he must believe that he will find the ground there under his every stride. That is, he must have beliefs and foregone conclusions, and conceptions of what the nature of life is, and the goal thereof. Only, as the land changes, his beliefs must change. It is no use charging on over the edge of a precipice. It is no use plunging on from stony ground into soft sand, and keeping the same hob-nailed boots on. Man is given mental intelligence in order that he may effect quick changes, quick readjustments, preserving himself alive and integral through a myriad environments and adverse circumstances which would exterminate a non-adaptable animal.

So now that the human soul is drawing near the conclusion of one of its great phases: now it has suddenly blundered out of Arabia Felix into Arabia Deserta, and is passing beyond the zone of grass and green trees altogether into the magic of the sands, it behoves us all to readjust ourselves. We can't go back to the fleshpots of the old fat peace, because the old fat peace is not within us. Let us go on, then, and adjust ourselves to the new stage.

We have got to discover a new mode of human relationship—for man is the world to man. We have blundered blind into a new world, and we don't know how to get on. It behoves us to find out.

We have got to discover a new mode of human relationship. Which means, incidentally, that we have got to get a new conception of man and of ourselves. And we have then to establish a new morality.

It is useless to think that we can go along with a conception of what man is, and without a belief in ourselves, and without the morality to support this belief. The only point is that our conception, our belief, and our morality, though valid for the time being, is valid only for the time being. We are a million things which we don't know we are. Now and again we make new and shocking discoveries in ourselves: our right hand suddenly becomes a new and monstrous-seeming member to us, our right eye has the iniquity to see those things which were never before seen. Hence a dilemma. We have either to cut off the hand and pluck out the eye, and remain virtuously *in statu quo*. Or we have to accept the eye and accept the hand, and admit that our virtue has lost its validity. In this latter issue, we must grow a new virtue as a snake grows a new skin. Which we can do, if we will, with much *éclat*.

Now the good old creed we have been suckled in teaches us that man is *essentially* and *finally* an ideal being: essentially and finally a pure spirit, an abstraction, a term of abstract consciousness. As such he has his immortality and his identity with the infinite. This identity with the infinite is the goal of life. Arid it is reached through love, self-abandoning love. All that is truly love is good and holy, all that is not truly love is evil.

There is the creed, in a nutshell. And any creed which is to be found in a nutshell is a creed which has dropped off the tree of life, and is finished.

Now it is according to this creed that we proceed, at present, to educate our children. Sentimentally, we like to assume that a child is a little pure spirit arrived out of the infinite and clothed in innocent, manna-like flesh. This pure little spirit only needs to be fed on beauty, truth, and light, and it will grow up into a creature so near the angels that we'd best not mention it. Little stories full of love and sacrifice, little acts full of grace, little productions, little models in plasticine more spiritual than Donatello, little silver-point drawings more ethereal than Botticelli, little water-colour blobs that will suggest the world's dawn: all these things we quite seriously expect of small children, and in this expectation Whitehall gravely elaborates the educational system.

Ideal and innocent little beings, their minds only need to be *led* into the Canaan of their promise, and we shall have a world of *blameless* Shelleys and *superior* Botticellis. The degree of blamelessness and ideal superiority we set out to attain, in educating our children, is unimaginable. Pure little spirits, unblemished darlings! So sad that as they grow up some of the grossness of the world creeps in! *How* it creeps in, heaven knows, unless it is through the Irish stew and rice pudding at dinner. Or perhaps *somewhere* there are evil communications to corrupt good manners: time itself seems the great corrupter.

Whatever the end may be—and the end is bathos—our children *must* be regarded as ideal little beings, and their little minds must be *led* into blossom. Of course their little bodies are important: most important. Because, of course, their little bodies are the instruments of their dear little minds. And therefore you can't have a good sweet mind without a sweet healthy body. Give *every* attention to the body, for it is the sacred ark, the holy vessel which contains the holy of holies, the *mind* of the ideal little creature. *Mens sana in corpore sano.*

And therefore the child is taught to cherish its own little body, to do its little exercises and its little drill, so that it can become a fine man, or a fine woman. Let it only turn its *mind* to its own physique, and it will produce a physique that would shame Phidias. Let only the mind take up the body, and it will produce a body as a show gardener produces carrots, something to take your breath away. For the mind, the ideal reality, this is omnipotent and everything. The body is but a lower extension from the mind, diminishing in virtue as it descends. What is noble is near the brain: the ignoble is near the earth. A child is an ideal little creature, a term of ideal consciousness, pure spirit.

Any ideal, once it is really established, becomes ridiculous, so ridiculous that we begin to feel a certain mistrust of mankind's collective sense of humour. A man is never half such a fool as mankind makes of him. Mankind is a sententious imbecile without misgiving. When an individual reaches this stage, we put him away.

Well, our ideal little darlings, our innocents from the infinite, our sweet and unspoiled little natures, our little spirits straight from the hands of the Maker, our idealised little children, what are we making of them, as we lead their pure little minds into the Canaan of promise, as we educate them up to all that is pure and spiritual and ideal? What are we making of them? Fools, bitter fools. Bitter fools. If you want to know, ask them.

What is a child? A breath of the spirit of God? Well then, the breath of the spirit of God is something that still needs defining. It isn't like the waft of a handkerchief perfumed with Ess-Bouquet.

But seriously, before we can dream of pretending to educate a child, we must get a different notion of the nature of children. When we see a seed putting forth its fat cotyledon do we rhapsodise about the pure beauty of the divine issue? When we see a foal on stalky legs creaking after its mother are we smitten with dazzled revelation of the hidden God? If we want to be dazzled with revelation, look at a mature tree in full blossom, a mature stallion in the full pride of spring. Look at a man or a woman in the magnificence of their full-grown power, not at a tubby infant.

What is an infant? What is its holy little mind? An infant is a new clue to an as-yet-unformed human being, and its little mind is a pulp of undistinguished memory and cognition. A little child has one clue to itself, central within itself. For the rest it is new pulp, busy with differentiation towards the great goal of fulfilled being. Instead of worshipping the child, and seeing in it a divine emission which time will stale, we ought to realise that here is a new little clue to a human being, laid soft and vulnerable on the face of the earth. Here is our responsibility, to see that this unformed thing shall come to its own final form and fulness, both physical and mental.

Which is a long and difficult business. We have to feed the little creature in more ways than one: not only its little stomach and its little mind, but its little passions and will, its senses. Long experience has taught us that a baby should be fed on milk and pap: though we're not *quite* sure even now, whether carrot-water wouldn't be better. Our ancient creed makes us insist on awaking the little "mind." We are all quite agreed that we have serious responsibilities with regard to the infant stomach and the infant mind. But we don't even know, yet, that there is anything else.

We think that all the reaction goes on within the stomach and the little brain. All that is wonderful, under the soft little skull; all that is tiresome, under the tubby wall of the abdomen. A set of organs which *ought* to work beautifully and

251

automatically, considering the care we take: and a marvellous little mind which, we are sure, is full of invisible celestial blossoms of consciousness.

Poor baby: no wonder it is queer. That self-same little stomach isn't half so automatic as we and our precious doctors would like to have it. The "instrument" of the human body isn't half so instrumental as it might be. Imagine a kettle, for instance, suddenly refusing to sit on the fire, and not to be persuaded. Think of a sewing-machine that insisted on sewing cushions, nothing but cushions, and would not be pacified. What a world! And yet we go on expecting the baby's stomach to cook the food and boil the water automatically, as if it were a kettle. And when it refuses, we still talk to it as if it *were* a kettle. Anything rather than depart from our foregone conclusion that the human body is a complicated instrument, a sort of system of retorts and generators which will finally produce the electric messages of ideas.

The body is not an instrument, but a living organism. And the goal of life is not the idea, the mental consciousness is not the sum and essence of a human being. Human consciousness is not only ideal; cognition or knowing, is not only a mental act. Acts of emotion and volition are acts of primary cognition, and may be almost entirely non-mental.

Even apart from this, it is obvious to anyone who handles a baby that the vital activity is neither mental nor stomachic. Wherein lies the mystry of a baby, for us adults? From what has grown the legend of the adoration of the infant? From the fact that in the infant the great affective centres, volitional and emotional, act direct and spontaneous, without mental cognition or interference. When mental cognition starts, it only puts a spoke in the wheel of the great affective centres.

This forever baffles us. We can see that it is not mental reaction which constitutes the true consciousness of a baby. Neither perception, nor apperception, nor conception, nor any form of cognition, such as is recognised by our psychology, is to be ascribed to the infant mind. And yet there *is* consciousness, and even cognition: here, as in the mindless animals.

What kind of consciousness is it? We must look to the great affective centres, emotional and volitional. And we shall find that in the tiny infant there are two emotional centres primal and intensely active, with two two corresponding volitional centres. We need go through no tortures of scientific psychology to get at the truth. We need only take direct heed of the infant.

And then we shall realise that the busy business of consciousness is not taking place beneath the soft little skull, but beneath the little navel, and in the midst of the little breast. Here are the two great affective centres of the so-called emotional consciousness. Which emotional consciousness, according to our idealistic psychology, is onlt some sort of *force,* like magnetism, heat, or electric current. This force which arises and acts from the primal emotional-affective centres is supposed to be impersonal, general, truly a mechanical universal force like electricity or heat or any kinetic force.

Impersonal, and having nothing to do with the individual. The personal and the individual element does not enter until we reach mental consciousness. Personality, individuality, depends on mentality. So our psychology assumes. In the *mind,* a child is personal and individual, it is itself Outside the mind, it is an instrument, a dynamo if you like, a unit of difficult kinetic force betraying a sort of automatic consciousness, the same in every child, undifferentiated. In the same way, according to our psychology animals have no personality and no individuality, because they have no mental cognition. They have a certain psyche which they hold in common. What is true of one rabbit is true of another. All we can speak of is "the psychology of the rabbit," one rabbit having just the same psyche as another. Why? Because it has no recognisable cognition: it has only instinct.

We know this is all wrong because, having met a rabbit or two, we have seen quite clearly that each separate rabbit was a separate distinct rabbit-individual, with a specific nature of his own. We should be sorry to attribute a *mind* to him. But he has consciousness, and quite an individual consciousness too. It is notorious that human beings see foreigners all alike. To an English sailor the faces of a crowd of Chinese are all alike. But that is because the English sailor doesn't *see* the difference, not because the difference doesn't exist. Why, each fat domestic sheep, mere clod as it seems, has a distinct individual nature of its own, known to a shepherd after a very brief acquaintance.

So here we are with the great affective centres, volitional and emotional. The two chief emotional centres in the baby are the solar plexus of the abdomen, and the cardiac plexus of the breast. The corresponding ganglia of the volitional system are the lumbar ganglion and the thoracic ganglion.

And we may as well leave off at once regarding these great affective centres as merely instrumental, like little dynamos and accumulators and so on. Nonsense. They are primary, integral *mind-centres,* each of a specific nature. There is a specific form of *knowing* takes place at each of these centres, without any mental reference at all. And the specific form of knowing at each of the great affective centres in the infant is of an individual and personal nature, peculiar to the very *soul* and being of that infant.

That is, at the great solar plexus an infant *knows,* in primary, mindless knowledge; and from this centre he acts and re-acts directly, individually, and self-responsibly. The same from the cardiac plexus, and the two corresponding ganglia, lumbar and thoracic. The brain at first acts only as a switch-board which keep these great active centres in circuit of communication. The proces of idealisation, mental consciousness is a subsidiary process. It is a second form of conscious activity. Mental activity, final cognition, ideation, is only set up secondarily from the perfect interaction and intercommunication of the primary affective centres, which remain all the time our dynamic first-minds.

VI

How to begin to educate a child.—First rule, leave him alone. Second rule, leave him alone. Third rule, leave him alone. That is the whole beginning.

Which doesn't mean we are to let him starve, or put his fingers in the fire or chew broken glass. That is mere neglect. As a little organism he must have his proper environment. As a little individual he has his place and his limits: we also are individuals, and as such cannot allow him to make an unlimited nuisance of himself.—But as a little person and a little mind, if you please, he does not exist. Personality and mind, like moustaches, belong to a certain age. They are a deformity in a child.

It is in this respect that we repeat, *leave him alone.* Leave his sensibilities, his emotions, his spirit and his mind severely alone. There is the devil in mothers, that they must try to provoke *personal* recognition and *personal* response from their infants. They might as well start rubbing Tatcho on the tiny chin, to provoke a beard. Except that the Tatcho provocation will have no effect—unless perhaps a blister: whereas the emotional or psychic provocation has, alas, only too much effect.

For this reason babies should invariably be taken away from their modern mothers and given, not to yearning and maternal old maids, but to rather stupid fat women who can't be bothered with them. There should be a league for the prevention of maternal love, as there is a society for the prevention of cruelty to animals. The stupid fat woman may not guard so zealously against germs. But all the germs in the list of bacteriology are not so dangerous for a child as love.

And why? Not for any thrilling Freudian motive, but because our now deadly idealism insists on idealising every human relationship, but particularly that of mother and child. Heaven, how we all prostrate ourselves before the mother-child relationship, in all the grovelling degeneracy of Mariolatry! Highest, purest, most ideal of relationships, mother and child!

What nasty drivel! The mother-child relationship is certainly deep and important, but to make it high, or pure, or ideal is to make a nauseous perversion of it. A healthy, natural child has no high nature, no purity, and no ideal being. To stimulate these qualities in the infant is to produce psychic deformity, just as ugly as if we stimulated the growth of a beard on the baby face.

As far as all these high and personal matters go, *leave the child alone.* Personality and spiritual being mean with us our mental *consciousness* of our *own self.* A mother is to a high degree, alas, mentally conscious of her own self, her own exaltedness, her own mission, in these miserable days. And she wants her own mental consciousness reciprocated in the child. The child must *recognise* and respond. Alas that the child cannot give her the greatest smack in the eye, every time she smirks and yearns for recognition and response If we are to save the ultimate sanity of our children, it is *down with mothers! A bas les mères!*

Down to the right level. Pull them down from their exalted perches. No more of this Madonna smirking and yearning. No more soul. A mother should have ten strokes with the birch every time she "comes over" with soul or yearning love or aching responsibility. Ten hard, keen, stinging strokes on her bare back, each time. Because White Slave Traffic is a cup of tea compared with yearning mother-love. It should be knocked out of her, for it is a vice which threatens the ultimate sanity of our race.

The relation between mother and child is not personal at all, until it becomes perverted. Personal means mental consciousness of self. And a child has *no* mental consciousness and *no* self, and ten times less than no mental consciousness of self, until that fiend, its mother, followed by a string of personally-affected females, proceeds to provoke this mental consciousness in the small psyche. Worst luck of all, the emotional female fiends succeed. Sometimes they produce an *obvious* derangement in the psyche of the infant, and then they receive all the pity in the world, instead of a good barbaric thrashing. Usually the derangement is only incipient, due to develop later as morbid self-consciousness and neurosis. How can we help being neurotic when our mother provoked self-consciousness in us at the breast: provoked our self-conscious reciprocity, in order to satisfy her own spiritual and ideal lust for communion in self consciousness.

Down with exalted mothers, and down with the exaltation of motherhood, for it threatens the sanity of our race. The relation of mother and child, while it remains natural, is non-personal, non-ideal, non-spiritual. It is effective at the great primary centres, the solar plexus and the cardiac plexus, and from these centres it acts *direct,* without the so-called conscious knowledge: that is, without any transfer into the mind. Nothing is so strange as the remote look of recognition, remote, heavy, and potent, which is seen in the eyes of an infant. This wonderful remote look should be magic and sacred to a mother. Her whole instinct should revolt against disturbing it.

But no creature so perverse as the human mother today. No creature so delights in the traducing of the deepest instincts. Show me a woman who can be satisfied with the remote, deep, far-off baby-recognition. Show me the woman who can rest without provoking the look of *present* recognition in the eyes of a baby; that winsome, pathetic smile of infant recognition which is murder to a child so young. Why even in the eyes of a child of seven, the look of recognition is still remote and impersonal, it has a certain heavy far-offnesss which is its beauty. The self does not stand full present in the eyes until maturity, look does not actually meet look until then.

The old, instinctive mother instinctively cast off her personal consciousness in her communication with her child, and entered into that state of deep, unformed or untranslated consciousness, non-mental, on a lower, more primal plane For this the idealists despised her, and hence the idealising, the making mental and self-conscious of the naturally non-mental, spontaneous state of motherhood.

Remains now for the perverted, idealised mother deliberately to cast off her ideal, self-conscious motherhood, to return to the old deeps. Or else man must drag her ideal robes off her, by force. But back she must go, to the old mindlessness, the old unconsciousness, the despised animality of motherhood. Our spiritualising processes have been sheer perversion, when they have influenced the basic human affections.

The true relation between mother and child is established between the primary affective centres in each, without mental, self-concious intervention. At the primary centres, the solar plexus and the cardiac plexus, the dynamic individual consciousness stirs and flushes and seeks an object. The primary dynamic consciousness is like a living force which moves from its own polarised centre seeking an object, the object being chiefly some other corresponding pole of vitality in another living being So, from the solar plexus of the infant sympathetic centre moves a pristine conscious-force, seeking an object, a corresponding pole. This corresponding pole is found in the solar plexus of the mother.

As a matter of fact, the first polarity between the essential clue of the infant and the essential clue of the mother, located in the solar plexus, was established long before birth, at the moment of conception. But during all the period of ingestion, the infant had no actual separate existence. It is only after birth, after the break of the navel-string, that the child's polar vitality becomes separate and distinct.

And at the same time, as soon as the child is liberated into separate and distinct existence, it craves at once for the re-adjustment of the old connection, the fitting together of the wound of the navel with its origin in the mother. We don't mean that the child has any idea of what has happened. We don't mean that it summons its little wits to effect the desired restitution.

What actually happens is that, once the child is born and divided into separate existence, then at the solar plexus there surges a current of free vital consciousness, like a wave of electricity seeking its correspondent pole. The correspondent pole is found naturally in the great affective centre, the solar plexus of the mother. But failing the mother, the corresponding pole may be found in another being, or even, as in the legend, in a she-wolf. Suffice it that the two great dynamic centres, the solar plexus in the infant and the solar plexus in some external being, are seized into correspondence, and a vital circuit set up.

The vital circuit, we remark, is set up between two extraneous and individual beings, each separately existing. Yet the circuit embraces the two into a perfectly balanced unison. The mother and child are on the same plane. The mother is one in vital correspondence with the child. That is, in all her direct intercourse with the child she is as rudimentary as the child itself, her dynamic consciousness is as undeveloped and non-mental as the child's.

Herein we have the true mother: she who corresponds with her child on the deep, rudimentary plane of the first dynamic consciousness. This correspondence is a sightless, mindless correspondence of touch and sound. The two dark poles of vital being must be kept constant in mother and infant, so that the flow is uninterrupted. This constancy is preserved by intimacy of contact, physical immediacy. But this physical immediacy does not make the two beings any less distinct and separate. It makes them more so. The child develops its own single, incipient self at its own primary centre, the mother develops her own separate, matured female self. The circuit of dynamic polarity which keeps the two equilibrised also produces each of them, produces the infant's developing body and psyche, produces the perfected womanhood of the mother.

All this, so long as the circuit is not broken, the flow perverted. The circuit, the flow is kept as the child lies against the bosom of its mother, just as the circle of magnetic force is kept constant in a magnet by the "keeper" which unites the two poles. The child which sleeps in its mother's arms, the child which sucks at its mother's breast, the child which screams and kicks on its mother's knee is established in a vital circuit with its parent, out of which circuit its being arises and develops. From pole to pole, direct, the current flows: from the solar plexus in the abdomen of the child to the solar plexus in the abdomen of the mother, from the cardiac plexus in the breast of the child to the cardiac plexus in the breast of the mother. The mouth which sucks, the little voice which calls and cries, both issue from the deep centres of the breast and bowels, giving expression from these centres, and not from the brain. The baby is not mentally vocal. It utters itself from the great affective centres. And this is why it has such power to charm or to madden us. The mother in her response utters herself from the same affective centres, her coos and callings also are unintelligible. Not the mind speaks, but the deep, happy bowels, the lively breast.

Introduce one grain of self-consciousness into the mother, as she chuckles and coos to her baby, and what then? The good life-flow instantly breaks. The sounds change. She begins to produce them deliberately, under mental control.— And what then? The deep affective centre in the baby is suddenly robbed, as when the mouth still sucking is suddenly snatched from the full breast. The vital flow is suddenly interrupted, and a new stimulus is applied to the child. There is a new provocation, a provocation for mental response from the infantile self-consciousness. And what then? The child either howls or turns pale and makes this convulsed effort at mental-conscious, or self-conscious response. After which it is probably sick.

The same with the baby's eyes. They do not see, mentally. Mentally, they are sightless and dark. But they have the remote deep vision of the deep affective centres. And so a mother, laughing and clapping to her baby, has the same half-sightless, glaucous look in her eyes, vision non-mental and non-critical, the primary affective centres corresponding through the eyes, void of idea or mental cognition.

But rouse the devil of the woman's self-conscious will, and she, clapping and cooing and laughing apparently just as before, will try to force a personal, *conscious* recognition into the eyes of the baby She will try and try and try, fiendishly. And the child will blindly, instinctively resist. But with the cunning of seven legions of devils and the persistency of hell's most hellish fiend, the cooing, clapping devilish modern mother traduces her child into the personal mode of consciousness. She succeeds, and starts this hateful "personal" love between herself and her excited child, and the unspoken but unfathomable hatred between the violated infant and her own assaulting soul, which together make the bane of human life, and give rise to all the neurosis and neuritis and nervous troubles we are all afflicted with.

With children, we must absolutely leave out the self-conscious and personal note. Communication must be remote and impersonal, a correspondence direct between the deep affective centres. And this is the reason why we must kick out all the personal fritter from the elementary schools. Stories must be *tales,* fables. They may have a flat *moral* if you like. But they must never have a personal, self-conscious note, the little-Mary-who-dies-and-goes-to-heaven touch, or the little-Alice-who-saw-a-fairy. This is the most vicious element in our canting infantile education today. "And you will all see fairies, dears, if you know how to look for them."

It is perversion of the infant mind at the start. This continual introduction of a little child heroine or hero, with whom the little boy or the little girl can self-consciously identify herself or himself stultifies all development at the true centres. Fairies are not a personal, *mental* reality. Alice Jenkinson who lives in "The Laburnums," Leslie Road, Brixton knows quite well that fairies are all my-eye. But she is quite content to smirk self-consciously and say "Yes Miss" when teacher asks her if she'd like to see a fairy. It's all very well playing games of pretence, so long as you enter right into the game, robustly, and forget your own pretensive self. But when, like the little Alices of today, you keep a constant self-conscious smirk on your nose all the time you're "playing fairies," then to hell with you and your fairies. And ten times to hell with the smirking self-conscious "teacher" who encourages you. A hateful self-tickling self-abusive affair, the whole business.

And this is what is wrong, first and foremost, with our education: this attempt deliberately to provoke reactions in the great affective centers and to dictate these reactions from the mind. Fairies are true embrylogical realities of the human psyche. They are true and real for the great affective centres, which see as through a glass, darkly, and which have direct correspondence with living and naturalistic influences in the surrounding universe, correspondence which cannot have mental, rational utterance, but must express itself, if it be expressed, in preternatural forms. Thus fairies are true, and Little Red Riding Hood is most true.

But they are not true for Alice Jenkinson, smirking little minx. Because Alice Jenkinson is an incurably self-conscious little piece of goods, and she *cannot* act direct from the great affective centres, she *can* only act perversely, by reflection, from her *personal* consciousness. And therefore, for her, all fairies and princesses and Peters and Wendys should be put on the fire, and she should be spanked and transported to Newcastle, to have some of her self-consciousness taken out of her.

An inspector should be sent round *at once* to burn all pernicious Little Alice and Little Mary literature in the elementary schools, and empowered to cut down to one-half the salary of any teacher found smirking or smugging or indulging in any other form of pretty self-conciousness and personal graces. Abolish all the bunkum, go back to the three R's. Don't cultivate any more imagination at all in children: it only means pernicious self-consciousness. Let us for heaven's sake have children without imagination and without "nerves" for the two are damnably inseparable.

Down with imagination in school, down with self-expression. Let us have a little severe hard work, good, clean, well-written exercises, well pronounced words, well-set-down sums: and as far as head-work goes, no more. No more self-conscious dabblings and smirkings and lispings of "The silver birch is a dainty lady" (so is little Alice of course). The silver birch must be finely downcast to see itself transmogrified into a smirky little Alice. The owl and the pussy-cat may have gone to sea in the pea-green boat, and the little girl may well have said: "What long teeth you've got, Grand-mother! This is well within the bounds of natural pristine experience But that dainty-lady business is only self-conscious smirking.

It will be a long time before we know how to act or speak again from the deep affective centres, without self-conscious perversion. And therefore, in the interim, whilst we learn, let us abolish all pretence at naïveté and childish self-expression. Let us have a bit of solid, hard, tidy work. And for the rest, *leave the children alone*. Pitch them out into the street or the playgrounds and take no notice of them. Drive them savagely away from their posturings.

There must be an end to the self-conscious attitudinising of our children. The self-consciousness and all the damned high-flowness must be taken out of them, and their little personalities must be nipped in the bud. Children shall be regarded as young *creatures,* not as young affected persons. Creatures, not persons.

VII

As a matter of fact, our private hope is that by a sane system of education we may release the coming generations from our own nasty disease of self-consciousness: a disease quite as rampant among the working classes as among the well-to-do classes; and perhaps even more malignant there, because, having fewer forms of expression it tends to pivot in certain ideas, which fix themselves in the psyche and become little less than manias. The wage is the mania of the moment: the working-man's consciousness of himself as a working-man, which has now become an *idée fixe,* excluding any possibility of his remaining a lively human being.

What do we mean by self-consciousness? If we will realise that all spontaneous life, desire, impulse, and first-hand individual consciousness arises and is effective at the great nerve-centres of the body, and *not* in the brain, we shall begin to understand. The great nerve-centres are in pairs, sympathetic and volitional.

Again, they are polarised in upper and lower duality, above and below the diaphragm. Thus the solar plexus of the abdomen is the first great affective centre, sympathetic, and the lumbar ganglion, volitional, is its partner. At these two great centres arises our first consciousness, our primary impulses, desires, motives. These are our primal minds, here located in the dual great affective centres below the diaphragm. But immediately above the diaphragm we have the cardiac plexus and the thoracic ganglion, another great pair of conjugal affective centres, acting in immediate correspondence with the two lower centres. And these four great nerve-centres establish the first field of our consciousness, the first plane of our vital being. They are the four corner-stones of our psyche, the four powerful vital poles which, flashing darkly in polarised interaction one with another, form the fourfold issue of our individual life. At these great centres, primarily, we live and move and have our being. Thought and idea do not enter in. The motion arises spontaneous, we know not how, and is emitted in dark vibrations. The vibration goes forth, seeks its object, returns, establishing a life-circuit. And this life-circuit, established internally between the four first poles, and established also externally between the primal affective centres in two different beings or creatures, this complex life-circuit or system of circuits constitutes in itself our profound primal consciousness, and contains all our radical knowledge, knowledge non-ideal, non-mental, yet still knowledge, primary cognition, individual and potent.

The mental cognition or consciousness is as it were distilled or telegraphed from the primal consciousness into a sort of written, final script, in the brain. If we imagine the infinite currents and meaningful vibrations in the world's atmosphere: and if we realise how some of these, at the great wireless stations, are ticked off and written down in fixed script, we shall form some sort of inkling of how the primary consciousness centralised in the great affective centres, and circulating in vital circuits of primary cognition, is captured by the supremely delicate registering-apparatus in the brain and registered there like some strange code, the newly-rising mental consciousness. The brain itself, no doubt, is a very tissue of memory, every smallest cell is a vast material memory which only needs to be roused, quickened by the vibration coming from the primary centres, only needs the new fertilisation of a new quiver of experience, to blossom out as a mental conception, and idea. This power for the transfer of the pure affective experience, the primary consciousness, into final mental experience, ideal consciousness, varies extremely according to individuals. It would seem as if, in negroes for example, the primary affective experience, the affective consciousness is profound and intense, but the transfer into mental consciousness is comparatively small. In ourselves, in modern Europeans, on the other hand, the primal experience, the vital consciousness grows weaker and weaker, the mind fixes the control and *limits* the life-activity. For let us realise once and for all that the whole mental consciousness and the whole sum of the mental content of mankind is never, and can never be more than a mere tithe of all the vast surging primal consciousness, the affective consciousness of mankind.

Yet we presume to limit the potent spontaneous consciousness to the poor limits of the mental consciousness. In us, instead of our life issuing spontaneously at the great affective centres, the mind the mental consciousness, grown unwieldy, turns round upon the primary affective centres, seizes control, and proceeds to evoke our primal motions and emotions, didactically. The mind subtly, without knowing, provokes and dictates our own feelings and impulses. That is to say, a man helplessly and unconsciously *causes* from his mind every one of his own important reactions at the great affective centres. He can't help himself. It isn't his own fault. The old polarity has broken down. The primal centres have collapsed from their original spontaneity, they have become subordinate, neuter, negative, waiting for the mind's provocation, waiting to be worked according to some secondary idea. Thus arises our pseudo-spontaneous modern living.

We are in the toils of helpless self-consciousness. We can't help ourselves. It is like being in a boat with no oars. What can we do but drift. We know we are drifting, but we don't know how or where. Because there is no primary *resistance* in us, nothing that resists the helpless but fatal flux of ideas which streams us away. The resistant spontaneous centres have broken down in us.

Why does this happen? Because we have become too conscious? Not at all. Merely because we have become too fixedly conscious. We have limited our consciousness, tethered it to a few great ideas, like a goat to a post. We insist over and over again on what we know from one mere centre of ourselves, the mental centre. We insist that we are essentially spirit, that we are ideal beings, conscious personalities, mental creatures. As far as ever possible we have resisted the independence of the great affective centres. We have struggled for some thousands of years, not only to get our passions under control, but absolutely to eliminate certain passions, and to give all passions an ideal nature.

And so, at last we succeed. We do actually give all our passions an ideal nature. Our passions at last are nothing more or less than ideas auto-suggested into practice. We try to persuade ourselves that it all fine and grand and flowing. And for quite a long time we manage to take ourselves in. But we can't continue, *ad infinitum,* this life of self-satisfied auto-suggestion.

Because, if you think of it, everything which is provoked or originated *by an idea* works automatically or mechanically. It works by principle. So that even our wickedness today, being ideal in its origin, a sort of deliberate reaction to the *accepted* ideal, amounts to the same mechanism. It is an ideal working of the affective centres in the *opposite direction* from the accepted direction: opposite and opposite and opposite, till murder itself becomes an ideal at last. But it is all auto-affective. No matter which way you *work* the affective centres, once you work them from the mental consciousness you automatise them. And the human being craves for change in his automatism. Sometimes it seems to him horrible that he must, in a fixed routine, get up in the morning and put his clothes on, day in, day out. He can't bear his automatism. He is beside himself in his self-consciousness. But he is a damned little Oliver Twist: nothing but twist: and always wanting "more." He doesn't want to drop his self-consciousness. He wants more, always more. The damned little ideal being, he wants to work his own little psyche till the end of time, like a clever little god-in-the-machine that he is. And he despises any real spontaneity with all the street-arab insolence of depraved idealism. Man would rather be the ideal god inside his own automaton than anything else on earth. And woman is ten times worse. Woman as the goddess in the machine of the human psyche is a heroine who will drive us, like a female chauffeur, through all the avenues of hell, till she pitches us eventually down the bottomless pit. And even then she'll save herself, she'll kilt her skirts and look round for new passengers. She has a million more dodges for automatic self-stimulation than man has. When man has finished, woman can still cadge a million more sensational reactions out of herself and her co-respondent.

Man is accursed once he falls into the trick of ideal self-automatism. But he is infinitely conceited about it. He really works his own psyche! He really *is* the god of his own creation! Isn't this enough to puff him out? Here he is, tricky god and creator of himself at last! And he's not going to be ousted from his at-last-acquired godhead. Not he! The triumphant little god sits in the machine of his own psyche and turns on the petrol. It is like a story by H. G. Wells —too true to life, alas. There sits every man ensconced upon the engine of his own psyche, turning on the ideal taps and opening the ideal valves of his own nature, and so proud of himself, it's a wonder he hasn't set off to fly to the sun in one of his aeroplanes, like a new Icarus. But he lacks the fine boldness for such a flight. He wants to sit tight in his little hobby machine, near enough to his little hearth and home, this tubby, domestic little mechanical godhead.

A curse on idealism. A million curses on self-conscious automatic humanity, men and women both. Curses on their auto-suggestive self-reactions, from which they derive such inordinate self-gratification. Most curses of all upon the women, the self-conscious provokers of infinite sensations, of which man is the instrument Let there be a fierce new Athanasian Creed, to damn and blast all idealists. But let spiritual, ideal self-conscious women be the most damned of all. Men after all don't get much more than aeroplane thrills and political thrills out of their god-in-the-machine reactions. But women get soul-thrills and sexual thrills, they float and squirm on clouds of self-glorification, with a lot of knock-kneed would-be saints and apostles of the male sort goggling sanctified eyes upwards at them, as in some sickening Raphael picture.

It is enough to send a sane person mad, to see this goggling squirming, self-glorifying idealised humanity carrying on its self-conscious little games. And how it loves its little games. Just heaven, how it wallows in them, ideally!

What is to be done? We talk about new systems of education, and here we have a civilised mankind sucking its own fingers avidly, as if its own fingers were so many sticks of juicy barley-sugar. It loves itself so much, this ideal self-conscious humanity, that it could verily eat itself. And so it nibbles gluttishly at itself.

Is it the slightest good doing anything but join in with the sucking and self-nibbling? Probably not. We'll throw stones at them none the less, even if every stone boomerangs back in our own teeth. Perhaps once we shall catch humanity one in the eye.

The question is, don't our children get this self-conscious self-nibbling habit in the very womb of their travesty mothers, before they are even born? We are afraid it is so. Our miserable offspring, churned in the abdomen of insatiable self-conscious woman, woman self-consciously every moment seeking and watching her own reactions, her own pregnancy and her own everything, grinding all her sensations from her head and reflecting them all back into her head, all her physical churnings ground exceeding small in the hateful self-conscious mills of her female mind, ideal and unremitting; do not our miserable offspring issue from the ovens of such a womb writhing and crisping with self-conscious morbid hunger of self? Alas and alack, to all appearance they do. The self-conscious devil is in them, either smirking and smarming, or preening prancing, or irritably self-nibbling and sentimentalising, or stolidly *suffisant,* or hostile. But there it is, the hateful devil of self-conscious self-importance born with them, simmered into them in the acid-seething irritable womb.

What's to be done? Why of course, keep the game up. Tickle the poor little wretches into ecstasies of self-consciousness. Gather round them and stare at them and mouth over them and sentimentalise and rhapsodise over them. Get the doctor to paw them, the nurse to expose them naked to a horde of ideal prurient females, get to preach over them and roll his eyes to heaven over their sanctity. Then send them to school to "express themselves," in the hopes that they'll turn out infant prodigies. For oh dear me, *what* a feather in the cap of a mortal mother is an infant prodigy!

If *one* healthily sensitive mother in these days bore one healthy-souled, simple child she'd pick him up and bolt for her life from the mobs of our ghoulish "charming" women, and the mobs of goggling adoring men. She'd run, poor Hagar, to some desert with her Ishmael. And there she'd give him to a she-wolf, or a she-bear, or a she-lion to suckle. She'd never trust herself. Verily she'd have more faith in a rattle-snake, as far as motherhood is concerned.

Would God a she-wolf had suckled me, and stood over me with her paps, and kicked me back into a rocky corner when she'd had enough of me. It might have made a man of me.

But it's no use sighing. Romulus and Remus had all the luck. We see now why they bred a great, great race: because they had no mother: a race of men. Christians have no fathers: only these ogling woman-worshipping saints, and the self-conscious friction of exalted mothers.

Let us rail, why shouldn't we! It is subject enough for railing. But what about these infants? Alas, there isn't a wild she-wolf in the length and breadth of Britain. There isn't a crevice in the British Isles where you could suckle a brat undisturbed by the village constable. And therefore, no hope with us of heroic twins.

What are we going to do? Presumably, nothing: except carry on the pretty process of smirking and goggling which we call education. —The sense of futility overwhelms us.—The thought of all the exalted mothers of England, and of all the knock-kneed smug God-besprinkled fathers is too much for us: all the hosts of the sentimental self-conscious ones, the sensational self-conscious ones, the free-and-easy self-conscious ones, the downright no-nonsense-about-me self-conscious ones, the elegant self-conscious ones, the would-be-dissolute self-conscious ones, the very-very-naughty self-conscious ones, the *chic* self-conscious ones, and *spiritual* self-conscious ones, and the *nuancy* self-conscious ones (those full of *nuances),* and the self-sacrificial self-conscious ones, and the do-all-you-can-for-others self-conscious ones, the do-your-bit self-conscious ones, the yearning, the aspiring, the sighing, the leering, the tip-the-winking self-conscious ones, females, and so-called men: all the lot of them: ad nauseam and ad nauseissimam: they are too much for me. All of them like so many little barrel-organs grinding their own sensations, nay, their own very natures, out of their own little heads: and become so automatic at it they don't even know they're doing it. They think they are fine spontaneous angels these little automata. And they are automata, self-turning little barrel-organs, all of them, from the millionaire down to the dustman. The dustman grinds himself off according to his own dustman-ideal prescription.

We've got to get on to a different tack: snap! off the old tack and veer onto a new one. No more seeing ourselves as others see us. No more seeing ourselves at all. A fig for such sights.

The primary conscious centres, the very first and deepest, are in the lower body. A button for your brain, whoever you are. If you are not darkly potent below the belt, you are nothing.

Let go the upper consciousness. Switch it off for a time. Release the cramped and tortured lower consciousness. Drop this loving and merging business. Fall back into your own isolation and the insuperable pride thereof. Break off the old polarity, the merging into oneness with others, with everything. Snap the old connections. Break clean away from the old yearning navel-string of love, which unites us to the body of everything. Break it, and be born. Fall apart into your own isolation; set apart single and potent in singularity for ever. One is one and all alone and ever more shall be so. Exult in it. Exult in the fact that you are yourself, and alone for ever. Exult in your own dark being. Across the gulf are strangers, myriad-faced dancing strangers like midges and like Pleiades. One draws near, there is a thrill and a fiery contact. But never a merging. A withdrawal, a bond of knowledge, but no identification. Recognition across space: across a dark and bottomless space: two beings, who recognise each other across the chasm, who occasionally cross and meet in a fiery contact, but who find themselves invariably withdrawn afterwards, with dark, dusky-glowing faces glancing across the insuperable chasm which intervenes between two beings.

Have done, let go the old connections. Fall apart, fall asunder, each into his own unfathomable dark bath of isolation. Break up the old incorporation. Finish for ever the old unison into homogeneity. Let every man fall apart into a fathomless, single isolation of being, exultant at his own core, and apart. Then, dancing magnificent in our own space, as the spheres dance in space, we can set up the extra-individual communication. Across the space comes the thrill ~of communication. There is an approach, a flash and blaze of contact, and then the sheer fiery purity of a purer isolation, a more exultant singleness. Not a mass of homogeneity, like sunlight. But a fathomless multiplicity, like the stars at night, each one isolate in the darkly-singing space. This symbol of Light, the homogeneous and universal Day, the daylight, symbolises our universal mental consciousness, which we have in common. But our *being* we have in integral separateness, as the stars at night. To think of lumping the stars together into one mass is hideous. Each one separate, each one his own peculiar ray. So the universe is made up.

And the sun only hides all this. Imagine, if the sun shone all the time, we should never know there was anything but ourselves in the universe. Everything would be limited to the plane superficies of ourself and our own mundane nature. Everything would be as we see it and as we think it.

Which is what ails us. Living as we do entirely in the light of the mental consciousness, we think everything is as we see it and as we think it. Which is a vast illusion. Imagine a man who all his life has been shut up in a hermetically dark room, between sundown and sunrise, and let out only when light was full in the heavens. He would imagine that everything, all the time, was light, that the firmament was a vast blue space screened from us sometimes by our own vapours, but otherwise a blue unblemished void occupied by ourselves and the sun, one blue unchanging blaze of eternal light, with ourselves for the only inhabitants, under the sun.

Which, in spite of Galileo, that star-master, is what we actually do think. If we proceed to imagine other worlds, we cook up a few distortions of our own world and scatter them into space. A Martian may have long ears and horns on his forehead, but he is only ourselves dressed up, busy making super-zeppelins. We are convinced, as a matter of fact, that the stars and ourselves are all seed of one sort.

And what holds true cosmologically holds much more true psychologically. The man sealed up during twilight and night-time would have a rare shock the first time he was taken out under the stars. To see all the blue heavens crumpled and shrivelled away! To see the pulsation of myriad orbs proudly moving in the endless darkness, insouciant, sunless, taking a stately path we know not whither or how. Ha, the day-time man would feel his heart and brain burst to a thousand shivers, he would feel himself falling like a seed into space. All that he counted *himself* would be suddenly dispelled. All that he counted eternal, infinite, *Everything,* suddenly shrivelled like a vast, burst roof of paper, or a vast paper lantern: the eternal light gone out: and behold, multiplicity, twinkling, proud multiplicity, utterly indifferent of oneness, proud far-off orbs taking their lonely way beyond the bounds of knowledge, emitting their own unique and untransmutable rays, pulsing with their own isolate pulsation.

This is what must happen to us. We have kept up a false daylight all through our nights. Our sophistry has intervened like a lamp between us and the slow-stepping stars, we have turned our cheap lanterns on the dark and wizard face of Galileo, till lo and behold, his words are as harmless as butterflies. Of course the orbs are manifold: we admit it easily. But *light* is one and universal and infinite.

Put it in human terms, men are manifold, but Wisdom and Understanding are one and universal. Men are manifold, but the Spirit, the consciousness, is one, as sunlight is one. And therefore, because the consciousness of mankind is really one and universal, therefore mankind is one and universal. Therefore each individual is a term of the Infinite.

A pretty bit of sophistry. Because the sunlight covers all the stars, therefore the stars are one, each is a homogeneous bit of light. Behold, how oneness achieves its ridiculous triumph, by self deception. It is a famous dodge, this of self-deception. The popes couldn't squash Galileo. But clever mankind has succeeded in smearing out his star-shine, by a trick of the psyche.

Mankind is an ostrich with its head in the bush of the infinite. This doesn't prevent the stars all trooping past with a superb smile at the rump of the bird.

We don't find fault with the mental consciousness, the daylight consciousness of mankind. Not at all. We only find fault with the One-and-Allness which is attributed to it. It isn't One-and-All, any more than the sun is one and all. Has it never occurred to us that the sun serves no more than as a great lantern and bonfire to the ambulating intermediary worlds? Has it never occurred to us that the sun is not *superior* to our little earth, and to the other little stars, but just instrumental, a bonfire and a lamp and an axle-tree. After all, it is the little spheres which *live,* and the great sun is instrumental to their living, even as the powerful arc-lamps high over Piccadilly only serve to illuminate the little feet of foot-passengers.

So there we are. All our Oneness and our infinite, which does but mount up to the sum-total of human mentality or consciousness, is merely intrumental to the small individual consciousnesses of individual beings. Bigness as a rule means departure from life. Things vividly living are never so very big. Vastness is a term which applies to the non-vital universe. The moment we consider the vital universe, vastness and extensiveness cease to be terms of merit, and become terms of demerit. Whatever is vast and extensive in the *living* world is less quick, less alive than that which creates no impression of superlative size. In the *living* world, appreciation is intensive, not extensive. A small fowl like a lark or a kestrel is more to us than a flock of rooks or an ostrich or a condor. One is one and all alone and ever more shall be so.

Hence the little stellar orbs, living as we feel they must be, are more than the great sun they hover round: just as the shadowy human men are more than the great fire round which they squat and move in the dark camp. So, the universe is a great living camp squatted round the sun. We warm ourselves and prepare our food at the fire. But after all, the fire is only the means to our living. So the sun. It is but the means to the living of the little mid-way spheres, the great fire camped in the middle of the sky, at which they warm themselves and prepare their meat.

And so with human beings. One is one, and as such, always more than an aggregation. Vitally, intensively, one human being is always more than six collective human beings. Because, in the collectivity, what is gained in bulk or number is lost in intrinsic being. The *quick* of any collective group is some consciousness they have in common. But the quick of the individual is the integral soul, forever indescribable and unstateable. That which is *in common* is never any more than some mere property of the vital, individual soul.

Away then with the old system of valuation, that many is more than one. In the static material world it is so. But in the living world, the opposite is true. One is more than many. The Japanese know that one flower is lovelier than many flowers. Alone, one flower lives and has its own integral wonder. Massed with other flowers, it has a being-in-common, and this being-in-common is always inferior to the single aloneness of one creature. Being-in-common means the summing up of one element held in common by many individuals. But this one common element, however many times multiplied is never more than one mere part in any individual, and therefore much *less* than any individual. The more common the element, the smaller is its part in the individual, and hence, the greater its vital insignificance. So with humanity, or mankind, or the infinite, as compared with one individual.

All of which is not mere verbal metaphysic, but an attempt to get in human beings a new attitude to life. Instead of finding our highest reality in an ever-extending aggregation with the rest of men, we shall realise at last that the highest reality for every living creature is in its purity of singleness and its perfect solitary integrity, and that everything else should be but a means to this end. All communion, all love, and all communication, which is all consciousness, are but a means to the perfected singleness of the individual being.

Which doesn't mean anarchy and disorder. On the contrary it means the most delicately and inscrutably established order, delicate, intricate, complicate as the stars in heaven, when seen in their strange groups and goings. Neither does it mean what is nowadays called individualism. The so-called individualism is no more than a cheap egotism, every self-conscious little ego assuming unbounded rights to display his self-consciousness. We mean none of this. We mean in the first place the recognition of the exquisite arresting *manifoldness* of being, multiplicity, plurality, as the stars are plural in their starry singularity. Lump the green flashing Sirius with red Mars, and what will you get? A muddy orb. Aggregate them, and what then? A mere smudgy cloudy nebula. One is one and all alone and ever more shall be so. Enveloped each one in its fathomless abyss of isolation. Magically, vitally alone, flashing with singleness.

Towards *this,* then, we are to educate our children and ourselves. Not towards any infinitely extended consciousness. Not towards any vastness or unlimitedness of any sort. Not towards any inordinate range of understanding or consciousness. Not towards any merging in any whole whatsoever. But delicately, through all the processes of communion and communication, love and consciousness, to the perfect singleness of a full and flashing, orb-like maturity.

And if this is the goal of all our striving and effort, then let us take the first stride by *leaving the child alone,* in his own soul. Take all due care of him, materially; give him all love and tenderness and wrath which the spontaneous soul emits: but always, always, at the very quick, leave him alone. Leave him alone. He is not you and you are not him. He is never to be merged into you nor you into him. Though you love him and he love you, this is but a communion in unfathomable difference, not an identification into oneness. There is *no* living oneness, for two people: only a deadly oneness, of merged human beings.

Leave the child *alone*. Alone! that is the great word and world. Suppose the moon went through the sky, loving all the stars, hugging them to her breast, and crushing them into one beam with her. O vile thought! Like a swollen leper the dead moon would roll out of a void and corpse-like sky. Supposing she even caught the star Sirius as he passes low and embraced him into oneness with herself, so that he merged amorphous into her. Immediately Orion would fall to pieces in the ruined heavens, the planets would drop from their orbits, a vast cataclysm and a rain of ruin in the cosmos.

Sirius must move and flash in his own circumambient space, single. Who knows what strange relation and intercommunion he has with Aldebaran, with the Pole Star, even with ourselves? But whatever his intercommunion, he is never raped from his own singleness he never falls from his own isolate self.

The same for the child. Since the navel string breaks, he is alone in the aura of his own exquisite and mystic solitariness, and there must be no trespass into this solitariness. He is alone. *Leave* him alone. Never forget. Never forget to leave him alone, within his own souls inviolability.

Do not be afraid, either, to *drive* him into his own soul's inviolable singleness. A child will trespass. It is born nowadays with an irritable craving to trespass into the nature of the mother. Nay, the parent-child relationship in these nervous days resolves itself into one series of trespasses across the confines of the two natures, till there is some unholy arrest.

Now the *seeking* centres of the human system are the great sympathetic centres. It is from these, and primarily from the solar plexus that the individual goes forth seeking communion with another being or creature or thing. At the solar plexus the child yearns avidly for the mother, for contact, for unison, for absorption even. A nervous child yearns and frets ceaselessly for complete identification. It wants to merge, to merge back into the mother, with the ceaseless craving of morbid love.

What are we to do, when a child of a few weeks old is so smitten, nervously craving for the mother and for re-identification with her? What on earth are we to do?

It is quite simple. *Break* the spell. Set up the activity of the volitional centres. For at the volitional centres a creature keeps itself apart, integral, centred in its own isolation. Living as we have done in one mode only, the mode of love, praising as we have done the single mode of unification and identification through love with the beloved, and with all the rest of the universe, we have used all the strength of the upper, mentally-directed *will* to break the power of these dark, proud, integral volitional centres of the lower body. And we have almost succeeded. So that human life is born now creeping, parasitic in its tendency. The proud volitional centres of the lower body, those which maintain a human being integral and distinct, these have collapsed, so that the whole individual crawls helplessly and parasitically from the sympathetic centres, to establish himself in a permanent life-oneness with another being, usually the mother. And the mother too rejoices in this horrible parasitism of her child, she feels exalted, like God, now she is the host of the parasite.

Break the horrible circle of this lust. Break it. Seize babies away from their mothers, with hard, fierce, terrible hands. Send the volts of fierce anger and severing force violently into the child. Volts of hard, violent anger, that shock the feeble volitional centres into life again. Smack the whimpering child. Smack it sharp and fierce on its small buttocks. With all the ferocity of a living, healthy anger, spank the little tail, till at last the powerful dynamic centres of the spinal system vibrate into life, out of their atrophied torture. It is not too late. Quick, quick, mothers of England, spank your wistful babies. Good God, spank their little bottoms, with sharp, red anger spank them and make men of them. Drive them back. Drive them back from their yearning loving parasitism, startle them forever out of their pseudo-angelic wistfulness, cure them with a quick wild yell of all their wonder-child spirituality. Sharp, sharp, before it is too late. Be *fierce* with the little darling, and put hell's temper into its soft little soul. Quick, before we are lost.

Let us get this wide, wistful look out of our children's eyes, this oh-so-spiritual look, varied by an oh-so-spiteful look. Let us cure them of their inordinate sensitiveness and consciousness. Kick the cat out of the room when the cat is a nuisance, and let the baby see you do it. And if the baby whimpers, kick the baby after the cat. In just mercy do it. And then maybe you'll have a slim-muscled independent cat that can walk with a bit of moon-devilish defiance, instead of the ravel of knitting-silk with a full belly and a sordid *meeau* which is "Pussy" of our dear domestic hearth. More important than the cat, you'll get a healthily-reacting human infant, animal and fierce and not-to-be-coddled, the first signs of a proud man whose neck won't droop like a weak lily, nor reach forward forever like a puppy reaching to suck, and whose knees won't be aching all his life with a luscious loose desire to slip into some woman's lap, dear darling, and feel her caress his brow.

This instant moment we've got to start to put some fire into the backbones of our children. Do you know what the backbone is? It is the long sword of the vivid, proud, *dark* volition of man, something primal and creative. Not that

267

miserable mental obstinacy which goes in the name of *will* nowadays. Not a will-to-power or a will-to-goodness or a will-to-love or a will *to* anything else. All these wills to this and the other are only so many obstinate mechanical directions given to some chosen mental idea. You may choose the idea of power, and fix your mechanical little will on that, as the Germans did; or the idea of love, and fix your equally mechanical and still more obstinate little will on *that,* as we do, privately. And all you'll get is some neurotic automaton or parasite, materialistic as hell. You must be automatic and materialistic once you substitute an ideal pivot for the spontaneous centres.

But at the centres of the primal will, situate in the spinal system, the great volitional centres, here a man arises in his own dark pride and singleness, his own sensual magnificence in single being. Here the flashing indomitable man himself takes rise. It is not any tuppeny mechanical instrumental thing, a will-to-this or a will-to-that.

And these, these great centres of primal proud volition, these, especially in the lower body, are the life-centres that have gone soft and rotten in us. Here we need sharp, fierce reaction: sharp discipline, rigour, fierce, fierce severity. We, who are willing to operate surgically on our physical sick, my God, we must be quick and operate psychically on our psychic sick, or they are done for.

Whipping, beating, yes, these alone will thunder into the moribund centres and bring them to life. Sharp, stinging whipping, keen, fierce smacks, and all the roused fury of reaction in the child, these alone will restore us to psychic health. Away with all mental punishments and reprobation. You *must* rouse the powerful physical reaction of anger, dark flushing rage in the child. You must. You *must* fight him, tooth and nail, if you're going to keep him healthy and alive. And if you're going to be able to love him with warm, rich bowels of love, my heaven, how you must fight him, how openly and fiercely and with no nonsense about it.

Rouse the powerful volitional centres at the base of the spine, and those between the shoulders. Even with stinging rods, rouse them.

IX

In the early years a child's education should be entirely non-mental. Instead of trying to attract an infant's attention, trying to arouse its *notice,* to make it *perceive,* the mother or nurse should mindlessly put it into contact with the physical universe. What is the first business of the baby? To ascertain the physical reality of its own context, even of its own very self. It has to learn to wave its little hands and feet. To a baby it is for a long time a startling thing, to find its own hand waving. It does not know what is moving, nor how it moves. It is quite unconscious of having inaugurated the motion, as a cat is unconscious of what makes the shadow after which it darts, or in what its own elusive tail-tip consists. So a baby marvels over the transit of this strange *something* which moves again and again across its own little vision. Behold, it is only the small fist. So it watches and watches. What is it doing?

When a baby absorbedly, almost painfully watches its own vagrant and spasmodic fist, is it trying to form a concept of that fist? Is it trying to formulate a little idea? "That is *my* fist: it is *I* who move it: I wave it *so,* and *so—!*"—Not at all. The concept of *I* is quite late forming. Some children do not realise that they are themselves until they are four or five years old. They are something objective to themselves: "Jackie wants it"—"Baby wants it"—and not "*I* want it." In the same way with the hand or the foot. A child for some years has no *conception* of its own foot as part of itself. It is "*the* foot." In most languages it is always "the foot, the hand" and not "my foot, my hand." But in English the ego is very insistent. We put it self-consciously in possession as soon as possible.

None the less, it is some time before a child is possessed of its own ego. A baby watches its little fist waving through the air, perilously near its nose. What is it doing, thinking about the fist? NO! It is establishing the "rapport" or connection between the primary affective centres which control the fist. From the deep sympathetic plexus leaps out an impulse. The fist waves, wildly, to the peril of the little nose. It waves, does it! It leaps, it moves! And from the fountain of impulse deep in the little breast, it moves. But there is also a quiver of fear because of this spasmodic, convulsive motion. Fear! And the first volitional centre of the upper body struggles awake, between the shoulders. It moves, the arm moves, ah, convulsively, wildly, wildly! Ah look, beyond control it moves, spurting from the wild source of impulse. Fear and ecstasy! Fear and ecstasy.—But the other dawning power obtrudes. Shall it move, the wildly waving little arm? Then look, it shall move soothly, it shall not flutter abroad. So! And so! Such a swing means such a balance, such an explosion of force means a leap in such and such a direction.

The volitional centre in the shoulders establishes itself bit by bit in relation to the sympathetic plexus in the breast, and forms a circuit of spontaneous-voluntary intelligence. The volitional centres are those which put us primarily into line with the earth's gravity. The wildly waving infant fist does not know how to swing attuned to the earth's gravity, the omnipresent force of gravity. Life flutters broadcast in the baby's arm. But at the thoracic ganglion acts a new vital power, which gradually seizes the motor energy that comes explosive from the sympathetic centre, and ranges it in line with all kinetic force, in line with the mysterious, omnipresent centre-pull of the earth's gravity great gravity. There is a true circuit now between the earth's centre and the centre of ebullient energy in the child. Everything depends on these true, polarised or orbital circuits. There is no disarray, no haphazard.

Once the flux of life from the spontaneous centres is put into its true kinetic relation with the earth's centre, adjusted to the force of gravity; once the gravitation of the baby's hand is spontaneously accepted and realised in the primary affective centres of the baby's psyche, then that little hand can take true and voluntary direction. The volitional centre is the pole that relates us, kinetically, to the earth's centre. The sympathetic plexus is the source whence the movement-impulse leaps out. Connect the two centres into a perfect circuit, and then, the moment the baby's fist leaps out for the tassel on its cradle, the volitional ganglion swings the leaping fist truly to its goal.

But this requires practice, for a baby. And in the course of the practice the infant bangs its own nose and swings its arm too far So that it hurts, and brings a fair amount of trouble upon itself. But in the end, the fluttering palpitating movement of the first days becomes a true and perfect flight, a gesture, a motion.

Has the mind got anything to do with all this? Does there enter any *idea* of movement into the baby's head, does the child form any conception of what it is doing? NONE. This whole range of activity and consciousness is non-mental, effective at the primary centres. It is not mere automatism. Far from it. It is *spontaneous consciousness,* effective and perfect in itself.

And it is in this spontaneous consciousness that education arises. One of the reasons why uneducated peasant nurses are on the whole so much better for infants than over-conscious mothers is that an uneducated nurse does not introduce any *idea* into her attitude towards the child. When she claps her hands before the child, again and again, nods, smiles, coos, and claps again, she is stimulating the infant to motion, pure, mindless motion. She wants the child to clap too. She wants its one little hand to find the other little hand, she wants to start the quick touch-and-go in the little shoulders. When you see her, time after time, making a fierce wild gesture with her arm, before the eyes of the baby, and the baby laughing and chuckling, she is rousing the infant to the same fierce, free, reckless *geste!* Fierce, free, wild, reckless *geste!* How it excites the child to a quaint reckless chuckle. How it wakes in him the desire, the impulse for free, sheer motion! It starts the proud *geste* of independence.

This is the clue to early education: movement, physical motion, the attuning of the kinetic energy of the motor centres to the vast sway of the earth's centre. Without this we are nothing: clumsy mechanical clowns, or pinched little automata.

But if you are going to make use of this form of education you must find teachers full of physical life and zest, of fine physical, motor intelligence, and mentally rather stupid, or at least quiescent. Above all things the *idea,* like a strangling worm, must not creep into the motor centres. It must be excluded. If we move, we must move primarily like a bird in the sky, which swings in supreme adjustment to the multiple forces of the winds of heaven and the pull of earth, mindless, idealess, a speck of perfect physical animation. That is the whole point of real physical life: its joy in spontaneous mindless animation, in motion sheer and superb, like a leaping fish or a hovering hawk or a deer which bounds away, creatures which have never known the pride and the blight of the idea. The idea is a glorious thing in its place. But interposed in all our living, interpolated into our every gesture, it is like some fatal mildew crept in, some vile blight.

Let children be taught the pride of clear, clean movement. If it only be putting a cup on the table, or a book on a shelf, let it be a fine pure motion, not a slovenly shove. Parents and teachers should be keen as hawks, watching their young in motion. Do we imagine that a young hawk learns to fly and stoop, does a young swallow learn to skim or a hare to dash uphill, or a hound to turn and seize him in full course, without long keen pain of learning? Where there is no pain of effort there is a wretched drossy degeneration, like the hateful cluttered sheep of our lush pastures. Look at the lambs, how they explode with new life, and skip up into the air. Already a *little* bit gawky! And then look at their mothers.—Whereas a wild sheep is a fleet fierce thing, leaping and swift like the sun.

So with our children. We, parents and teachers, must prevent their degenerating into physical cloddishness or mechanical affectation or fluttered nervousness. We must be after them, fiercely, sharpen and chasten their movements, their bearing, their walk. If a boy slouches out of a door, throw a book at him, like lightning. That will make him jump into keen and handsome alertness. And if a girl comes creeping, whining in, seize her by her pigtail and run her out again, full speed. That will bring the fire to her eyes and the poise to her head: if she's got any fire in her: and if she hasn't, why, give her a good knock to see if you can drive some in.

Anything, anything rather than the nervous, twisting, wistful, pathetic centreless children we are cursed with: or the fat and self-satisfied, sheep-in-the-pasture children who are becoming more common: or the impudent, I'm-as-good-as-anybody smirking children who are far too numerous. But it's all our own fault. We're afraid to *fight* with our children, and so we let them degenerate. Poor loving parents *we* are!

There must be a fight. There must be an element of danger, always. How do the wild animals get their grace, their beauty, their allure? Through being on the *qui vive,* always on the *qui vive.* A lark on a sand-dune springs up to heaven in song. She leaps up in a pure, fine strength. She trills out in triumph, she is beside herself in mid-heaven. But let her mind her p's and q's. In the first place, if she doesn't flick her wings finely and rapidly, with exquisite skilful energy, she'll come a cropper to earth. Let her mind the winds of heaven, in the first place. And in the second, let her mind the shadow of Monsieur the kestrel. And in the third place, let her be wary how she drops. And in the fourth place, let her be wary of who sees her dropping. For the moment she alights on this bristling earth she's got to dart to cover, and cut some secret track to her nest, or she's likely to be in trouble. It's all very well climbing a ladder of song to heaven But you've got to have your wits about you all the time, even while you're cock-a-lorying on your ladder: and *inevitably* you've got to climb down. Mind you don't give your enemies too good a chance, that's all. And watch it that you don't indicate where your nest is, or your ladder of song will have been a sore business. On the *qui vive,* bright lark!

So with our children. On the *qui vine.* The old-fashioned parents were right, when they made their children watch what they were about. But old-fashioned parents were a bore, dragging in moral and religious justification. If we are to chase our children, and chasten them too, it must be because they make our blood boil, not because some ethical or religious code sanctifies us.

"Miss, if you eat in that piggish, mincing fashion, you shall go without a meal or two."

"*Why!*"

"Because you're an objectionable sight."

"Well, you needn't look at me."

Here Miss should get a box on the ear.

"Take that! And know that I *need* look at you, since I'm responsible for you. And since I'm responsible for you, I'll watch it you don't behave like a mincing little pig."

Observe, no morals, no "What will people think of you?" or "What would your Daddy say?" or "What if Aunt Lucy saw you now!" or "It's wrong for little girls to be mincing and ugly!" or "You'll be sorry for it when you grow up!" or "I thought you were a good little girl!" or *"Now,* what did teacher say to you in Sunday school?" None of all these old dodges for shifting responsibility somewhere else. The plain fact is that parents and teachers *are* responsible for the bearing and developing of their children, so they may as well accept the responsibility flatly, and without dodges.

"I am responsible for the way you grow up, milady, and I'll fulfil my responsibility. So stop pushing your food about on your plate and looking like a self-conscious cockatoo, or leave the table and walk well out of my sight."

This is the tone that any honourable parent would take, seeing his little girl mincing and showing off at dinner. Let us keep the bowels of our compassion alive, and also the bowels of our wrath. No priggish brow-beating and mechanical authority, nor any disapproving superiority, but a plain, open anger when anger is aroused, and pleasure when this is waked.

The parent who sits at table in pained but disapproving silence while the child makes a nuisance of itself, and says: "Dear, I should be *so* glad if you would try to like your pudding: or if you don't like it, have a little bread and butter"—and who goes on letting the brat be a nuisance, this ideal parent is several times at fault. First she is assuming a pained ideal aloofness which is the worst form of moral bullying, a sort of *Of course I won't interfere, but I am in the right* attitude which is insufferable. If a parent is in the right, then she *must* interfere otherwise why does she bring up her child at all. If she doesn't interfere, what right has she to assume any virtue of superiority? Then when she is angry with the child, what right has she to say "Dear," which term implies a state of affectionate communion? This prefixing of the ideal rebuke with the term "Dear" or "Darling" is a hateful travesty of all good feeling. It is using love or affection as a bullying weapon: which vile sordid act the idealist is never afraid to commit. It is assuming authority of love, when love, as an emotional relationship, can have no authority. Authority must rest on responsible wisdom, and love must be a spontaneous thing or nothing: an emotional rapport. Love and authority have nothing to do with one another. "Whom the Lord loveth, he chasteneth. True! But the Lord's love is not supposed to be an emotional business, but a sort of divine responsibility and purpose. And so is parental love, a responsibility and a living purpose, not an emotion. To make the *emotion* responsible for the purpose is a fine falsification. One says "Dear" or "Darling" when the heart opens with spontaneous cherishment, not when the brow draws with anger or irritation. But the deep purpose and responsibility of parenthood remains unchanged no matter how the emotions flow. The emotions should flow unfalsified, in the very strength of that purpose.

Therefore parents should *never* seek justification outside themselves. They should never say "I do this for your good." You *don't* do it for the child's good. Parental responsibility is much deeper than an ideal responsibility. It is a vital connection. Parent and child are polarised together still, somewhat as before birth. When the child in the womb kicks it may almost hurt the parent. And the reaction is just as direct during all the course of childhood and parenthood. When a child is loose or ugly it is a direct *hurt* to the parent. The parent reacts and retaliates spontaneously. There is no justification, save the bond of parenthood, and certainly there is no ideal intervention.

We must accept the bond of parenthood primarily as a vital mindless conjunction, non-ideal, passional. A parent *owes* the child all the natural passional reactions provoked. If a child provokes anger, then to deny it this anger, the open, passional anger, is as bad as to deny it food or love. It causes an atrophy in the child, at the volitional centres, and a perversion of the true life flow.

Why are we so afraid of anger, of wrath, and clean fierce rage? What cowardice possesses us. Why would we reduce a child to a nervous irritable wreck, rather than spank it wholesomely? Why do we make such a fuss about a row. A row, a fierce storm in a family is a natural and healthy thing, which we ought even to have the courage to enjoy and exult in, as we can enjoy and exult in a storm of the elements. What makes us so namby-pamby? We ought all to fight: husbands and wives, parents and children, sisters and brothers and friends, all ought to fight, fiercely, freely, openly: and they ought to enjoy it. It stiffens the backbone and makes the eyes flash. Love without a fight is nothing but degeneracy. But the fight must be spontaneous and natural, without fixities and perversions.

The same with parenthood: spontaneous and natural, without any ideal taint.

And this is the beginning of true education: first, the stimulus to physical motion, physical trueness and élan, which is given to the infant. And this is continued during the years of early childhood *not by deliberate instruction,* but by the keen, fierce, unremitting swiftness of the parent, whose warm love opens the valves of glad motion in the child, so that the child plays in delicious security and freedom, and whose fierce vigilant anger sharpens the child to a trueness and boldness of motion and bearing such as are impossible save in children of strong-hearted parents.

Open the valves of warm love so that your child can play in serene joy by itself, or with others, like young weasels safe in a sunny nook of a wood or young tiger-cubs whose great parents lie grave and apart, on guard. And open also the sharp valves of wrath, that your child may be alert, keen, proud, and fierce in his turn. Let parenthood and childhood be a spontaneous, animal relationship, non-ideal, swift, a continuous interplay of shadow and light, ever-changing relationship and mood. And parents, keep in your heart, like tigers, the grave and vivid responsibility of parenthood, remote and natural in you, not fanciful and self-conscious.

X

From earliest childhood, let us have independence, independence, self-dependence. Every child to do all it can for itself, wash and dress itself, clean its own boots, brush and fold its own clothes, fetch and carry for itself, mend its own stockings, boy or girl alike, patch its own garments, and as soon as possible make as well as mend for itself. Man and woman are happy when they are busy, and children the same. But there must be the right motive behind the work. It must not always, for a child, be "Help mother" or "Help father" or "Help somebody." This altruism becomes tiresome, and causes disagreeable reaction.—Neither must the motive be the idea of work.—"Work is service, hence work is noble. *Laborare est orare.*" — Never was a more grovelling motto than this, that work is prayer. Work is not prayer at all: not in the same category. Work is a practical business, prayer is the soul's yearning and desire. Work is not an ideal, save for slaves. But work is quite a pleasant occupation for a human creature, a natural activity.

And the aim of work is neither the emotional helping of mother and father, nor the ethical-religious service of mankind. Nor is it the greedy piling up of stupid possessions. An individual works for his own pleasure and independence: but chiefly in the happy pride of personal independence, personal liberty. No man is free who depends on servants. Man can never be quite free. Indeed he doesn't want to be. But in his *personal* immediate life he can be vastly freer than he is.

How?—By doing things for himself. Once we wake the quick of personal pride, there is a pleasure in performing our own personal service, every man sweeping his own room, making his own bed, washing his own dishes—or in proportion: just as a soldier does. We have got a mistaken notion of ourselves. We conceive of ourselves as ideal beings, nothing but consciousness, and therefore actual work has become degrading, menial to us. But let us change our notion of ourselves. We are only in part ideal beings. For the rest we are lively physical creatures whose life consists in motion and action. We have two feet which need tending, and which need socks and shoes. This is our own personal affair, and it behoves us to see to it. Let me look after my own socks and shoes, since these are private to me. Let me tend to my own apparel and my own personal service. Every bird builds its own nest and preens its own feathers: save perhaps a cuckoo or a filthy little sparrow which likes to oust a swallow, or a crazy ostrich which squats in the sand. Proud personal privacy, personal liberty, gay individual self-dependence. Awake in a child the gay, proud sense of its own aloof individuality, and it will busy itself about its own affairs happily. It all depends what centre you try to drive from, what motive is at the back of all your movement.

It is just as irksome to *have* a servant as to *be* a servant: particularly a personal servant. A servant moving about me, or even anybody moving about me, doing things for me, is a horrible drag on my freedom. I feel it as a sort of prostitution. *Noli me tangere.* It is our motto as it is the motto of a wild wolf or deer. I want about me a clear cool space across which nobody trespasses. I want to remain intact within my own natural isolation, save at those moments when I am drawn to a rare and significant intimacy. The horrible personal promiscuity of our life is extremely ugly and distasteful. As far as possible, let *nobody* do anything for me, personally, save those who are near and dear to me: and even then as little as possible. Let me be by myself, and leave me my native distance. Sono io—and not a thing of public convenience.

Self-dependence is independence. To be free one must be self-sufficient, particularly in small, material, personal matters. In the great business of love, or friendship, or living human intercourse one meets and communes with another free individual, there is no service. Service is degrading, both to the servant and the one served: a promiscuity, a sort of prostitution. No one should do for me that which I can reasonably do for myself. Two individuals may be intimately interdependent on one another, as man and wife, for example. But even in this relation each should be as self-dependent, as self-supporting as ever possible. We should be each as single in our independence as the wild animals are. That is the only true pride. To have a dozen servants is to be twelve times prostituted in human relationship, sold and bought and automatised, divested of individual singleness and privacy.

The actual doing things is in itself a joy. If I wash the dishes I learn a quick light touch of china and earthenware, the feel of it, the weight and roll and poise of it, the peculiar hotness, the quickness or slowness of its surface. I am at the middle of an infinite complexity of motions and adjustments and quick, apprehensive contacts. Nimble faculties hover and play along my nerves, the primal consciousness is alert in me. Apart from all the moral or practical satisfaction derived from a thing well done, I have the *mindless* motor activity and reaction in primal consciousness, which is a pure satisfaction. If I am to be well and satisfied, as a human being, a large part of my life must pass in mindless motion, quick, busy activity in which I am neither bought nor sold, but acting alone and free from the centre of my own active isolation. Not self-consciously, however. Not watching my own reactions. If I wash dishes I wash them to get them clean, nothing else.

Every man must learn to be proud and single and alone, and after that, will be worth knowing. Mankind has degenerated into a conglomerate mass, where everybody strives to look and to be as much as possible an impersonal, non-individual, abstracted unit, a standard. A high *standard* of perfection: that's what we talk about. As if there could be any *standard* among living people, all of whom are separate and single, each one natively distinguished from every other one. Yet we all wear boots made for the abstract "perfect" or standard foot, and coats made as near as possible for the abstract shoulders of Mr Everyman.

I object to the abstract Mr Everyman being clapped over me like an extinguisher. I object to wearing his coat and his boots and his hat. Me, in a pair of "Lotus" boots, and a "Burberry," and "Oxonian" hat, why, I might just as well be anybody else. And I strenuously object. I am myself, and I don't want to be rigged out as a poor specimen of Mr Everyman. I don't want to be standardised, or even idealised.

If I could, I would make my own boots and my own trousers and coats. I suppose even now I could if I would. But in Rome one must do as Rome does: the *bourgeois* is not worth my while, I can't demean myself to *épater* him, and I am much too sensitive to my own isolation to want to draw his attention.

Although, however, in Rome one must do as Rome does; and although all the world is Rome today; yet even Rome falls. Rome fell and Rome will fall again. That is the point.

And it is to prepare for this fall of Rome that we conjure up a new system of education. When I say that every boy shall be taught cobbling and boot-making, it is in the hopes that before long a man will make his own boots to his own fancy. If he likes to have Maltese sandals, why, he'll have Maltese sandals; and if he likes better high laced buskins, why, he can stalk like an Athenian tragedian. Anyhow he'll sit happily devising his own covering for his own feet, and machine-made boots be hanged. They even hurt him, and give him callosities. And yet, so far, he thinks their machine-made standardised nullity is perfection. But wait till we have dealt with him. He'll be gay-shod to the happiness and vanity of his own toes and to the satisfaction of his own desire. And the same with his trousers. If he fancies his legs, and likes to flutter on his own elegant stem, like an Elizabethan, here's to him. And if he has a hankering after scarlet trunk-hose, I say hurray. *Chacun à son goût*: or ought to have. Unfortunately nowadays nobody has his own taste, everybody is trying to turn himself into a eunuch Mr Everyman, standardised to his collar-stud. A woman is a little different. She wants to look ultra-smart and chic beyond words. And so she knows that if she can set all women bitterly asking "Isn't her dress Paquin?" or "Surely it's Poiret," or Lucile or Chéruit or somebody *very* Parisian, why, she's done it. She wants to create an *effect*: not the effect of being just *herself*, her one and only self, as a flower in all its spots and frills is its own candid self. Not at all. A modern woman wants to hit you in the eye with her get-up. She wants to be a picture. She wants to derive her own nature from her accoutrements. Put her in a khaki uniform and she's a man shrilly whistling *K-K-K-Katie*. Let her wear no bodice at all, but just a row of emeralds and an aigrette, and she's a cocotte before she's eaten her hors d'œuvres, even though she was a Bible Worker all her life. She lays it all on from the outside, powders her very soul.

But of course, when the little girls from *our* schools grow up they will really consider the lily, and put forth their flowers from their own roots. See them, the darlings, the women of the future, silent and rapt spinning their own fabric out of their own instinctive souls,—and cotton and linen and silk and wool into the bargain, of course—and delicately unfolding the skirts and bodices, or the loose Turkish trousers and little vests, or whatever else they like to wear, evolving and unfurling them in sensitive form, according to their own instinctive desire. She puts on her clothes as a flower unfolds its petals, as an utterance from her own nature, instinctive and individual.

Oh if only people can learn to do as they like and to have what they like, instead of madly aspiring to do what everybody likes and to look as everybody would like to look. Fancy everybody looking as everybody else likes, and nobody looking like anybody. It sounds like Alice in Wonderland. A well-dressed woman before her mirror says to herself, if she is satisfied: "Every woman would like to look as I look now. Every woman will envy me."

Which is absurd. Fancy a petunia leaning over to a geranium and saying: "Ah miss, *wouldn* 't you just love to be in mauve and white, like me instead of that common turkey red." To which the geranium: "You! In your cheap material! You don't look more than one-and-a-ha'penny a yard. You'd thank your lucky stars if you had an inch of *chiffon velvet* to your name."

Of course, a petunia is a petunia, and a geranium is a geranium. And I'll bet Solomon in all his glory was not arrayed like one of these. Why? Because he was trying to cut a dash and look like something beyond nature, overloading himself. Without doubt Solomon in all his nakedness was a lovely thing. But one has a terrible misgiving about Solomon in all his glory. David probably unfolded his nakedness into clothes that came naturally from him. But that Jewish glory of Solomon's suggests diamonds in lumps. Though we may be wrong, and Solomon in all his glory may have moved in fabrics that rippled naturally from him as his own hair, and his jewels may have glowed as his soul glowed, intrinsic. Let us hope so, in the name of wisdom.

All of which may seem a long way from the education of the people. But it isn't really. It only means to say, don't set up standards and regulation patterns for people. Don't have criteria. Let every individual be single and self-expressive: not self-expressive in the self-conscious smirking fashion, but busy making something he *needs* and wants to have just so, according to his own soul's desire. Everyone individually and spontaneously busy, like a bird that builds its own nest and preens its own feathers, busy about its own business, alone and unaware.

The fingers must almost live and think by themselves. It is no good working from the idea, from the fancy: the creation must evolve itself from the vital activity of the fingers. Here's the difference between living evolving work and that ideal mental business we call "handi-craft instruction" or "handwork" in school today.

Dozens of high-souled idealists sit today at hand-looms and spiritually weave coarse fabrics. It is a high-brow performance. As a rule it comes to an end. But sometimes it achieves another effect. Sometimes actually the mind is lulled, by the steady repetition of mechanical, productive labour, into a kind of swoon. Gradually the idealism moults away, the high-brow resolves into a busy, unconscious worker, perhaps even a night and day slogger, absorbed in the process of work.

One should go to the extremity of any experience. But that one should stay there, and make a habit of the extreme, is another matter. A good part of the life of every human creature should pass in mindless, active occupation. But not all the days. There is a time to work, and a time to be still, a time to think, and a time to forget. And they are all different times.

The point about any handwork is that it should not be mindwork. Supposing we are to learn to solder a kettle. The theory is told in a dozen words. But it is not a question of applying a theory. It is a question of *knowing,* by direct physical contact, your kettle-substance, your kettle-curves, your solder, your soldering-iron, your fire, your resin, and all the fusing, slipping interaction of all these. A question of direct knowing by contact, not a question of understanding. The mental understanding of what is happening is quite unimportant to the job. If you are of an inquiring turn of mind, you can inquire afterwards. But while you are at the job, *know* what you're doing, and don't bother about understanding. Know by immediate sensual contact. Know by the tension and reaction of the muscles, know, know profoundly but forever untellably, at the spontaneous primary centres. Give yourself in an intense, mindless attention, almost as deep as sleep, but not charged with random dreams, charged with potent effectiveness. Busy, intent, absorbed work, forgetfulness, this is one of the joys of life. Thoughts may be straying through the mind all the time. But there is no attention to them. They stream on like dreams, irrelevant. The soul is attending with joy and active purpose to the kettle and the soldering-iron, the mindless psyche concentrates intent on the unwilling little rivulet of solder which runs grudgingly under the nose of the hot tool. To be or not to be— Being isn't a conscious effort, anyhow.

So we realise that there must be a deep gulf, an oblivion, between pedagogy and handwork. Don't let a pedagogue come fussing about in a workshop. He will only muddle up the instincts.

Not that a school-master is necessarily a pedagogue. Poor devil, he starts by being a man, and it isn't always easy to turn a man into that thing. And therefore many a school-master is a thousand times happier turning a lathe or soldering a kettle than expounding long division. But the two activities are incompatible. Not incompatible in the same individual, but incompatible with each other. So, separate the two activities. Let the pedagogue of the morning disappear in the afternoon. If he appears in a workshop, let it be before children who have not known him as a school-teacher.

And in the workshop, let real jobs be done. Workshops may be mere tin sheds, or wooden sheds. Let parents send the household kettles, broken chairs, boots and shoes, simple tailoring and sewing and darning and even cooking, to the workshop. Let the family business of this sort be given to the children, who will set off to the workshed and get the job done, under supervision, in the hours of occupation. A good deal can be done that way, instead of the silly theoretic fussing making fancy nick-nacks or specimen parts, such as goes on at present.

What we want is for every child to be *handy*: physically adaptable, and handy. If a boy shows any desire to go forward in any craft, he will have his opportunity. He can go on till he becomes an expert. But he must start by being, like Jack at sea, just a handy man. The same with a girl.

Let the handwork be a part of the family and communal life, an extension of family life. Don't muddle it up with the mindwork. Mindwork at its best is theoretic. Our present attempt to make mindwork "objective" and physical, and to instil theoretic mathematics through carpentry and joinering is silly. If we are teaching arithmetic, let us teach pure arithmetic, without bothering with sham pennies and shillings and pounds of sham sugar. In actual life, when we do our shopping, every one of our calculations is made quickly in abstraction: a pure mental act, everything abstracted. And let our mental acts be pure mental acts, not adulterated with "objects." What ails modern education is that it is trying to cram primal physical experience into mental activity—with the result of mere muddledness. Pure physical experience takes place at the great affective centres, and is *de facto* pre-mental, non-mental. Mental experience on the other hand is pure and different, a process of abstraction, and therefore *de facto* not physical.

If our consciousness is dual, and active in duality; if our human activity is of two incompatible sorts, why try to make a moshy oneness of it? The rapport between the mental consciousness and the affective or physical consciousness is always a polarity of contradistinction. The two are never one, save in their incomprehensible duality. Leave the two modes of activity separate. What connection is necessary will be effected spontaneously.

XI

The essence of most games, let us not forget, lies in the element of *contest*: contest in force, contest in skill, contest in wit. The essence of work, on the other hand, lies in single, absorbed, mindless productivity. Now here again we have done our best to muck up the natural order of things. All along the line we have tried to introduce the mean and impoverishing factor of *emulation* into work-activities, and we have tried to make games as little as possible contests, and as much as possible fanciful self-conscious processes.

Work is an absorbed and absorbing process of productivity. Introduce this mean motive of emulation, and you cause a flaw at once in the absorption. You introduce a worm-like *arrière-pensée,* you corrupt the true state. Pah, it makes us sick to think of the glib spuriousness which is doled out to young school-teachers, purporting to be "theory of education." The whole system seems to be a conspiracy to falsify and corrupt human nature, introduce an element of meanness, duplicity and self-consciousness. Emulation is a dirty spirit, introduced into work, a petty, fostered jealousy and affectation. And this is true whether the work be mental or physical.

On the other hand, rivalry is a natural factor in all sport and in practically all games, simple, natural rivalry, the spirit of contest.

Again let us draw attention to a duality in the human psychic activity. There is the original duality between the physical and the mental psyche. And now there is another duality, a duality of mode and direction chiefly: the natural distinction between productive and contestive activities. The state of soul of a man engaged in productive activity is, when pure, quite distinct from that of the same man engaged in some competitive activity.

Let us note here another fatal defect in our modern system.

Having attempted, according to ideal, to convert all life and all living into one mode only, the productive mode, we have been forced to introduce into our productive activities the spirit of contest which is original and ineradicable in us. This spirit of contest takes the form of competition: commercial, industrial, spiritual, educational, and even religious competition.

Was ever anything more humiliating than this spectacle of a mankind active in nothing but productive competition, all idea of pure, single-hearted production lost entirely, and all honest fiery contest condemned and tabooed. Here is the clue to the *bourgeois.* He will have no honest fiery contest. He will have only the mean, Jewish competition in productivity, in money-making. He won't have any single absorbed production. All work must be a scramble of contest against some other worker.

Is anything more despicable to be conceived? How make an end of? By separating the two modes. By realising that man is in at least one-half his nature a pure fighter—not a competitor competing for some hideous silver mug, or some pot of money—but a fighter, a contester, a warrior.

We must wake again the flashing centres of volition in the fierce, proud backbone, there where we should be superb and indomitable, where we are actually so soft. We can move in herds of self-sacrificing heroism. But laughing defiance has gone out of our shop-keeping world.

And so for the third part of education, games and physical instruction and drill. We are all on the wrong track again. In the elementary schools physical instruction is a pitiful business: this Swedish drill business. It is a mere pettifogging attempt to turn the body into a mental instrument, and seems warranted to produce nothing but a certain sulky hatred of physical command, and a certain amount of physical self-consciousness.

Physical training and Sandowism altogether is a ridiculous and puerile business. A man sweating and grunting to get his muscles up is one of the maddest and most comical sights. And the modern athlete parading the self-conscious mechanism of his body, reeking with a degraded physical, muscular self-consciousness and nothing but self-consciousness, is one of the most stupid phenomena mankind has ever witnessed. The physique is all right in itself. But to have your physique in your head, like having sex in the head, is unspeakably repulsive. To have your own physique on your mind all the time: why, it is a semi-pathological state, the exact counterpoise to the querulous peevish invalid.

To have one's mind full of one's own physical self, and to have one's own physical self pranking and bulging under one's own mental direction is a good old perversion. The athlete is perhaps of all the self-conscious objects of our day, the most self-consciously objectionable.

It is all wrong to mix up the two modes of consciousness. To the physique belongs the mindless, spontaneous consciousness of the great plexuses and ganglia. To the mind belongs pure abstraction, the *idea.* To drag down the idea into a bulging athletic physique; and to drag the body up into the head, till it becomes an obsession: horror.

Let the two modes of consciousness act in their duality, reciprocal, but polarised in difference, not to be muddled and transfused. If you are going to be physically active, physically strenuous and conscious, then *put off your mental attention,* put off all idea, and become a mindless physical spontaneous Consciousness.

Away with all physical culture. Banish it to the limbo of human prostitutions: self-prostitution as it is: the prostitution of the primary self to the secondary idea.

If you will have the gymnasium: and certainly let us have the gymnasium: let it be to get us ready for the great *contests* and games of skill. Never, never let the motive be self-produced, the act self-induced. It is as bad as masturbation. Let there be the profound motive of *battle.* Battle, battle, let that be the word that rouses us to pure physical efforts.

Not Mons or Ypres of course. Ah, the horror of machine explosions! But living, naked battle, flesh to flesh contest. Fierce tense struggle of man with man, struggle to the death. That is the spirit of the gymnasium. Fierce, unrelenting, honorable contest.

Let all physical culture be pure *training,* training for the contest, and training for the expressive dance. Let us have a gymnasium as the Greeks had it, and for the same purpose: the purpose of pure, perilous delight in contest, and profound, mystic delight in motion. Drop morality. But don't drop morality until you've dropped ideal self-consciousness.

Set the boys one against the other like young bantam cocks. Let them fight. Let them hurt one another. Teach them again to fight with gloves and fists, egg them on, spur them on, let it be fine balanced contest in skill and fierce pride. Egg them on, and look on the black eye and the bloody nose as insignia of honor, like the Germans of old.

Bring out the foils and teach fencing. Teach fencing, teach wrestling, teach jiu-jitsu, every form of fierce hand to hand contest. And praise the wounds. And praise the valour that will be killed rather than yield. Better fierce and unyielding death than our degraded creeping life.

We are all fighters. Let us fight. Has it come down to chasing a poor fox and kicking a leather ball. Heaven, what a spectacle we should be to the Lacedaemonian. Rouse the old male spirit again. The male is always a fighter. The human male is a superb and godlike fighter, unless he is contravened in his own nature. In fighting to the death he has one great crisis of his being.

What, are we going to revoke our own being? Are we going to soften and soften in self-sacrificial ardour till we are white worms? Are we going to get our battle out of some wretched competition in trade or profession?

We will have a new education, where a black eye is a sign of honor, and where men strip stark for the fierce business of the fight.

What is the fight? It is a primary physical thing. It is not a horrible obscene ideal process, like our last war. It is not a ghastly and blasphemous translation of ideas into engines, and men into cannon-fodder. Away with such war. A million times away with such obscenity. Let the desire of it die out of mankind.

But let us keep the real war, the real fight. And what is the fight? It is a sheer immediate conflict of physical men: that, and that best of all. What does death matter, if a man die in a flame of passionate conflict. He goes to heaven, as the ancients said: somehow, somewhere his soul is at rest, for death is to him a passional consummation.—But to be blown to smithereens while you are eating a sardine: horrible and monstrous abnormality. The soul should leap fiery into death, a

280

consummation. Then nothing is lost. But our horrible cannon-fodder!—let us go the right way about making an end of it.

And the right way, and the only way, is to rouse new, living, passionate desires and activities in the soul of man. Your universal-brotherhood, league-of-nations smoshiness and pappiness is no good. It will end in foul hypocrisy, and nothing can prevent its so ending.

It is a sort of idiocy to talk about putting an end to all fighting and turning all energy into some commercial or trades-union competition. What is a fight? It's not an ideal business. It is a physical business. Perhaps up to now, in our ideal world war was necessarily a terrific conflict of ideas, engines and explosives derived out of man's cunning ideas. But now we know we are not ideal beings only: now we know that it is hopeless and wretched to confuse the ideal conscious activity with the primal physical conscious activity: and now we know that true contest belongs to the primal physical self, that ideas, *per se,* are static; why, perhaps we shall have sense enough to fight once more hand to hand as fierce naked men. Perhaps we shall be able to abstain from the unthinkable baseness of pitting one ideal engine against another ideal engine, and supplying human life as the fodder for these ideal machines.

Death is glorious. But to be blown to bits by a machine is mere horror. Death, if it be violent death, should come as a grand passional climax and consummation, and then all is well with the soul of the dead.

The human soul is really capable of honor, once it has a true choice. But when it has a choice only of war with explosive engines and poison gases, and a universal peace which consists in the most sordid commercial and industrial competition, why, believe me, the human soul will choose war, in the long run, inevitably it will; if only with a remote hope of at last destroying utterly this stinking industrial-competitive humanity.

Man *must* have the choice of war. But, raving insane idealist as he is, he must no longer have the choice of bombs and poison gases and Long Berthas. That must not be. Let us beat our soldering-irons into swords, if we will. But let us blow all guns and explosives and poison gases sky-high. Let us shoot every man who makes one more grain of gunpowder, with his own powder.

After all, we are masters of our own inventions. Are we really so feeble and inane that we cannot get rid of the monsters we have brought forth? Why not? Because we are afraid of somebody else's preserving them? Believe me, there's nothing which every man—except insane criminals, and these we ought to hang right off; there's nothing which every man would be so glad to think had vanished out of the world as guns, explosives, and poison gases. I don't care when my share in them goes sky-high. I'll take every risk of the Japanese or the Germans having a secret store.

Pah, men are all human, till you drive them mad. And for centuries we have been driving each other mad with our idealism and universal love. Pretty weapons they have spawned, pretty fruits of our own madness. But the British people tomorrow could destroy all guns, explosives, all poison gases, and all apparatus for the making of these things. Perhaps you might leave one-barrelled pistols: but not another thing.—And the world would get on its sane legs the very next day. And we should run no danger at all: danger, perhaps, of the loss of some small property. But nothing at all compared with the great sigh of relief.

It's the only way to do it. Melt down *all* your guns of all sorts. Destroy all your explosives, save what bit you want for quarries and mines. Keep no explosive weapon in England bigger than a one-barrel pistol, which may live for one year longer. At the end of one year no explosive weapon shall exist.

The world at once starts afresh.—Well, do it. Your confabs and your meetings, your discussions and your international agreements will serve you nothing. League of Nations is all bilberry jam: bilge: and you know it. Put your guns in the fire and drown your explosives, and you've done your share of the League of Nations.

But don't pretend you've abolished war. Send your soldiers to Ireland if you must send them, armed with swords and shields, but with no *engines* of war. Trust the Irish to come out with swords and shields as well: they'll do it. And then have a rare old lively scrap, the heart can rejoice in. But in the name of human sanity, never point another cannon: never. And it lies with Britain to take the lead. Nobody else will.

Then, when all your explosive weapons are destroyed—which may be before Christmas—then introduce a proper system of martial training in the schools. Let every boy and every citizen be a soldier, a fighter. Let him have sword and spear and shield, and know how to use them. Let him be determined to use them, too.

For what does life consist in? Not in being some ideal little monster, a superman. It consists in remaining inside your own skin, and living inside your own skin, and not pretending you're any bigger than you are. And so, if you've got to go in for a scrap, go in your own skin. Don't turn into some ideal-obscene monster, and invent explosive engines which will blow up an ideal enemy whom you've never set eyes on and probably never will set eyes on. Loathsome and hateful insanity that.

If you have an enemy, even a national enemy, go for him in your own skin. Meet him, see him, come into contact and fierce struggle with him. What good is an enemy if he's only abstract and invisible? That's merely ideal. If he is an enemy he is a flesh and blood fellow whom I meet and fight with, to the death. I don't blow bombs into the vast air, hoping to scatter a million bits of indiscriminate flesh. God save us, no more of that.

Let us get back inside our own skins, sensibly and sanely. Let us fight when our dander is up: but hand to hand, hand to hand, always hand to hand. Let us meet a man like a man, not like some horrific idea-born machine.

Let us melt our guns. Let us just simply do it as an act of reckless defiant sanity. Why be afraid? It is such fear that has caused all the bother. Spit on such fear. After all, it can't do anything so vile as it has done already. Let us have a national holiday, melting the guns and drowning the powder. Let us make a spree of it. Let's have it on the Fifth of November: bushels of squibs and rockets. If we're quick we can have them ready. And as a squib fizzes away, we say "There goes the guts out of a half-ton bomb."

And then let us be soldiers, hand to hand soldiers. Lord, but it is a bitter thing to be born at the end of a rotten, idealistic machine-civilisation. Think what we've missed: the glorious bright passion of anger and pride, recklessness and dauntless cock-a-lory.

XII

Our life today is a sort of sliding scale of shifted responsibility. The man, who is supposed to be the responsible party, as a matter of fact flings himself either at the feet of a woman, and makes her his conscience keeper; or at the feet of the public. The woman, burdened with the lofty importance of man's conscience and decision, turns to her infant and says "It is all for you, my sacred child. For *you* are the future!" And the precious baby, saddled with the immediate responsibility of all the years, puckers his poor face and howls: as well he may.—Or the public, meaning the ordinary working man, being told for the fifty-millionth time that everything is for him, every effort and every move is made for his sake, naturally inquires at length: "Then why doesn't everything come my way?" To which, under the circumstances, there is no satisfactory answer.

So here we are, grovelling before two gods, the baby in arms and the people. In the sliding scale of shirked responsibility, man puts the golden crown of present importance on the head of the woman, and the nimbus of sanctity round the head of the infant, and then grovels in an ecstasy of worship and self-exoneration before the double idol. A disgusting and shameful sight. After which he gets up and slinks off to his money making and his commercial competition, and feels holy-holy-holy about it. "It is all for sacred woman and her divine child." The most disillusioning part about woman is that she sits on the Brummagem throne and laps up this worship. The baby, poor wretch, gets a stomach-ache. The other god, poor Demogorgon, the gorgon of the People, is even in a worse state. He sees the idealist kneeling before him crying: "You are Demos, you are the People, you are All in All. You have ten million heads and ten million voices and twenty million hands. Ah, how wonderful you are! Hail to you! Hail to you! Hall to you!"

Poor Demogorgon Briareus scratches his ten million heads with ten million of his hands, and feels a bit bothered, like. Because every one of the ten million heads is slow and flustered.

"Do you mean it, though?" he says.

"Ah shrieks the idealist. "Listen to the divine voice. Ten million throats, and one message! Divine, divine!"

Unfortunately each of the ten million throats is a little hoarse, each voice a little clumsy and mistrustful.

"All right then," mumbles Briareus Demogorgon; "fob out then."

"Certainly! Certainly! Ah the bliss with which we sacrifice our all to thee" And he flings a million farthings at the feet of the many-headed.

Briaeus picks up a farthing with one million out of his twenty million hands, turns over the coin, spits on it for luck, and puts it in his pocket. Feels however that this isn't everything.

"Now work a little harder for us, Great One, Supreme One," cajoles the idealist.

And Demogorgon, not knowing any better, but with some misgiving rumbling inside him, sets to for a short spell, whilst the idealist shrills out:

Behold him, the worker, the producer, the provider! Our Providence, our Great One, our God of Gods. Demos! Demo-gorgon!"

All of which flatters Briareus for a long time, till he realises once more that if he's as divine as all that he ought to see a few more Bradburys fluttering his way. So he strikes, and says: "Look here what do you mean by it?"

"You're quite right, O Great one," replies the idealist. "you are *always* right, Almighty Demos. Only don't stop working, otherwise the whole universe, which is *yours* mind you, will stop working too. And *then* where will you be?"

Demos thinks there's something in it, so he slogs at it again. But always with a bee buzzing in his bonnet. Which bee stings him from time to time, and then he jumps, and the world jumps with him.

It's time to get the bee out of the bonnet of Briareus, or he'll be jumping right on top of us, he'll become a real Demogorgon.

"Keep still, Demos my dear. You've got a nasty wasp in your bowler. Keep still, it's dangerous if it stings you. Let me get it out for you."

And so we begin to remove the lie which the idealist has slipped in.

"You're big, Briareus, my dear fellow. You've got ten million heads. But every one of your ten million heads works rather slowly, and not one of your twenty million eyes sees much further than the end of your nose: which is only about an inch and a half, and not ten-million times an inch and a half. And your great ten-million-times voice, rather rough and indistinct, though of course *very* loud, doesn't really tell me anything, Briareus, Demos, oh Democracy. Your wonderful cross which you make with your ten million hands when you vote, it's a stupid and meaningless little mark. You don't know what you're doing: and anyhow it's only a choice of evils, on whose side you put your little cross.—A thing repeated ten million times isn't any more important for the repetition: it's a weary, stupid little thing. So now be still, Briareus, and let a better man than yourself think for you, with his one clear head. For you must admit that ten million muddled heads are not better than one muddled head, and have no more right to authority. So just be quiet, Briareus, and listen with your twenty million ears to one clear voice, and one bit of sense, and one word of truth.—No, don't ramp and gnash your ten million sets of teeth. You won't come it over us with any of your Demogorgon turns. We shan't turn to stone. We shall think what a fool you are—."

The same with the infant.

"My poor, helpless child, let's get this nimbus off, so that you can sleep in comfort. There now, play with your toes and digest your pap in peace, the future isn't yours for many a day. We'll look after the present. And that's all *you* will be able to do. Take care of the present and the past and future can take care of themselves."

After which, to woman enthroned:

I'm sorry to trouble you, my dear, but do you mind coming down. We want that throne for a pigeon-place. And do you mind if I put a bottom in your crown; it'll make a good cake-tin. You can bake a nice dethronement cake in it.—You and I, my dear, we've had enough of this worship farce. You're nothing but a woman, a human female creature and I'm nothing but a man, a human male creature, and there's absolutely no call for worship on either hand. The fact that you're female doesn't mean that I ought to set about worshipping you, and the fact that I'm male doesn't intend to start you worshipping me. It's all bunkum and lies, this worshipping process, anyhow. We're none of us gods: just two-legged human creatures. You're just yourself and I'm just myself; we're different, and we'll agree to differ. No more of this puffing-up business. It makes us sick.

"You are yourself, a woman, and I'm myself, a man: and that makes a breach between us. So let's leave the breach, and walk across occasionally on some suspension bridge. But you live on one side, and I live on the other. Don't let us interfere with each other's side. We can meet and have a chat and swing our legs mid-stream on the bridge. But you live on that side and I on this. You're not a man and I'm not a woman. Don't let's pretend we are. Let us stick to our own side, and meet like the magic foreigners we are. There's much more fun in it. Don't bully me, and I won't bully you.

"I've got most of the thinking, abstracting business to do, and most of the mechanical business, so let me do it. I hate to see a woman trying to be abstract, and being abstract, just as I hate and loathe to see a woman doing mechanical work. You hate me when I'm feminine. So I'll let you be womanly, you let me be manly. You look after the immediate personal life, and I'll look after the further, abstracted and mechanised life. You remain at the centre, I scout ahead. Let us agree to it, without conceit on either side. We're neither better nor worse than each other, we're an equipoise in difference—but in difference, mind, not in sameness."

And then, beyond this, let the men scout ahead. Let them go always ahead of their women, in the endless trek across life. Central, with the wagons, travels the woman, with the children and the whole responsibility of immediate, personal living. And on ahead, scouting, fighting, gathering provision, running on the brink of death and at the tip of the life advance, all the time hovering at the tip of life and on the verge of death, the men, the leaders, the outriders.

And between men let there be a new spontaneous relationship, a new fidelity. Let men realise that their life lies ahead, in the dangerous wilds of advance and increase. Let them realise that they must go beyond their women, projected into a region of greater abstraction, more inhuman activity.

There, in these womanless regions of fight, and pure thought, and abstracted instrumentality, let men have a new attitude to one another. Let them have a new reverence for their heroes, a new regard for their comrades: deep, deep as life and death.

Let there be again the old passion of deathless friendship between man and man. Humanity can never advance into the new regions of unexplored futurity otherwise. Men who can only hark back to woman become automatic, static. In the great move ahead, in the wild hope which rides on the brink of death, men go side by side, and faith in each other alone stays them. They go side by side. And the extreme bond of deathless friendship supports them over the edge of the known and into the unknown.

Friendship should be a rare, choice, immortal thing, sacred and inviolable as marriage. Marriage and deathless friendship, both should be inviolable and sacred: two great creative passions, separate, apart, but complementary: the one pivotal, the other adventurous: the one, marriage, the centre of human life; and the other the leap ahead.

Which is the last word in the education of a people.

If no man lives for ever, neither does any precept. And if even the weariest river winds somewhere safe to sea, so also does the weariest wisdom. And there is lost. Also incorporated.

> "Know then thyself, presume not God to scan.
> The proper study of mankind is man."

It was Alexander Pope who absolutely struck the note of our particular epoch: not Shakespeare or Luther or Milton. A man of first magnitude never fits his age perfectly.

> Know then thyself, presume not God to scan.
> The proper study of mankind is Man—" with a capital M.

This stream of wisdom is very weary now: weary to death. It started such a gay little trickle, and is such a spent muddy ebb by now. It will take a big sea to swallow all its alluvia.

"Know then thyself." All right! I'll do my best. Honestly I'll do my best, sincerely to know myself. Since it is the great commandment to conciousness of our long era, let us be men, and try to obey it. Jesus gave the emotional commandment. "Love thy neighbour." But the But the Greeks set the even more absolute motto, in its way, a more deeply religious motto: "Know thyself."

Very well! Being man, and the son of man, I find it only honorable to obey. To do my best. To do my best to know myself. And particularly that part, or those parts of myself that have not yet been admitted into consciousness. Man is nothing, less than a tick stuck in a sheep's back, unless he adventures. Either into the unknown of the world of his environment. Or into the unknown of himself.

Allons! the road is before us. Know thyself! Which means, *really*, know thine own *unknown* self. It's no good knowing something you know already. The thing is to discover the tracts as yet unknown. And as the only unknown now lies deep in the passional soul, allons! The road is before us. We write a novel or two, we are called erotic or depraved or idiotic or boring. What does it matter, we go the road just the same. If you see the point of the great old commandment, *Know thyself* then you see the point of all art.

But knowing oneself, like knowing anything else, is not a process that can continue to infinity, in the same direction. The fact that I myself *am* only myself makes me very specifically finite. True, I may argue that my Self is a mystery that impinges on the infinite.

Admitted. But the moment my Self impinges on the infinite, it ceases to be just myself.

The same is true of all knowing. You start to find out the chemical composition of a drop of water, and before you know where you are, your river of knowledge is winding very unsatisfactorily into a very vague sea, called the ether. You start to study electricity, you track the wretch down till you get some mysterious and misbehaving atom of energy or unit of force that goes pop under your nose and leaves you with the dead body of a mere word.

You sail down your stream of knowledge, and you find yourself absolutely at sea. Which may be safety for the weary river, but is a sad look-out for you, who are a land animal.

Now all science starts gaily from the inland source of *I Don't Know.* Gaily it says: I don't know, but I'm going to know. It's like a little river bubbling up cheerfully in the determination to dissolve the whole world in its waves. And science, like the little river, winds wonderingly out again into the final *I Don't Know* of the last ocean.

All this is platitudinous as regards science. Science has learned an uncanny lot, *by the way.*

Apply the same to the Know Thyself motto. We have learned something by the way. But as far as I'm concerned, I see land receding, and the great ocean of the last *I Don't Know* enveloping me.

But the human consciousness is never allowed finally to say: "I Don't Know." It has *got* to know, even if it must metamorphose to do so.

"Know then thyself, presume not God to scan."

Now as soon as you come across a Thou Shalt Not commandment, you may be absolutely sure that sometime or other, you'll have to break this commandment. You needn't make a practice of breaking it. But the day will come when you'll have to break it. When you'll have to take the name of the Lord Your God in vain, and have other gods, and worship idols, and steal, and kill, and commit adultery, and all the rest. A day will come. Because, as Oscar Wilde says, what's a temptation for, except to be succumbed to!

There comes a time, to every man, when he has to break one or other of the Thou Shalt Not commandments. And then is the time to Know Yourself just a bit different from what you thought you were There is no escape.

So that in the end, this Know Thyself commandment brings me up against the Presume-Not-God-to-Scan fence. Trespassers will be prosecuted. Know then thyself, presume not God to scan.

It's a dilemma. Because this business of knowing myself has led me slap up against the forbidden enclosure where, presumably, this God mystery is kept in corral. It isn't my fault. I followed the road. And it leads over the edge of a precipice on which stands up a Danger! Don't go over the edge!

But I've *got* to go over the edge. The way lies that way.

Flop over we go, and into the endless sea. There drown.

No! Out of the drowning something else gurgles awake. And that's the best of the human consciousness. When you fall into the final sea of *I Don't Know,* then, if you can but gasp *Teach Me,* you turn into a fish and twiddle your fins and twist your tail and gorp in amazement, in a new element.

That's why they called Jesus: The Fish. Pisces. Because he fell, like the weariest river, into the great Ocean that is outside the shore, and there took on a new way of knowledge.

The proper Study is Man, sure enough. But the proper study of man, like the proper study of anything else, will in the end leave you no option. You'll have to presume to study God. Even the most hard-boiled scientist, if he is a brave and honest man, is landed in this unscientific dilemma. Or rather, he is all at sea in it.

287

The river of human consciousness, like ancient Ocean, goes in a circle. It starts gaily, bubblingly, fiercely from an inland source which it invariably calls God. A bubbling, mysterious inland pool, where it surges up in obvious mystery and Godliness, the human conciousness. And here is the God of the Beginning, call him Jehovah or Ra or Ammon or Jupiter or what you like. One bubbles up in Greece, one in India, one in Jerusalem. From their various God-sources the streams of human consciousness rush variously down. Then begin to meander and to doubt. Then fall slow. Then start to silt up. Then pass into the great Ocean, which is the God of the End.

In the great ocean of the End, most men are lost. But Jesus turned into a fish, he had the other consciousness of the Ocean which is the divine End of us all. And then like a salmon he beat his way up stream again, to speak from the source.

And this is the greater history of man, as distinguished from the lesser history, in which figures Mr Lloyd George and Monsieur Poincaré.

We are in the deep, muddy estuary of our era, and terrified of the emptiness of the sea beyond. Or we are at the end of the great road, that Jesus and Francis and Whitman walked. We are on the brinks of a precipice, and terrified at the great void below.

No help for it. We are men, and for men there is no retreat. Over we go.

Over we must and shall go, so we may as well do it voluntarily, keeping our soul alive; and as we drown in our terrestial nature, transmogrify into fishes. Pisces. That which knows the Oceanic Godliness of the End.

The proper study of mankind is man .—Agreed entirely! But in the long run, it becomes again as it was before, man in his relation to the deity. The proper study of mankind is man in his relation to the deity.

And yet not as it was before. Not the specific deity of the inland source. The vast deity of the End, Oceanus whom you can only know by becoming a Fish. Let us become Fishes, and try.

They talk about the sixth sense. They talk as if it were an extension of the other senses. A mere *dimensional* sense. It's nothing of the sort. There is a sixth sense right enough. Jesus had it. The sense of the God that is the End and the Beginning. And the proper study of mankind is man in his relation to this Oceanic God.

We have come to the end, for the time being, of the study of man in his relation to man. Or man in his relation to himself. Or man in his relation to woman. There is nothing more of importance to be said, by us or for us, on this subject. Indeed, we have no more to say.

Of course, there is the literature of perversity. And there is the literature of little playboys and playgirls, not only of the western world. But the literature of perversity is a brief weed. And the playboy playgirl stuff, like the movies, though a very monstrous weed, won't live long.

As the weariest river winds by no means safely to sea, all the muddy little individuals begin to chirrup: Let's play! Let's play at something! We're so godlike when we *play*.

But it won't do, my dears. The sea will swallow you up, and all your play and perversions and personalities.

You can't get any more literature out of man in his relation to man. Which of course should be writ large, to mean man in his relation to woman, to other men, and to the whole environment of men: or woman in her relation to man, or other women, or the whole environment of women. You can't get any more literature out of that. Because as any new book must needs be a new stride. And the next stride lands you over the sand-bar in the open ocean, where the first and greatest relation of every man and woman is to the Ocean itself, the great God of the End, who is the All-Father of all sources, as the sea is father of inland lakes and springs of water.

But get a glimpse of this new relation of men and women to the great God of the End, who is the father, not the Son, of all our beginnings: and you get a glimpse of the new literature. Think of the true novel of St. Paul, for example. Not the sentimental looking-backward Christian novel, but the novel looking out to sea, to the great Source, and End, of all beginnings. Not the St. Paul with his human feelings repudiated, to give play to the new divine feelings. Not the St. Paul violent in reaction against worldliness and sensuality therefore a dogmatist with his sheaf of Shalt-Nots ready. But a St. Paul two thousand years older, having his own epoch behind him, and having again the great knowledge of the deity, the Jesus knew, the vast Ocean God which is at the end of all our consciousness.

Because, after all, if chemistry winds wearily to sea in the ether, or some such universal, don't we also, not as chemists but as conscious men, also wind wearily to sea in a divine ether, which means nothing to us but space and words and emptiness? We wind wearily to sea in words and emptiness.

But man is a mutable animal. Turn into the Fish, the Pisces of man's final consciousness, and you'll start to swim again in the great life which is so frighteningly godly that you realise your previous presumption.

And then you realise the new relation of man. Men like fishes lifted on a great wave of the God of the End, swimming together, and apart, in a new medium. A new relation, in a new whole.

ON COMING HOME

"Breathes there a man with soul so dead
Who never to himself hath said
—This is my own, my native land—"

With a vengeance!

It is four years since I saw, under a little winter snow, the death-grey coast of Kent go out. After four years, down, down on the horizon, with the last sunset still in the west, right down under the eyelid of the shut cold sky, the faintest spark, like a message. It is the Land's End light. And I, who am a bit short-sighted, saw it almost first. One sees by divination. The infinitesimal sparking of the Land's End light, so absolutely remote, as one approaches from over the sea, from the Gulf of Mexico, after sunset.

I won't pretend my heart was dead. It exploded again in my chest. "This is my own, my native land!" My God, what lies behind that spark of light!

One goes out on deck again, two hours later, to find a vast light towering out of the dark, as if someone were swinging an immense white beam of communication in the black boughs of the tree of night. And the ship creeps invisible under the pure white branches of the light of men, down on the little lustre of the sea. We are entering Plymouth Sound.

"Breathes there a man with soul so dead—?"

There are the small lights on the soft blackness that must be land. Far off, ahead, a tiny row of lights that must be the Hoe. And the ship slowly pulses forward, at half speed, venturing in.

England! So still! So remote-seeming! Across what mysterious belt of isolation does England lie! "It doesn't seem like a big civilised country," says the Cuban behind me. "It seems as if there were no people in it."

"Yes!" cries the German woman. "So still! So still! As if one could never come to it."

And that is how it seems, as you slowly steam up the Sound in the night, and watch the little lights that must be land, on the unspeaking darkness. The darkness doesn't speak, as the darkness of the coast of America, or Spain for example, speaks in the night when you are passing.

Slowly the ship lapses to silence in mid-water. A tender lit up with red and white and yellow lights—the German woman calls it the Christmas-tree boat— hovers round the stern and comes up on the leeward side. It looks curiously empty, in spite of its lights. And with strange quick quietness, the English sailors make fast. Queer to hear English voices below on the tender, so curiously quiet and withheld, against the noise of Spanish and German we are used to on board.

It is the same with English voices of sailors making fast the ropes as with the sight of land. They do not stir the darkness. They do not come through. Quickly, quietly, the ladder is put up. Quickly, quietly, the police and passport people come on board. All is strangely still, and the ship, which at tea-time was still lively with mixed nationalities, seems deserted. England is on board—everything has fallen silent.

Quietly, quickly, softly, everything is done, and we are landed. There is a strange absence of something, an absentness is felt in everything and in everybody. I think, in the ordinary come-and-go of life, only the Englishman is really civilised. So, the soft, quiet, vague landing, the vague looking at the luggage, the vague finding oneself in the hotel in Plymouth. Everything soft, vague, with the quiet of accomplished civilisation. Accomplished, that is, in these matters of landing from a ship and finding oneself in an hotel.

And it is the first night ashore, in the curious stillness. I cannot say wherein lies the almost deathly sense of stillness one gets, returning to England from the west. Landing in San Francisco gave me the feeling of intolerable crackling noise. But London gives me a dead muffled sense of stillness, as if nothing had any resonance. Everything muffled, or muted, and no sharp contact, no sharp reaction anywhere. As if all the traffic went on deep sand, heavily, straining the heart, and hushed.

I must confess, this curious mutedness of my native land frightens me more than the noise of New York or of Mexico City. Since the sparking of the Land's End light, and the great strong beaming of the lighthouse overhead, tall overhead like a great tree, at the entrance to the Sound, I have not had one single sharp impression in England. Everything seems sand-bagged, like when a ship hangs bags of sand over her side to deaden the bump with the wharf. So it is here. Every impact, every contact is sand-bagged, deadened. Everything that everybody says is modified beforehand, to prevent any kind of bump. Everything that everybody feels is keyed down, and muted, so as not to impinge on anybody else's feelings.

And this, in the end, becomes a madness. One sits in the breakfast car in the train, coming to London. There is a strange tension. What is the curious unease that holds the car spell-bound? In America the Pullmans, being much heavier, don't shake like our cars. And there seems more room, inside and out, morally and physically. It is possible the American manners are not so good, though I doubt if I agree even there. The silent bad manners of the Englishman when it happens to decide that he is not among his own "sort," take a lot of beating. But of course, he never says or does anything, so he is perfectly safe and proper in his circumstance.

But there one sits in a breakfast car on the Great Western. The train shakes terribly. The waiters are quick and soft and attentive, but the food isn't very good, and one feels as if one were some sort of ghost being waited on by men who have long ago gone to sleep, and are serving one in their sleep. The place feels tight: one would like to smash something. Outside, a tight little landscape goes by, just unbelievable, with sunshine like thin water, a horizon half a mile away, and everything crowded forward into one's face till one gasps for space and breath, and tries to jerk one's head back, as one does when someone pushes his face right under one's hat-brim. Too close!

Inside, we eat kippers and bacon. The place is full. The other people, mostly men, all keep themselves modified and muted, as if they didn't want their aura to stray beyond the four legs of their chair. Inside this charmed circle of their self-constraint they seem to sit and smile with pleasant English faces. And, of course, they are all trying to be a bit "grander" than they really are: to give the impression that they have more servants in the kitchen than they really have, and so on. That is part of the English naïveté. If they have two servants, they want to give the impression of four: not less than four.

Essentially, however, and apart from being "grand," each one of them sits complacent inside a crystal bubble, smiling and eating and sprinkling sugar on porridge, and then half-furtively glancing through the transparency of their bubble, to see if there is anything outside. They will never allow anything outside: except, of course, other bubbles of varying "grandness."

In the small things of life, the Englishman is the only perfectly civilised being. But God save me from such civilisation. God in heaven deliver me. The trick lies in tensely withholding oneself, tensely withholding one's aura, till it forms a perfect and transparent little globe around one. At the centre of this little globe sits the Englishman, his own little god unto himself, terribly complacent and at the same time, terribly self-deprecating. He seems to say: My dear man, I know I am no more than what I am. I wouldn't trespass on what you are, not for worlds. Oh, not for worlds! Because when all's said and done, what you are means nothing to me. I am god inside my own crystal world, the strictly limited domain of myself, which after all no-one can deny is my own. I am only god within the bubble of my own self-contained being, dear sir; but there, god I am, so how could I possibly desire to trespass. I only urge that all other people shall be as self-contained and as little inclined to trespass. And they may be gods inside their own bubbles if they like.

Hence the feeling of intolerable shut-in-edness. One enters from the open sea, to the Channel: first box. Into Plymouth Sound: second box. Into the customs place: third box. Into the hotel: fourth. Into the dining car of the train: fifth. And so on and so on, like those Chinese boxes that fit one inside the other, and at the very middle is a tiny porcelain figure half an inch long. That is how one feels. Like a tiny porcelain figure shut in inside box after box of repeated and intensified shut-in-edness. It is enough to send one mad.

That is coming home, home to one's fellow countrymen! In one sense—the small ways of life—they are the nicest and most civilised people in the world. But there they are: each one of them a perfect little accomplished figure, enclosed first and foremost within the box, or bubble, of his own self-contained ego, and afterwards in all the other boxes he has made for himself, for his own safety.

At the centre of himself he is complacent, and even "superior." It strikes one very hard, coming home, that every Englishman sits there feeling subtly "superior." He wouldn't impose anything on anybody, dear me no. That is part of his own superiority. He is too superior to make any imposition of himself in any way. But like a pleased image, there he sits at the centre of his own bubble, and feels superior. Superior to what? Oh, nothing in particular, don't you know. Just damn superior.—And well—if you press him—superior to everything. Just damn superior to everything. There inside the bubble of his own self-constraint, his own illusion, the strange germ of his unnatural conceit.

"This is my own, my native land."

He seems to have accomplished the trick of appearing to be at his ease, the gentleman in the breakfast car, sprinkling sugar on his porridge. He knows he has a pretty way of sprinkling sugar on porridge: he knows he can put the spoon back prettily into the sugar-bowl: he knows his voice is cultured and his smile charming, compared to the rest of the world. It is quite obvious he means no-one ill. Surely it is obvious he would like to give every man the best that man could have. If it were his to give, which it isn't.—And finally he knows he is able to contain himself. He is an Englishman and he is himself, he is able to contain and to constrain himself, and to live within the unbroken bubble of his own self-constraint, without letting his aura stray and get at cross-purposes with other people's auras. The dear, dangerless patrician!

Yet something does stray out of him. Look into his nice, bright, apparently-smiling English eyes. They are not smiling. And look again at his nice fresh English face, that seems so pleased with life. It also is not smiling, any more than Mr Lloyd George is really smiling. The eyes are not really at ease, and the nice, fresh face is not at ease either. At the centre of the eyes, where the smile twinkles, there is fear. Even at the middle of this amiable and all-tolerant English complacency, there is fear. And the smile-wrinkles on the fresh, pleased face, they give odd quivers, and look like spite wrinkles. There strays out of him, in spite of all his self-constraining, the faint effluence of fear, and the sense of impotence, and a quiver of spite, of subdued malice. Underneath the soft civilisedness of him, fear, impotence, and malice.

"Whose heart within him ne'er hath burned

292

As home his wandering steps he turned
From travelling in a foreign land."

That's how one finds the Englishman at home. And then one understands the bitterness of Englishmen abroad in the world, especially Englishmen in responsible positions.

There is no denying this: that since the war, England's prestige has declined terribly, all over the world. Ah, says the Englishman, that's because America has the dollars.—And there you hear the voice of England's own downfall.

England's prestige wasn't based on money. It was based on the imagination of men. England was supposed to be proud, and at the same time, free. Proud in her freedom, and free, to a certain extent generous, truly generous, in her pride.

This was the England that led the world. Myself, I think this was a true conception of England, at her best. This was how the other nations accepted her: at her best. And the individual Englishman got his certain honour, in the world, on the strength of it.

Now? Now he still receives the remnants of honour, but mockingly, as poor Russian counts receive a little mocking distinction, now that they have to sell newspapers. The real English pride has gone, and "superiority" takes its place: a really imbecile superiority, which the world laughs at.

As far as the wide world is concerned, England is anything but superior. She is just humiliated. From day to day she makes a more humiliating spectacle of herself in the eyes of the world. Weak, vacillating, without purpose or policy, without even the last vestige of pride, she continues to apologise and deprecate on the platform of the world.

And of course individual Englishmen abroad feel it. You rarely meet an Englishman far from home, but he is burning with impatience, disgust, and even contempt, of home. Home seems a shoddy place. And when you get here, it's even shoddier than it seems from afar.

If, abroad, you meet an Englishman in office, he is speechless, almost cynical with rage. "What can I do!" he says. "What can I do, against the orders from home. I get orders that I must give no loop-hole for offence against America. All I have to do is to guard against giving offence, above all to America. I must be on my knees all the time, in front of America, begging her not to take offence, when she hasn't the faintest intention even of taking offence."

This is from a man who has lived out in the world, and who knows that the moment you go down on your knees to a man, he spits on you: and quite right too. Men have no business on their knees.

"I have an Englishman wants to go into the United States. Washington has given him a visa, and said: Yes, you can enter whenever you like. Comes a cable from London: Prevent this man from crossing into the United States, Washington might not like it. What can one do?"

The same story everywhere. A man is building a railway with nigger labour. Some insolent Jamaica nigger—British Subject, larger than life—brings a charge against his boss. Solemn trial by the British, influence from the government, the Englishman is reprimanded, the nigger smiles and spits in his face.

Long live the bottom dog! May he devour us all.

Same story from India, from Egypt, from China. At home, a lot of queer, inane, half-female-seeming men, not quite men at all, and certainly not women. The women would be far braver.—Then abroad a few Englishmen still struggling.

England seems to me the one really soft spot, the rotten spot in the empire. If ever men had to think in world terms, they have to think in world terms today. And here you get an island no bigger than a back garden, chock-full of people who never realise there is anything outside their back garden, pretending to direct the destinies of the world. It is pathetic and ridiculous. And the "superiority" is bathetic to lunacy.

These poor "superior" gentry, all that is left to them is to blame the Americans. It amazes me, the rancour with which English people speak of Americans. Just because the republican eagle of the west doesn't choose to be a pelican for other people's convenience. Why should it?

After all, rancour is a bad sign in a superior person. It is a sign of impotence. The superior Englishman feels impotent against the American dollar, so he is wildly rancorous, in private, when America can't hear him.

Now I am an Englishman. And I know, that if my countrymen still have a soul to sell, they'll sell it for American dollars, and drive a hard bargain.

Which is what I call being truly superior to the dollar.

"This is my own, my native land."

It was such a brave country, for so many years: the old brave, reckless, manly England. Even a man with dyed whiskers, like Palmerston. Too brave and reckless to be treacherous. My England.

Look at us now. Not a man left inside all the millions of pairs of trousers. Not a man left. A host of would-be-amiable cowards shut up each one in his own bubble of conceit, and the whole lot within box after box of safeguards.

One could shout with laughter at the figures inside these endless safety boxes. Except that one is still English, and therefore flabber-gasted. My own, my native land just leaves me flabbergasted.

ON BEING RELIGIOUS

The problem is not, and never was, whether God exists or doesn't exist. Man is so made, that the word God has a special effect on him, even if only to afford a safety valve for his feelings when he must swear or burst. And there ends the vexation of questioning the existence of God. Whatever the queer little word means, it means something we can none of us ever quite get away from, or at; something connected with our deepest explosions.

It isn't really quite a word. It's an ejaculation and a glyph. It never had a definition. "Give a definition of the word God," says somebody, and everybody smiles, with just a trifle of malice. There's going to be a bit of sport.

Of course nobody can define it. And a word nobody can define isn't a word at all. It's just a noise and a shape, like pop! or Ra or Om.

When a man says: *There is a God,* or *There is no God,* or *I don 't know whether there's a God or not,* he is merely using the little word like a toy to announce that he has taken an attitude. When he says: *There is no God,* he just means to say: *Nobody knows any better about life than I know myself; so nobody need try to chirp it over me.* Which is the democratic attitude. When he says: *There is a God,* he is either sentimental or sincere. If he is sincere, it means he refers himself back to some undefinable pulse of life in him, which gives him his direction and his substance. If he is sentimental, it means he is subtly winking to his audience to imply: *Let's make an arrangement favourable to ourselves.* That's the conservative attitude. Thirdly and lastly, when a man says: *I don't know whether there's a God or not,* he is merely making the crafty announcement: *I hold myself free to run with the hare and hunt with the hounds, whichever I feel like at the time.—And* that's the so-called artistic or pagan attitude.

In the end, one becomes bored by the man who believes that nobody, ultimately, can tell him anything. One becomes very bored by the men who wink a God into existence for their own convenience. And the man who holds himself free to run with the hare and hunt with the hounds doesn't hold interest any more. All these three classes of men bore us even to the death of boredom.

Remains the man who sincerely says: *I believe in God.* He may still be an interesting fellow.

I: *How* do you believe in God?

He: I believe in goodness.

Basta! Turn him down and try again.

I: *How* do you believe in God?

He: I believe in love.

Exit. Call another.

I: *How* do you believe in God?

He: I don't know.

I: What difference does it make to you, whether you believe in God or not?

He: It makes a difference, but I couldn't quite put it into words.

I: Are you sure it makes a difference? Does it make you kinder or fiercer?

He: Oh—I think it makes me more tolerant.

Retro me—

Enter another believer.

He: Hullo!

I: Hullo!

He: What's up?

I: Do you believe in God?

He: What the hell is that to you?

I: Oh, I'm just asking.

He: What about yourself?

I: Yes, I believe.

He: D'you say your prayers at night?

I: No.

He: When d'you say 'em then?

I: I don't.

He: Then what use is your god to you?

I: He merely isn't the sort you pray to.

He: What do you do with him then?

I: It's what he does with me.

He: And what does he do with you?

I: Oh, I don't know. He uses me as the thin end of the wedge.

He: Thin enough! What about the thick end?

I: That's what we're waiting for.

He: You're a funny customer.

I: Why not? Do you believe in God?

He: Oh, I don't know. I might, if it looked like fun.

I: Right you are.

This is what I call a conversation between two true believers. Either believing in a real God looks like fun, or it's no go at all. The Great God has been treated to so many sighs, supplications, prayers, tears and yearnings that, for the time, He's had enough. There is, I believe a great strike on in heaven. The Almighty has vacated the throne, abdicated, climbed down. It's no good your looking up into the sky. It's empty. Where the Most High used to sit listening to woes, supplications and repentances, there's nothing but a great gap in the empyrean. You can still go on praying to that gap, if you like. The Most High has gone out.

He has climbed down. He has just calmly stepped down the ladder of the angels, and is standing behind you. You can go on gazing and yearning up the shaft of hollow heaven if you like. The Most High just stands behind you, grinning to Himself.

Now this isn't a deliberate piece of blasphemy. It's just one way of stating an everlasting truth: or pair of truths. First, there is always the Great God. Second, as regards man, He shifts His position in the Cosmos. The Great God departs from the heaven where man has located Him, and plumps His throne down somewhere else. Man, being an ass, keeps going to the same door to beg for his carrot, even when the Master has gone away to another house. The ass keeps on going to the same spring, to drink, even when the spring has dried up, and there's nothing but clay and hoof-marks. It doesn't occur to him to look round, to see where the water has broken out afresh, somewhere else, out of some live rock. Habit! God has become a human habit, and Man expects the Almighty habitually to lend Himself to it. Whereas the Almighty—it's one of His characteristics—won't. He makes a move, and laughs when man goes on praying to the gap in the Cosmos.

"Oh little hole in the wall! Oh little gap, holy little gap!" as the Russian peasants are supposed to have prayed, making a deity of the hole in the wall."

Which makes me laugh. And nobody will persuade me that the Lord Almighty doesn't roar with laughter, seeing all the Christians still rolling their imploring eyes to the skies where the hole is, which the Great God left when He picked up His throne and walked.

I tell you, it isn't blasphemy. Ask any philosopher or theologian, he'll tell you that the real problem for humanity isn't, whether God exists or not. God always is, and we all know it. But the problem is, how to get at Him. That is the greatest problem ever set to our habit making humanity. The theologians try to find out: How shall man put himself into relation to God, into a living relation? Which is, How shall man *find* God?—That's the real problem.

Because God doesn't just sit still somewhere in the Cosmos Why should He? He too wanders His Own strange way down the avenues of time, across the intricacies of space. Just as the heavens shift. Just as the pole of heaven shifts. We know now that, in the strange widdishins movement of the heavens, called precession, the great stars and constellations and planets are all the time slowly, invisibly but absolutely shifting their positions, even the pole-star is silently stealing away from the pole. Four thousand years ago, our pole-star wasn't a pole-star. The earth had another one. Even at the present moment, Polaris has side-stepped. He doesn't really stand at the axis of the heavens. Ask any astronomer. We shall soon have to have another pole-star.

So it is with the Great God. He slowly and silently and invisibly shifts His throne, inch by inch, across the Cosmos. Inch by inch, across the blue floor of heaven, till He comes to the stairs of the angels. Then step by step down the ladder.

Where is He now? Where is the Great God now? Where has He put His throne?

We have lost Him! We have lost the Great God! Oh God, Oh God, we have lost our Great God! Jesus, Jesus, Thou art the Way! Jesus, Jesus, Thou art the Way to the Father, to the Lord Everlasting.

But Jesus shakes his head. In the great wandering of the heavens, the foot of the Cross has shifted. The great and majestic movement of the heavens has slowly carried away even the Cross of Jesus from its place on Calvary. And Jesus, who was our Way to God, has stepped aside, over the horizon, with the Father.

So it is. Man is only Man. And even the Gods and the Great God go their way; stepping slowly, invisibly across the heavens of time and space, going somewhere, we know not where. They do not stand still. They go and go, till they pass below the horizon of man.

Till man has lost his Great God, and there remains only the Gap, and images, and hollow words. The Way, even the Great Way of Salvation, leads only to the pit, the nothingness, the gap.

It is not our fault. It is nobody's fault. It is the mysterious and sublime fashion of the Almighty, who travels too. At least, as far as we are concerned, He travels. Apparently He is the same today, yesterday, and forever. Like the pole-star.—But now we know the pole-star slowly but inevitably side-steps. Polaris is no longer at the pole of the heavens.

Gradually, gradually God travels away from us, on His mysterious journey. And we, being creatures of obstinacy and will, we insist that He cannot move. God gave us a way to Himself. God gave us Jesus, and the way of repentance and love, the way to God. The salvation through Christ Jesus our Lord.

And hence, we assert that the Almighty cannot go back on it. He can never get away from us again. At the end of the way of repentance and love, there God *is*, and *must be*. Must be, because God himself said that He would receive us at the end of the road of repentance and love.

And he *did* receive men at the end of this road. He received our fathers even, into peace and salvation.

Then he must receive us.

And he doesn't. The road no longer leads to the Throne.

We are let down.

Are we? Did Jesus ever say: *I am the way, and there is no other way*? At the moment, there was no other way. For many centuries, there was no other way. But all the time, the heavens were mysteriously revolving, and God was going His own unspeakable way. All the time, men had to be making the road afresh. Even the road called Jesus, the way of the Christian to God, had to be subtly altered, century by century. At the Renaissance, in the Eighteenth Century, great curves in the Christian road to God, new strange directions.

As a matter of fact, never did God or Jesus say that there was one straight way of salvation, forever and ever. On the contrary, Jesus plainly indicated the changing of the way. And what is more, he indicated the only means to the finding of the right way. The Holy Ghost. The Holy Ghost is within you. And it is a Ghost, forever a Ghost, never a Way or a Word. Jesus is a Way and a Word. God is the Goal. But the Holy Ghost is forever Ghostly, unrealisable. And against this unsubstantial unreality, you may never sin, or woe betide you.

Only the Holy Ghost within you can scent the new tracks of the Great God across the Cosmos of Creation. The Holy Ghost is the dark hound of Heaven whose baying we ought to listen to, as he runs ahead into the unknown, tracking the mysterious everlasting departing of the Lord God, who is forever departing from us.

And now the Lord God has gone over our horizon. The foot of the Cross is lifted from the Mound, and moved across the heavens. The pole-star no longer stands on guard at the true polaric centre. We are all disorientated, all is gone out of gear.

All right, the Lord God left us neither blind nor comfortless nor helpless. We've got the Holy Ghost. And we hear him baying down strange darknesses, in other places.

The Almighty has shifted His throne, and we've got to find a new road. Therefore we've got to get off the old road. You can't stay on the old road, and find a new road. We've got to find our way to God. From time to time Man wakes up and realises that the Lord Almighty has made a great removal, and passed over the known horizon. Then starts the frenzy, the howling, the despair. Much better listen to the dark hound of Heaven, and start off into the dark of the unknown, in search.

From tithe to time, the Great God sends a new saviour. Christians will no longer have the pettiness to assert that Jesus is the only Saviour ever sent by the everlasting God. There have been other saviours, in other lands, at other times, with other messages. And all of them Sons of God. All of them sharing the Godhead with the Father. All of them showing the Way of Salvation and of Right Different Saviours. Different Ways of Salvation. Different pole-stars, in the great wandering Cosmos of time. And the Infinite God, always changing, and always the same infinite God, at the end of the different Ways.

Now, if I ask you if you believe in God, I do not ask you if you know the Way to God. For the moment, we are lost. Let us admit it. None of us knows the way to God. The Lord of time and space has passed over our horizon, and here we sit in our mundane creation, rather flabbergasted. Let us admit it.

Jesus, the Saviour, is no longer our Way of Salvation. He *was* the Saviour, and is not. Once it was Mithras: and has not been Mithras for these many years. It never *was* Mithras for us. God sends different Saviours to different peoples at different times.

Now, for the moment, there is no Saviour. The Jews have waited for three thousand years. They preferred just to wait. We do not. Jesus taught us what to do, when He, Christ, could no longer save us.

We go in search of God, following the Holy Ghost, and depending on the Holy Ghost. There is no Way. There is no Word. There is no Light. The Holy Ghost is ghostly and invisible. The Holy Ghost is nothing, if you like. Yet we hear his strange calling, the strange calling like a hound on the scent, away in the unmapped wilderness. And it seems great fun to follow. Oh great fun, God's own good fun.

Myself, I believe in God. But I'm off on a different road.

Adiós! And, if you like, *au revoir*!

BOOKS

Are books just toys? the toys of consciousness?

Then what is man? the everlasting brainy child?

Is man nothing but a brainy child, amusing himself forever with the printed toys called books?

That also. Even the greatest men spend most of their time making marvellous fine toys. Like *Pickwick* or *Two on a Tower*.

But there is more to it.

Man is a thought-adventurer.

Man is a great venture in consciousness.

Where the venture started, and where it will end, nobody knows. Yet here we are—a long way gone already, and no glimpse of any end in sight. Here we are, miserable Israel of the human consciousness, having lost our way in the wilderness of the world's chaos, giggling and babbling and pitching camp. We needn't go any further.

All right, let us pitch camp, and see what happens. When the worst comes to the worst, there is sure to be a Moses to set up a serpent of brass. And then we can start off again.

Man is a thought-adventurer. He has thought his way down the far ages. He used to think in little images of wood or stone: then in hieroglyphs on obelisks and clay rolls and papyrus. Now he thinks in books, between two covers.

The worst of a book is the way it shuts up between covers. When men had to write on rocks and obelisks, it was rather difficult to lie. The daylight was too strong. But soon he took his venture into caves and secret holes and temples, where he could create his own environment and tell lies to himself. And a book is an underground hole with two lids to it. A perfect place to tell lies in.

Which brings us to the real dilemma of man in his long adventure into consciousness. He is a liar. Man is a liar unto himself. And once he has told himself a lie, round and round he goes after that lie, as if it was a bit of phosphorus on his nose-end. The pillar of cloud and the pillar of fire wait for him to have done. They stand silently aside, waiting for him to rub the ignis fatuus off the end of his nose. But man, the longer he follows a lie, becomes all the surer he sees a light.

The life of man is an endless venture into consciousness. Ahead goes the pillar of cloud by day, the pillar of fire by night, through the wilderness of time. Till man tells himself a lie, another lie. Then the lie goes ahead of him, like the carrot before the ass.

There are, in the consciousness of man, two bodies of knowledge. the things he tells himself, and the things he finds out. The things he tells himself are nearly always pleasant, and they are lies. The things he finds out are usually rather bitter to begin with.

Man is a thought-adventurer. But by thought we mean, of course, discovery. We don't mean this telling himself stale facts and drawing false deductions, which usually passes as thought. Thought is an adventure, not a trick.

And of course it is an adventure of the whole man, not merely of his wits. That is why one cannot quite believe in Kant, or Spinoza. Kant thought with his head and his spirit, but he never thought with his blood. The blood also thinks, inside a man, darkly and ponderously. It thinks in desires and revulsions, and it makes strange conclusions. The conclusion of my head and my spirit is that it would be perfect, this world of man, if men all loved one another. The conclusion of my blood says nonsense, and finds the stunt a bit disgusting. My blood tells me there is no such thing as perfection. There is the long, endless venture into consciousness down an ever-dangerous valley of days.

Man finds that his head and his spirit have led him wrong. We are at present terribly off the track, following our spirit, which says how nice it would be if everything was perfect, and listening to our head, which says we might have everything perfect if we would only eliminate the tiresome reality of our obstinate blood-being.

We are sadly off the track, and we're in a bad temper, like a man who has lost his way. And we say: I'm not going to bother. Fate must work it out.

Fate doesn't work things out. Man is a thought-adventurer, and only his adventuring in thought re-discovers a way.

Take our civilisation. We are in a tantrum because we don't really like it now we've got it. There we've been building it for a thousand years, and built so big we can't shift it. And we hate it after all.

Too bad! What's to be done?

Why, there's nothing to be done! Here we are, like sulky children, sulking because we don't like the game we're playing, feeling that we've been *made* to play it against our will. So play it we do: badly: in the sulks.

We play the game badly, so of course it goes from bad to worse. Things go from bad to worse.

All right, let 'em! Let 'em go from bad to worse. Après moi le déluge.

By all means. But a deluge presupposes a Noah and an ark. The old adventurer on the old adventure.

When you come to think of it, Noah matters more than the deluge, and the ark is more than all the world washed out.

Now we've got the sulks, and are waiting for the flood to come and wash out our world and our civilisation. All right, let it come. But somebody's got to be ready with Noah's Ark.

We imagine, for example, that if there came a terrible crash, and terrible bloodshed over Europe, then out of the crash and bloodshed a remnant of regenerated souls would inevitably arise.

We are mistaken. If you look at the people who escaped the terrible times of Russia, you don't see much regenerated souls. They are more scared and senseless than ever. Instead of the great catastrophe having restored them to manhood, they are finally unmanned.

What's to be done? If a huge catastrophe is going only to unman us more than we are already unmanned, then there's no good in a huge catastrophe. Then there's no good in anything, for us poor souls who are trapped in the huge trap of our civilisation.

Catastrophes alone never helped man. The only thing that ever avails is the living adventurous spark in the souls of men. If there is no living adventurous spark, then death and disaster are as meaningless as tomorrow's newspaper.

Take the fall of Rome. During the Dark Ages of the Fifth, Sixth, Seventh centuries A.D., the catastrophes that befell the Roman Empire didn't alter the Romans a bit. They went on just the same, rather as we go on today, having a good time when they could get it, not caring. Meanwhile Huns, Goths, Vandals, Visigoths and all the rest wiped them out.

With what result? The flood of barbarism rose and covered Europe from end to end.

But, bless your life, there was Noah in his ark with the animals. There was young Christianity. There were the lonely fortified monasteries, the little arks floating and keeping the adventure afloat. There is no break in the great adventure in consciousness. Throughout the howlingest deluge, some few brave souls are steering the ark under the rainbow.

The monks and bishops of the early Church carried the soul and spirit of man unbroken, unabated, undiminished over the howling flood of the Dark Ages. Then this spirit of undying courage was fused into the barbarians, in Gaul, in Italy, and the new Europe began. But the germ had never been allowed to die.

Once *all* men in the world lost their courage and their newness, the world would come to an end. The old Jews said the same: unless in the world there was at least one Jew passionately praying, the race was lost.

So we begin to see where we are. It's no good leaving everything to fate. Man is an adventurer, and he must never give up the adventure. The venture is the venture: fate is the circumstance around the adventurer. The adventurer at the quick of his venture is the living germ inside the chaos of circumstance. But for the living germ of Noah in his ark, chaos would have redescended on the world in the waters of the flood. But chaos *couldn't* redescend, because Noah was afloat with all the animals.

The same with the Christians when Rome fell. In their little fortified monasteries they defended themselves against howling invasions, being too poor to excite much covetousness. When wolves and bears prowled through the streets of Lyons, and a wild boar was grunting and turning up the pavement of Augustus' temple, the Christian bishops also roved intently and determinedly, like poor forerunners, along the ruined streets, seeking a congregation. It was the great adventure, and they did not give it up.

But Noah, of course, is always in an unpopular minority. So, of course, were the Christians, when Rome began to fall. The Christians now are in a hopelessly popular majority, so it is their turn to fall.

I know the greatness of Christianity: it is a past greatness. I know that, but for those early Christians, we should never have emerged from the chaos and hopeless disaster of the Dark Ages. If I had lived in the year four hundred, pray God I should have been a true and passionate Christian. The adventurer.

But now I live in 1924, and the Christian venture is done. The adventure is gone out of Christianity. We must start on a new venture towards God.

Man is a thought-adventurer.

Which isn't the same as saying that man has intellect. In intellect there is skill, and tricks. To the intellect the terms are given, as the chessmen and rules of the game are given in chess. Real thought is an experience. It begins as a change in the blood, a slow convulsion and revolution in the body itself. It ends as a new piece of awareness, a new reality in mental consciousness.

On this account, thought is an adventure, and not a practice. In order to think, man must risk himself. He must risk himself doubly. First, he must go forth and meet life in the body. Then he must face the result in his mind.

It is bad enough going out like a little David to meet the giant of life bodily. Take the war as an example of that. It is still harder, and bitterer, after a great encounter with life, to sit down and face out the result. Take the war again. Many men went out and faced the fight. Who dared to face his own self afterwards?

The risk is double, because man is double. Each of us has two selves. First is this body which is vulnerable and never quite within our control. The body with its irrational sympathies and desires and passions, its peculiar direct communication, defying the mind. And second is the conscious ego, the self I KNOW I am.

The self that lives in my body I can never finally know. It has such strange attractions, and revulsions, and it lets me in for so much irrational suffering, real torment, and occasional frightening delight. The me that is in my body is a strange animal to me, and often a very trying one. My body is like a jungle in which dwells an unseen me, like a black panther in the night, whose two eyes glare green through my dreams, and, if a shadow falls, through my waking day.

Then there is this other me, that is fair-faced and reasonable and sensible and complex and full of good intentions. The known me, which can be seen and appreciated. I say of myself: "Yes, I know I am impatient and rather intolerant in ideas. But in the ordinary way of life I am quite easy and really rather kindly. My kindliness makes me sometimes a bit false. But then I don't believe in mechanical honesty. There is an honesty of the feelings, of the sensibilities, as well as of the mind. If a man is lying to me, and I know it, it is a matter of choice whether I tell him so or not. If it would only damage his real feelings, and my own, then it would be *emotionally* dishonest to call him a liar to his face. I would rather be a bit mentally dishonest, and pretend to swallow the lie."

This is the known me, having a talk with itself. It sees a reason for everything it does and feels. It has a certain unchanging belief in its own good intentions. It tries to steer a sensible and harmless course among all the other people and "personalities" around itself.

To this known me, everything exists as a term of knowledge. A man is what I know he is. England is what I know it to be. I am what I know I am. And Bishop Berkeley is absolutely right: things only exist in our own consciousness. To the known me, nothing exists beyond what I know. True, I am always adding to the things I know. But this is because, in my opinion, knowledge begets knowledge. Not because anything has entered *from the outside*. There *is* no outside. There is only more knowledge to be added.

If I sit in the train and a man enters my compartment, he is already, in a great measure, known to me. He is, in the first place, A Man, and I know what that is. Then, he is old. And Old, I know what that means. Then he is English and middle class, and so on, and so on. And I know it all.

There remains a tiny bit that is not known to me. He is a stranger. As a personality I don't yet know him. I glance at him quickly. It is a very small adventure, still an adventure in knowledge, a combination of certain qualities grouped in a certain way. At a glance I know as much about him as I want to know. It is finished, the adventure is over.

This is the adventure of knowing. People go to Spain, and "know" Spain. People study entomology, and "know" insects. People meet Lenin and "know" Lenin. Lots of people "know" me.

And this is how we live. We proceed from what we know already to what we know next. If we don't know the Shah of Persia, we think we have only to call at the palace in Teheran to accomplish the feat. If we don't know much about the moon, we have only to get the latest book on that orb, and we shall be *au courant*.

We know we know all about it, really. *Connu! Connu!* Remains only the fascinating little game of *understanding*, putting two and two together and being real little gods in the machine.

All this is the adventure of knowing and understanding. But it isn't the thought-adventure.

The thought-adventure starts in the blood, not in the mind. If an Arab or a negro or even a Jew sits down next to me in the train, I cannot proceed so glibly with my knowing. It is not enough for me to glance at a black face and say: He is a negro. As he sits next to me, there is a faint uneasy movement in my blood. A strange vibration comes from him, which causes a slight disturbance in my own vibration. There is a slight odour in my nostrils. And above all, even if I shut my eyes, there is a strange *presence* in contact with me.

I now can no longer proceed from what I am and what I know I am, to what I know him to be. I am not a nigger and so I can't quite know a nigger, and I can never fully "understand" him.

What then? It's an *impasse*.

Then, I have three courses open. I can just plank down the word Nigger, and having labelled him, finish with him! Or I can try to track him down in terms of my own knowledge. That is, understand him as I understand any other individual.

Or I can do a third thing. I can admit that my blood is disturbed, that something comes from him and interferes with my normal vibration. Admitting so much, I can either put up a resistance and insulate myself. Or I can allow the disturbance to continue, because, after all, there is some peculiar alien sympathy between us.

In almost every case, of course, the nigger among white men will insulate himself, and not let his black aura reach the white neighbours. If I find myself in a train full of niggers, I shall no doubt do the same.

But apart from this, I shall admit a certain strange and incalculable reaction between me and him. This reaction causes a slight but unmistakable change in the vibration of my blood and nerves. This slight change in my blood develops in dreams and unconsciousness till, if I allow it, it struggles forward into light as a new bit of realisation, a new term of consciousness.

Take the much commoner case of men and women. A man, proceeding from his known self, likes a woman because she is in sympathy with what he knows.

He feels that he and she know one another. They marry. And then the fun begins. In so far as they know one another they can proceed from their known selves, they are as right as ninepence. Loving couple, etc. But the moment there is real blood contact, as likely as not a strange discord enters in. She is not what he thought her. He is not what she thought him. It is the other, primary or bodily self—appearing, very often like a black demon, out of the fair creature who was erst the beloved.

The man who before marriage seemed everything that is delightful, after marriage begins to come out in his true colours, a son of the old and rather hateful Adam. And she, who was an angel of loveliness and desirability, gradually emerges as an almost fiendlike daughter of the snake-frequenting Eve.

What has happened?

It is the invariable crucifixion. The Cross, as we know, stands for the body, for the dark self which lives in the body. And on the Cross of this bodily self is crucified the self which I know I am, my so-called *real* self. The Cross, as an ancient symbol, has an inevitable phallic reference. But it is far deeper than sex. It is the self which darkly inhabits our blood and bone, and for which the ithyphallus is but a symbol. This self which lives darkly in my blood and bone is my *alter ego*, my other self, the homunculus, the second one of the Kabiri, the second of the Twins, the Gemini. And the sacred black stone at Mecca stands for this: the dark self that dwells in the blood of a man and of a woman. Phallic if you like. But much more than phallic. And on this cross of division in the whole self is crucified the Christ. We are all crucified on it.

Marriage is the great puzzle of our day. It is our sphinx-riddle. Solve it, or to be torn to bits, is the decree.

We marry from the known self, taking the woman as an extension of our knowledge—an extension of our known self. And then, almost invariably, comes the jolt and the crucifixion. The woman of the known self is fair and lovely. But the woman of the dark blood looks, to man, most malignant and horrific. In the same way, the fair daytime man of courtship days leaves nothing to be desired. But the husband, horrified by the serpent-advised Eve of the blood, obtuse and arrogant in his Adam obstinacy, is an enemy pure and simple.

Solve the puzzle. The quickest way is for the wife to smother the serpent-advised Eve which is in her, and for the man to talk himself out of his old arrogant Adam. Then they make a fair and above-board combination, called a successful marriage.

But Nemesis is on our track. The husband forfeits his arrogance, the wife has her children and her way to herself. But lo, the son of one woman is husband to the woman of the next generation! And oh, women, beware the mother's boy! Or else the wife forfeits the old serpent-advised Eve from her nature and becomes the instrument of the man. And then, oh, young husband of the next generation, prepare for the daughter's revenge.

What's to be done?

The thought-adventure! We've got to take ourselves as we are, not as we know ourselves to be. I am the son of the old red-earth Adam, with a black touchstone at the centre of me. And all the fair words in the world won't alter it. Woman is the strange serpent-communing Eve, inalterable. We are a strange pair, who meet, but never mingle. I came, in the bath of birth, out of a mother. But I arose the old Adam, with the black old stone at the core of me. She had a father who begot her, but the column of her is pure enigmatic Eve.

In spite of all the things I know about her, in spite of my knowing her so well, the serpent knows her better still. And in spite of my fair words, and my goodly pretences, she runs up against the black stone of Adam which is in the middle of me.

Know thyself means knowing at last that you *can't* know yourself. I can't know the Adam of red-earth which is me. It will always do things to me, beyond my knowledge. Neither can I know the serpent-listening Eve which is the woman, beneath all her modern glibness. I have to take her at that. And we have to meet as I meet a jaguar between the trees in the mountains, and advance, and touch, and risk it. When. man and woman *actually* meet, there is always terrible risk to both of them. Risk for her, lest her womanhood be damaged by the hard dark stone which is unchangeable in his soul. Risk for him, lest the serpent drag him down, coiled round his neck, and kissing him with poison.

There is always risk, for him and for her. Take the risk, make the adventure. Suffer and enjoy the change in the blood. And, if you are a man, slowly, slowly make the great experience of realising. The final adventure and experience of realisation, if you are man. Fully conscious realisation. If you are a woman, the strange, slumbrous serpentine realisation, which knows without thinking.

But with man, it is a thought-adventure. He risks his body and blood. He withdraws and touches the black stone of his inner conscience. And in a new adventure he dares take thought. He dares take thought for what he has done and what has happened to him. And daring to take thought, he ventures on, and realises at last.

To. be a man! To risk your body and your blood first, and then to risk your mind. All the time, to risk your known self, and become once more a self you could never have known or expected.

To be a man, instead of being a mere personality. To-day men don't risk their blood and bone. They go forth, panoplied in their own idea of themselves. Whatever they do, they perform it all in the full armour of their own idea of themselves. Their unknown bodily self is never for one moment unsheathed. All the time, the only protagonist is the known ego, the self-conscious ego. And the dark self in the mysterious labyrinth of the body is cased in a tight armour of cowardly repression.

Men marry and commit all their adulteries from the head. All that happens to them, all their reactions, all their experiences, happen only in the head. To the unknown man in them nothing happens. He remains shut up in armour, lest he might be hurt and give pain. And inside the armour he goes quite deranged.

All the suffering to-day is psychic: it happens in the mind. The red Adam only suffers the slow torture of compression and derangement. A man's wife is a mental thing, a known thing to him. The old Adam in him never sees her. She is just a thing of his own conscious ego. And not for one moment does he risk himself under the strange snake-infested bushes of her extraordinary Paradise. He is afraid.

He becomes extraordinarily clever and agile in his self-conscious panoply. With his mind he can dart about among the emotions as if he really felt something. It is all a lie, he feels nothing. He is just tricking you. He becomes extraordinarily acute at recognising real feelings from false ones, knowing for certain the falsity of his own. He has always the touchstone of his own conscious falseness against which to test the reality or the falseness of others. And he is always exposing falseness in others. But not for the sake of liberating the real Adam and Eve. On the contrary. He is more terrified even than the ordinary frightened man in the street, of the real Adam and Eve. He is a greater coward still. But his greater cowardice makes him strive to appear a greater man. He denounces falsity in order to triumph in his own greater falsity. He praises the real thing in order to establish his own superiority even to the real thing. He must, must, must be superior. Because he knows himself absolutely and unspeakably and irremediably false. His spurious emotions are more like the real thing than genuine emotions, and they have, for a time, greater effect. But all the time, somewhere, he knows they are false.

And this is his one point of power. Instead of having inside him, like the Adam of red earth, that heavy and immutable black stone which is the eternal touchstone of false and true, good and evil, he has this awful little tombstone of the knowledge of his own falsity. And in this ghastly little white tombstone which he erects to himself lies his peculiar infallibility among a false and mental people.

That's the widdishins way of being a man. To know so absolutely that you are *not* a man, that you dare almost anything on the strength of it. You dare anything, except being a man. So intense and final is the modern white man's conviction, his internal conviction, that he is *not* a man, that he dares anything on earth except be a man. There his courage drops to its grave. He daren't be a man: the old Adam of red earth, with the black touchstone at the middle of him.

He knows he's not a man. Hence his creed of harmlessness. He knows he is not a man of living red earth, to live onward through strange weather into new springtime. He knows there is extinction ahead: for nothing but extinction lies in wait for the conscious ego. Hence his creed of harmlessness, of relentless kindness. A little less than kin, and more than kind. There should be no danger in life *at all*, even no friction. This he asserts, while all the time he is slowly, malignantly undermining the tree of life.

All a man has to do is to live and let live. Absolutely live and let live. This is his harmless creed. And he gets so angry because the Germans actually start a war; and when the war is over, he gets angrier because the French won't forget it, and the Americans won't wipe the reckoning slate clean.

Poor harmless Englishman, he's not allowed to carry out his amiable programme. Not allowed to sell his milk of human kindness at sixpence a quart. Cheaper even than in America. Too, too bad. Not allowed to sell it.

These are the heroes of the Great War. They went and fought like heroes, truly, to prove their manhood. And having fought like heroes, they thought they had proved it, in the eyes of the world, Once and for all. Perhaps they have. The trouble is, they never proved it in their own eyes.

Because, as a matter of fact, they never really *did* fight, as men. As heroes, as martyrs, as saviours saving Belgian babies from the bayonet, etc etc: as all this they fought and died. But as men, as the old Adam of red earth, they never fought. And the Adam of red earth is manhood to man, not any martyrdom or saviourism.

They fought, the heroes, from their self-conscious known selves: to save democracy, to make the world safe for something or other, called democracy. As a matter of fact, to make it safe for the cowardice of modern men.

They fought and risked their lives for this; partly out of idealism, partly out of desire to vindicate their own manhood. And the best men died, knowing they'd better seek their lost manhood in the grave, since idealism obviously would never give it back to them. And certainly democracy wouldn't.

Those that lived, came back disillusioned. They hadn't vindicated their manhood. They didn't really feel they'd saved anything, except just their own meaningless life. The war hadn't made men of them, as it was supposed to do. It had only put the final touch to their disillusion and to their hopelessness about their own manhood. And it made them cocky because, in the eyes of the world at least, they were men and heroes.

Men and heroes!

Men and heroes soon were cheap. The old brotherhood of the trenches seemed to wash off like trench dirt. That too was nothing. And when a man and a hero came home to earn his living, he found that an admiring public and a saved democracy hardly thought it worthwhile to keep him alive any longer. So much for his manly heroism. They take off their hats to a lump of stone in Whitehall, and let a one-armed *living* hero try to sell them matches in the street. And they won't even buy his matches; he is a nuisance.

So much for war-heroes and disillusion. They have saved democracy, to find that democracy considers them a snake in its withered bosom. They have vindicated the brotherhood of man, by overthrowing Tyranny, and they come home to find that sixpence is brother to sixpence, there is no other kinship in the world. And they are not in the least surprised. They knew it all the time.

They are not really disillusioned. Their disillusion is made conscious, that is all. They were disillusioned all the while. They never *really* believed in anything. The self-conscious ego *can't* believe in anything. Only the old Adam of the red earth, with the black stone inside him, has the faculty and splendour of belief. And they had strangled their old Adam long ago, before ever they went to war, to be war-heroes.

Disillusioned! If a man goes out as a man, to fight, he may be beaten, but he cannot be disillusioned. There is no illusion to start with. These men went out in the illusion that their own self-conscious ego was their own manhood. They were disillusioned. But they turned the blame on democracy and other abstractions. They refused to realise the actuality.

As men, as responsible, sincerely-conscious men they never fought. As heroic automata, as servants of their country, as heroes and saviours they fronted the guns. But as men, isolated men, they never faced the strange war-passions that came up in themselves. As thought-adventurers, they never for one moment faced the issues of the war inwardly. They were all of them popular darlings, so they just sweltered in horrors and popularity, without ever taking the last manly adventure of realisation. Strange, strange feelings they had; and they funked them all. Pinned their faith to the happy days when they would once more be sitting on an office-stool keeping books, or digging in their allotment garden, and going home to a heavy Sunday dinner. Oh holy Peace!

Out of the strange passion that arose in men during the war, there should have risen the germ of a new idea, and the nucleus of a new way of feeling. Out of the strange revulsion of the days of horror, there should have resulted a fierce revision of existing values, and a final repudiation of the non-valid. From the previously unknown passion, and the fierce repudiation of false values should have ripened the seed of a whole new way of experience, the clue to a whole new era. For the way of our era was proved useless in the war, the Great Word of our day a dead letter.

But men funked realising. Heroes, statesmen, civilians, all of them funked the thought-adventure, they crept like tame cats back to their warm corners, pretended that everything was the same as before, and howled if it wasn't. This was their way of being men. And still is.

For a thousand years man has been pushing his civilisation, like a great snowball, uphill. All the time he has pushed it uphill, while it got huger and huger. In the belief that he would come at last to the happy top.

Now he no longer believes there is any top. And as a matter of fact, there isn't. So he has fallen into a funk, the go has gone out of him. And the snowball of his own accumulation begins slowly to roll back on him, slowly at first, but with gathering momentum, forcing him downhill. This is what is happening today.

We had a war, and beat the Germans, and lost our own manhood. We made the mechanical, automatic adventure, but not the soul adventure nor the thought-adventure. Passions came upon us, and we smirked and remembered the happy days of peace and plenty of pudding. Strange feelings and glimpses of weird realisation we had. But we twisted it all into a Sunday School address on "Peace, Sweet Peace, and How Nice It Is."

It was an alarming apple we pulled from the Tree of Life that time. With a weird, new flavour of experience. But we spat it out. We spat out the apple of a tremendous experience, and glibly announced ourselves unchanged. *We are not changed, Oh no!* Instead of knowing, like Adam, a new nakedness of ourselves, waking to a new knowledge altogether, we simply wallowed in dead, wet fig-leaves, till we were plastered all over with platitudes.

Now, in the evening cool, the Lord is walking in the garden and looking with amazement on our glib, platitudinously over-plastered imbecility. And all kinds of serpents are waking from a winter sleep and smiling to themselves as they yawn, along our paths.

We never fought the great fight, we never made the last adventure. We played with guns and horror and death, and funked realising. The German war-machine is broken. But is the world therefore *less* mechanical, or more?

Now the ball is rolling back on us, and in spite of all efforts, is driving us downward, downward. And we are getting more and more scared. But still we say: *We are unchanged. We are awfully nice fellows, too good to change.*

The backward-rolling ball of civilisation will change us, with a vengeance!

Heroes, heroes, heroes, and never a man among 'em! We even seem to know it. We erect a great lump of stone to the Unknown Warrior, who, if he ever existed, is grimly smiling at our imbecility, and preparing our doom. It is like the altar to the Unknown God in Athens. That self-same Unknown God was preparing to wipe out all Greece. And our own Unknown Warrior is preparing to attack us and annihilate us in the full flower of our own imbecility.

Because, whatever the war-heroes were and are, they were not warriors. Warrior! Warrior! I love that lump of blank stone to the Unknown Warrior. It's like the Unknown God, who is always a God of Vengeance to those that don't know Him.

Amigos, I pledge you the Unknown Warrior, with a vengeance. And the only incense he can accept, the sweat of a man's adventure into life. And the burnt offering of a sacrificed old idea.

Warrior! Warrior! The tomb isn't empty, any more than that old altar was barren. Beware of the occupant, that's all.

Warrior! Warrior! In the day of tame cats and cosy pussies!

ON HUMAN DESTINY

Man is a domesticated animal that must think. His thinking makes him a little lower than the angels. And his domestication makes him, at times, a little lower than the monkey.

It is no use retorting that most men *don't* think. It is quite true, most men don't have any original thoughts. Most men, perhaps, are incapable of original thought, or original thinking. This doesn't alter the fact that they are all the time, all men, all the time, thinking. Man cannot even sleep with a blank mind. The mind refuses to be blank. The millstones of the brain grind on while the stream of life runs. And they grind on the grist of whatever ideas the mind contains.

The ideas may be old and ground to powder already. No matter. The mill of the mind grinds on, grinds the old grist over and over and over again. The blackest savage in Africa is the same, in this respect, as the whitest Member of Parliament in Westminster. His risk of death, his woman, his hunger, his chieftain, his lust, his immeasurable fear, all these are fixed ideas in the mind of the black African savage. They are ideas based on certain sensual reactions in the black breast and bowels, that is true. They are none the less ideas, however "primitive." And the difference between a primitive idea and a civilised one is not very great. It is remarkable how little change there is in man's rudimentary ideas.

Nowadays we like to talk about spontaneity, spontaneous feeling, spontaneous passion, spontaneous emotion. But our very spontaneity is just an idea. All our modern spontaneity is fathered in the mind, gestated in self-consciousness.

Since man became a domesticated, thinking animal, long, long ago, a little lower than the angels, he long, long ago left off being a wild instinctive animal. If he ever was such, which I don't believe. In my opinion, the most prognathous cave-man was an ideal beast. He ground on his crude, obstinate ideas. He was no more like the wild deer or the jaguar among the mountains than we are. He ground his ideas in the slow ponderous mill of his heavy cranium.

Man is never spontaneous, as we imagine the thrushes or the sparrow-hawk, for example, to be spontaneous. No matter how wild, how savage, how apparently untamed the savage may be, Dyak or Hottentot, you may be sure he is grinding upon his own fixed, peculiar ideas, and he's no more spontaneous than a London 'bus conductor: probably not as much.

The simple innocent child of nature does not exist. If there be an occasional violet by a mossy. stone in the human sense, a Wordsworthian Lucy, it is because her vitality is rather low, and her simple nature is very near a simpleton's. You may, like Yeats, admire the simpleton, and call him God's Fool. But for me the village idiot is a cold egg.

No, no, let man be as primitive as primitive can be, he still has a mind. Give him at the same time a certain passion in his nature, and between his passion and his mind he'll beget himself ideas, ideas more or less good, more or less monstrous, but whether good or monstrous, absolute.

The savage grinds on his fetish or totem or taboo ideas even more fixedly and fatally than we on our Jove and salvation and making-good ideas.

Let us dismiss the innocent child of nature. He does not exist, never did, never will, and never could. No matter at what level man may be, he still has a mind, he has also passions. And the mind and the passions between them beget the scorpion brood of ideas. Or, if you like, call it the angelic hosts of the ideal.

Let us accept our own destiny. Man *can't* live by instinct, because he's got a mind. The serpent, with a crushed head, learned to brood along his spine, and take poison in his mouth. He has a strange sapience. But even he doesn't have ideas. Man has a mind, and ideas, so it is just puerile to sigh for innocence and naive spontaneity. Man is never spontaneous. Even children aren't spontaneous; not at all. It is only that their few and very dominant young ideas don't make logical associations. A child's ideas are ideas hard enough, but they hang together in a comical way, and the emotion that rises jumbles them ludicrously.

Ideas are born from a marriage between mind and emotion. But surely, you will say, it is possible for emotions to run free, without the dead hand of the ideal mind upon them.

It is impossible. Because, since man ate the apple and became endowed with mind, or mental consciousness, the human emotions are like a wedded wife; lacking a husband she is only a partial thing. The emotions cannot be "free." You can let your emotions run loose, if you like. You can let them run absolutely "wild." But their wildness and their looseness are a very shoddy affair. They leave nothing but boredom afterwards.

Emotions by themselves become just a nuisance. The mind by itself becomes just a sterile thing, making everything sterile. So what's to be done?

You've got to marry the pair of them. Apart, they are no good. The emotions that have not the approval and inspiration of the mind are just hysterics. The mind without the approval and inspiration of the emotions is just a dry stick, a dead tree, no good for anything unless to make a rod to beat and bully somebody with.

So, taking the human psyche, we have this simple trinity: the emotions, the mind, and then the children of this venerable pair, ideas. Man is controlled by his own ideas: there's no doubt about that.

Let us argue it once more. A pair of emancipated lovers are going to get away from the abhorred old ideal suasion. They're just going to fulfil their lives. That's all there is to it. They're just going to live their lives.

And then look at them! They do all the things that they know people do, when they are "living their own lives." They play up to their own ideas of being naughty instead of their ideas of good. And then what? It's the same old treadmill. They are just enacting the same set of ideas, only in the widdishins direction, being naughty instead of being good, treading the old circle in the opposite direction, and going round in the same old mill, even if in a reversed direction.

A man goes to a *cocotte*. And what of it? He does the same thing he does with his wife, but in the reverse direction. He just does everything naughtily instead of from his good self. It's a terrible relief perhaps, at first, to get away from his good self. But. after a little while he realises, rather drearily, that he's only going round in the same old treadmill, in the reversed direction. The Prince Consort turned us giddy with goodness, plodding round and round in the earnest mill. King Edward drove us giddy with naughtiness, trotting round and round in the same mill, in the opposite direction. So that the Georgian era finds us flummoxed, because we know the whole cycle back and forth.

At the centre is the same emotional idea. You fall in love with a woman, you marry her, you have bliss, you have children, you devote yourself to your family and to the service of mankind, and you live a happy life. Or, same idea but in the widdishins direction, you fall in love with a woman, you don't marry her, you live with her under the rose and enjoy yourself in spite of society; you leave your wife to swallow her tears or spleen, as the case may be; you spend the dowry of your daughters, you waste your substance, and you squander as much of mankind's heaped-up corn as you can.

The ass goes one way, and threshes out the corn from the chaff. The ass goes the other way and kicks the corn into the mud. At the centre is the same idea: love, service, self-sacrifice, productivity. It just depends upon which way round you run.

So there you are, poor man! All you can do is to run round like an ass, either in one direction or another, round the fixed pole of a certain central idea, in the track of a number of smaller, peripheral ideas. This idea of love, these peripheral ideals of service, marriage, increase, etc.

Even the vulgarest self-seeker trots in the same tracks and gets the same reactions, minus the thrill of the centralised passion.

What's to be done? What is being done?

The ring is being tightened. Russia was a complication of mixed ideas, old barbaric ideas of divine kingship, of irresponsible power, of sacred servility, conflicting with modern ideas of equality, serviceableness, productivity, etc. This complication had to be cleaned up. Russia was a great and bewildering but at the same time fascinating circus, with her splendours and miseries and brutalities and mystery. *Il faut changer tout cela.* So modern men have changed it. And the bewildering, fascinating circus of human anomalies is to be turned into a productive threshing-floor, an ideal treadmill. The treadmill of the one accomplished idea.

What's to be done? Man is an ideal animal: an idea-making animal. In spite of all his ideas, he remains an animal, often a little lower than the monkey. And in spite of all his animal nature, he can only act in fulfilment of disembodied ideas. What's to be done?

That too is quite simple. Man is not pot-bound in his ideas. Then let him burst the pot that contains him. Ideally he is pot-bound. His roots are choked, squeezed, and the life is leaving him, like a plant that is pot-bound and is gradually going sapless.

Break the pot, then.

But it's no good waiting for the slow accumulation of circumstance to break the pot. That's what men are doing to-day. They know the pot's got to break. They know our civilisation has got to smash, sooner or later. So they say : "Let it ! But let me live my life first !"

Which is all very well, but it's a coward's attitude. They say glibly: "Oh, well, every civilisation must fall at last. Look at Rome!" Very good, look at Rome. And what do you see? A mass of "civilised" so-called Romans, airing their *laissez-faire* and *laissez-aller* sentiments. And a number of barbarians, Huns, etc., coming down to wipe them out, and expending themselves in the effort.

What of it, the Dark Ages? What about the Dark Ages, when the fields of Italy ran wild as the wild wastes of the undiscovered world, and wolves and bears roamed in the streets of the grey city of Lyons?

Very nice!' But what else?' Look at the other tiny bit of a truth. Rome was pot-bound, the pot was smashed to atoms, and the highly developed Roman tree of life lay on its side and died. But not before a new young seed had germinated. There in the spilt soil, small, humble, almost indiscernible, was the little tree of Christianity. In the howling wilderness of slaughter and debacle, tiny monasteries of monks, too obscure and poor to plunder, kept the eternal light of man's undying effort at consciousness alive. A few poor bishops wandering through the chaos, linking up the courage of these men of thought and prayer. A scattered, tiny minority of men who had found a new way to God, to the life-source, glad to get again into touch with the Great God, glad to know the way and to keep the knowledge burningly alive.

That is the essential history of the Dark Ages, when Rome fell. We talk as if the flame of human courage and perspicacity had, in this time, gone out entirely, and that it miraculously popped into life again, out of nowhere, later on. Fusion of races, new barbaric blood, etc. Blarney! The fact of the matter is, the exquisite courage of brave men goes on in an unbroken continuity, even if sometimes the thread of flame becomes very thin. The exquisite delicate light of ever-renewed human consciousness is never blown, out. The lights of great cities go out, and there is howling darkness to all appearance. But always, since .men began, the light of the pure, God-knowing human consciousness has kept alight; sometimes, as in the Dark Ages, tiny but perfect flames of purest God-knowledge here and there; sometimes, as in our precious Victorian era, a huge and rather ghastly glare of human "understanding." But the light never goes out.

And that's the human destiny. The light shall never go out till the last day. The light of the human adventure into consciousness, which is, essentially, the light of human God-knowledge.

And human God-knowledge waxes and wanes, fed, as it were, from different oil. Man is a strange vessel. He has a thousand different essential oils in him, .to keep the light of consciousness fed. Yet, apparently, he can only draw on one source at a time. And when the source he has been drawing on dries up, he has a bad time sinking a new well of oil, or guttering to extinction.

So it was in Roman' times. The great old pagan fire of knowledge gradually died, its sources dried up. Then Jesus started a new, strange little flicker.

To-day, the long light of Christianity is guttering to go out and we have to get at new resources in ourselves.

It is no use waiting for the debacle. It's no use saying: "Well, I didn't make the world, so it isn't up to me to mend it. Time and the event must do the business."—Time and the event will do nothing. Men are worse after a great debacle than before. The Russians who have "escaped" from the horrors of the revolution are most of them extinguished as human beings. The real manly dignity has gone, all that remains is a collapsed human creature saying to himself: "Look at me! I am alive. I can actually eat more sausage."

Debacles don't save men. In nearly every case, during the horrors of a catastrophe the light of integrity and human pride is extinguished in the soul of the man or the woman involved, and there is left a painful, unmanned creature, a thing of shame, incapable any more. It is the great danger of debacles, especially in times of unbelief like these. Men lack the faith and courage to keep their souls alert, kindled and unbroken. Afterwards there is a great smouldering of shamed life.

Man, poor, conscious, forever-animal man, has a very stern destiny, from which he is never allowed to escape. It is his destiny that he must move on and on, in the thought-adventure. He is a thought-adventurer, and adventure he must. The moment he builds himself a house and begins to think he can sit still in his knowledge, his soul becomes deranged, and he begins to pull down the house over his own head.

Man is now house-bound. Human consciousness to-day is too small, too tight to let us live and act naturally. Our dominant idea, instead of being a pole-star, is a millstone round our necks, strangling us. Old tablets of stone.

That is part of our destiny. As a thinking being, man is destined to seek God and to form some conception of Life. And since the invisible God *cannot* be conceived, and since Life is always more than any idea, behold, from the human conception of God and of Life, a great deal of necessity is left out. And this God whom we have left out and this Life that we have shut out from our living, must in the end turn against us and rend us. It is our destiny.

Nothing will alter it. When the Unknown God whom we ignore turns savagely to rend us, from the darkness of oblivion, and when the Life that we exclude from our living turns to poison and madness in our veins, then there is only one thing left to do. We have to struggle down to the heart of things, where the everlasting flame is, and kindle ourselves another beam of light. In short, we have to make another bitter adventure in pulsating thought, far, far to the one central pole of energy. We have to germinate inside us, between our undaunted mind and our reckless, genuine passions, a new germ. The germ of a new idea. A new germ of God-knowledge, or Life-knowledge. But a new germ.

And this germ will expand and grow; and flourish to a great tree, maybe. And in the end die again. Die like all the other human trees of knowledge.

But what does that matter? We walk in strides, we live by days and nights. A tree slowly rises to a great height, and quickly falls to dust. There is a long life-day for the individual. Then a very dark, spacious death-room— I live and I die. I ask no other. Whatever proceeds from me lives and dies. I am glad, too. God is eternal, but my idea of Him is my own, and perishable. Everything human, human knowledge, human faith, human emotions, all perishes. And that is very good; if it were not so, everything would turn to cast-iron. There is too much of this cast-iron of permanence to-day.

Because I know the tree will ultimately die, shall I therefore refrain from planting a seed? Bah! it would be conceited cowardice on my part. I love the little sprout and the weak little seedling. I love the thin sapling, and the first fruit, and the falling of the first fruit. I love the great tree in its splendour. And I am glad that at last, at the very last, the great tree will go hollow, and fall on its side with a crash, and the little ants will run through it, and it will disappear like a ghost back into the humus.

It is the cycle of all things created, thank God. Because, given courage, it saves even eternity from staleness.

Man fights for a new conception of life and God, as he fights to plant seeds in the spring: because he knows that is the only way to harvest. If after harvest there is winter again, what does it matter? It is just seasonable.

But you have to fight even to plant seed. To plant seed you've got to kill a great deal of weeds and break much ground. You must labour to reap.

CLIMBING DOWN PISGAH

Sometimes one pulls oneself up short, and asks: "What am I doing this for?" One writes novels, stories, essays: and then suddenly:

"What on earth am I doing it for?"

What indeed?

For the sake of humanity?

Pfui! The very words *human, humanity, humanism* make one sick. For the sake of humanity as such, I wouldn't lift a little finger, much less write a story.

For the sake of the Spirit?

Tampoco!—But what do we mean by the Spirit? Let us be careful. Do we mean that One Universal Intelligence of which every man has his modicum? Or further, that one cosmic Soul, or Spirit, of which every individual is a broken fragment, and towards which every individual strives back, to escape the raw edges of his own fragmentariness, and to experience once more the sense of wholeness?

The sense of wholeness! Does one write books in order to give one's fellow-men a sense of wholeness: first, a oneness with all men, then a oneness with all things, then a oneness with our cosmos, and finally a oneness with the vast invisible universe? Is that it? Is that our achievement and our peace?

Anyhow, it would be a great achievement. And this has been the aim of the great ones. It was the aim of Whitman, for example.

Now it is the aim of the little ones, since the big ones are all gone. Thomas Hardy, a last big one, rings the knell of our Oneness. Virtually, he says: Once you achieve the great identification with the One, whether it be the One Spirit, or the Oversoul, or God, or whatever name you like to give it, you find that this God, this One, this Cosmic Spirit isn't human at all, hasn't any human feelings, doesn't concern itself for a second with the individual, and is, all told, a gigantic cold monster. It is a machine. The moment you attain that sense of Oneness and Wholeness, you become cold, dehumanised, mechanical, and monstrous. The greatest of all illusions is the Infinite of the Spirit.

Whitman really rang the same knell. (I don't expect anyone to agree with me.)

The sense of wholeness is a most terrible let-down. The big ones have already decided it. But the little ones, sneakingly too selfish to care, go on sentimentally tinkling away at it.

This we may be sure of: all talk of brotherhood, universal love, sacrifice, and so on, is a sentimental pose for us. We reached the top of Pisgah, and looking down, saw the graveyard of humanity. Those meagre spirits who could never get to the top, and are careful never to try, because it costs too much sweat and a bleeding at the nose, they sit below and still snivellingly invent Pisgah-sights. But strictly, it is all over. The game is up.

The little ones, of course, are writing at so many cents a word—or a line, according to their success. They may say I do the same. Yes, I demand my cents, a Shylock. Nevertheless, if I wrote for cents I should write differently, and with far more "success."

What, then, does one write for? There must be some imperative. Probably it is the sense of adventure, to start with. Life is no fun for a man, without an adventure.

The Pisgah-top of spiritual oneness looks down upon a hopeless squalor of industrialism, the huge cemetery of human hopes. This is our Promised Land. "There's a good time coming, boys, a good time coming." Well, we've rung the bell, and here it is.

Shall we climb hurriedly down from Pisgah, and keep the secret? Mum's the word!

This is what our pioneers are boldly doing. We used, as boys, to sing parodies of most of the Sunday-school hymns.

> "They climbed the steep ascents to heaven
> Through peril, toil and pain.
> Oh God to us may grace be given
> To scramble down again—"

This is the grand hymn of the little ones. But it's harder getting down from a height, very often, than getting up. It's a predicament. Here we are, cowering on the brinks of precipices half-way up, or down, Pisgah. The Pisgah of Oneness, the Oneness of Mankind, the Oneness of Spirit.

Hie, boys, over we go! Pisgah's a fraud, and the Promised Land is Pittsburgh, the Chosen Few, there are billions of 'em, and Canaan smells of kerosene. Let's break our necks if we must, but let's get down, and look over the brink of some other horizon. We're like the girl who took the wrong turning: thought it was the right one.

It's an adventure. And there's only one left, the venture in consciousness. Curse these ancients, they have said everything for us. Curse these moderns, they have done everything for us. The aeroplane descends and lays her egg-shells of empty tin cans on the top of Everest, in the Ultimate Thule, and all over the North Pole; not to speak of tractors waddling across the inviolate Sahara and over the jags of Arabia Petraea, laying the same addled eggs of our civilisation, tin cans, in every camp-nest.

Well then, they can have the round earth. They've got it, anyhow. And they can have the firmament: they've got that too. The moon is a cold egg in the astronomical nest. *Heigho! for the world well lost!* That's the Known World, the world of the One Intelligence. That's the Human World! I'm getting out of it. *Homo sum. Omnis a me humanum alienum puto.*

Of the thing we call human, I've had enough. And enough is as good as a feast.

Inside of me, there's a little demon—maybe he's a big demon— that says *Basta! Basta!* to all my oneness. "Farewell, a long farewell to all my greatness." In short, come off the perch, Polly, and look what a mountain of droppings you're crouched upon.

Are you human, and do you want me to sympathise with you for that? Let me hand you a roll of toilet paper.

After looking down from the Pisgah-top onto the oneness of all mankind safely sealed these several years in Canaan, I admit myself dehumanised.

> "Fair waved the golden corn
> In Canaan's pleasant land—"

The factory smoke waves much higher. And in the sweet smoke of industry I don't care a button who loves who, nor what babes are born. The sight of all of it *en masse* was a little too much for my human spirit, it dehumanised me. Here I am, without a human sympathy left. Looking down on Human Oneness was too much for my human stomach, so I vomited it away.

Remains a demon which says *Ha-ha! So you've conquered the earth, have you, oh man! Now swallow the pill.*

For if the proof of the pudding is in the eating, the proof of a Conquest is in digesting it. Humanity is an ostrich. But even the ostrich thinks twice before it bolts a rolled-up hedgehog. The earth is conquered as the hedgehog is conquered when he rolls himself up into a ball, and the dog spins him with his paw.

But that is not the point, at least for anyone except the Great Dog of Humanity. The point for us is, *What then?*

> "Whither, oh splendid ship, they white sails crowding—?"

To have her white sail dismantled and a gasoline engine fitted into her guts. That is whither, oh Poet!

When you've got to the bottom of Pisgah once more, where are you? Sitting on a sore posterior, murmuring: *Oneness is all bunk. There is no Oneness, till you've invented it and killed your goose to get it out of her belly. It takes millions of little people to lay the egg of the Universal Spirit, and then it's an addled omelette, and stinks in our nostrils. And all the millions of little people have over-reached themselves, trying to lay the mundane egg of oneness. They're all damaged inside, and they can't face the addled omelette they've laid. What a mess!*

What then?

Heigho! Whither, oh patched canoe, your kinked keel thrusting!

We've been over the rapids, and the creature that crawls out of the whirlpool feels that most things human are foreign to him. *Homo sum!* means a vastly different thing to him, from what it meant to his father.

Homo sum! a demon who knows nothing of oneness or of perfection. *Homo sum!* a demon who knows nothing of any First Creator who created the universe from His own perfection. *Homo sum!* a man who knows that all creation lives like some great demon inhabiting space, and pulsing with a dual desire, a desire to give himself forth into creation, and a desire to take himself back, in death.

Child of the great inscrutable demon, *Homo sum!* Adventurer from the first Adventurer, *Homo sum!* Son of the blazing-hearted father who wishes beauty and harmony and perfection, *Homo sum!* Child of the raging-hearted demon-father who fights that nothing shall surpass his crude and demonish range, *Homo sum!*

Whirling in the midst of Chaos, the demon of the beginning, who is forever willing and unwilling to surpass the *status quo.* Like a bird he spreads wings to surpass himself. Then like a serpent he coils to strike at that which would surpass him. And the bird of the first desire must either soar quickly, or strike back with his talons at the snake, if there is to be any surpassing of the thing that was, the *status quo.*

It is the joy forever, the agony forever, and above all, the fight forever. For all the universe is alive, and whirling in the same fight, the same joy and anguish. The vast demon of life has made himself habits, which except in the whitest heat of desire and rage, he will never break. And these habits are the laws of our scientific universe. But all the laws of physics, dynamic, kinetic, static, all are but the settled habits of a vast living incomprehensibility, and they can all be broken, superseded, in a moment of great extremity.

Homo sum! child of the demon. *Homo sum!* willing and unwilling. *Homo sum!* giving and taking. *Homo sum!* hot and cold. *Homo sum!* loving and loveless. *Homo sum!* the adventurer.

This we see, this we know as we crawl down the dark side of Pisgah, or slip down on a sore posterior. *Homo sum!* has changed its meaning for us.

That is, if we are young men. Old men and elderly will sit tight on heavy posteriors in some crevice upon Pisgah, babbling about "all for love, and the world well saved." Young men with hearts still for the life adventure will rise up with their trouser-seats scraped away, after the long slither from the heights down to the well-nigh bottomless pit, having changed their minds. They will change their minds and change their pants. Wisdom is sometimes in a sore bottom, and the new pants will no longer be neutral.

Young men will change their minds and their pants, having done with Oneness and neutrality. Even the stork meditates on an orange leg, and the bold drake pushes the water behind him with a red foot. Young men are the adventurers.

Let us scramble out of this ash-hole at the foot of Pisgah. The universe isn't a machine after all. It's alive and kicking. And in spite of the fact that man with his cleverness has discovered some of the habits of our old earth, and so lured him into a trap; in spite of the fact that man has trapped the great forces, and they go round and round at his bidding like a donkey in a gin; the old demon isn't quite nabbed. We didn't quite catch him napping. He'll turn round on us with bare fangs, before long. He'll swallow us with the very forces that go round and round at our bidding. They'll turn into a python, coiling, coiling, coiling till we're nicely mashed. Then they'll bolt us.

Let's get out of the vicious circle. Put on new bright pants to show that we're meditative fowl who have thought the thing out and decided to migrate. To assert that our legs are not grey machine-sections, but live and limber members who know what it is to have their rear well scraped and punished, in the slither down

317

Pisgah, and are not going to be diddled any more into mechanical service of mountain-climbing up to the great summit of Wholeness and of Bunk.

RESURRECTION

"Touch me not! I am not yet ascended unto the Father."

We have all the time been worshipping a dead Christ: or a dying. The Son of Man on the Cross.

Yet we know well enough, the Cross was only the first step into achievement. The second step was into the tomb. And the third step, whither?—"I am not yet ascended unto the Father."

I have just read, for the first time, Tolstoy's *Resurrection*. Tolstoy writhed very hard, on the Cross. His Resurrection is the step into the tomb. And the stone was rolled upon him.

Now, as Christians, we have died. The War was the Calvary of all real Christian men. Since the War, it has been the tomb, with no rule at all. As the peasants in Italy used to say, after Christ was put in the tomb, on Good Friday eve: Now we can sin. There is no Lord on earth to see us.

Since the War, the world has been without a Lord. What is the Lord within us, has been walled up in the tomb. But three days have fully passed, and it is time to roll away the stone. It is time for the Lord in us to arise.

With the stigmata healed up, and the eyes full open.

Rise as the Lord. No longer the Man of Sorrows. The Crucified Uncrucified. The Crown of Thorns removed, and the tongues of fire round the brows. The Risen Lord.

Man has done his worst, and crucified his God. Men will always crucify their god, given the opportunity. Christ proved that, by giving them the opportunity.

But Christ is not put twice on the Cross. Not a second time. And this is the great point that Tolstoy missed. It seemed to him, Christ would go on being crucified, everlastingly.

Bad doctrine. As man puts off his clothes when he dies, so the Cross is put off. Like a garment. And the Son of Man will not be twice crucified. That, never again.

He is risen. And now beware! Touch me not.

Put away the Cross, it is obsolete. Stare no more after the Stigmata. They are more than healed up. The Lord is risen, and ascended unto the Father. There is a new Body, and a new Law.

Christ and the Father are at one again. There is a new Law. The Man has disappeared into the God again. The column of fire shoots up, from the nadir to the zenith, and there is a new fierce light on our faces.

Men who can rise with the Son of Man, and ascend unto the Father, will see the new day. Many men will perish in the tomb, unable to roll the stone away. But the stone that is rolled away will roll on. It too has a course to run.

Christ has re-entered into the Father, and the pillar of flame shoots up, anew, from the nadir to the zenith. The world and the cosmos stagger to the new axis. There is a new light upon the hills, the valleys groan and are wrenched.

The Tree shivers, and sheds its leaves. Never was the Tree so vast in stature and so full of leaves. But the new fire spurts at its roots, the boughs writhe, the twigs crackle from within, and the old leaves fall thick and red to the ground. That is how a new day enters the Tree of Life.

The Cross has taken root again, and is putting forth buds. Slim branches sprout out where the nails went in, there is a tuft of sprouts like tongues of flame at the top, where the inscription was. Even *Consummatum est* is dissolved in a rising sap.

When Christ rejoins the Father, the Cross is again a Tree, the wheel of fire flares up and spins in the opposite way. And little wheels of fire are seen round the brows of men who have ascended, re-ascended to the Father. There are kings in the cosmos once more, there are lords among men again.

It is the day of the Risen Lord. Touch me not! I am the Lord Arisen.

Men of the Risen Lord, rise up. The wheel of fire is starting to spin in the opposite way, to throw off the mud of the world. Deep mud is on the staggering wheel, mud of the multitudes. But Christ has rejoined the Father at the axis, the flame of the hub spurts up. The wheel is beginning to turn in the opposite way, and woe to the multitudes.

Men of the Risen Lord, the many ways are one. Down the spokes of flame there are many paths which are one way still, to the core of the wheel. Turn round, turn round, away from the mud of the rim to the flame of the core, and walk down the spokes of fire to the Whole, where God is One.

For the multitudes shall be shaken off as a dog shakes off his fleas. And only the risen lords among men shall stand on the wheel and not fall, being fire as the wheel is Fire, facing in to the inordinate Flame.

The Lord is risen. Let us rise as well and be lords. The multitudes rolled the stone upon us. Let us roll it back.

Men in the tomb, rise up, the time is expired. The Lord is risen. Quick! let us follow Him.

The Lord is risen as Lord Indeed, let us follow, as lords in deed. The Lord has rejoined the Father, in the flame at the hub of the wheel. Let us look that way, and cry Behold! down the spokes of fire. Let us turn our backs on the tomb, and the stone that is rolling upon the multitude. It is more than finished, it is begun again.

The lords are out of prison, with the Risen Lord. Let the multitudes tremble and fall down, as the black stone rolls towards them, back from the mouth of the tomb. Except you died with the Lord, you shall surely die. Except you rise with the Lord, and roll the stone from the mouth of the tomb, the stone shall surely crush you. The greater the stone you rolled upon the mouth of the tomb, the greater the destruction overtakes you.

It is not given to you twice, oh multitudes, to put the Lord on the Cross. It was given you once, and once and for all, and now it is more than finished. If you have not died, you shall die. If you cannot rise, you shall fall. If you cannot note the coming day, if you're blind to the morning-star, it is because the shadow of the stone is upon you, rolling down from the mouth of the tomb.

More blessed to give than to receive. So you gave the Judas kiss. Now it rolls back on you, huge, an increasingly huge black stone, as big as the world, that kiss.

You thought *Consummatum est* meant *all is over*. You were wrong. It means: *The step is taken.*

Rise then, men of the Risen Lord, and push back the stone. Who rises with the Risen Lord rises himself as a lord. Come, stand on the spokes of fire, as the wheel begins to revolve. Face inward to the flame of Whole God, that plays upon the zenith. And be lords with the Lord, with bright, and brighter, and brightest, and most-bright faces.

ACCUMULATED MAIL

If there is one thing I don't look forward to, it's my mail.

"Look out! Look Out! Look out!
Look out! The postman comes!
His double knocking makes us start,
It rouses echoes in the heart,
It wakens expectation, and hope and agitation etc etc. —"

So we used to sing, in school.

Now, the postman is no knocker. He pitches the mail-bag into a box on a tree, and kicks his horse forward.

And when one has been away, and a heap of letters and printed stuff slithers out under one's eyes, there is neither hope nor expectation in the heart, but only repulsion, as if it were something nauseous one had to eat.

Business letters—all rather dreary. Bank letters, with the nasty green used-up cheques, and a dwindling small balance. Family letters: *we are so disappointed you are not coming to England. We wanted you to see the baby, he is so bonny: the new house, it is awfully nice: the show of daffodils and crocuses down the garden—* Friends' letters: *The winter has been very trying.* And then the unknown correspondents. They are the *worst.—If you saw my little blue-eyed darling, you could not refuse her anything—*not even an autograph.—The high-school students somewhere in Massachusetts or in Maryland are in the habit of choosing by name some known man, whom they accept as a sort of guide. A group has chosen me. Will I send them a letter of encouragement or of help in the battle of life?—Well, I would willingly, but what on earth am I to say to them?—*My dear young People: I daren't advise you to do as I do, for it's no fun, writing unpopular books. And I won't advise you, for your own sakes, to do as I say. For in details I'm sure I'm wrong. My dear young people, perhaps I need your encouragement more than you need mine.—*Well, that's no message!

Then there's the letter signed "A Mother"—from Lenton, Nottingham: telling me she has been reading *Sons and Lovers,* and is there not misery enough in Nottingham (my home town) without my indicating where vice can be found, and (to cut short) how it can be practised? She saw a young woman reading *Sons and Lovers,* but was successful in preventing her from finishing the book. And the book was so well written, it was a pity the author could not have kept it clean. "As it is, although so interesting, it cannot be mentioned in polite society." Signed. A

Mother.—(Let us hope the young woman who was saved from finishing *Sons and Lovers* may also be saved from becoming, in her turn, *A Mother!*)

Then the letter from some gentleman in New York beginning: *I am afraid you may consider this letter an impertinence.*—If *he* was afraid, then what colossal impertinence to carry on to two sheets, and then post his impudence to me. The substance was: *I should like to know, in the controversy between you and Norman Douglas,* (I didn't know myself that there *was* a controversy)—*how it was the Magnus manuscript came into your hands, and you came to publish it, when clearly it was left to Douglas? In this case, why should you be making a lot of money out of another man's work? —Of course, I know it is your Introduction which sells the book. Magnus' manuscript is trash, and not worth reading. Still, for the satisfaction of myself and many of my readers, I wish you could make it clear how you come to be profiting by a work that is not your own—*

Apparently this gentleman's sense of his own impertinence only drove him deeper in. He has obviously read neither Magnus' work nor my Introduction: else he would plainly have seen that this MS. was detained by Magnus' creditors, at his death, and handed by them to me, in the poor hope of recovering some of the money lost with that little adventurer.—Moreover, if I wrote the only part of the book that is worth reading, *(I* don't say so)—the only part for which people buy the book, (they're not *my* words)—then it is my work they buy! This out of my genteel correspondent's own mouth. Because I do *not* consider Magnus' work trash.— Finally, if I get half proceeds for a book of which practically half was written by me, and the other half sells on my account, who in heaven's name is going to be impertinent to me? Nobody, without a kick in the pants.—As for Douglas, if he could have paid the dead man's debts, he might have "executed" the dead man's literary works to his heart's content. Why doesn't he do something with the rest of the remains? Was this poor Foreign Legion MS. the only egg in the nest?— Anyhow, let us hope that those particular debts for which this MS. was detained, will now be paid. And R.I.P.—Anyhow I shan't be a rich man on the half profits.

But this is not all my precious mail.—From a London editor, and friend (soi-disant): *Perhaps you would understand other people better if you did not think that you were always* right.—How one learns things about oneself!—Or is it, really, about the other person?—I always find that my critics, pretending to criticise me, are analyzing themselves.—My own private opinion is that I have been, as far as people go, almost every time wrong! Anyhow my desire to "understand other people better" is turning to dread of finding out any more about them.—This "friend" goes on to say, will I ask my literary agent to let him have some articles of mine at a considerably cheaper figure than the agent puts on them.

It is not done yet. There is Mr Muir's article about me in *The Nation.* Never did I feel so baffled, confronting myself in my worst moments, as I feel when I read this "elucidation" of myself I hope it isn't my fault that Mr Muir plays such havoc between two stools. I think I read that he is a young man, and younger critic. It seems a pity he hasn't "A Mother" to take the books from him before he can do himself any more harm. Truly, I don't want him to read them. "There remain his gifts, splendid in their imperfection"—this is Mr Muir about me—"thrown recklessly into a dozen books, fulfilling themselves in none. His chief title to greatness is that he has brought a new mode of seeing into literature, a new beauty which is also one of the oldest things in the world. It is the beauty of the ancient instinctive life which civilised man has almost forgotten. Mr Lawrence has picked up a thread of life left behind by mankind; and at some time it will be woven in with the others, making human life more complete, as all art tends to. — Life has come to him fresh from the minting at a time when it seemed to everyone soiled and banal. — He has many faults, and many of these are wilful. He has not fulfilled the promise shown in *Sons and Lovers* and *The Rainbow. He has not submitted himself to any discipline —" "The will (in Mr Lawrence's characters) is not merely weak and inarticulate, it is in abeyance; it does not come into action. To this tremendous extent the tragedy in Mr Lawrence's novels fails in significance.—"——"We remember the scenes in his novels; we forget the names of his men and women. We should not know any of them if we met them in the street, as we should know Anna Karenina, or Crevel, or Soames Forsyte—" (Who is Crevel?)

Now listen, you, Mr Muir, and my dear readers. You read me for your own sakes, not for mine. You do me no favour by reading me. I am not indebted to you in the least, if you spend two dollars on a book. You do it entirely for your own delectation. Spend the dollars on chewing-gum, it keeps the mouth busy and doesn't fly to the brain. I shall live just as blithely, unbought and unsold. When you buy chewing-gum, do you feel you acquire divine rights over the mind and soul of Mr Wrigley? If you do, it's like your impudence. Therefore get it out of your heads, the idea that you are throned aloft like the gods, called upon to utter divine judgment. Your lofty seats, after all, are more like tall baby-chairs than thrones of the gods of judgment.—But here goes, for an answer.

1.. I have lunched with Mr Galsworthy, and I'm sure I should know him if I met him in the street.—Is that my fault, or his?—Alas that I recognise people in the street, by their noses or their bonnets! I don't care about their noses, bonnets, or beauty. Does nothing exist beyond that which is recognisable in the street?—How does my cat recognise me in the dark?—Ugh, thank God there are more, and other sorts of vision than the kodak sort which Mr Muir esteems above all others.

2. "The will is not merely weak and inarticulate, it is in abeyance."—Ah, my dear Mr Muir, the will of the modern young gentleman may not be in your opinion weak and inarticulate, but certainly it is as mechanical as a Ford car engine. To this extent is the tragedy of modern young men insignificant.—Oh, you little gods in the machine, stop the engine for a bit, do!

3. "He has not submitted himself to discipline—"——Try, Mr Muir et al., putting your little iron wills into abeyance for one hour daily, and see if it doesn't need a harder discipline than this doing of your "daily dozen," and all your other mechanical repetitions. Believe me, today, the little god in a Ford machine cannot get at the thing worth having, not even with the most praiseworthy little engine of a will.

4. "He has not fulfilled the promise of *Sons and Lovers* and *The Rainbow*—" Just after *The Rainbow* was published, the most eminent figure in English letters told me to my nose that this work was a failure. Now, after ten years, Mr Muir finds it "promising." Go ahead, oh youth! But whatever promise you read into *The Rainbow,* remember it's like the little boy who "promised" his mother to be good if she'd "promise" to take him to the pantomime. I, I promise nothing, inside or out of *The Rainbow.*

5. "Life has come to him fresh from the minting, at a time when it seemed to everyone stale and banal."—Come! Come! Mr Muir! With all that "spirit" of

yours, and all that "intellect," and all that "will," and all that "discipline," do you dare to confess that (I suppose you lump yourself in among everyone) life seemed to you stale and banal?—If so, something must be badly wrong with you and your psychic equipment, and Mr Lawrence wouldn't be in your shoes, for all the money and the "cleverness" in the world.

6. "Mr Lawrence has picked up a thread of life left behind by mankind—" Darn your socks with it, Mr Muir?

7. "It is the beauty of the ancient instinctive life which civilised man has almost forgotten—"—He may have forgotten it, but he can put a label on it, and price it at a figure, and let it go cheap, in one-and-a-half minutes.—Ah, my dear Mr Muir, when do you consider "ancient" life ended, and "civilised" life began? And which is stale and banal? Wherein does staleness lie, Mr Muir?—As for "ancient life," it may be ancient to you, but it is still alive and kicking in some people. And "ancient life" is far more deeply conscious than you can even imagine. And its discipline goes into regions where you have no existence.

8. "His chief title to greatness is that he has brought a new mode of seeing into literature, a new beauty etc etc—"—Easy, of course, as re-trimming an old hat. Michael Arlen does it better! Looks more modish, the old hat.—But shouldn't it be a new mode of "feeling" or "knowing," rather than of "seeing"? Since none of my characters would be recognisable in the street?

9. "There remain his gifts, splendid in their imperfection—" —Ugh, Mr Muir, think how horrible for us all, if I were perfect! Or even if I had "perfect" gifts!—Isn't splendour enough for you, Mr Muir? Or do you find the peacock more "perfect" when he is moulting, and has lost his tail, and therefore isn't so exaggerated, but is more "down to normal."—For "perfection" is only one of the attributes of "the normal" and "the average," in modern thought.

Well, I don't want to be just or to be kind. There is a further justice and a greater kindness, than this niggling tolerance business, and suffering fools gladly. Fools bore me.—But I don't mean Mr Muir. He is a phoenix, compared to most.

I often wonder what it is that the rainbow—I mean the natural phenomenon—stands for, in my own consciousness. I don't know all it means to me.—Is this lack of intellectual capacity on my part? Or is it because the rainbow is somehow not quite "normal," and therefore not quite fit for intellectual appreciation?—Of course white light passing through prisms of falling rain-drops makes a rainbow. Let us therefore sell it by the yard.

For me, give me a little splendour, and I'll leave perfection to the small fry.

Other scraps from the mail-bag: Mr Clive Bell, saying: "Half-educated people like Mr Lawrence—"

Retort simple: "People who only half exist, like Mr Bell."

Bertrand Russell: "What a pity Lawrence is obsessed by sex!"

Retort simple: "He's not! But mind yourself Bertie!"

But oh, my other anonymous little critic, what shall I say to thee? *Mr Lawrence's horses are all mares or stallions.*

Honi soit qui mal y pense, my dear. Though I'm sure the critic is a gentleman (I daren't say *man)* and not a lady.

Little critics' horses (sic) are all geldings.

Another little critic: "Mr Lawrence's introspective intelligence is too feeble to balance this melodramatic fancy in activities which cater for a free play of mind;——"

Retort simple: Mr Lawrence's intelligence would prevent his writing such a sentence down, and sending it to print.—What can those activities be which "cater for a free play of mind"?—whatever that may mean—and at the same time have "introspective intelligence"—(what quite is this?)—balancing "melodramatic fancy"—(what is this either?) within them?

Same critic, finishing the same sentence: "and so, since criticism begins at home, his (Mr Lawrence's) latter-day garment of philosopher and preacher is shot through with the vulgarity of aggressive self-ignorance.——"

Retort simple: If criticism begins at home, then the professional, and still more so the amateur critic (I suspect this gentleman to be the latter) is never by any chance at home. He is always out, sponging on some author.—As for a "latter-day garment of philosopher and preacher" (I never before knew a philosopher and preacher transmogrified into a garment)—being "shot through with the vulgarity of aggressive self-ignorance"—was it grape-shot, or duck-shot, or just a shot-silk effect?

Alas, this young critic is "shot through" with ignorance even more extensive than that of self. Or perhaps it is only his garment of critic and smart little fellow which is so shot through, *percé* or *miroité,* according to fancy;— "melodramatic fancy" balanced by "introspective intelligence" "in activities which cater for a free play of mind."

"We Cater to the Radical Trade," says Jimmie Higgins' advertisement.

Another friend and critic: "Lawrence is an artist, but his intellect is not up to his art."

You might as well say: Mr Lawrence rides a horse, but he doesn't wear his stirrups round his neck. And the accusation is just. Because, he hopes to heaven he is riding a horse that is alive of itself, not a wooden hobby horse suitable for the nursery.—And he does his best to keep his feet in the stirrups, and to leave his intellect under his hat, when he is riding his naughty steed. No my dears! I guess, as an instrument, my intellect is as good as yours. But instead of sitting in my own wheelbarrow (the intellect is a sort of wheelbarrow about the place) and whipping it ecstatically over the head, I just wheel out what dump I've got, and forget the old barrow again, till next time.

And now, thank God, I can throw all my mail, letters, used cheques, pamphlets, periodicals, clippings from the "press," Ave Marias, Pater Nosters, and bunk, into the fire.—When I get a particularly smelly bit of sentiment, I always burn it slowly, invoking the Lord thus: "Lord, Herrgott, nimm Du diesen Opfer-rauch! Take thou this smoke of sacrifice.—The sacrifice of blood is no longer acceptable, for blood has turned to water.—All is vapour! Therefore, Oh Lord, this choice tit-bit of the spirit, this kidney-fat of sentiment, accept it, Oh Lord, from thy servant.— This firstling of the sentimental herd, this young ram without spot or blemish, from the aesthetic flock, this adamantine young he-goat, from the troops of human 'stunts'—see Lord, I cut their throats and burn the cardboard fat of them. Lord of the Spirit, Lord of the Universal Mind, Lord of the cosmic will, snuff up the smoke of this burnt-paper offering, for it makes my eyes smart—"

I wish they'd make his eyes smart as well, this Lord of Sentimentalism, aestheticism, and stunts! One day I'll make a sacrifice of him too: to my own Lord, who broods at the centre of all the worlds, over his own fathomless Desire.

THE CROWN

I

The Lion and the Unicorn
Were fighting for the Crown

What is it then, that they want, that they are forever rampant and unsatisfied, the king of beasts and the defender of virgins? What is this Crown that hovers between them, unattainable? Does either of them ever hope to get it?

But think of the king of beasts lying serene with the crown on his head! Instantly the unicorn prances from every heart. And at the thought of the lord of chastity with the crown ledged above his golden horn, lying in virgin lustre of sanctity, the lion springs out of his lair in every soul, roaring after his prey.

It is a strange and painful position, the king of beasts and the beast of purity, rampant for ever on either side of the crown. Is it to be so for ever?

Who says lion?—who says unicorn? A lion, a lion!! Hi, a unicorn! Now they are at it, they have forgotten all about the crown. It is a greater thing to have an enemy than to have an object. The lion and the unicorn were fighting, it is no question any more of the crown. We know this, because when the lion beat the unicorn, he did not take the crown and put it on his head, and say "Now Mr. Purity, I'm king." He drove the unicorn out of town, expelled him, obliterated him, expurgated him from the memory, exiled him from the kingdom. Instantly the town was all lion, there was no unicorn at all, no scent nor flavour of unicorn.

"Unicorn!" they said in the city. "That is a mythological beast that never existed."

There was no question any more of rivalry. The unicorn was erased from the annals of fact.

Why did the lion fight the unicorn? Why did the unicorn fight the lion? Why must the one obliterate the other? Was it the *raison d'être* of each of them, to obliterate the other?

But think, if the lion really destroyed, killed the unicorn; not merely drove him out of town, but annihilated him! Would not the lion at once expire, as if he had created a vacuum around himself? Is not the unicorn necessary to the very existence of the lion, is not each opposite kept in stable equilibrium by the opposition of the other.

This is a terrible position: to have for a *raison d'être* a purpose which, if once fulfilled, would of necessity entail the cessation from existence of both opponents. They would both cease to be, if either of them really won in the fight which is their sole reason for existing. This is a troublesome thought.

It makes us at once examine our own hearts. What do we find there?—a want, a need, a crying out, a divine discontent. Is it the lion, is it the unicorn?—one, or both? But certainly there is this crying aloud, this infant crying in the night, born into a blind want.

What do we find at the core of our hearts?—a want, a void, a hollow want. It is the lion that must needs fight the unicorn, the unicorn that must needs fight the lion. Supposing the lion refuses the obligation of his being, and says, "I won't fight, I'll just lie down. I'll be a lion couchant."

What *then* is the lion? A void, a hollow ache, a want. "What am I?" says the lion, as he lies with his head between his paws, or walks by the river feeding on raspberries, peacefully, like a unicorn. "I am a hollow void, my roaring is the resonance of a hollow drum, my strength is the power of the vacuum, drawing all things within itself"

Then he groans with horrible self-consciousness. After all, there is nothing for it but to set upon the unicorn, and so forget, forget, obtain the precious self-oblivion.

Thus are we, then, rounded upon a void, a hollow want, like the lion. And this want makes us draw all things into ourselves, to fill up the void. But it is a bottomless pit, this void. If ever it were filled, there would be a great cessation from being, of the whole universe.

Thus we portray ourselves in the field of the royal arms. The whole history is the fight, the whole *raison d'être*. For the whole field is occupied by the lion and the unicorn. These alone are the living occupants of the immortal and mortal field.

We have forgotten the Crown, which is the keystone of the fight. We are like the lion and the unicorn, we go on fighting underneath the Crown, entirely oblivious of its supremacy.

It is modest common sense for us to acknowledge, all of us, nowadays, that we are built round a void and hollow want which, if satisfied, would imply our collapse, our utter ceasing to be. Therefore we regard our craving with complacence, we feel the great aching of the Want, and we say, with conviction "I know I exist, I know I am I, because I feel the divine discontent which is personal to me, and eternal, and present always in me."

That is because we are incomplete, we stand upon one side of the shield, or on the other. On the one side we are in darkness, our eyes gleam phosphorescent like cat's eyes. And with these phosphorescent gleaming eyes we look across at the opposite pure beast, and we say, "Yes, I am a lion, my *raison d'être* is to devour that unicorn, I am moulded upon an eternal void, a Want," Gleaming bright, we see ourselves reflected upon the surface of the darkness and we say: "I am the pure unicorn, it is for me to oppose and resist for ever that avid lion. If he ceased to exist, I should be supreme and unique and perfect. Therefore I will destroy him."

But the lion will not be destroyed. If he were, if he were swallowed into the belly of the unicorn, the unicorn would fly asunder into chaos.

This is like being a creature who walks by night, who says: "Men see by darkness, and in the darkness they have their being." Or like a creature that walks by day, and says: "Men live by the light."

We are enveloped in the darkness, like the lion: or like the unicorn, enveloped in the light.

For the womb is full of darkness, and also flooded with the strange white light of eternity. And we, the peoples of the world, we are enclosed within the womb of our era, we are there begotten and conceived, but not brought forth.

326

A myriad, myriad people, we roam in the belly of our era, seeking, seeking, wanting. And we seek and want deliverance. But we say we want to overcome the lion that shares with us this universal womb, the walls of which are shut, and have no window to inform us that we are in prison. We roam within the vast walls of the womb, unnourished now, because the time of our deliverance is ripe, even overpast, and the body of our era is lean and withered because of us, withered and inflexible.

We roam unnourished, moulded each of us around a core of want, a void. We stand in the darkness of the womb and we say: "Behold, there is the light, the white light of eternity, which we want." And we make war upon the lion of darkness, annihilate him, so that we may be free in the eternal light. Or else, suddenly, we admit ourselves the lion, and we rush rampant on the unicorn of chastity.

We stand in the light of Virginity, in the wholeness of our unbroached immortality, and we say: "Lo the darkness surrounds us, to envelop us. Let us resist the powers of darkness." Then like the bright and virgin unicorn we make war upon the ravening lion. Or we cry: "Ours is the strength and glory of the Creator, who precedes Creation, and all is unto us." So we open a ravening mouth, to swallow back all time has brought forth.

And there is no rest, no cessation from the conflict. For we are two opposites which exist by virtue of our inter-opposition. Remove the opposition and there is collapse, a sudden crumbling into universal nothingness.

The darkness, this has nourished us. The darkness, this is a vast infinite, an origin, a Source. The Beginning, this is the great sphere of darkness, the womb wherein the universe is begotten.

But this universal, infinite darkness conceives of its own opposite. If there is universal infinite darkness, then there is universal infinite light, for there cannot exist a specific infinite save by virtue of the opposite and equivalent specific infinite. So that if there be universal infinite darkness in the beginning, there must be universal infinite light in the end. And these are two relative halves.

Into the womb of the primary darkness enters the ray of ultimate light, and time is begotten, conceived, there is the beginning of the end. We are the beginning of the end. And there, within the womb, we ripen upon the beginning, till we become aware of the end.

We are fruit, we are an integral part of the tree. Till the time comes for us to fall, and we hang in suspense, realising that we are an integral part of the vast beyond, which stretches under us and grasps us even before we drop into it.

We are the beginning, which has conceived us within its womb of darkness, and nourished us to the fulness of our growth. This is ours that we adhere to. This is our God, Jehovah, Zeus, the Father of Heaven, this that has conceived and created us, in the beginning, and brought us the fulness of our strength.

And when we have come to the fulness of our strength, like lions which have been fed till they are full grown, then the strange necessity comes upon us, we must travel away, roam like falling fruit, fall from the initial darkness of the tree, of the cave which has reared us, into the eternal light of germination and begetting, the eternal light, shedding our darkness like the fruit that rots on the ground.

We travel across between the two great opposites of the Beginning and the End, the eternal night and everlasting day, and the transit is a stride taken, the night gives us up for the day to receive us. And what are we between the two?

But before the transit is accomplished, whilst we are yet like fruit heavy and ripe on the tree, we realise the delirious freedom of the end, the goal, and we cry: "Behold, I, who am here within the darkness, I am the light! I am the light, I am Unicorn, the beam of chastity. Behold, the beam of Virginity gleams within my loins, in this circumambient darkness. Behold, I am not the Beginning, I am the End. The End is universal light, the achieving again of infinite unblemished being, the infinite oneness of the Light, the escape from the infinite not-being of the darkness."

All the time, these cries take place within the womb, these are the myriad unborn uttering themselves as they come towards maturity, cry after cry as the darkness develops itself over the sea of light, and flesh is born, and limbs; cry after cry as the light develops within the darkness, and mind is born, and the consciousness of that which is inside my own flesh and limbs, and the desire for everlasting life grows more insistent.

These are the cries of the two adversaries, the two opposites.

First of all the flesh develops in splendour and glory out of the prolific darkness, begotten by the light it develops to a great triumph, till it dances naked in glory of itself, before the Ark, naked in glory of itself in the procession of heroes travelling towards the wise goodness, the white light, the Mind, the light which the vessel of living darkness has caught and captured within itself, and holds in triumph. The flesh of darkness triumphant circles round the treasure of light which it has enveloped, which it calls Mind, and this is the ecstasy, the dance before the Ark, the Bacchic delirium.

And then, within the womb, the light grows stronger and finds voice, it cries out: "Behold, I am free, I am not enveloped within this darkness. Behold, I am the everlasting light, the Eternity that stretches forward for ever, utterly the opposite of that darkness which departs backward, backward for ever. Come over to me, to the light, to the light that streams into the glorious eternity. For now the darkness is revoked for ever."

It is the voice of the unicorn crying in the wilderness, it is the Son of Man. And behold, in the fight, the unicorn beats the lion, and drives him out of town.

But all this is within the Womb. The darkness builds up the warm shadow of the flesh in splendour and triumph, enclosing the light. This is the zenith of David and Solomon, and of Assyria and Egypt. Then the light, wrestling within the vessel, throws up a white gleam of universal love, which is St. Francis of Assisi, and Shelley.

Then each has reached its maximum of self-assertion. The flesh is made perfect within the womb, the spirit is at last made perfect also, within the womb. They are equally perfect, equally supreme, the one adhering to the infinite darkness of the beginning, the other adhering to the infinite light of the end.

Yet, within the womb, they are eternally opposite. Darkness stands over against light, light stands over against dark. The lion is reared against the unicorn, the unicorn is reared against the lion. One says, "Behold, the darkness which gave us birth is eternal and infinite: this we belong to." The other says, "We are of the Light, which is everlasting and infinite."

And there is no reconciliation, save in negation. From the present, the stream flows in opposite directions, back to the past, on to the future. There are two goals, at opposite ends of time. There is the vast original dark out of which Creation issued, there is the Eternal light into which all mortality passes. And both are equally infinite, both are equally the goal, and both equally the beginning.

And we, fully equipped in flesh and spirit, fully built up of darkness, perfectly composed out of light, what are we but light and shadow lying together in opposition, or lion and unicorn fighting, the one to vanquish the other. This is our eternal life, in these two eternities which nullify each other. And we, between them both, what are we but nullity.

But this is because we see in part, always in part. We are enclosed within the womb, we are the seed from the loins of the eternal light, or we are the darkness which is enveloped by the body of the past, by our era.

Unless the sun were enveloped in the body of darkness, would a cast shadow run with me as I walk? Unless the night lay within the embrace of light, would the fish gleam phosphorescent in the sea, would the light break out of the black coals of the hearth, would the electricity gleam out of itself, suddenly declaring an opposite being?

Love and power, light and darkness, these are the temporary conquest of the one infinite by the other. In love, the Christian love, the End asserts itself supreme: in power, in strength like the lion's, the Beginning re-establishes itself unique. But when the opposition is complete on either side, then there is perfection. It is the perfect opposition of dark and light that brindles the tiger with gold flame and dark flame. It is the surcharge of darkness that opens the ravening mouth of the tiger, and drives his eyes to points of phosphorescence. It is the perfect balance of light and darkness that flickers in the stepping of a deer. But it is the conquered darkness that flares and palpitates in her eyes.

There are the two eternities fighting the fight of Creation, the light projecting itself into the darkness, the darkness enveloping herself within the embrace of light. And then there is the consummation of each in the other, the consummation of light in darkness and darkness in light, which is absolute: our bodies cast up like foam of two meeting waves, but foam which is absolute, complete, beyond the limitation of either infinity, consummate over both eternities. The direct opposites of the Beginning and the End, by their very directness, imply their own supreme relation. And this supreme relation is made absolute in the clash and the foam of the meeting waves. And the clash and the foam are the Crown, the Absolute.

The lion and the unicorn are not fighting *for* the Crown. They are fighting beneath it. And the Crown is upon their fight. If they made friends and lay down side by side, the Crown would fall on them both and kill them. If the lion really beat the unicorn, then the Crown pressing on the head of the king of beasts alone would destroy him. Which it has done and is doing. As it is destroying the unicorn who has achieved supremacy in another field.

So that now, in Europe, both the lion and the unicorn are gone mad, each with a crown tumbled on his bound-in head. And without rhyme or reason they tear themselves and each other, and the fight is no fight, it is a frenzy of blind things dashing themselves and each other to pieces.

Now the unicorn of virtue and virgin spontaneity has got the Crown slipped over the eyes, like a circle of utter light, and has gone mad with the extremity of light: whilst the lion of power and splendour, its own Crown of supreme night settled down upon it, roars in an agony of imprisoned darkness.

329

Now within the withered body of our era, within the husk of the past, the seed of light has come to supreme self-consciousness and has gone mad with the flare of eternal light in its eyes, whilst the fruit of darkness, unable to fall from the tree, has turned round towards the tree and is become mad, clinging faster upon the utter night whence it should have dropped away long ago.

For the stiffened, exhausted, inflexible loins of our era are too dry to give us forth in labour, the tree is withered, we are pent in, fastened, and now have turned round, some to the source of darkness, some to the source of light, and gone mad, purely given up to frenzy. For the dark has travelled to the light, and the light towards the dark. But then they reached the bound, neither could leap forth. The fruit could not fall from the tree, the lion just full grown could not get out of the cave, the unicorn could not enter the illimitable forest, the lily could not leap out of the darkness of her bulb straight into the sun. What then? The road was stopped. Whither then? Backward, back to the known eternity. There was a great, horrible huddle backwards. The process of birth had been arrested, the inflexible, withered loins of the mother-era were too old and set, the past was taut around us all. Then began the chaos, the going asunder, the beginning of nothingness. Then we leaped back, by reflex from the bound and limit, back upon ourselves, into madness.

There is a dark beyond the darkness of the womb, there is a light beyond the light of knowledge. There is the darkness of all the heavens for the seed of man to invest, and the light of all the heavens for the womb to receive. But we don't know it. How can the unborn within the womb know of the heavens outside; how can they?

How can they know of the tides beyond? On the one hand murmurs the utter, infinite sea of darkness, full of unconceived creation: on the other the infinite light stirs with eternal procreation. They are two seas which eternally attract and oppose each other, two tides which eternally advance to repel each other, which foam upon one another, as the ocean foams on the land, and the land rushes down into the sea.

And we, in the great movement, are begotten, conceived and brought forth, like the waves which meet and clash and burst up into foam, sending the foam like light, like shadow, into the zenith of the absolute, beyond the grasp of either eternity.

We are the foam and the foreshore, that which, between the oceans, is not, but that which supersedes the oceans in utter reality, and gleams in absolute Eternity.

The Beginning is-not, nor the eternity which lies behind us, save in part. Partial also is the eternity which lies in front. But that which is not partial, but whole, that which is not relative, but absolute, is the clash of the two into one, the foam of being thrown up into consummation.

It is the music which comes when the cymbals clash one upon the other: this is absolute and timeless. The cymbals swing back in one or the other direction of time, towards one or the other relative eternity. But absolute, timeless, beyond time or eternity, beyond space or infinity, is the music that was the consummation of the two cymbals in opposition.

It is that which comes when night clashes on day, the rainbow, the yellow and rose and blue and purple of dawn and sunset, which leaps out of the breaking of light upon darkness, of darkness upon light, absolute beyond day or night; the rainbow, the iridescence which is darkness at once and light, the two-in-one; the crown that binds them both.

It is the lovely body of foam that walks forever between the two seas, perfect and consummate, the revealed consummation, the oneness that has taken being out of the two.

We say the foam is evanescent, the wind passes over it and it is gone, he who would save his life must lose it.

But if indeed the foam were-not, if the two seas fell apart, if the sea fell departed from the land, and the land from the sea, if the two halves, day and night, were ripped asunder, without attraction or opposition, what then? Then there would be between them nothingness, utter nothingness. Which is meaningless.

So that the foam and the iridescence, the music that comes from the cymbals, all formed things that come from perfect union in opposition, all beauty and all truth and being, all perfection, these are the be-all and the end-all, absolute, timeless, beyond time or eternity, beyond the Limit or the Infinite.

This lovely body of foam, this iris between the two floods, this music between the cymbals, this truth between the surge of facts, this supreme reason between conflicting desires, this holy spirit between the opposite divinities, this is the Absolute made visible between the two Infinities, the Timelessness into which are assumed the two Eternities.

It is wrong to try to make the lion lie down with the lamb. This is the supreme sin, the unforgivable blasphemy of which Christ spoke. This is the creating of nothingness, the bringing about, or the striving to bring about the nihil which is pure meaninglessness.

The great darkness of the lion must gather into itself the little, feeble darkness of the lamb. The great light of the lamb must absorb elsewhere, in the whole world, the small, weak light of the lion. The lamb indeed will inherit the world, rather than the lion. It is the triumph of the meek. But the meek, like the merciless, shall perish in their own triumph. Anything that *triumphs,* perishes. The consummation comes from perfect relatedness. To this a man may *win.* But he who triumphs, perishes.

The crown is upon the perfect balance of the fight, it is not the fruit of either victory. The crown is not prize of either combatant. It is the *raison d'être* of both. It is the absolute within the fight.

And those alone are evil, who say, "The lion shall lie down with the lamb, the eagle shall mate with the dove, the lion shall munch in the stable of the unicorn." For they blaspheme against the *raison d'être* of all life, they try to destroy the essential, intrinsic nature of God.

But it is the fight of opposites which is holy. The fight of like things is evil. For if a thing turn round upon itself, in blind frenzy of destruction, this is to say: "The lamb shall roar like the lion, the dove strike down her prey like the eagle, and the unicorn shall devour the innocent virgin in her path." Which is precisely the equivalent blasphemy to the blasphemy of universal meekness, or peace.

And this, this last, is our blasphemy of the war. We would have the lamb roar like the lion, all doves turn into eagles.

The Lion beat the Unicorn
And drove him out of town

Life is a travelling to the edge of knowledge, then a leap taken. We cannot know beforehand. We are driven from behind, always as over the edge of the precipice.

It is a leap taken, into the beyond, as a lark leaps into the sky, a fragment of earth which travels to be fused out, sublimated, in the shining of the heavens.

But it is not death. Death is neither here nor there. Death is a temporal, relative fact. In the absolute, it means nothing. The lark falls from the sky and goes running back to her nest. This is the ebb of the wave. The wave of earth flung up in spray, a lark, a cloud of larks, against the white wave of the sun. The spray of earth and the foam of heaven are one, consummated, a rainbow mid-way, a song. The larks return to earth, the rays go back to heaven. But these are only the shuttles that weave the iris, the song, mid-way, in absoluteness, timelessness.

Out of the dark, original flame issues a tiny green flicker, a weed coming alive. On the edge of the bright, ultimate, spiritual flame of the heavens is revealed a fragment of iris, a touch of green, a weed coming into being. The two flames surge and intermingle, casting up a crest of leaves and stems, their battlefield, their meeting-ground, their marriage bed, the embrace becomes closer, more unthinkably vivid, it leaps to climax, the battle grows fiercer, fiercer, intolerably, till there is the swoon, the climax, the consummation, the little yellow disk gleams absolute between heaven and earth, radiant of both eternities, framed in the two infinities. Which is a weed, a sow-thistle bursting into blossom. And we, the foreshore in whom the waves of dark and light are unequally seething, we can see this perfection, this absolute, as time opens to disclose it for a moment, like the Dove that hovered incandescent from heaven, before it is closed again in utter timelessness.

"But the wind passeth over it and it is gone."

The wind passes over it and *we* are gone. It is time which blows in like a wind, closing up the clouds again upon the perfect gleam. It is the wind of time, out of either eternity, a wind which has a source and an issue, which swirls past the light of this absolute, like waves past a lighted buoy. For the light is not temporal nor eternal, but absolute. And we, who are temporal and eternal, at moments only we cease from our temporality. In these our moments we see the sow-thistle gleaming, light within darkness, darkness within light, consummated, we are with the song and the iris.

And then it is we, not the iris, not the song, who are blown away. We are blown for a moment against the yellow light of the window, the flower, then on again into the dark turmoil.

We have made a mistake. We are like travellers travelling in a train who watch the country pass by and pass away; all of us who watch the sun setting, sliding down into extinction, we are mistaken. It is not the country which passes by and fades, it is not the sun which sinks to oblivion. Neither is it the flower that withers, nor the song that dies out.

It is we who are carried past in the seethe of mortality. The flower is timeless and beyond condition. It is we who are swept on in the condition of time. So we shall be swept as long as time lasts. Death is part of the story. But we have being also in timelessness, we shall become again absolute, as we have been absolute, as we are absolute.

We know that we are purely absolute. We know in the last issue we are absolved from all opposition. We know that in the process of life we are purely relative. But timelessness is our fate, and time is subordinate to our fate. But time is eternal.

And the life of man is like a flower that comes into blossom and passes away. In the beginning, the light touches the darkness, the darkness touches the light, and the two embrace. They embrace in opposition, only in their desire is their unanimity. There are two separate statements, the dark wants the light, and the light wants the dark. But these two statements are contained within the one: "They want each other." And this is the condition of absoluteness, this condition of their wanting each other, that which makes light and dark consummate even in opposition. The interrelation between them, this is constant and absolute, let it be called love or power or what it may. It is all the things that it can be called.

In the beginning, light touches darkness and darkness touches light. Then life has begun. The light enfolds and implicates and involves the dark, the dark receives and interpenetrates the light, they come nearer, they are more finely combined, till they burst into the crisis of oneness, the blossom, the utter being, the transcendent and timeless flame of the iris.

Then time passes on. Out of the swoon the waves ebb back, dark towards the dark, light towards the light. They ebb back and away, the leaves return unto the darkness of the earth, the quivering glimmer of substance returns into the light, the green of the last wavering iris disappears, the waves ebb apart, further, further, further.

Yet they never separate. The whole flood recedes, the tides are going to separate. And they separate entirely, save for one enfolded ripple, the tiny, silent, scarce-visible enfolded pools of the seeds. These lie potent, the meeting-ground, the well-head wherein the tides will surge again, when the turn comes.

This is the life of man. In him too the tide sweeps together towards the utter consummation, the consummation with the darkness, the consummation with the light, flesh and spirit, one culminating crisis, when man passes into timelessness and absoluteness.

The residue of imperfect fusion and unfulfilled desire remains, the child, the well-head where the tides will flow in again, the seed. The absolute relation is never fully revealed. It leaps to its maximum of revelation in the flower, the mature life. But some of it rolls aside, lies potent in the enfolded seed. *My* desire is fulfilled, I, as individual am become timeless and absolute, perfect. But the whole desire of which I am part remains yet to be consummated. In me the two waves clash to perfect consummation. But immediately upon the clash come the next waves of the tide rippling in, the ripples, forerunners, which tinily meet and enfold each other, the seed, the unborn child. For we are all waves of the tide. But the tide contains all the waves.

It may happen that waves which meet and mingle come to no consummation, only a confusion and a swirl and a falling away again. These are the myriad lives of human beings which pass in confusion of nothingness, the uncreated lives. There are myriads of human lives that are not absolute nor timeless, myriads that just waver and toss temporarily, never become more than relative, never come into being. They have no being, no immortality. There are myriads of plants that never come to flower, but which perish away for ever, always separated in the fringe of time, never united, never consummated never brought forth.

I know I am compound of two waves, I, who am temporal and mortal. When I am timeless and absolute, all duality has vanished. But whilst I am temporal and mortal, I am framed in the struggle and embrace of the two opposite waves of darkness and of light.

There is the wave of light in me which seeks the darkness, which has for its goal the Source and the Beginning, for its God the Almighty Creator to Whom is all power and glory. Thither the light of the seed of man struggles and aspires, into the infinite darkness, the womb of all creation.

What way is it that leads me on to the Source, to the Beginning? It is the way of the blood, the way of power. Down the road of the blood, further and further into the darkness, I come to the Almighty God Who was in the beginning, is now, and ever shall be. I come to the Source of Power. I am received back into the utter darkness of the Creator, I am once again with Him.

This is a consummation, a becoming eternal. This is an arrival into eternity. But eternity is only relative.

I can become one with God, consummated into eternity, by taking the road down the senses into the utter darkness of power, till I am one with the darkness of initial power, beyond knowledge of any opposite.

It is thus, seeking consummation in the utter darkness, that I come to the woman in desire. She is the doorway, she is the gate to the dark eternity of power, the creator's power. When I put my hand on her, my heart beats with a passion of fear and ecstasy, for I touch my own passing away, my own ceasing-to-be, I apprehend my own consummation in a darkness which obliterates me in its infinity. My veins rock as if they were being destroyed, the blood takes fire on the edge of oblivion, and beats backward and forward. I resist, yet I am compelled; the woman resists, yet she is compelled. And we are the relative parts dominated by the strange compulsion of the absolute.

Gradually my veins relax their gates, gradually the rocking blood goes forward, quivers on the edge of oblivion, then yields itself up, passes into the borderland of oblivion. Oh, and then I would die, I would quickly die, to have all power, all life at once, to come instantly to pure, eternal oblivion, the source of life. But patience is fierce at the bottom of me; fierce, indomitable, abiding patience. So my blood goes forth in shock after shock of delirious passing-away, in shock after shock entering into consummation, till my soul is slipping its moorings, my mind, my will fuses down, I melt out and am gone into the eternal darkness, the primal creative darkness reigns, and I am not, and at last *I am*.

Shock after shock of ecstasy and the anguish of ecstasy, death after death of trespass into the unknown, till I fall down into the flame, I lapse into the intolerable flame, a pallid shadow I am transfused into the flux of unendurable darkness, and am gone. No spark nor vestige remains within the supreme dark flow of the flame, I am contributed again to the immortal source. I am with the dark Almighty of the beginning.

Till, new-created, I am thrown forth again on the shore of creation, warm and lustrous, goodly, new-born from the darkness out of which all time has issued.

And then, new-born on the knees of darkness, new-issued from the womb of creation, I open my eyes to the light and know the goal, the end, the light which stands over the end of the journey, the everlasting day, the oneness of the spirit.

The new journey, the new life has begun, the travelling to the opposite eternity, to the infinite light of the Spirit, the consummation in the Spirit.

My source and issue is in two eternities, I am founded in the two infinities. But absolute is the rainbow that goes between; the iris of my very being.

It may be, however, that the seed of light never propagates within the darkness, that the light in me is sterile, that I am never re-born within the womb, the Source, to be issued towards the opposite eternity.

It may be there is a great inequality, disproportion, within me, that I am nearly all darkness, like the night, with a few glimmers of cold light, moonlight, like the tiger with white eyes of reflected light brindled in the flame of darkness. Then I shall return again and again to the womb of the darkness, avid, never satisfied, my spirit will fall unfertile into the womb, will never be conceived there, never brought forth. I shall know the one consummation, the one direction only, into the darkness. It will be with me forever the almost, almost, almost, of satisfaction, of fulfilment. I shall know the one eternity, the one infinite, the one immortality, I shall have partial being; but never the whole, never the full. There is an infinite which does not know me. I am always relative, always partial, always, in the last issue, unconsummate.

The barren womb can never be satisfied, if the quick of darkness be sterile within it. But neither can the unfertile loins be satisfied, if the seed of light, of the spirit, be dead within them. They will return again and again and again to the womb of darkness, asking, asking, and never satisfied.

Then the unconsummated soul, unsatisfied, uncreated in part, will seek to make itself whole by bringing the whole world under its one order, will seek to make itself absolute and timeless by devouring its opposite. Adhering to the one eternity of darkness, it will seek to devour the eternity of light. Realising the one infinite of the Source, it will endeavour to absorb into its oneness the opposite infinite of the Goal. This is the infinite with its tail in its mouth.

Consummated in one infinite, and one alone, this soul will assert the oneness of all things, that all things are one in the One Infinite of the Darkness, of the Source. One is one and all alone and ever more shall be so. This is the cry of the Soul consummated in one eternity only.

There is one eternity, one infinite, one God. "Thou shalt have no other god before me.

But why this Commandment, unless there were in truth another god, at least the equal of Jehovah?

Consummated in the darkness only, having not enough strength in the light, the partial soul cries out in a convulsion of insistence that the darkness alone is infinite and eternal, that all light is from the small, contained sources, the lamps lighted at will by the desire of the Creator, the sun, the moon and stars. These are the lamps and candles of the Almighty, which He blows out at will. These are little portions of special darkness, darkness transfigured, these lights.

There is one God, one Creator, one Almighty; there is one infinite and one eternity, it is the infinite and the eternity of the Source. There is One Way: it is the

Way of the Law. There is One Life, the Life of Creation, there is one Goal, the Beginning, there is one immortality, the immortality of the great I AM. All is God, the One God. Those who deny this are to be stamped out, tortured, tortured for ever.

It is possible then to deny it?

Having declared the One God, then the partial soul, fulfilled of the darkness only, proceeds to establish this God on earth, to devour and obliterate all else.

Rising from the darkness of consummation in the flesh, with the woman, it seeks to establish its kingdom over all the world. It strides forth, the lord, the master, strong for mastery. It will dominate all, all, it will bring all under the rules of itself, of the One, the Darkness lighted with the lamps of its own choice.

This is the heroic tyrant, the fabulous king-warrior, like Sardanapalus or Caesar, like Saul even. These warrior kings seek to pass beyond all relatedness, to become absolute in might and power. And they fall inevitably. Their Judas is a David, a Brutus: the individual who knows something of both flames, but commits himself to neither. He holds himself, in his own ego, superior either to the creative dark power-flame, or the conscious love-flame. And so, he is the small man slaying the great. He is virtuous egoistic Brutus, or David: David slaying the preposterous Goliath, overthrowing the heroic Saul, taking Bathsheba and sending Uriah to death: David dancing naked before the Ark, asserting the oneness, his own oneness, the one infinity, *himself* the egoistic God, I AM. And David never went in unto Michal any more, because she jeered at him. So that she was barren all her life.

But it was David who really was barren. Michal, when she mocked, mocked the sterility of David. For the spirit in him was blasted with unfertility; he could not become born again, he could not be conceived in the spirit. Michal, the womb of profound darkness, could not conceive to the overweak seed of David's spirit. David's seed was too impure, too feeble in sheer spirit, too egoistic, it bred and begot preponderant egoists. The flood of vanity set in after David, the lamps and candles began to gutter.

Power is sheer flame, and spirit is sheer flame, and between them is the clue of the Holy Ghost. But David put a false clue between them: the clue of his own ego, cunning and *triumphant.*

It is unfertility of spirit which sends man raging to the woman, and sends him raging away again, unsatisfied. It is not the woman's barrenness: it is his own. It is sterility in himself which makes a Don Juan.

And the course of the barren spirit is dogmatically to assert One God, One Way, one Glory, one exclusive salvation. And this One God is indeed God, this one Way is the way, but it is the way of egoism and the One God is the reflection, inevitably, of the worshipper's ego.

This is the sham Crown, which the victorious lion and the victorious unicorn alike puts on his own head. When either *triumphs,* the true crown disappears, and the triumphant puts a false crown on his own head: the crown of sterile egoism. The true Crown is above the fight itself, and above the embrace itself, not upon the brow of either fighter or lover. Or, if you like, in the true fight it shines equally upon the brow of the defeated and the winner. For sometimes it is blessed to be beaten in a fight.

He who triumphs, perishes. As Caesar perished, and Napoleon. In the fight they were wonderful, and the power was with them. But when they would be supreme, sheer triumphers, exalted in their own ego they fell. Triumph is a false absolution, the winner salutes his enemy, and the light of victory is on *both* their brows, since both are consummated.

In the same way, Jesus triumphant perished. Any individual who will triumph, in love or in war, perishes. There is no triumph. There is but consummation, in either case.

So Shelley also perishes. He wants to be love triumphant, as Napoleon wanted to be power triumphant. Both fell.

In both, there is the spuriousness of the *ego* trying to seize the Crown that belongs only to the consummation.

In the Roman "Triumph" itself lay the source of Rome's downfall. And in the arrogance of England's dispensation of Liberty in the world lies the downfall of England. When Liberty triumphs, as in Russia, where then is the British Empire? Where then is the British Lion, crowned *Fidei Defensor,* Defender of the Faith of Liberty and Love? When Liberty needs no more defending, then the protective lion had better look out.

Take care of asserting any absolute, either of power or love, of empire or of democracy. The moment power *triumphs,* it becomes spurious with sheer egoism, like Caesar and Napoleon. And the moment democracy triumphs, it too becomes hideous with egoism, like Russia now.

Either lion or unicorn, triumphant, turns into a sheer beast of prey. Foe it has none: only prey: or victims.

So we have seen in the world, every time that power has triumphed: every time the lion and the eagle have jammed the crown down on their heads. Now it will be given us to see democracy triumphant, the unicorn and the dove seizing the crown, and on the instant turning into beasts of prey.

The true crown is upon the consummation itself, not upon the triumph of one over another, neither in love nor in power. The ego is the false absolute. And the ego crowned with the crown is the monster and the tyrant, whether it represent one man, an Emperor, or a whole mass of people, a Demos. A million egos summed up under a crown are not *better* than one individual crowned ego. They are a million times worse.

III

The Flux of Corruption

The tiger blazed transcendent into immortal darkness. The unique phoenix of the desert grew up to maturity and wisdom. Sitting upon her tree, she was the only one of her kind in all creation, supreme, the zenith, the perfect aristocrat. She attained to perfection, eagle-like she rose in her nest and lifted her wings, surpassing the zenith of mortality; so she was translated into the flame of eternity, she became one with the fiery Origin.

It was not for her to sit tight, and assert her own tight ego. She was gone as she came.

In the nest was a little ash, a little flocculent grey dust wavering upon a blue-red, dying coal. The red coal stirred and gathered strength, gradually it grew white with heat, it shot forth sharp gold flames. It was the young phoenix within the

337

nest, with curved beak growing hard and crystal, like a scimitar, and talons hardening into pure jewels.

Wherein, however, is the immortality, in the constant occupation of the nest, the widow's cruse, or in the surpassing of the phoenix? She goes gadding off into flame, into her consummation. In the flame she is timeless. But the ash within the nest lies in the restless hollow of time, shaken on the tall tree of the desert. It will rise to the same consummation, become absolute in flame.

In a low, shady bush, far off, on the other side of the world, where the rains are cold and the mists wrap the leaves in a chillness, the ring-dove presses low on the bough, while her mate sends forth the last ru-cuooo of peace. The mist darkens and ebbs-in in waves, the trees are melted away, all things pass into a universal oneness, with the last re-echoing dove, peace, all pure peace, ebbing in softer, softer waves to a universal stillness.

The dark blue tranquillity is universal and infinite, the doves are asleep in the sleeping boughs, all fruits are fallen and are silent and cold, all the leaves melt away into pure mist of darkness.

It is strange, that away on the other side of the world, the tiger gleams through the hot-purple darkness, and where the dawn comes crimson, the phoenix lifts her wings in a yawn like an over-sumptuous eagle, and passes into flame above the golden palpable fire of the desert.

Here are the opposing hosts of angels, the ruddy choirs, the upright, rushing flames, the lofty Cherubim that palpitate about the Presence, the Source; and then the tall, still angels soft and pearly as mist, who await round the Goal, the attendants that hover on the edge of the last Assumption.

And from the seed two travellers set forth, in opposite directions, the one concentrating towards the upper, ruddy, blazing sun, the zenith, the creative fire, the other towards the blue, cold silence, dividing itself and ever dividing itself till it is infinite in the universal darkness.

And at the summit, the zenith, there is a flash, a flame, as the traveller enters into infinite, there is a red splash as the poppy leaps into the upper, fiery eternity. And far below there is unthinkable silence as the roots ramify and divide and pass into the oneness of unutterable silence.

The flame is gone, the flower has leapt away, the fruit ripens and falls. Then dark ebbs back to dark, and light to light, hot to hot, and cold to cold. This is death and decay and corruption. And the worm, the maggot, these are the ministers of separation, these are the tiny clashing ripples that still ebb together, when the chief tide has set back, to flow utterly apart.

This is the terror and wonder of dark returning to dark, and of light returning to light, the two departing back to their Sources. This we cannot bear to think of. It is the temporal flux of corruption, as the flux together was the temporal flux of creation. The flux is temporal. It is only the perfect meeting, the perfect utter interpenetration into oneness, the kiss, the blow, the two-in-one, that is timeless and absolute.

And dark is not willing to return to dark till it has known the light, nor light to light till it has known the dark, till the two have been consummated into oneness. But the act of death may itself be a consummation, and life may be a state of negation.

It may be that our state of life is itself a denial of the consummation, a prevention, a negation; that this life is our nullification, our not-being.

It may be that the flower is held from the search of the light, and the roots from the dark, like a plant that is pot-bound. It may be that, as in the autumnal cabbage, the light and the dark are made prisoners in us, their opposition is overcome, the ultimate moving has ceased. We have forgotten our goal and our end. We have enclosed ourselves in our exfoliation, there are many little channels that run out into the sand.

This is evil, when that which is temporal and relative asserts itself eternal and absolute. This I, which I am, has no being save in timelessness. In my consummation, when that which came from the Beginning and that which came from the End are transfused into oneness, then I come into being, I have existence. Till then I am only a part of nature: I *am* not.

But as part of nature, as part of the flux, I have my instrumental identity, my inferior I, my self-conscious ego.

If I say that *I am,* this is false and evil. I am not. Among us all, how many have being?—too few. Our ready-made individuality, our identity is no more than an accidental cohesion in the flux of time. The cohesion will break down and utterly cease to be. The atoms will return into the flux of the universe. And that unit of cohesion which I was will vanish utterly. Matter is indestructible, spirit is indestructible. This of us remains, in any case, general in the flux. But the soul that has not come into being has no being for ever. The soul does not come into being at birth. The soul comes into being in the midst of life, just as the phoenix in her maturity becomes immortal in flame. That is not her perishing: it is her becoming absolute: a blossom of fire. If she did not pass into flame, *she* would never really exist. It is by her translation into fire that she is the phoenix. Otherwise she were only a bird, a transitory cohesion in the flux.

It is absurd to talk about all men being immortal, all having souls. Very few men have being at all. They perish utterly, as individuals. Their endurance afterwards is the endurance of Matter within the flux, non-individual: and spirit within the flux. Most men are just transitory natural phenomena. Whether they live or die does not matter: except in so far as every failure in the part is a failure in the whole. Their death is of no more matter than the cutting of a cabbage in the garden, an act utterly apart from grace.

They assert themselves as important, as absolute mortals. They are just liars. When one cuts a fat autumnal cabbage, one cuts off a lie, to boil it down in the pot.

They are all just fat lies, these people, these many people, these mortals They are innumerable cabbages in the regulated cabbage plot. And our great men are no more than Mrs. Wiggs of the Cabbage Patch.

The cabbage is a nice fat lie. That is why we eat it. It is the business of the truthful to eat up the lies. A fatted cow is a lie, and a fat pig is a lie, and a fatted sheep is a lie, just the same: these sacrificial beasts, lambs and calves, become fat lies when they are merely protected and fed full.

The cabbage is a lie because it asserts itself as a permanency, in the state wherein it finds itself. In the swirl of the Beginning and the End, stalk and leaves take place. But the stalk and leaves are only the swirl of the waves. Yet they say, they are absolute, they have achieved a permanent form. It is a lie. Their universal absolute is only the far-off dawning of the truth, the false dawn which in itself is nothing, nothing except in relation to that which comes after.

But they say, "We are the consummation and the reality, we are the fulfilment." This is pure amorphousness. Each one becomes a single, separate entity, a single separate nullity. Having started along the way to eternity, they say, "We are there, we have arrived," and they enclose themselves in the nullity of the falsehood.

And this is the state of man, when he falls into self-sufficiency and asserts that his self-conscious ego is It. He falls into the condition of fine cabbages.

Then they are wealthy and fat. They go no further, so they become wealthy. All that great force which would carry them naked over the edge of time, into timelessness, into being, they convert into fatness, into having. And they are full of self-satisfaction. Having no being, they assert their artificial completeness, and the life within them becomes a will-to-have; which is the expression of the will-to-persist, in the temporary unit. Selfishness is the subjugating of all things to a false entity, and riches is the great flux over the edge of the bottomless pit, the falsity, the nullity. For where is the rich man who is not the very bottomless pit? Travel nearer, nearer, nearer to him, and one comes to the gap, the hole, the abyss where his soul should be. He *is* not. And to stop up his hollowness, he drags all things unto himself.

And what are we all, all of us, collectively, even the poorest, now, in this age? We are only *potentially* rich men. We are all alike. The distinction between rich and poor is purely accidental. Rich and poor alike are only, each one, a pit-head surrounding the bottomless pit. But the rich man, by pouring vast quantities of matter down his void, gives himself a more pleasant illusion of fulfilment than the poor man can get: that is all. Yet we would give our lives, every one of us, for this illusion.

There are no rich or poor, there are no masses and middle classes and aristocrats. There are myriads of framed gaps, people, and a few timeless fountains, men and women. That is all.

Myriads of framed gaps! Myriads of little egos, all wearing the crown of life! Myriads of little Humpty-Dumpties, self-satisfied emptinesses, all about to have a great fall.

The current ideal is to be a gap with a great heap of matter around it, which can be sent clattering down. The most sacred thing is to give all your having so that it can be put on the heaps that surround all the other bottomless pits. If you give away all your having, even your life, then, you are a bottomless pit with no sides to it. Which is infinite. So that to become infinite, give away all your having, even to your life. So that you will achieve immortality yourself. Like the heroes of the war, you will become the bottomless pit itself; but more than this, you will be contributing to the public good, you will be one of those who make blessed history: which means, you will be heaping goods upon the dwindling heaps of superfluity that surrounds these bottomless lives of the myriad people. If we poor can each of us hire a servant, then the servant will be like a stone tumbling always ahead of us down the bottomless pit. Which creates an almost perfect illusion of having a solid earth beneath us.

Long ago we agreed that we had fulfilled all purpose and that our only business was to look after other people. We said; "It is marvellous, we are really complete." If the regulation cabbage, hide-bound and solid, could walk about on his stalk, he would be very much as we are. He would think of himself as we think of ourselves, he would talk as *we* talk, of the public good.

But inside him, proper and fine, the heart would be knocking and urgent, the heart of the cabbage. Of course for a long time he would not hear it. His good, enveloping green leaves outside, the heap round the hole, would have closed upon him very early, like Wordsworth's "Shades of the prison house," very close and complete and gratifying.

But the heart would beat within him, beat and beat, grow louder and louder, till it was threshing the whole of his inside rotten, threshing him hollow, till his inside began to devour his consciousness.

Then he would say: "I must do something." Looking round, he would see little dwindly cabbages struggling in the patch, and would say: "So much injustice, so much suffering and poverty in the world, it cannot be." Then he would set forth to make dwindly cabbages into proper, fine cabbages. So he would be a reformer.

He would kick, kick, kick against the conditions which make some cabbages poor and dwindly, most cabbages poorer and more dwindly than himself. He would but be kicking against the pricks.

But it is very profitable to kick against the pricks. It gives one a sensation, and saves one the necessity of bursting. If our reformers had not had the prickly wrongs of the poor to kick, so that they hurt their toe quite sorely, they might long ago have burst outwards from the enclosed form in which we have kept secure.

Let no one suffer, they have said. No mouse shall be caught by a cat, no mouse. It is a transgression. Every mouse shall become a pet, and every cat shall lap milk in peace, from the saucer, of utter benevolence.

This is the millennium, the golden age that is to be, when all shall be domesticated, and the lion and the leopard and the hawk shall come to our door to lap milk and to peck the crumbs, and no sound shall be heard but the lowing of fat cows and the baa-ing of fat sheep.

This is the Green Age that is to be, the age of the perfect cabbage. This was our hope and our fulfilment, for this, in this hope, we lived and we died.

So the virtuous, public-spirited ones have suffered bitterly from the aspect of their myriad more-or-less blighted neighbours, whom they love as themselves. They have lived and died to right the wrong conditions of social injustice.

Meanwhile, the threshing has continued at the core of us, till our entrails are threshed rotten. We are a wincing mass of self-consciousness and corruption, within our plausible rind. The most unselfish, the most humanitarian of us all, he is the hollowest and fullest of rottenness. The more rotten we become, the more insistent and insane becomes our desire to ameliorate the conditions of our poorer, and maybe healthier neighbours.

Fools, vile fools! Why cannot we acknowledge and admit the horrible pulse and thresh of corruption within us. What *is* this self-consciousness that palpitates within us like a disease? What is it that threshes and threshes within us, drives us mad if we see a cat catch a sparrow?

We dare not know. Oh, we are convulsed with shame long before we come to the point. It is indecent beyond endurance to think of it.

Yet here let it be told. It was the living desire for immortality, for *being,* which urged us ceaselessly. It was the bud within the cabbage, threshing, threshing,

threshing. And now, oh our convulsion of shame, when we must know this! We would rather die.

Yet it shall be made known. It was the struggling of the light and darkness within us, towards consummation, towards absoluteness, towards flowering. Oh, we shriek with anger of shame as the truth comes out: that the cabbage is rotten within because it wanted to straddle up into weakly fiery flower, wanted to straddle forth in a spire of ragged, yellow, inconsequential blossom.

Oh God, it is unendurable, this revelation, this disclosure, it is not to be borne. Our souls perish in an agony of self-conscious shame, we will not have it.

Yet had we listened, the hide-bound cabbage might have burst, might have opened apart, for a venturing forth of the tender, timid, ridiculous cluster of aspirations, that issue in little yellow tips of flame, the flowers naked in eternity, naked above the staring unborn crowd of amorphous entities, the cabbages: the myriad egos.

But the crowd of assertive egos, of tough entities, they were too strong, too many. Quickly they extinguished any shoot of tender immortality from among them, violently they adhered to the null rind and to the thresh of rottenness within.

Still the living desire beat and threshed at the heart of us, relentlessly. And still the fixed will of the temporal form we have so far attained, the static, mid-way form, triumphed in assertion.

Still the false I, the ego, held down the real, unborn I, which is a blossom with all a blossom's fragility.

Yet constantly the rising flower pushed and thrust at the belly and heart of us, thrashed and beat relentlessly. If it could not beat its way through into being, it must thrash us hollow. Let it do so then, we said. This also we enjoy, this being threshed rotten inside. This is sensationalism, reduction of the complex tissue back through rottenness to its elements. And this sensationalism, this reduction back, has become our very life, our only form of life at all. We enjoy it, it is our lust.

It became at last a collective activity, a war, when, within the great rind of virtue we thresh destruction further and further, till our whole civilisation is like a great rind full of corruption, of breaking down, a mere shell threatened with collapse upon itself.

And the road of corruption leads back to one eternity. The activity of utter going apart has, in eternity, a result equivalent to the result of utter coming together. The tiger rises supreme, the last brindled flame upon the darkness; the deer melts away, a blood-stained shadow received into the utter pallor of light; each having leapt forward into eternity, at opposite extremes. Within the closed shell of the Christian conception, we lapse utterly back, through reduction, back to the Beginning. It is the triumph of death, of decomposition.

And the process is that of the serpent lying prone in the cold, watery fire of corruption, flickering with the flowing-apart of the two streams. His belly is white with the light flowing forth from him, his back is dark and brindled where the darkness returns to the Source. He is the ridge where the two floods flow apart. So in the orange-speckled belly of the newt, the light is taking leave of the darkness, and returning to the light; the imperious, demon-like crest is the flowing home of the darkness. He is the god within the flux of corruption, from him proceeds the great retrogression back to the Beginning and back to the End. These are our gods.

There are elsewhere the golden angels of the Kiss, the golden, fiery angels of strife, those that have being when we come together, as opposites, as complements coming to consummation. There is delight and triumph elsewhere, these angels sound their loud trumpets. Then men are like brands that have burst spontaneously into flame, the phoenix, the tiger, the glistening dove, the white-burning unicorn.

But here are only the angels that cleave asunder, terrible and invincible. With cold, irresistible hands they put us apart, they send like unto like, darkness unto darkness. They thrust the seas backward from embrace, backward from the locked strife. They set the cold phosphorescent flame of light flowing back to the light, and cold heavy darkness flowing back to the darkness. They are the absolute angels of corruption, they are the snake, the newt, the water-lily, as reflected from below.

I cease to be, my darkness lapses into utter, stone darkness, my light into a light that is keen and cold as frost.

This goes on within the rind. But the rind remains permanent, falsely absolute, my false absolute self, my self-conscious ego. Till the work of corruption is finished; then the rind also, the public form, the civilisation, the established consciousness of mankind disappears as well in the mouth of the worm, taken unutterably asunder by the hands of the angels of separation. It ceases to be, all the civilisation and all the consciousness, it passes utterly away, a temporary cohesion in the flux. It was this, this rind, this persistent temporary cohesion, that was evil, this alone was evil. And it destroys us all before itself is destroyed.

IV

Within the Sepulchre

Within the womb of the established past, the light has entered the darkness, the future is conceived. It is conceived, the beginning of the end has taken place. Light is within the grip of darkness, darkness within the embrace of light, the Beginning and the End are closed upon one another.

They come nearer and nearer, till the oneness is full grown within the womb of the past, within the belly of Time, it must move out, must be brought forth, into timelessness.

But something withholds it. The pregnancy is accomplished, the hour of labour has come. Yet the labour does not begin. The loins of the past are withered, the young unborn is shut in.

All the time, within the womb, light has been travelling to the dark, the interfusion of the two into a oneness has continued. Now that it is fulfilled, it meets with some arrest. It is the dry walls of the womb which cannot relax.

There is a struggle. Then the darkness, having overcome the light, reaching the dead null wall of the womb, reacts into self-consciousness, and recoils upon itself. At the same time the light has surpassed its limit, become conscious, and starts in reflex to recoil upon itself. Thus the false I comes into being: the I which thinks itself supreme and infinite, and which is, in fact, a sick foetus shut up in the walls of an unrelaxed womb.

Here, at this moment when the birth pangs should begin, when the great opposition between the old and the young should take place, when the young should beat back the old body that surrounds it, and the old womb and loins should expel the young body, there is a deadlock. The two cannot fight apart. The walls of the old body are inflexible and insensible, the unborn does not know that there can be any travelling forth. It conceives itself as the whole universe, surrounded by dark nullity. It does not know that it is in prison. It believes itself to have filled up the whole of the universe, right to the extremes where is nothing but blank nullity.

T is tremendously conceited. It can only react upon itself. And the reaction can only take the form of self-consciousness. For the self is everything, universal, the surrounding womb is just the outer darkness in which that which *is,* exists. Therefore there remains either to die, to pass into the outer darkness, or to enter into self-knowledge.

So the unborn recoils upon itself, dark upon dark, light upon light. This is the horror of corruption begun already within the unborn, already dissolution and corruption set in before birth. And this is the triumph of the ego.

Mortality has usurped the Crown. The unborn, reacting upon the null walls of the womb, assumes that it has reached the limit of all space and all being. It concludes that its self is fulfilled, that all consummation is achieved. It takes for certain that itself has filled the whole of space and the whole of time.—And this is the glory of the ego.

There is no more fight to be fought, there is no more to be sought and embraced. All is fought and overcome, all is embraced and contained. It is all concluded, there is nothing remains but the outer nothingness. The only activity is the reaction against the outer nothingness, into the achieved being of the self, all else is fulfilled and concluded. To die is merely to assume nothingness. The limit of all life is reached.

And this is the apotheosis of the ego.

So there is the great turning round upon the self, dark upon dark, light upon light, the flux of separation, corruption within the unborn. The tides which are set towards each other swirl back as from a promontory which intervenes. There has been no consummation. There can be no consummation. The only thing is to return, to go back, that which came from the Beginning to go back to the Beginning, that which came from the End to return to the End. In the return lies the fulfilment.

And this is the unconscious undoing of the ego.

That which we *are* is absolute. There is no adding to it, no superseding this accomplished self. It is final and universal. All that remains is thoroughly to explore it.

That is, to analyse it. Analysis presupposes a corpse.

It is at this crisis in the human history that tragic art appears again, that Art becomes the only absolute, the only watchword among the people. This achieved self, which we are, is absolute and universal. There is nothing beyond. All that remains is to state this self, and the reactions upon this self, perfectly. And the perfect statement presumes to be art. It is aestheticism.

At this crisis there is a great cry of loneliness. Every man conceives himself as a complete unit surrounded by nullity. And he cannot bear it. Yet his pride is in this also. The greatest conceit of all is the cry of loneliness.

At this crisis, emotion turns into sentiment, and sentimentalism takes the place of feeling. The ego has no feeling, it has only sentiments. And the myriad egos sway in tides of sentimentalism.

But the *tacit* utterance of every man, when this state is reached, is "Après moi le Deluge." And when the Deluge begins to set in, there is profound secret satisfaction on every hand. For the ego in a man secretly hates every other ego. In a democracy where every little ego is crowned with the false crown of its own supremacy, every other ego is a false usurper, and nothing more. We can only tolerate those whose crowns are not yet manufactured, because they can't *afford* it.

And again, the supreme little ego in man hates an unconquered universe. We shall never rest till we have heaped tin cans on the North Pole and the South Pole, and put up barb-wire fences on the moon. Barb-wire fences are our sign of conquest. We have wreathed the world with them. The back of creation is broken. We have killed the mysteries and devoured the secrets. It all lies now within our skin, within the ego of humanity.

So, circumscribed within the outer nullity, we give ourselves up to the flux of death, to analysis, to introspection, to mechanical war and destruction, to humanitarian absorption in the body politic, the poor, the birth-rate, the mortality of infants, like a man absorbed in his own flesh and members, looking for ever at himself. It is the continued activity of disintegration, disintegration, separating, setting apart, investigation, research, the resolution back to the original void.

All this goes on within the glassy, insentient, insensible envelope of nullity. And within this envelope, like the glassy insects within their rind, we imagine we fill the whole cosmos, that we contain within ourselves the whole of time, which shall tick forth from us as from a clock, now everlastingly.

We are capable of nothing but reduction within the envelope. Our every activity is the activity of disintegration, of corruption, of dissolution, whether it be our scientific research, our social activity—(the social activity is largely concerned with reducing all the parts contained within the envelope to an equality, so that there shall be no unequal pressure, tending to rupture the envelope, which is divine)—our art, or our anti-social activity, sensuality, sensationalism, crime, war. Everything alike contributes to the flux of death, to corruption, and liberates the static data of the consciousness.

Whatever single act is performed by any man now, in this condition, it is an act of reduction, disintegration The scientist in his laboratory, the artist in his study, the statesman, the artizan, the sensualist obtaining keen gratification, every one of these is reducing down that which is himself to its simpler elements, reducing the compound back to its parts. It is the pure process of corruption in all of us. The activity of death is the only activity. It is like the decay of our flesh, and every new step in decay liberates a sensation, keen, momentarily gratifying, or a conscious knowledge of the parts that made a whole, knowledge equally gratifying.

It is like Dmitri Karamazov, who seeks and experiences sensation after sensation, reduction after reduction, till finally he is stripped utterly naked before the police, and the quick of him perishes. There *is* no more any physical or integral Dmitri Karamazov. That which is in the hospital, afterwards, is a conglomeration of qualities, strictly an idiot, a nullity.

And Dostoevsky has shown us perfectly the utter subjection of all human life to the flux of corruption. That is his theme, the theme of reduction through sensation after sensation, consciousness after consciousness, until nullity is reached, all complexity is broken down, an individual becomes an amorphous heap of elements, qualities.

There are the two types, the dark Dmitri Karamazov, or Rogozhin; and the Myshkin on the other hand. Dmitri Karamazov and Rogozhin will each of them plunge the flesh within the reducing agent, the woman, obtain the sensation and the reduction within the flesh, add to the sensual experience, and progress towards utter dark disintegration, to nullity. Myshkin on the other hand will react upon the achieved consciousness or personality or ego of every one he meets, disintegrate this consciousness, this ego, and his own as well, obtaining the knowledge of the factors that made up the complexity of the consciousness, the ego, in the woman and in himself, reduce further and further back, till himself is a babbling idiot, a vessel full of disintegrated parts, and the woman is reduced to a nullity.

This is real death. The actual physical fact of death is part of the life-stream. It is an incidental point when the flux of light and dark has flowed sufficiently apart for the conjunction, which we call life, to disappear.

We live with the pure flux of death, it is part of us all the time. But our blossoming is transcendent, beyond death and life.

Only when we fall into egoism do we lose all chance of blossoming, and then the flux of corruption is the breath of our existence.

From top to bottom, in the whole nation, we are engaged, fundamentally engaged in the process of reduction and dissolution. Our reward is sensational gratification in the flesh, or sensational gratification within the mind, the utter gratification we experience when we can pull apart the whole into its factors. This is the reward in scientific and introspective knowledge, this is the reward in the pleasure of cheap sensuality.

In each case, the experience remains as it were absolute. It is the statement of what is, or what was. And a statement of what *is,* is the absolute footstep in the progress backward towards the starting place, it is the *undoing* of a complete unit into the factors which previously went to making its oneness. It is the reduction of the iris back into its component waves.

There was the bliss when the iris came into being. There is now the bliss when the iris passes out of being, and the whole is torn apart. The secret of the whole is never captured. Certain data are captured. The secret escapes down the sensual or the sensational or intellectual thrill of pleasure.

So there goes on reduction after reduction within the shell. And we who find our utmost gratification in this process of reduction, this flux of corruption, this retrogression of death, we will preserve with might and main the glassy envelope, the insect rind, the tight-shut shell of the cabbage, the withered, null walls of the womb. For by virtue of this null envelope alone do we proceed uninterrupted in this process of gratifying reduction.

And this is utter evil, this secret, silent worship of the null envelope that preserves us intact for our gratification with the flux of corruption.

Intact within the null envelope, which we have come to worship as the preserver of this our life-activity of reduction, we re-act back upon what we are. We do not seek any more the consummation of union. We seek the consummation of reduction.

And this is utter evil, this secret, silent worship of the null envelope that preserves us intact for our gratification with the flux of corruption.

Intact within the null envelope, which we have come to worship as the preserver of this our life-activity of reduction, we re-act back upon what we are. We do not seek any more the consummation of union. We seek the consummation of reduction.

When a man seeks a woman in love, or in positive desire, he seeks a union, he seeks a consummation of himself with that which is not himself, light with dark, dark with light.

But within the glassy, null envelope of the enclosure, no union is sought, no union is possible; after a certain point, only reduction. Ego reacts upon ego only in friction. There are small egos, many small people, who have not reached the limit of the confines which we worship. They may still have small consummation in union. But all those who are strong and have travelled far have met and reacted from the nullity.

And then, when a man seeks a woman, he seeks not a consummation in union, but a frictional reduction. He seeks to plunge his compound flesh into the cold acid that will reduce him, in supreme sensual experience, down to his parts. This is Rogozhin seeking Nastasia Filippovna, Dmitri his Grushenka, or D'Annunzio in *Fuoco* seeking his Foscarina. This is more or less what happens when a soldier, maddened with lust of pure destructiveness, violently rapes the woman of his captivity. It is that he may destroy another being by the very act which is called the act of creation, or procreation. In the brute soldier it is cruelty-lust: as it was in the Red Indian. But when we come to civilised man, it is not so simple. His cruelty-lust is directed almost as much against himself as against his victim. He is destroying, reducing, breaking down that of himself which is within the envelope. He is immersing himself within a keen, fierce, terrible reducing agent. This is true of the hero of Edgar Allan Poe's tales, *Ligeia,* or the *Fall of the House of Usher.* The man seeks his own sensational reduction, but he disintegrates the woman even more, in the name of love. In the name of love, what horrors men perpetrate, and are applauded!

It is only in supreme crises that man reaches the supreme pitch of annihilation. The difference, however, is only a difference in degree, not in kind. The bank-clerk performs in a mild degree what Poe performed intensely and deathlily.

These are the men in whom the development is rather low, whose souls are coarsely compounded, so that the reduction is coarse, a sort of activity of coarse hate.

But the men of finer sensibility and finer development, sensuous or conscious, they must proceed more gradually and subtly and finely in the process of reduction. It is necessary for a finely compounded nature to reduce itself more finely, to know the subtle gratification of its own reduction.

A subtle nature like Myshkin's would find no pleasure of reduction in connection with Grushenka, scarcely any with Nastasia. He must proceed more delicately. He must give up his soul to the reduction. It is his mind, his conscious self he wants to reduce. He wants to dissolve it back. He wants to become infantile, like a child, to reduce and resolve back all the complexity of his consciousness, to the rudimentary condition of childhood. That is his ideal.

So he seeks mental contacts, mental re-actions. It is in his mental or conscious contacts that he seeks to obtain the gratification of self-reduction. He reaches his crisis in his monologue of self-analysis, self-dissolution, in the drawing-room scene where he falls in a fit.

And of course, all this reducing activity is draped in alluring sentimentalism. The most evil things in the world, today, are to be found under the chiffon folds of sentimentalism. Sentimentality is the garment of our vice. It covers viciousness as inevitably as greenness covers a bog.

With all our talk of advance, progress, we are all the time working backwards. Our heroines become younger and younger. In the movies, the heroine is becoming more and more childish, and touched with infantile idiocy. We cannot bear honest maturity. We want to reduce ourselves back, back to the *corruptive* state of childishness.

Now it is all very well for a child to be a child. But for a grown person to be slimily, pornographically reaching out for child-gratifications is disgusting. The same with the prevalent love of boys. It is the desire to be reduced back, reduced back, in our accomplished ego: always within the unshattered rind of our completeness and complacency, to go backwards, in sentimentalised disintegration, to the states of childhood.

And no matter *what* happens to us, now, we sentimentalise it and use it as a means of sensational reduction. Even the great war does not alter our civilisation one iota, in its total nature. The form, the whole form, remains intact. Only inside the complete envelope we writhe with sensational experiences of death, hurt, horror, reduction.

The goodness of anything depends on the direction in which it is moving. Childhood, like a bud, striving and growing and struggling towards blossoming full maturity, is surely beautiful. But childhood as a *goal*, for which grown people aim: childishness futile and sentimental, for which men and women lust, and which always retreats when grasped, like the *ignis fatuus* of a poisonous marsh of corruption: this is disgusting.

While we live, we are balanced between the flux of life and the flux of death. All the while, our bodies are being composed and decomposed. But while ever man fully lives, all the time the two streams keep fusing into the third reality, of real creation. Every new gesture, every fresh smile of a child is a new emergence into creative being: a glimpse of the Holy Ghost.

But when grown people start grimacing with childishness, or lusting after child-gratifications, it is corruption pure and simple.

And the still clear look on an old face, and the stillness of old, withered hands, which have gathered the long repose of autumn, this is the purity of the two streams consummated, and the bloom, like autumn crocuses, of age.

But the painted, silly child-face that old women make nowadays: or the harpy's face that many have, lusting for the sensations of youth: the hard, voracious, selfish faces of old men, seeking their own ends, devouring the shoots of young life: this is vile.

While we live, we are balanced between the flux of life and the flux of death. But the real clue is the Holy Ghost, that moves us on into the state of blossoming. And each year the blossoming is different: from the delicate blue speedwells of childhood, to the equally delicate, frail farewell flowers of old age: through all the poppies and sunflowers: year after year of difference.

While we live, we change, and our flowering is a constant change. But once we fall into the state of egoism, we cannot change. The ego, the self-conscious ego remains fixed, a final envelope around us. And we are then safe inside the mundane egg of our own self-consciousness and self-esteem.

Safe we are! Safe as houses! Shut up like unborn chickens that cannot break the shell of the egg. That's how safe we are! And as we can't be born, we can only rot. That's how safe we are!

Safe within the everlasting walls of the egg-shell we have not the courage, or the energy, to crack, we fall, like the shut-up chicken, into a pure flux of corruption, and the worms are our angels.

And mankind falls into the state of innumerable little worms bred within the unbroken shell: all clamoring for food, food, food, all feeding on the dead body of creation, all crying peace! peace! universal peace! brotherhood of man! Everything must be "universal," to the conquering worm. It is only *life* which is different.

V

The Nuptials of Death and the Attendant Vulture

To those who are in prison, whose being is prisoner within the walls of unliving fact, there are only two forms of triumph: the triumph of inertia, or the triumph of the will. There is no flowering possible.

And the experience *en route* to either triumph, is the experience of sensationalism.

Stone walls need not a prison make: that is, not an *absolute* prison. If the great sun has shone into a man's soul, even prison-walls cannot blot it out. Yet prison-walls, unless they be a temporary shelter, are deadly things.

So, if we are imprisoned within walls of accomplished fact, experience, or knowledge, we are prisoned indeed. The living sun is shut out finally. A false sun, like a lamp, shines.

All absolutes are prison-walls. These "laws" which science has invented, like conservation of energy, indestructibility of matter, gravitation, the will-to-live, survival of the fittest: and even these absolute facts, like—the earth goes round the sun—or the doubtful atoms, electrons, or ether—they are all prison-walls, unless we realize that we don't know what they mean. We don't know what we mean, ultimately, by *conservation,* or *indestructibility*. Our atoms, ether, are caps that fit exceeding badly. And our will-to-live contains a germ of suicide, and our survival-of-the-fittest the germ of degeneracy. As for the earth going round the sun: it goes round like the blood goes round my body, absolutely mysteriously, with the rapidity and hesitation of life.

But the human ego, in its pettifogging arrogance, sets up these things for you as absolutes, and unless you kick hard and kick in time, they are your prison-walls for ever. Your spirit will be like a dead bee in a cell.

349

Once you are in prison, you have no experience left, save the experience of reduction, destruction going on inwardly. Your sentimentalism is only the smell of your own rottenness.

This reduction within the self is sensationalism. And sensationalism, of course, is progressive. You can't have your cake and eat it. To get a sensation, you eat your cake. That is, to get a sensation, you reduce down some part of your complex psyche, physical and psychic. You get a flash, like when you strike a match. But a match once struck can never be struck again. It is finished.— Sensationalism is exhaustive process.

The resolving down is progressive. It can apparently go on *ad infinitum.* But in infinity it means what we call utter death, utter nothingness, opposites released from opposition, and from conjunction, till there *is* nothing left at all, only nullity itself.

Sensationalism progresses in the individual. This is the doom of it. This is the doom of egoistic sex. Egoistic sex-excitement means the reacting of the sexes against one another in a purely reducing activity. The reduction progresses. When I have finally reduced one complexity, one unit, I must proceed to the next, the lower. It is the progressive activity of dissolution within the soul.

And the climax of this progression is in perversity, degradation and death. But only the very powerful and energetic ego can go through all the phases of its own violent reduction. The ordinary crude soul, after having enjoyed the brief reduction in the sex, is finished there, blasé, empty. And alcohol is slow and crude, and opium is only for the imaginative, the somewhat spiritual nature. Then remain the opium-drugs, for a finisher, a last reducer.

There remains only the reduction of the contact with death. So that as the sex is exhausted, gradually, a keener desire, the desire for the touch of death follows on, in an intense nature. Then come the fatal drugs. Or else those equally fatal wars and revolutions which really create nothing at all, but destroy, and leave emptiness.

When a man is cleaving like a fly with spread arms upon the face of a rock, with infinite space beneath him, and he feels his foothold going, and he cries out to the men on the rope, and falls away, dangling into endless space, jerked back by the thin rope, then he perishes, he is fused in the reducing flame of death. He knows another keen anguish of reduction. What matters to that man, afterwards? Does any of the complex life of the world below matter? None. All that is left is the triumph of his will, in having gone so far and recovered. And all that lies ahead is another risk, another slip, another agony of the fall, or a demonish triumph of the will. And the *final* consummation of such a man is the last fall of all, the few horrible seconds whilst he drops, like a meteorite, to extinction. This is his final and utter satisfaction, the smash of extinction at the bottom.

But even this man is not a pure egoist. This man still has his soul open to the mystery of the mountains, he still feels the passion of the *contact* with death.

If he wins, however, in the contest: if his will triumphs in the test: then there is danger of his falling into final egoism, the more-or-less inert complacency of a self-satisfied old man.

The soul is still alive, while it has passion: any sort of passion, even for the brush with death, or for the final and utter reduction. And in the brush with death it may be released again into positive life. A man may be sufficiently released by a fall on the rope and the dangling for a few minutes of agony, in space. That may finally reduce his soul to its elements, set it free and child-like, and break down that egoistic entity which had developed upon it from the past. The near touch of death may be a release into life; if only it will break the egoistic will, and release that other flow.

But if a man, having fallen very near to death, gets up at length and says: I did it! It's my triumph! I beat the mountains that time!—then, of course, his ego has only pulled itself in triumph out of the menace, and the individual will go on more egoistic and barrenly complacent.

If a man says: "I fell! But the unseen goodness helped me, when I struggled for life, and so I was saved,"—then this man will go on in life unimprisoned, the channels of his heart open, and passion still flowing through him.

But if the brush with death only gave the brilliant sensational thrill of fear followed immediately by the *gamin* exultance: Yah! I got myself out all right!—then the ego continues intact, having enjoyed the sensation, and remaining vulgarly triumphant in the power of the Will. And it will continue inert and complacent, till the next thrill.

So it is with war. Whoever goes to war in his own might alone, will, even if he comes out victorious, come out barren: a barren triumpher, whose strength is in inertia. A man must do his own utmost: but even then, the final stroke will be delivered, or the final strength will be given from the unseen, and the man must feel it. If he doesn't feel it, he will be an inert victor, or equally inert vanquished, complacent and sterile in either case.

There must be a certain faith. And that means, an ultimate reliance on that which is beyond our will, and not contained in our ego.

We have gone to war. For a hundred years we have been piling up safety upon safety, we have grown enormously within the shell of our civilisation, we have rounded off our own ego and grown almost complacent about our own triumphs of will. Till we come to a point where sex seems exhausted, and passion falls flat. When even criticism and analysis now only fatigue the mind and weary the soul.

Then we gradually, gradually formulate the desire: Oh, give us the brush with death, and let us see if we can win out all right!

We go into a war like this, in order to get once more the final reduction under the touch of death. That the death is so inhuman, cold, mechanical, sordid, the giving of the body to the grip of cold, stagnant mud and stagnant water, whilst one awaits for some falling death, the knowledge of the gas clouds that may lacerate and reduce the lungs to a heaving mass, this, this sort of self-inflicted Sadism, brings almost a final satisfaction to our civilised and still passionate men.

Almost! And when it is over, and we have won out, shall we be released into a new lease of life? Or shall we only extend our dreary lease of egoism and complacency? Shall we know the barren triumph of the will?—or the equally barren triumph of inertia, helplessness, barren irresponsibility.

And still, as far as there is any passion in the war, it is a passion for the embrace with death. The desire to deal death and to take death. The enemy is the bride, whose body we will reduce with a rapture of agony and wounds. We are the bridegroom, engaged with him in the long, voluptuous embrace, the giving of agony, the rising and rising of the slow, unwilling transport of misery, the soaking-in of day after day of wet mud, in penetration of the heavy, sordid, unendurable cold, on and on to the climax, the laceration of the blade, like a frost through the tissue, blasting it.

This is the desire and the consummation, this is the war. But at length, we shall be satisfied, at length we shall have consummation. Then the war will end. And what then?

It is not really a question of victories or defeats. It is a question of fulfilment, and release from the old prison-house of a dead form. The war is one bout in the terrific, horrible labour, our civilisation laboring in child-birth, and unable to bring forth.

How will it end? Will there be a release, a relaxation of the horrible walls, and a real issuing, a birth?

Or will it end in nothing, all the agony going to stiffen the old form deader, to enclose the unborn more helplessly and drearily.

It may easily be. For behind us all, in the war, stand the old and the elderly, complacent with egoism, bent on maintaining the old form. Oh, they are the monkey grinning with anxiety and anticipation, behind us, waiting for the burnt young cat to pull the chestnut out of the fire. And in the end, they will thrill with the triumph of their egoistic will, and harden harder still with vulture-like inertia, rapacious inertia.

In sex, we have plunged the quick of creation deep into the cold flux of reduction, corruption, till the quick is extinguished. In war we have plunged the whole quick of the living, sentient body into a cold, cold flux. Much has died and much will die. But if the whole quick dies, and there remain only the material, mechanical, unquickened tissue, acting at the bidding of the mechanical will, and the sterile ego triumphant, then it is a poor tale, a barrenly poor tale.

I have seen a soldier at the seaside who was maimed. One leg was only a small stump, with the trouser folded back on it. He was a handsome man of about thirty, finely built. His face was sun-browned, and extraordinarily beautiful, still, with a strange placidity, something like perfection, abstract, complete. He had known his consummation. It seemed he could never desire corruption or reduction again, he had had his satisfaction of death. He was become almost impersonal, a simple abstraction, all his personality loosed and undone. He was now like a babe just born, new to begin life. Yet in a sense, still-born. The newness and candour, like a flower just unloosed, was something strange and rare in him. Yet unloosed, curiously, into the light of death.

So he came forward down the pier, in the sunshine, slowly on his crutches. Behind, the sea was milk-white and vague, as if full of ghosts, and silent, except when a long white wave plunged to silence the smooth, milky silence of the sea, coming from very far out of the ghostly stillness.

The maimed soldier, strong and handsome, with some of the frail candour of a newly-wakened child in his face, came slowly down the pier on his crutches, looking at everybody who looked at him. He was naïve like a child, wondering. The people stared at him with a sort of fascination. So he was rather vain, rather proud, like a vain child.

He did not know he was maimed, it had not entered his consciousness. His soul, so clean and new and fine, could not conceive of such a thing. He was rather vain and slightly ostentatious as a man with a wound, a trophy, more as a child who is conspicuous among envious elders.

The women particularly were fascinated. They could not look away from him. The strange abstraction of horror and death was so perfect in his face, like the horror of birth on a new-born infant, that they were almost hysterical. They gravitated towards him, helplessly, they could not move away from him.

They wanted him, they wanted him so badly, that they were almost beside themselves. They wanted his consummation, his perfect completeness in horror and death. They too wanted the consummation. They followed him, they made excuses to talk to him. And he, strange, abstract, glowing still from the consummation of destruction and pain and horror, like a bridegroom just come from the bride, seemed to glow before the women, to give off a strange unearthly radiance, which was like an embrace, a most poignant embrace to their souls.

But still his eyes were looking, looking, looking for someone who was not eager for him, to know him, to devour him, like women round a perfect child. He had not realised yet what all the attention meant, which he received. He was so strong in his new birth. And he was looking for his own kind, for the living, the new-born, round about. But he was surrounded by greedy, voracious people, like birds seeking the death in him, pecking at the death in him.

It was horrible, rather sinister, the women round the man, there on the pier stretched from the still, sunny land over the white sea, noiseless and inhuman.

The spirit of destruction is divine, when it breaks the ego and opens the soul to the wide heavens. In corruption there is divinity. Aphrodite is, on one side, the great goddess of destruction in sex, Dionysus in the spirit. Moloch and some gods of Egypt are gods also of the knowledge of death. In the soft and shiny voluptuousness of decay, in the marshy chill heat of reptiles, there is the sign of the Godhead. It is the activity of departure. And departure is the opposite equivalent of coming together; decay, corruption, destruction, breaking down is the opposite equivalent of creation. In infinite going-apart there is revealed again the pure absolute, the absolute relation: this time truly as a Ghost: the ghost of what was.

We who live, we can only live or die. And when, like the maimed soldier on the pier, with the white sea behind, when we have come right back into life, and the wonder of death fades off our faces again, what then?

Shall we go on with wide, careless eyes and the faint astonished smile waiting all our lives for the accomplished death? Waiting for death finally? And continuing the sensational reduction process? Or shall we fade into a dry, empty egoism? Which will the maimed soldier do? He cannot remain as he is, clear and peaceful.

Are we really doomed, and smiling with the wonder of doom?

Even if we are, we need not say: *It is finished*! It is never finished. That is one thing where Jesus spoke a fatal half-truth, in his *Consummatum Est*! Death consummates nothing. It can but abruptly close the individual life. But Life itself, and even the forms men have given it, will persist and persist and persist. There is no consummation into death. Death leaves still further deaths.

Leonardo knew this: he knew the strange endlessness of the flux of corruption. It is Mona Lisa's ironic smile. Even Michael Angelo knew it. It is in his Leda and the swan. For the swan is one of the symbols of divine corruption. With its reptile feet buried in the ooze and mud, its voluptuous form yielding and embracing the ooze of water, its beauty white and cold and terrifying, like the dead beauty of moon, like the water-lily, the sacred lotus, its neck and head like the snake, it is for us a flame of the cold white fire of flux, the phosphorescence of corruption, the salt, cold burning of the sea which corrodes all it touches, coldly reduces every sun-built form to ash, to the original elements. This is the beauty of the swan, the lotus, the snake, this cold white salty fire of infinite reduction. And there was some suggestion of this in the Christ of the early Christians, the Christ who was the Fish.

So that, when Leonardo and Michael Angelo represent Leda in the embrace of the swan, they are painting mankind in the clasp of the divine flux of corruption, the singing death. Mankind *turned back*, to cold bygone consummations.

When the swan first rose out of the marshes, it was a glory of creation. But when we turn back, we seek its consummation again, it is a fearful flower of corruption.

And corruption, like growth, is only divine when it is pure, when all is given up to it. If it be experienced as a controlled activity within an intact whole, this is vile. When the cabbage flourishes round a hollow rottenness, this is vile. When corruption goes on within the living womb, this is unthinkable. The chicken dead in the egg is an abomination. We cannot subject a divine process to a static will, not without blasphemy and loathsomeness. The static will must be subject to the process of reduction, also. For the pure absolute, the Holy Ghost, lies also in the relationship which is made manifest by the departure, the departure *ad infinitum,* of the opposing elements.

Corruption will at last break down for us the deadened forms, and release us into the infinity. But the static ego, with its will-to-persist, neutralises both life and death, and utterly defies the Holy Ghost. The unpardonable sin!

It is possible for this static will, this vile rind of nothingness, to triumph for a long while over the divine relation in the flux, to assert an absolute nullity of static form.

This we do who preserve intact our complete null concept of life, as an envelope around this flux of destruction, the war. The whole concept and form of life remains absolute and static, around the gigantic but contained seething of the fight. It is the rottenness seething within the cabbage, corruption within the old, fixed body. The cabbage does not relax, the body is not broken open. The reduction is sealed and contained.

That is our attitude now. It is the attitude of the women who flutter round and peck at death in us. This is the carrion process set in, the process of obscenity, the baboon, the vulture in us.

In so far as we fight to remain ideally intact, in so far as we seek to give and to have the experience of death, so that we may remain unchanged in our whole conscious form, may preserve the static entity of our conception, around the fight, we are obscene. We are like vultures and obscene insects.

We may give ourselves utterly to destruction. Then our conscious forms are destroyed along with us, and something new must arise. But we may not have corruption within ourselves as sensationalism, our skin and outer form intact. To destroy life for the preserving of a static, rigid form, a shell, a glassy envelope, this is the lugubrious activity of the men who fight to save democracy and to end all fighting. The fight itself is divine, the relation betrayed in the fight is absolute. But the glassy envelope of the established concept is only a foul nullity.

Destruction and Creation are the two relative absolutes between the opposing infinites. Life is in both. Life may even, for a while be almost entirely in

354

one, or almost entirely in the other. The end of either oneness is death. For life is really in the two, the absolute is the pure relation, which is both.

If we have our fill of destruction, then we shall turn again to creation. We shall need to live again, and live hard, for once our great civilised form is broken, and we are at last born into the open sky, we shall have a whole new universe to grow up into, and to find relations with. The future will open its delicate, dawning aeons in front of us, unfathomable.

But let us watch that we do not preserve an enveloping falsity around our destructive activity, some nullity of virtue and self-righteousness, some conceit of the "general good" and the salvation of the world by bringing it all within our own conceived whole form. This is the utter lie and obscenity. The ego, like Humpty Dumpty, sitting forever on the wall.

The vulture was once, perhaps, an eagle. It became a supreme strong bird, almost like the phoenix. But at a certain point, it said: "I am It." And then it proceeded to preserve its own static form crystal about the flux of corruption, fixed, absolute as a crystal, about the horrible seethe of corruption. Then the eagle became a vulture.

And the dog, through cowardice, arrested itself at a certain point and became domestic, or a hyaena, preserving a glassy, fixed form about a voracious seethe of corruption.

And the baboon, almost a man, or almost a high beast, arrested himself and became obscene, a grey, hoary rind closed upon an activity of strong corruption.

And the louse, in its little glassy envelope, brings everything into the corrupting pot of its little belly.

And these are all perfectly-arrested egoists, asserting themselves static and foul, triumphant in inertia and in will.

Let us watch that we do not turn either into carrion or into carrion eaters. Let us watch that we do not become, in the vulgar triumph of our will, and the obscene inertia of our ego, vultures who feed on putrescence. The lust for death, for pain, for torture, is even then better than this fatal triumph of inertia and the egoistic will. Anything is better than that. The Red Indians, full of Sadism and self-torture and death, destroyed themselves. But the eagle, when it gets stuck and can know no more blossoming turns into a vulture with a naked head, and becomes carrion-foul.

There must always be some balance between the passion for destruction and the passion for creation, in every living activity: for in the race to destruction we can utterly destroy the vital quick of our being, leave us amorphous, undistinguished, vegetable; and in the race for creation we can lose ourselves in mere production, and pile ourselves over with dead null monstrosities of obsolete form. All birth comes with the reduction of old tissue. But the reduction is not the birth. That is the fallacy of all of us, who represent the old tissue now. In this fallacy we go careering down the slope in our voluptuousness of death and horror, careering into oblivion, like Hippolytus trammelled up and borne away in the traces of his maddened horses.

Who says that the spirit of destruction will outrun itself? Not till the driver be annihilated. Then the destructive career will run itself out.

And then what?

But neither destruction nor production is, in itself, evil. The danger lies in the fall into egoism, which neutralises both. When destruction and production alike are mechanical, meaningless.

The race of destruction may outrun itself But still the form may remain intact, the old imprisoning laws. Only those who have not travelled to the confines will be left, the mean, the average, the laborers, the slaves: all of them little crowned egos.

Still the ancient mummy will have the people within its belly, There they will be slaves: not to the enemy, but to themselves, the concept established about them: being slaves, they will be happy enclosed within the tomb-like belly of a concept, like gold-fish in a bowl, which think themselves the centre of the universe.

This is like the vultures of the mountains. They have kept the form and height of eagles. But their souls have turned into the souls of slaves and carrion eaters. Their size, their strength, their supremacy of the mountains, remains intact. But they have become carrion eaters.

This is the tomb, the whited sepulchre, this very form, this liberty, this ideal for which we are fighting. The Germans are fighting for another sepulchre. Theirs is the sepulchre of the Eagle become vulture, ours is the sepulchre of the lion become dog: soon to become hyaena.

But we would have our own sepulchre, in which we shall dwell secure when the rage of destruction is over. Let it be the sepulchre of the dog or the vulture, the sepulchre of democracy or aristocracy, what does it matter! Inside it, the worms will jig the same jazz dances, and heave and struggle to get hold of vast and vaster stores of carrion, or its equivalent, gold.

The carrion birds, aristocrats, sit up high and remote, on the sterile rocks of the old absolute, their obscene heads gripped hard and small like knots of stone clenched upon themselves for ever. The carrion dogs and hyaenas of the old, arid, democratic absolute prowl among the bare stones of the common earth, in numbers, their loins cringing, their heads sharpened to stone.

Those who will hold power, afterwards, they will sit on their rocks and heights of inalterable morality, which have become foul through the course of ages, like vultures upon the unchangeable mountain-tops. The fixed, existing form will persist for ever beneath them, about them, they will have become the spirit incarnate of the fixed form of life. They will eat carrion, having become a static hunger for keen putrescence. This alone will support the incarnation of hoary fixity which they are. And beside the carrion they will fight the multitudes of hoary, obscene dogs, which also persist. It is the mortal form become null and fixed and enduring, glassy, horrible, beyond life and death, beyond consummation, the awful, stony nullity. It is timeless, almost as the rainbow.

But it is not utterly timeless. It is only unthinkably slow, static in its passing away, perpetuated.

Its very aspect of timelessness is a fraud.

What is evil?—not death, nor the blood-devouring Moloch, but this spirit of perpetuation and apparent timelessness, this obscenity which holds the great carrion birds, and the carrion dogs. The tiger, the hawk, the weasel, are beautiful things to me; and as they strike the dove and the hare, that is the will of God, it is a consummation, a bringing together of two extremes, a making perfect one from the duality.

But the baboon, and the hyaena, the vulture, the condor, and the carrion crow, these fill me with fear and horror. These are the highly developed life-forms, now arrested, petrified, frozen, falsely timeless. The baboon was almost as man, the hyaena as the lion: the vulture and the condor are greater than the eagle, the carrion crow is stronger than the hawk. And these obscene beasts are not ashamed. They are stark and static, they are not mixed. Their will is hoary, ageless. Before us, the Egyptians have known them and worshipped them.

The baboon, with his intelligence and his unthinkable loins, the cunning hyaena with his cringing, stricken loins, these are the static form of one achieved ego, the egoistic Christian, the democratic, the unselfish. The vulture, with her naked neck and naked, small, stony head, this is the static form of the other achieved ego, the eagle, the Self, aristocratic, lordly, pagan.

It is unthinkable and unendurable. Yet we are drawn more and more in this direction. After the supreme intelligence, the baboon, after the supreme pride, the vulture. The millionaire: the international financier: the bankers of this world. The baboons, the hyaenas, the vultures.

The snake is the spirit of the great corruptive principle, the festering cold of the marsh. This is how he seems, as we look back. We revolt from him. But we share the same life and tide of life as he. He struggles as we struggle, he enjoys the sun, he comes to the water to drink, he curls up, hides himself to sleep. And under the low skies of the far past aeons, he emerged a king out of chaos, a long beam of new life. But the vulture looms out in sleep like a rock, invincible within the hoary, static form, invincible against the flux of both eternities.

One day there was a loud, terrible scream from the garden, tearing the soul. Oh, and it was a snake lying on the warm garden bed, and in his teeth the leg of a frog, a frog spread out, screaming with horror. We ran near. The snake glanced at us sharply, holding fast to the frog, trying to get further hold. In so trying, it let the frog escape, which leaped convulsed away. Then the snake slid noiselessly under cover, sullenly, never looking at us again.

We were all white with fear. But why? In the world of twilight as in the world of light, one beast shall devour another. The world of corruption has its stages, where the lower shall devour the higher, *ad infinitum.*

So a snake, also, devours the fascinated bird, the little, static bird with its tiny skull. Yet is there no great reptile that shall swallow the vulture.

As yet, the vulture is beyond life or change. It stands hard, immune within the principle of corruption, and the principle of creation, unbreakable. It is kept static by the fire of putrescence, which makes the void within balance the void without. It is a changeless tomb wherein the latter stages of corruption take place, counteracting perfectly the action of life. Life devours death to keep the static nullity of the form.

So the ragged, grey-and-black vulture sits hulked, motionless, like a hoary, foul piece of living rock, its naked head and neck sunk in, only the curved beak protruding, the naked eyelids lowered. Motionless, beyond life, it sits on the sterile heights.

It does not sleep, it stays utterly static. 'When it spreads its great wings and floats down the air, still it is static, still this is the sleep, a dream-floating. When it rips up carrion and swallows it, it is still the same dream-motion, static, beyond the inglutination. The naked, obscene head is always fast locked, like stone.

It is this naked, obscene head of a bird, sleep-locked, a petrified knot of sleep, that I cannot bear to think of. When I think of it, I neither live nor die, I am petrified into foulness. The knot of volition, the will knotted upon a perpetuated moment, will not now be unloosed for ever. It will remain hoary, unchanging, timeless. Till it disappears, suddenly. Amid all the flux of time, of the two eternities, this head remains unbroken in a cold, rivetted sleep. But one day it will be broken.

I am set utterly against this small, naked, stone-clinched head, it is a foul vision I want to wipe away. But I am set utterly also against the loathsome, cringing, imprisoned loins of the hyaena, that cringe down the hind legs of the beast with their static weight. Again the static will has knotted into rivetted, endless nullity, but here upon the loins. In the vulture, the head is turned to stone, the fire is in the talons and the beak. In the hoary, glassy hyaena, the loins are turned to stone, heavy, sinking down to earth, almost dragged along, the fire is in the white eyes, and in the fangs. The hyaena can scarcely see and hear the living world; it draws back on to the stony fixity of its own loins, draws back upon its own nullity, sightless save for carrion. The vulture can neither see nor hear the living world, it is one supreme glance, the glance in search of carrion, its own absolute quenching, beyond which is nothing.

This is the end, and beyond the end. This is beyond the beginning and the end. Here the beginning and the end are revoked. The vulture, revoking the end, the end petrified upon the beginning, is a nullity. The hyaena, the beginning petrified beneath the end, is a nullity. This is beyond the beginning and the end, this is aristocracy gone beyond aristocracy, the I gone beyond the I; the other is democracy gone beyond democracy, the not-me surpassed upon itself.

This is the changelessness of the kingdoms of the earth, null, unthinkable.

This is the last state into which man may fall, in the triumph of will and the triumph of inertia. The state of the animated sepulchre.

VI

To be and to be Different

Behind me there is time stretching back forever, on to the unthinkable beginnings, infinitely. And this is eternity. Ahead of me, where I do not know, there is time stretching on infinitely, to eternity. These are the two eternities.

We cannot say, they are one and the same. They are two and utterly different. If I look at the eternity ahead, my back is towards the other eternity, this latter is forgotten, it *is* not. Which is the Christian attitude. If I look at the eternity behind, back to the source then there is for me one eternity, one only. And this is the pagan eternity, the eternity of Pan. This is the eternity some of us are veering round to, in private life, during the past few years.

The two eternities are *not* one eternity. It is only by denying the very meaning of speech itself, that we can argue them into oneness. They are two, relative to one another.

They are only *one* in their mutual relation, which relation is timeless and absolute. The eternities are temporal and relative. But their relation is constant, absolute without mitigation.

The motion of the eternities is dual: they flow together, and they flow apart, they flow forever towards union, they start back forever in opposition, to flow forever back to the issue, back into the unthinkable future, back into the unthinkable past.

We have known both directions. The Pagan, aristocratic, lordly, sensuous, has declared the Eternity of the Origin, the Christian, humble, spiritual, unselfish, democratic, has declared the Eternity of the Issue, the End. We have heard both declarations, we have seen each great ideal fulfilled, as far as is possible, at this time, on earth.

And now we say: "There is no eternity, there is no infinite, there is no God, there is no immortality."

And all the time we know we are cutting off our nose to spite our face. Without God, without some sort of immortality, not necessarily life-everlasting, but without *something* absolute, we are nothing. Yet now, in our spitefulness of self-frustration, we would rather be nothing than listen to our own being.

God is not the one infinite, nor the other, our immortality is not in the Original eternity, neither in the Ultimate eternity. God is the utter relation between the two eternities, He is in the flowing together and the flowing apart.

This utter relation is timeless, absolute and perfect. It is in the Beginning and the End, just the same. Whether it be revealed or not, it is the same. It is the Unrevealed God: what Jesus called the Holy Ghost.

My immortality is not from the beginning, in my endless ancestry. Nor is it on ahead in life everlasting. My life comes to me from the great Creator, the Beginner. And my spirit runs towards the Comforter, the Goal far ahead. But I, what am I between?

These two halves I always am. But I am never *myself* until they are consummated into a spark of oneness, the gleam of the Holy Ghost. And in this spark is my immortality, my non-mortal being, that which is not swept away down either direction of time.

I am not immortal till I have achieved immortality. And immortality is not a question of time, of everlasting life. It is a question of consummate being. Most men die and perish away, unconsummated, unachieved. It is not easy to achieve immortality, to win a consummate being. It is supremely difficult. It means undaunted suffering and undaunted enjoyment, both. And when a man has reached his ultimate of enjoyment and his ultimate of suffering, *both,* then he knows the two eternities, then he is made absolute, like the iris created out of the two. Then he is immortal. It is not a question of time. It is a question of being. It is not a question of submission, submitting to the divine grace: it is a question of submitting to the divine grace, in suffering and self-obliteration, and it is a question of conquering by divine grace, as the tiger leaps on the trembling deer, in utter satisfaction of the Self, in complete fulfilment of desire. The fulfilment is dual. And having known the dual fulfilment, then within the fulfilled soul is established the divine relation, the Holy Spirit dwells there, the soul has achieved immortality, it has attained to absolute being.

So the body of man is begotten and born in an ecstasy of delight and suffering. It is a flame kindled between the opposing confluent elements of the air. It is the battle-ground and marriage-bed of the two invisible hosts. It flames up to its full strength, and is consummate, perfect, absolute, the human body. It is a revelation of God, it is the foam-burst of the two waves, it is the iris of the two eternities. It is a flame flapping and travelling in the winds of mortality.

Then the pressure of the dark and the light relaxes, the flame sinks. We watch the slow departure, till only the wick glows. Then there is the dead body, cold, rigid, perfect in its absolute form, the revelation of the consummation of the flux, a perfect jet of foam that has fallen and is vanishing away. The two waves are fast going asunder, the snow-wreath melts, corruption's quick fire is burning in the achieved revelation.

We cannot bear it, that the body should decay. We cover it up, we cannot bear it. It is the revelation of God, it is the most holy of all revealed things. And it melts into slow putrescence.

We cannot bear it. We wish above all to preserve this achieved and perfect form, this revelation of God. And despair comes over us when it passes away. "Sic transit," we say, in agony.

The perfect form was not achieved in time, but in timelessness. It does not belong to today or tomorrow, or to eternity. It just *is*.

It is we who pass away, we and the whole flux of the two eternities, these pass. This is the eternal flux. But the God-quick, which is the constant within the flux, this is neither temporal nor eternal, it is truly timeless. And this perfect body was a revelation of the timeless God, timeless as He. If we in our mortality are temporal, if we are part of the flux of the eternities, then we swirl away in our living flux, the flesh decomposes and is lost.

But all the time, whether in the glad warm confluence of creation or in the cold flowing-apart of corruption, the same quick remains absolute and timeless, the revelation is in God, timeless. This alone of mortality does not belong to the passing away, this consummation, this revelation of God within the body, or within the soul. This revelation of God *is* God. But we who live, we are of the flux, we belong to the two eternities.

Only perpetuation is a sin. The perfect relation is perfect. But it is therefore timeless. And we must not think to tie a knot in Time, and thus to make the consummation temporal or eternal. The consummation is timeless, and we belong to Time, in our process of living.

Only Matter is a very slow flux, the waves ebbing slowly apart. So we engrave the beloved image on the slow, slow wave. We have the image in marble, or in pictured colour.

This is art, this transferring to a slow flux the form that was attained at the maximum of confluence between the two quick waves. This is art, the revelation of a pure, an absolute relation between the two eternities.

Matter is a slow, big wave flowing back to the Origin. And Spirit is a slow, infinite wave flowing back to the Goal, the ultimate Future. On the slow wave of matter and spirit, on marble or bronze or colour or air, and on the consciousness, we imprint a perfect revelation, and this is art: whether it reveal the relation in creation or in corruption, it is the same, it is a revelation of God: whether it be Piero della Francesca or Leonardo da Vinci, or the *Garçon qui pisse* or Phidias, or Christ or Rabelais. Because the revelation is imprinted on stone or granite, on the slow, last-receding wave, therefore it remains with us for a long long time, like the sculptures of Egypt. But it is all the time slowly passing away, unhindered, in its own time.

It passes away, but it is not in any sense lost. Our souls are established upon all the revelations, upon all the timeless achieved relationships, as the seed contains a convoluted memory of all the revelation in the plant it represents. The

360

flower is the burning of God in the bush: the flame of the Holy Ghost: the actual Presence of accomplished oneness, accomplished out of twoness. The true God is *created* every time a pure relationship, or a consummation out of twoness into oneness takes place. So that the poppy flower is God come red out of the poppy-plant. And a man, if he win to a sheer fusion in himself of all the manifold creation, a pure relation, a sheer gleam of oneness out of manyness, then this man is God created where before God was uncreate. He is the Holy Ghost in tissue of flame and flesh, whereas before, the Holy Ghost was but Ghost. It is true of a man as it is true of a dandelion or of a tiger or of a dove. Each creature, by some mystery, achieved a consummation in itself of all the wandering sky and sinking earth, and leaped into the other kingdom, where flowers are, of the gleaming Ghost.

So it is for ever. The two waves of Time flow in from the eternities, towards a meeting, a consummation. And the meeting, the consummation, is heaven, is absolute. All the while, as long as time lasts, the shock of the two waves passes into oneness, there is a new heaven. All the while, heaven is created from the flux of time, the galaxies between the night. And we too may be heavenly bodies, however we swirl back in the flux. When we have surged into being, when we have caught fire with friction, we are the immortals of heaven, the invisible stars that make the galaxy of night, no matter how the skies are tossed about. We can forget, but we cannot cease to be. Life nor death makes any difference, once we *are*.

For ever the kingdom of Heaven is established more perfectly, more beautifully, between the flux of the two eternities. One by one, in our consummation, we pass, a new star, into the galaxy that arches between the night-fall and the dawn, one by one, like the bushes in the desert, we take fire with God, and burn timelessly: and within the flame is heaven that has come to pass. Every flower that comes out, every bird that sings, every hawk that drops like a blade on her prey, every tiger flashing his paws, every serpent hissing out poison, every dove bubbling in the leaves, this is timeless heaven established from the flood, in this we have our form and our being. Every night new Heaven may ripple into being, every era a new Cycle of God may take place.

But it is all timeless. The error of errors is to try to keep heaven fixed and rocking like a boat anchored within the flux of time. Then there is sure to be shipwreck: "Die Wellen verschlingen am Ende Schiffer und Kahn." From the flux of time Heaven takes place in timelessness. The flux must go on.

This is sin, this tying the knot in Time, this anchoring the ark of eternal truth upon the waters. There is no ark, there is no eternal system, there is no rock of eternal truth. In Time and in Eternity all is flux. Only in the other dimension, which is not the time-space dimension, is there Heaven. We can no more *stay* in this heaven, than the flower can stay on its stem. We come and go.

So the body that came into being and walked transfigured in heavenliness must lie down and fuse away in the slow fire of corruption. Time swirls away, out of sight of the heavenliness. Heaven is not here nor there nor anywhere. Heaven is in the other dimension. In the young, in the unborn, this kingdom of Heaven which was revealed and has passed away, is established; of this Heaven the young and the unborn have their being. And if in us the Heaven be not revealed, if there be no transfiguration, no consummation, then the infants cry in the night, in want, void, strong want.

This is evil, this desire for constancy, for fixity in the temporal world. This is the denial of the absolute good, the revocation of the Kingdom of Heaven.

We cannot know God, in terms of the permanent, temporal world: we cannot. We can only know the *revelation* of God in the physical world. And the revelation of God is God. But it vanishes as the rainbow. The revelation is a condition in the whole flux of time. When this condition has passed away, the revelation is no more revealed. It has gone. And then God is gone, except to memory, a remembering of a critical moment within the flux. But there is no revelation of God in memory. Memory is not truth. Memory is persistence, perpetuation of a momentary cohesion in the flux. God is gone, until next time. But the next time will come. And then again we shall *see* God, and once more, it will be different. It is always different.

And we are all, now, living on the stale memory of a revelation of God. Which is a purely repetitive and temporal thing. But it contains us, it is our prison.

Whereas, there is nothing for a man to do but to behold God, and to become God. It is no good living on memory. When the flower opens, see him, don't remember him. When the sun shines, *be* him, and then cease again.

So we seek war, death, to kill this memory within us. We hate this imprisoning memory so much, we will kill the whole world rather than remain in prison to it. But why do we not create a new revelation of God, instead of seeking merely the destruction of the old revelations? We do this, because we are cowards. We say "The great revelation cannot be destroyed, but I, who am a failure, I can be destroyed." So we destroy the individual stones rather than decide to pull down the whole edifice. The edifice must stand, but the individual bricks must sacrifice themselves. So carefully we remove single lives from the edifice, and we destroy these single lives, carefully, supporting the edifice in the weakened place.

And the soldier says: "I die for my God and my Country." When, as a matter of fact, in his death his God and his country are so much destroyed.

But we must always lie, always convert our action to a lie. We know that we are living in a state of falsity, that all our social and religious form is dead, a crystallised lie. Yet we say: "We will die for our social and religious form."

In truth, we proceed to die because the whole frame of our life is a falsity, and we know that, if we die sufficiently, the whole frame and form and edifice will collapse upon itself. But it were much better to pull it down and have a great clear space, than to have it collapse on top of us. For we shall be like Samson, buried under the ruins.

And moreover, if we are like Samson, trying to pull the temple down, we must remember that the next generation will be none the less slaves, sightless, in Gaza, at the mill. And they will be by no means eager to commit suicide by bringing more temple beams down with a bang on their heads. They will say: It is a very nice temple, quite weather-tight. What's wrong with it?—They will be near enough to extinction to be very canny and cautious about imperilling themselves.

No, if we are to break through, it must be in the strength of life bubbling inside us. The chicken does not break the shell out of animosity against the shell. It bursts out in its blind desire to move under a greater heavens.

And so must we. We must burst out, and move under a greater heavens. As the chicken bursts out, and has a whole new universe to get into relationship with.

362

Our universe is not much more than a mannerism with us now. If we break through, we shall find that man is not man, as he seems to be, nor woman woman. The present seeming is a ridiculous travesty. And even the sun is not the sun as it appears to be. It is something tingling with magnificence.

And then starts the one glorious activity of man: the getting himself into a new relationship with a new heaven and a new earth. Oh, if we knew, the earth is everything and the sun is everything that we have missed knowing. But if we persist in our attitude of parasites on the body of earth and sun, the earth and the sun will be mere victims on which we feed our louse-like complacency for a long time yet: we, a myriad myriad little egos, five billion feeding like one.

The thing in itself! Why I never yet met a man who was anything but what he had been *told* to be. Let a man be a man-in-himself, and *then* he can begin to talk about the *Ding an Sich.* Men may be utterly different from the things they now seem. And then they will behold, to their astonishment, that the sun is absolutely different from the thing they now see, and that they call "sun."

HIM WITH HIS TAIL IN HIS MOUTH

Answer a fool according to his folly, philosophy ditto.

Solemnity is a sign of fraud.

Religion and philosophy both have the same dual purpose: to get at the beginning of things, and at the goal of things. They have both decided that the serpent has got his tail in his mouth, and that the end is one with the beginning.

It seems to me time somebody gave that serpent of eternity another dummy to suck.

They've all decided that the beginning of all things is the life-stream itself, energy, ether, libido, not to mention the Sanskrit joys of Purusha, Pradhana, Kala.

Having postulated the serpent of the beginning, now see all the heroes, from Moses and Plato to Bergson, wrestling with him might and main, to push his tail into his mouth.

Jehovah creates man in His Own Image, according to His Own Will. If man behaves according to the ready-made Will of God, formulated in a bunch of somewhat unsavoury commandments, then lucky man will be received back into the bosom of Jehovah.

Man isn't very keen. And that is Sin, original and perpetual.

Then Plato discovers how lovely the intellectual idea is: in fact, the only perfection is ideal.

But the old dragon of creation, who fathered us all, didn't have an idea in his head.

Plato was prepared. He popped the Logos into the mouth of the dragon, and the serpent of eternity was rounded off. The old dragon, ugly and venomous, wore yet the precious jewel of the Platonic idea in his head.

Unable to find the dragon wholesale, modern philosophy sets up a retail shop. You can't lay salt on the old scoundrel's tail, because, of course, he's got it in his mouth, according to postulate. He doesn't seem to be sprawling in his old lair, across the heavens. In fact, he appears to have vamoosed. Perhaps, instead of being one big old boy, he is really an infinite number of little tiny boys: atoms, electrons, units of force or energy, tiny little birds all spinning with their tails in their beaks. Just the same in detail as in the gross. Nothing will come out of the egg that isn't in it. Evolution sings away at the same old song. Out of the amoeba, or some such old-fashioned entity, the dragon of evolved life stretches himself enormous and more enormous, only, at last, to return each time, and put his tail into his mouth, and be an amoeba once more. The amoeba, or the electron or whatever it may lately be—the rose would be just as scentless—is the constant, from which all manifest living creation starts out, and to which it all returns.

There was a time when man was not, nor monkey, nor cow, nor catfish. But the amoeba (or the electron, or the atom, or whatever it is) always was and always will be.

Boom! tiddy-ra-ta! Boom!
Boom! tiddy-ra-ta! BOOM!!!

How do you know? How does anybody know, what always was or wasn't? Bunk of geology, and strata, and all that, biology or evolution.

"One, two, three four five,
Catch a little fish alive.
Six, seven, eight nine ten,
I have let him go again..

Bunk of beginnings and of ends, and heads and tails. Why does man always want to know so damned much? Or rather, so damned little. If he can't draw a ring round creation, and fasten the serpent's tail into its mouth with the padlock of one final clinching idea, then creation can go to hell, as far as man is concerned.

There is such a thing as life, or life-energy. We know, because we've got it, or had it. It isn't a constant. It comes and it goes. But we *want* it.

This, I think, is incontestable.

More than anything else in the world, we want to have life, and life-energy abundant in us. We think if we eat yeast, vitamines and proteids, we're sure of it. We're had. We diddle ourselves for the millionmillionth time.

What we want is life, and life-energy inside us. Where it comes from, or what it is, we don't know, and never shall. It is the capital X of all our knowledge.

But we want it, we must have it. It is the all in all.

This we know, now, for good and all: that which is good, and moral, is that which brings into us a stronger, deeper flow of life and life-energy: evil is that which impairs the life-flow.

But man's difficulty is, that he can't have life for the asking. "He asked life of Thee, and Thou gayest it him: even length of days for ever and ever.—There's a pretty motto for the tomb!

It isn't length of days for ever and ever that a man wants. It is strong life within himself, while he lives.

But how to get it? You may be as healthy as a cow, and yet have fear inside you, because your life is not enough.

We know, really, that we can't have life for the asking, nor find it by seeking, nor get it by striving. The river flows into us from behind and below. We must turn our backs to it, and go ahead. The faster we go ahead, the stronger the river rushes into us. The moment we turn round to embrace the river of life, it ebbs away, and we see nothing but a stony fiumara.

We must go ahead.

But which way is ahead?

We don't know.

We only know that, continuing in the way we are going, the river of life flows feebler and feebler in us, and we lose all sense of vital direction. We begin to talk about vitamines. We become idiotic. We cunningly prepare our own suicide.

This is the philosophic problem: to find the way ahead.

Allons!—there is no road before us.

Plato said that ahead, ahead was the perfect Idea, gleaming in the brow of the dragon.

We have pretty well caught up with the perfect Idea, and we find it a sort of vast, white, polished tomb-stone.

If the mouth of the serpent is the open grave, into which the tail disappears, then three cheers for the Logos, and down she goes.

We, children of a later Pa, know that Life is real, Life is earnest, and the Grave is not its Goal.

Let us side-step.

All goals become graves.

Every goal is a grave, when you get there.

Well, I came out of an egg-cell, like an amoeba, and I go into the grave. I can't help it. It's not my fault, and it's not my business.

I don't want eternal life, nor length of days for ever and ever. Nothing so long drawn out.

I give up all that sort of stuff.

Yet while I live, I want to live. Death, no doubt, solves its own problems. Let Life solve the problem of living.

"Teach me to live that so I may
Rise glorious at the Judgment Day."

I have no desire to rise glorious at any Judgment Day, when the serpent finally chokes himself with his own tail.

"Teach me to live that so I may
Go gaily on from day to day"

Nay, in all the world, I feel the life-urge weakening. It may be there are too many people alive. I feel it is, because there is too much automatic consciousness and self-consciousness in the world.

We can't live by loving life, alone. Life is like a capricious mistress: the more you woo her the more she despises you. You have to get up and go to something more interesting. Then she'll pelt after you.

Life is the river, darkly sparkling, that enters into us from behind when we set our faces towards the unknown. Towards some goal!!!

But there is no eternal goal. Every attempt to find an eternal goal puts the tail of the serpent into his mouth again, whereby he chokes himself in one more last gasp.

What is there then, if there is no eternal goal?

By itself, the river of life just gets nowhere. It sinks into the sand.

The river of life follows the living. If the living don't get anywhere, the river of life doesn't. The old serpent lays him down and goes into a torpor, instead of dancing at our heels and sending the life-sparks up our legs and spine, as we travel.

So we've got to get somewhere.

Yet there is no goal.

"Oh man! on your four legs, your two, and your three, where are you going?"—says the Sphinx.

"I'm just going to say *How-do-you-do?* to Susan, replies the man. And he passes without a scratch.

When the cock crows, he says *How-do-you-do?*
How-do-you-do, Peter? How-do-you-do? old liar!
How-do -you-do, Oh Sun!
A challenge and a greeting.

We live in a multiple universe. I am a chick that absolutely refuses to chirp inside the monistic egg. See me walk forth, with a bit of the egg-shell sticking to my tail!

When the cuckoo, the cow, and the coffee-plant chipped the Mundane Egg, at various points, they stepped out, and immediately set off in different directions. Not different directions of space and time, but different directions in creation: within the fourth dimension. The cuckoo went cuckoo-wards, the cow went cow-wise, and the coffee-plant started *coffing*. Three very distinct roads across the fourth dimension.

The cow was dumb, and the cuckoo too.
They went their ways, as creatures do,
Till they chanced to meet, in the Lord's green Zoo.

The bird gave a cluck, the cow gave a coo,
At the sight of each other the pair of them flew
Into tantrums, and started their hullabaloo.

They startled creation; and when they were through
Each said to the other: Till I came across you
I wasn't aware of the things I could do!
Cuckoo!
Moo!
Cuckoo!

And this, I hold, is the true history of evolution.

The Greeks made equilibrium their goal. Equilibrium is hardly a goal you travel towards. Yet it's something to attain. You travel in the fourth dimension, not in yards and miles, like the eternal serpent.

366

Equilibrium argues either a dualistic or a pluralistic universe. The Greeks, being sane, were pantheists and pluralists, and so am I.

Creation is a fourth dimension, and in it there are all sorts of things, gods and what-not. That brown hen, scratching with her hind leg in such a common fashion, is a sort of goddess in the creative dimension. Of course, if you stay outside the fourth dimension, and try to measure creation in length, breadth and height, you've set yourself the difficult task of measuring up the Monad, the Mundane Egg. Which is a game, like any other. The solution is, of course (let me whisper): *Put his tail in his mouth!*

Once you realise that, willy nilly, you're *inside* the Monad, you give it up. You're inside it, and inside it you always will be. Therefore, Jonah, sit still in the whale's belly, and have a look round. For you'll *never* measure the whale, since you're inside him.

And then you see it's a fourth dimension, with all sorts of gods and goddesses in it. That brown hen, who, being a Rhode Island Red, is big and stuffy like plush-upholstery, is of course, a goddess in her own rights. If I myself had to make a poem to her, I should begin:

> "Oh my flat-footed plush arm-chair
> So commonly scratching in the yard—!"

But this poem would only reveal my own limitations.

Because Flatfoot is the favorite of the white leghorn cock and he shakes the tit-bit for her with a most wooing noise, and when she lays an egg, he bristles like a double white poppy, and rushes to meet her, as she flounders down from the chicken-house, and his echo of her *I've-laid-an-egg* cackle is rich and resonant. Every pine-tree on the mountain hears him:
She's / I've laid an egg!
And his poem to her would be:

> Oh you who make me feel so good, when you sit next me on the perch,
> At night! (temporarily, of course!)
> Oh you who make my feathers bristle with the vanity of life!
> Oh you whose cackle makes my throat go off like a rocket!
> Oh you who walk so slowly, and make me feel swifter
> Than the boss!
> Oh you who bend your head down, and move in the under
> Circle, while I prance in the upper!
> Oh you, come! come! come! for here is a bit of fat from
> The roast veal, I am shaking it for you.

In the fourth dimension, in the creative world, we live in a pluralistic universe, full of gods and strange gods and unknown gods; a universe where that Rhode Island Red hen is a goddess in her own rights, and the white cock is a god indisputable, with a little red ring on his leg: which the boss put there.

Why? Why, I mean, is he a god?

Because he is something that nothing else is. Certainly he is something that I am not.

And she is something that neither he is nor I am.

When she scratches and finds a bug in the earth, she seems fairly to gobble down the monad of all monads; and when she lays, she certainly thinks she's put the mundane egg in the nest.

Just part of her naïve nature!

As for the goal, which doesn't exist, but which we are always coming back to: well, it doesn't spatially, or temporally, or eternally exist: but in the fourth dimension, it does.

What the Greeks called equilibrium: what I call relationship. Equilibrium is just a bit mechanical. It became very mechanical, with the Greeks: an intellectual nail put through it.

I don't *want* to be "good," or "righteous"—and I won't even be "virtuous," unless "vir" means a man, and "vis" means the life-river.

But I *do* want to be alive. And to be alive, I must have a goal: in the *creative,* not in the spatial universe.

I want, in the Greek sense, an equilibrium between me and the rest of the universe. That is, I want a relationship between me and the brown hen.

The Greek equilibrium took too much for granted. The Greek never asked the brown hen, nor the horse, nor the swan, if it would kindly be equilibrated with him. He took it for granted that hen and horse would only be too delighted.

You can't take it for granted. That brown hen is extraordinarily callous to my god-like presence. She doesn't even choose to know me to nod to. If I've got to strike a balance between us, I've got to   work at it.

But that is what I want: that she shall nod to me, with a *Howdy!*—*and* I shall nod to her, more politely: *How-do-you-do, Flatfoot?* And between us there shall exist the third thing, the *connaissance.* That is the goal.

I shall not betray myself nor my own life-passion for her. When she walks into my bedroom and makes droppings in my shoes, I shall chase her with disgust, and she will flutter and squawk. And I shall not ask her to be human for my sake.

That is the mistake the Greeks made. They talked about equilibrium, and then, when they wanted to equilibrate themselves with a horse, or an ox, or an acanthus, then horse, ox, and acanthus had to become nine-tenths human, to accommodate them. Call that equilibrium? The same with woman. When the Greek wanted to equilibrate with a woman, she had to become more and more a man, approximate to the man. Call that equilibrium?

As a matter of fact, we don't call it equilibrium, we call it anthropomorphism. And anthropomorphism is a bore. Too much anthropos makes the world a dull hole.

So Greek sculpture tends to become a bore. If it's a horse, it's an anthropomorphised horse. If it's a Praxiteles *Hermes,* it's a Hermes so Praxitelised, that it begins sugarily to bore us.

Equilibrium, in its very best sense—in the sense the Greeks *originally* meant it—stands for the strange spark that flies between two creatures, two things that are equilibrated, or in living relationship. It is a goal: to come to that state when the spark will fly from me to Flatfoot, the brown hen, and from her to me.

I shall leave off addressing her: *Oh my flat-footed plush arm-chair*! I realise that is only impertinent anthropomorphism on my part. She might as well address me: *Oh my skin-flappy split pole!* Which would be like her impudence.—

Skin-flappy, of course, would refer to my blue shirt and baggy cord trousers. How would *she* know I don't grow them like a loose skin!

In the early Greeks, the spark between man and man, stranger and stranger, man and woman, stranger and strangeress, was alive and vivid. Even those Doric Apollos.

In the Egyptians, the spark between man and the living universe remains alight for ever in those early, silent, motionless statues of Pharaohs. They say, it is the statue of the soul of the man. But what is the soul of a man, except *that* in him which is himself alone, suspended in immediate relation to the sum of things? Not isolated or cut off. The Greeks began the cutting apart business. Rodin's re-merging was only an intellectual tacking on again.

The serpent hasn't got his tail in his mouth. He is on the alert with lifted head like a listening, sparky flower. The Egyptians knew.

But when the oldest Egyptians carve a hawk or a Sekhet-cat, or paint birds or oxen or people: and when the Assyrians carve a she-lion: and when the cave-men drew the charging bison, or the reindeer, in the caves of Altamira: or when the Hindoo paints geese or elephants or lotus, in the great caves of India whose name I forget—Ajanta!—then how marvellous it is! How marvellous is the living relation between man and his object! be it man or woman, bird, beast, flower or rock or rain: the exquisite frail moment of pure conjunction, which, in the fourth dimension, is timeless. An Egyptian hawk, a Chinese painting of a camel, an Assyrian sculpture of a lion, an African fetish-idol of a woman pregnant, an Aztec rattle snake, an early Greek Apollo, a cave-man's painting of a prehistoric mammoth, on and on, how perfect the timeless moments between man and the other Pan-creatures of this earth of ours!

And by the way, speaking of cave-men, how did those prognathous semi-apes of Altamira come to depict so delicately, so beautifully, a female bison charging, with swinging udder, or deer stooping feeding, or an antediluvian mammoth deep in contemplation It is art on a pure, high level, beautiful as Plato, far, far more "civilised" than Burne Jones.—Hadn't somebody better write Mr Wells' History backwards, to prove how we've degenerated, in our stupid visionlessness, since the cave-men?

The pictures in the cave represent moments of purity which are the quick of civilisation. The pure relation between the cave-man and the deer: fifty per-cent man, and fifty per-cent bison, or mammoth, or deer. It is not ninety-nine per-cent man, and one per-cent horse: as in a Raphael horse. Or hundred per-cent fool, as when G. F. Watts sculpts a bronze horse and calls it Physical Energy.

If it is to be life, then it is fifty per-cent me, fifty per-cent thee: and the third thing, the spark, which springs from out of the balance, is timeless. Jesus, who saw it a bit vaguely, called it The Holy Ghost.

Between man and woman, fifty per-cent man, fifty per-cent woman: then the pure spark. Either this, or less than nothing.

As for ideal relationships, and pure love, you might as well start to water tin pansies with carbolic acid (which is pure enough, in the antiseptic sense) in order to get the Garden of Paradise.

The reign of love is passing, and the reign of power is coming again.

The day of popular democracy is nearly done. Already we are entering the twilight, towards the night that is at hand.

Before the darkness comes, it is as well to take our directions.

It is time to enquire into the nature of power, so that we do not crassly blunder into a new era: or fall down the gulf of anarchy, in the dark, as we cross the borders.

We have a confused idea, that *will* and power are somehow identical. We think we can have a will-to-power.

A will-to-power seems to work out as bullying. And bullying is something despicable and detestable.

Tyranny, too, which seems to us the apotheosis of power, is detestable.

It comes from our mistaken idea of power. It comes from the ancient mistake, old as Moses, of confusing power with *will*. The *power* of God, and the *will* of God, we have imagined identical. We need only think for a moment, and we can see the vastness of difference between the two.

The Jews, in Moses' time, and again particularly in the time of the Kings, came to look upon Jehovah as the apotheosis of arbitrary *will*. This is the root of a very great deal of evil; an old, old root.

Will is no more than an attribute of the ego. It is, as it were, the accelerator of the engine: or the instrument which increases the pressure. A man may have a strong will, an iron will, as we say, and yet be a stupid mechanical instrument, useful simply as an instrument, without any *power* at all.

An instrument, even an iron one, has no power. The power has to be put into it. This is true of men with iron wills, just the same.

The Jews made the mistake of deifying Will, the ethical Will of God. The Germans again made the mistake, of deifying the egoistic Will of Man: the will-to-power.

There is a certain inherent stupidity in apotheosised Will, and a consequent inevitable inferiority in the devotees thereof. They all have an inferiority complex.

Because power is not in the least like Will. Power comes to us, we know not how, from beyond. Whereas our will is our own.

When a man prides himself on something that is just in himself, part of his own ego, he falls into conceit, and conceit carries an inferiority complex as its shadow.

If a man, or a race, or a nation is to be anything at all, he must have the generosity to admit that his strength comes to him from beyond. It is not his own, self-generated. It comes as electricity comes, out of nowhere into somewhere.

It is no good trying to intellectualise about it. All attempts to argue and intellectualise merely strangle the passages of the heart. We wish to keep our hearts open. Therefore we brush aside argument and intellectual haggling.

The intellect is one of the most curious instruments of the psyche. But, like the will, it is only an instrument. And it works only under pressure of the will.

By willing and by intellectualising we have done all we can, for the time being. We only exhaust ourselves, and lose our lives—that is our livingness, our power to live—by any further straining of the will and the intellect. It is time to take our hands off the throttle: knowing well enough what we are about, and choosing our course of action with a steady heart.

To take one's hand off the throttle is not the same as to let go the reins.

Man lives to live, and for no other reason. And life is not mere length of days. Many people hang on, and hang on, into a corrupt old age, just because they have *not* lived, and therefore cannot let go.

We must live. And to live, life must be in us. It must come to us, the power of life, and we must not try to get a strangle-hold upon it. From beyond comes to us the life, the power to live, and we must wisely keep our hearts open.

But the life will not come *unless* we live. That is the whole point.

"To him that hath shall be given." To him that hath life shall be given life: on condition, of course, that he lives.

And again, life does not mean length of days. Poor old Queen Victoria had length of days. But Emily Brontë had life. She died of it.

And again "living" doesn't mean just doing certain things: running after women, or digging a garden, or working an engine, or becoming a member of Parliament. Just because, for Lord Byron, to sleep with a "crowned head" was life itself, it doesn't follow that it will be life for *me* to sleep with a crowned head, or even a head uncrowned. Sleeping with heads is no joke, anyhow. And living won't even consist in jazzing or motoring or going to Wembley, just because most folks do it. Living consists in doing what you really, vitally want to do: what the *life* in you wants to do, not what your ego imagines you want to do. And to find out *how* the life in you wants to be lived, and to live it, is terribly difficult. Somebody has to give us a clue.

And this is the real *exercise* of power.

That settles two points. First, power is life rushing in to us. Second, the exercise of power is the setting of life in motion.

And this is very far from *Will*.

If you want a dictator, whether it is Lenin, or Mussolini, or Primo de Rivera, ask, not whether he can set money in circulation, but if he can set life in motion, by dictating to his people.

Now, although we hate to admit it, Lenin did set life a good deal in motion, for the Russian proletariat. The Russian proletariat was like a child that had been kept under too much. So it was dying to be free. It was crazy to keep house for itself.

Now, like a child, it is keeping house for itself, without Papa or Mama to interfere. And naturally it enjoys it. For the time it's a game.

But for us, English or American or French or German people, it would not be a game. We have more or less kept house for ourselves for a long time, and it's not very thrilling, after years of it.

So a Lenin wouldn't do us any good. He wouldn't set any life going in us at all.

The Gallic and Latin blood isn't thrilled about keeping house, anyhow. It wants Glory, or else ɴᴏ Glory on horse-back, or Glory upset. If there was any Glory to upset, either in France or Italy or Spain, then communism might flourish. But since there isn't even a spark of Glory to blow out—Alfonso! Victor Emmanuel! Poincaré!—what's the good of blowing?

So they set up a little harmless Glory in baggy trousers—Papa Mussolini—or a bit of fat, self-loving but amiable elder-brother Glory in General de Rivera: and they call it power. And the democratic world holds up its hands, and moans: *Dictators! Tyranny!* While the conservative world cheers loudly, and cries: *The Man! The Man! El hombre! L'uomo! L'homme! Hooray!!!*

Bunk!

We want life. And we want the power of life. We want to feel the power of life in ourselves.

We're sick of being soft, and amiable, and harmless. We're sick to death of even enjoying ourselves. We're a bit ashamed of our own existence. Or if we aren't we ought to be.

But what then? Shall we exclaim, in a fat voice: *Aha! Power! Glory! Force! The Man!*—and proceed to set up a harmless Mussolini, or a fat Rivera?—Well, let us, if we want to. Only it won't make the slightest difference to our real living. Except it's probably a good thing to have the press, —the newspaper press—crushed under the up-to-date rubber heel of a tyrannous but harmless dictator.

We won't speak of poor old Hindenburg.—Except, why didn't they set up his wooden statue with all the nails knocked into it, for a President? For surely they drove *something* in, with those nails!

We had a harmless dictator, in Mr Lloyd George. Better go ahead with the Houses of Representatives, than have another shot in that direction.

Power! How can there be power in politics, when politics is money?

Money is power, they say. Is it? Money is to power what margarine is to butter: a nasty substitute.

No, power is something you've got to respect, even revere, before you can have it. It isn't bossing, or bullying, hiring a manservant or Salvationising your social inferior, issuing loud orders and getting your own way, doing your opponent down. That isn't power.

Power is *pouvoir* to be able to.

Might: the ability to make: to bring about that which may-be.

And where are we to get Power, or Might, or Glory, or Honour, or Wisdom?

Out of Lloyd George, or Lenin, or Mussolini, or Rivera, or anything else political?

Bah! It has to be in the people, before it can come out in politics.

Do we *want* Power, Might, Glory, Honour, and Wisdom?

If we do, we'd better start to get them, each man for himself.

But if we don't, we'd better continue our lick-spittling course of being as happy, as happy as Kings.

"The world is so full of a number of things
We ought all to be happy, as happy as Kings."

Which Kings, might we ask?—Better be careful!

Myself I want Power. But I don't want to boss anybody.

I want Honour. But I don't see any existing nation or government that could give it me.

I want Glory. But heaven save me from mankind.

I want Might. But perhaps I've got it.

The first thing, of course, is to open one's heart to the source of Power, and Might, and Glory, and Honour. It just depends, which gates of one's heart one opens. You can open the humble gate, or the proud gate. Or you can open both, and see what comes.

Best open both, and take the responsibility. But set a guard at each gate, to keep out the liars, the snivellers, the mongrel and the greedy.

However smart we be, however rich and clever or loving or charitable or spiritual or impeccable, it doesn't help us at all. The real power comes in to us from beyond. Life enters us from behind, where we are sightless, and from below, where we do not understand.

And unless we yield to the beyond, and take our power and might and honour and glory from the unseen, from the unknown, we shall continue empty. We may have length of days. But an empty tin can lasts longer than Alexander lived.

So, anomalous as it may sound, if we want power, we must put aside our own will, and our own conceit, and *accept* power, from the beyond.

And having admitted the power from the beyond into us, we must abide by it, and not traduce it. Courage, discipline, inward isolation, these are the conditions upon which power will abide in us.

And between brave people there will be the communion of power, prior to the communion of love. The communion of power does not exclude the communion of love. It includes it. The communion of love is only a part of the greater communion of power.

Power is the supreme quality of God and man: the power to cause, the power to create, the power to make, the power to do, the power to destroy. And then, between those things which are created or made, love is the supreme binding relationship. And between those who, with a single impulse, set out passionately to destroy what must be destroyed, joy flies like electric sparks, within the communion of Power.

Love is simply and purely a relationship, and in a pure relationship there can be nothing but equality; or at least equipoise.

But Power is more than a relationship. It is like electricity, it has different degrees. Men are powerful or powerless, more or less: we know not how or why. But it is so. And the communion of power will always be a communion in inequality.

In the end as in the beginning, it is always Power that rules the world! There *must be* rule. And only Power can rule. Love cannot should not, does not seek to. The statement that love rules the camp, the court, the grove, is a lie; and the fact that such love has to rhyme with "grove," proves it. Power rules and will always rule. Because it was Power that created us all. The act of love itself is an act of power, original as original sin. The power is given us.

As soon as there is an *act,* even in love, it is power. Love itself is purely a relationship.

But in an age that, like ours, has lost the mystery of power, and the reverence for power, a false power is substituted: the power of money. This is a power based on the force of human envy and greed, nothing more. So nations naturally become more envious and greedy every day. While individuals ooze away in a cowardice that they call love. They call it love, and peace, and charity, and benevolence, when it is mere cowardice. Collectively they are hideously greedy and envious.

True power, as distinct from the spurious power, which is merely the force of certain human vices directed and intensified by the human will: true power never belongs to us. It is given us, from the beyond.

Even the simplest form of power, physical strength, is not our own, to do as we like with. As Samson found.

But power is given differently, in varying degrees and varying kind to different people. It always was so, it always will be so. There will never be equality in power. There will always be unending inequality.

Nowadays, when the only power is the power of human greed and envy, the greatest men in the world are men like Mr Ford, who can satisfy the modern lust, we can call it nothing else, for owning a motor-car: or men like the great financiers, who can soar on wings of greed to uncanny heights, and even can spiritualise greed.

They talk about "equal opportunity": but it is bunk, ridiculous bunk. It is the old fable of the fox asking the stork to dinner. All the food is to be served in a shallow dish, levelled to perfect equality, and you get what you can.

If you're a fox, like the born financier, you get a bellyful and more. If you're a stork, or a flamingo, or even a man, you have the food gobbled from under your nose, and you go comparatively empty.

Is the fox, then, or the financier, the highest animal in creation? Bah!

Humanity never bunked itself so thoroughly as with the bunk of equality, even qualified down to "equal opportunity."

In living life, we are all born with different powers, and different degrees of power: some higher, some lower. The only thing to do is honorably to accept it, and to live in the communion of power. Is it not better to serve a man in whom power lives, than to clamour for equality with Mr Motor-car Ford, or Mr Shady Stinnes? Pfui! To your equality with such men! It gives me gooseflesh.

How much better it must have been, to be a colonel under Napoleon, than to be a Marshal Foch! Oh! how much better it must have been, to live in terror of Peter the Great—who was great—than to be a member of the proletariat under Comrade Lenin: or even to *be* Comrade Lenin: though even he was greatish, far greater than any extant millionaire.

Power is beyond us. Either it is given us from the unknown, or we have not got it. And better to touch it in another, than never to know it. Better be a Russian and shoot oneself out of sheer terror of Peter the Great's displeasure, than to live like a well-to-do American, and never know the mystery of Power at all. Live in blank sterility.

For Power is the first and greatest of all mysteries. It is the mystery that is behind all our being, even behind all our existence. Even the Phallic erection is a first blind movement of power. Love is said to call the power into motion: but it is probably the reverse: that the slumbering *power* calls love into being.

Power is manifold. There is physical strength, like Samson's. There is racial power, like David's or Mahomet's. There is mental power, like that of Socrates, and ethical power, like that of Moses, and spiritual power, like Jesus' or like Buddha's, and mechanical power, like that of Stephenson, or military power, like Napoleon's, or political power, like Pitt's. These are all true manifestations of power, coming out of the unknown.

374

Unlike the millionaire power, which comes out of the known forces of human greed and envy.

Power puts something new into the world. It may be Edison's gramophone, or Newton's Law or Caesar's Rome or Jesus' Christianity, or even Attila's charred ruins and emptied spaces. Something new displaces something old, and sometimes room has to be cleared beforehand.

Then power is obvious. Power is much more obvious in its destructive than in its constructive activity. A tree falls with a crash. It grew without a sound.

Yet true destructive power is power just the same as constructive.

Even Attila, the Scourge of God, who helped to scourge the Roman world out of existence, was great with power. He was the scourge of *God:* not the scourge of the League of Nations, hired and paid in cash.

If it must be a scourge, let it be a scourge of God. But let it be power, the old divine power. The moment the divine power manifests itself, it is right: whether. it be Attila or Napoleon or George Washington. But Lloyd George, and Woodrow Wilson, and Lenin, they never had the right smell. They never even roused real fear: no real passion. Whereas a manifestation of real power arouses passion, and always will.

Time it should again.

Blessed are the powerful, for theirs is the kingdom of earth.

LOVE WAS ONCE A LITTLE BOY

Collapse, as often as not, is the result of persisting in an old attitude towards some important relationship, which, in the course of time, has changed its nature.

Love itself is a relationship, which changes as all things change, save abstractions. If you want something really more durable than diamonds, you must be content with eternal truths like "twice two are four."

Love is the relationship between things that live, holding them together in a sort of unison. There are other vital relationships. But love is this special one.

In every living thing there is the desire, for love, or for the relationship of unison with the rest of things. That a tree should desire to develop itself between the power of the sun, and the opposite pull of the earth's centre, and to balance itself between the four winds of heaven, and to unfold itself between the rain and the shine, to have roots and feelers in blue heaven and innermost earth, both, this is a manifestation of love: a knitting together of the diverse cosmos into a oneness, a tree.

At the same time, the tree must most powerfully exert itself and defend itself, to maintain its own integrity against the rest of things.

So that even love, as a desire, is balanced against the opposite desire, to maintain the integrity of the individual self.

Hate is not the opposite of love. The real opposite of love is individuality.

We live in the age of individuality, we call ourselves the servants of love. That is to say, we enact a perpetual paradox.

Take the love of a man and a woman, today. As sure as you start with a case of "true love" between them, you end with a terrific struggle and conflict of the two opposing egos or individualities. It is nobody's fault: it is the inevitable result of trying to snatch an intensified individuality out of the mutual flame.

Love, as a relationship of unison, means, and must mean, *to some extent,* the sinking of the individuality. Hence the insistence on sacrifice. Woman for centuries was expected to sink her individuality into that of her husband and family. Nowadays, the tendency is to insist that a man shall sink his individuality into his job, or his business, primarily, and secondarily into his wife and family.

At the same time, education and the public voice urges man and woman into intenser individualism. The sacrifice takes the old symbolic form of throwing a few grains of incense on the altar. A certain amount of time, labor, money, emotion are sacrificed on the altar of love, by man and woman: especially emotion. But each calculates the sacrifice. And man and woman alike, each saves his individual ego, her individual ego, intact, as far as possible, in the scrimmage of love. Most of our talk about love is cant, and bunk. The treasure of treasures to man and woman today is his own or her own ego. And this ego, each hopes it will flourish like a salamand, in the flame of love and passion. Which it well may: but for the fact that there arc two salamanders in the same flame, and they fight till the flame goes out. Then they become grey cold lizards of the vulgar ego.

It is much easier, of course, when there *is* no flame. Then there is no serious fight.

You can't worship love and individuality in the same breath. Love is a mutual relationship, like a flame between wax and air. If either wax or air insists on getting its own way, or getting its own back too much, the flame goes out and the unison disappears. At the same time, if one yields itself up to the other entirely, there is a guttering mess. You have to balance love and individuality, and actually sacrifice a portion of each.

You have to have some sort of balance.

The Greeks said equilibrium. But whereas you can quite nicely balance a pound of butter against a pound of cheese, it is quite another matter to balance a rose and a ruby. Still more difficult is it to put male man in one scale, female woman in the other, and equilibrate that little pair of opposites.

Unless, of course, you abstract them. It's easy enough to balance a citizen against a citizeness, a Christian against a Christian, a spirit against a spirit, or a soul against a soul. There's a formula for each case. Liberty, Equality, Fraternity etc. etc.

But the moment you put young Tom in one scale, and young Kate in the other: why, not God Himself has succeeded as yet in striking a nice level balance. Probably doesn't intend to, ever.

Probably it's one of the things that are most fascinating because they are *nearly* possible, yet absolutely impossible. Still, a miss is better than a mile. You can at least draw blood.

How can I equilibrate myself with my black cow Susan? I call her daily at six o'clock. And sometimes she comes. But sometimes again, she doesn't, and I have to hunt her away among the timber. Possibly she is lying peacefully in cowy inertia, like a black Hindu statue, among the oak-scrub. Then she rises with a sighing heave. My calling was a mere nothing against the black stillness of her cowy passivity. Or possibly she is away down in the bottom corner, lowing *sotto voce* and blindly to some far-off, inaccessible bull. Then when I call at her, and approach, she screws round her tail and flings her sharp, elastic haunches in the air with a kick and a flick, and plunges off like a buck rabbit, or like a black demon among the pine trees, her udder swinging like a chime of bells. Or possibly the coyotes have been howling in the night along the top fence. And then I can call in vain. It's a question of saddling a horse and sifting the bottom timber. And there at last the horse suddenly winces, starts: and with a certain pang of fear I too catch sight of something black and motionless and alive, and terribly silent, among the tree-trunks. It is Susan, her ears apart, standing like some spider suspended motionless by a thread, from the web of the eternal silence. The strange faculty she has, cow-given, of becoming a suspended ghost, hidden in the very crevices of the atmosphere! It is something in her *will*. It is her tarnhelm. And then, she doesn't know me. If I am afoot, she knows my voice, but not the advancing me, in a blue shirt and cord trousers. She waits, suspended by the thread, till I come close. Then she reaches forward her nose, to smell. She smells my hand: gives a little snirt, exhaling her breath, with a kind of contempt, turns, and ambles up towards the homestead, perfectly assured. If I am on horseback, although she knows the grey horse perfectly well, at the same time she *doesn't* know what it is. She waits till the wicked Azul, who is a born cow-punching pony, advances mischievously at her. Then round she swings, as if on the blast of some sudden wind, and with her ears back, her head rather down, her black back curved, up she goes, through the timber, with surprising, swimming swiftness. And the Azul, snorting with jolly mischief, dashes after her. And when she is safely in her milking place, still she watches with her great black eyes as I dismount. And she has to smell my hand before the cowy peace of being milked enters her blood. Till then, there is something *roaring* in the chaos of her universe. When her cowy peace comes, then her universe is silent, and like the sea with an even tide, without sail or smoke: nothing.

That is Susan, my black cow.

And how am I going to equilibrate myself with her? Or even if you prefer the word, to get into harmony with her?

Equilibrium? Harmony? with that black blossom! Try it!

She doesn't even know me. If I put on a pair of white trousers, she wheels away as if the devil was on her back. I have to go behind her, talk to her, stroke her, and let her smell my hand; and smell the white trousers. She doesn't know they are trousers. She doesn't know that I am a gentleman on two feet. Not she. Something mysterious happens in her blood and her being, when she smells me and my nice white trousers.

Yet she knows me, too. She likes to linger, while one talks to her. She knows quite well she makes me mad when she swings her tail in my face. So sometimes she swings it, just on purpose: and looks at me out of the black corner of her great, pure-black eye, when I yell at her. And when I find her, away down the timber, when she is like a ghost, and lost to the world, like a spider dangling in the void of chaos, then she is relieved. She comes to, out of a sort of trance, and is relieved, trotting up home: with a queer, jerky cowy gladness. But she is never *really* glad, as the horses are. There is always a certain untouched chaos in her.

Where she is when she's *in* the trance, heaven only knows.

That's Susan! I have a certain relation to her. But that she and I are in equilibrium, or in harmony, I would never guarantee while the world stands. As for her individuality being in balance with mine, one can only feel the great blank of the gulf.

Yet a relationship there is. She knows my touch, and she goes very still and peaceful, being milked. I too, I know her smell and her warmth and her feel, and I share some of her cowy silence, when I milk her. There *is* a sort of relation between us. And this relation is part of the mystery of love: the individuality on each side, mine and Susan's, suspended in the relationship.

> "Cow Susan by the forest's rim
> A black-eyed Susan was to him
> And nothing more—"

One understands Wordsworth and the primrose and the yokel. The yokel had no relation at all—or next to none—with the primrose. Wordsworth gathered it into his own bosom and made it part of his own nature. "I, William, am also a yellow primrose blossoming on a bank." This, we must assert, is an impertinence on William's part.

He ousts the primrose from its own individuality. He doesn't allow it to call its soul its own. It must be identical with *his* soul. Because, of course, by begging the question, there is but One Soul in the universe.

This is bunk. A primrose has its own peculiar primrosy identity, and all the oversouling in the world won't melt it out into a Williamish oneness. Neither will the yokel's remarking: "Nay, boy, that's nothing. It's only a primrose!"—turn the primrose into nothing. The primrose will neither be assimilated nor annihilated, and Boundless Love breaks on the rock of one mere flower. It has its own individuality, which it opens with very lovely naïveté to sky and wind and William and yokel, bee and beetle alike. It *is* itself. But its very floweriness is a kind of communion with all things: the love unison.

In this lies the eternal absurdity of Wordsworth's lines. His own behaviour, primrosely, was as foolish as the yokel's.

> "A primrose by the river's brim
> A yellow primrose was to him
> And nothing more—"
>
> A primrose by the river's brim
> A yellow primrose was to him
> And a great deal more—
>
> A primrose by the river's brim
> Lit up its pallid yellow glim
> Upon the floor—
>
> And watched old Father William trim
> His course beside the river's brim
> And trembled sore—
>
> The yokel, going for a swim
> Had very nearly trod on him
> An hour before.
>
> And now the poet's fingers slim

Were reaching out to pluck at him
And hurt him more.

Oh gentlemen, hark to my hymn!
To be a primrose is my whim
Upon the floor,
And nothing more,
As you said before.

The sky is with me, and the dim
Earth clasps my roots. Your shadows skim
My face once more.
Leave me therefore
Upon the floor,
Say *au revoir*

Ah William! The "something more" that the primrose was to you, was yourself in the mirror. And if the yokel actually got as far as beholding a "yellow primrose," he got far enough.

You see, it is not so easy even for a poet to equilibrate himself even with a mere primrose. He didn't leave it with a soul of its own. It had to have his soul. And Nature had to be sweet and pure, Williamish Sweet-Williamish at that! Anthropomorphised! Anthropomorphism, that allows nothing to call its soul its own, save anthropos: and only a special brand, even of him.

Poetry can tell alluring lies, when we let our feelings, or our ego, run away with us.

And we must always beware of romance: of people who love Nature, or flowers, or dogs, or babies, or pure adventure. It means they are getting into a love-swim where everything is easy and nothing opposes their own egoism. Nature, babies, dogs are *so* lovable, because they can't answer back. The primrose, alas! couldn't pipe up and say: Hey! Bill! Get off the barrow!

That's the best of men and women. There's bound to be a lot of back chat. You can *Lucy Gray* your woman as hard as you like, one day she's bound to come back at you: Who are *you* when you're at home?

A man isn't going to spread his own ego over a woman, as he has done over Nature, and primroses, and dogs, or horses, or babies, or "the people" or the proletariat or the poor-and-needy. The old hen takes the cock by the beard, and says: *That's me, mind you!*

Man is an individual, and woman is an individual. Which sounds easy.

But it's not as easy as it seems. These two individuals are as different as chalk and cheese. True, a pound of chalk weighs as much as a pound of cheese. But the proof of the pudding is in the eating, not in the scales.

That is to say, you can announce that men and women should be equal, and *are* equal. All right. Put them in the scales.

Alas! my wife is about twenty pounds heavier than I am.

Nothing to do but to abstract. *L'homme est né libre*: with a napkin round his little tail—

379

Nevertheless, I am a citizen, my wife is a citizeness: I can vote, she can vote, I can be sent to prison, she can be sent to prison, I can have a passport, she can have a passport, I can be an author, she can be an authoress. OOray! OO-bloomin-ray!

You see, we are both British Subjects.—Everybody bow!

Subjects! Subjects! Subjects!

Madame is already shaking herself like a wet hen.

But yes, my dear! we are both subjects. And as subjects, we enjoy a lovely equality. Liberty, my dear! Equality! Fraternity or Sorority my dear!

Aren't you pleased?

But it is no use talking to a wet hen. That "subjects" was a cold douche.

As subjects, men and women may be equal.

But as objects, it's another pair of shoes.—Where, I ask you, is the equality between an arrow and a horseshoe? or a serpent and a squash-blossom? Find me the equation that equates the cock and the hen.

You can't.

As inhabitants of my backyard, as loyal subjects of my rancho, they, the cock and the hen, are equal. When he gets wheat, she gets wheat. When sour milk is put out, it is as much for him as for her. She is just as free to go where she likes, as he is. And if she likes to crow at sunrise, she may. There is no law against it. And he can lay an egg, if the fit takes him. Absolutely nothing forbids.

Isn't that equality? If it isn't, what is?

Even then, they're two very different objects.

As equals, they are just a couple of barnyard fowls, chickens! Generalised!

But dear me, when he comes prancing up with his red beard shaking, and his eye gleaming, and she comes slowly pottering after, with her nose to the ground, they're two very different objects. You never think of equality: or of inequality, for that matter. They're a cock and a hen, and you accept them as such.

You don't think of them as equals, or as unequals. But you think of them *together*.

Wherein, then, lies the togetherness?

Would you call it love?

I wouldn't.

Their two egos are absolutely separate. He's a cock, she's a hen. He never thinks of her for a moment, as if she were a cock like himself; and she never thinks for a moment that he is a hen like herself. I never hear anything in her squawk which would seem to say: *Aren't I fowl as much as you are, you brute!* Whereas I always hear women shrieking at their men: Aren't I a human being as much as you?

It seems so beside the point.

I always answer my spouse, with sweet reasonableness: My dear, we are both British Subjects. What can I say more, on the score of our equality! You are a British Subject as much as I am.

Curiously, she hates to have it put that way. She wants to be a human being as much as I am. But absolutely, and honestly, I don't know what a human being is. Whereas I do know what a British Subject is. It can be defined.

And I can see how a Civis Romanum, or a British Subject can be free, whether it's he or she. The he-ness or the she-ness doesn't matter. But how a *man* can consider himself free, I don't know. Any more than a cock-robin or a dandelion.

Imagine a dandelion suddenly hissing: *I am free and I will be free*! Then wriggling on his root like a snake with its tail pegged down!

What a horrifying sight!

So it is when a man, with two legs and a penis, a belly and a mouth, begins to shout about being free. One wants to ask: Which bit do you refer to?

There's the cock and there's the hen, and their two egos or individualities seem to stay apart without friction. They never coo at one another, nor hold each other's hand. I never see her sitting on his lap and being petted. True, sometimes he calls for her to come and eat a titbit. And sometimes he dashes at her and walks over her for a moment. She doesn't seem to mind. I never hear her squawking: *Don't you think you can walk over me*!

Yet she's by no means downtrodden. She's just herself, and seems to have a very good time: and she doesn't like it if he is missing.

So there is this peculiar togetherness about them. You can't call it love. It would be too ridiculous.

What then?

As far as I can see, it is desire: just desire. And the desire has a fluctuating intensity, but it is always there. His desire is always towards her, even when he's absolutely forgotten her. And by the way she puts her feet down, I can see she always walks in her plumes of desirableness, even when she's going broody.

The mystery about her, is her strange undying desirableness. You can see it in every step she takes. She is desirable, and this is the breath of her life.

It is the same with Susan. The queer cowy mystery of her is her changeless cowy desirableness. She is far, alas, from any bull. She never even remotely dreams of a bull, save at rare and brief periods. Yet her whole being and motion is that of being desirable: or else fractious. It seems to unite her with the very air, and the plants and trees. Even to the sky and the trees and the grass and the running stream, she is subtly, delicately and *purely* desirable, in cowy desirability. It is her cowy mystery. Then her fractiousness is the fireworks of her desirableness.

To me she is fractious, tiresome, and a faggot. Yet the same subtle desirableness is in her, for me. As it is in a brown hen, or even a sow. It is a peculiar charm: the creature's femaleness, her desirableness. It is sex, no doubt: but so subtle as to have nothing to do with function. It is a mystery, like a delicate flame. It would be false to call it love, because love complicates the ego. The ego is always concerned in love. But in the frail, subtle desirousness of the true male, towards everything female, and the equally frail, indescribable desirability of every female for every male, lies the real clue to the equating, or the *relating,* of things which otherwise are incommensurable.

And this, this desire, is the reality which is inside love. The ego itself plays a false part in it. The individual is like a deep pool, or tarn, in the mountains, fed from beneath by unseen springs, and having no obvious inlet or outlet. The springs which feed the individual at the depths are sources of power, power from the unknown. But it is not until the stream of desire overflows and goes running downhill into the open world, that the individual has his further, secondary existence.

Now we have imagined love to be something absolute and personal. It is neither. In its essence, love is no more than the stream of clear and unmuddied, subtle desire which flows from person to person, creature to creature, thing to thing.

The moment this stream of delicate but potent desire dries up, the love has dried up, and the joy of life has dried up. It's no good trying to turn on the tap. Desire is either flowing, or gone, and the love with it, and the life too.

This subtle streaming of desire is beyond the control of the ego. The ego says: This is *my* love, to do as I like with! This is *my* desire given me for my own pleasure.

But the ego deceives itself. The individual cannot possess the love which he himself feels. Neither should he be entirely possessed by it. Neither man nor woman should sacrifice individuality to love, nor love to individuality.

If we lose desire out of our life, we become empty vessels. But if we break our own integrity, we become a squalid mess, like a jar of honey dropped and smashed.

The individual has nothing, really, to do with love. That is, his individuality hasn't. Out of the deep silence of his individuality runs the stream of desire, into the open squash-blossom of the world. And the stream of desire may meet and mingle with the stream from a woman. But it is never *himself* that meets and mingles with *herself*: any more than two lakes, whose waters meet to make one river, in the distance, meet in themselves.

The two individualities stay apart, for ever and ever. But the two streams of desire, like the Blue Nile and the White Nile, from the mountains one and from the low hot lake the other, meet and at length mix their strange and alien waters, to make Nilus Flux.

See then the childish mistake we have made, about love. We have insisted that the two individualities should "fit." We have insisted that the "love" between man and woman must be "perfect." What on earth that means, is a mystery. What would a perfect Nilus Flux be?—one that never overflowed its banks? Or one that always overflowed its banks? Or one that had exactly the same overflow every year, to a hair's-breadth?

My dear, it is absurd. Perfect love is an absurdity. As for casting out fear, you'd better be careful. For fear, like curses and chickens, will also come home to roost.

Perfect love, I suppose, means that a married man and woman never contradict one another, and that they both of them always feel the same thing at the same moment, and kiss one another on the strength of it. What blarney! It means, I suppose, that they are absolutely intimate: this precious intimacy that lovers insist on. They tell each other *everything* and if she puts on chiffon knickers, he ties the strings for her: and if he blows his nose, she holds the hanky.

Pfui! Is anything so loathsome as intimacy, especially the married sort, or the sort that "lovers" indulge in!

It's a mistake, and ends in disaster. Why? Because the individualities of man and woman are incommensurable, and they will no more meet than the Mountains of Abyssinia will meet with Lake Victoria Nyanza. It is far more important to keep them distinct, than to try to join them. If they are to join, they will join in the third land where their two streams of desire meet.

Of course, as citizen and citizeness, as two persons, even as two spirits, man and woman can be equal and intimate. But this is in their outer, more general or common selves. The individual man himself, and the individual woman herself, this is another pair of shoes.

It is a pity that we have insisted on putting all our eggs in one basket: calling love the basket, and ourselves the eggs. It is a pity we have insisted on being individuals only in the communistic, semi-abstract or generalised sense: as voters, money-owners, "free" men and women: free in so far as we are all alike, and individual in so far as we are commensurable integers.

By turning ourselves into integers: every man to himself and every woman to herself a Number One; an infinite number of Number Ones; we have destroyed ourselves as desirous or desirable individuals, and broken the inward sources of our power, and flooded all mankind into one dreary marsh where the rivers of desire lie dead with everything else, except a stagnant unity.

It is a pity of pities women have learned to think like men. Any husband will say, *they haven 't.* But they have: they've all learned to think like some other beastly man, who is not their husband. Our education goes on and on, on and on, making the sexes alike, destroying the original individuality of the blood, to substitute for it this dreary individuality of the ego, the Number One. Out of the ego streams neither Blue Nile nor White. The infinite number of little human egos makes a mosquito marsh, where nothing happens except buzzing and biting, ooze and degeneration.

And they call this marsh, with its poisonous will-o'-the-wisps, and its clouds of mosquitoes, *democracy,* and the reign of love!!

You can have it.

I am a man, and the Mountains of Abyssinia, and my Blue Nile flows towards the desert. There should be a woman, somewhere far South, like a great lake, sending forth her White Nile towards the desert, too: and the rivers will meet among the slopes of the world, somewhere

But alas, every woman I've ever met spends her time saying she's as good as any man, if not better, and she can beat him at his own game. So Lake Victoria Nyanza gets up on end, and declares it's the Mountains of Abyssinia, and the Mountains of Abyssinia fall flat and cry: *You're all that, and more, my dear!*—and between them, you're bogged.

I give it up.

But at any rate it's nice to know *what's* wrong, since wrong it is.

If we were men, if we were women, our individualities would be lonely and a bit mysterious, like tarns, and fed with power, male power, female power, from underneath, invisibly. And from us the streams of desire would flow out in the eternal glimmering adventure, to meet in some unknown desert.

Mais nous avons changé tout cela.

I'll bet the yokel, even then, was more himself, and the stream of his desire was stronger and more gurgling, than William Wordsworth's. For a long time the yokel retains his own integrity, and his own real stream of desire flows from him. Once you break this, and turn him, who was a yokel, into still another Number One, an assertive newspaper-parcel of an ego, you've done it!

But don't, dear, darling reader, when I say "desire," immediately conclude that I mean a jungleful of rampaging Don Juans and raping buck niggers. When I say that a woman should be eternally desirable *don't* say that I mean, every man should want to sleep with her, the instant he sets eyes on her.

On the contrary. Don Juan was only Don Juan because he *had* no real desire. He had broken his own integrity, and was a mess to start with. No stream of desire, with a course of its own, flowed from him He was a marsh in himself. He mashed and trampled everything up and desired no woman, so he ran after every one of them, with an itch instead of a steady flame. And tortured by his own itch, he inflamed his itch more and more. That's Don Juan: the man who *couldn't* desire a woman. He shouldn't have tried. He should have gone into a monastery at fifteen.

As for the yokel, his little stream may have flowed out of commonplace little hills, and been ready to mingle with the stream of any easy, puddly little yokeless. But what does it matter! And men are far less promiscuous, even then, than we like to pretend. It's Don Juanery, sex-in-the-head, no real desire, which leads to profligacy or squalid promiscuity. The yokel usually met desire with desire: which is all right: and sufficiently rare to ensure the moral balance.

Desire is a living stream. If we gave free rein, or a free course, to our living flow of desire, we shouldn't go far wrong. It's quite different from giving a free rein to an itching, prurient imagination. That is our vileness.

The living stream of sexual desire itself does not often, in any man, find its object, its confluent, the stream of desire in a woman, into which it can flow. The two streams flow together, spontaneously, not often, in the life of any man or woman. Mostly, men and women alike rush into a sort of prostitution, because our idiotic civilisation has never learned to hold in reverence the true desire-stream. We force our desires, from our ego: and this is deadly.

Desire itself is a pure thing, like sunshine, or fire, or rain. It is desire that makes the whole world living to me, keeps me in the flow, connected. It is my flow of desire that makes me move as the birds and animals move through the sunshine and the night, in a kind of accomplished innocence, not shut outside of the natural paradise. For life is a kind of paradise, even to my horse Azul, though he doesn't get his own way in it, by any means, and is sometimes in a real temper about it. Sometimes he even gets a bellyache, with wet alfalfa. But even the bellyache is part of the natural paradise. Not like human *ennui*.

So a man can go forth in desire, even to the primrose. But let him refrain from falling all over the poor blossom, as William did. Or trying to incorporate it in his own ego, which is a sort of lust. Nasty anthropomorphic lust.

Everything that exists, even a stone, has two sides to its nature. It fiercely maintains its own individuality, its own solidity. And it reaches forth from itself in the subtlest flow of desire.

It fiercely resists all inroads. At the same time it sinks down in the curious weight, or flow, of that desire which we call gravitation. And imperceptibly, through the course of ages, it flows into delicate combination with the air and sun and rain.

At one time, men worshipped stones: symbolically, no doubt, because of their mysterious durability, their power of hardness, resistance, their strength of remaining unchanged. Yet even then, worshipping man did not rest till he had erected the stone into a pillar, a menhir, symbol of the eternal desire, as the phallus itself is but a symbol.

And we, men and women, are the same as stones: the powerful resistance and cohesiveness of our individuality is countered by the mysterious flow of desire, from us and towards us.

It is the same with the worlds, the stars, the suns. All is alive, in its own degree. And the centripetal force of spinning earth is the force of earth's individuality: and the centrifugal force is the force of desire. Earth's immense centripetal energy, almost a passion, balanced against her furious centrifugal force, holds her suspended between her moon and her sun, in a dynamic equilibrium.

So instead of the Greek: *Know Thyself*! we shall have to say, to every man: *Be thyself*! *Be desirous*!—and to every woman: *Be thyself*! *Be desirable*!

Be thyself! does not mean: *Assert thy ego*! It means, be true to your own integrity, as man, as woman: let your heart stay open, to receive the mysterious inflow of power from the unknown: know that the power comes to you from beyond, it is not generated by your own will: therefore, all the time, be watchful, and reverential towards the mysterious coming of power into you.

Be thyself! is the grand cry of individualism. But individualism makes the mistake of considering an individual as a fixed entity: a little windmill that spins without shifting ground or changing its own nature. And this is nonsense. When power enters us, it does not just move us mechanically. It changes us. When the unseen wind blows, it blows upon us, and through us. It carries us like a ship on a sea. And it roars to flame in us, like a draught in a fierce fire. Or like a dandelion in flower.

What is the difference between a dandelion and a windmill?

Heap on more wood!

Even the Nirvanists consider man as a fixed entity, a changeless ego, which is capable of nothing, ultimately, but re-merging into the infinite. A little windmill that can turn faster and faster and faster, till it becomes actually invisible, and nothing remains in nothingness, except a blur and a faint hum.

I am not a windmill. I am not even an ego. I am a man.

I am myself, and I remain myself only by the grace of the powers that enter me, from the unseen, and make me forever newly myself.

And I am myself, also, by the grace of the desire that flows from me, and consummates me with the other unknown, the visible, tangible creation.

The powers that enter me fluctuate and ebb. And the desire that goes forth from me waxes and wanes. Sometimes it is weak, and I am almost isolated. Sometimes it is strong, and I am almost carried away.

But supposing the cult of Individualism, Liberty, Freedom and so forth, has landed me in the state of egoism, the state so prettily and nauseously described by Henley in his *Invictus:* which, after all, is but the yelp of a house-dog, a domesticated creature with an inferiority complex!

> "It matters not how strait the gate,
> How charged with punishment the scroll:
> I am the master of my fate!
> I am the captain of my soul!"

Are you, old boy? Then why hippety-hop?
He was a cripple at that!"

As a matter of fact, it is the slave's bravado! The modern slave is he who does not receive his powers from the unseen, and give reverence, but who thinks he is his own little boss. Only a slave would take the trouble to shout: *I am free!* That is to say, to shout it in the face of the open heavens. In the face of men, and their institutions and prisons, Yes-yes! But in the face of the open heavens I would be ashamed to talk about freedom. I have no life, no real power, unless it will come to me. And I accomplish nothing, not even my own fulfilled existence, unless I go forth, delicately, desirous, and find the mating of my desire: even if it be only the sky itself, and trees, and the cow Susan, and the inexpressible consolation of a statue of an Egyptian Pharaoh, or the Old Testament, or even three rubies. These answer my desire with fulfilment. What bunk then, to talk about being master of my fate! when my fate depends upon these things:—not to mention the unseen reality that sends strength, or life into me, without which I am a gourd rattle.

The ego, the little conscious ego that I am, that doll-like entity, that mannikin made in ridiculous likeness of the Adam which I am: am I going to allow that that is *all of me*? And shout about it?

Of course, if I am nothing but an ego, and woman is nothing but another ego, then there is really no vital difference between us. Two little dolls of conscious entities, squeaking when you squeeze them. And with a tiny bit of an extraneous appendage, to mark which is which. 35

"Woman is just the same as man," loudly said the political speaker: "save for a very little difference."

"Three cheers for the very little difference!" says a vulgar voice from the crowd.

Though nowadays, a lady's chemise won't save her face.

In or out of her chemise, however, doesn't make much difference to the modern woman. She's a finished-off ego, an assertive conscious entity, cut off like a doll from any mystery. And her nudity is about as interesting as a doll's. If you can *be* interested in the nudity of a doll, then jazz on, jazz on!

The same with the men. No matter how they pull their shirts off, they never arrive at their own nakedness. They have none. They can only be undressed. Naked they cannot be. Without their clothes on, they are like a dismantled street-car without its advertisements: sort of public article that doesn't refer to anything.

The ego! Anthropomorphism! Love! What it works out to in the end, is that even anthropos disappears, and leaves a sawdust mannikin wondrously jazzing.

"My little sisters, the birds!" says Francis of Assisi.

"Whew!" goes the blackbird.

"Listen to me, my little sisters, you birds!"

"Whew!" goes the blackbird. *"I'm a cock, mister!"*

Love! What's the good of woman who isn't desirable, even though she's as pretty as paint, and the waves in her hair are as permanent as the pyramids!

"He buried his face in her permanent wave, and cried: Help! Get me out!"

Individualism! Read the advertisements! "Jewjew's hats give a man that individual touch he so much desires."—"No man could lack individuality in Poppem's pyjamas."—Poor devil! If he was left to his own skin, where would he be!

Pop goes the weasel!

REFLECTIONS ON THE DEATH OF A PORCUPINE

There are many bare places on the little pine-trees, towards the top, where the porcupines have gnawed the bark away and left the white flesh showing. And some trees are dying from the top.

Everyone says, porcupines should be killed; the Indians, Mexicans, Americans all say the same.

At full moon a month ago, when I went down the long clearing in the brilliant moonlight, through the poor dry herbage a big porcupine began to waddle away from me, towards the trees and the darkness. The animal had raised all its hairs and bristles, so that by the light of the moon it seemed to have a tall, swaying, moonlit aureole arching its back as it went. That seemed curiously fearsome, as if the animal were emitting itself demon-like on the air.

It waddled very slowly, with its white spiky spoon-tail steering flat, behind the round bear-like mound of its back. It had a lumbering, beetle's, squalid motion, unpleasant. I followed it into the darkness of the timber, and there, squat like a great tick, it began scrapily to creep up a pine-trunk. It was very like a great aureoled tick, a bug, struggling up.

I stood near and watched, disliking the presence of the creature. It is a duty to kill the things. But the dislike of killing him was greater than the dislike of him. So I watched him climb.

And he watched me. When he had got nearly the height of a man, all his long hairs swaying with a bristling gleam like an aureole, he hesitated, and slithered down. Evidently he had decided, either that I was harmless, or else that it was risky to go up any further, when I could knock him off so easily with a pole. So he slithered podgily down again, and waddled away with the same bestial, stupid motion of that white-spiky repulsive spoon-tail. He was as big as a middle-sized pig: or more like a bear.

I let him go. He was repugnant. He made a certain squalor in the moonlight of the Rocky Mountains. As all savagery has a touch of squalor, that makes one a little sick at the stomach. And anyhow, it seemed almost more squalid to pick up a pine-bough and push him over, hit him and kill him.

A few days later, on a hot, motionless morning when the pine-trees put out their bristles in stealthy, hard assertion; and I was not in a good temper, because Black-eyed Susan, the cow, had disappeared into the timber, and I had had to ride hunting her, so it was nearly nine o'clock before she was milked: Madame came in suddenly out of the sunlight, saying: "I got such a shock! There are two strange dogs, and one of them has got the most awful beard, all round his nose."

She was frightened like a child, at something unnatural.

"Beard! Porcupine quills, probably! He's been after a porcupine."

"Ah!" she cried in relief. "Very likely! Very likely!—" then with a change of tone; "Poor thing, will they hurt him?"

"They will.—I wonder when he came."

"I heard dogs bark in the night."

"Did you! Why didn't you say so? I should have known Susan was hiding—"

The ranch is lonely, there is no sound in the night, save the innumerable noises of the night, that you can't put your finger on cosmic noises in the far deeps of the sky, and of the earth.

I went out. And in the full blaze of sunlight in the field, stood two dogs, a black-and-white, and a big, bushy, rather handsome sandy-red dog, of the collie type. And sure enough, this latter did look queer and a bit horrifying, his whole muzzle set round with white spines, like some ghastly growth; like an unnatural beard.

The black-and-white dog made off as I went through the fence. But the red dog whimpered and hesitated, and moved on hot bricks. He was fat and in good condition. I thought he might belong to some shepherds herding sheep in the forest ranges, among the mountains.

He waited while I went up to him, wagging his tail and whimpering, and ducking his head, and dancing. He daren't rub his nose with his paws any more: it hurt too much. I patted his head and looked at his nose, and he whimpered loudly.

He must have had thirty quills, or more, sticking out of his nose, all the way round: the white, ugly ends of the quills protruding an inch, sometimes more, sometimes less, from his already swollen, blood-puffed muzzle.

The porcupines here have quills only two or three inches long. But they are devilish: and a dog will die if he does not get them pulled out. Because they work further and further in, and will sometimes emerge through the skin away in some unexpected place.

Then the fun began. I got him in the yard: and he drank up the whole half-gallon of the chickens' sour milk. Then I started pulling out the quills. He was a big, bushy, handsome dog, but his nerve was gone, and every time I got a quill out, he gave a yelp. Some long quills were fairly easy. But the shorter ones, near his lips, were deep in, and hard to get hold of, and hard to pull out when you did get hold of them. And with every one that came out, came a little spurt of blood and another yelp and writhe.

The dog wanted the quills out: but his nerve was gone. Every time he saw my hand coming to his nose, he jerked his head away. I quieted him, and stealthily managed to jerk out another quill, with the blood all over my fingers. But with every one that came out, he grew more tiresome. I tried and tried and tried to get hold of another quill, and he jerked and jerked, and writhed and whimpered, and ran under the porch floor.

It was a curiously unpleasant, nerve-trying job. The day was blazing hot. The dog came out and I struggled with him again for an hour or more. Then we blindfolded him. But either he smelled my hand approaching his nose, or some weird instinct told him. He jerked his head, this way, that way, up, down, sideways, roundwise, as one's fingers came slowly, slowly, to seize a quill.

The quills on his lips and chin were deep in, only about a quarter of an inch of white stub protruding from the swollen, blood-oozed, festering black skin. It was very difficult to jerk them out.

We let him lie for an interval, hidden in the quiet cool place under the porch floor. After half an hour, he crept out again. We got a rope round his nose, behind the bristles, and one held while the other got the stubs with the pliers. But it was too trying. If a quill came out, the dog's yelp startled every nerve. And he was frightened of the pain, it was impossible to hold his head still any longer.

After struggling for two hours, and extracting some twenty quills, I gave up. It was impossible to quiet the creature, and I had had enough. His nose on the top was clear: a punctured, puffy, blood-darkened mess; and his lips were clear. But just on his round little chin, where the few white hairs are, was still a bunch of white quills, eight or nine, deep in.

We let him go, and he dived under the porch, and there he lay invisible: save for the end of his bushy, foxy tail, which moved when we came near. Towards noon he emerged, ate up the chicken-food, and stood with that doggish look of dejection, and fear, and friendliness, and greediness, wagging his tail.

But I had had enough.

"Go home!" I said. "Go home! Go home to your master, and let him finish for you."

He would not go. So I led him across the blazing hot clearing, in the way I thought he should go. He followed a hundred yards, then stood motionless in the blazing sun. He was not going to leave the place.

And I! I simply did not want him.

So I picked up a stone. He dropped his tail, and swerved towards the house. I knew what he was going to do. He was going to dive under the porch, and there stick, haunting the place.

I dropped my stone, and found a good stick under the cedar tree. Already in the heat was that sting-like biting of electricity, the thunder gathering in the sheer sunshine, without a cloud, and making one's whole body feel dislocated.

I could not bear to have that dog around any more. Going quietly to him, I suddenly gave him one hard hit with the stick, crying: "Go home!" He turned quickly, and the end of the stick caught him on his sore nose. With a fierce yelp, he went off like a wolf, downhill, like a flash, gone. And I stood in the field full of pangs of regret, at having hit him, unintentionally, on his sore nose.

But he was gone.

And then the present moon came, and again the night was clear. But in the interval there had been heavy thunder-rains, the ditch was running with bright water across the field, and the night, so fair, had not the terrific, mirror-like brilliancy, touched with terror, so startling bright, of the moon in the last days of June.

We were alone on the ranch. Madame went out into the clear night, just before retiring. The stream ran in a cord of silver across the field, in the straight line where I had taken the irrigation ditch. The pine-tree in front of the house threw a black shadow. The mountain slope came down to the fence, wild and alert.

"Come!" said she excitedly. "There is a big porcupine drinking at the ditch. I thought at first it was a bear."

When I got out he had gone. But among the grasses and the coming wild sunflowers, under the moon, I saw his greyish halo, like a pallid living bush, moving over the field, in the distance, in the moonlit *clair-obscur.*

We got through the fence, and following, soon caught him up. There he lumbered, with his white spoon-tail spiked with bristles, steering behind almost as if he were moving backwards, and this was his head. His long, long hairs above the quills quivering with a dim grey gleam, like a bush.

And again I disliked him.

Should one kill him?"

She hesitated. Then with a sort of disgust:

"Yes!"

I went back to the house, and got the little twenty-two rifle. Now never in my life had I shot at any live thing: I never wanted to. I always felt guns very repugnant: sinister, mean. With difficulty I had fired once or twice at a target: but resented doing even so much. Other people could shoot if they wanted to. Myself, individually, it was repugnant to me even to try.

But something slowly hardens in a man's soul. And I knew now, it had hardened in mine. I found the gun, and with rather trembling hands, got it loaded. Then I pulled back the trigger and followed the porcupine. It was still lumbering through the grass. Coming near, I aimed.

The trigger stuck. I pressed the little catch with a safety-pin I found in my pocket, and released the trigger. Then we followed the porcupine. He was still lumbering towards the trees. I went sideways on, stood quite near to him, and fired, in the clear-dark of the moonlight.

And as usual I aimed too high. He turned, went scuttling back whence he had come.

I got another shell in place, and followed. This time I fired full into the mound of his round back, below the glistening grey halo. He seemed to stumble on to his hidden nose, and struggled a few strides, ducking his head under like a hedgehog.

"He's not dead yet! Oh fire again!" cried Madame.

I fired, but the gun was empty.

So I ran quickly, for a cedar pole. The porcupine was lying still, with subsiding halo. He stirred faintly. So I turned him and hit him hard over the nose; or where, in the dark, his nose should have been. And it was done. He was dead.

And in the moonlight, I looked down on the first creature I had ever shot.

"Does it seem mean?" I asked aloud, doubtful.

Again Madame hesitated. Then:

"No!" she said resentfully.

And I felt she was right. Things like the porcupine, one must be able to shoot them, if they get in one's way.

One must be able to shoot. I, myself, must be able to shoot, and to kill.

For me, this is a *volte-face*. I have always preferred to walk round my porcupine, rather than kill it.

Now, I know it's no good walking round. One must kill.

I buried him in the adobe hole. But some animal dug down and ate him; for two days later there lay the spines and bones spread out, with the long skeletons of the porcupine-hands.

The only nice thing about him—! or her, for I believe it was a female, by the dugs on her belly—were the feet. They were like longish alert black hands, paw-hands. That is why a porcupines tracks in the snow look almost as if a child had gone by, leaving naked little human foot-prints, like a little boy.

So, he is gone: or she is gone. And there is another one, bigger and blacker-looking, among the west timber. That too is to be shot. It is part of the business of ranching: even if it's only a little half-abandoned ranch like this one.

Wherever man establishes himself, upon the earth, he has to fight for his place, against the lower orders of life. Food, the basis of existence, has to be fought for even by the most idyllic of farmers. You plant, and you protect your growing crop with a gun. Food, food, how strangely it relates man with the animal and vegetable world! How important it is! And how fierce is the fight that goes on around it.

The same when one skins a rabbit, and takes out the inside, one realises what an enormous part of the animal, comparatively, is intestinal, what a big part of him is just for food-apparatus; for *living on* other organisms.

And when one watches the horses in the big field, their noses to the ground, bite-bite-biting at the grass, and stepping absorbedly on, and bite-bite-biting without ever lifting their noses, cropping off the grass, the young shoots of alfalfa, the dandelions, with a blind, relentless, unwearied persistence, one's whole life pauses. One suddenly realises again how all creatures devour, and *must* devour the lower forms of life.

So Susan, swinging across the field, snatches off the tops of the little wild sunflowers as if she were mowing. And down they go, down her black throat. And when she stands in her cowy oblivion chewing her cud, with her lower jaw swinging peacefully, and I am milking her, suddenly the camomilely smell of her breath, as she glances round with glaring, smoke-blue eyes, makes me realise it is the sunflowers that are her ball of cud. Sunflowers! And they will go to making her glistening black hide, and the thick cream on her milk.

And the chickens, when they see a great black beetle, that the Mexicans call a *toro,* floating past, they are after it in a rush. And if it settles, instantly the brown hen stabs it with her beak. It is a great beetle two or three inches long: but in a second it is in the crop of the chicken. Gone!

And Timsy, the cat, as she spies on the chipmunks, crouches in another sort of oblivion, soft, and still. The chipmunks come to drink the milk from the chickens' bowl. Two of them met at the bowl. They were little squirrely things with stripes down their backs. They sat up in front of one another, lifting their inquisitive little noses and humping their backs. Then each put its two little hands on the other's shoulders, they reared up, gazing into each other's faces; and finally they put their two little noses together, in a sort of kiss.

But Miss Timsy can't stand this. In a soft, white-and-yellow leap she is after them. They skip with the darting jerk of chipmunks, to the wood-heap, and with one soft, high-leaping sideways bound Timsy goes through the air. Her snow-flake of a paw comes down on one of the chipmunks. She looks at it for a second. It squirms. Swiftly and triumphantly she puts her two flowery little white paws on it, legs straight out in front of her, back arched, gazing concentratedly yet whimsically. Chipmunk does not stir. She takes it softly in her mouth, where it dangles softly, like a lady's tippet. And with a proud, prancing motion the Timsy sets off towards the house, her white little feet hardly touching the ground.

But she gets shooed away. We refuse to loan her the sitting-room any more, for her gladiatorial displays. If the chippy must be "butchered to make a Timsy holiday," it shall be outside. Disappointed, but still high-stepping, the Timsy sets off towards the clay oven by the shed.

There she lays the chippy gently down, and soft as a little white cloud lays one small paw on its striped back. Chippy does not move. Soft as thistle-down she raises her paw a tiny, tiny bit, to release him.

And all of a sudden, with an elastic jerk, he darts from under the white release of her paw. And instantly, she is up in the air and down she comes on him, with the forward-thrusting bolts of her white paws. Both creatures are motionless.

Then she takes him softly in her mouth again, and looks round, to see if she can slip into the house. She cannot. So she trots towards the wood-pile.

It is a game, and it is pretty. Chippy escapes into the wood-pile, and she softly, softly reconnoitres among the faggots.

Of all the animals, there is no denying it, the Timsy is the most pretty, the most fine. It is not her mere *corpus* that is beautiful; it is her bloom of aliveness. Her "infinite variety"; the soft, snowflakey lightness of her, and at the same time her lean, heavy ferocity. I had never realised the latter, till I was lying in bed one morning moving my toe, unconsciously, under the bedclothes. Suddenly a terrific blow struck my foot. The Timsy had sprung out of nowhere, with a hurling, steely force, thud upon the bedclothes where the toe was moving. It was as if someone had aimed a sudden blow, vindictive and unerring.

"Timsy!"

She looked at me with the vacant, feline glare of her hunting eyes. It is not even ferocity. It is the dilation of the strange, vacant arrogance of power. The power is in her.

And so it is. Life moves in circles of power and of vividness, and each circle of life only maintains its orbit upon the subjection of some lower circle. If the lower cycles of life are not *mastered,* there can be no higher cycle.

In nature, one creature devours another, and this is an essential part of all existence and of all being. It is not something to lament over, nor something to try to reform. The Buddhist who refuses to take life is really ridiculous, since if he eats only two grains of rice per day, it is two grains of life. We did not make creation, *we* are not the authors of the universe. And if we see that the whole of creation is established upon the fact that one life devours another life, one cycle of existence can only come into existence through the subjugating of another cycle of existence, then what is the good of trying to pretend that it is not so? The only thing to do is to realise, what is higher, and what is lower, in the cycles of existence.

It is nonsense to declare that there *is* no higher and lower. We know full well that the dandelion belongs to a higher cycle of existence than the hartstongue fern, that the ant's is a higher form of existence than the dandelion's, that the thrush is higher than the ant, that Timsy the cat, is higher than the thrush, and that I, a man, am higher than Timsy.

What do we mean by higher? Strictly, we mean more alive. More vividly alive. The ant is more vividly alive than the pine-tree. We know it, there is no trying to refute it. It is all very well saying that they are both alive in two different ways, and therefore they are incomparable, incommensurable. This is also true.

But one truth does not displace another. Even apparently contradictory truths do not displace one another. Logic is far too coarse to make the subtle distinctions life demands.

Truly, it is futile to compare an ant with a great pine-tree, in the absolute. Yet as far as *existence* is concerned, they are not only placed in comparison to one another, they are occasionally pitted against one another. And if it comes to a contest, the little ant will devour the life of the huge tree. If it comes to a contest.

And, in the cycles of *existence,* this is the test. From the lowest form of existence to the highest, the test question is: *Can thy neighbour finally overcome thee?*

If he can, then he belongs to a higher cycle of existence.

This is the truth behind the survival of the fittest. Every cycle of existence is established upon the overcoming of the lower cycles of existence. The real question is, wherein does *fitness* lie? Fittest for what? Fit merely to survive? That which is only fit to survive will survive only to supply food or contribute in some way to the existence of a higher form of life, which is able to do more than survive, which can really *vive,* live.

Life is more vivid in the dandelion than in the green fern, or than in a palm tree.

Life is more vivid in a snake than in a butterfly.

Life is more vivid in a wren than in an alligator.

Life is more vivid in a cat than in an ostrich.

Life is more vivid in the Mexican who drives the wagon, than in the two horses in the wagon.

Life is more vivid in me, than in the Mexican who drives the wagon for me.

We are speaking in terms of *existence:* that is, in terms of species, race, or type.

The dandelion can take hold of the land, the palm tree is driven into a corner, with a fern.

The snake can devour the fiercest insect.

The fierce bird can destroy the greatest reptile.

The great cat can destroy the greatest bird.

The man can destroy the horse, or any animal.

One race of man can subjugate and rule another race. All this in terms of *existence.* As far as existence goes, that life-species is the highest which can devour, or destroy, or subjugate every other life-species against which it is pitted in contest.

This is a law. There is no escaping this law. Anyone, or any race trying to escape it, will fall a victim: will fall into subjugation.

But let us insist and insist again, we are talking now of existence of species, of types, of races, of nations, not of single individuals, nor of *beings.* The dandelion in full flower, a little sun bristling with sun-rays on the green earth, is a nonpareil, a non-such. Foolish, foolish, foolish to compare it to anything else on earth. It is itself incomparable and unique.

But that is the fourth dimension, of *being.* It is in the fourth dimension, nowhere else.

Because, in the time-space dimension, any man may tread on the yellow sun-mirror, and it is gone. Any cow may swallow it. Any bunch of ants may annihilate it.

This brings us to the inexorable law of life.

1   Any creature that attains to its own fulness of being, its own *living* self, becomes unique, a nonpareil. It has its place in the fourth dimension, the heaven of existence, and there it is perfect, it is beyond comparison.

2   At the same time, every creature exists in time and space. And in time and space it exists relatively to all other existence, and can

393

never be absolved. Its existence impinges on other existences, and is itself impinged upon. And in the struggle for existence, if an effort on the part of any one type or species or order of life, can finally destroy the other species, then the destroyer is of a more vital cycle of existence than the one destroyed. (When speaking of existence we always speak in types, species, not of individuals. Species exist. But even an individual dandelion has *being.)*

3   The force which we call *vitality,* and which is the determining factor in the struggle for existence, is, however, derived also from the fourth dimension. That is to say, the ultimate source of all vitality is in that other dimension, or region, where the dandelion blooms, and which men have called heaven, and which now they call the fourth dimension: which is only a way of saying that it is not to be reckoned in terms of space and time.

4   The primary way, in our existence, to get vitality, is to absorb it from living creatures lower than ourselves. It is thus transformed into a new and higher creation. (There are many ways of absorbing: devouring food is one way, love is often another. The best way is a pure relationship, which includes the *being* on each side, and which allows the transfer to take place in a living flow, enhancing the life in both beings.)

5   No creature is fully itself till it is, like the dandelion, opened in the bloom of pure relationship to the sun, the entire living cosmos.

So we still find ourselves in the tangle of existence and being, a tangle which man has never been able to get out of, except by sacrificing the one to the other.

Sacrifice is useless.

The clue to all existence is being. But you can't have being without existence, any more than you can have the dandelion flower without the leaves and the long tap root.

Being is *not* ideal, as Plato would have it: nor spiritual. It is a transcendent form of existence, and as much material as existence is. Only the matter suddenly enters the fourth dimension.

All existence is dual, and surging towards a consummation into being. In the seed of the dandelion, as it floats with its little umbrella of hairs, sits the Holy Ghost in tiny compass. The Holy Ghost is that which holds the light and the dark, the day and the night, the wet and the sunny, united in one little clue. There it sits, in the seed of the dandelion.

The seed falls to earth. The Holy Ghost rouses, saying: *Come!* And out of the sky come the rays of the sun, and out of earth comes dampness and dark and the death-stuff. They are called in, like those bidden to a feast. The sun sits down at the hearth, inside the seed; and the dark, damp death-returner sits on the opposite side, with the host between. And the host says to them: *Come! Be merry together!* So the sun looks with desirous curiosity on the dark face from the earth, and the dark damp one looks with wonder on the bright face of the other, who comes from the sun. And the host says:

Here you are at home! Lift me up, between you, that I may cease to be a Ghost. For it longs me to look out, it longs me to dance with the dancers.

So the sun in the seed, and the earthy one in the seed take hands, and laugh, and begin to dance. And their dancing is like a fire kindled, a bonfire with leaping flame. And the treading of their feet is like the running of little streams, down into the earth. So from the dance of the sun-in-the-seed with the earthy death-returner, green little flames of leaves shoot up, and hard little trickles of roots strike down. And the host laughs, and says: *I am being lifted up! Dance harder! Oh wrestle, you two, like wonderful wrestlers, neither of which can win*. So sun-in-the-seed and the death-returner, who is earthy, dance faster and faster and the leaves rising greener begin to dance in a ring above-ground, fiercely overwhelming any outsider, in a whirl of swords and lions' teeth. And the earthy one wrestles , wrestles with the sun-in-the-seed, so the long roots reach down like arms of a fighter gripping the power of earth, and strangles all intruders, strangling any intruder mercilessly. Till the two fall in one strange embrace, and from the centre the long flower-stem lifts like a phallus, budded with a bud. And out of the bud the voice of the Holy Ghost is heard crying: *I am lifted up! Lo! I am lifted up! I am here!* So the bud opens, and there is the flower poised in the very middle of the universe, with a ring of green swords below, to guard it, and the octopus arms deep in earth, drinking and threatening. So the Holy Ghost, being a dandelion flower, looks round, and says: *Lo I am yellow! I believe the sun has lent me his body! Lo I am sappy with golden, bitter blood! I believe death out of the damp black earth has lent me his blood! I am incarnate! I like my incarnation! But this is not all. I will keep this incarnation. It is good! But oh! if I can win to another incarnation, who knows how wonderful it will be! This one will have to give place. This one can help to create the next.*

So the Holy Ghost leaves the clue of himself behind, in the seed, and wanders forth in the comparative chaos of our universe, seeking another incarnation.

And this will go on forever. Man, as yet, is less than half grown. Even his flower-stem has not appeared yet. He is all leaves and roots, without any clue put forth. No sign of a bud anywhere.

Either he will have to start budding, or he will be forsaken of the Holy Ghost: abandoned as a failure in creation, as the ichthyosaurus was abandoned. Being abandoned means losing his vitality. The sun and the earth-dark will cease rushing together in him. Already it is ceasing. To men, the sun is becoming stale, and the earth sterile. But the sun itself will never become stale, nor the earth barren. It is only that the *clue* is missing inside men. They are like flowerless, seedless fat cabbages, nothing inside.

Vitality depends upon the clue of the Holy Ghost inside a creature, a man, a nation, a race. When the clue goes, the vitality goes. And the Holy Ghost seeks forever a new incarnation, and subordinates the old to the new. You will know that any creature or race is still alive with the Holy Ghost, when it can subordinate the lower creatures or races, and assimilate them into a new incarnation.

No man, or creature, or race can have vivid vitality unless it be moving towards a blossoming: and the most powerful is that which moves towards the as-yet-unknown blossom.

Blossoming means the establishing of a pure, *new* relationship with all the cosmos. This is the state of heaven. And it is the state of a flower, a cobra, a jenny-wren in spring, a man when he knows himself royal and crowned with the sun, with his feet gripping the core of the earth.

This too is the fourth dimension: this state, this mysterious other reality of things in a perfected relationship. It is into this perfected relationship that every straight line curves, as if to some core, passing out of the time-space dimension.

But any man, creature, or race moving towards blossoming will have to draw immense supplies of vitality from men, or creatures below, passionate strength. And he will have to accomplish a perfected relation with all things.

There will be conquest, always. But the aim of conquest is a perfect relation of conquerors with conquered, for a new blossoming. Freedom is illusory. Sacrifice is illusory. Almightiness is illusory. Freedom, sacrifice, almightiness, these are all human side-tracks, cul-de-sacs, bunk. All that is real is the overwhelmingness of a new inspirational command, a new relationship with all things.

Heaven is always there. No achieved consummation is lost. Procreation goes on forever, to support the achieved revelation. But the torch of revelation itself is handed on. And this is all important.

Every living thing wants to procreate more living things.

But more important than this is the fact that every revelation is a torch held out, to kindle new revelations. As the dandelion holds out the sun to me, saying: *Can you take it!*

Every gleam of heaven that is shown—like a dandelion flower, or a green beetle—quivers with strange passion to kindle a new gleam, never yet beheld. This is not self-sacrifice: it is self-contribution: in which the highest happiness lies.

The torch of existence is handed on, in the womb of procreation.

And the torch of revelation is handed on, by every living thing from the protococcus to a brave man or a beautiful woman, handed to whomsoever can take it. He who can take it, has power beyond all the rest.

The cycle of procreation exists purely for the keeping alight of the torch of perfection, in any species: the torch being the dandelion in blossom, the tree in full leaf, the peacock in all his plumage, the cobra in all his colour, the frog at full leap, woman in all the mystery of her fathomless desirableness, man in the fulness of his power: every creature become its pure self.

One cycle of perfection urges to kindle another cycle, as yet unknown.

And with the kindling from the torch of revelation comes the inrush of vitality, and the need to consume and *consummate* the lower cycles of existence, into a new thing. This consuming and this consummating means conquest, and fearless mastery. Freedom lies in the honorable yielding towards the new flame, and the honorable mastery of that which shall be new, over that which must yield. As I must master my horses, which are in a lower cycle of existence. And they, they are relieved and *happy* to serve. If I turn them loose into the mountain ranges, to run wild till they die, the thrill of real happiness is gone out of their lives.

Every lower order seeks in some measure to serve a higher order: and rebels against being conquered.

It is always conquest, and it always will be conquest. If the conquered be an old, declining race, they will have handed on their torch to the conqueror: who will burn his fingers badly, if he is too flippant. And if the conquered be a barbaric race, they will consume the fire of the conqueror, and leave him flameless, unless he watch it. But it is always conquest, conquered and conqueror, forever. The kingdom of heaven is the kingdom of conquerors, who can serve the conquest forever, after their own conquest is made.

In heaven, in the perfected relation, is peace: in the fourth dimension. But there is getting there. And that, forever, is the process of conquest.

When the rose blossomed, then the great Conquest was made by the Vegetable Kingdom. But even this conqueror of conquerors, the rose, had to lend himself towards the caterpillar and the butterfly of a later conquest. A conqueror, but tributary to the later conquest.

There is no such thing as equality. In the kingdom of heaven, in the fourth dimension, each soul that achieves a perfect relationship with the cosmos, from its own centre, is perfect, and incomparable. It has no superior. It is a conqueror, and incomparable.

But every man, in the struggle of conquest towards his own consummation, must master the inferior cycles of life, and never relinquish his mastery. Also, if there be men beyond him, moving on to a newer consummation than his own, he must yield to their greater demand, and serve their greater mystery, and so be faithful to the kingdom of heaven which is within him, which is gained by conquest and by loyal service.

Any man who achieves his own being will, like the dandelion or the butterfly, pass into that other dimension which we call the fourth, and the old people called heaven. It is the state of perfected relationship. And here a man will have his peace for ever: whether he serve or command, in the process of living.

But even this entails his faithful allegiance to the kingdom of heaven, which must be forever and forever extended, as creation conquers chaos. So that my perfection will but serve a perfection which still lies ahead, unrevealed and unconceived, and beyond my own.

We have tried to build walls round the kingdom of heaven: but it's no good. It's only the cabbage rotting inside.

Our last wall is the golden wall of money. This is a fatal wall. It cuts us off from life, from vitality, from the alive sun and the alive earth, as *nothing* can. Nothing, not even the most fanatical dogmas of an iron-bound religion, can insulate us from the inrush of life and inspiration, as money can.

We are losing vitality: losing it rapidly. Unless we seize the torch of inspiration, and drop our moneybags, the moneyless will be kindled by the flame of flames, and they will consume us like old rags.

We are losing vitality, owing to money and money-standards. The torch in the hands of the moneyless will set our house on fire, and burn us to death, like sheep in a flaming corral.

ARISTOCRACY

Everything in the world is relative to everything else. And every living thing is related to every other living thing.

But creation moves in cycles, and in degrees. There is higher and lower, in the cycles of creation, and greater and less, in the degree of life.

Each thing that attains to purity in its own cycle of existence, is pure, and is itself, and, in its purity, is beyond compare.

But in relation to other things, it is either higher or lower, or greater or less degree.

We have to admit that a daisy is more highly developed than a fern, even if it be a tree-fern. The daisy belongs to a higher order of life. That is, the daisy is more alive. The fern is more torpid.

And a bee is more alive than a daisy: of a higher order of life. The daisy, pure as it is in its own being, yet, when compared with the bee, is limited in its being.

And birds are higher than bees: more alive. And mammals are higher than birds. And man is the highest, most developed, most conscious, most *alive* of the mammals: master of them all.

But even within the species, there is difference. The nightingale is higher, purer, even more alive, more subtly, delicately alive, than the sparrow. And the parrot is more highly developed, or more alive, than the pigeon.

Among men, the difference in *being* is infinite. And it is a difference in degree as well as in kind. One man *is,* in himself, more, more alive, more of a man, than another. One man has greater being than another: a purer manhood, a more vivid livingness. The difference is infinite.

And, seeing that the inferiors are so vastly more numerous than the superiors, when Jesus came, the inferiors, who are by no means the meek that they *should* be, set out to inherit the earth.

Jesus, in a world of arrogant Pharisees and egoistic Romans, thought that purity and poverty were one. It was a fatal mistake. Purity is often enough poor. But poverty is only too rarely pure. Poverty too often is only the result of *natural* poorness, poorness in courage, poorness in living vitality, poorness in manhood: poor life, poor character. Now the poor in life are the most impure, the most easily degenerate.

But the few men rich in life and pure in heart read purity into poverty, and Christianity started. "Charity suffereth long, and kind. Charity envieth not. Charity vaunteth not itself, is not puffed up."

They are the words of a noble manhood.

There happened what was bound to happen: the men with pure hearts left the scramble for money and power to the impure.

Still, the great appeal: the kingdom of heaven is within you, acted powerfully on the hearts of the poor, who were still full of life. The rich were more active, but less alive. The poor still wanted, most of all, the kingdom of heaven.

Until the pure men began to mistrust the figurative kingdom of heaven. "Not much kingdom of heaven for a hungry man," they said.

This was a mistake, and a fall into impurity. For even if I die of hunger, the kingdom of heaven is within me, and I am within it, if I truly choose.

But once the pure men said this: *Not much kingdom of heaven for a hungry man:* the soul began to die out of men.

By the old creed, every soul was equal in the sight of God. By the new creed, everybody should be equal in the sight of men. And being equal meant, having equal possessions. And possessions were reckoned in terms of money.

So that money became the one absolute. And man figures as a money-possessor and a money-getter. The absolute, the God, the kingdom of heaven itself, became money: hard, hard cash. "The kingdom of heaven is within you"—now means "The money is in your pocket."—"Then shall thy peace be as a river" now means: "Then shall thy investments bring thee a safe and ample income."

"L'homme est né libre," means, he is born without a sou. *"Et on le trouve partout enchainé* means: "He wears breeches, and must fill his pockets."

So now there is a new (a new-old) aristocracy, completely unmysterious and scientific: the aristocracy of money. Have you got a million *gold*? (for heaven's sake, the gold standard!) Then you are a *king.* Have you five hundred thousand? Then you are a lord.

"In *my* country, we're *all* kings and queens," as the American lady said, being a bit sick of certain British snobbery. She was quite right, they are all potential kings and queens. But until they come into their kingdom—five hundred thousand dollars minimum—they might just as well be commoners.

Yet even still, there is *natural* aristocracy.

Aristocracy of birth is bunk, when a Kaiser Wilhelm and an Emperor Franz-Josef and a Czar Nicolas is all that noble birth will do for you.

Yet the whole of life is established on a natural aristocracy. And aristocracy of birth is a *little* more natural than aristocracy of money. (Oh for God's sake, the gold standard!)

But a millionaire can do without birth, whereas birth cannot do without dollars. So, by the all-prevailing law of pragmatism, the dollar has it.

What then does *natural* aristocracy consist in?

It's not just *brains!* The mind is an instrument, and the *savant,* the professor, the scientist, has been looked upon since the Ptolemies, as a sort of upper servant. And justly. The millionaire has brains too: so does a modern President or Prime Minister. They all belong to the class of upper servants. They serve, forsooth, the public.

"Ca, Ca, Caliban!

Get a new master, be a new man.

What does a natural aristocracy consist in? Count Keyserling says: "Not in what a man can *do,* but what he i*s.*" Unfortunately, what a man *is,* is measured by what he can do, even in nature. A nightingale, *being* a nightingale, can sing: which a sparrow can't. If you *are* something you'll *do* something, *ipso facto.*

The question is, what *kind* of thing can a man do? Can he put more life into us, and release in us the fountains of our vitality? Or can he only help to feed us, and give us money or amusement.

The providing of food, money, and amusement belongs, truly, to the servant class.

The providing of *life* belongs to the aristocrat. If a man, whether by thought or action, makes *life,* he is an aristocrat. So Caesar and Cicero are both strictly aristocrats. Lacking these two, the first century B.C. would have been far less vital, less vividly alive. And Anthony, who seemed so much more vital, robust and robustious, was, when we look at it, comparatively unimportant. Caesar and Cicero lit the great flame.

How?—It is easier asked than answered.

But one thing they did, whatever else: they put men into a new relation with the universe. Caesar opened Gaul, Germany and Britain, and let the gleam of ice and snow, the shagginess of the north, the mystery of the menhir and the mistletoe in upon the rather stuffy soul of Rome, and of the Orient. And Cicero was discovering the moral nature of man, as citizen chiefly, and so putting man in new relation to man.

But Caesar was greater than Cicero. He put man in a new relationship to ice and sun.

Only Caesar was, perhaps, also too much an egoist; he never knew the mysteries he moved amongst. But Caesar was great *beyond* morality

Man's life consists in a connection with all things in the universe. Whoever can establish, or initiate a new connection between mankind and the circumambient universe is, in his own degree a saviour. Because mankind is always exhausting its human possibilities, always degenerating into repetition, torpor, ennui, lifelessness. When ennui sets in, it is a sign that human vitality is waning and the human connection with the universe is gone stale.

Then he who comes to make a new revelation, a new connection, whether he be soldier, statesman, poet, philosopher, artist, he is a saviour.

When George Stephenson invented the locomotive engine, he provided a *means of communication,* but he didn't alter in the slightest man's *vital* relation to the universe. But Galileo and Newton, *discoverers,* not inventors, they made a big difference. And the energy released in mankind because of them was enormous. The same is true of Peter the Great, Frederick the Great, and Napoleon. The same is true of Voltaire, Shelley, Wordsworth, Byron, Rousseau. They established a *new* connection between mankind and the universe, and the result was a vast release of energy. The *sun* was reborn to man, so was the moon.

To man, the very sun goes stale, becomes a habit. Comes a saviour, a seer, and the very sun dances new in heaven.

That is because the *sun* is always sun beyond sun beyond sun. The sun is every sun that has ever been, Helios or Mithras, the sun of China or of Brahma, or of Peru or of Mexico: great gorgeous suns, besides which our puny "envelope of incandescent gas" is a smoky candle-wick.

It is our fault. When man becomes stale and paltry, his sun is the mere stuff that our sun is. When man is great and splendid, the sun of China and Mithras blazes over him and gives him, not radiant energy in the form of heat and light, but life, life, life!

The world is to us what we take from it. The sun is to us what we take from it. And if we are puny, it is because we take punily from the superb sun.

Man is great according as his relation to the living universe is vast and vital.

Men are related to men: including women: and this, of course, is very important. But one would think it were everything. One would think, to read modern books, that the life of any tuppenny bank-clerk was more important than sun, moon, and stars; and to read the pert drivel of the critics, one would be led to imagine that every three-farthing whipper-snapper who lifts up his voice in approval or censure were the thrice-greatest Hermes speaking in judgment out of the mysteries.

This is the democratic age of cheap clap-trap, and it sits in jackdaw judgment on all greatness.

And this is the result of making, in our own conceit, man the measure of the universe. Don't you be taken in. The universe, so vast and profound, measures man up very accurately, for the yelping mongrel with his tail between his legs, that he is. And the great sun, and the moon, with a smile, will soon start dropping the mongrel down the vast refuse-pit of oblivion. Oh, the universe has a terrible hole in the middle of it, an oubliette for all of you, whipper-snappering mongrels.

Man, of course, being measure of the universe, is measured only against man. Has, of course, vital relationship only with his own cheap little species. Hence the cheap little twaddler he has become.

In the great ages, man has vital relation with man, with woman: and beyond that, with the cow, the lion, the bull, the cat, the eagle, the beetle, the serpent. And beyond these, with narcissus and anemone, mistletoe and oak-tree, myrtle, olive, and lotus. And beyond these, with humus and slanting water, cloud-towers and rainbow and the sweeping sun-limbs. And beyond that, with sun and moon, the living night and the living day.

Do you imagine the great realities, even the ram of Amon, are only sy*mbols* of something human? Do you imagine the great symbols, the dragon, the snake, the bull, only refer to bits, qualities or attributes of little man? It is puerile. The puerility, the puppyish conceit of modern white humanity is almost funny.

Amon, the great ram, do you think he doesn't stand alone in the universe, without your permission, oh cheap little man? Just because he's there, do you think *you* bred him, out of your own almightiness, you cheap-jack?

Amon, the great ram! Mithras, the great bull! The mistletoe on the tree. Do you think, you stuffy little human fool sitting in a chair and wearing lambswool underwear, and eating your mutton and beef under the Christmas decoration, do you think then that Amon, Mithras, mistletoe, and the whole Tree of Life were just invented to contribute to your complacency?

You fool! You dyspeptic fool, with your indigestion tablets! You can eat your mutton and your beef, and buy sixpenn'orth of the golden bough, till your belly turns sour, you fool. Do you think because you eat beef, that the Mithras fire is yours? Do you think, because you keep a fat castrated cat, the moon is on your knees? Do you think, in your woolen underwear, you are clothed in the might of Amon?

You idiot! You cheap-jack idiot!

Was not the ram created before you were, you twaddler? Did he not come in might out of chaos? And is he not still clothed in might?—To you, he is mutton. Your wonderful perspicacity relates you to him just that far. But any farther, he is— well, wool.

Don't you see, idiot and fool, that you have *lost* the ram out of your life entirely, and it is one great connection gone, one great life-flow broken? Don't you see you are so much the emptier, mutton-stuffed and wool-wadded, but lifeless, lifeless.

And the oak-tree, the slow great oak-tree, isn't he alive? Doesn't he live where you *don't* live, with a vast silence you shall never, never penetrate, though you chop him into kindling shred from shred. He is alive with life such as you have not got and will never have. And in so far as he is a vast, powerful, silent life, you should worship him.

You should seek a living relation with him. Didn't the old Englishman have a living, vital relation to the oak-tree, a *mystic* relation? Yes, mystic! Didn't the red-faced old admirals who *made* England, have a living relation in *sacredness,* with the oak-tree which was their ship, their ark? The last living vibration and power in pure connection, between man and tree, coming down from the Druids.

And all you can do now is to twiddle-twaddle about golden boughs, because you are empty, empty, empty, hollow, deficient, and cardboardy.

Do you think the tree is not, now and forever, sacred and fearsome? The trees have turned against you, fools, and you are running to imbecility to your own destruction.

Do you think the bull is at your disposal, you zenith of creation? Why, I tell you, the blood of the bull is indeed your poison. Your veins are bursting, with beef. You may well turn vegetarian. But even milk is bull's blood: or Hathor's.

My cow Susan is at my disposal indeed. But when I see her suddenly emerging, jet-black, sliding through the gate of her little corral into the open sun, does not my heart stand still, and cry out, in some long-forgotten tongue, salutation to the fearsome one? Is not even now my life widened and deepened in connection with her life, throbbing with the other pulse, of the bull's blood?

Is not this my life, this throbbing of the bull's blood in my blood?

And as the white cock calls in the doorway, who calls? Merely a barnyard rooster, worth a dollar-and-a-half. But listen! Under the old dawns of creation the Holy Ghost, the Mediator, shouts aloud in the twilight. And every time I hear him, a fountain of vitality gushes up in my body. It is life.

So it is! Degree after degree after degree widens out the relation between man and his universe, till it reaches the sun, and the night.

The impulse of existence, of course, is to *devour* all the lower orders of life. So man now looks upon the white cock, the cow, the ram, as good to eat.

But *living* and having *being* means the relatedness between me and all things. In so far as I am I, a being who is proud and in place, I have a connection with my circumambient universe, and I know my place. When the white cock crows, I do not hear myself, or some anthropomorphic conceit, crowing. I hear the not-me, the voice of the Holy Ghost. And when I see the hard, solid, longish green cones
        thrusting up at blue heaven from the high bluish tips of the balsam pine,
I say: Behold! Look at the strong, fertile silence of the thrusting tree! God is in the bush like a clenched dark fist, or a thrust phallus.

So it is with every natural thing. It has a vital relation with all other natural things. Only the machine is absolved from vital relation. It is based on the mystery of neuters. The neutralising of one great natural force against another, makes mechanical power. Makes the engine's wheels go round.

Does the earth go round like a wheel, in the same way? No! In the living, balanced, hovering flight of the earth, there is a strange leaning, an unstatic equilibrium, a balance that is non-balance. This is owing to the relativity of earth, moon, and sun, a vital, even sentient relatedness, never perpendicular: nothing neutral or neuter.

Every natural thing has its living relation to every other natural thing. So the tiger, striped in gold and black, lies and stretches his limbs in perfection between all that the day is, and all that is night. He has a by-the-way relatedness with trees, soil, water, man, cobras, deer, ants, and of course, the she-tiger. Of all these he is reckless as Caesar was, when he stretches himself superbly. When he stretches himself superbly, he stretches himself between the living day and the living night, the vast and inexhaustible duality of creation. And he is the fanged and brindled Holy Ghost, with ice-shiny whiskers.

The same with man. His life consists in a relation with all things: stone, earth, trees, flowers, water, insects, fishes, birds, creatures, sun, rainbow, children, woman, other men. But his greatest and final relation is with the sun, the sun of suns: and with the night, which is moon and dark and stars. In the last great connections, he lifts his body speechless to the sun, and, the same body, but so different, to the moon and the stars, and the spaces between the stars.

Sun! Yes, the actual sun! That which blazes in the day! Which scientists call a sphere of blazing gas;—what a lot of human gas there is, which has never been set ablaze!—and which the Greeks called Helios!

The sun, I tell you, is alive, and more alive than I am, or a tree is. It may have blazing gas, as I have hair, and a tree has leaves. But I tell you, it is the Holy Ghost in full raiment, shaking and walking, and alive as a tiger is, only more so, in the sky.

And when I can turn my body to the sun, and say: "Sun! Sun!"—and we meet—then I am come finally into my own. For the universe of day, finally, is the sun. And when the day of the sun is my day too, I am a lord of all the world.

And at night, when the silence of the moon, and the stars, and the spaces between the stars, is the silence of me too, then I am come into my own by night. For night is a vast untellable life, and the Holy Ghost starry, beheld as we only behold night on earth.

In his ultimate and surpassing relation, man is given only to that which he can never describe or account for; the sun, as it is alive, and the living night.

A man's supreme moment of active life is when he looks up and is with the sun, and is with the sun as a woman is with child. The actual yellow sun of morning.

This makes a man a lord, an aristocrat of life.

And the supreme moment of quiescent life is when a man looks up into the night, and is gone into the night, so the night is like a woman with child, bearing him. And this, a man has to himself.

The true aristocrat is the man who has passed all the relationships, and has met the sun, and the sun is with him as a diadem.

Caesar was like this. He passed through the great relationships, with ruthlessness, and came to the sun. And he became a sun-man. But he was too unconscious. He was not aware that the sun forever was beyond him, and that only in his *relation* to the sun was he deified. He wanted to be God.

Alexander was wiser. He placed himself a god among men. But when blood flowed from a wound in him, he said: Look! It is the blood of a man like other men.

The sun makes man a lord: an aristocrat: almost a deity. But in his consummation with night and the moon, man knows forever his own passing away.

But no man is man in all his splendour till he passes further than every relationship: further than mankind and womankind, in the last leap to the sun, to the night. The man who can touch both sun and night, as the woman touched the garment of Jesus, becomes a lord and a saviour, in his own kind. With the sun he has his final and ultimate relationship, beyond man or woman, or anything human or created. And in this final relation is he most intensely alive, surpassing.

Every creature at its zenith surpasses creation and is alone in the face of the sun, and the night: the sun that lives, and the night that lives and survives. Then we pass beyond every other relationship, and every other relationship, even the intensest passion of love, sinks into subordination and obscurity. Indeed, every relationship, even that of purest love, is only an approach nearer and nearer, to a man's last consummation with the sun, with the moon or night. And in the consummation with the sun, even love is left behind.

He who has the sun in his face, in his body, he is the pure aristocrat. He who has the sun in his breast, and the moon in his belly, he is the first: the aristocrat of aristocrats, supreme in the aristocracy of life.

Because he is *most alive.*

Being alive constitutes an aristocracy which there is no getting beyond. He who is most alive, intrinsically, is king, whether men admit it or not. In the face of the sun.

Life rises in circles, in degree. The most living is the highest. And the lower shall serve the higher, if there is to be any life among men.

More life! More *vivid* life! Not more safe cabbages, or meaningless masses of people.

Perhaps Dostoevsky was more vividly alive than Plato; culminating a more vivid life circle, and giving the clue towards a higher circle still. But the clue *hidden,* as it always is hidden, in every revelation, underneath what is stated.

All creation contributes, and must contribute to this: towards achieving of a vaster, vivider cycle of life. That is the goal of living. He who gets nearer the sun is leader, the aristocrat of aristocrats. Or he who, like Dostoevsky, gets nearest the moon of our not-being.

There is, of course, the power of mere conservatism and inertia. Deserts made the cactus thorny. But the cactus still is a rose of roses.

Whereas a sort of cowardice made the porcupine spiny. There is a difference between the cowardice of inertia, which now governs the democratic masses, particularly the capitalist masses: and the conservative fighting spirit which saved the cactus in the middle of the desert.

The democratic mass, capitalist and proletariat alike, are a vast, sluggish, ghastlily greedy porcupine, lumbering with inertia. Even Bolshevism is the same porcupine: nothing but greed and inertia.

The cactus had a rose to fight for. But what has democracy to fight for, against all the living elements, except money, money, money!

The world is stuck squalid inside an achieved form, and bristling with a myriad spines, to protect its hulking body as it feeds, feeds: gnawing the bark of the young tree of life, and killing it from the top downwards. Leaving its spines to fester and fester in the nose of the gay dog.

The actual porcupine, in spite of legend, cannot shoot its quills. But mankind, the porcupine out-pigging the porcupine, can stick quills in the face of the sun.

Bah! Enough of the squalor of democratic humanity. It is time to begin to recognise the aristocracy of the sun. The children of the sun shall be lords of the earth.

There will form a new aristocracy, irrespective of nationality, of men who have reached the sun. Men of the sun, whether Chinese or Hottentot or Nordic, or Hindu or Esquimo, if they touch the sun in the heavens, are lords of the earth. And together they will form the aristocracy of the world. And in the coming era they will rule the world; a confraternity of the living sun, making the embers of financial internationalism and industrial internationalism pale upon the hearth of the earth.

DOSTOEVSKY – A Fragment

Art is the evidence of the conscious and of the unconscious self in the artist, and nearly all drama, nearly all tragedy, consists in the conflict between this conscious and this unconscious self. In his consciousness, the great artist is, or has been, nearly always conservative, aristocratic. In his unconsciousness he is subversive to the old order.

This is evident in all the great tragedians: Aeschylus, Shakspere, Corneille. In Shakspere, the conscious, or the immediate man adheres to the established order; he reveres kingship and fatherhood as the supreme dignity and significance of man. God is King of the world, and Father of mankind. Manhood in the King and the father is likest, nearest to Godhood. This is the old belief on which the mediaeval world was established. It is also the root and blossoming of Shakspere's early plays, such as *Henry V.* And for this reason, *Henry V* and its equivalent plays are not tragedies: they are written entirely from the ready, immediate self of the artist.

In the later plays, however, *Hamlet, Lear, Macbeth,* the unconscious man has risen against the conscious, against the accepted formula, against the established order. It is the unconscious self of Shakspere—characterised as a woman—who really murders this king and father who represents almost all that is divine in man. It is Gertrude, Lady Macbeth, Goneril and Regan who destroy the supreme image of man, the image of God in man. The punishment is meted out to them severally, afterwards. But nevertheless, the king, the father is dead, killed, cast down from supremacy.

This is the dramatic portrayal of the whole change that took place at the Renaissance, and it is the presentiment of the execution of Charles I in actual life, just as *Le Cid* is the presentiment of the French Revolution.

The order in this case was, first the philosophic and religious departure from the old position, in the Humanists, in Erasmus, Savonarola, and Luther. Then came the personal and artistic departure, in the dramatists, Shakspere, Milton, then the political and social departure, of the Commonwealth.

It is these great philosophical and religious revolutions, the revolution in thought, the change in conception of the spiritual world, which divide and which make the great periods in history.

The mediaeval world believed in an Almighty and Everlasting God, Maker of Heaven and Earth, Lord of all life, in Whom was absolute power, Whose law was eternal, Who had however a Son Jesus, who would intercede with the Almighty God, and obtain mercy for repentant sinners. This on earth was carried out in the imperial state, an absolute monarch, invested with all power, yet open to clemency.

At the Renaissance all this collapsed, philosophically, even religiously. God was no longer the Almighty, the Wielder of Power, the Creator and the Destroyer. The mediaeval saints had modified this conception.

Christ was God, Christ, the Lamb, the Dove, Christ, who was all love, all mercy, all humility. The symbol now was the Shepherd carrying the lamb and leading the sheep to the fold. The people of the world were the sheep. And God was

Love for his people. For the sake of the sheep the Shepherd sought the green pastures, for the sake of the sheep, always for the sake of the sheep.

This was the very reverse of the old idea of Almighty God Who held the thunderbolt in His right hand, and balanced the firmament in His left. The fulfilling of this new conception meant the subversion of the established order, entirely.

In the dramatist, in Shakspere, there is no conception of the new order. Shakspere was not a thinker. His conscious self was slow and reluctant, he found it difficult, as every artist must, to attend to abstract propositions, or to think in generalisations. He could only *feel* supremely the things which reformers could settle in the mind. And he could only feel that his old self, his great, immediate, conscious and subconscious self, that which he conceived himself wholly to be, the whole establishment of his soul, was impeached, arraigned, condemned. His whole being was condemned to nullification.

> "It is a tale told by an idiot—"
> "How weary, stale, flat and unprofitable
> Seem to me all the uses of this world."

What was it but tragedy and annihilation, madness and horror? Shakspere is, in his dual self, Gertrude and Hamlet, Duncan and Banquo on the one hand, and Lady Macbeth and Macbeth on the other, Lear and Lear's fool and Cordelia, and then Goneril and Regan. He is the murdered and the murderer, the King and the regicide, the father and the patricide. And as such he ends in a convulsion of horror and self-annihilation, self-obliteration.

This is the whole condition of tragedy, when the formed soul of the artist is to be destroyed by the unconscious, unformed will. This will, being unconscious, as yet is purely destructive. It must destroy the old consciousness before itself can rise to occupy the field.

The condition of tragedy occurs naturally half way between the change in the philosophical and spiritual conception of life and the world, and the change in the actual living frame of life to fit this new conception. The first change is made in the minds and in the spirit of the few. It is a purely personal thing, and not necessarily in its first form at all subversive to the existing order, because it has no immediate relation to it. It is only when the new light, the new spirit, the new conception soaks through into the blood, and the actual feelings of the simple, not-intellectual people are changed, set in a new order, a new category, that a new system is created on the face of the earth: is created, or takes place.

But this process, of the gradual infusing and informing of the very blood of a people, by a new light, a new spiritual conception, is very slow. It is the artist who is first submitted to the change. Just as the philosopher's is the first mind into which the new idea penetrates, so the artist's is the first *soul* to be affected. And it is affected first, necessarily, with a sense of death, of its own subversion, destruction. For the form of the existing soul must be broken before the new soul can have being.

The Greek tragedians came between the real philosophic revolution, of Heraclitus and the Pythagoreans, and Pannenides and Anaxagoras, and the later social and political revolution, when the spirit of democracy supplanted the spirit of kingship. Aeschylus, who leaned back to the conservative form, ended in confidence of the conservative order: but Agamemnon was murdered, nevertheless. Euripides, who leaned to the advanced thought, ended in a spirit of pure death, pure not-being, of complete passing-away.

Turgenev, Tolstoi, and Dostoevsky occupy somewhat the position in the crisis of late European history that Shakspere and Corneille and Cervantes occupied with relation to the Renaissance, the crisis of middle European history, and that Aeschylus and Sophocles and Euripides occupied in the Grecian era.

[end of manuscript]

POLITE TO ONE ANOTHER ...

polite to one another—through the glass partitions.

Don't you dare to step through a glass partition. The whole fabric of England will collapse if you do. It's a crystal prison, horribly brittle.

If you happen to walk unconsciously through the glass partition-walls, the Englishmen curl up like caterpillars in salt. They just can't bear it. Each kind of social fish can swim only in its own glass tank. It will gorp through the partition-wall, mouthing words to the fishes on the other side, and feeling *very* social and brotherly, don't you know. But if a young hot-blooded porpoise happens to run with a bump against a wall of glass, all the fish in that social tank reel and swoon on the wave.

You can't just simply talk to an Englishman, as if he were a man and nothing but a man. He may be an English working man, and then don't you dare to treat him as anything else. English working man, salt of the earth, awfully decent fellow, nature's home-made gentleman, most intelligent proletarian on the face of the earth. That's the tone you've got to take with him. That or nothing. Treat him as if he were just a man, answering from his own fearless man's self, and he'll gasp like a hooked fish. He's *not* a mere man: he's British working man, so you needn't try to confuse him with all the rest of mammals that are not British Working Men.

The same with the British professional man: he's another special kind of fish, endowed with his own markings and his own special brand of dumbness. Then there's the lower middle class, and middle middle class, and the upper middle class. Then there's artistic and literary people, in their various tanks. Then the several tanks of the aristocracy. Sometimes an aristocratic trout will jump over the low division between the aristocratic tanks, and swim for while with the aristocratic perch. Sometimes a rich fat carp will come flopping into the upper waters. But back to their own tanks they go at evening.

It is a land of fishes in a complicated arrangement of tanks. Outsiders, of course, are always running with a bump against invisible partition walls. Thank goodness the partitions will stand, any amount of casual bumps. Only a concentrated kick from the working-class herrings is frightfully dangerous. Oh frightfully! then the British herring is such a decent fish. Decent is the word: the very English word.

If you happen to be a sort of dolphin, and in the usual way of dolphins you go jumping about on the surface of the waters, then you find yourself suddenly in a strange tank, with all the spotted trout or the striped carp looking at you aghast, wondering if you're a pike, and wishing to heaven you were on the other side of the glass partition.

Then, being a dolphin of many dyes, you hastily assume trout-spots or carp-stripes, to put your hosts at their ease. Because, poor darlings, their embarrassment at finding a strange fish in their midst is acute. The strange fish himself doesn't mind. He's used to being a strange fish. But the hosts of his hosts mind terribly: they are cramped with nervous embarrassment and fear. They hang suspended, paralysed in their own tank.

So the strange fish quickly changes his spots, and becomes middle-middle-class, or working-class, or pseudo-aristocratic, as the case may be. And a hush of relief comes over his hosts: "He is one of ourselves! Thank God!"

You must always assert your harmlessness, first thing, in England. Harmless you must be.

Yet they always keep an uneasy eye on you.

You must be one of them—whoever "they" happen to be. Otherwise "they" suffer so. It is cruelty to animals.

The English are so acutely socially sensitive, and so temperamentally tough, leathery. If you can't speak with a certain well-bred accent, and sit in a chair in a certain way, you'd better die, you'll cause so much suffering to "them." In England domestication is carried to excess. People are domestic in families, in groups, in cliques, in parties, in classes. The clue to English life is the domesticated clique. The clique is a class within a class within a class.

The members of a clique feel "comfortable" with one another: safe from all harm or possibility of harm. Temperamentally the toughest of people, English people nowadays are almost morbidly socially sensitive. It's like fish swimming thick in a pool, yet slipping past one another by miracle, without touching. You mustn't come into contact with anybody. There must be no impact. You mustn't butt into anybody's feelings, you really mustn't. An occasional innuendo, perhaps, to show that you're not such a fool as you look. And an innuendo which will reveal you with a soul as tough and impervious as shoe-leather. But a delicate outside social skin—oh, a marvellously sensitive social epidermis.

If you are one of the upper classes, you wouldn't hurt a working man's feelings—honest working man—not for worlds and worlds At the same time, your tough, leathery indifference to his bewilderment, his penniless and humiliated bewilderment, is amazing. Tough, leathery, insentient inside. Oh dear me, so sensitive on the outside! The Working Man, the generalised, abstract article, is so much nicer than Bill Smith, don't you know.

It is always the same, when a people develops its social side at the expense of its own living blood. Comes a white-blooded kind of callousness. And a marvellous squeamishness. Squeamish the English are, to excess. And as insensitive as celluloid.

Over-developed socially. Anemic and insentient inside. Concerned supremely with protecting themselves. Only afraid.

The old gentry armed themselves in iron armour and went out with lances. The modern gentry of England arm themselves in the armour of their class, which has grown into them like transparent horn, and with a transparent, horny smile on their faces, they go gingerly forth, waving the tentacles or the antennae of their class instinct to scent the approach of danger. Danger means anything that is not "one of ourselves." And the means of protection is to curl up deprecatingly inside the transparent horn armour, and when driven to extremity, spit a little poison or call a policeman.

The extreme of danger, of course, lies in being approached as if you were a naked human man. You have long ago left off being naked or nakedly human. Your armour has grown into you, layer on layer, and in the middle you are largely pulp. The armour of your nationality, the armour of your social class, the armour of your profession, your clique, your family. All these layers upon layers of safeguard against your own nakedness.

The Englishman firmly believes that when the Lord gave him a soul, the Lord breathed the first breath into him saying: *It's got to be an Englishman, so let's make it superior to start with.* At the second breath: *it's born into the upper middle classes, so we'd better put a superior kind of gas into it.* At the third breath: *Its father's a successful barrister, so it had better have brains and a bit of wit.* At the third breath: *Let's see,* is *it a boy or a girl? Doesn't matter anyhow.*

So down descends the baby, a ready-made English Subject of the Upper Middle Classes born into the professional class (parliamentary bar). As long as this English two-legged animal lives, it must be spoken to as an Englishman of the upper
[end of manuscript]

THERE IS NO REAL BATTLE ...

There is no real battle between me and Christianity. Perhaps there is a certain battle between me and nonconformity, because, at the depth, my nature is catholic. But I believe in the all-overshadowing God. I believe that Jesus is one of the Sons of God: not, however, the only Son of God. I think that the men who believe in the all-overshadowing God will naturally form a Church of God. That is, I believe in a Church. And I believe in secret doctrine, as against the vulgarity of nonconformity. I believe in an initiated priesthood, and in cycles of esoteric knowledge. I believe in the authority of the Church, and in the power of the priest to grant absolution.

So that on the religious fundamentals, there is no breach between me and the Catholic Church.

But I cannot believe in a Church of Christ. Jesus is only one of the Sons of Almighty God. There are many saviours—there is only one God. There will be more saviours: but God is one God.

So that the great Church of the future will know other saviours: men are saved variously, in various lands, in various climes, in various centuries. A church established on the Almighty God, but having temples to the various saviours, is the true [church] of man.

The great disaster of religion is that each religion tends to assert one exclusive saviour. One hates Christianity because it declares there is only one God. A true Church would know that there are a few great roads to God, and many, many small tracks.

"I am the way" — Not even Jesus can declare this to *all* men. To very many men, Jesus is no longer the way. He is no longer the way for me. But what does it matter? He is one of the Sons of God. And I will gladly light a candle for him also.

Yet I must seek another way. God, the great God is always God. But we have always to find our way to him. The way was Jesus. And the way is no longer Jesus.

So, for the moment, we have no way. God is God — but we cannot come to him. God is God — but he has not yet sent us a prophet.

That does not mean we leave off seeking, or trying, or adventuring.

[end of manuscript]

ON BEING IN LOVE

Man is a thinking animal—domesticated—instincts gone. He is thought-bound—his emotions limited by his thoughts. New thoughts liberate new emotions.

Instinctive animal Russia, with its miseries and splendours, gone: now a thinking, or pseudo-thinking Russia, enacting a few old thoughts, the best spontaneity destroyed.

Man is a thought adventurer—he's got to advance in thought across the ages, or wither. Because his thoughts, willy nilly, dominate his emotions.

Love—sacred and profane. Sacred makes a great offering. Two sorts—an offering up of self—or an act of dominion, the offering up of the other.

Profane is just self-centred and momentary.

[end of manuscript]

ON TAKING THE NEXT STEP

When we moderns are sent down to hell, as we shall all be sent, it will be for our sins of omission, not for our sins of commission. We shall be damned because we never really did anything.

We just mark time on the brink.

Brink of what? We are on a brink, we all seem agreed about it. But we none of us decide what brink it is.

What is it we don't know? What is it we should have realised, or begun to realise, in the war, and didn't. What is it we funked?

What about the next step? Whither? Towards what? And what will it land us in.

Brink! That means the edge of something. A river, a gulf, a chasm, a precipice, a barranca, a sea, an ocean. What is it then that lies over the brink? What is this mysterious beyond?

But don't let us hurry. We are on the verge, on the brink. And the war brought us there.

A brink is the end of an old journey, the edge of a jump of some sort. This brink then is the end of a journey.

End of what?

Why, the end of democracy, the end of the ideal of liberty and freedom, the end of the brotherhood of man, the end of the idea of the perfectibility of man, the end of the belief in the reign of love, the end of the belief that man desires peace, harmony, tranquility, love, and lovingkindness all the while. The end of

Christianity, the end of the Church of Jesus. The end of idealism, the end of the idealistic ethic. The end of Plato and Kant, as well as of Jesus. The end of science, as an absolute knowledge. The end of the absolute power of the Word. The end, the end, the end.

We're at the end of all these things.

And at the beginning of what?

A gulf. A gulf, a gulf! What's a gulf?

Nay, you can't look into the gulf till you've run to the real edge of it. And you very rarely come to the brink of one sheer precipice. No, you come to a steep place, and look down to another level: not very far. You scramble down to this level: your old paths will get you down so far. And you look over. And still you can't see into the gulf. You look down to another ledge, rather narrower.

And that's how one comes to a brink. It's not really very dramatic. You don't pull up sharp before a yawning gulf three thousand feet in sheer depth. No no! The gulf is there, three thousand feet. But when you come to the first brink, it is only a sort of bank, with a sloping rocky descent of three hundred feet. And you can make it. You can scramble down.

So, bit by bit you scramble down, from level to level, from brink to brink. And every brink looks final, before you get to it. You think *there is the verge!* But it isn't. Not quite.

And yet it's all part of the gulf: the great chasm.

These various preliminary falls are all ends. They are all departures from the old way. The broad old way ends at the first drop. But there are paths, continuations.

The broad old way, what is that? What is it we leave when we leave the broad old way, at the first brink?

[end of manuscript]

MAN IS ESSENTIALLY A SOUL

Man is essentially a soul. The soul is neither the body nor the spirit, but the central flame that burns between the two, as the flame of a lamp burns between the oil of the lamp and the oxygen of the air.

The soul is to be obeyed, by the body, by the spirit, by the mind.

The mind is the instrument for registering the soul in consciousness.

The soul is instinctive. Real education is the learning to recognize and obey the instincts of the soul.

The most subtle and sensitive thing in life, is the recognising and responding directly to the instinctive soul. All men do it in their own degree. But to catch the finest and ultimate flickers of intimation that can come from within needs a rare, pure, burning soul, a pure body, a sensitive, strong spirit, and a quick, imaginative mind.—And this is rare.

So men are really arranged in hierarchies of the soul, from the finest down to the dullest, in hierarchies of the soul.

This is the new order of aristocracy, and it is a world-order. The finest soul in the world is the first man in the world, and the rest form themselves naturally into hierarchies.

By the movement of his soul within himself, a man knows the soul within another man, and whether it be a purer, stronger flame, whether the man belong to a higher hierarchy or not. Man knows at first hand, *if he will.*

Body and spirit both must learn to obey the soul, since both are consummated in the soul. The soul is a flame that forever quivers between oil and air, between body and spirit, between substance and non-substance, between the senses and the mind. It is born of both and partakes of both and consummates both and surpasses both. But it is always midmost between the two.

If the flame of the soul dies out, or is blown out by perverse living, the body begins to go corrupt in life, and the spirit takes on its murderous aspect.

So that there must be *authority* and *discipline.—The* soul itself is the source of all authority, and the man of the purest, strongest soul-flame is the highest authority in the world. But even he must discipline his senses, his spirit, his mind and body, all the time, to the fulfilment of the soul. And every man's life, in so far as it is truly lived, is a long self-discipline.

If the body is disciplined to the soul, then the senses are consummated in the soul, and pleasure is transmuted into joy. And when the spirit is disciplined to the soul, then delight and ecstasy likewise fall into the deeper harmony of joy, without shrillness.

There is no such thing as absolute freedom. True, soul is the only authority, and each man primarily obeys his own soul. But obeying his own soul means, to every man, realising that he cannot know his own soul or come at its intimations without help from a purer stronger being, to whose authority he must submit himself. Yet he only submits because his own soul tells him to. And this is freedom. Freedom in the sense of escape from all authority is illusion and disintegration. There is *always* authority imposed from the soul within, and obedience and discipline exacted. This we cannot escape, without falling into corruption and running into disintegration.

There is no absolute Word or Logos, even no *absolute* Law. All depends on the soul.

Neither is there any One Way. The soul takes many and different ways, all of them right.

Neither is there one supreme passion, like love and sacrifice. No sacrifice is final, not even Christ's. And every sacrifice man can make will in its turn have to be sacrificed, when the time comes. And every supreme passion will yield in its turn to another passion, which will then be supreme for its own time. So pride yielded before love, and love will yield before the passion of integrity.

[end of manuscript]

412

RETURN TO BESTWOOD

I came home to the Midlands for a few days, at the end of September. Not that there is any home, for my parents are dead. But there are my sisters, and the district one calls home; that mining district between Nottingham and Derby.

It always depresses me to come to my native district. Now I am turned forty, and have been more or less a wanderer for nearly twenty years, I feel more alien, perhaps, in my home place than anywhere else in the world. I can feel at ease in Canal Street, New Orleans, or in the Avenue Madero, in Mexico City, or in George Street, Sydney, in Trincomalee Street, Kandy, or in Rome or Paris or Munich or even London. But in Nottingham Road, Bestwood, I feel at once a devouring nostalgia and an infinite repulsion. Partly, I want to get back to the place as it was when I was a boy, and I waited so long to be served in the Co-op——I remember our Co-op number, 1533 A. L. better than the date of my birth—and when I came out lugging a string net of groceries. There was a little hedge across the road from the Co-op then, and I used to pick the green buds which we called bread-and-cheese. And there were no houses in Gabes Lane. And at the corner of Queen Street, Butcher Bob was huge and fat and taciturn.

Butcher Bob is long dead, and the place is all built up, I am never quite sure where I am, in Nottingham Rd. Walker Street is not very much changed though—because the ash tree was cut down when I was sixteen, when I was ill. The houses are still only on one side the street, the fields on the other. And still one looks across at the amphitheatre of hills which I still find beautiful, though there are new patches of reddish houses, and a darkening of smoke. Crich is still on the sky line to the west, and the woods of Annesley to the north, and Coney Grey Farm still lies in front. And there is still a certain glamour about the country-side. Curiously enough, the more motor-cars and tram-cars and omnibuses there are rampaging down the roads, the more the country retreats into its own isolation, and becomes more mysteriously inaccessible.

When I was a boy, the whole population lived very much more *with* the country. Now, they rush and tear along the roads, and have joy-rides and outings, but they never seem to touch the reality of the country-side. There are many more people, for one thing: and all these new contrivances, for another.

The country seems, somehow, fogged over with people, and yet not really touched. It seems to lie back, away, unreached and asleep. The roads are hard and metalled and worn with everlasting rush. The very field-paths seem wider and more trodden and squalid. Wherever you go, there is the sordid sense of humanity.

And yet the fields and the woods in between the roads and paths sleep as in a heavy, weary dream, disconnected from the modern world.

This visit, this September, depresses me peculiarly. The weather is soft and mild, mildly sunny in that hazed, dazed, uncanny sunless sunniness which makes the Midlands peculiarly fearsome to me. I cannot, cannot accept as sunshine this thin luminous vapourousness which passes as a fine day in the place of my birth. Oh Phœbus Apollo! Surely you have turned your face aside!

But the special depression this time is the great coal strike, still going on. In house after house, the families are now living on bread and margarine and potatoes. The colliers get up before dawn, and are away into the last recesses of the countryside, scouring the country for blackberries, as if there were a famine. But they will sell the blackberries at fourpence a pound, and so they'll be fourpence in pocket.

But when I was a boy, it was utterly *infra dig.* for a miner to be picking blackberries. He would never have demeaned himself to such an unmanly occupation. And as to walking home with a little basket—he would almost rather have committed murder. The children might do it, or the women, or even the half-grown youths. But a married, manly collier!

But nowadays, their pride is in their pocket, and the pocket has a hole in it.

It is another world. There are policemen everywhere, great, big strange policemen with faces like a leg of mutton. Where they come from, heaven only knows: Ireland or Scotland, presumably, for they are no Englishmen. And they exist, along the countryside, in thousands. The people call them "blue-bottles," and "meat-flies." And you can hear a woman call across the street to another: "Seen any blow-flies about?"—Then they turn to look at the alien policemen, and laugh shrilly.

And this in my native place! Truly, one no longer knows the palm of his own hand. When I was a boy, we had our own police-sergeant, and two young constables. And the women would as leave have thought of calling Sergeant Mellor a blue-bottle as calling Queen Victoria one. The Sergeant was a quiet, patient man, who spent his life trying to keep people out of trouble. He was another sort of shepherd, and the miners and their children were a flock to him. The women had the utmost respect for him.

But the women seem to have changed most in this, that they have no respect for anything. There was a scene in the market-place yesterday, a Mrs Hafton and a Mrs Rowley being taken off to court to be tried for insulting and obstructing the police. The police had been escorting the black-legs from the mines, after a so-called day's work, and the women had made the usual row. They were two women from decent homes. In the past they would have died of shame, at having to go to court. But now, not at all.

They had a little gang of women with them in the market-place, waving red flags and laughing loudly and using occasional bad language. There was one, the decent wife of the post-man. I had known her and played with her as a girl. But she was waving her red flag, and cheering as the motor-bus rolled up.

The two culprits got up, hilariously, into the bus.

"Good luck, old girl! Let 'em have it! Give it the blue-bottles in the neck! Tell me what for! Three cheers for Bestwood! Strike while the iron's hot, girls!"

"So long! So long, girls! See you soon! Merry home-coming, what, eh?"

"Have a good time, now! Have a good time! Stick a pin in their fat backsides, if you can't move 'em any other road. We s'll be thinking of you!"

"So long! So long! See you soon! Who says Walker!"

"E-eh! E—eh!——"

The bus rolled heavily off, with the shouting women, amid the strange hoarse cheering of the women in the little market-place. The draughty little market-place where my mother shopped on Friday evenings, in her rusty little black bonnet, and where now a group of decent women waved little red flags and hoarsely cheered two women going to court!

O mamma mia!—as the Italians say. My dear mother, your little black bonnet would fly off your head in horrified astonishment, if you saw it now. You were so keen on progress: a decent working man, and a good wage! you paid my father's union pay for him, for so many years! you believed so firmly in the Co-op! you were at your Women's Guild when they brought you word your father, the old tyrannus, was dead! At the same time, you believed so absolutely in the ultimate benevolence of all the masters, of all the upper classes. One had to be grateful to them, after all!

Grateful! You can have your cake and eat it, while the cake lasts. When the cake comes to an end, you can hand on your indigestion. Oh my dear and virtuous mother, who believed in a Utopia of goodness, so that your own people were never quite good enough for you—not even the spoiled delicate boy, myself!—oh my dear and virtuous mother, behold the indigestion we have inherited, from the cake of perfect goodness you baked too often! Nothing was good enough! We must all rise into the upper classes! Upper! Upper! Upper!

Till at last the boots are all uppers, the sole is worn out, and we yell as we walk on stones.

My dear, dear mother, you were so tragic, because you had nothing to be tragic about! We, on the other side, having a moral and social indigestion that would raise the wind for a thousand explosive tragedies, let off a mild crepitus ventrist and shout: Have a good time, old girl! Enjoy yourself, old lass!

Never-the-less, we have all of us "got on." The reward of goodness, in my mother's far-off days, less than twenty years ago, was that you should "get on." *Be good, and you'll get on in life.*

Myself, a snotty-nosed little collier's lad, I call myself at home when I sit in a heavy old Cinque-cento Italian villa, of which I rent only half, even then—surely I can be considered to have "got on." When I wrote my first book, and it was going to be published—sixteen years ago—and my mother was dying, a fairly well-known editor wrote to my mother and said, of me: "By the time he is forty; he will be riding in his carriage!"

To which my mother is supposed to have said, sighing: "Ay, if he lives to be forty!"

Well, I am forty-one, so there's one in the eye for that sighing remark. I was always weak in health, but my life was strong. Why had they all made up their minds that I was to die? Perhaps they thought I was too good to live. Well, in that case they were had!

And when I was forty, I was not even in my own motor-car. But I *did* drive my own two horses in a light buggy (my own) on a little ranch (also my own, or my wife's, through me) away on the western slope of the Rocky Mountains. And sitting in my corduroy trousers and blue shirt, calling: "Get up Aaron! *Ambrose!*" then I thought of Austin Harrison's prophecy. Oh Oracle of Delphos! Oracle of Dodona! "Get up, Ambrose!" Bump! went the buggy over a rock, and the pine-needles slashed my face! See him driving in his carriage, at forty!—driving it pretty badly too! Put the brake on!

So I suppose I've got on, snotty-nosed little collier's lad, of whom most of the women said: "He's a *nice* little lad!" They don't say it now: if ever they say anything, which is doubtful. They've forgotten me entirely.

But my sister's "getting on" is much more concrete than mine. She is almost on the spot. Within six miles of that end dwelling in The Breach, which is the house I first remember—an end house of hideous rows of miners' dwellings, though I loved it, too—stands my sister's new house, "a lovely house!"—and her garden: "I wish mother could see my garden in June!"

And if my mother did see it, what then? It is wonderful the flowers that bloom in these Midlands, in June. A northern Persephone seems to steal out from the Plutonic, coal—mining depths and give a real hoot of blossoms. But if my mother *did* return from the dead, and see that garden in full bloom, and the glass doors open from the hall of the new house, what then? Would she then say: It is reached! Consummatum est!

When Jesus gave up the ghost, he cried: It is finished! Consummatum est! But was it? And if so, what? What was it that was consummate?

Likewise, before the war, in Germany I used to see advertised in the newspapers a moustache-lifter, which you tied on at night and it would make your moustache stay turned up, like the immortal moustache of Kaiser Wilhelm II, whose moustache alone is immortal. This moustache-lifter was called: Es ist erreicht! In other words: It is reached! Consummatum est!

Was it? Ws it reached? With the moustache lifter?

So the ghost of my mother, in my sister's garden. I see it each time I am there, bending over the violas, or looking up at the almond tree. Actually an almond tree! And I always ask, of the grey-haired, good little ghost: "Well what of it, my dear? What is the verdict?"

But she never answers, though I press her:

"Do look at the house, my dear! Do look at the tiled hall, and the rug from Mexico, and the brass from Venice, seen through the open doors, beyond the lilies and the carnations of the lawn beds! Do look! And do look at me, and see if I'm not a gentleman! Do say that I'm almost upper class!"

But the dear little ghost says never a word.

"Do say we've got on! Do say, we've arrived. Do say, it is reached, es ist erreicht, consummatum est!"

But the little ghost turns aside, she knows I am teasing her. She gives me one look, which is a look I know, and which says: "I shan't tell you, so you can't laugh at me. You must find out for yourself" And she steals away, to her place, wherever it may be.—"In my father's house are many mansions. If it were not so, I would have told you."

The black slate roofs beyond the wind-worn young trees at the end of the garden are the same thick layers of black roofs of blackened brick houses, as ever. There is the same smell of sulphur from the burning pit bank. Smuts fly on the white violas. There is a harsh sound of machinery. Persephone couldn't quite get out of hell, so she let spring fall from her lap along the upper workings.

But no! There are no smuts, there is even no smell of the burning pit bank. They cut the bank, and the pits are not working. The strike has been going on for months. It is September, but there are lots of roses on the lawn beds.

"Where shall we go this afternoon? Shall we go to Hardwick?"

416

Let us go to Hardwick. I have not been for twenty years. Let us go to Hardwick.

"Hardwick Hall
More window than wall."

Built in the days of good Queen Bess, by that other Bess, termagant and tartar, Countess of Shrewsbury.

Butterley, Alfreton, Tibshelf—what was once the Hardwick district is now the Notts-Derby coal area. The country is the same, but scarred and splashed all over with mines and mining settlements. Great houses loom from hill-brows, old villages are smothered in rows of miners' dwellings, Bolsover Castle rises from the mass of the colliery village of Bolsover.—Böwser, we called it, when I was a boy.

Hardwick is shut. On the gates, near the old inn, where the atmosphere of the old world lingers perfect, is a notice: "This park is closed to the public and to all traffic until further notice. No admittance."

Of course! The strike! They are afraid of Vandalism.

Where shall we go? Back into Derbyshire, or to Sherwood Forest.

Turn the car. We'll go on through Chesterfield. If I can't ride in my own carriage, I can ride in my sister's motor-car.

It is a still September afternoon. By the ponds in the old park, we see colliers slowly loafing, fishing, poaching, in spite of all notices.

And at every lane-end there is a bunch of three or four policemen, blue-bottles, big, big-faced, stranger policemen. Every field path, every stile is to be guarded. There are great pits, coal mines, in the fields.

And at the end of the paths coming out of the field from the colliery, along the high-road, the colliers are squatted on their heels, on the wayside grass, silent and watchful. Their faces are clean, white, and all the months of the strike have given them no colour and no tan. They are pit-bleached. They squat in silent remoteness, as if in the upper galleries of hell. And the policemen, alien, stand in a group near the stile. Each lot pretends not to be aware of the others.

It is past three. Down the path from the pit come straggling what my little nephews calls "the dirty ones." They are the men who have broken strike, and gone back to work. They are not many: their faces are black, they are in their pit-dirt. They linger till they have collected, a group of a dozen or so "dirty ones", near the stile, then they trail off down the road, the policemen, the alien blue-bottles, escorting them. And the "clean ones", the colliers still on strike, squat by the wayside and watch without looking. They say nothing. They neither laugh nor stare. But there they are, a picket, and with their bleached faces they see without looking, and they register with the silence of doom, squatted down in rows by the road-side.

The "dirty ones" straggle off in the lurching, almost slinking walk of colliers, swinging their heavy feet and going as if the mine-roof were still over their heads. The big blue policemen follow at a little distance. No voice is raised: nobody seems aware of anybody else. But there is the silent, hellish registering in the consciousness of all three groups, clean ones, dirty ones, and blue-bottles.

So it is now all the way into Chesterfield, whose crooked spire lies below. The men who have gone back to work—they seem few, indeed— are lurching and slinking in quiet groups, home down the high-road, the police at their heels. And the pickets, with bleached faces, squat and lean and stand, in silent groups, with a certain pale fatality, like Hell, Upon them.

And I, who remember the homeward-trooping of the colliers when I was a boy, the ringing of the feet, the red mouths and the quick whites of the eyes, the swinging pit-bottles, and the strange voices of men from the underworld calling back and forth, strong and, it seemed to me, gay with the queer, absolved gaiety of miners—I shiver, and feel I turn into a ghost myself. The colliers were noisy, lively with strong underworld voices such as I have never heard in any other men, when I was a boy. And after all, it is not so long ago. I am only forty-one.

But after the war, the colliers went silent: after 1920. Till 1920 there was a strange power of life in them, something wild and urgent, that one could hear in their voices. They were always excited, in the afternoon, to come up above-ground: and excited, in the morning, at going down. And they called in the darkness with strong, strangely evocative voices. And at the little local foot-ball matches, on the damp, dusky Saturday afternoons of winter, great, full-throated cries came howling from the football field, in the zest and the wildness of life.

But now, the miners go by to the football match in silence like ghosts, and from the field comes a poor, ragged shouting. These are the men of my own generation, who went to the board school with me. And they are almost voiceless. They go to the welfare clubs, and drink with a sort of hopelessness.

I feel I hardly know any more the people I come from, the colliers of the Erewash Valley district. They are changed, and I suppose I am changed. I find it so much easier to live in Italy. And they have got a new kind of shallow consciousness, all newspaper and cinema, which I am not in touch with. At the same time, they have, I think an underneath ache and heaviness very much like my own. It must be so, because when I see them, I feel it so strongly.

They are the only people who move me strongly, and with whom I feel myself connected in deeper destiny. It is they who are, in some peculiar way, "home" to me. I shrink away from them, and I have an acute nostalgia for them.

And now, this last time, I feel a doom over the country, and a shadow of despair over the hearts of the men, which leaves me no rest. Because the same doom is over me, wherever I go, and the same despair touches my heart.

Yet it is madness to despair, while we still have the course of destiny open to us.

One is driven back to search one's own soul, for a way out into a new destiny.

A few things I know, with inner knowledge.

I know that what I am struggling for is life, more life ahead, for myself and the men who will come after me: struggling against fixations and corruptions.

I know that the miners at home are men very much like me, and I am very much like them: ultimately, we want the same thing. I know they are, in the life sense of the word, good.

I know that there is ahead the mortal struggle for property.

I know that the ownership of property has become, now, a problem, a religious problem. But it is one we can solve.

I know I want to own a few things: my personal things. But I also know that I want to own no more than those. I don't want to own a house, nor land, nor a motor-car, nor shares in anything. I don't want a fortune—not even an assured income.

At the same time, I don't want poverty and hardship. I know I need enough money to leave me free in my movements, and I want to be able to earn that money without humiliation.

I know that most decent people feel very much the same in this respect: and the indecent people must, in their indecency, be subordinated to the decent.

I know that we could, if we would, establish little by little a true democracy in England: we could nationalise the land and industries and means of transport, and make the whole thing work infinitely better than at present, *if we would.* It all depends on the spirit in which the thing is done.

I know we are on the brink of a class war.

I know we had all better hang ourselves at once, than enter on a struggle which shall be a fight for the ownership or non-ownership of property, pure and simple, and nothing beyond.

I know the ownership of property is a problem that may have to be fought out. But beyond the fight must lie a new hope, a new beginning.

I know our vision of life is all wrong. We must be prepared to have a new conception of what it means, *to live.* And everybody should try to help to build up this new conception, and everybody should be prepared to destroy bit by bit, our old conception.

I know that man cannot live by his own will alone. With his soul, he must search for the sources of the power of life. It is life we want.

I know that where there is life, there is essential beauty. Genuine beauty, which fills the soul, is an indication of life, and genuine ugliness, which blasts the soul, is an indication of morbidity.—But prettiness is opposed to beauty.

I know that, first and foremost, we must be sensitive to life and to its movements. If there is power, it must be sensitive power.

I know that we must look after the quality of life, not the quantity. Hopeless life should be put to sleep, the idiots and the hopeless sick and the true criminal. And the birth-rate should be controlled.

I know we must take up the responsibility for the future, now. A great change is coming, and must come. What we need is some glimmer of a vision of a world that shall be, beyond the change. Otherwise we shall be in for a great débâcle.

What is alive, and open, and active, is good. All that makes for inertia, lifelessness, dreariness, is bad. This is the essence of morality.

What we should live for is life and the beauty of aliveness, imagination, awareness, and contact. To be perfectly alive is to be immortal.

I know these things, along with other things. And it is nothing very new to know these things. The only new thing would be to act on them. And what is the good of saying these things, to men whose whole education consists in the fact that twice two are four?—which, being interpreted, means that twice tuppence is fourpence. All our education, the whole of it, is formed upon this little speck of dust.

They talk about home, but what is home? I went this autumn once more to the place of my birth, a little mining town eight miles out of Nottingham. And once more I was on hot bricks, to get away. I find I can be at home anywhere, except at home. I feel perfectly calm in London or Paris or Rome or Munich or Sydney or San Francisco. The one place where I feel absolutely not at home, is my home place, where I lived for the first twenty-one years of my life.

"I remember, I remember

The house where I was born" —very vaguely that is, because we left it when I was a year old. It was at a corner of the ugly streets of miners' dwellings known as The Buildings, and it was stuck on to Henry Saxton's shop. Henry Saxton was a burly bullying fellow with fair curly hair, and though he never pronounced an 'h' in the right place, he had a great opinion of Henry. I knew him well enough, because he was the afternoon Sunday-school superintendent for many years, and he kept us in order. And without knowing him, I disliked him, the loud and vulgar way he spoke.

My mother seemed, however, to have a respect for him. She, after all, was only a collier's wife, and at that, wife of a collier who drank, who never went to church, who spoke broad dialect, and was altogether one of the common colliers. My mother, of course, spoke good English and was not of the colliery class. She came from Nottingham, was a city girl, had been a sort of clerk to a lace manufacturer whom she probably adored.

A queer woman, my mother. Why, in heaven's name, did she have such a respect for a man like Henry Saxton? She was far more intelligent than he, better educated, in that he wasn't educated at all, and infinitely better bred. Yet she spoke of him with an absolute, almost a tender, respect. And this puzzled my earliest childhood. As a tiny child, I had no instinctive respect for him, and no liking. He was loud-mouthed, aggressive, a pusher, a man who wore his gold watch and chain on his full stomach as if it gave off royal rays. My mother was a shrewd and ironical woman. Yet she looked up to Henry Saxton with tender respect. And, since I was foreordained to accept all her values, I had to look up to Henry Saxton too.

He was, of course, terribly respectable. He was Sunday School Superintendent, he was a deacon at the Congregational Chapel, where he managed to make the life of each succeeding minister a misery, with his hectoring impudence. He criticised the sermons, he who hardly knew A from B: and if the congregation fell off a little, so that the collection on Sundays went down a few shillings, then he sacked the clergyman. The Chapel was another sort of shop to Henry, and the minister was his hired shopman. I remember only two ministers, both good, honest men, whose memory I respect. And each of them was humiliated to the quick by Henry.

And my mother knew it all, yet she admired him. She thought him an infinitely more wonderful man than my father, Why, in heaven's name? Because he was a chapel man, and far more than that, because he was successful. I can see now, that my mother found it so bitter to be very poor, with a husband who came home drunk and who was by no means "respected" in the village, and a dreary family of young children to bring up, that she had really just one idol, success. She felt herself humiliated beyond endurance by her conditions. Successful men succeeded in making money and passing beyond such conditions. Then let us have success at any price.

Now I am forty I realise that my mother deceived me. She stood for all that was lofty and noble and delicate and sensitive and pure, in my life. And all the time, she was worshipping success, because she hadn't got it. She was worshipping a golden calf of a Henry Saxton.

I must say, it was not her *nature* to worship Henry Saxton. She could say very cutting things about him, very jeering. She would pull the tail of the golden calf very shrewdly. For instance, she would tell of people who came to his shop for sugar. Sugar in those days was very cheap. "What else do yer want besides sugar?" said Henry.—"Nothing."—"Then you can go. I shan't serve sugar to them as buys nothing else."—And off went the unfortunate collier's wife. Henry lost a tiny bit on sugar.

I think my mother admired even that in him. She thought it "strength." I remember the story from my very small childhood. Even then *I* thought it rudeness. But it is what makes success.

My mother was all the time sitting down between two stools: My father had charm and a certain warm, uncurbed vitality that made a glow in the house, when he was not in an evil temper. He loved my mother, in his own way, and thought her a much higher being than himself. She loved him physically, felt his charm always, and hated him for being false and mean in money matters. There was so little money. And he kept so much for himself, selfishly. He made "conditions" so wretched. So she despised him, and fought him tooth and nail.

She even fought her love for him, and hated him for his charm. At the same time, she had five children by him. And when she was well over forty, and he must have been forty-seven or more, and came back home at last from a convalescent home, after his leg had been smashed in a bad mining accident, she was in love with him like any girl, and he sat ruddy and resplendent on the sofa, being made much of: though this state of things didn't last, unfortunately. I was about fourteen, and for the first time my eyes were opened a little. I had thought he made her life an agony pure and simple. For years I prayed that he might either be converted into a chapel man, or die. They were not my own prayers. They were a child's prayers for his mother, who has captured him and in whom he believes implicitly.

My mother fought with deadly hostility against my father, all her life. He was not hostile, till provoked, then he too was a devil. But my mother began it. She seemed to begrudge his very existence. She begrudged and hated her own love for him, she fought against his natural charm, vindictively. And by the time she died, at the age of fifty-five, she neither loved him nor hated him any more. She had got over her feeling for him, and was "free." So she died of cancer.

Her feeling for us, also, was divided. We were her own, therefore she loved us. But we were "his," so she despised us a little—I was the most delicate: a pale-faced, dirty-nosed frail boy. So she devoted a great love to me. And she also despised me. I was one of the inferior brats her love for my father—or her disastrous marriage with him—had thrust upon her. She loved me tenderly. And for me, of course, she was the one being on earth: or so I *thought*, anyhow. But now, in the after-years, I realise that she had decided I was going to die, and that was a great deal to her. Also, from many little things I remember, and from things my sisters tell me she said, I realise that she also despised the delicate brat with a chest catarrh and an abnormal love for her. She looked on us all as her lower class inferiors.

She admired me when I won a scholarship and went to the High school in Nottingham, and knew the swells. I was going to be a little gentleman!—But I made no friends among the little gentlemen, and went on quite amiably, quite pleasantly at school, without making the slightest connection with the middle-class boys. I never felt any connection, so it never occurred to me there might be any. We just lived with different outlooks.

It was Miriam who gave me my first incentive to write—when I was about eighteen or nineteen. She was a poor girl on a little farm. Her people were poorer even than we. But it was they who roused me to consciousness. And it was for her, Miriam, I wrote scraps of poems and bits of a novel. I wrote them furtively at home, pretending it was study: writing in the kitchen where all the household affairs were going on, My father hated study and books—he hated to see us poring. My mother liked to see us submissively studying, to "get on." She wanted to be proud of us. And of course, I know she twigged when I was writing poems or bits of a novel. She was so shrewd. I wrote in a college exercise book, and pushed the book in the shelf among the others. But she knew, and she read the things when I wasn't there. Never did she say anything to me. Nor did I say anything to her. She knew also I always took the scraps of writing to Miriam. Poor Miriam, she always thought them wonderful: otherwise I should never have gone on. But for her, I should probably never have written—I never thought of myself as a writer, or of anything special at all. I thought myself rather clever, after I had passed examinations, but because I was not strong, I thought myself of rather less account than most people: the weakling in health! And if I had never written, I probably should have died soon. The being able to express one's soul keeps one alive.

At last, when I was twenty-two, and going to college in Nottingham, one sunny warm day, half-day at college, when my mother loved me to come home and we were two together and alone, she took the exercise-book in which I had re-written the scene in the *White Peacock* where the bride runs up the church path. She put on her spectacles, and read with an amused look on her face.

"But my boy," she said, amused and a bit mocking, as she put down the book and took off her spectacles, "how do you *know* it was like that?"

How did I know? My heart stood still. She treated it as if it were a school essay and she were the teacher: kindly and sceptical. And then I saw in her the slight contempt she had for me: nay, even more, the slight hostility to my presumptuousness. I might "get on" in the ordinary rut, and even become a school-master at three pounds a week. Which would be a great rise above my father. But that I should presume to "know" things off my own bat!—things I had not learned at school!—well, it was presumption in me.

So I became a school-teacher, and went down to Croydon, London, to teach boys in an elementary school, at ninety pounds a year. I hated it: I am no teacher. I wrote in the evenings, but never looked on myself as a writer. There was a burning sort of pleasure in writing: and Miriam loved everything I wrote. I never showed anything to my mother. She would have had an amused feeling about it all, and have felt sceptical. To this day my family is annoyed that I write unpleasant books that nobody really wants to read: certainly *they* don't, although they work through them,

I suppose, because they still "love" me so dearly: me, the brother Bertie, not the embarrassing D. H. Lawrence.

It was Miriam who first sent poems of mine to the English Review: when I was twenty-three. It was she who got back the answer, accepting them. And she was still at home in Underwood, I was in London, far away. Ford Madox Hueffer, who had just begun to edit the English Review—and he did it so well—immediately told me I was a genius: which was a mere phrase to me. Among the working classes, geniuses don't enter. Hueffer was very kind to me, so was Edward Garnett. They were the first literary men I ever met—and the first men *really* outside my own class. They were very kind, very generous. Hueffer read the Manuscript of the *White Peacock*. I had by now finished the novel, having struggled for five years to get it out of the utterly unformed chaos of my consciousness, having written some of it eleven times, and all of it four times. I hewed it out with infinitely more labour than my father hewed out coal. But once it was done, I knew more or less what I had to do.

Hueffer said the *White Peacock* had every fault that an English novel can have—"but you are a genius." That is how they have always been with me. I have every fault that a writer can have—but I have genius. I used to say: For God's sake, don't insult me by calling me a genius. Now I let them talk.

Heinemann the publisher accepted *The White Peacock* at once, and gave me fifty pounds. My mother was dying of cancer: I was twenty-five. Heinemann's kindly sent me an advance copy of my novel. My mother held it in her hands, opened it—then it was enough. She died two days later. Perhaps she thought it spelled success. Perhaps she thought it helped to justify her life. Perhaps she only felt terribly, terribly bitter that she was dying, just as the great adventure was opening before her. Anyhow she died.

A few months before she died, Austin Harrison, who had taken over the English Review, which published all my early things, wrote to her: "By the time he is forty, he will be riding in his own carriage—" And my mother is supposed to have said: "Ay! if he lives to be forty!"—She was so sure of my not living, it seems! I might even ride in my carriage, if I lived! But I was not to live.—I don't know why. I always had more vitality than all the rest put together. My very vitality wore me thin. But vitality doesn't kill a man till it is dammed up.

Well, I am forty-one, and am not dead, neither have I yet ridden in my own carriage, not even in my own motor-car: only in my own buggy driving my own two horses down the rocky trail of my own little ranch in New Mexico. That is all. Whether it justifies the oracle, who knows.

And what my mother would say to it all, I don't know. She would have hated my "sexual" writing, and have felt I had brought deep shame on her, when the "Rainbow" was suppressed. Or perhaps not. Perhaps she would have decided I was worth her backing. But she would have been chagrined at my lack of "real" success: that I don't make more money; that I am not *really* popular, like *Michael Arlen,* or *really* genteel, like Mr Galsworthy: that I have a had reputation as an improper writer, so that she couldn't discuss me complacently with my aunts: that I don't make any "real" friends among the upper classes: that I don't *really* rise in the world, only drift about without any *real* status. All this would have been a chagrin to her. It is perhaps as well she did not live to take part in the adventure.

WHICH CLASS I BELONG TO

It seems to me now, that the gulf between the classes of society, in all the white world, is infinitely deeper than the gulf between nations. As a matter of fact, consciousness is above all things international, and any man of culture, no matter what nation he belongs to, has a permanent contact with any other conscious individual of the white race. One must stick to the white race, and not include the Hindus, even, because with them the European culture is super-imposed, as a sort of mimicry of the ruling races. But among the white race, educated people are very much alike, and can understand one another at once, even though their language be different. There are national idiosyncrasies and national biases. But the dynamic ideas and the conventional emotions and the behaviour are almost identical in the middle-class individuals of any European nation, or of America. There is no true upper class left.

The point is that the content of the consciousness is almost homogeneous in all people of the European culture: and in them all, the consciousness functions in very much the same way. In great things as in small, domestic politics or international finance, internal commerce or a world war, each nation behaves in almost the same way as each other nation: and what is more, thinks the same thoughts, says the same things, re-acts to the same stimuli.

This is, we repeat, the oneness of middle-class Europe. And in all the world there are today only two classes: middle-class and working class.

The cleavage is not vertical: it is horizontal. And there is one line of cleavage only. The middle-class has absorbed the upper class entirely. Kings now belong to the "best" bourgeoisie. The line of cleavage is horizontal. And it cuts through the whole civilised world, horizontally; dividing mankind into two layers, the upper and the lower.

It may be argued that the working classes today are only lower-middle-class. All are striving towards the same goal, to become richer and to have the disposing of riches. Seen from the outside, this is true. Seen from the inside, it is a great fallacy.

Myself, I was born among the working class. My father was a collier, and only a collier. He went down into the pit at twelve years old, and down the pit he went till he was nearly seventy. He could with great difficulty write a few words for a letter, and he could spell down the columns of the local newspaper. But though he always read some bit of the newspaper, he very rarely knew what it meant, the bit he had read. It never occurred to me that it was strange, that he should almost invariably say to my mother: "Lass, what's meanin' o' this 'ere about Canada?" Even when it was explained, a little impatiently, he knew no more. Canada, to him, was somewhere in America, and America was merely somewhere where you went when you were discontented at home. It was all words, and "talk." But he liked to appear to know something about it, because the colliers talked in the public-house, politics and newspaper-stuff, garbled into a sort of fairy-tale.

My father earned, I suppose, on an average, from thirty to thirty-five shillings a week. In summer, however, there were bad times, when the pits were not turning, and the wages would go down to twenty-five, twenty, even fifteen shillings. But though there was a family of children, my father always kept his own share. He never gave my mother more than thirty-shillings: in bad times, when he earned thirty shillings, he kept five for himself: out of twenty-five, he kept the same—or perhaps four shillings. He *had* to have money in his pocket, to go the public-house.

My mother belonged potentially to the middle-classes. She spoke kings English, never could speak a sentence of the dialect correctly; wrote a fine Italian hand and an amusing, clever letter, and preferred the novels of the two discrepant Georges, George Eliot and George Meredith.

Nevertheless, ours was an absolutely working class home. My mother, in a shabby little black bonnet, was a working-man's wife, in spite of her shrewd, "different" face. And we were brought up as working-class children, pure and simple.

Till I was twelve, when I got a County Council scholarship, and went to Nottingham High School. This richly endowed school is supposed to be one of the best day schools in England. It was then under, Dr Gow, later of Westminster.

Well, there was I suddenly figuring as a clever boy, and a pride to my mother. I suppose she was as surprised as I was.—We were a tiny batch of scholarship boys—"common" boys—among the rest of the truly middle-class lads, whose fathers were professors or lace-manufacturers or shop-keepers: anyhow, rich enough to pay the fees. But there was no very marked snobbishness. In Nottingham High School, I never had any sense of being looked down on, because I was a scholarship boy, of the working people. And yet there was a difference. There was a gap. It was nothing voluntary. I remember the better-class boys as having been kindly, almost always, and always ordinarily respectful. But there was a peculiar, indefinable difference. It was as if, boys of the same race, the same locality, the same everything, still we were, in some way, different *animals.*

After the High School, and a brief spell in an office, I became a school-teacher, responsible for a class of boys, at half-a-crown a week for the first year. Then, as a school-teacher, I went to Nottingham University to take the normal course. We who had matriculated were allowed to take the degree course, along with the paying students. And the first year, I took the Arts work.

But it was the same again. The "normal" youths kept together, the paying students were apart. We met, we talked, we exchanged a modicum of ideas. But there was the indefinable gulf between the two sets. It was not snobbism, exactly. It was something deeper. It was something in the very way the heart beat. I remember I sent two poems to the college paper, *On dit!* and they refused them in exactly the same way the middle-class monthlies still would refuse them.

The mysterious difference in vibration between the working-class nature and that of the middle-class I never analysed, just accepting it as a fact. But there it was. Even one had no real pleasure listening to the professors. They had that other peculiar vibration which caused them to be uninteresting, and in some curious way, *outside* one's own life. By the end of the first year I was bored by the university, dropped the degree work, went on with the normal course, did no work at all, and wrote bits of the White Peacock or read novels during lectures.

Again, no one was unfriendly. The professors were lenient, even made slight advances, very kindly. But it was no good. Unless one were by nature a climber, one could not respond in kind. The middle-class seemed quite open, quite willing for one to climb into it. And one turned away, ungratefully.

It was the same with the rest of the normal students. Only one climbed in among the other class, and he was a Jew. The cleverest man of my own year—also a normal student, and a cleverer fellow than myself, by far—was expelled, went loose, drank, and died. So it was.

After college, I went down to Croydon, near London, to teach—at a hundred pounds a year. It was a new school, and hard work. The actual teaching I didn't mind, and the boys, on the whole, I liked very much—they were of all sorts— but the so-called school discipline, the bossiness, the false sort of power one was obliged to assume, all that I hated.

It was when I was at Croydon, when I was twenty-three, that a girl-friend sent some poems of mine to the English Review. Ford Madox Hueffer was then editor, for a brief, brilliant while. He wrote to me, and asked me to come and see him. And he was most kind. He got Heinemann's to publish "The White Peacock" at once. Hueffer said to me "Your book has got every fault that the English novel can have, but you have genius."—They never seemed to grudge me genius, because, perhaps, it is something that can be legitimately patronised. But published I was, and always have been, without any effort on my part. They always allowed me "genius", and every other fault the English novelist can have.

Hueffer introduced me to Edward Garnett, and no-one could have been kinder than he was, helping, advising, asking me down for the week-end to his house in Kent. In those school-teaching days, it was an adventure. And London was an adventure. Ezra Pound was another adventure, and the Bayswater world he introduced me to. And then Austin Harrison, who took over the English Review, would ask me to dinner or to a theatre, and I met all kinds of people.

And that I have not got a thousand friends, and a place in England among the esteemed, is entirely my own fault. The door to "success" has been held open to me. The social ladder has been put ready for me to climb. I have known all kinds of people, and been treated quite well by everyone, practically, whom I have known personally.

Yet here I am, nowhere, as it were, and infinitely an outsider. And of my own choice.

It is only this year, since coming back to Europe from America that I have asked myself why. Why why why could I never go through the open door, into the other world? Why am I forever on the outskirts?

And it seems to me the answer is banal enough: class! I cannot go into the middle-class world. I have, as far as circumstances go left the working-class world. So I have no world at all, and am content.

What is it, then, that prevents so many capable men from moving on in the apparently natural order of progress from the lower class into the upper class? Why can I not follow in the footsteps of Barrie, who is a son of the working-class?—or of Wells?—and become well-to-do middle-class?

What is the peculiar repugnance one feels, towards entering the middle-class world? It is not that there is anything very difficult about it, it seems to me. On the contrary; nothing is so easy as to be a middle-class man among middle-class men: or call it upper-class, if you like. For one who can bring himself to it.

What is the obstacle? I have looked for it in myself, as a clue to this dangerous cleavage between the classes. And I find it is a very deep obstacle. It is in the manner of contact. The contact, among the lower classes—as perhaps, in the past, among the aristocracy—is much more immediate, more physical, between man and man, than it ever is among the middle classes. The middle class can be far more *intimate,* yet never so *near* to one another. It is the difference between the animal, physical affinity that can govern the lives of men, and the other, the affinity of culture and purpose, which actually does govern the mass today.

But the affinity of culture and purpose that holds the vast middle-class world together seems to me to be an intensification today, of the acquisitive and possessive instinct. The dominant instinct of the middle-class world, that is, of the whole world to day, is the possessive instinct, which in its active form is the acquisitive instinct.

It may be said that the working people are *more* acquisitive and more possessive by instinct, than the other class. This may be true of many. But any individual of the lower class who has the dominant acquisitive instinct will automatically pass into the middle or upper class.

The essential working man, like my father, for example, is far too vague to be really acquisitive. He will take sixpence, never thinking that he might have had a pound. And why? Because he wants the sixpence to go to the public-house, to be with the other men, in that queer physical contact which is the affinity of the blood, and is, in the long run, more deeply necessary to men than the affinity of the mind, but which, none the less, can be a prison either to man or woman who is confined to it. So that I myself could never go back into the working class, to the blindness, the obtuseness, the prejudice, the mass-emotions. But neither can I adapt myself to the middle-class, to sacrifice the old, deep blood-affinity between myself and my fellows.

Here, in Italy my environment, my *ambiente* is formed by the peasants who work the *podere.* I am not intimate with them, hardly say anything to them beyond Good-day!—yet they are there, they are present for me, and I for them. If I had to live with them in their cottage, it would be a prison to me. And yet, if I had to choose between two evils, I should choose that, rather than to be imprisoned in the circle of the *intelligentsia* and the middle-class.

Because, it seems to me, one *could* have both affinities, the physical affinity with one's fellow-men, and the mental or spiritual or "conscious" affinity. Yet you can't have them equally. One or the other must predominate. And the mental affinity, in its insistence on predominating, insists on the destruction and the sacrifice of the physical affinity. Even here in Italy, it is bad form to make gestures with your hands when you speak: and an Italian has to murder a good part of himself before he can suppress his gestures. But the middle class insists on it, and so it is done.

To enter the middle class, a man has to sacrifice something that is very deep and necessary to him, his natural physical affinity with other men and women. That is, *if he's got it.* If he hasn't got it, he is bastard middle-class already.

But it is the loss of the old, deep physical affinity between man and man, and man and woman, which causes the great gulf between the classes. And it is down this gulf that our civilisation will collapse: is already rapidly collapsing.

"To me, dancing," said Romeo, "is just making love to music."

"That's why you never will dance with me, I suppose," replied Juliet.

Well, you know, you are a bit too much of an individualist—"

It is a curious thing, but the ideas of one generation become the instincts of the next. We are all of us, largely, the embodied ideas of our grandmothers, and without knowing it, we behave as such. It is odd that the grafting works so quickly, but it seems to. Let the ideas change rapidly, and there follows a correspondingly rapid change in humanity. We become what we think. Worse still, we have become what our grandmothers thought. And our children's children will become the lamentable things that we are thinking. Which is the psychological visiting of the sins of the fathers upon the children. For we do not become just the lofty or beautiful thoughts of our grandmothers. Alas no! We are the embodiment of the most potent ideas of our progenitors, and these ideas were mostly private ones, not to be admitted in public, but to be transmitted as instincts and as the dynamics of behaviour to the third and fourth generation. Alas for the thing that our grandmothers brooded over in secret, and wished and willed in private. That thing are we.

What did they wish and will? One thing is certain: they wished to be made love to, to music. They wished man were not a coarse creature, jumping to his goal, and finished. They wanted heavenly strains to resound, while he held their hand, and a new musical movement to burst forth, as he put his arm round their waist. With infinite variations the music was to soar on, from level to level of love-making, in a delicious dance, the two things inextricable, the two persons likewise.

To end, of course, before the so-called consummation of love-making, which, to our grandmothers in their dream, and therefore to us in actuality, is the grand anti-climax. Not a consummation, but a humiliating anti-climax.

This is the so-called act of love itself, the actual knuckle of the whole bone of contention: a humiliating anti-climax. The bone of contention, of course, is sex. Sex is very charming and very delightful, so long as you make love to music, and you tread the clouds with Shelley, in a two-step. But to come at last to the grotesque bathos of copulation: no Sir! Nay-nay!

Even a man like Maupassant, an apparent devotee of sex, says the same thing: and Maupassant is grandfather, or great-grandfather, to very many of us. Surely, he says, the act of copulation is the Creator's cynical joke against us. To have created in us all these beautiful and noble sentiments of love, to set the nightingale and all the heavenly spheres singing, merely to throw us into this grotesque posture, to perform this humiliating act, is a piece of cynicism worthy, not of a benevolent Creator, but of a mocking demon.

Poor Maupassant, there is the clue to his own catastrophe! He wanted to make love to music. And he realised, with rage, that copulate to music you cannot. So he divided himself against himself, and damned his eyes in disgust, then copulated all the more.

We, however, his grandchildren, are shrewder. Men *must* make love to music, and woman *must* be made love to, to a string and saxophone accompaniment. It is our inner necessity. Because our grandfathers, and especially our great-grandfathers, left the music most severely out of their copulations. So now we leave the copulation most severely out of our musical love-making. We *must* make love to music: it is our grandmothers' dream, become an inward necessity in us, an unconscious motive force. Copulate you cannot, to music. So cut out that part, and solve the problem.

The popular modern dances, far from being "sexual," are distinctly anti-sexual. But there again, we must make a distinction. We should say, the modern jazz and tango and Charleston, far from being an incitement to copulation, are in direct antagonism to copulation. Therefore it is all nonsense for the churches to raise their voice against dancing, against "making love to music." Because the Church, and society at large, has no particular antagonism to sex. It would be ridiculous, for sex is so large and all-embracing, that the religious passion itself is largely sexual. But, as they say, "sublimated." This is the great recipe for sex: only sublimate it! Imagine the quicksilver heated and passing off in weird, slightly poisonous vapour, instead of heavily rolling together and fusing: and there you have the process: sublimation: making love to music! Morality has really no quarrel at all with "sublimated" sex Most "nice" things are "sublimated sex." What morality hates, what the Church hates, what modern *mankind* hates—for what, after all, is "morality" except the instinctive revulsion of the majority?—is just copulation. The modern youth especially just have an instinctive aversion from copulation. They love sex. But they inwardly loathe copulation, even when they play at it. As for playing at it, what else are they to do, given the toys? But they don't like it. They do it in a sort of self-spite. And they turn away, with disgust and relief, from this bedridden act, to make love once more to music.

And really, surely this is all to the good. If the young don't really *like* copulation, then they are safe. As for marriage, they will marry, according to their grandmothers' dream, for quite other reasons. Our grandfathers, or great-grandfathers, married crudely and unmusically, for copulation. That was the actuality—So the dream was all of music. The dream was the mating of two souls, to the faint chiming of the Seraphim—We, the third and fourth generation, we are the dream made flesh. They dreamed of a marriage with all things gross—meaning especially copulation—left out, and only the pure harmony of equality and intimate companionship remaining. And the young live out the dream. They marry: they copulate in a perfunctory and half-disgusted fashion, merely to show they can do it—And so they have children. But the marriage is made to music, the gramophone and the wireless orchestrate each small domestic act, and keep up the jazzing jig of connubial felicity, a felicity of companionship, equality, forbearance, and mutual sharing of everything the married couple have in common. Marriage set to music! The worn-out old serpent in this musical Eden of domesticity is the last, feeble instinct for copulation, which drives the married couple to clash upon the boring organic differences in one another, and prevents from being twin souls in almost identical bodies.—But we are wise, and soon learn to leave the humiliating act out altogether. It is the only wisdom.

We are such stuff as our Grandmothers' dreams were made on, and our little life is rounded by a band.

The thing you wonder, as you watch the modern dancers making love to music in a dance-hall, is what kind of dances will our children's children dance? Our mothers' mothers danced quadrilles and sets of Lancers, and the waltz was almost an indecent thing to them. Our mothers' mothers' mothers danced minuets and Roger de Coverleys, and smart and bouncing country dances which worked up the blood and danced a man nearer and nearer to copulation.

But Lo! even while she was being whirled round in the dance, our great-grandmother was dreaming of soft and throbbing music, and the arms of "one person," and the throbbing and sliding unison of this one, more elevated person, who would never coarsely bounce her towards bed and copulation, but would slide on with her forever, down the dim and sonorous vistas, making love without end to music without end, and leaving out entirely that disastrous, music-less full-stop of copulation, the end of ends.

So she dreamed, our great-grandmother, as she crossed hands and was flung around, and buffeted and busked towards bed, and the bouncing of the *bête à deux dos*. She dreamed of men that were only embodied souls, not tiresome and gross males, lords and masters. She dreamed of "one person" who was all men in one, universal, and beyond narrow individualism.

So that now the great-granddaughter is made love to by all men—to music—as if it were one man. To music, all men, as if it were one man, make love to her, and she sways in the arms, not of an individual, but of the modern species. It is wonderful. And the modern man makes love, to music, to all women, as if she were one woman. All woman, as if she were one woman! It is almost like Baudelaire making love to the vast thighs of Dame Nature herself: except that that dream of our great-grandfather is still too copulative, though all-embracing.

But what is the dream that is simmering at the bottom of the soul of the modern young woman, as she slides to music across the floor, in the arms of the species, or as she waggles opposite the species, in the Charleston? If she is content, there is no dream. But woman is never content. If she were content, the Charleston and the Black Bottom would not oust the tango.

She is not content. She is even less content, in the morning after the night before, than was her great-grandmother, who had been bounced by copulatory attentions. She is even less content, therefore her dream, though not risen yet to consciousness, is even more devouring and more rapidly subversive.

What is her dream, this slender, tender lady just out of her teens, who is varying the two-step with the Black Bottom? What can her dream be? Because what her dream is, that her children, and my children, or children's children, will become. It is the very ovum of the future soul, as my dream is the sperm.

There is not much left for her to dream of, because whatever she wants she can have. All men or no men, this man or that, she has the choice, for she has no lord and master. Sliding down the endless avenues of music, having an endless love endlessly made to her: she has this too. If she wants to be bounced into copulation, at a dead end, she can have that too: just to prove how monkeyish it is, and what a fumbling in the *cul de sac*.

Nothing is denied her, so there is nothing to want. And without desire, even dreams are lame. Lame dreams! Perhaps she has lame dreams, and wishes, last wish of all, she had no dreams at all.

But while life lasts, and is an affair of sleeping and waking, this is the one wish that will never be granted. From dreams no man escapeth, no woman either. Even the little blonde who is preferred by gentlemen has a dream somewhere, if she, and we, and he, did but know it. Even a dream beyond emeralds and dollars.

What is it? What is the lame and smothered dream of the lady?— Whatever it is, she will never know: not till somebody has told it her, and then gradually, and after a great deal of spiteful repudiation, she will recognise it, and it will pass into her womb.

Myself, I do not know what the frail lady's dream may be. But depend upon one thing, it will be something very different from the present business. The dream and the business! — an eternal antipathy. So the dream, whatever it may be, will *not* be "making love to music." It will be something else.

Perhaps it will be the re-capturing of a dream that started in mankind, and never finished, was never fully unfolded. The thought occurred to me suddenly when I was looking at the remains of paintings on the walls of Etruscan tombs at Tarquinia. There the painted women dance, in their transparent linen with heavier, coloured borders, opposite the naked-limbed men, in a splendour and an abandon which is not at all abandoned. There is a great beauty in them, as of life which has not finished. The dance is Greek, if you like, but not finished off like the Greek dancing. The beauty is not so pure, if you will, as the Greek beauty; but also it is more ample, not so narrowed. And there is not the slight element of abstraction, of inhumanity, which underlies all Greek expression, the tragic will.

The Etruscans, at least before the Romans smashed them, do not seem to have been tangled up with tragedy, as the Greeks were from the first. There seems to have been a peculiar-large carelessness about them, very human and non-moral. As far as one can judge, they never said: certain acts are immoral, just because we say so! They seem to have had a strong feeling for taking life sincerely as a pleasant thing. Even death was a gay and lively affair.

Moralists will say: Divine law wiped them out—The answer to that is, divine law wipes everything out in time, even itself. And if the smashing power of the all-trampling Roman is to be identified with divine law, then all I can do is to look up another divinity.

No, I do believe that the unborn dream at the bottom of the soul of the shingled, modern young lady is this Etruscan young woman of mine, dancing with such abandon opposite her naked-limbed, strongly-dancing young man, to the sound of the double flute. They are wild with a dance that is heavy and light at the same time, and not a bit anti-copulative, yet not bouncingly copulative either.

That was another nice thing about the Etruscans: there was a phallic symbol everywhere, so everybody was used to it, and they no doubt all offered it small offerings, as the source of inspiration. Being part of the everyday life, there was no need to get it on the brain, as we tend to do. And apparently the men, the men slaves at least, went gaily and jauntily round with no clothes on at all, and being therefore of a good brown colour, wore their skin for livery. And the Etruscan ladies thought nothing of it. Why should they? We think nothing of a naked cow, and we still refrain from putting our pet dogs into pants or petticoats: marvellous to relate: but then our ideal is Liberty, after all! So if the slave was stark naked, who gaily piped to the lady as she danced, and if her partner was three parts naked, and herself nothing but a transparency, well, nobody thought anything about it, there was nothing to shy off from, and all the fun was in the dance.

There it is, the delightful quality of the Etruscan dance. They are neither making love to music, to avoid copulation, nor are they bouncing towards copulation with a brass band accompaniment. They are just dancing a dance with the elixir of life. And if they have made a little offering to the stone phallus at the door, it is because when one is full of life one is full of possibilities, and the phallus gives life. And if they have made an offering also to the queer ark of the female symbol, at the door of a woman's tomb, it is because the womb too is the source of life, and a great fountain of dance-movements.

It is we who have narrowed the dance down to two movements: either bouncing towards copulation, or sliding and shaking and waggling, to elude it. Surely it is ridiculous to make love to music, and to music to be made love to! Surely the music is to dance to! And surely the modern young woman feels this, somewhere deep inside.

To the music one should dance, and dancing, dance. The Etruscan young woman is going gaily at it, after two-thousand five hundred years. She is not making love to music, nor is the dark-limbed youth, her partner. She is just dancing her very soul into existence, having made an offering on one hand to the lively phallus of man, on the other hand, to the shut womb-symbol of woman, and put herself on real good terms with both of them. So she is quite serene, and dancing herself as a very fountain of motion and of life, the young man opposite her dancing himself the same, in contrast and balance, with just the double flute to whistle round their naked heels.

And I believe this is, or will be, the dream of our pathetic music-stunned young girl of today, and the substance of her children's children, unto the third and fourth generation.

THE "JEUNE FILLE" WANTS TO KNOW

If you are a writer, nothing is more confusing than the difference between the things you have to say and the things you are allowed to print. Talking to an intelligent girl, the famous *"jeune fille"* who is the excuse for the great Hush ! Hush! in print, you find, not that you have to winnow your words and leave out all the essentials, but that she, the innocent girl in question, is flinging all sorts of fierce questions at your head, in all sorts of shameless language, demanding all sorts of impossible answers. You think to yourself: "My heaven, *this* is the innocent young thing on whose behalf books are suppressed!" And you wonder "How on earth am I to answer her?"

You decide the only way to answer her is straight-forward. She smells an evasion in an instant, and despises you for it. She is no fool, this innocent maiden. Far from it. And she loathes an evasion. Talking to her father in the sanctum of his study, you have to winnow your words and watch your step, the old boy is so nervous, so tremulous lest anything be said that should hurt his feelings. But once away in the drawing-room or the garden, the innocent maiden looks at you anxiously, and it is all you can do to prevent her saying crudely, "Please don't be annoyed with daddy. You see, he *is* like that, and we have to put up with him"—or else from blurting out, "Daddy's an old fool, but he *is* a dear, isn't he?"

It is a queer reversal of the Victorian order. Father winces and bridles and trembles in his study or his library, and the innocent maiden knocks you flat with her outspokenness in the conservatory. And you have to admit that she is the man of the two; of the three, maybe. Especially when she says, rather sternly, "I hope you didn't let daddy see what you thought of him!" "But what *do* I think of him?" I gasp. "Oh, it's fairly obvious!" she replies coolly, and dismisses the point.

I admit the young are a little younger than I am; or a little older, which is it? I really haven't spent my years cultivating prunes and prisms, yet, confronted with a young thing of twenty-two, I often find myself with a prune-stone in my mouth, and I don't know what to do with it.

"Why *is* daddy like that?" she says, and there is genuine pain in the question. "Like what?" you ask. "Oh, you know what I mean! Like a baby ostrich with its head in the sand! It only makes his rear so much the more conspicuous. And it's a pity, because he's awfully intelligent in other ways."

Now, what is a man to answer? "*Why* are they like that?" she insists. "Who?" say I. "Men!" she says; "men like daddy!" "I suppose it's a sort of funk," say I. "*Exactly*!" she pounces on me like a panther. "But what is there to be in a funk about?"

I have to confess I don't know. "Of course not!" she says. "There's nothing at all to be in a funk about. So why can't we make him see it?"

When the younger generation, usually the feminine half of it in her early twenties, starts firing off Whys? at me, I give in. Anything crosses her in the least—and she takes aim at it with the deadly little pistol of her inquiring spirit, and says "*Why*?" She is a deadly shot: Billy the Kid is nothing to her; she hits the nail on the head every time. "Now, why can't I talk like a sensible human being to daddy?" "I suppose he thinks it is a little early for you to be quite so sensible," say I mildly. "Cheek! What *cheek* of him to think he can measure out the amount of sense I ought to have!" she cries. "Why does he think it?"

Why indeed? But once you start whying, there's no end to it. A hundred years ago, a few reformers piped up timorously, "Why is man so infinitely superior to woman?" And on the slow years came the whisper "He isn't!" Then the poor padded young of those days roused up. "Why are fathers *always* in the right?" And the end of the century confessed that they weren't. Since then, the innocent maiden has ceased to be anæmic; all maidens were more or less anæmic thirty years ago; and though she is no less innocent, but probably more so, than her stuffy grandmother or mother before her, there isn't a thing she hasn't shot her Why? at, or her Wherefore?—the innocent maiden of to-day. And digging implements are called by their bare, their barest names. "Why should daddy put his foot down upon love? He's been a prize muff at it himself, judging from mother."

It's terrible, if all the sanctifications have to sit there like celluloid Aunt Sallies, while the young take pot shots at them. A real straight Why? aimed by sweet-and-twenty goes clean through them. Nothing but celluloid! and looking so important! Really, *why* . . .?

The answer seems to be, bogey! The elderly to-day seem to be ridden by a bogey, they grovel before the fetish of human wickedness. Every young man is out to "ruin" every young maiden. Bogey! The young maiden knows a thing or two about that. She's not quite the raw egg she's supposed to be, in the first place. And as for most young men, they're only too nice, and it would grieve them bitterly to "ruin" any young maid, even if they knew exactly how to set about it. Of which the young maiden is perfectly aware, and "Why can't daddy see it?" He can, really. But he is so wedded to his bogey, that once the young man's back is turned, the old boy can see in the young boy nothing but a danger, a danger to my daughter!

433

Wickedness in other people is an *idée fixe* of the elderly. "Ah, my boy, you will find that in life every man's hand is against you!" As a matter of fact, my boy finds nothing of the sort. Every man has to struggle for himself, true. But most people are willing to give a bit of help where they can. The world may really be a bogey. But that isn't because individuals are wicked villains. At least ninety-nine per cent. of individuals in this country, and in any other country as far as we have ever seen, are perfectly decent people who have a certain amount of struggle to get along, but who don't want to do anybody any harm, if they can help it.

This seems to be the general experience of the young, and so they can't appreciate the bogey of human wickedness which seems to dominate the minds of the old, in their relation to the succeeding generation. The young ask "What, exactly, is this bogey, this wickedness we are to be shielded from?" And the old only reply, "Of course, there is no danger to *us*. But to you, who are young and inexperienced . . . !"

And the young, naturally, see nothing but pure hypocrisy. They have no desire to be shielded. If the bogey exists, they would like to set eyes on him, to take the measure of this famous "wickedness." But since they never come across it, since they find meanness and emptiness the worst crimes, they decide that the bogey doesn't and never did exist, that he is an invention of the elderly spirit, the last stupid stick with which the old can beat the young and feel self-justified. "Of course, it's perfectly hopeless with mother and daddy, one has to treat them like mental infants," say the young. But the mother sententiously reiterates, "I don't mind, as far as I am concerned. But I have to protect my children."

Protect, that is, some artificial children that only exist in parental imagination, from a bogey that likewise has no existence outside that imagination, and thereby derive a great sense of parental authority, importance and justification.

The danger for the young is that they will question everything out of existence, so that nothing is left. But that is no reason to stop questioning. The old lies must be questioned out of existence, even at a certain loss of things worth having. When everything is questioned out of existence, then the real fun will begin putting the right things back. But nothing is any good till the old lies are got rid of.

LAURA PHILIPPINE

When you find two almonds in one shell, that's a Philippine. So when Philippa Homes had twins she called them Laura Philippine and Philip Joseph. And she went on calling them Laura Philippine and Philip Joseph till it fixed, and they are it to this day, and Laura Philippine is twenty.

She is quite a lovely girl, tall and white-skinned, but except when she's dancing, or driving a car, or riding a horse, she's languid. Having had what is called a good education, she drawls in slang. She has rather wonderful blue eyes, asleep rather than sleepy, with the oddest red-gold lashes coming down over them; close, red-gold lashes. You notice the lashes because most of the daytime she doesn't trouble to raise them.

At about half-past eleven in the morning you suddenly come across her reclining on a lounge in the drawing-room, smoking a cigarette, showing several yards of good leg and turning over a periodical without looking at it.

"Hello, Laura Philippine, just got up?"

" This minute."

"How are you?"

"Same."

And she's nothing more to say. She turns over the periodical without looking at it, lights another cigarette, and time, since it can't help it, passes. At half-past twelve you find her in the hall in an elegant wrap, and a nut of a little blue hat, looking as if she might possibly be drifting out of doors to commit suicide in some half-delicious fashion.

"Where are you going, Laura Philippine?"

"Out."

"Where's that?"

"Oh, meet some of the boys—"

"Well, lunch is half-past one—"

But she is gone, with a completeness that makes it seem impossible she will ever come back. Yet back she comes, about two, when we are peeling our apple. She is the image of freshness, in her bit of a putty-coloured frock, her reddish petals of hair clinging down over her ears, her cheeks pink by nature, till she almost powders them out of spite, her long white limbs almost too languid to move, and her queer fiery eyelashes down over her dark blue eyes.

"I told her not to serve me soup till I came."

"And I told her to serve it when she served us. Lunch is half-past one."

Laura Philippine sits down in front of her soup, which Philippa always has for lunch, out of spite. The parlourmaid comes in again.

"I won't have soup," says Laura Philippine. "What else is there?" And when she is told, she replies: " I won't take that either. I'll just take salad, and• will you find me something to eat with it?"

The parlourmaid looks at Philippa, and Philippa says:

"I suppose you'd better bring the galantine."

So Laura Philippine, with pure indifference, eats galantine and salad, and drinks burgundy, which almost shows ruddy as it goes down her white throat.

"Did you find the boys?" I ask.

"Oh, quite!"

"Did you drink cocktails?"

"Not before lunch. Gin and bitters."

I got no more out of her. But we went out in the afternoon in the car. As we went through Windsor Park, I said:

"It is rather lovely, isn't it?"

"Oh, quite!"

"But you don't look at it."

"What am I to look at it for?"

"Pleasure."

"No pleasure to me."

She looked at nothing—unless it might be at a well-dressed woman. She was interested in nothing: unless it were the boys, just at meal-times.

So she came with Philippa to Rome.

"Doing the sights of Italy with your mother, are you?" said I.

"Mother'll have a swell time taking me to see sights."

Mother did. Laura Philippine just smoked cigarettes and lowered her reddish-gold lashes over her dark blue eyes, and said languidly: Is that so? We drove down to Ostia over the Campagna. Oh, look, Laura Philippine, there are still a few buffaloes! Laura Philippine knocked cigarette ash over the other side of the car in order not to look, and said yes! Look at the old fortifications of Ostia, Laura Philippine!—Yes, I've seen 'em!—We came to the sea, got out of the car and walked on to the shingle shore. Call that the sea? said Laura Philippine. I said I did: the Mediterranean, at least. Is it always that way? Why, it must have something the matter with it!—And Laura Philippine reclined on the shingle, lit another cigarette, and was gone into a special void of her own, leaving the sea to take care of itself. Where shall we have tea, Laura Philippine?—Oh, anywhere!—At the Castle of the Cæsars ?—Suit me all right!—If one had said in the cemetery, she would have answered the same.

She appeared at dinner looking very, very modern.

"Where are you going to-night, Laura Philippine?"

"There's a dance at the Hotel de Russie."

"But you're not going alone."

"Oh, I shan't be alone. I know a whole crowd of 'em."

"But does your mother let you go off like that?"

"My mother! Imagine if she had to come along!" Laura Philippine was animated. Her red-gold lashes lifted, her dark blue eyes flashed.

"Do you Charleston?" she said. It was the day before yesterday, when people still said it. And she started wriggling in the middle of the drawing-room. She was flushed, animated, flashing, a weird sort of Bacchanal on the hills of Rome, wriggling there, and her white teeth showing in an odd little smile.

She was gone for good again. But next day about lunch-time, there she was, lying down, faintly haunted by the last vestiges of life, otherwise quite passed out.— Have a good time?—Yes!—What time did you get home?—About four. Dance all night?—Yes! Isn't it too much for you?—Not a bit. If I could dance all day as well, I might keep going. It's this leaving off that does me in.—And she lapsed out.

One day Philippa said to her: "Show him your poems. Yes, let him see them. He won't think you a fool."

They were really nice poems, like little sighs. They were poems to yellow leaves, then to a grey kitten, then to a certain boy. They were ghostly wisps of verse, somehow touching and wistful. You should care for somebody, Laura Philippine, said I.—Oh, come! Not that old bait! she replied— But you've got to live, said I.—I know it! she said. Why mention it?—But you're only twenty. Think of your future. The only single thing you care about is jazz—Exactly. But what are boys for, 'xcept to jazz with?—Quite! But what about when you're thirty, and forty?—and fifty?—I suppose they'll invent new dances all the, time, she said mildly. I see old birds trotting like old foxes, so why shouldn't I, if I'm ninety?—But you'll wear out, said I.— Not if anybody's a good dancer, and will wind me up, she said.—But are you happy? said I.—Mother's always saying that. Why should anybody on earth want to be happy? I say to mother: *Show* me somebody happy, then! And she shows me some guy, or some bright young thing, and gets mad when I say: See the pretty monkey! I'm not happy, thank God, because I'm not anything. Why should I be?

THAT WOMEN KNOW BEST

When I was a small boy, I remember my father shouting at my mother: I'll make you tremble at the sound of my footstep! To me it seemed a very terrible, but *still* perfectly legitimate thing to say, and though I'm sure I wept, I secretly felt it rather splendid and right. Women and very small children should by nature tremble at the sound of the approaching wrath of the lord and master.

But alas! My mother, even though she was furious, only gave one of her peculiar amused little laughs and replied: Which boots will you wear?

It was done. No use my father storming: Never you mind which boots I shall wear!—Away flew one of the pigeons of illusion that fill the dovecot of a child's fancy Supposing he wore his rubber-heeled shoes! or worse, his house-slippers, which always shuffled! No, it was no good. She wasn't going to tremble. What a pity! The lordly male could no longer make the dependent female tremble at the sound of his footstep. What a pity!

At a very tender age, I realised with regret that *that* particular game was up. A man was not lord and master any more; and why? because he no longer dictated what was right and what was wrong. He left that to the women: and that is the big stick. From my early childhood it puzzled me, between my two parents: Why does my mother care so much for what is right against what is wrong, and why doesn't my father care a bit?—For it was obvious he didn't care. If we broke the teapot or dodged Sunday School or said we'd been to Brinsley when we hadn't, all my father would remark was: Ay, an' what will your mother say!—What indeed! Certainly all there was to be said, so my father was excused from saying anything.

Which perhaps was what he wanted. He put the big stick of right and wrong in my mother's hands, and said: Use it, you know best!—If, after that, he occasionally got a crack on the head himself, he might storm and rave, but he accepted it really. He knew she was right.

Which led me to wonder, as a small child, why God was a man, and not a woman. In heaven, God was the fount of right and wrong, and on earth, woman. Women knew best. Men didn't care. God knows best of all—That was my childish arrangement of the moral scheme.

So naturally one listened to women. They knew best. My elder brothers both loved football and ruffling round. One of them was by way of being a champion footballer. Also he was considered very clever, and learned French and Latin and worked at law, and the young women adored him. All of which was very manly and fine, and I was a little boy.

But nevertheless, he caved in in a minute before my mother—My boy, there's been a young woman asking for you. Tell them not to come to the house, for I won't have it.—But mother, who was she?—I didn't enquire.—And my poor brother left on thorns. As a matter of fact the event had been thus: a very attractive (to me) young woman on the doorstep.—Is Mr Lawrence at home, please?—No, my husband is out.—Er—I meant the young Mr Lawrence.—I have three sons.—Oh—er—-I meant Mr William.—My son William is not at home.—The door is shut firmly, and to me my mother, pink with indignation, says: The brazen huzzy!—To which I reply: But *why,* mother? She was nice. That's why! says my mother, and slams the question shut.

Clearly a question of right and wrong. Rather mysterious, but apparently very important. In fact, the real power lies in the hands of the one who really knows the difference between the two. My mother seemed a dead cert. In fact the knowing one seems to be always a woman. Clergymen pretend to be ministers and administers, but they are in the hands of the women. No, the moral big stick is wielded by gentle woman, and red-faced men like my father, and footballing young champions like my brother knuckle under when she waves her moral sceptre.

So I started early to study the only vivid and lively power which is left on earth, the power of earnest women. Of course there is the power of money, mostly in the hands of men. But that is only materially, and not *vitally* interesting.

It seemed to me that only in women could one find the grand uncanny courage of saying confidently what was right and what was wrong. And with that courage they seized the sceptre of the real power in life.

But did they really know? That was the burning point. Had they a mysterious gift, an inner voice, which infallibly told them? If so, that was the thing to learn from them. That was the secret of power.

Alas, after many years the truth comes out: they don't know. The courage is largely bravado. Even my mother, when she was older, realised that she didn't know. She had stood like a lighthouse for so many years. But when one put it to her: Are you quite sure you're showing the real way of life? she had to admit, she wasn't quite sure. The lighthouse wavered its beams and went out. It wasn't really sure of itself. It didn't absolutely know right from wrong.

Yet how splendid in the woman, that she put up such a superb bravado, while the men sat round on their hams and said: Isn't she wonderful! We'll abide by what she says!

And how sad, that after all, the good earnest woman has been deceiving herself! There is no *absolute* right and wrong. But a decent, working right and wrong there has to be. And woman, who seemed so sure and exalted, didn't hit on the right sort after all. She's been hammering the wrong nail on the head, so the muddle is terrible. Perhaps the things that one can unlearn from women are more effective than the things one can learn. How not to be too sure of right and wrong, for example.

ALL THERE

What you want to do, said Jimmy to Ciss, is to forget yourself —So I can think of you all the time, I suppose, said Cecilia—Well, not necessarily all the time. Now and then would do. But it'd do you a lot of good to forget yourself, persisted Jim.—I agree, snapped Cecilia. But why don't you make me? Why don't you give a girl a bit of a lift? You don't exactly sweep me off my feet, or lift me clean out of myself, I must say!—Dash it all, a fellow might as well try to sweep the Albert Memorial off its feet. Seems to me you're cemented in! cried the exasperated Jim.—In what?— Eh?——What am I cemented in? demanded Cecilia—Oh, how should I know? In your own idea of yourself! cried he, desperately;

Silence! One of those fatal and Egyptian silences that can intervene between the fair sex and the unfair.

I should love to forget myself, if I were allowed, resumed Cecilia.— Who prevents you?—You do!—I wish I knew how.—You throw me back on myself, every time.—Throw you back on yourself! cried the mortified Jim. Why I've never seen you come an inch forward, away from yourself, yet.—I'm always coming forward to you, and you throw me back on myself, she declared—Coming forward to me! he cried, in enraged astonishment. I wish you'd tell me when the movement begins—You wouldn't see it, if I hooted like a bus.—I believe you, he groaned, giving up.

The gulf yawned between them. I, miserable ostrich, hid my head in the sands of the Times. The clock had the impertinence to tick extra-cheerfully.

Don't you think it's a boy's duty to make a girl forget herself? she asked of me, mercilessly.—If there's a good band, said I—Precisely! cried Jim. The minute the saxophone lets on, she's as right as rain.—Of course! she said. Because then I don't have to forget myself, I'm all there.—We looked at her in some astonishment, and Jim, being a cub, did the obvious.—Do you mean to say that the rest of the time you're not all there? he asked, with flat-footed humour—Witty boy!, she said witheringly No, naturally I leave my wits at home, when I go out with you.— Sounds like it! said Jim.

Now look here, said I. Do you mean to say you only feel quite yourself when you're dancing?—Not always then, she retorted.—And never any other time?—Never!—The word fell on top of us with a smack, and left us flat. Oh go on! cried Jimmy. What about the other day at Cromer?—What about it? said she.—Ah! What were the wild waves saying! Cried he knowingly—You may ask me, she replied. They hummed and hawed, but they never got a word out, as far as I'm concerned. —Do you mean to say you weren't happy! cried he, mortified.—I certainly never forgot myself, not for a moment, she replied. He made a gesture of despair.

But which do you mean? said I. Do you mean you were never all there, or that you were too much there? Which?—She became suddenly attentive, and Jimmy looked at her mockingly, with a sort of got-her-on-toast look.—Why? she drawled languidly I suppose when you can't forget yourself, it's because some of you's left out, and you feel it—So you are only painfully aware of yourself when you're not altogether yourself—like a one-legged man trying to rub his missing toes, because they ache? said I. —She pondered a moment.—I suppose that's about the size of it, she admitted.—And nothing of you is left out in jazz? Jimmy demanded. —Not in good jazz—if the boy can dance, she replied.—Well I think you'll grant me that, said Jim. To which she did not reply.

So it takes a jazz band to get you all there? I asked.—Apparently! she replied.—Then why aren't you content to be only half there, till the band toots up?—Oh, I am. It's only friend James gets the wind up about the missing sections— Hang it all! cried James—but I held up my hand like a high-church clergyman, and hushed him off—Then why don't you marry a boy who will prefer you only half there? I demanded of her.—What! marry one of those coat-hangers? You see me! she said, with cool contempt.

Then the point, said I, is that Jimmy leaves some of you out, and so he never sweeps you off your feet. And so you can't forget yourself, because part of you isn't embraced by Jimmy, and that part stands aside and gibbers.—Gibbers is the right word, like a lucky monkey! said Jim spitefully—Better a whole monkey than half a man! said she.—So what's to be done about it? said I. Why not think about it? Which bit of the woman does Jimmy leave out of his manly embrace?—Oh, about nine-tenths of her! said she.—Nine-tenths of her being too conceited for nuts! said Jimmy.

Look here! said I. This is vulgar altercation.—What do you expect, with a whipper-snapper like Jimmy? said she.—My stars! if that two-stepping Trissie says another word—! cried Jim.

Peace! said I. And give the last word to me, for I am the latter-day Aristotle, who has more to say even than a woman. Next time, Oh James, when you have your arms, both of them, around Cecilia—Which will be never! said Cecilia—then, I continued, you must say to yourself: I have here but one-tenth of my dear Ciss, the remaining nine-tenths being mysteriously elsewhere. Yet this one-tenth is a pretty good armful, not to say handful, and will do me very nicely; so forward the light brigade! And you, Cecilia, under the same circumstance, will say to yourself: Alas, so little of me is concerned, that why should I concern myself? Jimmy gets his tenth. Let's see him make the most of it.

THINKING ABOUT ONESELF

After all, we live most of our time alone, and the biggest part of our life is the silent yet busy stream of our private thoughts. We think about ourselves, and about the things that most nearly concern us, during the greater part of the day and night, all our lifelong. A comparatively small period is really spent in work or actual activity, where we say we "don't think." And a certain space is spent in sleep, where we don't know what we think, but where, in some sense, we keep on thinking. But the bulk of the time we think, or we muse or we dully brood about ourselves and the things that most nearly concern us.

Perhaps it is a burden, this consciousness. Perhaps we don't want to think. That is why people devote themselves to hobbies, why men drink and play golf, and women jazz and flirt, and everybody goes to the brainless cinema: all just to "get away from themselves" as they say. *Oh, forget it!* is the grand panacea. "You want to forget yourself," is the cry. The joy of all existence is supposed to be this "forgetting oneself."

Well perhaps it is! and perhaps it isn't. While a boy is getting "gloriously drunk" in the evening, in the process of forgetting himself, he knows perfectly well all the time that he'll remember himself next morning quite painfully. The same with the girls who jazz through the gay night. The same even with the crowd that comes out of the cinema. They've been forgetting themselves. But if you look at them, it doesn't seem to have been doing them much good. They look rather like the cat that has swallowed the stuffed canary, and feels the cotton-wool in its stomach.

You would think, to hear people talk, that the greatest bugbear you can possibly have is yourself. If you can't get away from yourself, if you can't forget yourself, you're doomed. The millstone is round your neck, so you might as well jump in and drown yourself.

It seems curious. Why should I myself be the greatest bugbear to myself? Why should I be so terrified of being in my own company only, as if some skeleton clutched me in its horrid arms, the moment I am lone with myself?

It's all nonsense. It's perfectly natural for every man and every woman to think about himself or herself most of the time. What is there to be afraid of?—And yet people as a mass are afraid. You'd think everybody had a skeleton in the cupboard of their inside. Which of course they have.

I've got a skeleton, and so have you. But what's wrong with him? He's quite a good solid wholesome skeleton. And what should I do without him? No no, I'm quite at home with my good and bony skeleton. So if he wants to have a chat with me, let him.

We all seem to be haunted by some spectre of ourselves, that we daren't face. "By Jove, that's me!"—And we bolt.—"Oh heaven, there's an escaped tiger in Piccadilly! Let's rush up Bond Street!"—"Look out! There's a tiger! Make for Maddox Street!"—"My God, there's a tiger here too! Let's get in the underground."—And underground we go, forgetting that we have to emerge somewhere, and whether it's Holland Park or the Bank, there'll be a tiger.

The only thing to do is: "All right! If there's a tiger, let's have a look at him."—As everybody knows, all you have to do with a tiger is to look him firmly in the eye. So with this alter ego, this spectral me that haunts my thoughts.

"I'm a poor young man and nobody loves me," says the spectre, the tiger. Look him firmly in the eye and reply: "Really! That's curious. In what way are you poor? Are you nothing *but* poor? Do you *want* to be loved? *How* do you want to be loved, and by whom, for example? And why *should* you be loved?"—Answering these questions is really amusing, far greater fun than running away from yourself and listening-in and being inert.

If the tiger is a tigress, she mews wofully: "I'm such a nice person, and nobody appreciates me. I'm so unhappy!"—Then the really sporting girl looks her tigress in the eye and says: "Oh! What makes you so sure you're nice? *Where* are you nice? Are there no other ways of being nice but *your* way? Perhaps people are pining for a different sort of niceness from your sort. Better do something about it."

If it's a young married couple of tigers they wail: "We're so hard up, and there's no prospect."—Then the young he and she, if they've any spunk, fix their two tigers. "Prospect! What do you mean by prospect? Sufficient unto the day is the dinner thereof. What is a prospect? Why should we need one? What sort of a one do we need? What's it all about?"

And answering these questions is fun, fun for a life-time. It's the essential fun of life, answering the tiger back. Thinking, thinking about oneself and the things that really concern one is the greatest fun of all, especially when, now and then, you feel you've really spoken to your skeleton.

INSOUCIANCE

My balcony is on the east side of the hotel, and my neighbours on the right are a Frenchman, white-haired, and his white-haired wife; my neighbours on the left are two little white-haired English ladies. And we are all mortally shy of one another.

When I peep out of my room in the morning and see the matronly French lady in a purple silk wrapper, standing like the captain on the bridge surveying the morning, I pop in again before she can see me. And whenever I emerge during the day, I am aware of the two little white-haired ladies popping back like two white rabbits, so that literally I only see the whisk of their skirt-hems.

This afternoon being hot and thundery, I woke up suddenly and went out on the balcony barefoot. There I sat serenely contemplating the world, and ignoring the two bundles of feet of the two little ladies which protruded from their open doorways, upon the end of the two *chaises longues*. A hot, still afternoon! the lake shining rather glassy away below, the mountains rather sulky, the greenness very green, all a little silent and lurid, and two mowers mowing with scythes, downhill just near: *slush! slush!* sound the scythe-strokes.

The two little ladies become aware of my presence. I become aware of a certain agitation in the two bundles of feet wrapped in two discreet steamer rugs and protruding on the end of two *chaises longues* from the pair of doorways upon the balcony next me. One bundle of feet suddenly disappears; so does the other. Silence

Then lo! with odd sliding suddenness a little white-haired lady in grey silk, with round blue eyes, emerges and looks straight at me, and remarks that it is pleasant now. A little cooler, say I, with false amiability. She quite agrees, and we speak of the men mowing; how plainly one hears the long breaths of the scythes

By now we are *tête-a-tête*. We speak of cherries, strawberries, and the promise of the vine crop. This somehow leads to Italy, and to Signor Mussolini. Before I know where I am, the little white-haired lady has swept me off my balcony, away from the glassy lake, the veiled mountains, the two men mowing, and the cherry trees, away into the troubled ether of international politics.

I am not allowed to sit like a dandelion on my own stem. The little lady in a breath blows me abroad. And I was so pleasantly musing over the two men mowing: the young one, with long legs in bright blue cotton trousers, and with bare black head, swinging so lightly downhill, and the other, in black trousers, rather stout in front, and wearing a new straw hat of the boater variety, coming rather stiffly after, crunching the end of his stroke with a certain violent effort.

I was watching the curiously different motions of the two men, the young thin one in bright blue trousers, the elderly fat one in shabby black trousers that stick out in front, the different amount of effort in their mowing, the lack of grace in the elderly one, his jerky advance, the unpleasant effect of the new "boater" on his head—and I tried to interest the little lady.

But it meant nothing to her. The mowers, the mountains, the cherry trees, the lake, all the things that were *actually* there, she didn't care about. They even seemed to scare her off the balcony. But she held her ground, and instead of herself being scared away, she snatched me up like some ogress, and swept me off into the empty desert spaces of right and wrong, politics, Fascism and the rest.

The worst ogress couldn't have treated me more villainously. I don't care about right and wrong, politics, Fascism, abstract liberty or anything else of the sort. I want to look at the mowers, and wonder why fatness, elderliness and black trousers should inevitably wear a new straw hat of the boater variety, move in stiff jerks, shove the end of the scythe-stroke with a certain violence, and win my hearty disapproval, as contrasted with young long thinness, bright blue cotton trousers, a bare black head, and a pretty lifting movement at the end of the scythe-stroke.

Why do modern people almost invariably ignore the things that are actually present to them? Why, having come out from England to find mountains, lakes, scythe-mowers and cherry trees, does the little blue-eyed lady resolutely close her blue eyes to them all, now she's got them, and gaze away to Signor Mussolini, whom she hasn't got, and to Fascism, which is invisible anyhow? Why isn't she content to be where she is? Why can't she be happy with what she's got? Why must she *care*?

I see now why her round blue eyes are so round, so noticeably round. It is because she "cares." She is haunted by that mysterious bugbear of "caring." For everything on earth that doesn't concern her she "cares." She cares terribly because far-off, invisible, hypothetical Italians wear black shirts, but she doesn't care a rap that one elderly mower whose stroke she can hear, wears black trousers instead of bright blue cotton ones. Now if she would descend from the balcony and climb the grassy slope and say to the fat mower: "*Cher monsieur, pourquoi porte-vous les pantalons noirs?* Why, oh, why do you wear black trousers?" —then I should say: What an on-the-spot little lady!—But since she only torments me with international politics, I can only remark: What a tiresome off-the-spot old woman!

They care! They simply are eaten up with caring. They are so busy caring about Fascism or Leagues of Nations or whether France is right or whether Marriage is threatened, that they never know where they are. They certainly never live on the spot where they are. They inhabit abstract space, the desert void of politics, principles, right and wrong, and so forth. They are doomed to be abstract. Talking to them is like trying to have a human relationship with the letter x in algebra.

There simply is a deadly breach between actual living and this abstract caring. What is actual living? It is a question mostly of direct contact. There was a direct sensuous contact between me, the lake, mountains, cherry trees, mowers, and a certain invisible but noisy chaffinch in a clipped lime tree. All this was cut off by the fatal shears of that abstract word Fascism, and the little old lady next door was the Atropos who cut the thread of my actual life this afternoon. She beheaded me, and flung my head into abstract space. Then we are supposed to love our neighbours!

When it comes to living, we live through our instincts and our intuitions. Instinct makes me run from little over-earnest ladies; instinct makes me sniff the lime blossom and reach for the darkest cherry. But it is intuition which makes me feel the uncanny glassiness of the lake this afternoon, the sulkiness of the mountains, the vividness of near green in thunder-sun, the young man in bright blue trousers lightly tossing the grass from the scythe, the elderly man in a boater stiffly shoving his scythe-strokes, both of them sweating in the silence of the intense light.

MASTER IN HIS OWN HOUSE

We still are ruled too much by ready-made phrases. Take, for example: A man must he master in his own house. There's a good old maxim; we all believe it in theory. Every little boy sees himself a future master in his own house. He grows up with the idea well fixed. So naturally, when his time comes and he finds, as he does pretty often, that he's *not* master in his own house, his nose is conventionally out of joint. He says: These overbearing modern women, they insist on bossing the show, and they're absolutely in the wrong.

What we have to beware of is mass thinking. The idea that a man must be master in his own house is just a mass idea. No man really thinks it for himself. He accepts it *en bloc*, as a member of the mass. He is born, so to speak, tightly swaddled up in it, like a lamb in its wool. In fact, we are born so woolly and swaddled up in mass ideas, that we hardly get a chance to move, to make a real move of our own. We just bleat foolishly out of a mass of woolly cloud, our mass-ideas, and we get no further. A man must be master in his own house. Feed the brute. An Englishman's home is his castle. Two servants are better than one. Happy is the bride who has her own little car in her own little garage. It is the duty of a husband to give his wife what she wants. It is the duty of a wife to say "Yes, darling!" to her husband; all these are mass ideas, often contradicting one another, but always effective. If you want to silence a man, or a woman, effectively, trot out a mass idea. The poor sheep is at once mum. Now the thing to do with a mass idea is to individualise it. Instead of massively asserting: A man must be master in his own house, the gentleman in question should particularise and say: I, Jim, must be master in my own house, The Rosebud, or The Doves' Nest, over my wife, Julia.—And as soon as you make it personal, and drag it to earth, you will feel a qualm about it. You can storm over the breakfast coffee: A man must be master in his own house! But it takes much more courage to say: My name's Jim, and I must be master in this house, The Rosebud, over you, Julia, my spouse!—This is bringing things to an issue. And things are rarely so brought. The lord and master fumes with a mass idea, and the spouse and helpmeet fumes with a mass resentment, and their mingled fumings make a nice mess of The Rosebud.

As a matter of fact, when Jim begins to look into his own heart, and also to look The Rosebud, which is his own house, firmly in the eye, he finds—O shattering discovery!—that he has very little desire to be master in The Rosebud. On the contrary, the idea rather nauseates him. And when he looks at Julia calmly pouring the coffee, he finds, if he's the usual Jim, that his desire to be master over that young dame is curiously non-existent.

And there's the difference between a mass idea and real individual thinking. A man must be master in his own house. But Jim finds the idea of being master in The Rosebud rather feeble, and the idea of being master over the cool Julia somehow doesn't inspire him. He doesn't really care whether The Rosebud has pink bows on the curtains or not. And he doesn't care really what Julia does with her day, while he's away at his job. He wants her to amuse herself and not bother him.—That is, if he's the ordinary Jim.

So that man being master in his own house falls flat when the man is indifferent to his mastery. And that's the worst of mass ideas: they remain, like fossils, when the life that animated them is dead. The problem of a man being master in his own house is to-day no problem, really, because the man is helplessly indifferent about it. He feels mere indifference; only now and then he may spout up the mass idea, and make an unreal fume which does a lot of harm.

We may take it for granted, that wherever woman bosses the show, it is because man doesn't want to. It is not rapacity and pushing on the woman's part. It is indifference on the man's. Men don't really care. Wherever they *do* care, there is no question of the intrusion of women. Men really care still about engineering and mechanical pursuits, so there is very little intrusion of women there. But men are sadly indifferent to clerking pursuits; and journalistic pursuits, and even to parliamentary pursuits. So women flood in to fill the vacuums. If we get a House of Commons filled with women Members, it will be purely and simply for the reason that men, energetic men, are indifferent; they don't care any more about being Members of Parliament and making laws.

Indifference is a strange thing. It lies there under all the mass thinking and the mass activity, like a gap in the foundations. We still make a great fuss about Parliament—and underneath, most men are indifferent to Parliament. All, the fuss about a home of your own and a wife of your own: and underneath, the men are only too often indifferent to the house and the wife both. They are only too willing for the wife to do the bossing and the caring, so that they need neither care nor boss.

Indifference is not the same as insouciance. Insouciance means not caring about things that don't concern you; it also means not being pinched by anxiety. But indifference is inability to care; it is the result of a certain deadness or numbness. And it is nearly always accompanied by the pinch of anxiety. Men who can't care any more, feel anxious about it. They have no insouciance. They are thankful if the woman will care. And at the same time they resent the women's caring and running the show.

The trouble is not in the women's bossiness, but in the men's indifference. This indifference is the real malady of the day. It is a deadness, an inability to care about anything. And it is always pinched by anxiety.

And whence does the indifference arise? It arises from having cared too much, from having cared about the wrong thing, in the immediate past. If there is a growing indifference to politics on the part of men, it is because men have cared far too much about politics. If Jim is really indifferent to his little home, The Rosebud, if he leaves it all to Julia, that is because his father and grandfather cared far too much about their little homes, made them a bit nauseating. If men don't care very vitally about their jobs, nowadays, and leave them to women, it is because our fathers and grandfathers considered the job sacrosanct—which it isn't—and so wore out the natural feeling for it, till it became repulsive.

Men leave the field to women, when men become inwardly indifferent to the field. What the women take over is really an abandoned battle. They don't pick up the tools and weapons of men till men let them drop.

And then men, gnawed by the anxiety of their own very indifference, blame women and start reiterating like parrots such mass ideas as: "Man must be master in his own house."

MATRIARCHY

Whether they are aware of it or not, the men of to-day are a little afraid of the women of to-day; and especially the younger men. They not only see themselves in the minority, overwhelmed by numbers, but they feel themselves swamped by the strange unloosed energy of the silk-legged hordes. Women, women everywhere, and all of them on the warpath! The poor young male keeps up a jaunty front, but his masculine soul quakes. Women, women everywhere, silk-legged hosts that are up and doing, and no gainsaying them. They settle like silky locusts on all the jobs, they occupy the offices and the playing-fields like immensely active ants, they buzz round the coloured lights of pleasure in amazing bare-armed swarms, and the rather dazed young male is, naturally, a bit scared. Tommy may not be scared of his own individual Elsie, but when he sees her with her scores of female "pals," let him bluff as he may, he is frightened.

Being frightened, he begins to announce: Man must be master again!—The *must* is all very well. Tommy may be master of his own little Elsie in the stronghold of his own little home. But when she sets off in the morning to her job, and joins the hosts of her petticoatless, silk-legged "pals," who is going to master her? Not Tommy!

It's not a question of petticoat rule. Petticoats no longer exist. The unsheathed silky legs of the modern female are petticoatless, and the modern young woman is not going to spend her life managing some little husband. She is not interested. And as soon as a problem ceases to contain interest, it ceases to be a problem. So that petticoat rule, which was such a problem for our fathers and grandfathers, is for us nothing. Elsie is not interested.

No, the modern young man is not afraid of being petticoat-ruled. His fear lies deeper. He is afraid of being swamped, turned into a mere accessory of bare-limbed, swooping woman; swamped by her numbers, swamped by her devouring energy. He talks rather bitterly about rule of women, monstrous regiment of women, and about matriarchy, and, rather feebly, about man being master again. He knows perfectly well that he will never be master again. John Knox could live to see the head of his monstrous regiment of women, the head of Mary of Scotland, just chopped off. But you can't chop off the head of the modern woman. As leave try to chop the head off a swarm of locusts. Woman has emerged, and you can't put her back again. And she's not going back of her own accord, not if she knows it.

So we are in for the monstrous rule of women, and a matriarchy. A matriarchy! This seems the last word of horror to the shuddering male. What it means, exactly, is not defined. But it rings with the hollow sound of man's subordination to woman. Woman cracks the whip, and the Spoor trained dog of a man jumps through the hoop. Nightmare!

Matriarchy, according to the dictionary, means mother-rule. The mother the head of the family. The children inherit the mother's name. The property is bequeathed from mother to daughter, with a small allowance for the sons. The wife, no doubt, swears to love and cherish her husband, and the husband swears to honour and obey his spouse.—It doesn't sound so very different from what already is: except that when Tommy Smith marries Elsie Jones, he becomes Mr. Jones; quite right, too, nine cases out of ten.

And this is the matriarchy we are drifting into. No good trying to stem the tide. Woman is in flood.

But in this matter of matriarchy, let us not be abstract. Men and women will always be men and women. There is nothing new under the sun, not even matriarchy. Matriarchies have been and will be. And what about them, in living actuality?—It is said that in the ancient dawn of history there was nothing but matriarchy: children took the mother's name, belonged to the mother's clan, and the man was nameless. There is supposed to be a matriarchy to-day among the Berbers of the Sahara, and in Southern India, and one or two other rather dim places.

Yet, if you look at photographs of Berbers, the men look most jaunty and cocky, with their spears, and the terrible matriarchal women look as if they did most of the work. It seems to have been so in the remote past. Under the matriarchal system that preceded the patriarchal system of Father Abraham, the men seem to have been lively sports, hunting and dancing and fighting, while the women did the drudgery and minded the brats.

Courage! Perhaps a matriarchy isn't so bad, after all. A woman deserves to possess her own children and have them called by her name. As for the household furniture and the bit of money in the bank, it seems naturally hers.

Far from being a thing to dread, matriarchy is a solution to our weary social problem. Take the Pueblo Indians of the Arizona desert. They still have a sort of matriarchy. The man marries into the woman's clan, and passes into *her* family house. His corn supply goes to *her* tribe. His children are the children of *her* tribe, and take *her* name, so to speak. Everything that comes into the house is hers, *her* property. The man has no claim on the house, which belongs to her clan, nor to anything within the house. The Indian woman's home is *her* castle.

So! And what about the man, in this dread matriarchy? Is he the slave of the woman? By no means. Marriage, with him, is a secondary consideration, a minor event. His first duty is not to his wife and children—they belong to the clan. His first duty is to the tribe. The man is first and foremost an active, religious member of the tribe. Secondarily, he is son or husband or father.

The real life of the man is not spent in his own little home, daddy in the bosom of the family, wheeling the perambulator on Sundays. His life is passed mainly in the khiva, the great underground religious meeting-house where only the males assemble, where the sacred practices of the tribe are carried on; then also he is away hunting, or performing the sacred rites on the mountains, or he works in the fields. But he spends only certain months of the year in his wife's house, sleeping there. The rest he spends chiefly in the great khiva, where he sleeps and lives, along with the men, under the tuition of the old men of the tribe.

The Indian is profoundly religious. To him, life itself is religion: whether planting corn or reaping it, scalping an enemy or begetting a child; even washing his long black hair is a religious act. And he believes that only by the whole united effort of the tribe, day in, day out, year in, year out, in sheer religious attention and practice, can the tribe be kept vitally alive. Of course, the religion is pagan, savage, and to our idea unmoral. But religion it is, and it is his charge.

Then the children. When the boys reach the age of twelve or thirteen, they are taken from the mother and given into the charge of the old men. They live now in the khiva, or they are taken to the sacred camps on the mountains, to be initiated into manhood. Now their home is the khiva, the great sacred meeting-house underground. They may go and eat in their mother's house, but they live and sleep with the men.

And this is ancient matriarchy. And this is the instinctive form that society takes, even now. It seems to be a social instinct to send boys away to school at the age of thirteen, to be initiated into manhood. It is a social instinct in a man to leave his wife and children safe in the home, while he goes out and foregathers with other men, to fulfil his deeper social necessities. There is the club and the public-house, poor substitutes for the sacred khiva, no doubt, and yet absolutely necessary to most men. It is in the clubs and public-houses that men have really educated one another, by immediate contact, discussed politics and ideas, and made history. It is in the clubs and public-houses that men have tried to satisfy their deeper social instincts and intuitions. To satisfy his deeper social instincts and intuitions, a man must be able to get away from his family, and from women altogether, and foregather in the communion of men.

Of late years, however, the family has got hold of a man, and begun to destroy him. When a man is clutched by his family, his deeper social instincts and intuitions are all thwarted, he becomes a negative thing. Then the woman, perforce, becomes positive, and breaks loose into the world.

Let us drift back to matriarchy. Let the woman take the children and give them her name—it's a wise child that knows its own father. Let the woman take the property—what has a man to do with inheriting or bequeathing a grandfather's clock! Let the women form themselves into a great clan, for the preservation of themselves and their children. It is nothing but just.

And so, let men get free again, free from the tight littleness of family and family possessions. Give woman her full independence, and with it, the full responsibility of her independence. That is the only way to satisfy women once more: give them their full independence and full self-responsibility as mothers and heads of the family. When the children take the mother's name, the mother will look after the name all right.

And give the men a new foregathering ground, where they can meet and satisfy their deep social needs, profound social cravings which can only be satisfied apart from women. It is absolutely necessary to find some way of satisfying these ultimate social cravings in men, which are deep as religion in a man. It is necessary for the life of society, to keep us organically vital, to save- us from the mess of industrial chaos and industrial revolt.

OWNERSHIP

The question of the possession of property, I read somewhere lately, has now become a religious question. On the other hand, the religious people assert that the possession of property can never be a religious question, because in his religious soul a man is indifferent to property either way. I only care about property, money, possessions of any sort, when I have no religion in me. As soon as real religion enters, out goes my interest in the things of this world.

This, I consider, is hard lines on a man; since I must spend the best part of my day earning my living and acquiring a modicum of possession, I must acknowledge myself a religionless wretch most of my time or else I must be a possessionless beggar and a parasite on industrious men.

There is something wrong with the arrangement. Work is supposed to be sacred, wages are slightly contemptible and mundane, and a savings bank account is distinctly irreligious, as far as pure religion goes. Where are we, quite?

No getting away from it, there is something rather mean about saving money. But still more fatal is the disaster of having no money at all, when you need it.

The trouble about this property business, money, possessions, is that we are most of us exceedingly and excruciatingly bored by it. Our fathers got a great thrill out of making money, building their own houses, providing for their old age and laying by something for their children. Children inherit their father's leavings; they never inherit their father's and mother's thrill; never more than the tail end of it: a point to which parents are consistently blind. If my father was thrilled by saving up, I shall be thrilled by blowing my last shilling. If my father gave all he had to the poor, I shall quite enjoy making things pleasant for my own little self. If my father wasted, I shall probably economise. Unless, of course, my father was a jolly waster.

But fathers for the last fifty years have been saving up, building their own houses, acquiring neat little properties, leaving small inheritances to their children, and preaching the sanctity of work. And they have pretty well worn it all out. The young don't believe in the sanctity of work, they are bored by the thought of saving up for their children. If they do build themselves a little house, they are tired of it in ten minutes. They want a car to run around in, and money to spend; but possessions, as possessions, are simply a bore to them. What's the fun owning things, anyway, unless you can do something with them?

So that the young are approaching the religious indifference to property, out of sheer boredom.

But being bored by property doesn't solve the problem. Because, no matter how bored you may be, you've got to live, and to do so you have to earn a living, and you have to own a certain amount of property. If you have wife and children, the earning and the property are a serious matter. So, many young men to-day drive themselves along in work and business, feeling a distinct inner boredom with it all, and bemoaning a thankless existence.

What's to be done about it? Why, nothing, all in a hurry. The thing to do is to face the situation. A young man to-day says to himself: I'm bored! I'm bored by making money slowly and meagrely, I'm bored at the thought of owning my own little bit. Why haven't I a maiden aunt who'll die and leave me a thousand a year? Why can't I marry a rich wife? Why doesn't somebody set me up for life? Why . . .?

This seems to be peculiarly the attitude of the young Englishman. He truly doesn't want much, it's not riches he's after. All he wants, he says, is independence. By which he means, not real independence at all, but freedom from the bore of having to make a living.

To make a living was to our fathers and grandfathers an adventure; to us it is no more an adventure, it is a bore. And the situation is serious. Because, after all, it is change in feelings which makes changes in the world.

When it says in *The Times*: The question of the possession of property has now become a religious question—it does not mean that the question whether I shall own my little six-roomed house or not has become a religious question. It is a vague hint at national ownership. It is becoming a religious question with us now, whether the nation or whether private individuals shall own the land and the industries. This is what is hinted at.

And perhaps national or private ownership is indeed becoming a religious question. But if so, like the question of a man and his own little house, it is becoming religious not because of our passionate interest in it, but because of our deadly indifference. Religion must be indifferent to the question of ownership, and we are, *au fond*, indifferent. Most men are inwardly utterly bored by the problem of individual ownership or national ownership; and therefore, at this point, they are inwardly utterly religious.

Ownership altogether has lost its point, its vitality. We are bored by ownership, public or private, national or individual. Even though we may hang on like grim death to what we've got, if somebody wants to snatch it—and the instinct

449

is perfectly normal and healthy—still, for all that, we are inwardly bored by the whole business of ownership. And the sooner we realise it, the better. It saves us from the bogey of Bolshevism.

If we could come to a fair unanimity on this point—the point that ownership is boring, making money is boring, earning a living is a bore—then we could wriggle out of a lot of the boredom. Take the land, for example. Nobody really wants it, when it comes to the point. Neither does anybody really want the coal mines. Even the nation doesn't want them. The men of the nation are fed stiff with mines and land and wages.

Why not hand it all over to the women? To the women of Britain! The modern excessive need of money is a female need. Why not hand over to the women the means of making the money which they, the women, mostly need? Men must admit themselves flummoxed. If we handed over to the women the means of making money, perhaps there might be a big drop in the feminine need of money. Which, after all, is the straight road to salvation.

AUTOBIOGRAPHY

David Herbert Lawrence—born 11 Sept. 1885 in Eastwood, Nottingham, a small mining town in the Midlands—father a coal-miner, scarcely able to read or write— Mother from the bourgeoisie, the cultural element in the house (read *Sons and Lovers,* the first part is all autobiography).__Fourth of five children—two brothers oldest—then a sister, then D. H.—then another sister—always delicate health but strong constitution—went to elementary school and was just like anybody else of the miners' children—at age of twelve won a scholarship for Nottingham High School, considered best day school in England—purely bourgeois school—quite happy there, but the scholarship boys were a class apart—D. H. made a couple of bourgeois friendships, but they were odd fish,—he instinctively recoiled away from the bourgeoisie, regular sort—left school at 16—had a severe illness—made the acquaintance of Miriam and her family; who lived on a farm, and who really roused him to critical and creative consciousness (see Sons and Lovers). Taught in a rough and fierce elementary school of mining boys: salary, first year, £5. — second year £10—third year £15—(from age of 17 to 21)—Next two years in Nottingham University, at first quite happy; then utterly bored.—Again the same feeling of boredom with the middle-classes, and recoil away from them instead of moving towards them and rising in the world. Took B. A. course, but dropped it; used to write bits of poems and patches of *The White Peacock* during lectures. These he wrote for Miriam, the girl on the farm, who was herself becoming a school-teacher. She thought it all wonderful—else, probably; he would never have written—His own family strictly "natural" looked on such performance as writing as "affectation." Therefore wrote in secret at home. Mother came upon a chapter of *White Peacock* — read it quizzically, and was amused. "But my boy; how do you know it was like that? You don't know —"—She thought one ought to *know*—and she hoped her son, who was "clever", might one day be a professor or a clergyman or perhaps even a little Mr Gladstone. That would have been rising in the world—on the ladder. Flights of genius were nonsense—you had to be clever and rise in the world, step by step.—D. H. however recoiled away from the world, hated its ladder, and refused to rise. He had proper bourgeois aunts with "library" and "drawing-room" to their houses—but didn't like that either—preferred the powerful life in a miners kitchen—and still more, the clatter of nailed boots in the little kitchen of Miriam's farm. Miriam was even poorer then he—but she loved poetry and consciousness and flights of fancy above all. So he wrote for her—still without any idea of becoming a literary man at all—looked on himself as just a school-teacher—and mostly hated school-teaching. Wrote *The White Peacock* in bits and snatches, between age of 19 and 24. Most of it written six or seven times.

At the age of twenty-three, left Nottingham college and went for the first time to London, to be a teacher in a boys school in Croydon, £90. a year. Already the intense physical dissatisfaction with Miriam. Miriam read all his writings—she alone. His mother, whom he loved best on earth, he never spoke to, about his writing. It would have been a kind of "showing-off", or affectation.—It was Miriam who sent his poems to Ford Madox Hueffer, who had just taken over *The English Review*. This was when D. H. was 24. Hueffer accepted, wrote to Lawrence, and was most kind and most friendly—Got Heinemann to accept the MS., a ragged and bulky mass, of *The White Peacock*—invited the school-teacher to lunch—introduced him to Edward Garnett—and Garnett became a generous and genuine friend. Hueffer and Garnett launched D. H. into the literary world. Garnett got Duckworth to accept the first book of poems: *Love Poems and Others.* When Lawrence was 25, *The White Peacock* appeared. But before the day of publication, his mother died—she just looked once at the advance copy, held it in her hand—

The death of his mother wiped out everything else—books published, or stories in magazines. It was the great crash, and the end of his youth. He went back to Croydon to the hated teaching—the £50 for the *White Peacock* paid the doctor etc for his mother.

Then a weary and bitter year—broke with Miriam—and again fell dangerously ill with pneumonia. Got slowly better. Was making a little money with stories, Austin Harrison who had taken over the *English Review,* being a staunch supporter, and Garnett and Hueffer staunch backers. In May, 1912, went away suddenly with his present wife, of German birth, daughter of Baron Friedrich von Richthofen. They went to Metz, then Bavaria, then Italy—and the new phase had begun. He was 26—his youth was over—there came a great gap between him and it.

Was in Italy and Germany the greater part of the time between 1912 and 1914. In England during the period of the war—pretty well isolated. In 1915 *The Rainbow* was suppressed for immorality—and the sense of detachment from the bourgeois world, the world which controls press, publication and all, became almost complete. He had no interest in it, no desire to be at one with it. Anyhow the suppression of *The Rainbow* had proved it impossible. Henceforth he put away any idea of "success," of succeeding with the British bourgeois public, and stayed apart.

Left England in 1919, for Italy—had a house for two years in Taormina, Sicily. In 1920 was published in America *Women in Love*— which every publisher for four years had refused to accept, because of *The Rainbow* scandal. In Taormina wrote *The Lost Girl, Sea and Sardinia,* and most of *Aaron's Rod.* In 1922 sailed from Naples to Ceylon, and lived in Kandy for a while—then on to Australia for a time—in each case taking a house and settling down. Then sailed from Sydney to San Francisco, and went to Taos, in New Mexico, where he settled down again with his wife, near the Pueblo of the Indians. Next year he acquired a small ranch high up on the Rocky Mountains, looking west to Arizona. Here, and in Old Mexico, where he travelled and lived for about a year, he stayed till 1926, writing *St. Mawr* in New Mexico, and the final version of *The Plumed Serpent* down in Oaxaca in Old Mexico,

Came to England 1926—but cannot stand the climate. For the last two years has lived in a villa near Florence, where *Lady Chatterley's Lover* was written.

WOMEN ARE SO COCKSURE

My destiny has been cast among cocksure women. Perhaps when man begins to doubt himself, woman, who should be nice and peacefully hen-sure, becomes instead insistently cocksure. She develops convictions, or she catches them. And then woe-betide everybody.

It began with my mother. She was convinced about some things: one of them being that a man ought not to drink beer. This conviction developed from the fact, naturally; that my father drank beer. He sometimes drank too much. He sometimes boozed away the money necessary for the young family. Therefore the drinking of beer became to my mother the cardinal sin. No other sin was so red, so red-hot. She was like a bull before this red sin. When my father came in tipsy, she saw scarlet.

We dear children were trained never, *never* to fall into this sin. We were sent to the Band of Hope, and told harrowing stories of drunkenness; we wept bitterly over the heroic youth who had taken the pledge and sworn never never to touch nor to taste, and who clenched his teeth when his cruel comrades tried to force beer down his throat: but alas, he had lost one of his front teeth, and through this narrow gap beer trickled even down his gullet. So he died of a broken heart.

My mother, though a woman with a real sense of humour, kept her face straight and stern while we recounted this fearsome episode. And we were rigidly sent to the Band of Hope.

Years passed. Children became young men. It was evident my mother's sons were not going to hell down the beer-mug: they didn't care enough about it. My mother relaxed. She would even watch with pleasure while I drank a glass of ale, the fearful enemy, at supper. There was no longer a serpent in the glass, dash it down, dash it down.

"But mother, if you don't mind if I drink a little beer, why did you mind so much about my father?"

"You don't realise what I had to put up with."

"Yes I do. But you made it seem a sin, a horror. You terrified our lives with the bogey of strong drink. You were absolutely sure it was utter evil. —Why isn't it utter evil any more?"

"You're different from your father—"

But she was just a little shame-faced. Life changes our feelings. We may get mellower, or we may get harsher, as time goes on. But we change. What outrages our feelings in the twenties will probably not outrage them in the fifties, not at all. And the change is much more striking in women than in men. Particularly in those women who are the moral force in the household, as my mother was.

My mother spoilt her life with her moral frenzy against John Barleycorn. To be sure she had occasion to detest the alcoholic stuff. But why the moral frenzy? It made a tragedy out of what was only a nuisance. And at fifty, when the best part of life was gone, she realised it. And then what would she not have given to have her life again, her young children, her tipsy husband, and a proper natural insouciance, to get the best out of it all. When woman tries to be too much mistress of fate, particularly of other people's fates, what a tragedy!

As sure as a woman has the whip-hand over her destiny and the destinies of those near her, so sure will she make a mess of her own destiny, and a muddle of the others'. And just as inevitably as the age of fifty will come upon her, so inevitably will come the realisation that she has got herself into a hole. *She ought not to have been so cocksure.*

Beware, oh modern woman, the age of fifty. It is then that the play is over, the theatre shuts, and you are turned out into the night. If you have been making a grand show of your life, all off your own bat, and being grand mistress of your destiny, all triumphant, the clock of years tolls fifty; and the play is over. You've had your turn on the stage. Now you must go, out into the common night, where you may or may not have a true place of shelter.

It is dangerous for any body to be cocksure. But it is peculiarly dangerous, for a woman. Being basically a creature of emotion, she will direct all her emotion force full on to what seems to her the grand aim of existence. For twenty, thirty years she may rush ahead to the grand goal of existence. And then—the age of fifty approaches—the speed slackens—the driving-force begins to fail—the grand goal is not only no nearer, it is all too near. It is all round about. It is a waste of unspeakable dreariness.

There were three sisters. One started out to be learned and to give herself to social reform. She was absolutely cocksure about being able to bring the world nearer salvation. The second obstinately decided to live her own life and to be herself "The aim of my life is to be myself." She was cocksure about what her self was and how to be it. The aim of the third was to gather roses, whilst she might. She had real good times with her lovers, with her dress-makers, with her husband and her children. All three had everything life could offer.

The age of fifty draws near. All three are in the state of vital bankruptcy of the modern woman of that age. The one is quite cynical about reform, the other begins to realise that the "self" she was so cocksure about doesn't exist, and she wonders what does exist. To the third the world is a dangerous and dirty place, and she doesn't know where to put herself

Of all things, the most fatal to a woman is to have an aim, and be cocksure about it.

DULL LONDON

It begins the moment you set foot ashore, the moment you step off the boat's gangway. The heart suddenly, yet vaguely, sinks. It is no lurch of fear. Quite the contrary. It is as if the life-urge failed, and the heart dimly sank. You trail past the benevolent policeman and the inoffensive passport officials, through the fussy and somehow foolish customs—we don't *really* think it matters if somebody smuggles in two pairs of false-silk stockings—and we get into the poky but inoffensive train, with poky but utterly inoffensive people, and we have a cup of inoffensive tea from a nice inoffensive boy, and we run through small, poky but nice and inoffensive country, till we are landed in the big but unexciting station of Victoria, when an inoffensive porter puts us into an inoffensive taxi and we are driven through the crowded yet strangely dull streets of London to the cosy yet strangely poky and dull place where we are going to stay. And the first half-hour in London, after some years abroad, is really a plunge of misery. The strange, the grey and uncanny, almost deathly sense of *dulness* is overwhelming. Of course, you get over it after a while, and admit that you exaggerated. You get into the rhythm of London again, and you tell yourself that it is *not* dull. And yet you are haunted, all the time, sleeping or waking, with the uncanny feeling: It is dull! It is all dull! This life here is one vast complex of dulness! I am dull! I am being dulled My spirit is being dulled! My life is dulling down to London dulness.

This is the nightmare that haunts you the first few weeks of London. No doubt if you stay longer you get over it, and find London as thrilling as Paris or Rome or New York. But the climate is against me. I cannot stay long enough. With pinched and wondering gaze, the morning of departure, I look out of the taxi upon the strange dulness of London's arousing; a sort of death; and hope and life only return when I get my seat in the boat-train, and I hear all the Good-byes! Good-bye! Good-bye! Thank God to say Good-bye!

Now to feel like this about one's native land is terrible. I am sure I am an exceptional, or at least an exaggerated case. Yet it seems to me most of my fellow-countrymen have the pinched, slightly pathetic look in their faces, the vague, wondering realisation: It is dull! It is always essentially dull My life is dull!

Of course, England is the easiest country in the world, easy, easy and nice. Everybody is nice, and everybody is easy. The English people on the whole are surely the *nicest* people in the world, and everybody makes everything so easy for everybody else, that there is almost nothing to resist at all. But this very easiness and this very niceness become at last a nightmare. It is as if the whole air were impregnated with chloroform or some other pervasive anæsthetic, that makes everything easy and nice, and takes the edge off everything, whether nice or nasty. As you inhale the drug of easiness and niceness, your vitality begins to sink. Perhaps not your physical vitality, but something else: the vivid flame of your individual life. England can afford to be so free and individual because no individual flame of life is sharp and vivid. It is just mildly warm and safe. You couldn't burn your fingers at it. Nice, safe, easy: the whole ideal. And yet under all the easiness is a gnawing uneasiness, as in a drug-taker.

It used not to be so. Twenty years ago London was to me thrilling, thrilling, thrilling; the vast and roaring heart of all adventure. It was not only the heart of the world, it was the heart of the world's living adventure. How wonderful the Strand, the Bank, Charing Cross at night, Hyde Park in the morning!

True, I am now twenty years older. Yet I have not lost my sense of adventure. But now all the adventure seems to. me crushed out of London. The traffic is too heavy! It used to be going somewhere, on an adventure. Now it only rolls massively and overwhelmingly, going nowhere, only dully and enormously *going*. There is no adventure at the end of the 'buses' journey. The 'bus lapses into an inertia of dulness, then dully starts again. The traffic of London used to roar with the mystery of man's adventure on the seas of life, like a vast seashell, murmuring a thrilling, half-comprehensible story. Now it booms like monotonous, far-off guns, in a monotony of crushing something, crushing the earth, crushing out life, crushing everything dead.

And what does one do, in London? I, not having a job to attend to, lounge round and gaze in bleak wonder on the ceaseless dulness. Or I have luncheons and dinners with friends, and talk. Now my deepest private dread of London is my dread of this talk. I spend most of my days abroad, saying little, or with a bit of chatter and a silence again. But in London I feel like a spider whose thread has been caught by somebody, and is being drawn out of him, so he must spin, spin, spin, and all to no purpose. He is not even spinning his own web, for his own reasons.

So it is in London, at luncheon, dinner or tea. I don't want to talk. I don't mean to talk. Yet the talk is drawn out of me, endlessly. And the others talk, endlessly also. It is ceaseless, it is intoxicating, it is the only real occupation of us who do not jazz. And it is purely futile. It is quite as bad as ever the Russians were: talk for talk's sake, without the very faintest intention of a result in action. Utter inaction and storms of talk. That again is London to me. And the sense of abject futility in it all only deepens the sense of abject dulness, so all there is to do is to go away.

COCKSURE WOMEN AND HEN-SURE MEN

It seems to me there are two aspects to women. There is the demure and the dauntless. Men have loved to dwell, in fiction at least, on the demure maiden whose inevitable reply is: Oh, yes, if you please, kind sir! The demure maiden, the demure spouse, the demure mother—this is still the ideal. A few maidens, mistresses and mothers *are* demure. A few pretend to be. But the vast majority are not. And they don't pretend to be. We don't expect a girl skilfully driving her car to be demure, we expect her to be dauntless. What good would demure and maidenly Members of Parliament be, inevitably responding: Oh, yes, if you please, kind sir!—Though of course there are masculine members of that kidney.—And a demure telephone girl? Or even a demure stenographer? Demureness, to be sure, is outwardly becoming, it is an outward mark of femininity, like bobbed hair. But it goes with inward dauntlessness. The girl who has got to make her way in life has got to be dauntless, and if she has a pretty, demure manner with it, then lucky girl. She kills two birds with two stones.

With the two kinds of femininity go two kinds of confidence: there are the women who are cocksure, and the women who are hensure. A really up-to-date woman is a cocksure woman. She doesn't have a doubt nor a qualm. She is the modern type. Whereas the old-fashioned demure woman was sure as a hen is sure, that is, without knowing anything about it. She went quietly and busily clucking around, laying the eggs .and mothering the chickens in a kind of anxious dream that still was full of sureness. But not mental sureness. Her sureness was a physical condition, very soothing, but a condition out of which she could easily be startled or frightened.

It is quite amusing to see the two kinds of sureness in chickens. The cockerel is, naturally, cocksure. He crows because he is *certain* it is day. Then the hen peeps out from under her wing. He marches to the door of the hen-house and pokes out his head assertively: *Ah ha! daylight, of course, just as I said!*—and he majestically steps down the chicken ladder towards *terra firma*, knowing that the hens will step cautiously after him, drawn by his confidence. So after him, cautiously, step the hens. He crows again: *Ha-ha! here we are!*—It is indisputable, and the hens accept it entirely. He marches towards the house. From the house a person ought to appear, scattering corn. Why does the person not appear? The cock will see to it. He is cocksure. He gives a loud crow in the doorway, and the person appears. The hens are suitably impressed, but immediately devote all their henny consciousness to the scattered corn, pecking absorbedly, while the cock runs and fusses, cocksure that he is responsible for it all.

So the day goes on. The cock finds a tit-bit, and loudly calls the hens. They scuffle up in henny surety, and gobble the tit-bit. But when they find a juicy morsel for themselves, they devour it in silence, hensure. Unless, of course, there are little chicks, when they most anxiously call the brood. But in her own dim surety, the hen is really much surer than the cock, in a different way. She marches off to lay her egg, she secures obstinately the nest she wants, she lays her egg at last, then steps forth again with prancing confidence, and gives that most assured of all sounds, the hensure cackle of a bird who has laid her egg. The cock, who is never so sure about anything as the hen is about the egg she has laid, immediately starts to cackle like the female of his species. He is pining to be hensure, for hensure is so much surer than cocksure.

Nevertheless, cocksure is boss. When the chicken-hawk appears in the sky, loud are the cockerel's calls of alarm. Then the hens scuffle under the veranda, the cock ruffles his feathers on guard. The hens are numb with fear, they say: Alas, there is no health in us! How wonderful to be a cock so bold!—And they huddle, numbed. But their very numbness is hensurety.

Just as the cock can cackle, however, as if he had laid the egg, so can the hen bird crow. She can more or less assume his cocksureness. And yet she is never so easy, cocksure, as she used to be when she was hensure. Cocksure, she is cocksure, but uneasy. Hensure, she trembles, but is easy.

It seems to me just the same in the vast human farmyard. Only nowadays all the cocks are cackling and pretending to lay eggs, and all the hens are crowing and pretending to call the sun out of bed. If women to-day are cocksure, men are hensure. Men are timid, tremulous, rather soft and submissive, easy in their very henlike tremulousness. They only want to be spoken to gently. So the women step forth with a good loud *cock-a-doodle-do!*

The tragedy about cocksure women is that they are more cocky, in their assurance, than the cock himself. They never realise that when the cock gives his loud crow in the morning, he listens acutely afterwards, to hear if some other wretch of a cock dare crow defiance, challenge. To the cock, there is always defiance, challenge, danger and death on the clear air; or the possibility thereof.

But alas, when the hen crows, she listens for no defiance or challenge. When she says *cock-a-doodle-do!* then it is unanswerable. The cock listens for an answer, alert. But the hen knows she is unanswerable. *Cock-a-doodle-do!* and there it is, take it or leave it!

And it is this that makes the cocksureness of women so dangerous, so devastating. It is really out of scheme, it is not in relation to the rest of things. So we have the tragedy of cocksure women. They find, so often, that instead of having laid an egg, they have laid a vote, or an empty ink-bottle, or some other absolutely unhatchable object, which means nothing to them.

It is the tragedy of the modern woman. She becomes cocksure, she puts all her passion and energy and years of her life into some effort or assertion, without ever listening for the denial which she ought to take into count. She is cocksure, but she is a hen all the time. Frightened of her own henny self she rushes to mad lengths about votes, or welfare, or sports, or business: she is marvellous, out-manning the man. But alas, it is all fundamentally disconnected. It is all an attitude, and one day the attitude will become a weird cramp, a pain, and then it will collapse. And when it has collapsed, and she looks at the eggs she has laid, votes, or miles of typewriting, years of business efficiency—suddenly, because she is a hen and not a cock, all she has done will turn into pure nothingness to her. Suddenly it all falls out of relation to her basic henny self and she realises she has lost her life. The lovely henny surety, the hensureness which is the real bliss of every female, has been denied her: she had never had it. Having lived her life with such utmost strenuousness and cocksureness, she has missed her life altogether. Nothingness!

HYMNS IN A MAN'S LIFE

Nothing is more difficult than to determine what a child takes in, and does not take in, of its environment and its teaching. This fact is brought home to me by the hymns which I learned as a child, and never forgot. They mean to me almost more than the finest poetry, and they have for me a more permanent value, somehow or other.

It is almost shameful to confess that the poems which have meant most to me, like Wordsworth's "Ode to Immortality" and Keats' Odes, and pieces of "Macbeth" or "As You Like It" or "Midsummer Night's Dream," and Goethe's lyrics, such as "Über allen Gipfeln ist Ruh," and Verlaine's "Ayant poussé la porte qui chancelle"—all these lovely poems which after all give the ultimate shape to one's life ; all these lovely poems woven deep into a man's consciousness, are still not woven so deep in me as the rather banal Nonconformist hymns that penetrated through and through my childhood.

"Each gentle dove
And sighing bough
That makes the eve
So fair to me
Has something far
Diviner now
To draw me back
To Galilee.
O Galilee, sweet Galilee,
Where Jesus loved so much to be,
O Galilee, sweet Galilee,
Come sing thy songs again to me!"

457

To me the word Galilee has a wonderful sound. The Lake of Galilee! I don't want to know where it is. I never want to go to Palestine. Galilee is one of those lovely, glamorous worlds, not places, that exist in the golden haze of a child's half-formed imagination. And in my man's imagination it is just the same. It has been left untouched. With regard to the hymns which had such a profound influence on my childish consciousness, there has been no crystallising out, no dwindling into actuality, no hardening into the commonplace. They are the same to my man's experience as they were to me nearly forty years ago.

The moon, perhaps, has shrunken a little. One has been forced to learn about orbits, eclipses, relative distances, dead worlds, craters of the moon, and so on. The crescent at evening still startles the soul with its delicate flashing. But the mind works automatically and says: "Ah, she is in her first quarter. She is all there, in spite of the fact that we see only this slim blade. The earth's shadow is over her." And, Willy-nilly, the intrusion of the mental processes dims the brilliance, the magic of the first apperception.

It is the same with all things. The sheer delight of a child's apperception is based on *wonder*; and deny it as we may, knowledge and wonder counteract one another. So that as knowledge increases wonder decreases. We say again: Familiarity breeds contempt. So that as we grow older, and become more familiar with phenomena, we become more contemptuous of them. But that is only partly true. It has taken some races of men thousands of years to become contemptuous of the moon, and to the Hindu the cow is still wondrous. It is not familiarity that breeds contempt: it is the assumption of knowledge. Anybody who looks at the moon and says, "I know all about that poor orb," is, of course, bored by the moon.

Now the great and fatal fruit of our civilisation, which is a civilisation based on knowledge, and hostile to experience, is boredom. All our wonderful education and learning is producing a grand sum-total of boredom. Modern people are inwardly thoroughly bored. Do as they may, they are bored.

They are bored because they experience nothing. And they experience nothing because the wonder has gone out of them. And when the wonder has gone out of a man he is dead. He is henceforth only an insect.

When all comes to all, the most precious element in life is wonder. Love is a great emotion, and power is power. But both love and power are based on wonder. Love without wonder is a sensational affair, and power without wonder is mere force and compulsion. The one universal element in consciousness which is fundamental to life is the element of wonder. You cannot help feeling it in a bean as it starts to grow and pulls itself out of its jacket. You cannot help feeling it in the glisten of the nucleus of the amoeba. You recognise it, willy-nilly, in an ant busily tugging at a straw; in a rook, as it walks the frosty grass.

They all have their own obstinate will. But also they all live with a sense of wonder. Plant consciousness, insect consciousness, fish consciousness, animal consciousness, all are related by one permanent element, which we may call the religious element inherent in all life, even in a flea: the sense of wonder. That is our sixth sense. And it is the *natural* religious sense.

Somebody says that mystery is nothing, because mystery is something you don't know, and what you don't know is nothing to you. But there is more than one way of knowing.

Even the real scientist works in the sense of wonder. The pity is, when he comes out of his laboratory he puts aside his wonder along with his apparatus, and tries to make it all perfectly didactic. Science in its true condition of wonder is as religious as any religion. But didactic science is as dead and boring as dogmatic religion. Both are wonderless and productive of boredom, endless boredom.

Now we come back to the hymns. They live and glisten in the depths of the man's consciousness in undimmed wonder, because they have not been subjected to any criticism or analysis. By the time I was sixteen I had criticised and got over the Christian dogma.

It was quite easy for me; my immediate forebears had already done it for me. Salvation, heaven, Virgin birth, miracles, even the Christian dogmas of right and wrong—one soon got them adjusted. I never could really worry about them. Heaven is one of the instinctive dreams. Right and wrong is something you can't dogmatise about; it's not so easy. As for my soul, I simply don't and never did understand how I could "save" it. One can save one's pennies. But how can one save one's soul? One can only *live* one's soul. The business is to live, really alive. And this needs wonder.

So that the miracle of the loaves and fishes is just as good to me now as when I was a child. I don't care whether it is historically a fact or not. What does it matter? It is part of the genuine wonder. The same with all the religious teaching I had as a child, *apart* from the didacticism and sentimentalism. I am eternally grateful for the wonder with which it filled my childhood.

"Sun of my soul, thou Saviour dear,
It is not night if Thou be near—"

That was the last hymn at the board school. It did not mean to me any Christian dogma or any salvation. Just the words, "Sun of my soul, thou Saviour dear," penetrated me with wonder and the mystery of twilight. At another time the last hymn was:

"Fair waved the golden corn
In Canaan's pleasant land—"

And again I loved "Canaan's pleasant land." The wonder of "Canaan," which could never be localised.

I think it was good to be brought up a Protestant: and among Protestants, a Nonconformist, and among Nonconformists, a Congregationalist. Which sounds pharisaic. But I should have missed bitterly a direct knowledge of the Bible, and a direct relation to Galilee and Canaan, Moab and Kedron, those places that never existed on earth. And in the Church of England one would hardly have escaped those snobbish hierarchies of class, which spoil so much for a child. And the Primitive Methodists, when I was a boy, were always having "revivals" and being "saved," and I always had a horror of being saved. So, altogether, I am grateful to my "Congregational" upbringing. The Congregationalists are the oldest Nonconformists, descendants of the Oliver Cromwell Independents. They still had the Puritan tradition of no ritual. But they avoided the personal emotionalism which one found among the Methodists when I was a boy.

I liked our chapel, which was tall and full of light, and yet still; and colour-washed pale green and blue, with a bit of lotus pattern. And over the organ-loft, "O worship the Lord in the beauty of holiness," in big letters.

That was a favourite hymn, too:

"O worship the Lord, in the beauty of holiness,
    Bow down before Him, His glory proclaim;
With gold of obedience and incense of lowliness
    Kneel and adore Him, the Lord is His name."

I don't know what the "beauty of holiness" is, exactly. It easily becomes cant, or nonsense. But if you don't think about it—and why should you?— it has a magic. The same with the whole verse. It is rather bad, really, "gold of obedience" and "incense of lowliness." But in me, to the music, it still produces a sense of splendour.

I am always glad we had the Bristol hymn-book, not Moody and Sankey. And I am glad our Scotch minister on the whole avoided sentimental messes such as "Lead, Kindly Light," or even "Abide With Me." He had a healthy preference for healthy hymns.

"At even, ere the sun was set,
    The sick, O Lord, around Thee lay.
Oh, in. what divers pains they met!
    Oh, in what joy they went away!"

And often we had "Fight the good fight with all thy might."

In Sunday School I am eternally grateful to old Mr. Remington, with his round white beard and his ferocity. He made us sing! And he loved the martial hymns:

"Sound the battle-cry,
See, the foe is nigh.
Raise the standard high
For the Lord."

The ghastly sentimentalism that came like a leprosy over religion had not yet got hold of our colliery village. I remember when I was in Class II in the Sunday School, when I was about seven, a woman teacher trying to harrow us about the Crucifixion. And she kept saying: "And aren't you sorry for Jesus? 'Aren't you sorry?" And most of the children wept. I believe I shed a crocodile tear or two, but very vivid is my memory of' saying to myself: "I don't *really* care a bit." And I could never go back on it. I never *cared* about the Crucifixion, one way or another. Yet the *wonder* of it penetrated very deep in me.

Thirty-six years ago men, even Sunday School teachers, still believed in the fight for life and the fun of it. "Hold the fort, for I am coming." It was far, far from any militarism or gun-fighting. But it was the battle-cry of a stout soul, and a fine thing too.

"Stand up, stand up for Jesus,
Ye soldiers of the Lord."

Here is the clue to the ordinary Englishman—in the Nonconformist hymns.

RED TROUSERS

A man wrote to me, in answer to my article in which I complained of London dulness: "Dear Sir,— Have you ever paused to consider that the cause of our dulness is the cigarette? This is the tubular white ant which is sapping our civilisation."

Now this man, at least, is not entirely dull. He is out on a crusade, a crusade against the "tubular white ant," from which he wants to rescue our holy civilisation. And whatever else a crusader may be, he is not, to himself at least, dull. He is inspired with a mission, and on the march, which, perhaps, is better than sitting still and being inert.

But, after all, a crusade may turn out ultimately dull, like the crusade of Votes for Women, or tee-totalism, or even the Salvation Army. When you've got the vote, it is dull. When people are merely teetotal, it is merely dull. When the Salvation Army has saved you, you may really feel duller than when you weren't saved. Or, of course, you may not.

So that there are two sides to a crusade. The good side is the activity. There was a thrill in the Votes for Women processions, even in the sight of suffragettes being marched off by stout and semiindignant policemen. When I hear the tambourine clashing, and see the poke bonnets of the Salvation Army lasses and the funny scarlet of the men, and hear the piercing music of "Marching to Zion" or "Throw Out the Lifeline," then I am invariably thrilled. Here is a crusade, of a sort, here is spunk! And even in the denunciative "tubular white ants" of my correspondent there is a certain pep, a certain "go."

But the bad side of these crusades is the disillusion when the mission is fulfilled. Take the cigarette and dulness. Which causes which? Does dulness cause the cigarette, or the cigarette the dulness? Apparently it is a vicious circle: each causes the other. But at the very beginning, dulness causes the cigarette, after which the cigarette may cause more dulness, or may not, as the case may be. Anyhow, that, is not my crusade, because it isn't really interesting.

What is really the point is that a crusade is a sovereign remedy against dulness, but you'd better watch out that the end of the crusade isn't a greater dulness still. Nothing is such fun as a crusade, it is the adventure of adventures. But it is no good setting out grandly to rescue some Zion from the clutch of the infidel, if you're not going to care a button about the Zion when you've rescued it.

That's the trouble with most of our modern crusades, like Votes or Socialism or politics, freedom of little nations, and the rest. In the flush of youth, I believed in Socialism, because I thought it would be thrilling and delightful. Now I no longer believe very deeply in Socialism, because I am afraid it might be dull, duller even than what we've got now. In the past, it seemed wildly thrilling to think of a free Poland, or a free Bohemia. Now we have a painful suspicion that free Czecho-Slovakia is possibly duller than when it was an Austrian province.

What we want is life, first and foremost: to live, and to know that we are living. And you can't have life without adventure of some sort. There are two sorts of adventure: the hairs-breadth escape sort, and the more inward sort. The hairs-breadth escape sort is nearly used up, though of course small boys still climb trees, and there is speeding on the roads, the traffic danger, aeroplanes, and the North Pole. But this is meagre, compared to the wild old days when the Turk held Jerusalem, and the world was flat.

What remains is the vast field of social adventure. In the ancient recipe, the three antidotes for dulness or boredom are sleep, drink, and travel. It is rather feeble. From sleep you wake up, from drink you become sober, and from travel you come home again. And then where are you? No, the two sovereign remedies for dulness are love or a crusade.

But love is a thing you can do nothing about. It's like the weather. Whereas a crusade can be carefully considered. When the Salvation Army march out with drum and brass to pitch a stand at the street corner, they are on a crusade, and full of adventure, though they run no risk except that of ridicule. Probably they get more out of life than those who ridicule them: and that's the chief point.

Yet, still, we can't all join the Salvation Army; there'd be nobody to save. And we sadly need a crusade. What are we going to do about it? Politics, Socialism, preaching of any sort: we feel there's not much in it. It is going to make greater dulness in the end. There is money, that is an adventure to a certain degree. But it is an adventure within definite limits, very definite limits. Besides, it is for his leisure that man needs a crusade.

Women, of course, are still thrilling in the last stages of their emancipation crusade. Votes, short skirts, unlimited leg, Eton crop, the cigarette, and see you damned first; these are the citadels captured by women, along with endless "jobs." Women, for a little while longer, have enough to thrill them in the triumphs of the emancipation crusade.

But the men, what are they going to do? The world of adventure is pretty well used up, especially for a man who has a wage to earn. He gets a little tired of being spoon-fed on wireless, cinema, and newspaper, sitting an inert lump while entertainment or information is poured into him. He wants to *do* something.

And what is there to be done? Thousands of things—and nothing. Golf, jazz, motoring—hobbies. But what we want is a crusade.

Find us a crusade. It is apparently impossible. There is no formula.

The thing to do is to decide 'that there is no crusade or holy war feasible at this moment, and to treat life more as a joke, but a good joke, a jolly joke. That would freshen us up a lot. Our flippant world takes life with a stupid seriousness. Witness the serious mock-morality of the film and the wireless, the spurious earnestness poured out. What a bore!

It is time we treated life as a joke again, as they did in the really great periods like the Renaissance. Then the young men swaggered down the street with one leg bright red, one leg bright yellow, doublet of puce velvet and yellow feather in silk cap.

Now that is the line to take. Start with externals, and proceed to internals, and treat life as a good joke. If a dozen men would stroll down the Strand and Piccadilly to-morrow, wearing tight scarlet trousers fitting the leg, gay little orange-brown jackets and bright green hats, then the revolution against dullness which we need so much would have begun. And, of course, those dozen men would be considerably braver, really, than Captain Nobile or the other arctic venturers. It is not particularly brave to do something the public wants you to do. But it takes a lot of courage to sail gaily, in brave feathers, right in the teeth of a dreary convention.

IS ENGLAND STILL A MAN'S COUNTRY?

They, that is men, Englishmen, get up and ask if England is still a man's country. The only answer is, it would be if there were any men in it. For what makes a man's country, do you imagine? Is it the landscape or the number of pubs or the rate of wages or the size of boots? Is it the fact that the women say: I obey you, my lord? If the men of England *feel* that England is no longer a man's country—for apparently it was so not long ago—then it isn't. And if it isn't a man's country, then what in heaven's name is it?

The men will say, it's a woman's country. The women will immediately reply: I *don't* think!— And so it's nobody's country. Poor England! The men say it's no longer a man's country, it has fallen into the hands of the women. The women give a shout of scorn, and say *Not half!*—and proceed to demonstrate that England would be a very different place if it *were* a woman's country—my word, a changed shop altogether. And between the two of them, men and women, Old England rubs her eyes and says: Where am I? What am I? Am I at all? In short, do I exist?—And there's never a man or a woman takes the trouble to answer, they're all so busy blaming one another.

If England is not a man's country, it isn't a woman's country either. That's obvious. Women didn't make England. And women don't run England to-day, in spite of the fact that nine-tenths of the voices on the telephone are female voices. Women to-day, wherever they are, show up; and they pipe up. They are heard and they are seen. No denying it. And it seems to get on the men's nerves. Quite! But that doesn't prove that the women own England and run England. They don't. They occupy, on the whole, rather inferior jobs, which they embellish with flowered voile and artificial silk stockings and a number of airs and graces, and they are apt to be a drain on a man's cigarettes. What then? Is this the cormorant devouring England, gobbling it up under the eyes of the squeaking herring-gulls of men? Do the men envy the women these rather inferior jobs? Or do they envy them the flowered voile and the silk stockings which decorate the jobs? Or is it the airs and graces they begrudge them, or the cigarettes?—that England is no more a man's country!

"When my father and my mother forsake me, then the Lord will take me up." I suppose that's how poor old England feels to-day. The men have certainly forsaken her. They pretend the women have usurped the land, so the men need do no more about it. Which is very comfortable for the men. Very soft and nice and comfortable. Which is what the men of to-day want. No responsibility.

Soft and nice and comfortable! Soft jobs, nice wives, comfortable homes—that is supposed. to be England to-day. And Englishmen are quite startled if you suggest that it might require more to make a real England.—What more could England be, they say, than soft and nice and comfortable?— And then they blame the women for being hard and unkind and uncomfortable, and usurping England.

England, we are told, has always been a fighting country, though never a military country. That is a *cliché*. But it seems true. The Englishman hated being bossed or bullied. So he hated being a soldier or a marine, because as such he was bossed and bullied. And when he felt anything or anybody coming to boss or to bully him, he got up and prepared to place his fist in the eye of the boss and bully. Which is a real man's spirit, and the only spirit that makes a country a man's country.

Nowadays, alas, a change has come over all that. The Englishman only wants to be soft and nice and comfortable, and to have no real responsibility, not even for his own freedom and independence. He's got all the political freedom he can manage, and so he cares nothing about it. He even won't mind if it's taken from him again, after his forefathers fought so hard for it. He's got political freedom, so he cares nothing about it; which is a bit despicable, after all.

He's got political freedom, but he hasn't got economical freedom. There's the rub. And the modern man feels it not right. He feels he *ought* to have an income. A man's parents *ought* to leave him a sufficient independent income, and if they don't, he bears them a lifelong grudge.—And worse still, he has to do a job.

Now this is the disaster that has happened to almost every Englishman— he's got to do a job. All day long and every day, all his life, he is condemned to a job. There's no getting away from it. Very few men can inherit a fortune or marry a fortune. A job!—That is the great inevitable. That is the boss and the bully. That is the treadmill; The job! Men secretly and silently hate the job to-day. They push it over to the women. Then they loudly and openly abuse the women for having taken it. And they ask: Is England a man's country? Or is it nothing but a dog-gone women's show?

The answer is obvious. When a man wants a plum off a plum tree, he climbs up and gets it. But if he won't face the climb, and stands under the tree with his mouth open, waiting for the plum to fall into it; and if while he stands waiting, he sees a woman picking up a few plums that he wasn't smart enough even to pick up; and if he then begins to yell that the women have snatched away all the plums from the impoverished men, then what are we to think of him?

If men find they've got political freedom only to realise most disastrously their economic enslavement, they'd better do something about it. It's no good despising their political freedom—that is ridiculous, for political freedom is a supremely valuable thing. And it's no good blaming the women. Women, poor things, have to live, just as much as men do. It's no good whining that England is no more a man's country.

It will be a man's country the instant there are men in it. And men will be men the instant they tackle their insuperable difficulty. The insuperable difficulty, the unsolvable problem, are only insuperable and unsolvable because men can't make up their minds to tackle them. The insuperable difficulty to modern man is economic bondage. Slavery! Well, history is the long account of the abolishing of endless forms of slavery, none of which we ever want back again. Now we've got a new form of slavery. If every man who feels the burden of it determined ultimately to abolish it, using all his wits and powers and accepting no ready-made formula— then England would be a man's country, sure as eggs.

It is a pity that *sex* is such an ugly little word. An ugly little word, and really almost incomprehensible. What *is* sex, after all? The more we think about it the less we know.

Science says it is an instinct; but what is an instinct? Apparently an instinct is an old, old habit that has become ingrained. But a habit, however old, has to have a beginning. And there is really no beginning to sex. Where life is, there it is. So sex is no "habit" that has been formed.

Again, they talk of sex as an appetite, like hunger. An appetite; but for what? An appetite for propagation? It is rather absurd. They say a peacock puts on all his fine feathers to dazzle the peahen into letting him satisfy his appetite for propagation. But why should the peahen not put on fine feathers, to dazzle the peacock, and satisfy *her* desire for propagation? She has surely quite as great a desire for eggs and chickens as he has. We cannot believe that her sex-urge is so weak that she needs all that blue splendour of feathers to rouse her. Not at all.

As for me, I never even saw a peahen so much as look at her lord's bronze and blue glory. I don't believe she ever sees it. I don't believe for a moment that she knows the difference between bronze, blue, brown or green.

If I had ever seen a peahen gazing with rapt attention on her lord's flamboyancy, I might believe that he had put on all those feathers just to "attract" her. But she never looks at him. Only she seems to get a little perky when he shudders all his quills at her, like a storm in the trees. Then she does seem to notice, just casually, his presence.

These theories of sex are amazing. A peacock puts on his glory for the sake of a wall-eyed peahen who never looks at him. Imagine a scientist being so naive as to credit the peahen with a profound, dynamic appreciation of a peacock's colour and pattern. Oh, highly æsthetic peahen!

And a nightingale sings to attract his female. Which is mighty curious, seeing he sings his best when courtship and honeymoon are over and the female is no longer concerned with him at all, but with the young. Well, then, if he doesn't sing to attract her, he must sing to distract her and amuse her while she's sitting.

How delightful, how naive theories are! But there is a hidden will behind them all. There is a hidden will behind all theories of sex, implacable. And that is the will to deny, to wipe out the mystery of beauty.

Because beauty is a mystery. You can neither eat it nor make flannel out of it. Well, then, says science, it is just a trick to catch the female and induce her to propagate. How naive! As if the female needed inducing. She will propagate in the dark, even—so where, then, is the beauty trick?

Science has a mysterious hatred of beauty, because it doesn't fit in the cause-and-effect chain. And society has a mysterious hatred of sex, because it perpetually interferes with the nice money-making schemes of social man. So the two hatreds made a combine, and sex and beauty are mere propagation appetite.

Now sex and beauty are one thing, like flame and fire. If you hate sex you hate beauty. If you love *living* beauty, you have a reverence for sex. Of course you can love old, dead beauty and hate sex. But to love living beauty you must have a reverence for sex.

Sex and beauty are inseparable, like life and consciousness. And the intelligence which goes with sex and beauty, and arises out of sex and beauty, is intuition. The great disaster of our civilisation is the morbid hatred of sex. What, for example, could show a more poisoned hatred of sex than Freudian psycho-analysis?—which carries with it a morbid fear of beauty, "alive" beauty, and which causes the atrophy of our intuitive faculty and our intuitive self.

The deep psychic disease of modern men and women is the diseased, atrophied condition of the intuitive faculties. There is a whole world of life that we might know and enjoy by intuition, and by intuition alone. This is denied us, because we deny sex and beauty, the source of the intuitive life and of the insouciance which is so lovely in free animals and in plants.

Sex is the root of which intuition is the foliage and beauty the flower. Why is a woman lovely, if ever, in her twenties? It is the time when sex rises softly to her face, as a rose to the top of a rose bush.

And the appeal is the appeal of beauty. We deny it wherever we can. We try to make the beauty as shallow and trashy as possible. But, first and foremost, sex appeal is the appeal of beauty.

Now beauty is a thing about which we are so uneducated we can hardly speak of it. We try to pretend it is a fixed arrangement: straight nose, large eyes, etc. We think a lovely woman must look like Lilian Gish, a handsome man must look like Rudolph Valentino. So we *think*.

In actual life we behave quite differently. We say: "She's quite beautiful, but I don't care for her." Which shows we are using the word *beautiful* all wrong. We should say: "She has the stereotyped attributes of beauty, but she is not beautiful to me."

Beauty is an *experience*, nothing else. It is not a fixed pattern or an arrangement of features. It is something *felt*, a glow or a communicated sense of fineness. What ails us is that our sense of beauty is so bruised and blunted, we miss all the best.

But to stick to the films—there is a greater essential beauty in Charlie Chaplin's odd face than ever there was in Valentino's. There is a bit of true beauty in Chaplin's brows and eyes, a gleam of something pure.

But our sense of beauty is so bruised and clumsy, we don't see it, and don't know it when we do see it. We can only see the blatantly obvious, like the so-called beauty of Rudolph Valentino, which only pleases because it satisfies some ready-made notion of handsomeness.

But the plainest person can look beautiful, can *be* beautiful. It only needs the fire of sex to rise delicately to change an ugly face to a lovely one. That is really sex appeal the communicating of a sense of beauty.

And in the reverse Way, no one can be quite so repellent as a really pretty woman. That is, since beauty is a question of experience, not of concrete form, no one can be as acutely ugly as a really pretty woman. When the sex-glow is missing, and she moves in ugly coldness, how hideous she seems, and all the worse for her externals of prettiness.

What sex is, we don't know, but it must be some sort of fire. For it always communicates a sense of warmth, of glow. And when the glow becomes a pure shine, then we feel the sense of beauty.

But the communicating of the warmth, the glow of sex, is true sex appeal. We all have the fire of sex slumbering or burning inside us. If we live to be ninety, it is still there. Or, if it dies, we become one of those ghastly living corpses which are unfortunately becoming more numerous in the world.

Nothing is more ugly than a human being in whom the fire of sex has gone out. You get a nasty clayey creature whom everybody wants to avoid.

But while we are fully alive, the fire of sex smoulders or burns in us. In youth it flickers and shines; in age it glows softer and stiller, but there it is. We have some control over it; but only partial control. That is why society hates it.

While ever it lives, the fire of sex, which is the source of beauty and anger, burns in us beyond our understanding. Like actual fire, while it lives it will burn our fingers if we touch it carelessly. And so social man, who only wants to be ."safe," hates the fire of sex.

Luckily, not many men succeed in being merely social men. The fire of the old Adam smoulders. And one of the qualities of fire is that it calls to fire. Sex-fire here kindles sex-fire there. It may only rouse the smoulder into a soft glow. It may call up a sharp flicker. Or rouse a flame; and then flame leans to flame, and starts a blaze.

Whenever the sex-fire glows through, it will kindle an answer somewhere or other. It may only kindle a sense of warmth and optimism. Then you say: "I like that girl; she's a real good sort." It may kindle a glow that makes the world look kindlier, and life feel better. Then you say: "She's an attractive woman. I like her."

Or she may rouse a flame that lights up her own face first, before it lights up the universe. Then you say: "She's a lovely woman. She looks lovely to me."

It takes a rare woman to rouse a real sense of loveliness. It is not that a woman is born beautiful. We say that to escape our own poor, bruised, clumsy understanding of beauty. There have been thousands and thousands of women quite as good-looking as Diane de Poitiers, or Mrs. Langtry, or any of the famous ones. There are to-day thousands and thousands of superbly good-looking women. But oh, how few lovely women!

And why? Because of the failure of their sex appeal. A good-looking woman becomes lovely when the fire of sex rouses pure and fine in her and flickers through her face and touches the fire in me.

Then she becomes a lovely woman to me, then she is in the living flesh a lovely woman: not a mere photograph of one. And how lovely a lovely woman! But, alas! how rare! How bitterly rare in a world full of unusually handsome girls and women!

Handsome, good-looking, but not lovely, not beautiful. Handsome and good-looking women are the women with good features and the right hair. But a lovely woman is an experience. It is a question of communicated fire. It is a question of sex appeal in our poor, dilapidated modern phraseology. Sex appeal applied to Diane de Poitiers, or even, in the lovely hours, to one's wife—why, it is a libel and a slander in itself. Nowadays, however, instead of the fire of loveliness, it is sex appeal. The two are the same thing, I suppose, but on vastly different levels.

The business man's pretty and devoted secretary is still chiefly valuable because of her sex appeal. Which does not imply "immoral relations" in the slightest.

Even to-day a girl with a bit of generosity likes to feel she is helping a man if the man will take her help. And this desire that he shall take her help is her sex appeal. It is the genuine fire, if of a very mediocre heat.

Still, it serves to keep the world of "business alive. Probably, but for the introduction of the lady secretary into the business man's office, the business man would have collapsed entirely by now. She calls up the sacred fire in her and she. communicates it to her boss. He feels an added flow of energy and optimism, and—business flourishes.

There is, of course, the other side of sex appeal. It can be the destruction of the one appealed to. When a woman starts using her sex appeal to her own advantage it is usually a bad moment for some poor devil. But this side of sex appeal has been overworked lately, so it is not nearly as dangerous as it was.

The sex-appealing courtesans who ruined so many men in Balzac no longer find it smooth running. Men have grown canny. They fight shy even of the emotional vamp. In fact, men are inclined to think they smell a rat the moment they feel the touch of feminine sex appeal to-day.

Which is a pity, for sex appeal is only a dirty name for a bit of life-flame. No man works so well and so successfully as when some woman has kindled a little fire in his veins. No woman does her housework with real joy unless she is in love—and a woman may go on being quietly in love for fifty years almost without knowing it.

If only our civilisation had taught us how to let sex appeal flow properly and subtly, how to keep the fire of sex clear and alive, flickering or glowing or blazing in all its varying degrees of strength and communication, we might, all of us, have lived all our lives in love, which means we should be kindled and full of zest in all kinds of ways and for all kinds of things. . .

Whereas, what a lot of dead ash there is in life now.

DO WOMEN CHANGE?

The tell of all the things that are going to happen in the future—babies bred in bottle, all the love-nonsense cut out, women indistinguishable from men. But it seems to me bosh. We like to imagine we are something very new on the face of the earth. But it seems to me we flatter ourselves. Motor-cars and aeroplanes are something novel, if not something new—one could draw a distinction. But the people in them are merely people, and not many steps up, if any, it seems to me, from the people who went in litters or palanquins or chariots, or who walked on foot from Egypt to Jordan, in the days of Moses. Humanity seems to have an infinite capacity for remaining the same—that is, human.

Of course, there are all kinds of ways of being human; but I expect almost every possible kind is alive and kicking to-day. There are little Cleopatras and Zenobias and Semiramises and Judiths and Ruths, and even Mother Eves, to-day just the same as in all the endless yesterdays. Circumstances make them little Cleopatras and little Semiramises instead of big ones, because our age goes in for quantity regardless of quality. But sophisticated people are sophisticated people, no matter whether it is Egypt or Atlantis. And sophisticated people are pretty well all alike. All that varies is the proportion of "modern" people to all the other unmodern

468

sorts, the sophisticated to the unsophisticated. And to-day there is a huge majority of sophisticated people. And they are probably very little different from all the other sophisticated people of all the other civilisations, since man was man.

And women are just part of the human show. They aren't something apart. They aren't something new on the face of the earth, like the logan-berry or artificial silk. Women are as sophisticated as men, anyhow, and they were never anything but women, and they are nothing but women to-day, whatever they may think of themselves. They say the modern woman is a new type. But is she? I expect, in fact I am sure, there have been lots of women like ours in the past, and if you'd been married to one of them, you wouldn't have found her any different from your present wife. Women are women. They only have phases. In Rome, in Syracuse, in Athens, in Thebes, more than two or three thousand years ago, there was the bob-haired, painted, perfumed Miss and Mrs. of to-day, and she inspired almost exactly the feelings that our painted and perfumed Misses and Mrses. inspire in the men.

I saw a joke in a German paper—a modern young man and a modern young woman leaning on an hotel balcony at night, overlooking the sea. *He*: "See the stars sinking down over the dark restless ocean!" *She*: "Cut it out! My room number is 32!"

That is supposed to be very modern: the very modern woman. But I believe women in Capri under Tiberias said "*Cut it out*" to their Roman and Campanian lovers in just the same way. And women in Alexandria in Cleopatras's time. Certain phases of history are "modern." As the wheel of history goes round women become "modern," then they become unmodern again. The Roman women of the late Empire were most decidedly "modern"—so were the women of Ptolemaic Egypt. True modern cut-it-out women. Only the hotels were run differently.

Modernity or modernism isn't something we've just invented. It's something that comes at the end of civilisations. Just as leaves in autumn are yellow, so the women at the end of every known civilisation—Roman, Greek, Egyptian, etc.—have been modern. They were smart, they were *chic*, they said cut-it-out, and they did as they jolly well pleased.

And then, after all, how deep does modernness go? Even in a woman? You give her a run for her money; and if you don't give it her, she takes it. The sign of modernness in a woman is that she says: Oh, cut it out, boy!—So the boy cuts it out—all the stars and ocean stuff.—My room number's thirty-two !—Come to the point!

But the point, when you come to it, is a very bare little place, a very meagre little affair. It's extraordinary how meagre the point is once you've come to it. It's not much better than a full-stop. So the modern girl comes to the point brutally and repeatedly, to find that her life is a series of fullstops, then a mere string of dots. Cut it out, boy . . . When she comes to dot number one thousand, she's getting about tired of dots, and of the plain point she's come to. The point is all too plain and too obvious. It is so pointed that it is pointless. Following the series of dots comes a blank—a dead blank. There's nothing left to cut out. Blank-eye!

Then the thoroughly modern girl begins to moan: Oh, boy, do put something in again!—And the thoroughly modern boy, having cut it out so thoroughly that it will never grow again, tunes up with: I can't give you anything but love, Baby!— And the thoroughly modern girl accepts it with unction. She knows it's nothing but a most crestfallen echo from the sentimental past. But when you've cut everything out so that it will never grow again, you are thankful even for echoes from a sentimental past. And so the game begins again. Having cut it out, and brought it down to brass tacks, you find brass tacks are the last thing you want to lie down on.—Oh, boy, aren't you going to do something about it ?—And the boy, having cut it all out so that it won't grow again, has no other bright inspiration but to turn the brass tacks round, when lo, they become the brass-headed nails that go around Victorian plush furniture. And there they are, the hyper-modern two.

No, women don't change. They only go through a rather regular series of phases. They are first the slave; then the obedient helpmeet; then the respected spouse; then the noble matron; then the splendid woman and citizen; then the independent female; then the modern girl, oh, cut-it-out, boy And when the boy has cut it all out, the mills of God grind on, and having nothing else to grind, they grind the cut-it-out girl down, down, down— back to—we don't know where—but probably to the slave once more, and the whole cycle starts afresh, on and on, till in the course of a thousand years or two we come once more to the really "modern" girl. Oh, cut it out, boy!

A lead-pencil has a point, an argument may have a point, remarks may be pointed, and a man who wants to borrow five pounds from you only comes to the point when he asks you for the fiver. Lots of things have points: especially weapons. But where is the point to life? Where is the point to love? Where, if it comes to the point, is the point to a bunch of violets? There is no point. Life and love are life and love, a bunch of violets is a bunch of violets, and to drag in the idea of a point is to ruin everything. Live and let live, love and let love, flower and fade, and follow the natural curve, which flows on, pointless.

Now women used to understand this better than men. Men, who were keen on weapons, which all have points, used to insist on putting points to life and love. But women used to know better. They used to know that life is a flow, a soft curving flow, a flowing together and a flowing apart and a flowing together again, in a long subtle motion that has no full-stops and no points, even if there are rough places. Women used to see themselves as a softly flowing stream of attraction and desire and beauty, soft quiet rivers of energy and peace. Then suddenly the idea changes. They see themselves as isolated things, independent females, instruments, instruments for love, instruments for work, instruments for politics, instruments for pleasure, this, that and the other. And as instruments they become pointed and they want everything, even a small child, even love itself, to have a point. When women start coming to the point, they don't hesitate. They pick a daisy, and they say: There must be a point to this daisy, and I'm going to get at it.—So they start pulling off the white petals, till there are none left. Then they pull away the yellow bits of the centre, and come to a mere green part, still without having come to the point. Then in disgust they tear the green base of the flower across, and say: I call that a fool flower. It had no point to it!

Life is not a question of points, but a question of flow. It's the *flow* that matters. If you come to think of it, a daisy even is like a little river flowing, that never for an instant stops. From the time when the tiny knob of a bud appears down among the leaves, during the slow rising up a stem, the slow swelling and pushing out the white petal-tips from the green, to the full round daisy, white and gold and gay, that opens and shuts through a few dawns, a few nights, poised on the summit of her stem, then silently shrivels and mysteriously disappears,—there is no stop, no

470

halt, it is a perpetual little streaming of a gay little life out into full radiance and delicate shrivelling, like a perfect little fountain that flows and flows, and shoots away at last into the invisible, even then without any stop.

So it is with life, and especially with love. There is no point. There is nothing you can cut out, except falsity, which isn't love or life. But the love itself is a flow, two little streams of feeling, one from the woman, one from the man, that flow and flow and never stop, and sometimes they twinkle with stars, sometimes they chafe, but still they flow on, intermingling; and if they rise to a floweriness like a daisy, that is part of the flow; and they will inevitably die down again, which is also part of a flow. And one relationship may produce many flowerinesses, as a daisy plant produces many daisies; but they will all die down again as the summer passes, though the green plant itself need not die. If flowers didn't fade they wouldn't be flowers, they'd be artificial things. But there are roots to faded flowers and in the root the flow continues and continues. And only the flow matters; live and let live, love and let love. There is no point to love.

ENSLAVED BY CIVILISATION

The one thing men have not learned to do is to stick up for their own instinctive feelings, against the things they are taught. The trouble is, we are all caught young. Little boys are trundled off to school at the age of five, and immediately the game begins, the game of enslaving the small chap. He is delivered over into the hands of schoolmistresses, young maids, middle-aged maids, and old maids, and they pounce on him, and with absolute confidence in their own powers, their own *rightness*, and their own superiority, they begin to "form" the poor little devil. Nobody questions for a moment the powers of these women to mould the life of a young man. The Jesuits say: Give me a child till he is seven, and I will answer for him for the rest of his life.—Well, schoolmistresses are not as clever as Jesuits, and certainly not as clear as to what they are about, but they do the trick, nevertheless. They make the little boy into an incipient man, the man of to-day.

Now I ask you, do you really think that school-mistresses are qualified to form the foundations of a *man*? They are almost all excellent women, and filled with the best of motives. And they have all passed some little exam. or other. But what, in the name of heaven, qualifies them to be the makers of men? They are all maids: young maids, middling maids, or old maids. They none of them know anything about men: that is to say, they are not *supposed* to know anything about men. What knowledge they have must be surreptitious. They certainly know nothing about manhood. Manhood, in the eyes of the schoolmistress, and especially the elderly schoolmistress, is something uncalled-for and unpleasant. Men, in the pleasant opinions of school-mistresses, are mostly grown-up babies. Haven't the babies all been through the mistress's hands, and aren't the men almost identically the same?

Well, it may be so! It may be that men nowadays are all grown-up babies. But if they are, it is because they were delivered over in their tenderest years, poor little devils, to absolute petticoat rule; mothers first, then schoolmistresses. But the mother very quickly yields to the schoolmistress. It is amazing what reverence ordinary women have for the excellent old-maid mistress of the infants' school. What the mistress says is gospel. Kings are no more kings by divine right, but queens are queens and mistresses mistresses straight from God. It is amazing. It is fetish-worship. And the fetish is goodness.

"Oh, but Miss Teacher is so *good*, she's awfully *good*," say the approving mothers, in luscious voices. "Now, Johnny, you must mind what Miss Teacher says, she knows what is best for you. You must always listen to her!"

Poor Johnny, poor little devil! On the very first day it is: "Now, Johnny dear, you must sit like a good little boy, like all the other good little boys." And when he can't stand it, it is: "Oh, Johnny dear, I wouldn't cry if I were you. Look at all the other good little boys, they don't cry, do they, dear? Be a good little boy, and teacher will give you a teddy-bear to play with. Would Johnny like a teddy-bear to play with? There, don't cry! Look at all the other good little boys. They are learning to write—to write! Wouldn't Johnny like to be a good little boy, and learn to write?"

As a matter of fact, Johnny wouldn't. At the bottom of his heart, he doesn't in the least want to be a good little boy and learn to write. But she comes it over him. Dear teacher, she starts him off in the way he must go, poor little slave. And once started, he goes on wheels, being a good little boy like all the other good little boys. School is a very elaborate railway system where good little boys are taught to run upon good lines till they are shunted off into life, at the age of fourteen, sixteen, or whatever it is. And by that age the running-on-lines habit it absolutely fixed. The good big boy merely turns off one set of rails on to another. And it is so easy, running on rails; he never realises that he is a slave to the rails he runs on. Good boy!

Now the funny thing is that nobody, not even the most conscientious father, ever questions the absolute rightness of these school-marms. It is all for dear little Johnny's own good. And these school-marms know absolutely what Johnny's own good is. It is being a good little boy like all the other good little boys.

But to be a good little boy like all the other good little boys is to be at last a slave, or at least an automaton, running on wheels. It means that dear little Johnny is going to have all his own individual manhood nipped out of him, carefully plucked out, every time it shows a little peep. Nothing is more insidiously clever than an old maid's fingers at picking off the little shoots of manhood as they sprout out from a growing boy, and turning him into that neutral object, a good little boy. It is a subtle, loving form of mutilation, and mothers absolutely believe in it. "Oh, but I *want* him to be a good boy!" She fails to remember how bored she gets with her good-boy husband. Good boys are very nice to mothers and schoolmistresses. But as men, they make a wishy-washy nation.

Of course, nobody wants Johnny to be a bad little boy. One would like him to be just a boy, with no adjective at all. But that is impossible. At the very best schools, where there is most "freedom," the subtle, silent *compulsion* towards goodness is perhaps strongest. Children are all silently, steadily, relentlessly bullied into being good. They grow up good. And then they are no good.

For what does goodness mean? It means, in the end, being like everybody else, and not having a soul to call your own. Certainly you mustn't have a feeling to call your own. You must be good, and feel exactly what is expected of you, which is just what other people feel. Which means that in the end you feel nothing at all, all your feeling has been killed out of you. And all that is left is the artificial stock emotion which comes out with the morning papers.

I think I belong to the first generation of Englishmen that was really broken in. My father's generation, at least among the miners where I was brought up, was still wild. But then my father had never been to anything more serious than a dame's school, and the dame, Miss Hight, had never succeeded in making him a good little boy. She had barely succeeded in making him able to write his name. As for his feelings, they had escaped her clutches entirely: as they escaped the clutches of his mother. The country was still open. He fled away from the women and rackapelted with his own gang. And to the end of his days his idea of life was to escape over the fringe of virtue and drink beer and perhaps poach an occasional rabbit.

But the boys of my generation were caught in time. We were sent at the ripe age of five to Board-schools, British schools, national schools, and though there was far less of the Johnny dear business, and no teddy-bear, we were forced to knuckle under. We were forced on to the rails. I went to the Board-school. Most of us, practically all, were miners' sons. The bulk were going to be miners themselves. And we all hated school.

I shall never forget the anguish with which I wept, the first day. I was captured. I was roped in. The other boys felt the same. They hated school because they felt captives there. They hated the masters because they felt them as jailers. They hated even learning to read and write. The endless refrain was: "When I go down pit you'll see what— sums I'll do." That was what they waited for: to go down pit, to escape, to be men. To escape into the wild warrens of the pit, to get off the narrow lines of school.

The schoolmaster was an excellent, irascible old man with a white beard. My mother had the greatest respect for him. I remember he flew into a rage with me because I did not want to admit my first name, which is David. "David! David!" he raved. "David is the name of a great and good man. You don't like the name of David? You don't like the name of David!" He was purple with indignation. But I had an unreasonable dislike of the name David, and still have, and he couldn't force me into liking it. But he wanted to. And there it was. David was the name of a great and good man, so I was to be *forced* to like it. If my first name had been Ananias or Ahab, I should have been excused. But David! no! My father, luckily, didn't know the difference between David and Davy of the safety-lamp.

But the old schoolmaster gradually got us under. There were occasional violent thrashings. But what really did the trick was not the thrashing, but the steady, persistent pressure of: Honest, decent lads behave in my way, and no other.—And he got the lads under. Because he was so absolutely sure he was right, and because mothers and fathers all agreed he was right, he managed pretty well to tame the uncouth colliery lads during the six or seven years he was responsible for them. They were the first generation to be really tamed.

With what result? They went down pit, but even pit was no more the happy subterranean warren it used to be. Down pit everything was made to run on lines, too, new lines, up-to-date lines; and the men became ever less men, more mere instruments. They married, and they made what the women of my mother's generation always prayed for, good husbands. But as soon as the men were good husbands, the women were a tiresome, difficult, unsatisfied lot of wives, so there you are! Without knowing it, they missed the old wildness, and were bored.

The last time I was back in the Midlands was during the great coal strike. The men of my age, the men just over forty, were there, standing derelict, pale, silent, with nothing to say, nothing to do, nothing to feel, and great hideous policemen from God-knows-where waiting in gangs to keep them on the lines. Alas, there was no need. The men of my generation were broken in; they'll stay on the lines and rust there. For wives, schoolmasters and employers of labour it is perhaps very nice to have men well broken in. But for a nation, for England, it is a disaster.

GIVE HER A PATTERN

The real trouble about women is that they must always go on trying to adapt themselves to men's theories of women, as they always have done. When a woman is thoroughly herself, she is being what her type of man wants her to be. When a woman is hysterical it's because she doesn't quite know what to be, which pattern to follow, which man's picture of woman to live up to.

For, of course, just as there are many men in the world, there are many masculine theories of what women should be. But men run to type, and it is the type, not the individual, that produces' the theory, or "ideal" of woman. Those very grasping gentry, the Romans, produced a theory or ideal of the matron, which fitted in very nicely with the, Roman property lust. "Cæsar's wife should be above suspicion."—So Cæsar's wife kindly proceeded to be above it, no matter how far below it the Cæsar fell. Later gentlemen like Nero produced the "fast" theory of woman, and later ladies were fast enough for everybody. Dante arrived with a chaste and untouched Beatrice, and chaste and untouched Beatrices began to march self-importantly through the centuries. The Renaissances discovered the learned woman, and learned women buzzed mildly into verse and prose. Dickens invented the child-wife, so child-wives have swarmed ever since. He also fished out his version of the chaste Beatrice, a chaste but marriageable Agnes. George Eliot imitated this pattern, and it became confirmed. The noble woman, the pure spouse, the devoted mother took the field, and was simply worked to death. Our own poor mothers were this sort. So we younger men, having been a bit frightened of our noble mothers, tended to revert to the child-wife. We weren't very inventive. Only the child-wife must be a boyish little thing—that was the new touch we added. Because young men are definitely frightened of the real female. She's too risky a quantity. She is too untidy, like David's Dora. No, let her be a boyish little thing, it's safer. So a boyish little thing she is.

There are, of course, other types. Capable men produce the capable woman ideal. Doctors produce the capable nurse. Business men produce the capable secretary. And so you get all sorts. You can produce the masculine sense of honour (whatever that highly mysterious quantity may be) in women, if you want to.

There is, also, the eternal secret ideal of men—the prostitute. Lots of women live up to this idea: just because men want them to.

And so, poor woman, destiny makes away with her. It isn't that she hasn't got a mind——she has. She's got everything that man has. The only difference is that she asks for a pattern. Give me a pattern to follow! That will always be woman's cry. Unless of course she has already chosen her pattern quite young, then she will declare she is herself absolutely, and no man's idea of women has any influence over her.

Now the real tragedy is not that women ask and must ask for a pattern of womanhood. The tragedy is not, even, that men give them such abominable patterns, child-wives, little-boy-baby-face girls, perfect secretaries, noble spouses, self-sacrificing mothers, pure women who bring forth children in virgin coldness, prostitutes who just make themselves low, to please the men; all the atrocious patterns of womanhood that men have supplied to woman; patterns all perverted from any real natural fulness of a human being. Man is willing to accept woman as an equal, as a man in skirts, as an angel, a devil, a baby-face, a machine, an instrument, a bosom, a womb, a pair of legs, a servant, an encyclopædia, an ideal or an obscenity; the one thing he won't accept her as, is a human being, a real human being of the feminine sex.

And, of course, women love living up to strange patterns, weird patterns— the more uncanny the better. What could be more uncanny than the present pattern of the Eton-boy girl with flower-like artificial complexion? It is just weird. And for its very weirdness women like living up to it. What can be more gruesome than the little-boy-baby-face pattern? Yet the girls take it on with avidity.

But even that isn't the real root of the tragedy. The absurdity, and often, as in the Dante-Beatrice business, the inhuman nastiness of the pattern—for Beatrice had to go on being chaste and untouched all her life, according to Dante's pattern, while Dante had a cosy wife and kids at home—even that isn't the worst of it. The worst of it is, as soon as a woman has really lived up to the man's pattern, the man dislikes her for it. There is intense secret dislike for the Eton-young-man girl, among the boys, now that she is actually produced. Of course, she's very nice to show in public, absolutely the thing. But the very young men who have brought about her production detest her in private and in their private hearts are appalled by her.

When it comes to marrying, the pattern goes all to pieces. The boy marries the Eton-boy girl, and instantly he hates the *type*. Instantly his mind begins to play hysterically with all the. other types, noble Agneses, chaste Beatrices, clinging Doras and lurid *filles de joie*. He is in a wild welter of confusion. Whatever pattern the poor woman tries to live up to, he'll want another. And that's the condition of modern marriage.

Modern woman isn't really a fool. But modern man is. That seems to me the only plain way of putting it. The modern man is a fool, and the modern young man a prize fool. He makes a greater mess, of his women than men have ever made. Because he absolutely doesn't know *what* he wants her to be. We shall see the changes in the woman-pattern follow one another fast and furious now, because the young men hysterically don't know what they want. Two years hence women may be in crinolines—there was a pattern for you!—or a bead flap, like naked negresses in mid-Africa—or they may be wearing brass armour, or the uniform of the Horse Guards. They may be anything. Because the young men are off their heads, and don't know what they want.

The women aren't fools, but they *must* live up to some pattern or other. They *know* the men are fools. They don't really respect the pattern. Yet a pattern they must have, or they can't exist.

Women are not fools. They have their own logic, even if it's not the masculine sort. Women have the logic of emotion, men have the logic of reason. The two are complementary and mostly in opposition. But the woman's logic of emotion is no less real and inexorable than the man's logic of reason. It only works differently.

And the woman never really loses it. She may spend years living up to a masculine pattern. But in the end, the strange and terrible logic of emotion will work out the smashing of that pattern, if it has not been emotionally satisfactory. This is the partial explanation of the astonishing changes in women. For years they go on being chaste Beatrices or child-wives. Then on a sudden—bash! The chaste Beatrice becomes something quite different, the child-wife becomes a roaring lioness! The pattern didn't suffice, emotionally.

Whereas men are fools. They are based on a logic of reason, or are supposed to be. And then they go and behave, especially with regard to women, in a more-than-feminine unreasonableness. They spend years training up the little-boy-baby-face type, till they've got her perfect. Then the moment they marry her, they want something else. Oh, beware, young women, of the young men who adore you! The moment they've got you they'll want something utterly different. The moment they marry the little-boy-baby-face, instantly they begin to pine for the noble Agnes, pure and majestic, or the infinite mother with deep bosom of consolation, or the perfect business woman, or the lurid prostitute on black silk sheets; or, most idiotic of all, a combination of all the lot of them at once. And that is the logic of reason! When it comes to women, modern men are idiots. They don't know what they want, and so they never want, permanently, what they get. They want a cream cake that is at the same time ham and eggs and at the same time porridge. They are fools. If only women weren't bound by fate to play up to them!

For the fact of life is that women *must* play up to man's pattern. And she only gives her best to a man when he gives her a satisfactory pattern to play up to. But to-day, with a stock of ready-made, worn-out idiotic patterns to live up to, what can women give to men but the trashy side of their emotions? What could a woman possibly give to a man who wanted her to be a boy-baby face? What could she possibly give him but the dribblings of an idiot?—And, because women aren't fools, and aren't fooled even for very long at a time, she gives him some nasty cruel digs with her claws, and makes him cry for mother dear!—abruptly changing his pattern.

Bah! men are fools. If they want anything from women, let them give women a decent, satisfying idea of womanhood—not these trick patterns of washed-out idiots.

INTRODUCTION TO PICTURES

Man is anything from a forked radish to an immortal spirit. He is pretty well everything that ever was or will be, absolutely human and absolutely inhuman. If we did but know it, we have every imaginable and unimaginable feeling streaking somewhere through us. Even the most pot-headed American judge who feels that his daughter will be lost forever if she hears the word *cunt,* has all the feelings of a satyr careering somewhere inside him, very much suppressed and distorted. And the reason that Puritans are so frightened of life is that they happen, unfortunately, to be alive in spite of themselves.

The trouble with poor, pig-headed man is that he makes a selection out of the vast welter of his feelings, and says: I *only* feel these excellent selected feelings,

and you, moreover, are allowed only to feel these excellent select feelings too.—
Which is all very well, till the pot boils over, or blows up.

When man fixes on a few select feelings and says that these feelings must
be felt exclusively, the said feelings rapidly become repellant. Because we've *got* to
love our wives, we make a point of loving somebody else. The moment the mind
fixes a feeling, that feeling is repulsive. Take a greedy person, who falls right into
his food. Why is he so distasteful? Is it because his stomach is asserting itself? Not
at all! It is because his *mind,* having decided that food is good, or good for him,
drives on his body to eat and eat and eat. The poor stomach is over-loaded in spite
of itself. The appetites are violated. The natural appetite says: I've had enough!—
But the fixed mind, fixed on feeding, forces the jaws, the gullet to go on working,
the stomach to go on receiving. And this is greed. And no wonder it is repulsive.

The same is precisely true of drinking, smoking, drug-taking, or any of the
vices. When did the *body* of a man ever like getting drunk? Never! Think how it
reacts, how it vomits, how it tries to repudiate the excess of drink, how utterly
wretched it feels when its sane balance is overthrown. But the mind or spirit of a
man finds in intoxication some relief, some escape, some sense of licence, so the
drunkenness is forced upon the unhappy stomach and bowels, which gradually get
used to it, but which are slowly destroyed.

If only we would realise that, until perverted by the mind, the human body
preserves itself continually in a delicate balance of sanity! That is what it is always
striving to do, and always it is shoved over by the pernicious mental consciousness,
called the spirit. As soon as even a baby finds something good, it howls for more,
till it is sick. That is the nauseating side of the human consciousness. But it is not the
body; It is the mind, the self aware of itself, which says: This is good, I will go on
and on and on eating it!—The human spirit is the self aware of itself. This self-
awareness *may* make us noble. More often it makes us worse than pigs. We need
above all things a curb upon this spirit of ours, this self aware of itself, which is our
spirituality and our vice.

As a matter of fact, we need to be a little more *radically* aware of
ourselves. When a man starts drinking, and his stomach simply doesn't want any
more, it is time he put a check on his independent spirit and obeyed his stomach.
When a man's body has reached one of its periods of loneliness, and with a sure
voice cries that it wants to be alone and intact, it is then, inevitably, that the accursed
perversity of the spirit, the self aware of itself, is bound to whip the unhappy senses
into excitement and to force them into fornication. It is then, when a man's body
cries to be left alone and intact, that man forces himself to be a Don Juan. The same
with women. It is the price we have to pay for our precious spirit, our self aware of
itself, which we don't yet know how to handle.

And when a man has forced himself to be a Don Juan, you may bet his
children will force themselves to be Puritans, with a nasty, *greedy* abstinence, as
greedy as the previous gluttony. Oh bitter inheritance, the human spirit, the self
aware of itself! The self aware of itself, that says: I like it, so I will have it all the
time!—and then, in revulsion, says: I don't like it, I will have *none* of it, and no man
shall have any of it.—Either way, it is sordid, and makes one sick. Oh lofty human
spirit, how sordid you have made us! What a viper Plato was, with his distinction
into body and spirit, and the exaltation of the spirit, the self aware of itself. The

human spirit, the self aware of itself, is only tolerable when controlled by the divine, or demonish sanity which is greater than itself.

It is difficult to know what name to give to that most central and vital clue to the human being, which clinches him into integrity. The best is to call it his vital sanity. We then escape the rather nauseating emotional suggestions of words like soul and spirit and holy ghost.

We can escape from the trap of the human spirit, the self aware of itself, in which we are entrapped, by going quite, quite still and letting our whole sanity assert itself inside us, and set us into rhythm.

But first of all we must know we are entrapped. We most certainly are. You may call it intellectualism, self-consciousness, the self aware of itself, or what you will: you can even call it just human consciousness, if you like: but there it is. Perhaps it is simplest to stick to a common word like self-consciousness. In modern civilisation we are all self-conscious. All our emotions are mental, self-conscious. Our passions are self-conscious. Our feelings are self-conscious. We are an intensely elaborate and intricate clock-work of nerves and brain. Nerves and brain! but still, a clock-work. A mechanism, and hence incapable of experience.

The nerves and brain are the apparatus by which we signal and *register* consciousness. Consciousness, however, does not take rise in the nerves and brain. It takes rise elsewhere: in the blood, in the corpuscles, somewhere very primitive and pre-nerve and pre-brain. Just as energy generates in the electron. Every speck of protoplasm, every living cell is *conscious.* All the cells of our body are conscious. And all the time, they give off a stream of consciousness which flows along the nerves and keeps us spontaneously alive. While the flow streams through us, from the blood to the heart, the bowels, the viscera, then along the sympathetic system of nerves into our spontaneous minds, making us breathe, and see, and move, and be aware, and *do* things spontaneously, while this flow streams as a flame streams ceaselessly, we are lit up, we glow, we live.

But there is another process. There is that strange switch-board of consciousness, the brain, with its power of transferring spontaneous energy into voluntary energy: or consciousness, as you please: the two are very closely connected. The brain can transfer spontaneous consciousness, which we are *unaware* of—into voluntary consciousness, which we *are* aware of, and which we call consciousness exclusively.

Now it is nonsense to say there cannot be a consciousness in us of which we are *always* unaware. We are never aware of sleep except when we awake. If we didn't sleep, we should never know we were awake. But we *are* very much aware of our "consciousness." We are aware that it is a state only. And we are aware that it displaces another state. The other state we may negatively call the unconscious. But it is a poor way of putting it. To say that a skylark sings unconsciously is feeble. The skylark of course sings consciously; But with the other, spontaneous or sympathetic consciousness, which flows up like a flame from the corpuscles of all the body to the gates of the body, through the muscles and nerves of the sympathetic system to the hands and eyes and all the organs of utterance. The skylark does *not* sing like the lady in the concert-hall, consciously; mentally, deliberately, with the voluntary consciousness.

Some very strange process takes place in the brain, the process of cognition. This process of cognition consists in the forming of ideas, which are units of transmuted consciousness. These ideas can then be stored in the memory; or wherever it is that the brain stores its ideas. And these ideas are alive: they are little batteries in which so much energy of consciousness is stored.

It is here that our secondary consciousness comes in, our mind, our mental consciousness, our cerebral consciousness. Our mind is made up of a vast number of live ideas, and a good number of dead ones. Ideas are like the little electric batteries of a flash-light, in which a certain amount of energy is stored, which expends itself and is not renewed. Then you throw the dead battery away.

But when the mind has a sufficient number of these little batteries of ideas in store, a new process of life starts in. The moment an idea forms in the mind, at that moment does the old integrity of the consciousness break. In the old myths, at that moment we lose our "innocence", we partake of the tree of knowledge, and we become "aware of our nakedness": in short, self-conscious. The self becomes aware of itself, and then the fun begins, and then the trouble starts.

The first thing the self-aware-of-itself realises is that it is a derivative, not a primary entity. The second thing it realises is that the spontaneous self with its sympathetic consciousness and non-ideal reaction is the original reality; the old Adam, over which the self-aware-of-itself has no originative power. That is, the self-aware-of-itself knows it can frustrate the conscious flow of the old Adam, divert it, but it cannot stop it: it knows, moreover, that as the moon is a luminary because the sun shines, so it, the self-aware-of-itself, the mental consciousness, the spirit, is only sort of reflection of the great primary consciousness of the old Adam.

Now the self-aware-of-itself has *always* the quality of egoism. The spirit is *always* egoistic. The greatest spiritual commands are *all* forms of egoism, usually inverted egoism, for deliberate humility, we are all well aware, is a rabid form of egoism. The Sermon on the Mount is a long string of utterances from the self-aware-of-itself, the spirit, and all of them are rabid aphorisms of egoism, back-handed egoism.

The moment the self-aware-of-itself comes into being, it begins egoistically to assert itself It cuts immediately at the wholeness of the pristine consciousness, the old Adam, and wounds it. And it goes on with the battle. The greatest enemy man has or ever can have is his own spirit, his own self-aware-of-itself.

This self-aware ego *knows* it is a derivative, a satellite. So it must assert itself. It knows it has no power over the original body, the old Adam, save the secondary power of the idea. So it begins to store up ideas, those little batteries which *always* have a moral, or good-and-bad implication.

For four thousand years man has been accumulating these little batteries of ideas, and using them on himself, against his pristine consciousness, his old Adam. The queen bee of all human ideas since 2000 B.C. has been the idea that the body, the pristine consciousness, the great sympathetic life-flow, the steady flame of the old Adam is *bad,* and must be conquered. Every religion taught the conquest: science took up the battle tooth and nail: culture fights in the same cause: and only art sometimes—or always—exhibits an internecine conflict and betrays its own battle-cry.

I believe that there was a great age, a great epoch when man did not make war: previous to 2000 B.C. Then the self had not really become aware of itself, it had not separated itself off, the spirit was not yet born, so there was no internal conflict, and hence no permanent external conflict. The external conflict of war, or of industrial competition is only a reflection of the war that goes on inside each human being, the war of the self-conscious ego against the spontaneous old Adam.

If the self-conscious ego once wins, you get immediate insanity, because our primary self is the old Adam, in which rests our sanity. And when man starts living from his self-conscious energy; women at once begin to go to pieces, all the "freedom" business sets in. Because women are only kept in equilibrium by the Old Adam. Nothing else can avail.

But the means which the spirit, the self-conscious ego, the personality; the self-aware-of—itself takes to conquer the vital self or Old Adam are curious. First it has an idea, a semi-truth in which some of the energy of the vital consciousness is transmuted and stored. This idea it projects down again on to the spontaneous affective body. The very first idea is the idea of shame. The spirit, the self-conscious ego looks at the body and says: You are shameful!—The body, for some mysterious reason (really, because it is so vulnerable) immediately feels ashamed. Ah-ha! Now the spirit has got a hold. It discovers a second idea. The second idea is work. The spirit says: Base body! you need all the time to eat food. Who is going to give you food? You must sweat for it, sweat for it, or you will starve.

Now before the spirit emerged white and tyrannous in the human consciousness, man had not concerned himself deeply about starving. Occasionally, no doubt, he starved: but no oftener than the birds do, and they don't often starve. Anyhow he cared no more about it than the birds do. But now he feared it, and fell to work.

And here we see the mysterious power of ideas, the power of raising emotion, primitive emotions of shame, fear, anger, and sometimes joy; but usually the specious joy over another defeat of the pristine self.

So the spirit, the self-aware-of-itself organised a grand battery of dynamic ideas, the pivotal idea being almost always the idea of self-sacrifice and the triumph of the self-aware-of-itself, that pale Galilean simulacrum of a man.

But wait! Wait! There is a nemesis. It is great fun overcoming the Old Adam while the Old Adam is still lusty and kicking: like breaking in a bronco. But nemesis, strange nemesis. The old Adam isn't an animal that you *can permanently* domesticate. Domesticated, he goes deranged.

We are the sad results of a four-thousand-year effort to break the Old Adam, to domesticate him utterly. He is to a large extent broken and domesticated.

But then what? Then, as the flow of pristine or spontaneous consciousness gets weaker and weaker, the grand dynamic ideas go deader and deader. We have got a vast magazine of ideas, all of us. But they are practically all dead batteries, played out. They can't provoke any emotion or feeling or reaction in the spontaneous body, the old Adam. Love is a dead shell of an idea—we don't react— for love is only one of the great dynamic ideas, now played out. Self-sacrifice is another dead shell. Conquest is another. Success is another. Making good is another.

In fact, I don't know of one great idea or ideal—they are the same— which is still alive today. They are all dead. You can turn them on, but you get no kick. You turn on love, you fornicate till you are black in the face—you get no real thing out of it. The old Adam plays his last revenge on you, and refuses to respond *at all* to any of your ideal pokings. You have gone dead. You can't feel anything, and you may as well know it. The mob, of course, will always deceive themselves that they are feeling things, even when they are not. To them, when they say: *I love you!* there

480

will be a huge imaginary feeling, and they will act up according to schedule. All the love on the film, the close-up kisses and the rest, and all the response in buzzing emotion in the audience, is *all* acting up, all according to schedule. It is all just cerebral, and the body is just forced to go through the antics.

And this deranges the natural body-mind harmony on which our sanity rests. Our masses are rapidly going insane.

And in the horror of nullity—for the human being comes to have his own nullity in horror, he is terrified by his own incapacity to feel anything at all, he has a mad fear, at last, of his own self-consciousness— the modern man sets up the reverse process of katabolism, destructive sensation. He can no longer have any living productive feelings. Very well, he will have destructive sensations, produced by katabolism on his most intimate tissues.

Drink, drugs, jazz, speed, "petting", all modern forms of thrill, are just the production of sensation by the katabolism of the finest conscious cells of our living body. We explode our own cells and release a certain energy and accompanying sensation. It is, naturally, a process of suicide. And it is just the same process as ever: the self-conscious ego, the spirit, attacking the pristine body, the old Adam. But now the attack is direct. All the wildest bohemians and profligates are only doing directly what their puritanical grandfathers did indirectly: killing the body of the Old Adam. But now the lust is direct self-murder. It only needs take a few more strides, and it is promiscuous murder, like the war.

But we see this activity rampant today: the process of the sensational katabolism of the conscious body. It is perhaps even more pernicious than the old conservative attack on the old Adam, certainly it is swifter. But it is the same thing. There is no volta face. There is no new spirit. It may be a *Life of Christ* or it may be a book on Relativity or a slim volume of lyrics or a novel like the telephone directory: it is still the same old attack on the living body. The body is still made disgusting. Only the moderns drag in all the excrementa and the horrors and put them under your nose and say: Enjoy that horror!—Or they write about love as if it were a process of endless pissing—except that they write kissing instead of pissing—and they say: Isn't it lovely!

MYSELF REVEALED

They ask me: "Did you find it very hard to get on and to become a success?" And I have to admit that if I can be said to have got on, and if I can be called a success, then I *did not* find it hard.

I never starved in a garret, nor waited in anguish for the post to bring me an answer from editor or publisher, nor did I struggle in sweat and blood to bring forth mighty works, nor did I ever wake up and find myself famous.

I was a poor boy. I *ought* to have wrestled in the fell clutch of circumstance, and undergone the bludgeonings of chance before I became a writer with a very modest income and a very questionable reputation. But I didn't. It all happened by itself and without any groans from me.

It seems a pity. Because I was undoubtedly a poor boy of the working classes, with no apparent future in front of me. But after all, what am I now?

I was born among the working classes and brought up among them. My father was a collier, and only a collier, nothing praiseworthy about him. He wasn't even respectable, in so far as he got drunk rather frequently, never went near a chapel, and was usually rather rude to his little immediate bosses at the pit.

He practically never had a good stall, all the time he was a butty, because he was always saying tiresome and foolish things about the men just above him in control at the mine. He offended them all, almost on purpose, so how could he expect them to favour him? Yet he grumbled when they didn't.

My mother was, I suppose, superior. She came from town, and belonged really to the lower bourgeoisie. She spoke King's English, without an accent, and never in her life could even imitate a sentence of the dialect which my father spoke, and which we children spoke out of doors.

She wrote a fine Italian hand, and a clever and amusing letter when she felt like it. And as she grew older she read novels again, and got terribly impatient with "Diana of the Crossways" and terribly thrilled by "East Lynne."

But she was a working man's wife, and nothing else, in her shabby little black bonnet and her shrewd, clear, "different" face. And she was very much respected, just as my father was not respected. Her nature was quick and sensitive, and perhaps really superior. But she was down, right down in the working class, among the mass of poorer colliers' wives.

I was a delicate pale brat with a snuffy nose, whom most people treated quite gently as just an ordinary delicate little lad. When I was twelve I got a county council scholarship, twelve pounds a year, and went to Nottingham High School.

After leaving school I was a clerk for three months, then had a very serious pneumonia illness, in my seventeenth year, that damaged my health for life.

A year later I became a school teacher, and after three years' savage teaching of collier lads I went to take the "normal" course in Nottingham University.

As I was glad to leave school, I was glad to leave college. It had meant mere disillusion, instead of the living contact of men. From college I went down to Croydon, near London, to teach in a new elementary school at a hundred pounds a year.

It was while I was at Croydon, when I was twenty-three, that the girl who had. been the chief friend of my youth, and who was herself a school teacher in a mining village at home, copied out some of my poems, and without telling me, sent them to the *English Review*, which had just had a glorious re-birth under Ford Madox Hueffer.

Hueffer was most kind. He printed the poems, and asked me to come and see him. The girl had launched me, so easily, on my literary career, like a princess cutting a thread, launching a ship.

I had been tussling away for four years, getting out "The White Peacock" in inchoate bits, from the underground of my consciousness. I must have written most of it five or six times, but only in intervals, never as a task or a divine labour, or in the groans of parturition.

I would dash at it, do a bit, show it to the girl; she always admired it; then realise afterwards it wasn't what I wanted, and have another dash. But at Croydon I had worked at it fairly steadily, in the evenings after school.

Anyhow, it was done, after four or five years' spasmodic effort. Hueffer asked at once to see the manuscript. He read it immediately, with the greatest cheery sort of kindness and bluff. And in his queer voice, when we were in an omnibus in London, he shouted in my ear: "It's got every fault that the English novel can have."

Just then the English novel was supposed to have so many faults, in comparison with the French, that it was hardly allowed to exist at all. "But," shouted Hueffer in the 'bus, "you've got GENIUS."

This made me want to laugh, it sounded so comical. In the early days they were always telling me I had got genius, as if to console me for not having their own incomparable advantages.

But Hueffer didn't mean that. I always thought he had a bit of genius himself. Anyhow, he sent the MS. of "The White Peacock" to William Heinemann, who accepted it at once, and made me alter only four little lines whose omission would now make anybody smile. I was to have £50 when the book was published.

Meanwhile Hueffer printed more poems and some stories of mine in the *English Review*, and people read them and told me so, to my embarrassment and anger. I hated being an author, in people's eyes. Especially as I was a teacher.

When I was twenty-five my mother died, and two months later "The White Peacock" was published, but it meant nothing to me. I went on teaching for another year, and then again a bad pneumonia illness intervened. When I got better I did not go back to school. I lived henceforward on my scanty literary earnings.

It is seventeen years since I gave up teaching and started to live an independent life of the pen. I have never starved, and never even felt poor, though my income for the first ten years. was no better, and often worse, than it would have been if I had remained an elementary school teacher.

But when one has been born poor a very little money can be enough. Now my father would think I am rich, if nobody else does. And my mother would think I have risen in the world, even if I don't think so.

But something is wrong, either with me or with the world, or with both of us. I have gone far and met many people, of all sorts and all conditions, and many whom I have genuinely liked and esteemed.

People, *personally*, have nearly always been friendly. ' Of critics we will not speak, they are different fauna from people. And I have *wanted* to feel truly friendly with some, at least, of my fellow-men.

Yet I have never quite succeeded. Whether I get on *in* the world is a question; but I certainly don't get on very well *with* the world. And whether I am a worldly success or not I really don't know. But I feel, somehow, not much of a human success.

By which I mean that I don't feel there is any very cordial or fundamental contact between me and society, or me and other people. There is a breach. 'And my contact is with something that is non-human, non-vocal.

I used to think it had something to do with the oldness and the worn-outness of Europe. Having tried other places, I know that is not so. Europe is, perhaps, the least worn-out of the continents, because it is the most lived in. A place that is lived in lives.

It is since coming back from America that I ask myself seriously: Why is there so little contact between myself and the people whom I know? Why has the contact no vital meaning?

And if I write the question down, and try to write the answer down, it is because I feel it is a question that troubles many men.

The answer, as far as I can see, has something to do with class. Class makes a gulf, across which all the best human flow is lost. It is not exactly the triumph of the middle classes that has made the deadness, but the triumph of the middle-class *thing*.

As a man from the working class, I feel that the middle class cut off some of my vital vibration when I am with them. I admit them charming and educated and good people often enough. *But they just stop some part of me from working.* Some part has to be left out.

Then why don't I live with my working people? Because their vibration is limited in another direction. They are narrow, but still fairly deep and passionate, whereas the middle class is broad and shallow and passionless. Quite passionless. At the best they substitute affection, which is the great middle-class positive emotion.

But the working class is narrow in outlook, in prejudice, and narrow in intelligence. This again makes a prison. One can belong absolutely to no class.

Yet I find, here in Italy, for example, that I live in a certain silent contact with the peasants who work the land of this villa. I am not intimate with them, hardly speak to them save to say good day. And they are not working for me; I am not their *padrone*.

Yet it is they, really, who form my *ambiente*, and it is from them that the human flow comes to me. I don't want to live with them in their cottages; that would be a sort of prison. But I want them to be there, about the place, their lives going on along with mine, and in relation to mine. I don't idealise them. Enough of that folly! It is worse than setting school-children to express themselves in self-conscious twaddle. I don't expect them to make any millennium here on earth, neither now nor in the future. But I want to live near them, because their life still flows.

And now I know, more or less, why I cannot follow in the footsteps even of Barrie or of Wells, who both came from the common people also and are both such a success. Now I know why I cannot rise in the world and become even a little popular and rich.

I cannot make the transfer from my own class into the middle class. I cannot, not for anything in the world, forfeit my passional consciousness and my old blood-affinity with my fellow-men and the animals and the land, for that other thin, spurious mental conceit which is all that is left of the mental consciousness once it has made itself exclusive.

INTRODUCTION TO THESE PAINTINGS

The reason the English produce so few painters is not that they are, as a nation, devoid of a genuine feeling for visual art: though, to look at their productions, and to look at the mess which has been made of actual English landscape, one might really conclude that they were, and leave it at that. But it is not the fault of the God that made them. They are made with æsthetic sensibilities the same as anybody else. The fault lies in the English attitude to life.

The English, and the Americans following them, are paralysed by fear. That is what thwarts and distorts the Anglo-Saxon existence, this paralysis of fear. It thwarts life, it distorts vision, and it strangles impulse: this overmastering fear. And fear what of, in heaven's name? What is the Anglo-Saxon stock to-day so petrified with fear about? We have to answer that before we can understand the English failure in the visual arts: for on the whole, it is a failure.

It is an old fear, which seemed to dig into the English soul at the time of the Renaissance. Nothing could be more lovely and fearless than Chaucer. But already Shakespeare is morbid with fear, fear of consequences. That is the strange phenomenon of the English Renaissance: this mystic terror of the consequences, the consequences of action. Italy too had her reaction, at the end of the sixteenth century, and showed a similar fear. But not so profound, so overmastering. Aretino was anything but timorous: he was bold as any Renaissance novelist, and went one better.

What appeared to take full grip on the northern consciousness at the end of the sixteenth century was a terror, almost a horror of sexual life. The Elizabethans, grand as we think them, started it. The real 'mortal coil' in Hamlet is all sexual, the young man's horror of his mother's incest, sex carrying with it a wild and nameless terror which, it seems to me, it had never carried before. Oedipus and Hamlet are very different in this respect. In Oedipus there is no recoil in horror from sex itself Greek drama never shows us that. The horror, when it is present in Greek tragedy, is against *destiny*, man caught in the toils of destiny. But with the Renaissance itself particularly in England, the horror is sexual. Orestes is dogged by destiny and driven mad by the Eumenides. But Hamlet is overpowered by horrible revulsion from his physical connection with his mother, which makes him recoil in similar revulsion from Ophelia, and almost from his father, even as a ghost. He is horrified at the merest suggestion of physical connection, as if it were an unspeakable taint.

This no doubt is all in the course of the growth of the 'spiritual-mental' consciousness, at the expense of the instinctive intuitive consciousness. Man came to have his own body in horror, especially in its sexual implications: and so he began to suppress with all his might his instinctive-intuitive consciousness, which is so radical, so physical, so sexual. Cavalier poetry, love poetry, is already devoid of body. Donne, after the exacerbated revulsion-attraction excitement of his earlier poetry, becomes a divine. 'Drink to me only with thine eyes,' sings the cavalier: an expression incredible in Chaucer's poetry. 'I could not love thee, dear, so much, loved I not honour more,' sings the cavalier lover. In Chaucer the 'dear' and the 'honour' would have been more or less identical.

But with the Elizabethans the grand rupture had started, in the human consciousness, the mental consciousness recoiling in violence away from the physical, instinctive-intuitive. To the Restoration dramatists sex is, on the whole, a dirty business, but they more or less glory in the dirt. Fielding tries in vain to defend the Old Adam. Richardson with his calico purity and his underclothing excitements sweeps all before him. Swift goes mad with sex and excrement revulsion. Sterne flings a bit of the same excrement humorously around. And physical consciousness gives a last song in Burns, then is dead Wordsworth, Keats, Shelley, the Brontës, all are post-mortem poets. The essential instinctive-intuitive body is dead, and worshipped in death—all very unhealthy. Till Swinburne and Oscar Wilde try to start a revival from the mental field. Swinburne's 'white thighs' are purely mental.

Now in England—and following, in America— the physical self was not just fig-leafed over or suppressed in public, as was the case in Italy and on most of the Continent. In England it excited a strange horror and terror. And this extra morbidity came, I believe, from the great shock of syphilis and the realization of the consequences of the disease Wherever syphilis, or 'pox', came from, it was fairly new in England at the end of the fifteenth century. But by the end of the sixteenth, its ravages were obvious, and the shock of them had just penetrated the thoughtful and the imaginative consciousness. The royal families of England and Scotland were syphilitic, Edward VI and Elizabeth born with the inherited consequences of the disease. Edward VI died of it, while still a boy. Mary died childless and in utter depression. Elizabeth had no eyebrows, her teeth went rotten, she must have felt herself, somewhere, utterly unfit for marriage, poor thing. That was the grisly horror that lay behind the glory of Queen Bess. And so the Tudors died out: and another syphilitic-born unfortunate came to the throne, in the person of James I. Mary Queen of Scots had no more luck than the Tudors, apparently. Apparently Darnley was reeking with the pox, though probably at first she did not know it. But when the Archbishop of St. Andrew's was christening her baby James, afterwards James I of England, the old clergyman was so dripping with pox that she was terrified lest he should give it to the infant. And she need not have troubled, for the wretched infant had brought it into the world with him, from that fool Darnley. So James I of England slobbered and shambled, and was the wisest fool in Christendom, and the Stuarts likewise died out, the stock enfeebled by the disease.

With the Royal families of England and Scotland in this condition, we can judge what the noble houses, the nobility of both nations, given to free living and promiscuous pleasure, must have been like. England traded with the East and with America; England, unknowing, had opened her doors to the disease. The English aristocracy travelled and had curious taste in loves. And pox entered the blood of the nation, particularly of the upper classes, who had more chance of infection. And after it had entered the blood, it entered the consciousness, and it hit the vital imagination.

It is possible that the effects of syphilis and the conscious realization of its consequences gave a great blow to the Spanish psyche, precisely at this period. And it is possible that Italian society, which was on the whole so untravelled, had no connection with America, and was so privately self-contained, suffered less from the disease. Someone ought to make a thorough study of the effects of 'pox' on the minds and the emotions and imagination of the various nations of Europe, at about the time of our Elizabethans.

The apparent effect on the Elizabethans and the Restoration wits is curious. They appear to take the whole thing as a joke. The common oath, 'Pox on you!' was almost funny. But how common the oath was! How the word 'pox' was in every mind, and in every mouth. It is one of the words that haunt Elizabethan speech. Taken very manly, with a great deal of Falstaffian bluff, treated as a huge joke! Pox! Why, he's got the pox! Ha-ha! What's he been after?

There is just the same attitude among the common run of men to-day with regard to the minor sexual diseases. Syphilis is no longer regarded as a joke, according to my experience. The very word itself frightens men. You could joke with the word 'pox'. You can't joke with the word 'syphilis'. The change of word has killed the joke. But men still joke about *clap*! which is a minor sexual disease. They pretend to think it manly, even, to have the disease, or to have had it. 'What! Never had a shot of clap!' cries one gentleman to another. 'Why, where have you been all your life!' If we changed the word and insisted on 'gonorrhoea', or

486

whatever it is, in place of 'clap', the joke would die. And anyhow I have had young men come to me green and quaking, afraid they've caught 'a shot of clap'.

Now, in spite of all the Elizabethan jokes about pox, pox was no joke to them. A joke may be a very brave way of meeting a calamity, or it may be a very cowardly way. Myself, I consider the Elizabethan pox joke a purely cowardly attitude. They didn't think it funny, for by God it *wasn't* funny. Even poor Elizabeth's lack of eyebrows and her rotten teeth were not funny. And they all knew it. They may not have known it was the direct result of pox though probably they did This fact remains, that no man can contract syphilis, or any deadly sexual disease, without feeling the most shattering and profound terror go through him, through the very roots of his being. And no man can look without a sort of horror on the effects of a sexual disease in another person. We are so constituted that we are all at once horrified and terrified. The fear and dread has been so great, that the pox joke was invented as an evasion, and following that, the great hush! hush! was imposed. Man was *too* frightened, that's the top and bottom of it.

But now, with remedies discovered, we need no longer be *too* frightened. We can begin, after all these years, to face the matter. After the most fearful damage has been done.

For an overmastering fear is poison to the human psyche. And this overmastering fear, like some horrible secret tumour, has been poisoning our consciousness ever since the Elizabethans, who first woke up with dread to the entry of the original syphilitic poison into the blood.

I know nothing about medicine and very little about diseases, and my facts are such as I have picked up in casual reading. Nevertheless I am convinced that the secret awareness of syphilis, and the utter secret terror and horror of it, has had an enormous and incalculable effect on the English consciousness, and on the American. Even when the fear has never been formulated, there it has lain, potent and overmastering. I am convinced that *some* of Shakespeare's horror and despair, in his tragedies, arose from the shock of his consciousness of syphilis. I don't suggest for one moment Shakespeare ever contracted syphilis. I have never had syphilis myself. Yet I know and confess how profound is my fear of the disease, and more than fear, my horror. In fact, I don't think I am so very much afraid of it. I am more horrified, inwardly and deeply, at the idea of its existence.

All this sounds very far from the art of painting. But it is not so far as it sounds. The appearance of syphilis in our midst gave a fearful blow to our sexual life. The real natural innocence of Chaucer was impossible after that. The very sexual act of procreation might bring as one of its consequences a foul disease, and the unborn might be tainted from the moment of conception. Fearful thought! It is truly a fearful thought, and all the centuries of getting used to it won't help us. It remains a fearful thought, and to free ourselves from this fearful dread we should use all our wits and all our efforts, not stick our heads in the sand of some idiotic joke or still more idiotic don't-mention-it. The fearful thought of the consequences of syphilis, or of any sexual disease, upon the unborn gives a shock to the impetus of fatherhood in any man, even the cleanest. Our consciousness is a strange thing, and the knowledge of a certain fact may wound it mortally, even if the fact does not touch us directly. And so I am certain that *some* of Shakespeare's father-murder complex, *some* of Hamlet's horror of his mother, of his uncle, of all old men, came from the feeling that fathers may transmit syphilis, or syphilis-consequences, to children. I don't know even whether Shakespeare was actually aware of the consequences to a child born of a syphilitic father or mother. He may not have been, though most probably he was. But he certainly was aware of the effects of syphilis itself, especially on men. And this awareness struck at his deep sex imagination, at his instinct for fatherhood, and brought in an element of terror and abhorrence there where man should feel anything but terror and abhorrence, into the procreative act.

The terror-horror element which had entered the imagination with regard to the sexual and procreative act was at least partly responsible for the rise of Puritanism, the beheading of the king-father Charles, and the establishment of the New England colonies. If America really sent us syphilis, she got back the full recoil of the horror of it, in her Puritanism.

But deeper even than this, the terror-horror element led to the crippling of the consciousness of man. Very elementary in man is his sexual and procreative being, and on his sexual and procreative being depend many of his deepest instincts and the flow of his intuition. A deep instinct of kinship joins men together, and the kinship of flesh-and-blood keeps the warm flow of intuitional awareness streaming between human beings. Our true awareness of one another is intuitional, not mental. Attraction between people is really instinctive and intuitional, not an affair of judgment. And in mutual attraction lies perhaps the deepest pleasure in life, mutual attraction which may make us 'like' our travelling companion for the two or three hours we are together, then no more, or mutual attraction that may deepen to powerful love, and last a lifetime.

The terror-horror element struck a blow at our feeling of physical communion. In fact it almost killed it. We have become ideal beings, creatures that exist in idea, to one another, rather than flesh-and-blood kin. And with the collapse of the feeling of physical, flesh-and-blood oneness, and the substitution of an ideal, social or political oneness, came the failing of our intuitive awareness, and the great unease, the *nervousness* of mankind. We are *afraid* of the instincts. We are *afraid* of the intuition within us. We suppress the instincts, and we cut off our intuitional awareness from one another and from the world. The reason being some great shock to the procreative self. Now we know one another only as ideal or social or political entities, fleshless, bloodless, and cold, like Bernard Shaw's creatures. Intuitively we are dead to one another, we have all gone cold.

But by intuition alone can man *really* be aware of man, or of the living, substantial world. By intuition alone can man love and know either woman or world, and by intuition alone can he bring forth again images of magic awareness which we call art. In the past men brought forth images of magic awareness, and now it is the convention to admire these images. The convention says, for example, we must admire Botticelli or Giorgione, so Baedeker stars the pictures, and we admire them. But it is all a fake. Even those that get a thrill, even when they call it ecstasy, from these old pictures, are only undergoing a cerebral excitation. Their deeper responses, down in the intuitive and instinctive body, are not touched. They cannot be, because they are dead. A dead intuitive body stands there and gazes at the corpse of beauty: and usually it is completely and honestly bored; sometimes it feels a mental coruscation which it calls an ecstasy or an æsthetic response.

Modern people, but particularly English and Americans, *cannot* feel anything with the whole imagination. They can see the living body of imagery as little as a blind man can see colour. The imaginative vision, which includes physical

488

intuitional perception, they *have not got*. Poor things, it is dead in them. And they stand in front of a Botticelli Venus, which they know is conventionally 'beautiful', much as a blind man might stand in front of a bunch of roses and pinks and monkey-mush, saying: 'Oh, do tell me which is red, let me feel red! Now let me feel white! Oh, let me feel it! 'What is this I am feeling? Monkey-mush? Is it white? Oh, do you say it is yellow blotched with orange-brown? Oh, but I can't feel it! What *can* it be? Is white velvety or just silky?'

So the poor blind man! Yet he may have an acute perception of alive beauty. Merely by touch and scent, his intuitions being alive, the blind man may have a genuine and soul-satisfying experience of imagery. But not pictorial images. These are forever beyond him.

So those poor English and Americans in front of the Botticelli Venus. They stare so hard, they do so *want* to see. And their eyesight is perfect. But all they can see is a sort of nude woman on a sort of shell on a sort of pretty greenish water. As a rule they rather dislike the 'unnaturalness' or 'affectation' of it. If they are highbrows they may get little self-conscious thrills of æsthetic excitement. But real imaginative awareness, which is so largely physical, is denied them. *Ils n'ont pas de quoi*, as the Frenchman said of the angels, when asked if they made love in heaven.

Ah, the dear highbrows who gaze in a sort of ecstasy and get a correct mental thrill! Their poor highbrow bodies stand there as dead as dust-bins, and can no more feel the sway of complete imagery upon them than they can feel any other real sway. *Ils n'ont pas de quoi*. The instincts and the intuitions are so nearly dead in them and they fear even the feeble remains. Their fear of the instincts and intuitions is even greater than that of the English Tommy who calls: 'Eh, Jack! Come an' look at this girl standin' wi' no clothes on, an' two blokes spittin' at 'er'. That is his vision of Botticelli's Venus. It is, for him, complete, for he is void of image-seeing imagination. But at least he doesn't have to work up a cerebral excitation, as the highbrow does, who is really just as void.

All alike, cultured and uncultured, they are still dominated by that unnamed, yet overmastering dread and hate of the instincts deep in the body, dread of the strange intuitional awareness of the body, dread of anything but ideas, which *can't* contain bacteria. And the dread all works back to a dread of the procreative body, and is partly traceable to the shock of the awareness of syphilis.

The dread of the instincts included the dread of intuitional awareness. 'Beauty is a snare'—'Beauty is but skin-deep'—'Handsome is as handsome does'—'Looks don't count'—'Don't judge by appearances'—if we only realized it, there are thousands of these vile proverbs which have been dinned into us for over two hundred years. They are all of them false. Beauty is not a snare, nor is it skin-deep, since it always involves a certain loveliness of modelling, and handsome doers are often ugly and objectionable people, and if you ignore the look of the thing you plaster England with slums and produce at last a state of spiritual depression that is suicidal, and if you don't judge by appearances, that is, if you can't trust the *impression* which things make on you, you are a fool. But all these base-born proverbs, born in the cash-box, hit direct against the intuitional consciousness. Naturally, man gets a great deal of his life's satisfaction from beauty, from a certain sensuous pleasure in the look of the thing. The old Englishman built his hut of a cottage with a childish joy in its appearance, purely intuitional and direct. The modern Englishman has a few borrowed ideas, simply doesn't know *what* to feel, and makes a silly mess of it. The intuitional faculty, which alone relates us in direct awareness to physical things and substantial presences, is atrophied and dead, and we don't know *what* to feel. We know we ought to feel something, but what?—oh, tell us what! And this is true of all nations, the French and Italians as much as the English. Look at new French suburbs! Go through the crockery and furniture departments in the *Dames de France* or any big shop. The blood in the body stands still, before such *crétin* ugliness. One has to decide that the modern bourgeois is a *crétin*.

This movement against the instincts and the intuition took on a moral tone in all countries. It started in hatred. Let us never forget that modern morality has its roots in hatred, a deep, evil hate of the instinctive, intuitional, procreative body. This hatred is made more virulent by fear, and an extra poison is added to the fear by unconscious horror of syphilis. And so we come to modern bourgeois consciousness, which turns upon the secret pole of fear and hate. That is the real pivot of all bourgeois consciousness in all countries: fear and hate of the instinctive, intuitional, procreative body in man or woman. But of course this fear and hate had to take on a righteous appearance, so it became moral, said that the instincts, intuitions and all the activities of the procreative body were evil, and promised a *reward* for their suppression. That is the great clue to bourgeois psychology: the reward business. It is screamingly obvious in Maria Edgeworth's tales, which must have done unspeakable damage to ordinary people—Be good and you'll have money. Be wicked, and you'll be utterly penniless at last, and the good ones will have to offer you a little charity. This is sound working morality in the world. And it makes one realize that, even to Milton, the true hero of *Paradise Lost* must be Satan. But by this baited morality the masses were caught and enslaved to industrialism before ever they knew it; the good ones got hold of the goods, and our modern 'civilization' of money, machines and wage-slaves was inaugurated. The very pivot of it, let us never forget, being fear and hate, the most intimate fear and hate, fear and hate of one's own instinctive, intuitive body, and fear and hate of every other man's and every other woman's warm, procreative body and imagination.

Now it is obvious what result this will leave on the plastic arts, which depend entirely on the representation of substantial bodies, and on the intuitional perception of the *reality* of substantial bodies. The reality of substantial bodies can only be preserved by the imagination, and the imagination is a kindled state of consciousness in which intuitive awareness predominates. The plastic arts are all imagery, and imagery is the body of our imaginative life, and our imaginative life is a great joy and fulfilment to us, for the imagination is a more powerful and more comprehensive flow of consciousness than our ordinary flow. In the flow of true imagination we know in full, mentally and physically at once, in a greater, enkindled awareness. At the maximum of our imagination we are religious. And if we deny our imagination, and have no imaginative life, we are poor worms who have never lived.

In the seventeenth and eighteenth centuries we have the deliberate denial of intuitive awareness, and we see the results on the arts. Vision became more optical, less intuitive, and painting began to flourish. But what painting! Watteau, Ingres, Poussin, Chardin have some imaginative glow still. They are still somewhat free. The puritan and the intellectual has not yet struck them down with his fear and hate obsessions. But look at England! Hogarth, Reynolds, Gainsborough, they all are

490

already bourgeois. The coat is really more important than the man. It is amazing how important clothes suddenly become, how they *cover* the subject. An old Reynolds colonel in a red uniform is much more a uniform than an individual, and as for Gainsborough, all you can say is: What a lovely dress and hat! What really expensive Italian silk! This painting of garments continued in vogue, till pictures like Sargent's seem to be nothing but yards and yards of satin from the most expensive shops, having some pretty head popped over the top. The imagination is quite dead. The optical vision, a sort of flashy coloured photography of the eye, is rampant.

In Titian, in Velasquez, in Rembrandt, the people are there inside their clothes all right, and the clothes are imbued with the life of individual, the gleam of the warm procreative body comes through all the time, even if it be an old, half-blind woman or a weird, ironic little Spanish princess. But modern people are nothing inside their garments, and a head sticks out at the top and hands stick out of the sleeves, and it is a bore. Or, as in Lawrence, or Raeburn, you have something very pretty but almost a mere cliché, with very little instinctive or intuitional perception to it. After this, and apart from landscape and watercolour, there is strictly no English painting that exists. As far as I am concerned, the pre-Raphaelites don't exist, Watts doesn't, Sargent doesn't, and none of the moderns.

There is the exception of Blake. Blake is the only painter of the first order that England has produced. And unfortunately there is so little Blake, and even in that little the symbolism is often artificially imposed. Nevertheless Blake paints with real intuitional awareness and solid instinctive feeling. He dares handle the living, sensuous human body: a thing which no other Englishman has dared to do. Painters of composition pictures in England, of whom perhaps the best is Watts, never quite get below the level of cliché, sentimentalism, and *funk*. Even Watts is a failure: and the others don't bear mention. They illustrate ideas with clichés in paint.

Landscape, however, is different. Here the English exist and hold their own. But, for me, personally, landscape is always waiting for something to occupy it. Landscape seems to be *meant* as a background to an intense vision of life, so to my feeling painted landscape is background with the real subject left out.

Nevertheless, it can be very lovely, especially in water-colour, which is a more bodiless medium, and doesn't aspire to very substantial existence, and is so small that it doesn't try to make a very deep seizure on the consciousness. Water-colour will always be more of a statement than an experience.

And landscape, on the whole, is the same. It doesn't call up the more powerful responses of the human imagination, the sensual, passional responses. Hence it is the favourite modern form of expression in painting. There is no deep conflict. The instinctive and intuitional consciousness is called into play, but lightly, superficially. It is not confronted with any living, procreated body.

Hence the English have delighted in landscape, and have succeeded in it well. It is a form of escape for them, from the actual human body they so hate and fear, and it is an outlet for their perishing æsthetic desires. For more than a century we have produced delicious water-colours, and Wilson, Crome, Constable, Turner are all great landscape painters. Some of Turner's landscape compositions are, to my feeling, the finest that exist. They still satisfy me more even than Van Gogh's or Cézanne's landscapes, which make a more violent assault on the emotions, and repel a little for that reason. Somehow I don't want landscape to make a violent assault on

491

my feelings. Landscape is background with the figures left out or reduced to the minimum, so let it stay back. Van Gogh's surging earth and Cézanne's explosive or rattling planes worry me. Not being profoundly interested in landscape, I prefer it to be rather quiet and unexplosive.

But of course the English delight in landscape is a delight in escape. It is always the same. The northern races are so innerly afraid of their own bodily existence, which they believe fantastically to be an evil thing—you could never find them feel anything but uneasy shame, or an equally shameful gloating, over the fact that a man was having intercourse with his wife, in his house next door—that all they cry for is an escape. And, especially, art must provide that escape.

It is easy in literature. Shelley is pure escape: the body is sublimated into sublime gas. Keats is more difficult—the body can still be *felt* dissolving in waves of successive death—but the death-business is very satisfactory. The novelists have even a better time. You can get some of the lasciviousness of Hetty Sorrell's 'sin', and you can enjoy condemning her to penal servitude for life. You can thrill to Mr. Rochester's *passion*, and you can enjoy having his eyes burnt out. So it is, all the way: the novel of 'passion'!

But in paint it is more difficult. You cannot paint Hetty Sorrell's sin or Mr. Rochester's passion without being really shocking. And you *daren't* be shocking. It was this fact that unsaddled Watts and Millais. Both might have been painters if they hadn't been Victorians. As it is, each of them is a wash-out.

Which is the poor feeble history of art in England, since we can lay no claim to the great Holbein. And art on the Continent, in the last century? It is more interesting, and has a fuller story. An artist *can* only create what he really religiously *feels* is truth, religious truth really *felt*, in the blood and the bones. The English could never think anything connected with the body *religious*—unless it were the eyes. So they painted the social appearance of human beings, and hoped to give them wonderful eyes. But they *could* think landscape religious, since it had no sensual reality. So they felt religious about it and painted it as well as it could be painted, maybe, from their point of view.

And in France? In France it was more or less the same, but with a difference. The French, being more rational, decided that the body had its place, but that it should be rationalized. The Frenchman of to-day has the most reasonable and rationalized body possible. His conception of sex is basically hygienic. A certain amount of copulation is good for you. *Ça fait du bien au corps!* sums up the physical side of a Frenchman's idea of love, marriage, food, sport and all the rest. Well, it is more sane, anyhow, than the Anglo-Saxon terrors. The Frenchman is afraid of syphilis and afraid of the procreative body, but not quite so deeply. He has known for a long time that you can take precautions. And he is not profoundly imaginative.

Therefore he has been able to paint. But his tendency, just like that of all the modern world, has been to get away from the body, while still paying attention to its hygiene, and still not violently quarrelling with it. Puvis de Chavannes is really as sloppy as all the other spiritual sentimentalizers. Renoir is jolly: *Ça fait du bien au corps!* is his attitude to the flesh. If a woman didn't have buttocks and breasts, she wouldn't be paintable, he said, and he was right. *Ça fait du bien au corps.* What do you paint with, Maître?—With my penis, and be damned! Renoir didn't try to get away from the body. But he had to dodge it in some of its aspects, rob it of its natural terrors, its natural demonishness. He is delightful, but a trifle banal. *Ça fait du bien au corps!* Yet how infinitely much better he is than any English equivalent.

Courbet, Daumier, Degas, they all painted the human body. But Daumier satirized it, Courbet saw it as a toiling thing, Degas saw it as a wonderful instrument. They all of them deny it its finest qualities, its deepest instincts, its purest intuitions. They prefer, as it were, to industrialize it. They deny it the best imaginative existence.

And the real grand glamour of modern French art, the real outburst of delight came when the body was at last dissolved of its substance, and made part and parcel of the sunlight-and-shadow scheme. Let us say what we will, but the real grand thrill of modern French art was the discovery of light, the discovery of light, and all the subsequent discoveries of the impressionists, and of the post-impressionists, even Cézanne. No matter how Cézanne may have reacted from the impressionists, it was they, with their deliriously joyful discovery of light and 'free' colour, who really opened his eyes. Probably the most joyous moment in the whole history of painting was the moment when the incipient impressionists discovered light, and with it, colour. Ah, then they made the grand, grand escape into freedom, into infinity, into light and delight. They escaped from the tyranny of solidity and the menace of mass-form. They escaped, they escaped from the dark procreative body which so haunts a man, they escaped into the open air, *plein air* and *plein soleil*: light and almost ecstasy.

Like every other human escape, it meant being hauled back later with the tail between the legs. Back comes the truant, back to the old doom of matter, of corporate existence, of the body sullen and stubborn and obstinately refusing to be transmuted into pure light, pure colour, or pure anything. It is not concerned with purity. Life isn't. Chemistry and mathematics and ideal religion are, but these are only small bits of life, which is itself bodily, and hence neither pure nor impure.

After the grand escape into impressionism and pure light, pure colour, pure bodilessness—for what is the body but a shimmer of lights and colours!—poor art came home truant and sulky, with its tail between its legs. And it is this return which now interests. We know the escape was illusion, illusion, illusion. The cat had to come back. So now we despise the 'light' blighters too much. We haven't a good word for them. Which is nonsense, for they too are wonderful, even if their escape was into *le grand néant*, the great nowhere.

But the cat came back. And it is the home-coming tom that now has our sympathy: Renoir, to a certain extent, but mostly Cézanne, the sublime little grimalkin, who is followed by Matisse and Gauguin and Derain and Vlaminck and Braque and all the host of other defiant and howling cats that have come back, perforce, to form and substance and *thereness*, instead of delicious nowhereness.

Without wishing to labour the point, one cannot help being amused at the dodge by which the Impressionists made the grand escape from the body. They metamorphosed it into a pure assemblage of shifting lights and shadows, all coloured. A web of woven, luminous colour was a man, or a woman—and so they painted her, or him: a web of woven shadows and gleams. Delicious! and quite true as far as it goes. A purely optical, *visual* truth: which paint is supposed to be. And they painted delicious pictures: a little too delicious. They bore us, at the moment. They bore people like the very modern critics intensely. But very modern critics need not be so intensely bored. There is something very lovely about the good impressionist pictures. And ten years hence critics will be bored by the present run of post-impressionists, though not so passionately bored, for these post-impressionists don't move us as the impressionists moved our fathers. We have to persuade ourselves, and we have to persuade one another to be impressed by the post-impressionists, on the whole. On the whole, they rather depress us. Which is perhaps good for us.

But modern art criticism is in a curious hole. Art has suddenly gone into rebellion, against all the canons of accepted religion, accepted good form, accepted everything. When the cat came back from the delicious impressionist excursion, it came back rather tattered, but bristling and with its claws out. The glorious escape was all an illusion. There *was* substance still in the world, a thousand times be damned to it! There *was* the body, the great lumpy body. There it was; you had it shoved down your throat. What really existed was lumps, lumps. Then paint 'em. Or else paint the thin 'spirit' with gaps in it and looking merely dishevelled and 'found out'. Paint had found the spirit out.

This is the sulky and rebellious mood of the post-impressionists. They still hate the body—hate it. But in a rage they admit its existence, and paint it as huge lumps, tubes, cubes, planes, volumes, spheres, cones, cylinders, all the 'pure' or mathematical forms of substance. As for landscape, it comes in for some of the same rage. It has also suddenly gone lumpy. Instead of being nice and ethereal and non-sensual, it was discovered by Van Gogh to be heavily, overwhelmingly substantial and sensual. Van Gogh took up landscape in heavy spadefuls. And Cézanne had to admit it. Landscape, too, after being, since Claude Lorraine, a thing of pure luminosity and floating shadows, suddenly exploded, and came tumbling back on to the canvases of artists in lumps. With Cézanne landscape 'crystallized', to use one of the favourite terms of the critics, and it has gone on crystallizing into cubes, cones, pyramids and so-forth ever since.

The impressionists brought the world at length, after centuries of effort, into the delicious oneness of light. At last, at last! Hail, Holy Light! the great natural One, the universal, the universalizer. We are not divided, all one body we—one in Light, lovely light! No sooner had this pæan gone up than the post-impressionists, like Judas, gave the show away. They exploded the illusion, which fell back to the canvas of art in a chaos of lumps.

This new chaos, of course, needed new apologists who therefore rose up in hordes to apologize, almost, for the new chaos. They felt a little guilty about it, so they took on new notes of effrontery, defiant as any Primitive Methodists, which indeed they are: the Primitive Methodists of art criticism. These evangelical gentlemen at once ran up their chapels in a Romanesque or Byzantine shape, as was natural for a primitive and a methodist, and started to cry forth their doctrines in the decadent wilderness. They discovered once more that the æsthetic experience was an ecstasy, an ecstasy granted only to the chosen few, the elect, among whom the said critics were, of course, the arch-elect. This was outdoing Ruskin. It was almost Calvin come to art. But let scoffers scoff, the æsthetic ecstasy was vouchsafed only to the few, the elect, and even then, only when they had freed their minds of false doctrine. They had renounced the mammon of 'subject' in pictures, they went whoring no more after the Babylon of painted 'interest', nor did they hanker after the flesh-pots of artistic 'representation'. Oh, purify yourselves, ye who would know the æsthetic ecstasy, and be lifted up to the 'white peaks of artistic inspiration'.

Purify yourselves of all base hankering for a tale that is told, and of all low lust for likenesses. Purify yourselves, and know the one supreme way, the way of Significant Form. I am the revelation and the way! I am Significant Form, and my unutterable name is Reality. Lo, I am Form and I am Pure, behold I am Pure Form. I am the revelation of Spiritual Life, moving behind the veil. I come forth and make myself known, and I am Pure Form, behold I am Significant Form.

So the prophets of the new era in art cry aloud to the multitude, in exactly the jargon of the revivalists, for revivalists they are. They will revive the Primitive-Method brethren, the Byzantines, the Ravennese, the early Italian and French primitives (which ones, in particular, we aren't told): these were Right, these were Pure, these were Spiritual, these were Real! and the builders of early Romanesque churches, Oh, my brethren! these were holy men, before the world went a-whoring after Gothic. Oh, return, my brethren, to the Primitive Method, lift up your eyes to Significant Form and be saved—

Now myself, brought up as a Nonconformist as I was, I just was never able to understand the language of salvation. I never knew what they were talking about, when they raved about being saved, and safe in the arms of Jesus, and Abraham's bosom, and seeing the great light, and entering into glory I just was puzzled, for what did it *mean?* It seemed to work out as a getting rather drunk on your own self-importance, and afterwards coming dismally sober again and being rather unpleasant. That was all I could see in actual experience of the entering-into-glory business The term itself, like something which ought to mean something but somehow doesn't, stuck on my mind like an irritating burr, till I decided that it was just an artificial stimulant to the individual self-conceit. How could I enter into glory, when glory is just an abstraction of a human state, and not a separate reality at all? If glory means anything at all, it means the thrill a man gets when a great many people look up to him with mixed awe, reverence, delight. To-day, it means Rudolf Valentino. So that the cant about entering into glory is just used fuzzily to enhance the individual sense of self-importance—one of the rather cheap cocaine-phrases.

And I'm afraid 'æsthetic ecstasy' sounds to me very much the same, especially when accompanied by exhortations. It sounds like another great uplift into self-importance, another apotheosis of personal conceit: especially when accompanied by a lot of jargon about the pure world of reality existing behind the veil of this vulgar world of accepted appearances, and of the entry of the elect through the doorway of visual art. Too evangelical altogether, too much chapel and Primitive Methodist, too obvious a trick for advertising one's own self-glorification. The ego, as an American says, shuts itself up and paints the inside of the walls sky-blue, and thinks it is in heaven.

And then the great symbols of this salvation. When the evangelical says: Behold the lamb of God?—what on earth does he want one to behold? Are we invited to look at a lamb, with woolly, muttony appearance, frisking and making its little pills? Awfully nice, but what *has* it got to do with God or my soul? Or the cross? What *do* they expect us to see in the cross? A sort of gallows? Or the mark we use to cancel a mistake? Cross it out! That the cross by itself was supposed to *mean* something always mystified me. The same with the Blood of the Lamb. Washed in the Blood of the Lamb! always seemed to me an extremely unpleasant suggestion. And when Jerome says: He who has once washed in the blood of Jesus

495

need never wash again!—I feel like taking a hot bath at once, to wash off even the suggestion.

And I find myself equally mystified by the cant phrases like Significant Form and Pure Form. They are as mysterious to me as the Cross and the Blood of the Lamb. They are just the magic jargon of invocation, nothing else. If you want to invoke an æsthetic ecstasy, stand in front of a Matisse and whisper fervently under your breath, 'Significant Form! Significant Form!' and it will come. It sounds to me like a form of masturbation, an attempt to make the body react to some cerebral formula.

No, I am afraid modern criticism has done altogether too much for modern art. If painting survives this outburst of ecstatic evangelicism, which it will, it is because people do come to their senses, even after the silliest vogue.

And so we can return to modern French painting, without having to quake before the bogey, or the Holy Ghost of Significant Form: a bogey which doesn't exist if we don't mind leaving aside our self-importance when we look at a picture.

The actual fact is that in Cézanne modern French art made its first tiny step back to real substance, to objective substance, if we may call it so. Van Gogh's earth was still subjective earth, himself projected into the earth. But Cézanne's apples are a real attempt to let the apple exist in its own separate entity, without transfusing it with personal emotion. Cézanne's great effort was, as it were, to shove the apple away from him, and let it live of itself. It seems a small thing to do; yet it is the first real sign that man has made for several thousands of years that he is willing to admit that matter *actually* exists. Strange as it may seem, for thousands of years, in short, ever since the mythological 'Fall', man has been preoccupied with the constant preoccupation of the denial of the existence of matter, and the proof that matter is only a form of spirit. And then, the moment it is done, and we realize finally that matter is only a form of energy, whatever that may be, in the same instant matter rises up and hits us over the head and makes us realize that it exists absolutely, since it is compact energy itself.

Cézanne felt it in paint, when he felt for the apple. Suddenly he felt the tyranny of mind, the white, worn-out arrogance of the spirit, the mental consciousness, the enclosed ego in its sky-blue heaven self-painted. He felt the sky-blue prison. And a great conflict started inside him. He was dominated by his old mental consciousness, but he wanted terribly to escape the domination. He wanted to *express* what he suddenly, convulsedly knew: the existence of matter. He terribly wanted to paint the real existence of the body, to make it artistically palpable. But he couldn't. He hadn't got there yet. And it was the torture of his life. He wanted to be himself in his own procreative body—and he couldn't. He was, like all the rest of us, so intensely and exclusively a mental creature, or a spiritual creature, or an egoist, that he could no longer identify himself with his phallus. He wanted to, terribly. At first he determined to do it by sheer bravado and braggadocio. But no good; it couldn't be done that way. He had, as one critic says, to become humble. But it wasn't a question of becoming humble. It was a question of abandoning his cerebral conceit and his 'willed ambition', and coming down to brass tacks. Poor Cézanne, there he is in his self-portraits, even the early showy ones, peeping out like a mouse and saying: I *am* a man of flesh, am I not?—for he was not quite, as none of us are. The man of flesh has been slowly destroyed through centuries, to give place to the man of spirit, the mental man, the ego, the self-conscious I. And in his artistic soul, Cézanne knew it, and wanted to rise in the flesh. He couldn't do it, and it embittered him. Yet, with his apple, he did shove the stone from the door of the tomb.

He wanted to be a man of flesh, a real man: to get out of the sky-blue prison into real air. He wanted to live, really live in the body, to know the world through his instincts and his intuitions, and to be himself in his procreative blood, not in his mere mind and spirit. He wanted it, he wanted it terribly. And whenever he tried, his mental consciousness, like a cheap fiend, interfered. If he wanted to paint a woman, his mental consciousness simply overpowered him and wouldn't let him paint the woman of flesh, the first Eve who lived before any of the fig-leaf nonsense. He couldn't do it. If he wanted to paint people, intuitively and instinctively, he couldn't do it. His mental concept shoved in front, and he *wouldn't* paint *them*—mere representations of what the *mind* accepts, not what the intuitions gather—and they, his mental concepts, wouldn't let him paint them from intuition; they shoved in between all the time, so he painted his conflict and his failure, and the result is almost ridiculous.

Woman he was not allowed to know by intuition; his mental self, his ego, that bloodless fiend, forbade him. Man, other men he was likewise not allowed to know—except by a few, few touches. The earth likewise he was not allowed to know: his landscapes are mostly acts of rebellion against the mental concept of landscape. After a fight tooth-and-nail for forty years, he did succeed in knowing an apple, fully; and, not quite so fully, a jug or two. That was all he achieved.

It seems little, and he died embittered. But it is the first step that counts, and Cézanne's apple is a great deal, more than Plato's Idea. Cézanne's apple rolled the stone from the mouth of the tomb, and if poor Cézanne couldn't unwind himself from his cerements and mental winding-sheet, but had to lie still in the tomb, till he died, still he gave us a chance.

The history of our era is the nauseating and repulsive history of the crucifixion of the procreative body for the glorification of the spirit, the mental consciousness. Plato was an arch-priest of this crucifixion. Art, that handmaid, humbly and honestly served the vile deed, through three thousand years at least. The Renaissance put the spear through the side of the already crucified body, and syphilis put poison into the wound made by the imaginative spear. It took still three hundred years for the body to finish: but in the eighteenth century it became a corpse, a corpse with an abnormally active mind: and to-day it stinketh.

We, dear reader, you and I, we were born corpses, and we are corpses. I doubt if there is even one of us who has even known so much as an apple, a whole apple. All we know is shadows, even of apples. Shadows of everything, of the whole world, shadows even of ourselves. We are inside the tomb, and the tomb is wide and shadowy like hell, even if sky-blue by optimistic paint, so we think it is all the world. But our world is a wide tomb full of ghosts, replicas. We are all spectres, we have not been able to touch even so much as an apple. Spectres we are to one another. Spectre you are to me, spectre I am to you. Shadow you are even to yourself. And by shadow I mean idea, concept, the abstracted reality, the ego. We are not solid. We don't live in the flesh. Our instincts and intuitions are dead, we live wound round with the winding-sheet of abstraction. And the touch of anything solid hurts us. For our instincts and intuitions, which are our feelers of touch and knowing through touch, they are dead, amputated. We walk and talk and eat and copulate and laugh and evacuate wrapped in our winding-sheets, all the time wrapped in our winding-sheets.

So that Cézanne's apple hurts. It made people shout with pain. And it was not till his followers had turned him again into an abstraction that he was ever accepted. Then the critics stepped forth and abstracted his good apple into Significant Form, and henceforth Cézanne was saved. Saved for democracy. Put safely in the tomb again, and the stone rolled back. The resurrection was postponed once more.

As the resurrection will be postponed *ad infinitum* by the good bourgeois corpses in their cultured winding-sheets. They will run up a chapel to the risen body, even if it is only an apple, and kill it on the spot. They are wide-awake, are the corpses, on the alert. And a poor mouse of a Cézanne is alone in the years. Who else shows a spark of awakening life, in our marvellously civilized cemetery? All is dead, and dead breath preaching with phosphorescent effulgence about æsthetic ecstasy and Significant Form. If only the dead would bury their dead. But the dead are not dead for nothing. Who buries his own sort? The dead are cunning and alert to pounce on any spark of life and bury it, even as they have already buried Cézanne's apple and put up to it a white tombstone of Significant Form.

For who of Cézanne's followers does anything but follow at the triumphant funeral of Cézanne's achievement? They follow him in order to bury him, and they succeed. Cézanne is deeply buried under all the Matisses and Vlamincks of his following, while the critics read the funeral homily.

It is quite easy to accept Matisse and Vlaminck and Friecsy and all the rest. They are just Cézanne abstracted again. They are all just tricksters, even if clever ones. They are all mental, mental, egoists, egoists, egoists. And therefore they are all acceptable now to the enlightened corpses of connoisseurs. You needn't be afraid of Matisse and Vlaminck and the rest. They will never give your corpse-anatomy a jar. They are just shadows, minds, mountebanking and playing charades on canvas. They may be quite amusing charades, and I am all for the mountebank. But of course it is all games inside the cemetery, played by corpses and *hommes d'esprit*, even *femmes d'esprit*, like Mademoiselle Laurencin. As for *l'esprit*, said Cézanne, I don't give a fact for it. Perhaps not! But the connoisseur will give large sums of money. Trust the dead to pay for their amusement, when the amusement is deadly!

The most interesting figure in modern art, and the only really interesting figure, is Cézanne: and that not so much because of his achievement as because of his struggle. Cézanne was born at Aix in Provence in 1839: small, timorous, yet sometimes bantam defiant, sensitive, full of grand ambition, yet ruled still deeper by a naïve, Mediterranean sense of truth or reality, imaginative, call it what you will. He is not a big figure. Yet his struggle is truly heroic. He was a bourgeois, and one must never forget it. He had a moderate bourgeois income. But a bourgeois in Provence is much more real and human than a bourgeois in Normandy. He is much nearer the actual people, and the actual people are much less subdued by awe of his respectable bourgeois money.

Cézanne was naïf to a degree, but not a fool. He was rather insignificant, and grandeur impressed him terribly. Yet still stronger in him was the little flame of life where he *felt* things to be true. He didn't betray himself in order to get success, because he couldn't: to his nature it was impossible: he was too pure to be able to betray his own small real flame for immediate rewards. Perhaps that is the best one can say of a man, and it puts Cézanne—small and insignificant as he is—among the heroes. He would *not* abandon his own vital imagination.

He was terribly impressed by physical splendour and flamboyancy, as people usually are in the lands of the sun. He admired terribly the splendid virtuosity of Paul Veronese and Tintoretto, and even of later and less good baroque painters. He wanted to be like that—terribly he wanted it. And he tried very, very hard, with bitter effort. And he always failed. It is a cant phrase with the critics to say 'he couldn't draw'. Mr. Fry says: 'With all his rare endowments, he happened to lack the comparatively common gift of illustration, the gift that any draughtsman for the illustrated papers learns in a school of commercial art.'

Now this sentence gives away at once the hollowness of modern criticism. In the first place, can one learn a 'gift' in a school of commercial art, or anywhere else? A gift surely is given, we tacitly assume by God or Nature or whatever higher power we hold responsible for the things we have no choice in.

Was then Cézanne devoid of this gift? Was he simply incapable of drawing a cat so that it would look like a cat? Nonsense! Cézanne's work is full of accurate drawing. His more trivial pictures, suggesting copies from other masters, are perfectly well drawn—that is, conventionally: so are some of the landscapes, so even is that portrait of M. Geffroy and his books, which is, or was so famous. Why these cant phrases about not being able to draw? Of course Cézanne could draw, as well as anybody else. And he had learned everything that was necessary in the art schools.

He *could* draw. And yet, in his terrifically earnest compositions in the late Renaissance or baroque manner, he drew so badly. Why? Not because he couldn't. And not because he was sacrificing 'significant form' to 'insignificant form', or mere slick representation, which is apparently what artists themselves mean when they talk about drawing. Cézanne knew all about drawing: and he surely knew as much as his critics do about significant form. Yet he neither succeeded in drawing so that things looked right, nor combining his shapes so that he achieved real form. He just failed.

He failed, where one of his little slick successors would have succeeded with one eye shut. And why? Why did Cézanne fail in his early pictures? Answer that, and you'll know a little better what art is. He didn't fail because he understood nothing about drawing or significant form or æsthetic ecstasy: he knew about them all, and didn't give a spit for them.

Cézanne failed in his earlier pictures because he was trying with his mental consciousness to do something which his living provençal body didn't want to do, or couldn't do. He terribly wanted to do something grand and voluptuous and sensuously satisfying, in the Tintoretto manner. Mr. Fry calls that his 'willed ambition', which is a good phrase, and says he had to learn humility, which is a bad phrase.

The 'willed ambition' was more than a mere willed ambition—it was a genuine desire. But it was a desire that thought it could be satisfied by ready-made baroque expressions, whereas it needed to achieve a whole new marriage of mind and matter. If we believed in reincarnation, then we should have to believe that after a certain number of new incarnations into the body of an artist, the soul of Cézanne *would* produce grand and voluptuous and sensually rich pictures—but not at all in the baroque manner. Because the pictures he actually did produce with undeniable success are the first steps in that direction, sensual and rich, with not the slightest hint of baroque, but new, the man's new grasp of substantial reality.

There was, then, a certain discrepancy between Cézanne's *notion* of what he wanted to produce, and his other, intuitive knowledge of what he *could* produce. For whereas the mind works in possibilities, the intuitions work in actualities, and what you *intuitively* desire, that is possible to you. Whereas what you mentally or 'consciously' desire is nine times out of ten impossible: hitch your wagon to a star, and you'll just stay where you are.

So the conflict, as usual, was not between the artist and his medium, but between the artist's *mind* and the artist's *intuition* and *instinct*. And what Cézanne had to learn was not humility—cant word!—but honesty, honesty with himself. It was not a question of any gifts of significant form or æsthetic ecstasy: it was a question of Cézanne being himself, just Cézanne. And when Cézanne is himself he is not Tintoretto nor Veronese nor anything baroque at all. Yet he is something *physical*, and even sensual: qualities which he had identified with the masters of virtuosity.

In passing, if we think of Henri Matisse, a real virtuoso, and imagine him possessed with a 'willed ambition' to paint grand and flamboyant baroque pictures, then we know at once that he would not have to 'humble' himself at all, but that he would start in and paint with great success grand and flamboyant modern-baroque pictures. He would succeed because he has the gift of virtuosity. And the gift of virtuosity simply means that you don't have to humble yourself, or even be honest with yourself, because you are a clever mental creature who is capable at will of making the intuitions and instincts subserve some mental concept: in short, you can prostitute your body to your mind, your instincts and intuitions you can prostitute to your 'willed ambition', in a sort of masturbation process, and you can produce the impotent glories of virtuosity. But Veronese and Tintoretto are real painters, they are not mere *virtuosi*, as some of the later men are.

The point is very important. Any creative act occupies the whole consciousness of a man. This is true of the great discoveries of science as well as of art. The truly great discoveries of science and real works of art are made by the whole consciousness of man working together in unison and oneness; instinct, intuition, mind, intellect all fused into one complete consciousness, and grasping what we may call a complete truth, or a complete vision, a complete revelation in sound. A discovery, artistic or otherwise, may be more or less intuitional, more or less mental; but intuition will have entered into it, and mind will have entered too. The whole consciousness is concerned, in every case. And a painting requires the activity of the whole imagination, for it is made of imagery, and the imagination is that form of complete consciousness in which predominates the intuitive awareness of forms, images, or *physical* awareness.

And the same applies to the genuine appreciation of a work of art, or the *grasp* of a scientific law, as to the production of the same. The whole consciousness is occupied, not merely the mind alone, or merely the body. The mind and spirit alone can never really grasp a work of art, though they may, in a masturbating fashion, provoke the body into an ecstasized response. The ecstasy will die out into ash and more ash. And the reason we have so many trivial scientists promulgating fantastic 'facts' is that so many modern scientists likewise work with the mind alone, and *force* the intuitions and instincts into a prostituted acquiescence. The very statement that water is H20 is a mental *tour de force*. With our bodies we know that water is *not* H20, our intuitions and instincts both know it is not so. But they are bullied by the impudent mind. Whereas if we said that water, under certain circumstances, produces two volumes of hydrogen and one of oxygen, then the intuitions and instincts would agree entirely. But that water *is composed* of two volumes of hydrogen to one of oxygen we cannot physically believe. It needs something else. Something is missing.

A parallel case is all this modern stuff about astronomy, stars, their distances and speeds and so on, talking of billions and trillions of miles and years and so forth: it is just occult. The mind is revelling in words, the intuitions and instincts are just left out, or prostituted into a sort of ecstasy. In fact the sort of ecstasy that lies in absurd figures such as 2,000,000,000,000,000,000,000,000,000 miles or years or tons, figures which abound in modern *scientific* books on astronomy, is just the sort of æsthetic ecstasy that the over-mental critics of art assert they experience to-day from Matisse's pictures. It is all poppy-cock. The body is either stunned to a corpse, or prostituted to ridiculous thrills, or stands coldly apart.

When I read how far off the suns are, and what they are made of, and so on, and so on, I believe all I am *able* to believe, with the true imagination. But when my intuition and instinct can grasp no more, then I call my mind to a halt. I am not going to accept mere mental asseverations. The mind can assert anything, and pretend it has proved it. My beliefs I test on my body, on my intuitional consciousness, and when I get a response there, then I accept. The same is true of great scientific 'laws' like the law of evolution. After years of acceptance of the 'laws' of evolution—rather desultory or 'humble' acceptance—now I realize that my vital imagination makes great reservations. I find I can't, with the best will in the world, believe that the species have 'evolved' from one common life-form. I just can't feel it, I have to violate my intuitive and instinctive awareness of something else, to make myself believe it. But since I know that my intuitions and instincts may still be held back by prejudice, I seek in the world for someone to make me intuitively and instinctively feel the truth of the 'law'—and I don't find anybody. I find scientists, just like artists, asserting things they are *mentally* sure of, in fact cocksure, but about which they are much too egoistic and ranting to be *intuitively*, *instinctively* sure. When I find a man, or a woman, intuitively and instinctively sure of anything I am all respect. But for scientific or artistic braggarts how can one have respect? The intrusion of the egoistic element is a sure proof of intuitive uncertainty. No man who is sure by instinct and intuition *brags*, though he may fight tooth-and-nail for his beliefs.

Which brings us back to Cezanne, why he couldn't draw, or why he couldn't paint baroque masterpieces. It is just because he was real, and could only believe in his own expression when it expressed a moment of wholeness or completeness of consciousness in himself. He could not prostitute one part of himself to the other. He *could* not masturbate, in paint or words. And that is saying a very great deal, to-day; to-day, the great day of the masturbating consciousness, when the mind prostitutes the sensitive, responsive body, and just forces the reactions. The masturbating consciousness produces all kinds of novelties, which thrill for the moment, then go very dead. It cannot produce a single genuinely new utterance.

What we have to thank Cézanne for is not his humility, but for his proud, high spirit that refused to accept the glib utterances of his facile mental self. He wasn't poor-spirited enough to be facile—nor humble enough to be satisfied with visual and emotional clichés. Thrilling as the baroque masters were to him in themselves, he realized that as soon as he reproduced them, he produced nothing but cliché. The mind is full of all sorts of memory, visual, tactile, emotional memory, memories, groups of memories, systems of memories. A cliché is just a worn-out memory that has no more emotional or intuitional root, and has become a habit. Whereas a novelty is just a new grouping of clichés, a new arrangement of accustomed memories. That is why a novelty is so easily accepted: it gives the little shock or thrill of surprise, but it does not *disturb* the emotional and intuitive self. It forces you to see nothing new, it is only a novel compound of clichés. The work of most of Cézanne's successors is just novel, just a new arrangement of clichés, soon growing stale. And the clichés are Cézanne-clichés, just as in Cézanne's own earlier pictures his clichés were all, or mostly, baroque-clichés.

Cézanne's early history as a painter is a history of his fight with his own cliché. His consciousness wanted a new realization. And his ready-made mind offered him all the time a ready-made expression. And Cézanne, far too inwardly proud and haughty to accept the ready-made clichés that came from his mental consciousness, stocked with memories, and which appeared mocking at him on his canvas, spent most of his time smashing his own forms to bits. To a true artist, and to the living imagination, the cliché is the deadly enemy. Cézanne had a bitter fight with it. He hammered it to pieces a thousand times. And still it reappeared.

Now again we can see why Cézanne's drawing was so bad. It was bad because it represented a smashed, mauled cliché, terribly knocked about. If Cézanne had been willing to accept his own baroque cliché, his drawing would have been perfectly conventionally 'all right', and not a critic would have had a word to say about it. But when his drawing was conventionally all right, to Cézanne himself it was mockingly all wrong, it was cliché. So he flew at it and knocked all the shape and stuffing out of it, and when it was so mauled that it was all wrong, and he was exhausted with it, he let it go; bitterly, because it still was not what he wanted. And here comes in the comic element in Cézanne's pictures. His rage with the cliché made him distort the cliché sometimes into parody as we see in pictures like *The Pashs* and *La Femme*. 'You *will* be cliché, will you?' he gnashes. 'Then *be* it!' And he shoves it in a frenzy of exasperation over into parody. And the sheer exasperation makes the parody still funny; but the laugh is a little on the wrong side of the face.

This smashing of the cliché lasted a long way into Cézanne's life: indeed, it went with him to the end. The way he worked over and over his forms was his nervous manner of laying the ghost of his cliché, burying it. Then, when it disappeared perhaps from his forms themselves, it lingered in his composition, and he had to fight with the *edges* of his forms and contours, to bury the ghost there. Only his colour he knew was not cliché. He left it to his disciples to make it so.

In his very best pictures, the best of the still-life compositions, which seem to me Cézanne's greatest achievement, the fight with the cliché is still going on. But it was in the still-life pictures he learned his final method of *avoiding* the cliché: just leaving gaps through which it fell into nothingness. So he makes his landscape succeed. In his art, all his life long, Cézanne was tangled in a twofold activity. He wanted to express something, and before he could do it, he had to fight the hydra-headed cliché, whose last head he could never lop off. The fight with the cliché is the most obvious thing in his pictures. The dust of battle rises thick, and the splinters fly wildly. And it is this dust of battle and flying of splinters which his imitators still so fervently imitate If you give a Chinese dressmaker a dress to copy, and the dress happens to have a darned rent in it, the dress-maker carefully tears a rent in the new dress, and darns it in exact replica. And this seems to be the chief occupation of Cézanne's disciples, in every land. They absorb themselves reproducing imitation mistakes. He let off various explosions, in order to blow up the stronghold of the cliché, and his followers make grand firework imitations of the explosions, without the faintest inkling of the true attack. They do, indeed, make an onslaught on representation, true-to-life representation: because the explosion in Cézanne's pictures blew them up. But I am convinced that what Cézanne himself wanted *was* representation. He *wanted* true-to-life representation. Only he wanted it *more* true to life. And once you have got photography, it is a very, very difficult thing to get representation *more* true-to-life: which it has to be.

Cézanne was a realist, and he wanted to be true to life. But he would not be content with the optical cliché. With the impressionists, purely optical vision perfected itself and fell *at once* into cliché, with a startling rapidity. Cézanne saw this. Artists like Courbet and Daumier were not purely optical, but the other element in these two painters, the intellectual element, was cliché. To the optical vision they added the concept of force-pressure, almost like a hydraulic brake, and this force-pressure concept is mechanical, a cliché, though still popular. And Daumier added mental satire, and Courbet added a touch of a sort of socialism, both cliché and unimaginative.

Cézanne wanted something that was neither optical nor mechanical nor intellectual. And to introduce into our world of vision something which is neither optical nor mechanical nor intellectual-psychological requires a real revolution. It was a revolution Cézanne began, but which nobody, apparently, has been able to carry on.

He wanted to touch the world of substance once more with the intuitive touch, to be aware of it with the intuitive awareness, and to express it in intuitive terms. That is, he wished to displace our present mode of mental visual consciousness, the consciousness of mental concepts, and substitute a mode of consciousness that was predominantly intuitive, the awareness of touch. In the past, the primitives painted intuitively, but *in the direction* of our present mental-visual, conceptual form of consciousness. They were working away from their own intuition. Mankind has never been able to trust the intuitive consciousness—and the decision to accept that trust marks a very great revolution in the course of human development.

Without knowing it, Cézanne, the timid little conventional man sheltering behind his wife and sister and the Jesuit father, was a pure revolutionary. When he said to his models: Be an apple! Be an apple! he was uttering the foreword to the fall not only of Jesuits and the Christian idealists altogether, but to the collapse of our whole way of consciousness, and the substitution of another way. If the human being is going to be primarily an Apple, as for Cézanne it was, then you are going to have a new world of men: a world which has very little to say, men that can sit still and just be physically there and be truly non-moral. That was what Cézanne meant with his: 'Be an apple!' He knew perfectly well that the moment the model began to

503

intrude her personality and her 'mind', it would be cliché, and moral, and he would have to paint cliché. The only part of her that was not banal, known *ad nauseam*, living cliché, the only part of her that was not living cliché was her appleyness. Her body, even her very sex was known, nauseously: *connu! connu!* the endless chain of known cause-and-effect, the infinite web of the hated cliché which nets us all down in utter boredom. He knew it all, he hated it all, he refined it all, this timid and 'humble' little man. He knew, as an artist, that the only bit of a woman which nowadays escapes being ready-made and ready-known cliché is the appley part of her. Oh, be an apple, and leave out all your thoughts, all your feelings, all your mind and all your soul, which we know all about and find boring beyond endurance. Leave it all out—and be an apple!— It is the appleyness of the portrait of Cézanne's wife that makes it so permanently interesting: the appleyness, which carries with it also the feeling of knowing the other side as well, the side you don't see, the hidden side of the moon. For the intuitive apperception of the apple is so *tangibly* aware of the apple that it is aware of it *all round*, not only just of the front. The eye sees all fronts, and the mind, on the whole, is satisfied with fronts. But intuition needs all-aroundness, and instinct needs insideness. The true imagination is forever curving round to the other side, to the back of presented appearance.

So to my feeling the portraits of Madame Cézanne, particularly the portrait in the red dress, are more interesting than the portrait of M. Geffroy, or the portraits of the housekeeper or the gardener. In the same way the *Card-players* with two figures please me more than those with four.

But we have to remember, in his figure paintings, that while he was painting the appleyness he was also deliberately painting *out* the so-called humanness, the personality, the 'likeness', the physical cliché. He had deliberately to paint it out, deliberately to make the hands and face rudimentary, and so on, because if he had painted them in fully, they would have been cliché. He *never* got over the cliché denominator, the intrusion and interference of the ready-made concept, when it came to people, to men and women. Especially to women he could only give a cliché response— and that maddened him. Try as he might, woman remained a known, ready-made cliché object to him, and he *could not* break through the concepted obsession to get at the intuitive awareness of her. Except with his wife—and in his wife he did at least know the appleyness. But with his house-keeper he failed somewhat. She is a bit cliché, especially the face. So really is M. Geffroy.

With men Cézanne often dodged it by insisting on the clothes, those stiff cloth jackets bent into thick folds, those hats, those blouses, those curtains. Some of the *Card-players*, the big ones with four figures, seem just a trifle banal, so much occupied with painted *stuff*, painted clothing, and the humanness a bit cliché. Nor good colour, nor clever composition, nor 'planes' of colour, nor anything else will save an emotional cliché from being an emotional cliché, though they may, of course, garnish it and make it more interesting.

Where Cézanne did sometimes escape the cliché altogether and really give a complete intuitive interpretation of actual objects is in some of the still-life compositions. To me, these good still-life scenes are purely representative and quite true-to-life. Here Cézanne did what he wanted to do: he made the things quite real, he didn't deliberately leave anything out, and yet he gave us a triumphant and rich intuitive vision of a few apples and kitchen pots. For once his intuitive consciousness triumphed, and broke into utterance. And here he is inimitable. His imitators imitate his accessories of tablecloths folded like tin, etc.—the unreal parts of his pictures—but they don't imitate the pots and apples, because they can't. It's the real appleyness, and you can't imitate it. Every man must create it new and different out of himself: new and different. The moment it looks 'like' Cézanne, it is nothing.

But at the same time that Cézanne was triumphing with the apple and appleyness, he was still fighting with the cliché. When he makes Madame Cézanne most *still*, most appley, he starts making the universe slip uneasily about her. It was part of his desire: to make the human form, the *life* form come to rest. Not static—on the contrary. Mobile but come to rest. And at the same time, he set the unmoving material world into motion. Walls twitch and slide, chairs bend or rear up a little, cloths curl like burning paper. Cézanne did this partly to satisfy his intuitive feeling that nothing is really *statically* at rest—a feeling he seems to have had strongly—as when he watched the lemons shrivel or go mildewed, in his still-life group, which he left lying there so long so that he *could* see that gradual flux of change: and partly to fight the cliché, which says that the inanimate world *is* static, and that walls *are* still. In his fight with the cliché, he denied that walls are still and chairs are static. In his intuitive self he *felt* for their changes.

And these two activities of his consciousness occupy his later landscapes. In the best landscapes, we are fascinated by the mysterious *shiftiness* of the scene under our eyes; it shifts about as we watch it. And we realize, with a sort of transport, how intuitively *true* this is of landscape. It is *not* still. It has its own weird anima, and to our wide-eyed perception it changes like a living animal under our gaze. This is a quality that Cézanne sometimes got marvellously.

Then again, in other pictures he seems to be saying: Landscape is not like this and not like this and not like this and not . . . etc.—and every *not* is a little blank space in the canvas, defied by the remains of an assertion. Sometimes Cézanne builds up a landscape essentially out of omissions. He puts fringes on the complicated vacuum of the cliché, so to speak, and offers us that. It is interesting in a *repudiative* fashion, but it is not the new thing. The appleyness, the intuition has gone. We have only a mental repudiation. This occupies many of the later pictures: and ecstasizes the critics.

And Cézanne was bitter. He had never, as far as his *life* went, broken through the horrible glass screen of the mental concepts, to the actual *touch* of life. In his art, he had touched the apple, and that was a great deal. He had intuitively known the apple and intuitively brought it forth on the tree of his life in paint. But when it came to anything beyond the apple, to landscape, to people, and above all to nude woman, the cliché had triumphed over him. The cliché had triumphed over him, and he was bitter, misanthropic. How not to be misanthropic, when men and women are just clichés to you, and you hate the cliché? Most people, of course, love the cliché—because most people *are* the cliché. Still, for all that, there is perhaps more appleyness in man, and even in nude woman, than Cézanne was able to get at. The cliché obtruded, so he just abstracted away from it. Those last water-colour landscapes are just abstractions from the cliché. They are blanks, with a few pearly-coloured sort of edges. The blank is vacuum, which was Cézanne's last word against the cliché. It is a vacuum. And the edges are there to assert the vacuity.

And the very fact that we can reconstruct almost instantly a whole landscape from the few indications Cézanne gives, shows what a cliché the landscape is, how it exists already, ready-made, in our minds, how it exists in a pigeon-hole of the consciousness, so to speak, and you need only be given its number to be able to get it out, complete. Cézanne's last water-colour landscapes, made up of a few touches on blank paper, are a satire on landscape altogether. *They leave so much to the imagination!*—that immortal cant phrase, which means they give you the clue to a cliché and the cliché comes. That's what the cliché exists for. And that sort of imagination is just a rag-bag memory stored with thousands and thousands of old and really worthless sketches, images, etc.— clichés.

We can see what a fight it means, the escape from the domination of the ready-made mental concept, the mental consciousness stuffed full of clichés that intervene like a complete screen between us and life. It means a long, long fight, that will probably last for ever. But Cézanne did get as far as the apple. I can think of nobody else who has done anything.

When we put it in personal terms, it is a fight in a man between his own ego, which is his ready-made mental self which inhabits either a sky-blue self-tinted heaven or a black, self-tinted hell, and his other free intuitive self. Cézanne never freed himself from his ego, in his life. He haunted the fringes of experience—'I who am so feeble in life'—but at least he knew it. At least he had the greatness to feel bitter about it. Not like the complacent bourgeois who now 'appreciate' him!

So now perhaps it is the English turn. Perhaps this is where the English will come in. They have certainly stayed out very completely. It is as if they had received the death-blow to their instinctive and intuitive bodies in the Elizabethan age, and since then they have steadily died, till now they are complete corpses. As a young English painter, an intelligent and really modest young man, said to me: But I do think we ought to begin to paint good pictures, now that we know pretty well all there is to know about how a picture should be made. You do agree, don't you, that technically we know almost all there is to know about painting?

I looked at him in amazement. It was obvious that a newborn babe was as fit to paint pictures as he was. He knew technically all there was to know about pictures: all about two-dimensional and three-dimensional composition, also the colour-dimension and the dimension of values in that view of composition which exists apart from form: all about the value of planes, the value of the angle in planes, the different values of the same colour on different planes: all about edges, visible edges, tangible edges, intangible edges: all about the nodality of form-groups, the constellating of mass-centres: all about the relativity of mass, the gravitation and the centrifugal force of masses, the resultant of the complex impinging of masses, the isolation of a mass in the line of vision: all about pattern, line pattern, edge pattern, tone pattern, colour pattern, and the pattern of moving planes: all about texture, impasto, surface, and what happens at the edge of the canvas: also which is the æsthetic centre of the canvas, the dynamic centre, the effulgent centre, the kinetic centre, the mathematical centre and the Chinese centre: also the points of departure in the foreground, and the points of disappearance in the background, together with the various routes between these points, namely, as the crow flies, as the mind intoxicated with knowledge reels and gets there; all about spotting, what you spot, which spot, on the spot, how many spots, balance of spots, recedence of spots, spots on the explosive vision and spots on the co-ordinative vision: all about literary interest and how to hide it successfully from the policeman: all about photographic representation, and which heaven it belongs to, and which hell: all about the sex-appeal of a picture, and when you can be arrested for solicitation, when for indecency: all about the psychology of a picture, which section of the mind it appeals to, which mental state it is intended to represent, how to exclude the representation of all other states of mind from the one intended, or how, on the contrary, to give a hint of complementary states of mind fringing the state of mind portrayed: all about the chemistry of colours, when to use Winsor and Newton and when not, and the relative depth of contempt to display for Lefranc on the history of colour, past and future, whether cadmium will really stand the march of ages, whether viridian will go black, blue, or merely greasy, and the effect on our great-great-grandsons of the flake white and zinc white and white lead we have so lavishly used: on the merits and demerits of leaving patches of bare, prepared canvas, and which preparation will bleach, which blacken: on the mediums to be used, the vice of linseed oil, the treachery of turps, the meanness of gums, the innocence or the unspeakable crime of varnish: on allowing your picture to be shiny, on insisting that it should be shiny, or weeping over the merest suspicion of gloss, and rubbing it with a raw potato: on brushes, and the conflicting length of the stem, the best of the hog, the length of bristle most to be desired on the many varying occasions, and whether to slash in one direction only: on the atmosphere of London, on the atmosphere of Glasgow, on the atmosphere of Rome, on the atmosphere of Paris, and the peculiar action of them all upon vermilion, cinnabar, pale cadmium yellow, mid-chrome, emerald green, veronese green, linseed oil, turps, and Lyalls's perfect medium: on quality, and the relation to light, and its ability to hold its own in so radical a change of light as that from Rome to London. All these things the young man knew—and out of it, God help him, he was going to make pictures.

Now such innocence and such naïveté, coupled with true modesty, must make us believe that we English have indeed, at least as far as paint goes, become again as little children: very little children: tiny children: babes: nay, babes unborn. And if we have really got back to the state of the unborn babe, we are perhaps almost ready to be born. The English *may* be born again, pictorially. Or, to tell the truth, they may begin for the first time to be born: since as painters of composition pictures they don't really exist. They have reached the stage where their innocent egos are entirely and totally enclosed in pale blue glass bottles of insulated inexperience. Perhaps now they *must* hatch out!

'Do you think we may be on the brink of a Golden Age again, in England?' one of our most promising young writers asked me, with that same half-timorous innocence and naïveté of the young painter. I looked at him—he was a sad young man—and my eyes nearly fell out of my head. A golden age! He looked so ungolden, and though he was twenty years my junior, he felt also like my grandfather. A golden age! In England! A golden age! Now, when even money is paper! When the enclosure in the ego is final, when they are hermetically sealed and insulated from all experience, from any *touch*, from anything *solid*.

'I suppose it's up to *you*,' said I.

And he quietly accepted it.

But such innocence, such naïveté must be a prelude to something. It's a *ne plus ultra*. So why shouldn't it be a prelude to a golden age? If the innocence and naïveté as regards artistic expression doesn't become merely idiotic, why shouldn't

507

it become golden. The young might, out of a sheer sort of mental blankness, strike the oil of their live intuition, and get a gusher. Why not? A golden gush of artistic expression! 'Now we know pretty well everything that can be known about the technical side of pictures.' A golden age! With the artists all in bottles! Bottled up!

THE STATE OF FUNK

What is the matter with the English, that they are so scared of everything? They are in a state of blue funk, and they behave like a lot of mice when somebody stamps on the floor. They are terrified about money, finance, about ships, about war, about work, about Labour, about Bolshevism, and funniest of all, they are scared stiff of the printed word. Now this is a very strange and humiliating state of mind, in a people which has always been so dauntless. And, for the nation, it is a very dangerous state of mind. When a people falls into a state of funk, then God help it. Because mass funk leads some time or other to mass panic, and then—one can only repeat, God help us.

There is, of course, a certain excuse for fear. The time of change is upon us. The need for change has taken hold of us. We are changing, we have got to change, and we can no more help it than leaves can help going yellow and coming loose in autumn, or than bulbs can help shoving their little green spikes out of the ground in spring. We are changing, we are in the throes of change, and the change will be a great one. Instinctively, we feel it. Intuitively, we know it. And we are frightened.

Because change hurts. And also, in the periods of serious transition, everything is uncertain, and living things are most vulnerable.

But what of it? Granted all the pains and dangers and uncertainties, there is no excuse for falling into a state of funk. If we come to think of it, every child that is begotten and born is a seed of change, a danger to its mother, at childbirth a great pain, and after birth, a new responsibility, a new change. If we feel in a state of funk about it, we should cease having children altogether. *If* we fall into a state of funk, indeed, the best thing is to have no children. But why fall into a state of funk?

Why not look things in the face like men, and like women? A woman who is going to have a child says to herself: Yes, I feel uncomfortable, sometimes I feel wretched, and I have a time of pain and danger ahead of me. But I have a good chance of coming through all right, especially if I am intelligent, and I bring a new life into the world. Somewhere I feel hopeful, even happy. So I must take the sour with the sweet. There is no birth without birth-pangs.

It is the business of men, of course, to take the same attitude towards the birth of new conditions, new ideas, new emotions. And sorry to say, most. modern men don't. They fall into a state of funk. We all of us know that ahead of us lies a great social change, a great social readjustment. A few men look it in the face and try to realise what will be best. We none of us *know* what will be best. There is no ready-made solution. Ready-made solutions are almost the greatest danger of all. A change is a slow flux, which must happen bit by bit. And it must *happen*. You can't drive it like a steam engine. But all the time you can be alert and intelligent about it, and watch for the next step, and watch for the direction of the main trend. Patience, alertness, intelligence, and a human goodwill and fearlessness, that is what you want in a time of change. Not funk.

Now England is on the brink of great changes, radical changes. Within the next fifty years the whole framework of our social life will be altered, will be greatly modified. The old world of our grandfathers is disappearing like thawing snow, and is as likely to cause a flood. What the world of our grandchildren will be, fifty years hence, we don't know. But in its social form it will be very different from our world of to-day. We've got to change. And in our power to change, in our capacity to make new intelligent adaptation to new conditions, in our readiness to admit and fulfil new needs, to give expression to new desires and new feelings, lies our hope and our health. Courage is the great word. Funk spells sheer disaster.

There is a great change coming, bound to come. The whole money arrangement will undergo a change: what, I don't know. The whole industrial system will undergo a change. Work will be different and pay will be different. The owning of property will be different. Class will be different, and human relations will be modified and perhaps simplified. If we are intelligent, alert and undaunted, then life will be much better, more generous, more spontaneous, more vital, less basely materialistic. If we fall into a state of funk, impotence and persecution, then things may be very much worse than they are now. It is up to us. It is up to men to be men. While men are courageous and willing to change, nothing terribly bad can happen. But once men fall into a state of funk, with the inevitable accompaniment of bullying and repression, then only bad things can happen. To be firm is one thing. But bullying is another. And bullying of any sort whatsoever can have nothing but disastrous results. And when the mass falls into a state of funk, and you have mass bullying, then catastrophe is near.

Change in the whole social system is inevitable not merely because conditions change—though partly for that reason—but because people themselves change. We change, you and I, we change and change vitally, as the years go on. New feelings arise in us, old values depreciate, new values arise. Things we thought we wanted most intensely we realise we don't care about. The things we built our lives on crumble and disappear, and the process is painful. But it is not tragic. A tadpole that has so gaily waved its tail in the water must feel very sick when the tail begins to drop off and little legs begin to sprout. The tail was its dearest, gayest, most active member, all its little life was in its tail. And now the tail must go. It seems rough on the tadpole; but the little green frog in the grass is a new gem, after all.

As a novelist, I feel it is the change inside the individual which is my real concern. The great social change interests me and troubles me, but it is not my field. I know a change is coming—and I know we must have a more generous, more human system based on the life values and not on the money values. That I know. But what steps to take I don't know. Other men know better.

My field is to know the feelings inside a man, and to make new feelings conscious. What really torments civilised people is that they are full of feelings they know nothing about; they can't realise them, they can't fulfil them, they can't *live* them. And so they are tortured. It is like having energy you can't use—it destroys you. And feelings are a form of vital energy.

I am convinced that the majority of people to-day have good, generous feelings which they can never know, never experience, because of some fear, some repression. I do not believe that people would be villains, thieves, murderers and sexual criminals if they were freed from legal restraint. On the contrary, I think the vast majority would be much more generous, good-hearted and decent if they felt they dared be. I am convinced that people want to be more decent, more good-hearted than our social system of money and grab allows them to be. The awful fight for money, into which we are all forced, hurts our good nature more than we can bear. I am sure this is true of a vast number of people.

And the same is true of our sexual feelings; only worse. There, we start all wrong. Consciously, there is supposed to be no such thing as sex in the human being. As far as possible, we never speak of it, never mention it, never, if we can help it, even think of it. It is disturbing. It is—somehow— wrong.

The whole trouble with sex is that we daren't speak of it and think of it naturally. We are not secretly sexual villains. We are not secretly sexually depraved. We are just human beings with living sex. We are all right, if we had not this unaccountable and disastrous *fear* of sex. I know, when I was a lad of eighteen, I used to remember with shame and rage in the morning the sexual thoughts and desires I had had the night before. Shame, and rage, and terror lest anybody else should have to know. And I *hated* the self that I had been, the night before.

Most boys are like that, and it is, of course, utterly wrong. The boy that had excited sexual thoughts and feelings was the living, warm-hearted, passionate me. The boy that in the morning remembered these feelings with such fear, shame and rage was the social mental me: perhaps a little priggish, and certainly in a state of funk. But the two were divided against one another. A boy divided against himself; a girl divided against herself; a people divided against itself; it is a disastrous condition.

And it was a long time before I was able to say to myself: I am *not* going to be ashamed of my sexual thoughts and desires, they are me myself, they are part of my life. I am going to accept myself sexually as I accept myself mentally and spiritually, and know that I am one time one thing, one time another, but I am always myself. My sex is me as my mind is me, and nobody will make me feel shame about it.

It is long since I came to that decision. But I remember how much freer I felt, how much warmer and more sympathetic towards people. I had no longer anything to hide from them, no longer anything to be in a funk about, lest they should find it out. My sex was me, like my mind and my spirit. And the other man's sex was him, as his mind was him, and his spirit was him. And the woman's sex was her, as her mind and spirit were herself too. And once this quiet admission is made, it is wonderful how much deeper and more real the human sympathy flows. And it is wonderful how difficult the admission is to make, for man or woman: the tacit, natural admission, that allows the natural warm flow of the blood-sympathy, without repression amid holding back.

I remember when I was a very young man I was enraged when with a woman, if I was reminded of her sexual actuality. I only wanted to be aware of her personality, her mind and spirit. The other had to be fiercely shut out. Some part of the natural sympathy for a woman had to be shut away, cut off. There was a mutilation in the relationship all the time.

Now, in spite of the hostility of society, I have learned a little better. Now I know that a woman is her sexual self too, and I can feel the normal sex sympathy with her. And this silent sympathy is utterly different from desire or anything rampant or lurid. If I can really sympathise with a woman in her sexual self, it is just a form of warm-heartedness and compassionateness, the most natural life-flow in the world. And it may be a woman of seventy-five, or a child of two, it is the same. But our civilisation, with its horrible fear and funk and repression and bullying, has almost destroyed the natural flow of common sympathy between men and men, and men and women.

And it is this that I want to restore into life: just the natural warm flow of common sympathy between man and man, man and woman. Many people hate it, of course. Many men hate it that one should tacitly take them for sexual, physical men instead of mere social and mental personalities. Many women hate it the same. Some, the worst, are in a state of rabid funk. The papers call me "lurid" and a "dirty-minded fellow." One woman, evidently a woman of education and means, wrote to me out of the blue: "You, who are a mixture of the missing-link and the chimpanzee, etc."—and told me my name stank in men's nostrils: though, since she was Mrs. Something or other, she might have said women's nostrils.—And these people think they are being perfectly well-bred and perfectly "right." They are safe inside the convention, which also agrees that we are sexless creatures and social beings merely, cold and bossy and assertive, cowards safe inside a convention.

Now I am one of the least lurid mortals, and I don't at all mind being likened to a chimpanzee. If there is one thing I don't like it is cheap and promiscuous sex. If there is one thing I insist on it is that sex is a delicate, vulnerable, vital thing that you mustn't fool with. If there is one thing I deplore it is heartless sex. Sex must be a real flow, a real flow of sympathy, generous and warm, and not a trick thing, or a moment's excitation, or a mere bit of bullying.

And if I write a book about the sex relations of a man and a woman, it is not because I want all men and women to begin having indiscriminate lovers and love affairs, off the reel. All this horrid scramble of love affairs and prostitution is only part of the funk, bravado and *doing it on purpose*. And bravado and *doing it on purpose* is just as unpleasant and hurtful as repression, just as much a sign of secret fear.

What you have to do is to get out of the state of funk, sex funk. And to do so, you've got to be perfectly decent, and you have to accept sex fully in the consciousness. Accept sex in the consciousness, and let the normal physical awareness come back, between you and other people. Be tacitly and simply aware of the sexual being in every man and woman, child and animal; and unless the man or woman is a bully, be sympathetically aware. It is the most important thing just now, this gentle physical awareness. It keeps us tender and alive at a moment when the great danger is to go brittle, hard, and in some way dead.

Accept the sexual, physical being of yourself and of every other creature. Don't be afraid of it. Don't be afraid of the physical functions. Don't be afraid of the so-called obscene words. There is nothing wrong with the words. It is your fear that makes them bad, your needless fear. It is your fear which cuts you off physically even from your nearest and dearest. And when men and women are physically cut off, they become at last dangerous, bullying, cruel. Conquer the fear of sex, and restore the natural flow. Restore even the so-called obscene words, which are part of the natural flow. If you don't, if you don't put back a bit of the old warmth into life, there is savage disaster ahead.

One has to eat one's own words. I remember I used to assert, perhaps I even wrote it: Everything that can possibly be painted has been painted, every brush-stroke that can possibly be laid on canvas has been laid on. The visual arts are at a dead end. Then suddenly, at the age of forty, I begin painting myself and am fascinated.

Still, going through the Paris picture shops this year of grace, and seeing the Dufys and Chiricos, etc., and the Japanese Ito with his wish-wash nudes with pearl-button eyes, the same weariness comes over one. They are all so would-be, they make such efforts. They at least have nothing to paint. In the midst of them a graceful Fricsz flower-piece, or a blotting-paper Laurencin, seems a masterpiece. At least here is a bit of *natural* expression in paint. Trivial enough, when compared to the big painters, but still, as far as they go, real.

What about myself, then! What am I doing, bursting into paint? I am a writer, I ought to stick to ink. I have found my medium of expression; why, at the age of forty, should I suddenly want to try another?

Things happen, and we have no choice. If Maria Huxley hadn't come rolling up to our house near Florence with four rather large canvases, one of which she had busted, and presented them to me because they had been abandoned in her house, I might never have started in on a real picture in my life. But those nice stretched canvases were too tempting. We had been painting doors and window-frames in the house, so there was a little stock of oil, turps and colour in powder, such as one buys from an Italian *drogheria*. There were several brushes for house-painting. There was a canvas on which the unknown owner had made a start—mud-grey, with the beginnings of a red-haired man. It was a grimy and ugly beginning, and the young man who had made it had wisely gone no further. He certainly had had no inner compulsion: nothing in him, as far as paint was concerned, or if there was anything in him, it had stayed in, and only a bit of the mud-grey "group" had come out.

So for the sheer fun of covering a surface and obliterating that mud-grey, I sat on the floor with the canvas propped against a chair—and with my house-paint brushes and colours in little casseroles, I disappeared into that canvas. It is to me the most exciting moment— when you have a blank canvas and a big brush full of wet colour, and you plunge. It is just like diving into a pond—then you start frantically to swim. So far as I am concerned, it is like swimming in a baffling current and being rather frightened and very thrilled, gasping and striking out for all you're worth. The knowing eye watches sharp as a needle; but the picture comes clean out of instinct, intuition and sheer physical action. Once the instinct and intuition gets into the brush-tip, the picture *happens*, if is to be a picture at all.

At least, so my first picture happened—the one I have called A *HOLY FAMILY*. In a couple of hours there it all was, man, woman, child, blue shirt, red shawl, pale room —all in the rough, but, as far as I am concerned, a picture. The struggling comes later. But the picture itself comes in the first rush, or not at all. It is only when the picture has come into being that one can struggle and make it *grow* to completion.

Ours is an excessively conscious age. We *know* so much, we feel so little. I have lived enough among painters and around studios to have had all the theories— and how contradictory they are — rammed down my throat. A man has to have a gizzard like an ostrich to digest all the brass-tacks and wire nails of modern art theories. Perhaps all the theories, the utterly indigestible theories, like nails in an ostrich's gizzard, do indeed help to grind small and make digestible all the emotional and aesthetic pabulum that lies in an artist's soul. But they can serve no other purpose. Not even corrective. The modern theories of art make real pictures impossible. You only get these expositions, critical ventures in paint, and fantastic negations. And the bit of fantasy that may lie in the negation — as in a Dufy or a Chirico—is just the bit that has escaped theory and perhaps saves the picture. Theorize, theorize all you like — but when you start to paint, shut your theoretic eyes and go for it with instinct and intuition.

Myself, I have always loved pictures, the pictorial art. I never went to an art school, I have had only one real lesson in painting in all my life. But of course I was thoroughly drilled in "drawing," the solid-geometry sort, and the plaster-cast sort, and the pin-wire sort. I think the solid-geometry sort, with all the elementary laws of perspective, was valuable. But the pin-wire sort and the plaster-cast light-and-shade sort was harmful. Plaster-casts and pin-wire outlines were always so repulsive to me, I quite early decided I "couldn't draw." I couldn't draw, so I could never do anything on my own. When I did paint jugs of flowers or bread and potatoes, or cottages in a lane, copying from Nature, the result wasn't very thrilling. Nature was more or less of a plaster-cast to me — those plaster-cast heads of Minerva or figures of Dying Gladiators which so unnerved me as a youth. The "object," be it what it might, was always slightly repulsive to me once I sat down in front of it, to paint it. So, of course, I decided I couldn't really paint. Perhaps I can't. But I verily believe I can make pictures, which is to me all that matters in this respect. The art of painting consists in making pictures — and so many artists accomplish canvases without coming within miles of painting a picture.

I learnt to paint from copying other pictures — usually reproductions, sometimes even photographs. When I was a boy, how I concentrated over it! Copying some perfectly worthless scene reproduction in some magazine. I worked with almost dry water-colour, stroke by stroke, covering half a square-inch at a time, each square-inch perfect and completed, proceeding in a kind of mosaic advance, with no idea at all of laying on a broad wash. Hours and hours of intense concentration, inch by inch progress, in a method entirely wrong — and yet those copies of mine managed, when they were finished, to have a certain something that delighted me: a certain glow of life, which was beauty to me. A picture lives with the life you put into it. If you put no life into it—no thrill, no concentration of delight or exaltation of visual discovery—then the picture is dead, like so many canvases, no matter how much thorough and scientific work is put into it. Even if you only copy a purely banal reproduction of an old bridge, some sort of keen, delighted awareness of the old bridge or of its atmosphere, or the image it has kindled inside you, can go over on to the paper and give a certain touch of life to a banal conception.

It needs a certain purity of spirit to be an artist, of any sort. The motto which should be written over every School of Art is: "Blessed are the pure in spirit, for theirs is the kingdom of heaven." But by "pure in spirit" we mean pure in spirit. An artist may be a profligate and, from the social point of view, a scoundrel. But if he can paint a nude woman, or a couple of apples, so that they are a living image, then he was pure in spirit, and, for the time being, his was the kingdom of heaven.

This is the beginning of all art, visual or literary or musical: be pure in spirit. It isn't the same as goodness. It is much more difficult and nearer the divine. The divine isn't only good, it is all things.

One may see the divine in natural objects; I saw it today, in the frail, lovely little camellia flowers on long stems, here on the bushy and splendid flower-stalls of the Ramblas in Barcelona. They were different from the usual fat camellias, more like gardenias, poised delicately, and I saw them like a vision. So now, I could paint them. But if I had bought a handful, and started in to paint them "from nature," then I should have lost them. By staring at them I should have lost them. I have learnt by experience. It is personal experience only. Some men can only get at a vision by staring themselves blind, as it were: like Cézanne; but staring kills my vision. That's why I could never "draw" at school. One was supposed to draw what one stared at.

The only thing one can look into, stare into, and see only vision, is the vision itself: the visionary image. That is why I am glad I never had any training but the self-imposed training of copying other men 's pictures. As I grew more ambitious, I copied Leader's landscapes, and Frank Brangwyn's cartoon-like pictures, then Peter de Wint and Girtin water-colours. I can never be sufficiently grateful for the series of English water-colour painters, published by the Studio in eight parts, when I was a youth. I had only six of the eight parts, but they were invaluable to me. I copied them with the greatest joy, and found some of them extremely difficult. Surely I put as much labour into copying from those water-colour reproductions as most modern art students put into all their years of study. And I had enormous profit from it. I not only acquired a considerable technical skill in handling water-colour—let any man try copying the English water-colour artists, from Paul Sandby and Peter de Wint and Girtin, up to Frank Brangwyn and the impressionists like Brabazon, and he will see how much skill he requires — but also I developed my visionary awareness. And I believe one can only develop one's visionary awareness by close contact with the vision itself: that is, by knowing pictures, real vision pictures, and by dwelling on them, and really dwelling in them. It is a great delight, to dwell in a picture. But it needs a purity of spirit, a sloughing of vulgar sensation and vulgar interest, and above all, vulgar contact, that few people know how to perform. Oh, if art schools only taught that! If, instead of saying: This drawing is wrong, incorrect, badly drawn, etc., they would say: Isn't this in bad taste? isn't it insensitive? Isn't that an insentient curve with none of the delicate awareness of life in it?—But art is treated all wrong. It is treated as if it were a science, which it is not. Art is a form of religion, minus the Ten Commandment business, which is sociological. Art is a form of supremely delicate awareness and atonement — meaning at-oneness, the state of being at one with the object. But is the great atonement in delight? —for I can never look on art save as a form of delight.

All my lie I have from time to time gone back to paint, because it gave me a form of delight that words can never give. Perhaps the joy in words goes deeper and is for that reason more unconscious. The conscious delight is certainly stronger in paint. I have gone back to paint for real pleasure — and by paint I mean copying, copying either in oils or waters. I think the greatest pleasure I ever got came from copying Fra Angelico's *FLIGHT INTO EGYPT* and Lorenzetti's big picture of the Thebaid, in each case working from photographs and putting in my own colour; or perhaps even more a Carpaccio picture in Venice. Then I really learned what life, what powerful life has been put into every curve, every motion of a great picture. Purity of spirit, sensitive awareness, intense eagerness to portray an inward vision, how it all comes. The English water-colours are frail in comparison —and the French and the Flemings are shallow. The great Rembrandt I never tried to copy, though I loved him intensely, even more than I do now; and Rubens I never tried, though I always liked him so much, only he seemed so spread out. But I have copied Peter de Hooch, and Vandyck, and others that I forget. Yet none of them gave me the deep thrill of the Italians, Carpaccio, or the lovely *DEATH OF PROCRIS* in the National Gallery, or that *WEDDING* with the scarlet legs, in the Uffizi, or a Giotto from Padua. I must have made many copies in my day, and got endless joy out of them.

Then suddenly, by having a blank canvas, I discovered I could make a picture myself. That is the point, to make a picture on a blank canvas. And I was forty before I had the real courage to try. Then it became an orgy, making pictures.

I have learnt now not to work from objects, not to have models, not to have a technique. Sometimes, for a water-colour, I have worked direct from a model. But it always spoils the picture. I can only use a model when the picture is already made; then I can look at the model to get some detail which the vision failed me with, or to modify something which I feel is unsatisfactory and I don 't know why. Then a model may give a suggestion. But at the beginning, a model only spoils the picture. The picture must all come out of the artist's inside, awareness of forms and figures. We can call it memory, but it is more than memory. It is the image as it lives in the consciousness, alive like a vision, but unknown. I believe many people have, in their consciousness, living images that would give them the greatest joy to bring out. But they don't know how to go about it. And teaching only hinders them.

To me, a picture has delight in it, or it isn't a picture. The saddest pictures of Piero della Francesca or Sodoma or Goya, have still that indescribable delight that goes with the real picture. Modern critics talk a lot about ugliness, but I never saw a real picture that seemed to me ugly. The theme may be ugly, there may be a terrifying, distressing, almost repulsive quality, as in El Greco. Yet it is all, in some strange way, swept up in the delight of a picture. No artist, even the gloomiest, ever painted a picture without the curious delight in image-making.

PORNOGRAPHY AND OBSCENITY

What they are depends, as usual, entirely on the individual. What is pornography to one man is the laughter of genius to another.

The word itself, we are told, means 'pertaining to harlots'—the graph of the harlot. But nowadays, what is a harlot? If she was a woman who took money from a man in return for going to bed with him—really, most wives sold themselves, in the past, and plenty of harlots gave themselves, when they felt like it, for nothing. If a woman hasn't got a tiny streak of a harlot in her, she's a dry stick as a rule. And probably most harlots had somewhere a streak of womanly generosity. Why be so cut and dried? The law is a dreary thing, and its judgments have nothing to do with life.

The same with the word *obscene*: nobody knows what it means. Suppose it were derived from *obscena*: that which might not be represented on the stage: how much further are you? None! What is obscene to Tom is not obscene to Lucy or Joe, and really, the meaning of a word has to wait for majorities to decide it. If a play shocks ten people in an audience, and doesn't shock the remaining five hundred, then it is obscene to ten and innocuous to five hundred; hence the play is not obscene, by majority. But *Hamlet* shocked all the Cromwellian Puritans, and shocks nobody to-day, and some of Aristophanes shocks everybody to-day, and didn't galvanize the later Greeks at all, apparently. Man is a changeable beast, and words change their meanings with him, and things are not what they seemed, and what's what becomes what isn't, and if we think we know where we are it's only because we are so rapidly being translated to somewhere else. We have to leave everything to the majority, everything to the majority, everything to the mob, the mob, the mob. They know what is obscene and what isn't, they do. If the lower ten million doesn't know better than the upper ten men, then there's something wrong with mathematics. Take a vote on it! Show hands, and prove it by count! Vox populi, vox Dei. Odi profanum vulgus! Profanum vulgus.

So it comes down to this: if you are talking to the mob, the meaning of your words is the mob-meaning, decided by majority. As somebody wrote to me: the American law on obscenity is very plain, and America is going to enforce the law. Quite, my dear, quite, quite, quite! The mob knows all about obscenity. Mild little words that rhyme with spit or farce are the height of obscenity. Supposing a printer put 'h' in the place of 'p', by mistake, in that mere word spit? Then the great American public knows that this man has committed an obscenity, an indecency, that his act was lewd, and as a compositor he was pornographical. You can't tamper with the great public, British or American. Vox populi, vox Dei, don't you know. If you don't we'll let you know it. At the same time, this vox Dei shouts with praise over moving-pictures and books and newspaper accounts that seem, to a sinful nature like mine, completely disgusting and obscene. Like a real prude and Puritan, I have to look the other way. When obscenity becomes mawkish, which is its palatable form for the public, and when the Vox populi, vox Dei, is hoarse with sentimental indecency, then I have to steer away, like a Pharisee, afraid of being contaminated. There is a certain kind of sticky universal pitch that I refuse to touch.

So again, it comes down to this: you accept the majority, the mob, and its decisions, or you don't. You bow down before the Vox populi, vox Dei, or you plug your ears not to hear its obscene howl. You perform your antics to please the vast public, Deus ex machina, or you refuse to perform for the public at all, unless now and then to pull its elephantine and ignominious leg.

When it comes to the meaning of anything, even the simplest word, then you must pause. Because there are two great categories of meaning, forever separate. There is mob-meaning, and there is individual meaning. Take even the word *bread*. The mob-meaning is merely: stuff made with white flour into loaves that you eat. But take the individual meaning of the word bread: the white, the brown, the corn-pone, the home-made, the smell of bread just out of the oven, the crust, the crumb, the unleavened bread, the shew-bread, the staff of life, sour-dough bread, cottage loaves, French bread, Viennese bread, black bread, a yesterday's loaf, rye, Graham, barley, rolls, Bretzeln, Kringeln, scones, damper, matsen—there is no end to it all, and the word bread will take you to the ends of time and space, and far-off down avenues of memory. But this is individual. The word bread will take the individual off on his own journey, and its meaning will be his own meaning, based

516

on his own genuine imaginative reactions. And when a word comes to us in its individual character, and starts in us the individual responses, it is a great pleasure to us. The American advertisers have discovered this, and some of the cunningest American literature is to be found in advertisements of soapsuds, for example. These advertisements are *almost* prose-poems. They give the word soapsuds a bubbly, shiny individual meaning, which is very skilfully poetic, would, perhaps, be quite poetic to the mind which could forget that the poetry was bait on a hook.

Business is discovering the individual, dynamic meaning of words, and poetry is losing it. Poetry more and more tends to far-fetch its word-meanings, and this results once again in mob-meanings, which arouse only a mob-reaction in the individual. For every man has a mob-self and an individual self in varying proportions. Some men are almost all mob-self, incapable of imaginative individual responses. The worst specimens of mob-self are usually to be found in the professions, lawyers, professors, clergymen and so on. The business man, much maligned, has a tough outside mob-self, and a scared, floundering, yet still alive individual self. The public, which is feeble-minded like an idiot, will never be able to preserve its individual reactions from the tricks of the exploiter. The public is always exploited and always will be exploited. The methods of exploitation merely vary. To-day the public is tickled into laying the golden egg. With imaginative words and individual meanings it is tricked into giving the great goose-cackle of mob-acquiescence. Vox populi, vox Dei. It has always been so, and will always be so. Why? Because the public has not enough wit to distinguish between mob-meanings and individual meanings. The mass is forever vulgar, because it can't distinguish between its own original feelings and feelings which are diddled into existence by the exploiter. The public is always profane, because it is controlled from the outside, by the trickster, and never from the inside, by its own sincerity. The mob is always obscene, because it is always secondhand.

Which brings us back to our subject of pornography and obscenity. The reaction to any word may be, in any individual, either a mob-reaction or an individual reaction. It is up to the individual to ask himself: Is my reaction individual, or am I merely reacting from my mob-self?

When it comes to the so-called obscene words, I should say that hardly one person in a million escapes mob-reaction. The first reaction is almost sure to be mob-reaction, mob-indignation, mob-condemnation. And the mob gets no further. But the real individual has second thoughts and says: am I really shocked? Do I *really* feel outraged and indignant? And the answer of any individual is bound to be: No, I am not shocked, not outraged, nor indignant. I know the word, and take it for what it is, and I am not going to be jockeyed into making a mountain out of a mole-hill, not for all the law in the world.

Now if the use of a few so-called obscene words will startle man or woman out of a mob-habit into an individual state, well and good. And word prudery is so universal a mob-habit that it is time we were startled out of it.

But still we have only tackled obscenity, and the problem of pornography goes even deeper. When a man is startled into his individual self he still may not be able to know, inside himself whether Rabelais is or is not pornographic: and over Aretino or even Boccaccio he may perhaps puzzle in vain, torn between different emotions.

One essay on pornography, I remember, comes to the conclusion that pornography in art is that which is calculated to arouse sexual desire, or sexual excitement. And stress is laid on the fact, whether the author or artist *intended* to arouse feelings. It is the old vexed question of intention, become so dull to-day, when we know how strong and influential our unconscious intentions are. And why a man should be held guilty of his conscious intentions, and innocent of his unconscious intentions, I don't know, since every man is more made up of unconscious intentions than of conscious ones. I am what I am, not merely what I think I am.

However! We take it, I assume, that *pornography* is something base, something unpleasant. In short, we don't like it. And why don't we like it? Because it arouses sexual feelings?

I think not. No matter how hard we may pretend otherwise, most of us rather like a moderate rousing of our sex. It warms us, stimulates us like sunshine on a grey day. After a century or two of Puritanism, this is still true of most people. Only the mob-habit of condemning any form of sex is too strong to let us admit it naturally. And there are, of course, many people who are genuinely repelled by the simplest and most natural stirrings of sexual feeling. But these people are perverts who have fallen into hatred of their fellow men: thwarted, disappointed, unfulfilled people, of whom, alas, our civilization contains so many. And they nearly always enjoy some unsimple and unnatural form of sex excitement, secretly.

Even quite advanced art critics would try to make us believe that any picture or book which had 'sex appeal' was *ipso facto* a bad book or picture. This is just canting hypocrisy. Half the great poems, pictures, music, stories of the whole world are great by virtue of the beauty of their sex appeal. Titian or Renoir, the *Song of Solomon* or *Jane Eyre*, Mozart or *Annie Laurie*, the loveliness is all interwoven with sex appeal, sex stimulus, call it what you will. Even Michael Angelo, who rather hated sex, can't help filling the Cornucopia with phallic acorns. Sex is a very powerful, beneficial and necessary stimulus in human life, and we are all grateful when we feel its warm, natural flow through us, like a form of sunshine.

So we can dismiss the idea that sex appeal in art is pornography. It may be so to the grey Puritan, but the grey Puritan is a sick man, soul and body sick, so why should we bother about his hallucinations? Sex appeal, of course, varies enormously. There are endless different kinds, and endless degrees of each kind. Perhaps it may be argued that a mild degree of sex appeal is not pornographical, whereas a high degree is. But this is a fallacy. Boccaccio at his hottest seems to me less pornographical than *Pamela* or *Clarissa Harlowe* or even *Jane Eyre*, or a host of modern books or films which pass uncensored. At the same time Wagner's *Tristan and Isolde* seems to me very near to pornography, and so, even, do some quite popular Christian hymns.

What is it, then? It isn't a question of sex appeal, merely: nor even a question of deliberate intention on the part of the author or artist to arouse sexual excitement. Rabelais sometimes had a deliberate intention, so in a different way did Boccaccio. And I'm sure poor Charlotte Brontë, or the authoress of *The Sheik* did *not* have any deliberate intention to stimulate sex feelings in the reader. Yet I find *Jane Eyre* verging towards pornography and Boccaccio seems to me always fresh and wholesome.

The late British Home Secretary, who prides himself on being a very sincere Puritan, grey, grey in every fibre, said with indignant sorrow in one of his outbursts on improper books: '—and these two young people, who had been perfectly pure up till that time, after reading this book went and had sexual intercourse together!!!' *One up to them!* is all we can answer. But the grey Guardian of British Morals seemed to think that if they had murdered one another, or worn each other to rags of nervous prostration, it would have been much better. The grey disease!

Then what is pornography, after all this? It isn't sex appeal or sex stimulus in art. It isn't even a deliberate intention on the part of the artist to arouse or to excite sexual feelings. There's nothing wrong with sexual feelings in themselves, so long as they are straightforward and not sneaking or sly. The right sort of sex stimulus is invaluable to human daily life. Without it the world grows grey. I would give everybody the gay Renaissance stories to read, they would help to shake off a lot of grey self importance, which is our modern civilized disease.

But even I would censor genuine pornography, rigorously. It would not be very difficult. In the first place, genuine pornography is almost always underworld, it doesn't come into the open. In the second, you can recognize it by the insult it offers, invariably, to sex, and to the human spirit.

Pornography is the attempt to insult sex, to do dirt on it. This is unpardonable. Take the very lowest instance, the picture post-card sold underhand, by the underworld, in most cities. What I have seen of them have been of an ugliness to make you cry. The insult to the human body, the to a vital human relationship! Ugly and cheap they make the human nudity, ugly and degraded they make the sexual act, trivial and cheap and nasty.

It is the same with the books they sell in the underworld. They are either so ugly they make you ill, or so fatuous you can't imagine anybody but a cretin or a moron reading them, or writing them.

It is the same with the dirty limericks that people tell after dinner, or the dirty stories one hears commercial travellers telling each other in a smoke-room. Occasionally there is a really funny one, that redeems a great deal. But usually they are just ugly and repellent, and the so-called 'humour' is just a trick of doing dirt on sex.

Now the human nudity of a great many modern people is just ugly and degraded, and the sexual act between modern people is just the same, merely ugly and degrading. But this is nothing to be proud of. It is the catastrophe of our civilization. I am sure no other civilization, not even the Roman, has showed such a vast proportion of ignominious and degraded nudity, and ugly, squalid dirty sex. Because no other civilization has driven sex into the underworld, and nudity to the W.C.

The intelligent young, thank heaven, seem determined to alter in these two respects. They are rescuing their young nudity from the stuffy, pornographical hole-and-corner underworld of their elders and they refuse to sneak about the sexual relation. This is a change the elderly grey ones of course deplore, but it is in fact a very great change for the better, and a real revolution.

But it is amazing how strong is the will in ordinary vulgar people, to do dirt on sex. It was one of my fond illusions, when I was young, that the ordinary healthy-seeming sort of men, in railway carriages, or the smoke-room of an hotel or a pullman, were healthy in their feelings and had a wholesome rough devil-may-care attitude toward sex. All wrong! All wrong! Experience teaches that common individuals of this sort have a disgusting attitude toward sex, a disgusting contempt of it, a disgusting desire to insult it. If such fellows have intercourse with a woman, they triumphantly feel that they have done her dirt, and now she is lower, cheaper, more contemptible than she was before.

It is individuals of this sort that tell dirty stories, carry indecent picture post-cards, and know the indecent books. This is the great pornographical class—the really common men-in-the-street and women-in-the-street. They have as great a hate and contempt of sex as the greyest Puritan, and when an appeal is made to them, they are always on the side of the angels. They insist that a film-heroine shall be a neuter, a sexless thing of washed-out purity. They insist that real sex-feeling shall only be shown by the villain or villainess, low lust. They find a Titian or a Renoir really indecent, and they don't want their wives and daughters to see it.

Why? Because they have the grey disease of sex-hatred, coupled with the yellow disease of dirt lust. The sex functions and the excrementory functions in the human body work so close together, yet they are, so to speak, utterly different in direction. Sex is a creative flow, the excrementory flow is towards dissolution, de-creation, if we may use such a word. In the really healthy human being the distinction between the two is instant, our profoundest instincts are perhaps our instincts of opposition between the two flows.

But in the degraded human being the deep instincts have gone dead, and then the two flows become identical. *This* is the secret of really vulgar and of pornographical people: the sex flow and the excrement flow is the same thing to them. It happens when the psyche deteriorates, and the profound controlling instincts collapse. Then sex is dirt and dirt is sex, and sexual excitement becomes a playing with dirt, and any sign of sex in a woman becomes a show of her dirt. This is the condition of the common, vulgar human being whose name is legion, and who lifts his voice and it is the Vox populi, vox Dei. And this is the source of all pornography.

And for this reason we must admit that *Jane Eyre* or Wagner's *Tristan* are much nearer to pornography than is Boccaccio. Wagner and Charlotte Bronte were both in the state where the strongest instincts have collapsed, and sex has become something slightly obscene, to be wallowed in, but despised. Mr. Rochester's sex passion is not 'respectable' till Mr. Rochester is burned, blinded, disfigured and reduced to helpless dependence. Then, thoroughly humbled and humiliated, it may be merely admitted. All the previous titillations are slightly indecent, as in *Pamela* or *The Mill on the Floss* or *Anna Karenina*. As soon as there is sex excitement with a desire to spite the sexual feeling, to humiliate it and degrade it, the element of pornography enters.

For this reason, there is an element of pornography in nearly all nineteenth-century literature, and very many so-called pure people have a nasty pornographical side to them, and never was the pornographical appetite stronger than it is to-day. It is a sign of a diseased condition of the body politic. But the way to treat the disease is to come out into the open with sex and sex stimulus. The real pornographer truly dislikes Boccaccio, because the fresh healthy naturalness of the Italian storyteller makes the modern pornographical shrimp feel the dirty worm he is. To-day Boccaccio should be given to everybody young or old, to read if they like. Only a natural fresh openness about sex will do any good, now we are being swamped by secret or semi-secret pornography. And perhaps the Renaissance story-tellers, Boccaccio, Lasca and the rest, are the best antidote we can find now, just as more plasters of Puritanism are the most harmful remedy we can resort to.

The whole question of pornography seems to me a question of secrecy. Without secrecy there would be no pornography. But secrecy and modesty are two utterly different things. Secrecy has always an element of fear in it, amounting very often to hate. Modesty is gentle and reserved. Today, modesty is thrown to the winds, even in the presence of the grey guardians. But secrecy is hugged, being a vice in itself. And the attitude of the grey ones is: Dear young ladies, you may abandon all modesty, so long as you hug your dirty little secret.

This 'dirty little secret' has become infinitely precious to the mob of people to-day. It is a kind of hidden sore or inflammation which, when rubbed or scratched, gives off sharp thrills that seem delicious. So the dirty little secret is rubbed and scratched more and more, till it becomes more and more secretly inflamed, and the nervous and psychic health of the individual is more and more impaired. One might easily say that half the love-novels and half the love-films to-day depend entirely for their success on the secret rubbing of the dirty little secret. You can call this sex-excitement if you like, but it is sex-excitement of a secretive, furtive sort, quite special. The plain and simple excitement, quite open and wholesome, which you find in some Boccaccio stories is not for a minute to be confused with the furtive excitement aroused by rubbing the dirty little secret in all secrecy in modern best-sellers. This furtive, sneaking, cunning rubbing of an inflamed spot in the imagination is the very quick of modern pornography, and it is a beastly and very dangerous thing. You can't so easily expose it, because of its very furtiveness and its sneaking cunning. So the cheap and popular modern love-novel and love-film flourishes and is even praised by moral guardians, because you get the sneaking thrill fumbling under all the purity of dainty underclothes, without one single gross word to let you know what is happening.

Without secrecy there would be no pornography. But if pornography is the result of sneaking secrecy, what is the result of pornography? What is the effect on the individual?

The effect on the individual is manifold, and always pernicious. But one effect is perhaps inevitable. The pornography of to-day, whether it be the pornography of the rubber-goods shop or the pornography of the popular novel, film and play, is an invariable stimulant to the vice of self-abuse, onanism, masturbation, call it what you will. In young or old, man or woman, boy or girl, modern pornography is a direct provocative of masturbation. It cannot be otherwise. When the grey ones wail that the young man and the young woman went and had sexual intercourse, they are bewailing the fact that the young man and the young woman didn't go separately and masturbate. Sex must go somewhere, especially in young people. So, in our glorious civilization, it goes in masturbation. And the mass of our popular literature, the bulk of our popular amusements just exists to provoke masturbation. Masturbation is the one thoroughly secret act of the human being, more secret even than excrementation. It is the one functional result of sex-secrecy, and it is stimulated and provoked by our glorious popular literature of pretty pornography, which rubs on the dirty secret without letting you know what is happening.

Now I have heard men, teachers and clergymen, commend masturbation as the solution of an otherwise insoluble sex problem. This at least is honest. The sex problem is there, and you can't just will it away. There it is, and under the ban of secrecy and taboo in mother and father, teacher, friend and foe, it has found its own solution, the solution of masturbation.

But what about the solution? Do we accept it? Do all the grey ones of this world accept it? If so, they must now accept it openly. We can none of us pretend any longer to be blind to the fact of masturbation, in young and old, man and woman. The moral guardians who are prepared to censor all open and plain portrayal of sex must now be made to give their only justification: We prefer that the people shall masturbate. If this preference is open and declared, then the existing forms of censorship are justified. If the moral guardians prefer that the people shall masturbate, then their present behaviour is correct, and popular amusements are as they should be. If sexual intercourse is deadly sin, and masturbation is comparatively pure and harmless, then all is well. Let things continue as they now are.

Is masturbation so harmless, though? Is it even comparatively pure and harmless? Not to my thinking. In the young, a certain amount of masturbation is inevitable, but not therefore natural. I think, there is no boy or girl who masturbates without feeling a sense of shame, anger and futility. Following the excitement comes the shame, anger, humiliation and the sense of futility. This sense of futility and humiliation deepens as the years go on, into a suppressed rage, because of the impossibility of escape. The one thing that it seems impossible to escape from, once the habit is formed, is masturbation. It goes on and on, on into old age, in spite of marriage or love affairs or anything else. And it always carries this secret feeling of futility and humiliation, futility and humiliation. And this is, perhaps, the deepest and most dangerous cancer of our civilization. Instead of being a comparatively pure and harmless vice, masturbation is certainly the most dangerous sexual vice that a society can be afflicted with, in the long run. Comparatively pure it may be—purity being what it is. But harmless!!!

The great danger of masturbation lies in its merely exhaustive nature. In sexual intercourse, there is a give and take. A new stimulus enters as the native stimulus departs. Something quite new is added as the old surcharge is removed. And this is so in all sexual intercourse where two creatures are concerned, even in the homosexual intercourse. But in masturbation there is nothing but loss. There is no reciprocity. There is merely the spending away of a certain force, and no return. The body remains, in a sense, a corpse, after the act of self-abuse. There is no change, only deadening. There is what we call dead loss. And this is not the case in any act of sexual intercourse between two people. Two people may destroy one another in sex. But they cannot just produce the null effect of masturbation.

The only positive effect of masturbation is that it seems to release a certain mental energy, in some people. But it is mental energy which manifests itself always in the same way, in a vicious circle of analysis and impotent criticism, or else a vicious circle of false and easy sympathy, sentimentalities. The sentimentalism and the niggling analysis, often self-analysis, of most of our modern literature is a sign of self-abuse. It is the manifestation of masturbation, the sort of conscious activity stimulated by masturbation, whether male or female. The outstanding feature of such consciousness is that there is no real object, there is only subject. This is just the same whether it be a novel or a work of science. The author never escapes from himself, he pads along within the vicious circle of himself. There is hardly a writer living who gets out of the vicious circle of himself—or a painter either. Hence the lack of creation, and the stupendous amount of production. It is a masturbation result, within the vicious circle of the self. It is self-absorption made public.

And of course the process is exhaustive. The real masturbation of Englishmen began only in the nineteenth century. It has continued with an increasing emptying of the real vitality and the real *being* of men, till now people are little more than shells of people. Most of the responses are dead, most of the awareness is dead, nearly all the constructive activity is dead, and all that remains is a sort of shell, a half-empty creature fatally self-preoccupied and incapable of either giving or taking. Incapable either of giving or taking, in the vital self. And this is masturbation result. Enclosed within the vicious circle of the self, with no vital contacts outside, the self becomes emptier and emptier, till it is almost a nullus, a nothingness.

But null or nothing as it may be, it still hangs on to the dirty little secret, which it must still secretly rub and inflame. Forever the vicious circle. And it has a weird, blind will of its own.

One of my most sympathetic critics wrote: 'If Mr. Lawrence's attitude to sex were adopted, then two things would disappear, the love lyric and the smoking-room story.' And this, I think, is true. But it depends on which love-lyric he means. If it is the: *Who is Sylvia, what is she?*—then it may just as well disappear. All that pure and noble and heaven-blessed stuff is only the counterpart to the smoking-room story. *Du bist wie eine Blume!* Jawohl! One can see the elderly gentleman laying his hands on the head of the pure maiden and praying God to keep her forever so pure, so clean and beautiful. Very nice for him! Just pornography! tickling the dirty little secret and rolling his eyes to heaven! He knows perfectly well that if God keeps the maiden so clean and pure and beautiful—in his vulgar sense of clean and pure— for a few more years, then she'll be an unhappy old maid, and not pure nor beautiful at all, only stale and pathetic. Sentimentality is a sure sign of pornography. Why should 'sadness strike through the heart' of the old gentleman, because the maid was pure and beautiful? Anybody but a masturbator would have been glad and would have thought: What a lovely bride for some lucky man!—But no, not the self-enclosed, pornographic masturbator. Sadness has to strike into his beastly heart!— Away with such love-lyrics, we've had too much of their pornographic poison, tickling the dirty little secret and rolling the eyes to heaven.

But if it is a question of the sound love-lyric, *'My love is like a red, red rose—!'* then we are on other ground. My love is like a red, red rose only when she's *not* like a pure, pure lily. And nowadays the pure, pure lilies are mostly festering, anyhow. Away with them and their lyrics. Away with the pure, pure lily lyric, along with the smoking-room story. They are counterparts, and the one is as pornographic as the other. *Du bist wie eine Blume*— is really as pornographic as a dirty story: tickling the dirty little secret and rolling the eyes to heaven. But oh, if only Robert Burns had been accepted for what he is, then love might still have been like a red, red rose.

The vicious circle, the vicious circle! The vicious circle of masturbation! The vicious circle of self-consciousness that is never *fully* self-conscious, never fully and openly conscious, but always harping on the dirty little secret. The vicious circle of secrecy, in parents, teachers, friends—everybody. The specially vicious circle of family. The vast conspiracy of secrecy in the press, and at the same time the endless tickling of the dirty little secret. The endless masturbation! and the endless purity! The vicious circle!

How to get out of it? There is only one way: Away with the secret! No more secrecy! The only way to stop the terrible mental itch about sex is to come out quite simply and naturally into the open with it. It is terribly difficult, for the secret is cunning as a crab. Yet the thing to do is to make a beginning. The man who said to his exasperating daughter: 'My child, the only pleasure I ever had out of you was the pleasure I had in begetting you'— has already done a great deal to release both himself and her from the dirty little secret.

How to get out of the dirty little secret! It is, as matter of fact, extremely difficult for us secretive moderns You can't do it by being wise and scientific about it, like Dr. Marie Stopes: though to be wise and scientific like Dr. Marie Stopes is better than to be utterly hypocritical, like the grey ones. But by being wise and scientific in the serious and earnest manner you only tend to disinfect the dirty little secret, and either kill sex altogether with too much seriousness and intellect, or else leave it a miserable disinfected secret. The unhappy 'free and pure' love of so many people who have taken out the dirty little secret and thoroughly disinfected it with scientific words is apt to be more pathetic even than the common run of dirty-little-secret love. The danger is, that in killing the dirty little secret, you kill dynamic sex altogether, and leave only the scientific and deliberate mechanism.

This is what happens to many of those who become seriously 'free' in their sex, free and pure. They have mentalized sex till it is nothing at all, nothing at all but a mental quantity. And the final result is disaster, every time.

The same is true, in an even greater proportion, of the emancipated bohemians: and very many of the young are bohemian to-day, whether they ever set foot in bohemia or not. But the bohemian is 'sex free'. The dirty little secret is no secret either to him or her. It is, indeed, a most blatantly open question. There is nothing they don't say: everything that can be revealed is revealed. And they do as they wish.

And then what? They have apparently killed the dirty little secret, but somehow, they have killed everything else too. Some of the dirt still sticks perhaps; sex remains still dirty. But the thrill of is gone. Hence the terrible dreariness and depression of modern Bohemia, and the inward mess and emptiness of so many young people to-day. They have killed, they imagine, the dirty little secret. The thrill of secrecy is gone. Some of the dirt remains. And for the rest, depression, inertia, lack of life. For sex is the fountain-head of our energetic life, and now the fountain ceases to flow.

Why? For two reasons. The idealists along the Marie Stopes line, and the young bohemians of today have killed the dirty little secret as far as their personal self goes. But they are still under its dominion socially. In the social world, in the press, in literature, film, theatre, wireless, everywhere purity and the dirty little secret reigns supreme.

At home, at the dinner table, it is just the same. It is the same wherever you go. The young girl, and the young woman is by tacit assumption pure, virgin, sexless. *Du bist wie eine Blume*. She, poor thing, knows quite well that flowers, even lilies, have tippling yellow anthers and a sticky stigma, sex, rolling sex. But to the popular mind flowers are sexless things, and when a girl is told she is like a flower, it means she is sexless and ought to be sexless. She herself knows quite well she isn't sexless and she isn't merely like a flower. But how bear up against the great social lie forced on her? She can't! She succumbs, and the dirty little secret triumphs. She loses her interest in sex, as far as men are concerned, but the vicious circle of masturbation and self-consciousness encloses her even still faster.

This is one of the disasters of young life to-day. Personally, and among themselves, a great many, perhaps a majority of the young people of to-day, have come out into the open with sex and laid salt on the tail of the dirty little secret. And this is a very good thing. But in public, in the social world, the young are still entirely under the shadow of the grey elderly ones. The grey elderly ones belong to the last century, the eunuch century, the century of the mealy-mouthed lie, the century that has tried to destroy humanity, the nineteenth century. All our grey ones are left over from this century. And they rule us. They rule us with the grey, mealy-mouthed, canting lie of that great century of lies which, thank God, we are drifting away from. But they rule us still with the lie, for the lie, in the name of the lie. And they are too heavy and too numerous, the grey ones. It doesn't matter what government it is. They are all grey ones, left over from the last century, the century of mealy-mouthed liars, the century of purity and the dirty little secret.

So there is one cause for the depression of the young; the public reign of the mealy-mouthed lie, purity and the dirty little secret, which they themselves have privately overthrown. Having killed a good deal of the lie in their own private lives, the young are still enclosed and imprisoned within the great public lie of the grey ones. Hence the excess, the extravagance, the hysteria, and then the weakness, the feebleness, the pathetic silliness of the modern youth. They are all in a sort of prison, the prison of a great lie and a society of elderly liars. And this is one of the reasons, perhaps the main reason why the sex-flow is dying out of the young, the real energy is dying away. They are enclosed within a lie, and the sex won't flow. For the length of a complete lie is never more than three generations, and the young are the fourth generation of the nineteenth-century lie.

The second reason why the sex-flow is dying is of course, that the young, in spite of their emancipation, are still enclosed within the vicious circle of self-conscious masturbation. They are thrown back into it, when they try to escape, by the enclosure of the vast public lie of purity and the dirty little secret. The most emancipated bohemians, who swank most about sex, are still utterly self-conscious and enclosed within the narcissus-masturbation circle. They have perhaps less sex even than the grey ones. The whole thing has been driven up into their heads. There isn't even the lurking hole of a dirty little secret. Their sex is more mental than their arithmetic; and as vital physical creatures they are more non-existent than ghosts. The modern bohemian is indeed a kind of ghost, not even narcissus, only the image of narcissus reflected on the face of the audience. The dirty little secret is most difficult to kill. You may put it to death publicly a thousand times, and still it reappears, like a crab, stealthily from under the submerged rocks of the personality. The French, who are supposed to be so open about sex, will perhaps be the last to kill the dirty little secret. Perhaps they don't want to. Anyhow mere publicity won't do it.

You may parade sex abroad, but you will not kill the dirty little secret. You may read all the novels of Marcel Proust, with everything there in all detail. Yet you will not kill the dirty little secret. You will perhaps only make it more cunning. You may even bring about a state of utter indifference and sex-inertia, still without killing the dirty little secret. Or you may be the most wispy and enamoured little Don Juan of modern days, and still the core of your spirit merely be the dirty little secret. That is to say, you will still be in the narcissus-masturbation circle, the vicious circle of self-enclosure. For whenever the dirty little secret exists, it exists as the centre of the vicious circle of masturbation self-enclosure. And whenever you have the vicious circle of masturbation self-enclosure, you have at the core the dirty little secret. And the most high-flown sex-emancipated young people to-day are perhaps the most fatally and nervously enclosed within the masturbation self-enclosure. Nor do they want to get out of it, for there would be nothing left to come out.

But some people surely do want to come out of the awful self-enclosure. To-day, practically everybody is self-conscious and imprisoned in self-consciousness. It is the joyful result of the dirty little secret. Vast numbers of people don't want to come out of the prison of their self-consciousness: they have so little left to come out with. But some people, surely, want to escape this doom of self-enclosure which is the doom of our civilization. There is surely a proud minority that wants once and for all to be free of the dirty little secret.

And the way to do it is, first, to fight the sentimental lie of purity and the dirty little secret wherever you meet it, inside yourself or in the world outside. Fight the great lie of the nineteenth century, which has soaked through our sex and our bones. It means fighting with almost every breath, for the lie is ubiquitous.

Then secondly, in his adventure of self-conciousness a man must come to the limits of himself and become aware of something beyond him. A man must be self-conscious enough to know his own limits, and to be aware of that which surpasses him. What surpasses me is the very urge of life that is within me, and this life urges me to forget myself and to yield to the stirring half-born impulse to smash up the vast lie of the world, and make a new world. If my life is merely to go on in a vicious circle of self-enclosure, masturbating self-consciousness, it is worth nothing to me. If my individual life is to be enclosed within the huge corrupt lie of society to-day, purity and the dirty little secret, then it is worth not much to me. Freedom is a very great reality. But it means, above all things, freedom from lies. It is first, freedom from myself; from the lie of myself, from the lie of my all-importance, even to myself; it is freedom from the self-conscious masturbating thing I am, self-enclosed And second, freedom from the vast lie of the social world, the lie of purity and the dirty little secret. All the other monstrous lies lurk under the cloak of this one primary lie. The monstrous lie of money lurks under the cloak of purity. Kill the purity-lie, and the money-lie will be defenceless.

We have to be sufficiently conscious, and self-conscious, to know our own limits and to be aware of the greater urge within us and beyond us. Then we cease to be primarily interested in ourselves. Then we learn to leave ourselves alone, in all the affective centres: not to force our feelings in any way, and never to force our sex. Then we make the great onslaught on to the outside lie, the inside lie being settled. And that is freedom and the fight for freedom.

The greatest of all lies in the modern world is the lie of purity and the dirty little secret. The grey ones left over from the nineteenth century are the embodiment of this lie. They dominate in society, in the press, in literature, everywhere. And, naturally, they lead the vast mob of the general public along with them.

Which means, of course, perpetual censorship of anything that would militate against the lie of purity and the dirty little secret, and perpetual encouragement of what may be called permissible pornography, pure, but tickling the dirty little secret under the delicate underclothing. The grey ones will pass and will commend floods of evasive pornography, and will suppress every outspoken word.

The law is a mere figment. In his article on the 'Censorship of Books', in the *Nineteenth Century*, Viscount Brentford, the late Home Secretary, says: 'Let it be remembered that the publishing of an obscene book, the issue of an obscene post-card or pornographic photograph—are all offences against the law of the land, and the Secretary of State who is the general authority for the maintenance of law and order most clearly and definitely cannot discriminate between one offence and another in discharge of his duty.'

So he winds up, *ex cathedra* and infallible. But only ten lines above he has written: 'I agree, that if the law were pushed to its logical conclusion, the printing and publication of such books as *The Decameron*, Benvenuto Cellini's *Life*, and Burton's *Arabian Nights* might form the subject of proceedings. But the ultimate sanction of all law is public opinion, and I do not believe for one moment that prosecution in respect of books that have been in circulation for many centuries would command public support.'

Ooray then for public opinion! It only needs that a few more years shall roll. But now we see that the Secretary of State most clearly and definitely *does* discriminate between one offence and another in discharge of his duty. Simple and admitted discrimination on his part! Yet what is this public opinion? Just more lies on the part of the grey ones. They would suppress Benvenuto tomorrow, if they dared. But they would make laughing-stocks of themselves, because *tradition* backs up Benvenuto. It isn't public opinion at all. It is the grey ones afraid of making still bigger fools of themselves. But the case is simple. If the grey ones are going to be backed by a general public, then every new book that would smash the mealy-mouthed lie of the nineteenth century will be suppressed as it appears. Yet let the grey ones beware. The general public is nowadays a very unstable affair, and no longer loves its grey ones so dearly, with their old lie. And there is another public, the small public of the minority, which hates the lie and the grey ones that perpetuate the lie, and which has its own dynamic ideas about pornography and obscenity. You can't fool all the people all the time, even with purity and a dirty little secret.

And this minority public knows well that the books of many contemporary writers, both big and lesser fry, are far more pornographical than the liveliest story in *The Decameron*: because they tickle the dirty little secret and excite to private masturbation, which the wholesome Boccaccio never does. And the minority public knows full well that the most obscene painting on a Greek vase—*Thou still unravished bride of quietness*—is not as pornographical as the close-up kisses on the film, which excite men and women to secret and separate masturbation.

And perhaps one day even the general public will desire to look the thing in the face, and see for itself the difference between the sneaking masturbation pornography of the press, the film, and present-day popular literature, and then the creative portrayals of the sexual impulse that we have in Boccaccio or the Greek vase-paintings or some Pompeian art, and which are necessary for the fulfilment of our consciousness.

As it is, the public mind is to-day bewildered on this point, bewildered almost to idiocy. When the police raided my picture show, they did not in the least know what to take. So they took every picture where the smallest bit of the sex organ of either man or woman showed. Quite regardless of subject or meaning or anything else: they would allow anything, these dainty policemen in a picture show, except the actual sight of a fragment of the human *pudenda*. This was the police test. The dabbing on of a postage stamp—especially a green one that could be called a leaf—would in most cases have been quite sufficient to satisfy this 'public opinion'.

It is, we can only repeat, a condition of idiocy. And if the purity-with-a-dirty-little-secret lie is kept up much longer, the mass of society will really be an idiot, and a dangerous idiot at that. For the public is made up of individuals. And each individual has sex, and is pivoted on sex. And if, with purity and dirty little secrets you drive every individual into the masturbation self-enclosure, and keep him there, then you will produce a state of general idiocy. For the masturbation self-enclosure produces idiots. Perhaps if we are all idiots, we shan't know it. But God preserve us.

PICTURES ON THE WALLS

Whether wall pictures are or are not an essential part of interior decoration in the home seems to be considered debatable. Yet since there is scarcely one house in a thousand which doesn't have them, we may easily conclude that they are, in spite of the snobbism, which pretends to prefer blank walls. The human race loves pictures. Barbarians or civilised, we are all alike, we straightway go to look at a picture if there is a picture to look at. And there are very few of us who wouldn't love to have a perfectly fascinating work hanging in our room, that we could go on looking at, if we could afford it. Instead, unfortunately, as a rule we have only some mediocre thing left over from the past, that hangs on the wall just because we've got it, and it must go somewhere. If only people would be firm about it, and rigorously burn *all* insignificant pictures, frames as well, how much more freely we should breathe indoors. If only people would go round their walls every ten years and say, Now, what about that oil-painting, what about that reproduction, what about that photograph? What do they mean? What do we get from them? Have they any point? Are they worth keeping ?—the answer would almost invariably be No. And then what? Shall we say, Oh, let them stay! They've been there ten years, we might as well leave them !—But that is sheer inertia and death to any freshness in the home. A woman might as well say: I've worn this hat for a year, so I may as well go on wearing it for a few more years.—A house, a home, is only a greater garment, and just as we feel we must renew our clothes and have fresh ones, so we should renew our homes and make them in keeping. Spring cleaning isn't enough. Why do fashions in clothes change? Because, really, we ourselves change, in the slow metamorphosis of time. If we imagine ourselves now in the clothes we wore six years ago, we shall see that it is impossible. We are, in some way, different persons now, and our clothes express our different personality.

And so should the home. It should change with us, as we change. Not so quickly as our clothes change, because it is not so close in contact. More slowly, but just as inevitably, the home should change around us. And the change should be more rapid in the more decorative scheme of the room: pictures, curtains, cushions; and slower in the solid furniture. Some furniture may satisfy us for a lifetime. Some may be quite unsuitable after ten years. But certain it is that the cushions and curtains and pictures will begin to be stale after a couple of years. And staleness in the home is stifling and oppressive to the spirit. It is a woman's business to see to it. In England especially we live so much indoors that our interiors must live, must change, must have their seasons of fading and renewing, must come alive to fit the new moods, the new sensations, the new selves that come to pass in us with the changing years. Dead and dull permanency in the home, dreary sameness, is a form of inertia, and very harmful to the modern nature, which is in a state of flux, sensitive to its surroundings far more than we really know.

And, do as we may, the pictures in a room are in some way the key to the atmosphere of a room. Put up grey photogravures, and a certain greyness will dominate in the air, no matter if your cushions be daffodils. Put up Baxter prints, and for a time you will have charm, after that, a certain stuffiness will ensue. Pictures are strange things. Most of them die as sure as flowers die, and, once dead, they hang on the wall as stale as brown withered bouquets. The reason lies in ourselves. When we buy a picture because we like it, then the picture responds fresh to some living feeling in us. But feelings change: quicker or slower. If our feeling for the picture was superficial, it wears away quickly—and quickly the picture is nothing but a dead rag hanging on the wall. On the other hand, if we can see a little deeper, we shall buy a picture that will at least last us a year or two, and give a certain fresh joy all the time, like a living flower. We may even find something that will last us a lifetime. If we found a masterpiece, it would last many lifetimes. But there are not many masterpieces of any sort in this world.

The fact remains there are pictures of every sort, and people of every sort to be pleased by them; and there is, perhaps, a limit to the length of time that even a masterpiece will please mankind. Raphael now occasionally bores us, after several centuries, and Michael Angelo begins to.

But we needn't bother about Raphael or Michael Angelo, who keep up their fresh interest for centuries. Our concern is rather with pictures that may be dead rags in six months, all the fresh feeling for them gone. If we think of Landseer, or Alma Tadema, we see how even traditional connoisseurs like Dukes of Devonshire paid large sums for momentary masterpieces that now hang on the ducal walls as dead and ridiculous rags. Only a very uneducated person nowadays would want to put those two Landseer dogs, "Dignity and Impudence," on the drawing-room wall. Yet they pleased immensely in their day. And the interest was sustained, perhaps, for twenty years. But after twenty years it has become a humiliation to keep them hanging on the walls of Chatsworth or wherever they hang. They should be burnt, of course. They only make an intolerable stuffiness wherever they are, and remind us of the shallowness of our taste.

And if this is true of "Dignity and Impudence" or Millais' "Bubbles," which have a great deal of technical skill in them, how much more true is it of cheap photogravures, which have none. Familiarity wears a picture out. Since Whistler's portrait of his mother was used for advertisement, it has lost most of its appeal, and become for most people a worn-out picture, a dead rag. And once a picture has been really popular, and then died into staleness, it never revives again. It is dead for ever. The only thing is to burn it.

Which applies very forcibly to photogravures and other such machine pictures. They may have fascinated the young bride twenty years ago. They may even have gone on fascinating her for six months or two years. But at the end of that time they are almost certainly dead, and the bride's pleasure in them can only be a reminiscent sentimental pleasure, or that rather vulgar satisfaction in them as pieces of property. It is fatal to look on pictures as pieces of property. Pictures are like flowers, that fade away sooner or later, and die, and must be thrown in the dustbin and burnt. It is true of all pictures. Even the beloved Giorgione will one day die to human interest—but he is still very lovely, after almost five centuries, still a fresh flower. But when at last he is dead, as so many pictures are that hang on honoured walls, let us hope he will be burnt. Let us hope he won't still be regarded as a piece of valuable property, worth huge sums, like lots of dead-as-doornails canvases today.

If only we could get rid of the idea of "property" in the arts! The arts exist to give us pleasure or joy. A yellow cushion gives us pleasure. The moment it ceases to do so, take it away, have done with it, give us another.—Which we do, and so cushions remain fresh and interesting, and the manufacturers manufacture continually new, fresh, fascinating fabrics. The natural demand causes a healthy supply.

In pictures it is just the opposite. A picture, instead of being regarded, like a flower or a cushion, as something that must be fresh and fragrant with attraction, is looked on as solid property. We may spend ten shillings on a bunch of roses, and throw away the dead stalks without thinking we have thrown away ten shillings. We may spend two guineas on the cover of a lovely cushion, and strip it off and discard it the moment it is stale, without for a moment lamenting the two guineas. We know where we are. We paid for æsthetic pleasure, and we have had it. Lucky for us that money can buy roses or lovely embroidery.—Yet if we pay two pounds for some picture, and are tired of it after a year, we can no more burn that picture than we can set the house on fire. It is uneducated folly on our part. We *ought* to burn the picture, so that we can have real fresh pleasure in a different one, as in fresh flowers and fresh cushions. In every school it is taught: Never leave stale flowers in a vase. Throw them away!—So it should be taught: Never leave stale pictures on the wall. Burn them! The value of a picture lies in the æsthetic emotion it brings, exactly as if it were a flower. The æsthetic emotion dead, the picture is a piece of ugly litter.

Which belies the tedious dictum that a picture should be part of the architectural whole, built into the room, as it were. This is fallacy. A picture is decoration, not architecture. The room exists to shelter us and house us, the picture exists only to please us, to give us certain emotions. Of course, there can be harmony or disharmony between the pictures and the whole *ensemble* of a room. But in any room in the world you could carry out dozens of different schemes of decoration, at different times, and to harmonise with each scheme of decoration there are hundreds of different pictures. The built-in theory is all wrong. A picture in a room is the gardenia in my buttonhole. If the tailor "built" a permanent and irremovable gardenia in my morning coat buttonhole, I should be done in.

Then there is the young school which thinks pictures should be kept in stacks like books in a library, and looked at for half an hour or so at a time, as we turn over the leaves of a book of reproductions. But this again entirely disregards the real psychology of pictures. It is true the great trashy mass of pictures are exhausted in half an hour. But then why keep them in a stack, why keep them at all? On the other hand, if I had a Renoir nude, or a good Fricsz flower-study, or even a Brabazon water-colour, I should want to keep it at least a year or two, and hang it up in a chosen place, to live with it and get all the fragrance out of it. And if I had the Titian "Adam and Eve," from the Prado, I should want to have it hanging in my room all my life, to look at: because I know it would give me a subtle rejoicing all my life, and would make my life delightful. And if I had some Picassos I should want to keep them about six months, and some Braques I should like to have for about a year: then, probably, I should be through with them. But I would not want a Romney even for a day.

And so it varies, with the individual and with the picture, and so it should be allowed to vary. But at present it is not allowed to vary. We all have to stare at the dead rags our fathers and mothers hung on the walls, just because they are *property*.

But let us change it. Let us refuse to have our vision filled with dust and nullity of dead pictures in the home. Let there be a grand conflagration of dead "art," immolation of canvas and paper, oil-colours, water-colours, photographs and all, a grand clearance.

Then what? Then ask Harrods about it. Don't for heaven's sake go and spend twenty guineas on another picture that will have to hang on the wall till the end of time just because it cost twenty guineas. Go to Harrods and ask them what about their Circulating Picture scheme. They have a circulating library—or other people have—huge circulating libraries. People hire books till they have assimilated their content. Why not the same with pictures?

Why should not Harrods have a great "library" of pictures? Why not have a great "pictuary," where we can go and choose a picture? There would be men in charge who knew about pictures, just as librarians know about books. We subscribe, we pay a certain deposit, and our pictures are sent home to us, to keep for one year, for two, for ten, as we wish: at any rate, till we have got all the joy out of them, and want a change.

In the pictuary you can have everything except machine-made rubbish that is not worth having. You can have big supplies of modern art, fresh from the artists, etchings, engravings, drawings, paintings; you can have the lovely new colour reproductions that most of us can't afford to buy; you can have frames to suit. And here you can choose, choose what will give you real joy and will suit your home for the time being.

There are few, very few great artists in any age. But there are hundreds and hundreds of men and women with genuine artistic talent and beautiful artistic feeling, who produce quite lovely works that are never seen. They are lovely works—not immortal, not masterpieces, not "great"; yet they are lovely, and will keep their loveliness a certain number of years; after which they will die, and the time will have come to destroy them.

Now it is a tragedy that all these pictures with their temporary loveliness should be condemned to a premature dust-heap. For that is what they are.

Contemporary art belongs to contemporary society. Society at large *needs* the pictures of its contemporaries, just as it needs the books. Modern people read modern books. But they hang up pictures that belong to no age whatever, and have no life, and have no meaning, but are mere, blotches of deadness on the walls.

The living moment is everything. And in pictures we never experience it. It is useless asking the public to "see" Matisse or Picasso or Braque. They will never see more than an odd horrific canvas, anyhow. But does the modern public read James Joyce or Marcel Proust? It does not. It reads the great host of more congenial and more intelligible contemporary writers. And so the modern public is more or less up-to-date and on the spot about the general run of modern books. It is conscious of the literature of its day, moderately awake and intelligent in that respect.

But of the pictures and drawings of its day it is blankly unaware. The general public feels itself a hopeless ignoramus when confronted with modern works of art. It has no clue to the whole unnatural business of modern art, and is just hostile. Even those who are tentatively attracted are uneasy, and they dare never *buy*. Prices are comparatively high, and you may so easily be let in for a dud. So the whole thing is a deadlock.

Now the only way to keep the public in touch with art is to let it get hold of works of art. It was just the same with books. In the old five-guinea and two-guinea days there was no public for literature, except the squire class. The great reading public came into being with the lending library. And the great picture-loving public would come into being with the lending pictuary. The public *wants* pictures hard enough. But it simply can't get them.

And this will continue so long as a picture is regarded as a piece of property, and not as a source of æsthetic emotion, of sheer pleasure, as a flower is. The great public was utterly deprived of books till books ceased to be looked on as lumps of real estate, and came to be regarded as something belonging to the mind and consciousness, a spiritual instead of a gross material property. To-day, if I say: "Doughty's 'Arabia Deserta' is a favourite book of mine," then the man I say it to won't reply: "Yes, I own a copy," he will say: "Yes, I have read it." In the eighteenth century he would probably have replied: "I have a fine example *in folio* in my library," and the sense of "property" would have overwhelmed any sense of literary delight.

The cheapening of books freed them from the gross property valuation and released their true spiritual value. Something of the same must happen for pictures. The public wants and needs badly all the real æsthetic stimulus it can get. And it knows it When books were made available, the vast reading public sprang into being almost at once. And a vast picture-loving public would arise, once the public could get at the pictures, personally.

There are thousands of quite lovely pictures, not masterpieces, of course, but with real beauty, *which belong to to-day*, and which remain stacked dustily and hopelessly in corners of artists' studios, going stale. It is a great shame. The public wants them, but it never sees them; and if it does see an occasional few, it daren't buy, especially as "art" is high-priced, for it feels incompetent to judge. At the same time, the unhappy, work-glutted artists of to-day want above all things to let the public have their works. And these works are, we insist, an essential part of the education and emotional experience of the modern mind. It is necessary that adults should *know* them, as they know modern books. It is necessary that children should be familiar with them, in the constant stream of creation. Our æsthetic education is become immensely important, since it is so immensely neglected.

And there we are, the pictures going to dust, for they don't keep their freshness, any more than books or flowers or silks, beyond a certain time; yet their freshness now is the breath of life to us, since it means hours and days of delight. And the public is pining for the pictures, but daren't buy, because of the money-property complex. And the artist is pining to let the public have them, but daren't make himself cheap. And so the thing is an *impasse*, simple state of frustration.

Now for Messrs. Harrods and their lending library —or pictuary—of modern works of art. Or, better still, an Artists' Co-operative Society, to supply pictures on loan or purchase, to the great public. To-day nobody buys pictures, except as a speculation. If a man pays a hundred pounds for a canvas, he does it in the secret belief that that canvas will be worth a thousand pounds in a few years' time. The whole attitude is disgusting. The reading public only asks of a book that it shall be entertaining, it doesn't give a hang as to whether the book will be considered a great book five years hence. The great public wants to be entertained and, sometimes, delighted, and literature exists to supply the demand. Now there is a great deal of delight in even a very minor picture, produced by an artist who has delicate artistic feeling and some skill, even if he be not wildly original. There are hundreds and hundreds of perfectly obscure pictures stuck away in corners of studios, which would, I know, give me a real delight if they were hung in my room for a year. After a while they would go stale; but not nearly as quickly as a bunch of lilac, which yet I love and set with pleasure on the table. As a tree puts beauty into a flower that will fade, so all the hosts of minor artists, one way and another, put beauty and delight into their pictures, that likewise will not last beyond their rhythmic season. But it is a wicked shame and waste that nearly all these pictures, with their modicum of beauty and their power of giving delight, should just be taken from the easel to be laid on the dust-heap, while a beauty-starved public doesn't even get a look at them. It is all very well saying the public should buy. A picture is cheap at twenty pounds, and very cheap at ten pounds, and "given away" at five pounds. And the public is not only shy, it has a complex about buying any picture that hasn't at least the chance of turning out a masterpiece of ultimate extraordinary value.

It is all nonsensical and futile. The only way now is for the hosts of small artists to club together and form an Artists' Co-operative Society, with proper business intelligence and business energy, to supply the public with pictures on the public's own terms. Or for the shrewd business men of the world to take the matter up and make a profitable concern of it, as publishers have made a profitable concern of publishing books.

THE RISEN LORD

"The risen lord, the risen lord
has risen in the flesh,
and treads the earth to feel the soil
though his feet are still nesh."

The Churches loudly assert: We preach Christ crucified!—But in so doing, they preach only half of the Passion, and do only half their duty. The Creed says : "Was crucified, dead, and buried . . . the third day He rose again from the dead." And again, "I believe in the resurrection of the body . . . So that to preach Christ Crucified is to preach half the truth. It is the business of the Church to preach Christ born among men—which is Christmas; Christ crucified, which is Good Friday; and Christ Risen, which is Easter. And after Easter, till November and All Saints, and till Annunciation, the year belongs to the Risen Lord: that is, all the full-flowering spring, all summer, and the autumn of wheat and fruit, all belong to Christ Risen.

But the Churches insist on Christ Crucified, and rob us of the blossom and fruit of the year. The Catholic Church, which has given us our images, has given us the Christ-child, in the lap of woman, and again, Christ Crucified: then the Mass, the mystery of atonement through sacrifice. Yet all this is really preparatory, these are the preparatory stages of the real living religion. The Christ-child, enthroned in the lap of the Mother, is obviously only a preparatory image, to prepare us for Christ the Man. Yet a vast mass of Christians stick there.

What we have to remember is that the great religious images are only images of our own experiences, or of our own state of mind and soul. In the Catholic countries, where the Madonna-and-Child image overwhelms everything else, the man visions himself all the time as a child, a Christ-Child, standing on the lap of a virgin mother. Before the war, if an Italian hurt himself, or suddenly fell into distress, his immediate cry was: *O mamma mia! mamma mia!—Oh, mother, mother!*—The same was true of many Englishmen. And what does this mean? It means that the man sees himself as a child, the innocent saviour-child enthroned on the lap of the all-pitying virgin mother. He lives according to this image of himself—the image of the guileless "good" child sheltered in the arms of an all-sheltering mother—until the image breaks in his heart.

And during the war, this image broke in the hearts of most men, though not in the hearts of their women. During the war, the man who suffered most bitterly suffered beyond the help of wife or mother, and no wife nor mother nor sister nor any beloved could save him from the guns. This fact went home in his heart, and broke the image of mother and Christ-child, and left in its place the image of Christ crucified.

It was not so, of course, for the woman. The image did not break for her. She visioned herself still as the all-pitying, all-sheltering Madonna, on whose lap the man was enthroned, as in the old pictures, like a Christ-child. And naturally the woman did not want to abandon this vision of herself. It gave her her greatest significance; and the greatest power. Break the image, and her significance and her power were gone. But the men came back from the war and denied the image—for them it was broken. So she fought to maintain it, the great vision of man, the Christ-child, enthroned in the lap of the all-pitying virginal woman. And she fought in vain, though not without disastrous result.

For the vision of the all-pitying and all-helpful Madonna was shattered in the hearts of men, during the war. The all-pitying and all-helpful Woman actually did not, whether she could or not, prevent the guns from blowing to pieces the men who called upon her. So her image collapsed, and with it the image of the Christ-child. For the man who went through the war the resultant image inevitably was

Christ Crucified, Christ tortured on the Cross. And Christ Crucified is essentially womanless.

True, many of the elderly men who never went through the war still insist on the Christ-child business, and most of the elderly women insist on their benevolent Madonna supremacy. But it is in vain. The guns broke the image in the hearts of middle-aged men, and the young were born, or are come to real consciousness, after the image was already smashed.

So there we are! We have three great image-divisions among men and women to-day. We have the old and the elderly, who never were exposed to the guns, still fatuously maintaining that man is the Christ-child and woman the infallible safeguard from all evil and all danger. It is fatuous, because it absolutely didn't work. Then we have the men of middle age, who were all tortured and virtually put to death by the war. They accept Christ Crucified as their image, are essentially womanless, and take the great cry: *Consummatum est!—It is finished!—* as their last word.—Thirdly, we have the young, who never went through• the war. They have no illusions about it, however, and the death-cry of their elder generation: *It is finished!* rings cold through their blood. They cannot answer. They cannot even scoff. It is no joke, and never will be a joke.

And yet, neither of the great images is *their* image. They cannot accept the child-and-mother position which the old buffers still pose in. They cannot accept the Christ Crucified finality of the generations immediately ahead. For they, the young, came into the field of life after the death-cry *Consummatum est!* had rung through the world, and while the body, so to speak, was being put into the tomb. By the time the young came on to the stage, Calvary was empty, the tombs were closed, the women had lost for ever the Christ-child and the virgin savour, and it was altogether the day after, cold, bleak, empty, blank, meaningless, almost silly.

The young came into life, and found everything finished. Everywhere the empty crosses, everywhere the closed tombs, everywhere the manless, bitter or over-assertive woman, everywhere the closed grey disillusion of Christ Crucified, dead, and buried, those grey empty days between Good Friday and Easter.

And the Churches, instead of preaching the Risen Lord, go on preaching the Christ-child and Christ Crucified. Now man cannot live without some vision of himself. But still less can he live with a vision that is not true to his inner experience and inner feeling. And the vision of Christ-Child and Christ Crucified are both untrue to the inner experience and feeling of the young. They don't feel that way. They show the greatest forbearance and tolerance of their elders, for whom the two images *are* livingly true. But for the post-war young, neither the Christ-child nor Christ Crucified means much.

I doubt whether the Protestant Churches, which supported the war, will ever have the faith and the power of life to take the great step onwards, and preach Christ Risen. The Catholic Church might. In the countries of the Mediterranean, Easter has always been the greatest of the holy days, the gladdest and holiest, not Christmas, the birth of the Child. Easter, Christ Risen, the Risen Lord, this, to the old faith, is still the first day in the year. The Easter festivities are the most joyful, the Easter processions the finest, the Easter ceremonies the most splendid. In Sicily the women take into church the saucers of growing corn, the green blades rising tender and slim like green light, in little pools, filling round the altar. It is Adonis. It is the re-born year. It is Christ Risen. It is the Risen Lord. And in the warm south still a great joy floods the hearts of the people on Easter Sunday. They feel it, they feel it everywhere. The Lord is risen. The Lord of the rising wheat and the plum blossoms is warm and kind upon earth again, after having been done to death by the evil and the jealous ones.

The Roman Catholic Church may still unfold this part of the Passion fully, and make men happy again. For Resurrection is indeed the consummation of all the passion. Not even Atonement, the being at one with Christ through partaking in His sacrifice, consummates the Passion finally. For even after Atonement men still must live, and must go forward with the vision. After we share in the body of Christ, we rise with Him in the body. And that is the final vision that has been blurred to all the Churches.

Christ risen in the flesh! We must accept the image complete, if we accept it at all. We must take the mystery in its fulness and in fact. It is only the image of our own experience. Christ rises, when He rises from the dead, in the flesh, not merely as spirit. He rises with hands and feet, as Thomas knew for certain: and if with hands and feet, then with lips and stomach and genitals of a man. Christ risen, and risen in the whole of His flesh, not with some left out.

Christ risen in the full flesh! What for? It is here the gospels are all vague and faltering, and the Churches leave us in the lurch. Christ risen in the flesh in order to lurk obscurely for six weeks on earth, then be taken vaguely up into heaven in a cloud? Flesh, solid flesh, feet and bowels and teeth and eyes of a man, taken up into heaven in a cloud, and never put down again?

It is the only part of the great mystery which is all wrong. The virgin birth, the baptism, the temptation, the teaching, Gethsemane, the betrayal, the crucifixion, the burial and the resurrection, these are all true according to our inward experience. They are what men and women go through, in their different ways. But floated up into heaven as flesh-and-blood, and never set down again—this nothing in all our experience will ever confirm. If aeroplanes take us up, they bring us down, or let us down. Flesh and blood belong to the earth, and only to the earth. We know it.

And Jesus was risen flesh-and-blood. He rose a man on earth to live on earth. The greatest test was still before Him: His life as a man on earth. Hitherto He had been a sacred child, a teacher, a messiah, but never a full man. Now, risen from the dead, He rises to be a man on earth, and live His life of the flesh, the great life, among other men. This is the image of our inward state to-day.

This is the image of the young: the Risen Lord. The teaching is over, the crucifixion is over, the sacrifice is made, the salvation is accomplished. Now comes the true life, man living his full life on earth, as flowers live their full life, without rhyme or reason except the magnificence of coming forth into fulness.

If Jesus rose from the dead in triumph, a man on earth triumphant in renewed flesh, triumphant over the mechanical anti-life convention of Jewish priests, Roman despotism, and universal money-lust; triumphant above all over His own self-absorption, self-consciousness, self-importance; triumphant and free as a man in full flesh and full, final experience, even the accomplished acceptance of His own death; a man at last full and free in flesh and soul, a man at one with death: then He rose to become at one with life, to live the great life of the flesh and the soul together, as peonies or foxes do, in their lesser way. If Jesus rose as a full man, in full flesh and soul, then He rose to take a woman to Himself, to live with her, and to know the tenderness and blossoming of the twoness with her; He who had been hitherto so limited to His oneness, or His universality, which is the same thing. If Jesus rose in the full flesh, He rose to know the tenderness of a woman, and the great pleasure of her, and to have children by her. He rose to know the responsibility and the peculiar delight of children, and also the exasperation and nuisance of them. If Jesus rose as a full man, in the flesh, He rose to have friends, to have a man-friend whom He would hold sometimes to His breast, in strong affection, and who would be dearer to Him than a brother, just out of the sheer mystery of sympathy. And how much more wonderful, this, than having disciples! If Jesus rose a full man in the flesh, He rose to do His share in the world's work, something He really liked doing. And if He remembered His first life, it would neither be teaching nor preaching, but probably carpentering again, with joy, among the shavings. If Jesus rose a full man in the flesh, He rose to continue His fight with the hard-boiled conventionalists like Roman judges and Jewish priests and money-makers of every sort. But this time, it would no longer be the fight of self-sacrifice that would end in crucifixion. This time it would be a freed man fighting to shelter the rose of life from being trampled on by the pigs. This time, if Satan attempted temptation in the wilderness, the Risen Lord would answer: Satan, your silly temptations no longer tempt me. Luckily, I have died to that sort of self-importance and self-conceit. But let me tell you something, old man! Your name's Satan, isn't it? And your name is Mammon? You are the selfish hog that's got hold of all the world, aren't you? Well, look here, my boy, I'm going to take it all from you, so don't worry. The world and the power and the riches thereof, I'm going to take them all from you, Satan or Mammon or what-ever your name is. Because you don't know how to use them. The earth is the Lord's, and the fulness thereof, and it's going to be. Men have risen from the dead and learned not to be so greedy and self-important. We left most of that behind in the late tomb. Men have risen beyond you, Mammon, they are your risen lords. And so, you hook-nosed, glisten-eyed, ugly, money-smelling anachronism, you've got to get out. Men have not died and risen again for nothing. Whom do you think the earth belongs to, you stale old rat? The earth is the Lord's and is given to the men who have died and had the power to rise again. The earth is given to the men who have risen from the dead, risen, you old grabber, and when did you ever rise? Never! So go you down to oblivion, and give your place to the risen men, and the women of the risen men. For man has been dispossessed of the full earth and the earth's fulness long enough. And the poor women, they have been shoved about manless and meaningless long enough. The earth is the Lord's and the fulness thereof, and I, the Risen Lord, am here to take possession. For now I am fully a man, and free above all from my own self-importance. I want life, and the pure contact with life. What are riches, and glory, and honour, and might, and power, to me who have died and lost my self-importance? That's why I am going to take them all from you, Mammon, because I care nothing about them. I am going to destroy all your values, Mammon; all your money values and conceit values, I am going to destroy them all.

Because only life is lovely, and you, Mammon, prevent life. I love to see a squirrel peep round a tree; and left to you, Mammon, there will soon be no squirrels to peep. I love to hear a man singing a song to himself, and if it is an old, improper song, about the fun between lads and girls, I like it all the better. But you, beastly mealy-mouthed Mammon, you would arrest any lad that sings a gay song. I love the movement of life, and the beauty of life, O Mammon, since I am risen, I love the beauty of life intensely; columbine flowers, for example, the way they dangle, or the delicate way a young girl sits and wonders, or the rage with which a man turns and kicks a fool dog that suddenly attacks him—beautiful that, the swift fierce turn and lunge of a kick, then the quivering pause for the next attack; or even the slightly silly glow that comes over some men as they are getting tipsy—it still is a glow, beautiful; or the swift look a woman fetches me, when she would really like me to go off with her, but she is troubled; or the real compassion I saw a woman express for a man who slipped and wrenched his foot: life, the beauty, the beauty of life! But that which is anti-life, Mammon, like you, and money, and machines, and prostitution, and all that tangled mass of self-importance and greediness and self-conscious conceit which adds up to Mammon, I hate it. I hate it, Mammon, I hate you and am going to push you off the face of the earth, Mammon, you great mob-thing, fatal to men.

MEN MUST WORK AND WOMEN AS WELL

Supposing that circumstances go on pretty much in the same way they're going on in now, then men and women will go on pretty much in the same way they are now going on in. There is always an element of change, we know. But change is of two sorts: the next step, or a jump in another direction. The next step is called progress. If our society continues its course of gay progress along the given lines, then men and women will do the same: always along the given lines.

So what is important in that case is not so much men and women, but the given lines. The railway train doesn't matter particularly in itself. What matters is where it is going to. If I want to go to Crewe, then a train to Bedford is supremely uninteresting to me, no matter how full it may be. It will only arouse a secondary and temporal interest if it happens to have an accident.

And there you are with men and women to-day. They are not particularly interesting, and they are not, in themselves, particularly important. All the thousands and millions of bowler hats and neat handbags that go bobbing to business every day may represent so many immortal souls, but somehow we feel that is not for us to say. The clergyman is paid to tickle our vanity in these matters. What all the bowler hats and neat handbags represent to you and me and to each other is business, my dear, and a job.

So that, granted the present stream of progress towards better business and better jobs continues, the point is, not to consider the men and women bobbing in the stream, any more than you consider the drops of water in the Thames—but where the stream is flowing. Where is the stream flowing, indeed, the stream of progress? Everybody hopes, of course, it is flowing towards bigger business and better jobs. And what does that mean, again, to the man under the bowler hat and the woman who clutches the satchel?

It means, of course, more money, more congenial labours, and fewer hours. It means freedom from all irksome tasks. It means, apart from the few necessary hours of highly paid and congenial labour, that men and women shall have nothing to do except enjoy themselves. No beastly housework for the women, no beastly homework for the men. Free! free to enjoy themselves. More films, more motor-cars, more dances, more golf, more tennis and more getting completely away from yourself. And the goal of life is enjoyment.

Now if men and women want these things with sufficient intensity, they may really get them, and go on getting them. While the game is worth the candle, men and women will go on playing the game. And it seems to-day as if the motor-car, the, film, the radio and the jazz were worth the candle. This being so, progress will continue from business to bigger business, and from job to better job. This is, in very simple terms, the plan of the universe laid down by the great magnates of industry like Mr. Ford. And they know what they are talking about.

But—and the "but" is a very big one—it is not easy' to turn business into bigger business, and it is sometimes *impossible* to turn uncongenial jobs into congenial ones. This is where science really leaves us in the lurch, and calculation collapses. Perhaps in Mr. Ford's super-factory of motor-cars all jobs may be made abstract and congenial. But the woman whose cook falls foul of the kitchen range, heated with coal, every day, hates that coal range herself even more darkly than the cook hates it. Yet many housewives can't afford electric cooking. And if everyone could, it still doesn't make housework entirely congenial. All the inventions of modern science fail to make housework anything but uncongenial to the modern woman, be she mistress or servant-maid. Now the only decent way to get something done is to get it done by somebody who quite likes doing it. In the past, cooks really enjoyed cooking and housemaids enjoyed scrubbing. Those days are over; like master, like man, and still more so, like mistress, like maid. Mistress loathes scrubbing; in two generations, maid loathes scrubbing. But scrubbing must be done. At what price?— raise the price. The price is raised, the scrubbing goes a little better. But after a while, the loathing of scrubbing becomes again paramount in the kitchen-maid's breast, and then ensues a general state of tension, and a general outcry: Is it worth it? Is it really worth it?

What applies to scrubbing applies to all labour that cannot be mechanised or abstracted. A girl will slave over shorthand and typing for a pittance because it is not muscular work. A girl will not do housework well, not for a good wage. Why? Because, for some mysterious or obvious reason, the modern woman and the modern man hate physical work. Ask your husband to peel the potatoes, and earn his deep resentment. Ask your wife to wash your socks, and earn the same. There is still a certain thrill about "mental" and purely mechanical work like attending a machine. But actual labour has become to us, with our education, abhorrent.

And it is here that science has not kept pace with human demand. It is here that progress is fatally threatened. There is an enormous, insistent demand on the part of the human being that mere labour, such as scrubbing, hewing and loading coal, navvying, the crude work that is the basis of all labour, shall be done away with. Even washing dishes. Science hasn't even learned how to wash dishes for us yet. The mistress who feels so intensely bitter about her maid who will not wash the dishes properly does so because she herself so loathes washing them. Science has rather left us in the lurch in these humble but basic matters. Before babies are conveniently bred in bottles, let the scientist find a *hey presto!* trick for turning dirty teacups into clean ones ; since it is upon science we depend for our continued progress.

Progress, then, which proceeds so smoothly, and depends on science, does not proceed as rapidly as human feelings change. Beef-steaks are beef-steaks still, though all except the eating is horrible to us. A great deal must be done about a beef-steak besides the eating of it. And this great deal is done, we have to face the fact, unwillingly. When the mistress loathes trimming and grilling a beef-steak, or paring potatoes, or wringing the washing, the maid will likewise loathe these things, and do them at last unwillingly, and with a certain amount of resentment.

The one thing we don't sufficiently consider, in considering the march of human progress, is also the very dangerous march of human feeling that goes on at the same time, and not always parallel. The change in human feeling! And one of the greatest changes that has ever taken place in man and woman is this revulsion from physical effort, physical labour and physical contact, which has taken place within the last thirty years. This change hits woman even harder than man, for she has always had to keep the immediate physical side going. And now it is repellent to her—just as nearly all physical activity is repellent to modern man. The film, the radio, the gramophone were all invented because physical effort and physical contact have become repulsive to man and woman alike. The aim is to abstract as far as possible. And science is our only help. And science still can't wash the dinner-things or darn socks, or even mend the fire. Electric heaters or central heating, of course! But that's not all.

What, then, is the result? In the abstract we sail ahead to bigger business and better jobs and babies bred in bottles and food in tabloid form. But meanwhile science hasn't rescued us from beef-steaks and dish-washing, heavy labour and howling babies. There is a great hitch. And owing to the great hitch, a great menace to progress. Because every day mankind hates the business of beefsteaks and dish-washing, heavy labour and howling babies more bitterly.

The housewife is full of resentment—she can't help it. The young husband is full of resentment—he can't help it, when he has to plant potatoes to eke out the family income. The housemaid is full of resentment, the navvy is full of resentment, the collier is full of resentment, and the collier's wife is full of resentment, because her man can't earn a proper wage. Resentment grows as the strange fastidiousness of modern men and women increases. Resentment, resentment, resentment—because the basis of life is still brutally physical, and that has become repulsive to us. Mr. Ford, being in his own way a genius, has realised that what the modern workman wants, just like the modern gentleman, is abstraction. The modern workman doesn't *want* to be "interested" in his job. He wants to be as little interested, as nearly perfectly mechanical as possible. This is the great will of the people, and there is no gainsaying it. It is precisely the same in woman as in man.. Woman demands an electric cooker because it makes no call on her attention or her "interest" at all. It is almost a pure abstraction, a few switches, and no physical contact, no *dirt*, which is the inevitable result of physical contact, at all. If only we could make housework a real abstraction, a matter of turning switches and guiding a machine, the house-wife would again be more or less content. But it can't quite be done, even in America.

And the resentment is enormous. The resentment against *eating*, in the breast of modern woman who has to prepare food, is profound. Why all this work and bother about *mere eating*? Why, indeed? Because neither science nor evolution has kept up with the change in human feeling, and beef-steaks are beef-steaks still, no matter how detestable they may have become to the people who have to prepare them. The loathsome fuss of food continues, and will continue, in spite of all talk about tabloids. The loathsome digging of coal out of the earth, by half-naked men, continues, deep underneath Mr. Ford's super-factories. There it is, and there it will be, and you can't get away from it. While men quite enjoyed hewing coal, which

540

they did, and while women really enjoyed cooking, even with a coal range, which they did—then all was well. But suppose society *en bloc* comes to hate the thought of sweating cooking over a hot range, or sweating hacking at a coal-seam, then what are you to do? You have to ask, or to demand that a large section of society shall do something they have come to hate doing, and which you would hate to do yourself. What then? Resentment and ill-feeling!

Social life means all classes of people living more or less harmoniously together. And private life means men and women, man and woman living together more or less congenially. If there is serious discord between the social classes, then society is threatened with confusion. If there is serious discord between man and woman, then the individual, and that means practically everybody, is threatened with internal confusion and unhappiness.

Now it is quite easy to keep the working classes in harmonious working order, so long as you don't ask them to do work they simply do not want to do. The board-schools, however, did the fatal deed. They said to the boys: Work is noble, but what you want is to *get on*, you don't want to stick down a coal-mine all your life. Rise up, and do *clean* work! become a school teacher or a clerk, not a common collier.

This is sound board-school education, and is in keeping with all the noblest social ideals of the last century. Unfortunately it entirely overlooks the unpleasant effect of such teaching on those who *cannot* get on, and who must perforce stick down a coal-mine all their lives. And these, in the board-school of a mining district, are at least 90 per cent. of the boys; it must be so. So that 90 per cent. of these board-school scholars are deliberately taught, at school, to be malcontents, taught to despise themselves for not having "got on," for not having "got out of the pit," for sticking down all their lives doing "dirty work" and being "common colliers." Naturally, every collier, doomed himself, wants to get his boys out of the pit, to be gentlemen. And since this again is *impossible* in 90 per cent. of the cases, the number of "gentlemen," or clerks and school teachers, being strictly proportionate to the number of colliers, there comes again the sour disillusion. So that by the third generation you have exactly what you've got to-day, the young malcontent collier. He has been deliberately produced by modern education coupled with modern conditions, and is logically, inevitably and naturally what he is: a malcontent collier. According to all the accepted teaching, he ought to have risen and bettered himself: equal opportunity, you know. And he hasn't risen and bettered himself. Therefore he is more or less a failure in his own eyes even. He is doomed to do dirty work. He is a malcontent, Now even Mr. Ford can't make coal-mines clean and shiny and abstract. Coal won't be abstracted. Even a Soviet can't do it. A coal-mine remains a hole in the black earth, where blackened men hew and shovel and sweat. You can't abstract it, or make it an affair of puffing levers, and, what is even worse, you can't abandon it, you can't do away with it. There it is, and it has got to be. Mr. Ford forgets that his clean and pure and harmonious super-factory, where men only pull shining levers or turn bright handles, has all had to be grossly mined and smelted before it could come into existence. Mr. Ford's is one of the various heavens of industry. But these heavens rest on various hells of labour, always did and always will. Science rather leaves us in the lurch in these matters. Science is supposed to remove these hells for us. And—it doesn't. Not at all!

If you had never taught the blackened men down in the various hells that they *were* in hell, and made them despise themselves for being there—a *common* collier, a *low* labourer—the mischief could never have developed so rapidly. But now we have it, all society resting on a labour basis of smouldering resentment. And the collier's question: How would *you* like to be a collier?—is unanswerable. We know perfectly well we should dislike it intensely.—At the same time, my father, who never went to a Board-school, quite liked it. But he has been improved on. Progress! Human feeling has changed, changed rapidly and radically. And science has not changed conditions to fit.

What is to be done? We all loathe brute physical labour. We all think it is horrible to have to do it. We consider those that actually do it low and vile, and we have told them so, for fifty years, urging them to get away from it and "better themselves," which would be very nice, if everybody *could* get on, and brute labour could be abandoned, as, scientifically, it ought to be. But actually, not at all. We are forced to go on forcing a very large proportion of society to remain "unbettered," "low and common," "common colliers, common labourers," since a very large portion of humanity must still spend its life labouring, now and in the future, science having let us down in this respect. You can't teach mankind to "better himself" unless you'll better the gross earth to fit him. And the gross earth remains what it was, and man its slave. For neither science nor evolution shows any signs of saving us from our gross necessities. The labouring masses are and will be, even if all else is swept away: because they must be. They represent the gross necessity of man, which science has failed to save us from.

So then, what? The only thing that remains to be done is to make labour as likeable as possible, and try to teach the labouring masses to like it: which, given the trend of modern feeling, not only sounds, but is, fatuous. Mankind *en bloc* gets more fastidious and more "nice" every day. Every day it loathes dirty work more deeply. And every day the whole pressure of social consciousness works towards making everybody more fastidious, more "nice," more refined, and more unfit for dirty work. Before you make all humanity unfit for dirty work, you should first remove the necessity for dirty work.

But such being the condition of men and women with regard to work—a condition of repulsion in the breasts of men and women for the work that has got to be done—what about private life, the relation between man and woman? How does the new fastidiousness and nicety of mankind affect this?

Profoundly! The revulsion from physical labour, physical effort, physical contact has struck a deathblow at marriage and home-life. In the great trend of the times, a woman cannot save herself from the universal dislike of housework, housekeeping, rearing children and keeping a home going. Women make the most unselfish efforts in this direction, because it is generally expected of them. But this cannot remove the *instinctive* dislike of preparing meals and scouring saucepans, cleaning baby's bottles or darning the man's underwear, which a large majority of women feel to-day. It is something which there is no denying, a real physical dislike of doing these things. Many women school themselves and are excellent housewives, physically disliking it all the time. And this, though admirable, is wearing. It is an exhaustive process, with many ill results.

Can it be possible that women actually ever did like scouring saucepans and cleaning the range?—I believe some few women still do. I believe that twenty years ago, even, the majority of women enjoyed it. But what, then, has happened? Can human instincts really change?

They can, and in the most amazing fashion. And this is the great problem for the sociologist: the violent change in human instinct, especially in women. Woman's instinct used to be all for home, shelter, the protection of the man, and the happiness of running her own house. Now it is all against. Woman *thinks* she wants a lovely little home of her own, but her instinct is all against it, when it means matrimony. She *thinks* she wants a man of her own, but her instinct is dead against having him around all the time. She would like him on a long string, that she can let out or pull in, as she feels inclined. But she just doesn't want him inevitably and insidiously there all the time—not even every evening— not even for week-ends, if it's got to be a fixture. She wants him to be merely intermittent in her landscape, even if he is always present in her soul, and she writes him the most intimate letters every day. All well and good! But her instinct is against him, against his permanent and perpetual physical presence. She doesn't want to feel his presence as something material, unavoidable and permanent. It goes dead against her grain, it upsets her instinct. She loves him, she loves, even, being faithful to him. But she doesn't want him substantially around. She doesn't want his actual physical presence—except in snatches. What she *really* loves is the thought of him, the idea of him, the *distant* communion with him—varied with snatches of actually being together, like little festivals, which we are more or less glad when they are over.

Now a great many modern girls feel like this, even when they force themselves to behave in the conventional side-by-side fashion. And a great many men feel the same—though perhaps not so acutely as the women. Young couples may force themselves to be conventional husbands and wives, but the strain is often cruel, and the result often disastrous.

Now then we see the trend of our civilisation, in terms of human feeling and human relation. It is, and there is no denying it, towards a greater and greater abstraction from the physical, towards a further and further physical separateness between men and women, and between individual and individual. Young men and women to-day are together all the time, it will be argued. Yes, but they are together as good sports, good chaps, in strange independence of one another, intimate one moment, strangers the next, hands-off! all the time, and as little connected as the bits in a kaleidoscope.

The young have the fastidiousness, the nicety, the revulsion from the physical, intensified. To the girl of to-day, a man whose physical presence she is aware of, especially a bit *heavily* aware of, is or becomes really abhorrent. She wants to fly away from him to the uttermost ends of the earth. And as soon as women or girls get a bit female physical, young men's nerves go all to pieces. The sexes can't stand one another. They adore one another as spiritual or personal creatures, all talk and wit and back-chat, or jazz and motor-cars and machines, or tennis and swimming—even sitting in bathing-suits all day on a beach. But this is all peculiarly non-physical, a flaunting of the body in its non-physical, merely optical aspect. So much nudity, fifty years ago, would have made man and woman quiver through and through. Now, not at all! People flaunt their bodies to show how unphysical they are. The more the girls are not desired, the more they uncover themselves.

543

And this means, when we analyse it out, repulsion. The young are, in a subtle way, physically repulsive to one another, the girl to the man and the man to the girl. And they rather enjoy the feeling of repulsion, it is a sort of contest. It is as if the young girl said to the young man to-day: I rather like you, you know. You are so thrillingly repulsive to me.— And as if the young man replied: Same here!— There may be, of course, an intense bodiless sort of affection between young men and women. But as soon as either becomes a positive physical presence to the other, immediately there is repulsion.

And marriages based on the thrill of physical repulsion, as so many are to-day, even when coupled with mental "adoring" or real wistful, bodiless affection, are in the long run—not so very long, either—catastrophic. There you have it, the great "spirituality," the great "betterment" or refinement; the great fastidiousness; the great "niceness" of feeling; when a girl must be a flat, thin, bodiless stick, and a boy a correct mannequin, each of them abstracted towards real caricature. What does it all amount to? What is its motive force?

What it amounts to, really, is physical repulsion. The great spirituality of our age means that we are all physically repulsive to one another. The great advance in refinement of feeling and squeamish fastidiousness means that we hate the *physical* existence of anybody and everybody, even ourselves. The amazing move into abstraction on the part of the whole of humanity—the film, the radio, the gramophone—means that we loathe the physical element in our amusements, we don't *want* the physical contact, we want to get away from it. We don't *want* to look at flesh and blood people—we want to watch their shadows on a screen. We don't *want* to hear their actual voices: only transmitted through a machine. We must get away from the physical.

The vast mass of the lower classes—and this is most extraordinary—are even more grossly abstracted, if we may use the term, than the educated classes. The uglier sort of working man to-day truly has no body and no real feelings at all. He eats the most wretched food, because taste has left him, he only *sees* his meal, he never *really* eats it. He drinks his beer by idea, he no longer tastes it at all. This must be so, or the food and beer could not be as bad as they are. And as for his relation to his women—his poor women—they are pegs to hang clothes on, and there's an end of them. It is a horrible state of feelingless depravity, atrophy of the senses.

But under it all, as ever, as everywhere, vibrates the one great impulse of our civilisation, physical recoil from every other being and from every form of 'physical existence. Recoil, recoil, recoil. Revulsion, revulsion, revulsion. Repulsion, repulsion, repulsion. This is the rhythm that underlies our social activity, everywhere, with regard to physical existence.

Now we are all basically and permanently physical. So is the earth, so even is the air. What then is going to be the result of all this recoil and repulsion, which our civilisation has deliberately fostered?

The result is really only one and the same: some form of collective social madness. Russia, being a very physical country, was in a frantic state of physical recoil and "spirituality" twenty years ago. We can look on the revolution, really, as nothing but a great outburst of anti-physical insanity; we can look on Soviet Russia as nothing but a logical state of society established in anti-physical insanity.— Physical and material are, of course, not the same in fact, they are subtly opposite. The machine is absolutely material, and absolutely anti-physical— as even our fingers know. And the Soviet is established on the image of the machine, "pure" materialism. The Soviet hates the real physical body far more deeply than it hates Capital. It mixes it up with the bourgeois. But it sees very little danger in it, since all western civilisation is now mechanised, materialised and ready for an outburst of insanity which shall throw us all into some purely machine-driven unity of lunatics.

What about it, then? What about it, men and women? The only thing to do is to get your bodies back, men and women. A great part of society is irreparably lost: abstracted into non-physical, mechanical entities whose motive power is still recoil, revulsion, repulsion, hate, and, ultimately, blind destruction. The driving force *underneath* our society remains the same: recoil, revulsion, hate. And let this force once run out of hand, and we know what to expect. It is not only in the working class. The well-to-do classes are just as full of the driving force of recoil, revulsion, which ultimately becomes hate. The force is universal in our spiritual civilisation. Let it once run out of hand, and then—

It only remains for some men and women, individuals, to try to get back their bodies and preserve the other flow of warmth, affection and physical unison. There is nothing else to do.

NOTTINGHAM AND THE MINING COUNTRYSIDE

I was born nearly forty-four years ago, in Eastwood, a mining village of some three thousand souls, about eight miles from Nottingham, and one mile from the small stream, the Erewash, which divides Nottinghamshire from Derbyshire. It is hilly country, looking west to Crich and towards Matlock, sixteen miles away, and east and north-east towards Mansfield and the Sherwood Forest district. To me it seemed, and still seems, an extremely beautiful countryside, just between the red sandstone and the oak-trees of Nottingham, and the cold limestone, the ash-trees, the stone fences of Derbyshire. To me, as a child and young man, it was still the old England of the forest and agricultural past; there were no motor-cars, the mines were, in a sense, an accident in the landscape, and Robin Hood and his merry men were not very far away.

The string of coal-mines of B.W. & Co. had been opened some sixty years before I was born, and Eastwood had come into being as a consequence. It must have been a tiny village at the beginning of the nineteenth century, a small place of cottages and fragmentary rows of little four-roomed miners' dwellings, the homes of the old colliers of the eighteenth century, who worked in the bits of mines, foot-rill mines with an opening in the hillside into which the miners walked, or windlass mines, where the men were wound up one at a time, in a bucket, by a donkey. The windlass mines were still working when my father was a boy and the shafts of some were still there, when I was a boy.

But somewhere about 1820 the company must have sunk the first big shafts—not very deep—and installed the first machinery, or the real industrial colliery. Then came my grandfather, a young man trained to be a tailor, drifting from the south of England, and got the job of company tailor for the Brinsley mine. In those days the Company supplied the men with the thick flannel vests, or singlets, and the mole-skin trousers lined at the top with flannel, in which the colliers worked. I remember the great rolls of coarse flannel and pit-cloth which stood in the corner of my grandfather's shop when I was a small boy, and the big, strange old sewing-machine, like nothing else on earth, which sewed the massive pit-trousers. But when I was only a child the company discontinued supplying the men with pit-clothes.

My grandfather settled in in an old cottage down in a quarry-bed, by the brook at Old Brinsley, near the pit. A mile away, up at Eastwood, the Company built the first miners' dwellings—it must be nearly a hundred years ago. Now Eastwood occupies a lovely position on a hill-top, with the steep slope towards Derbyshire and the long slope towards Nottingham. They put up a new church, which stands fine and commanding, even if it has no real form, looking across the awful Erewash Valley at the church of Heanor, similarly commanding, away on a hill beyond. What opportunities, what opportunities! These mining villages *might* have been like the lovely hill-towns of Italy, shapely and fascinating. And what happened?

Most of the little rows of dwellings of the old-style miners were pulled down, and dull little shops began to rise along the Nottingham Road, while on the down-slope of the north side, the Company erected what is still known as the New Buildings, or the Square. These New Buildings consist of two great hollow squares of dwellings planked down on the rough slope of the hill, little four-room houses with the "front" looking outward into the grim blank street, and the "back", with a tiny square brick yard, a low wall, and a W.C. and ash-pit, looking into the desert of the square, hard, uneven, jolting black earth tilting rather steeply down, with these little back yards all round, and openings at the corners. The squares were quite big, and absolutely desert save for the posts for clothes lines, and people passing, children playing on the hard earth. And they were shut in like a barracks enclosure, very strange.

Even fifty years ago the squares were unpopular. It was "common" to live in the Square. It was a little less common to live in The Breach, which consisted of six blocks of rather more pretentious dwellings erected by the Company in the valley below, two rows of three blocks, with an alley between. And it was most "common", most degraded of all to live in Dakins Row, two rows of the old dwellings, very old, black, four-roomed little places, that stood on the hill again, not far from the Squares.

So the place started. Down the steep street between the Squares, Scargill Street, the Wesleyan chapel was put up, and I was born in the little corner shop just above. Across the other side the square the miners themselves built the big barn-like Primitive Methodist Chapel. Along the hill-top ran the Nottingham Road, with its scrappy, ugly mid-Victorian shops. The little market-place, with a superb outlook, ended the village on the Derbyshire side, and was just left bare, with the Sun Inn on one side, the chemist across, with the gilt pestle-and-mortar, and a shop at the other corner, the corner of Alfreton Road and Nottingham Road.

In this queer jumble of the old England and the new, I came into consciousness. As I remember, little local speculators already began to straggle dwellings in rows, always in rows, across the fields: nasty red-brick flat-faced dwellings with dark slate roofs. The bay-window period only began when I was a child. But most of the country was untouched.

There must be three or four hundred Company houses in the Squares and the streets that surround the Squares, like a great barracks wall. There must be sixty or eighty Company houses in The Breach. The old Dakins Row will have thirty to forty little holes. Then counting the old cottages and rows left with their old gardens down the lanes and along the twitchells, and even in the midst of Nottingham Road itself, there were houses enough for the population, there was no need for much building. And not much building went on, when I was small.

We lived in the Breach, in a corner house. A field-path came down under a great hawthorn hedge. On the other side was the brook, with the old sheep-bridge going over into the meadows. The hawthorn hedge by the brook had grown tall as tall trees: and we used to bathe from there in the dipping-hole, where the sheep were dipped: just near the fall from the old mill-dam, where the water rushed. The mill only ceased grinding the local corn when I was a child. And my father, who always worked in Brinsley pit, and who always got up at five o'clock, if not at four, would set off in the dawn across the fields at Coney Grey, and hunt for mushrooms in the long grass, or perhaps pick up a skulking rabbit, which he would bring home at evening inside the lining of his pit-coat.

So that the life was a curious cross between industrialism and the old agricultural England of Shakespeare and Milton and Fielding and George Eliot. The dialect was broad Derbyshire, and always "thee" and "thou". The people lived almost entirely by instinct, men of my father's age could not really read. And the pit did not mechanise men. On the contrary. Under the butty system, the miners worked underground as a sort of intimate community, they knew each other practically naked, and with curious close intimacy, and the darkness and the underground remoteness of the pit "stall", and the continual presence of danger, made the physical, instinctive and intuitional contact between men very highly developed, a contact almost as close as touch, very real and very powerful. This physical awareness and intimate *togetherness* was at its strongest down pit. When the men came up into the light, they blinked. They had, in a measure, to change their flow Nevertheless they brought with them above-ground the curious dark intimacy of the mine, the naked sort of contact, and if I think of my childhood, it is always as if there was a lustrous sort of inner darkness, like the gloss of coal, in which we moved and had our real being. My father loved the pit. He was hurt badly, more than once, but he would never stay away, He loved the contact, the intimacy, as men in the war loved the intense male comradeship of the dark days. They did not know what they had lost till they lost it. And I think it is the same with the young colliers of today.

Now the colliers had also an instinct of beauty. The colliers' wives had not. The colliers were deeply alive, instinctively. But they had no daytime ambition, and no daytime intellect. They avoided, really, the rational aspect of life. They preferred to take life instinctively and intuitively. They didn't even care very profoundly about wages. It was the women, naturally, who nagged on this score. There was a big discrepancy when I was a boy, between the collier who saw, at the best, only a brief few hours of daylight, often no daylight at all, during the winter weeks: and the collier's wife, who had all the day to herself, when the man was down pit.

The great fallacy is, to pity the man. He didn't dream of pitying himself, till agitators and sentimentalists taught him to. He was happy: or more than happy, he was fulfilled. Or he was fulfilled on the receptive side, not on the expressive. The collier went to the pub and drank, in order to continue his intimacy with his mates. They talked endlessly, but it was rather of wonders and marvels, even in politics, than of facts. It was hard facts, in the shape of wife, money, and nagging home necessities, which they fled away from, out of the house to the pub: and out of the house to the pit.

The collier fled out of the house as soon as he could, away from the nagging materialism of the woman. With the women, it was always: This is broken, now you've got to mend it!—or else: We want this, that and the other, and where is the money coming from?—The collier didn't know and didn't care very deeply—his life was otherwise. So he escaped. He roved the countryside, with his dog, prowling for a rabbit, for nests, for mushrooms, anything. He loved the countryside, just the indiscriminating feel of it. Or he loved just to sit on his heels and watch—anything or nothing. He was not intellectually interested. Life for him did not consist in facts, but in a flow. Very often, he loved his garden. And very often, he had a genuine love of the beauty of flowers. I have known it often and often, in colliers.

Now the love of flowers is a very misleading thing. Most women love flowers as possessions, and as trimmings. They can't look at a flower, and wonder a moment, and pass on. If they see a flower that arrests their attention, they must at once pick it, pluck it. Possession! A possession! Something added on to me!—And most of the so-called love of flowers today is merely this reaching out of possession and egoism: something I've *got:* something that embellishes *me.* Yet I've seen many a collier stand in his back garden looking down at a flower with that odd, remote sort of contemplation which shows a *real* awareness of the presence of beauty. It would not even be admiration, or joy, or delight, or any of those things which so often have a root in the possessive instinct. It would be a sort of contemplation: which shows the incipient artist.

The real tragedy of England, as I see it, is the tragedy of ugliness. The country is so lovely: the man-made England is so vile. I know that the ordinary collier, when I was a boy, had a peculiar sense of beauty, coming from his intuitive and instinctive consciousness, which was awakened down pit. And the fact that he met with just cold ugliness and raw materialism when he came up into daylight, and particularly when he came to the Square or the Breach, and to his own table, killed something in him and in a sense, spoiled him as a man. The woman almost invariably nagged about material things. She was taught to do it, she was encouraged to do it. It was a mother's business to see that her sons "got on", and it was the man's business to provide the money, In my father's generation, with the old wild England behind them, and the lack of education, the man was not beaten down. But in my generation, the boys I went to school with, colliers now, have all been beaten down, what with the din-din-dinning of Board Schools, books, cinemas, clergymen, the whole national and human consciousness hammering on the fact of material prosperity above all things.

The men are beaten down, there is prosperity for a time, in their defeat— and then disaster looms ahead. The root of all disaster is disheartenment. And men are disheartened. The men of England, the colliers in particular, are disheartened. They have been betrayed and beaten.

Now though perhaps nobody knew it, it was ugliness which really betrayed the spirit of man, in the nineteenth century, The great crime which the moneyed classes and promoters of industry committed in the palmy Victorian days was the condemning of the workers to ugliness, ugliness, ugliness: meanness and formless and ugly surroundings, ugly ideals, ugly religion ugly hope, ugly love, ugly clothes, ugly furniture, ugly houses, ugly relationship between workers and employers. The human soul needs actual beauty even more than bread. The middle classes jeer at the colliers for buying pianos—but what is the piano, often as not, but a blind reaching out for beauty, To the woman it is a possession and a piece of furniture and something to feel superior about. But see the elderly colliers trying to learn to play, see them listening with queer alert faces to their daughter's execution of *The Maiden's Prayer,* and you will see a blind, unsatisfied craving for beauty, It is far more deep in the men than the women. The women want show. The men want beauty, and still want it.

If the Company, instead of building those sordid and hideous Squares, then, when they had that lovely site to play with, there on the hill top: if they had put a tall column in the middle of the small market-place, and run three parts of a circle of arcade round the pleasant space: where people could stroll or sit, and with handsome houses behind! If they had made big, substantial houses, in apartments of five or six rooms, and with handsome entrances. If above all, they had encouraged song and dancing—for the miners still sang and danced— and provided handsome space for these. If only they had encouraged some form of beauty in dress, some form of beauty in interior life— furniture, decoration. If they had given prizes for the handsomest chair or table, the loveliest scarf, the most charming room that the men or women could make! If only they had done this, there would never have been an industrial problem. The industrial problem arises from the base forcing of all human energy into a competition of mere acquisition.

You may say the working man would not have accepted such a form of life: the Englishman's home is his castle etc. etc.—"My own little home". But if you can hear every word the next-door people say, there's not much castle. And if you can see everybody in the square, if they go to the W.C.! And if your one desire is to get out of your "castle" and your "own little home"!—well, there's not much to be said for it. Anyhow it's only the woman who idolises "her own little home"—and it's always the woman at her worst, her most greedy, most possessive, most mean. There's nothing to be said for the "little home" any more: a great scrabble of ugly pettiness over the face of the land.

As a matter of fact, till 1800 the English people were strictly a rural people—very rural. England has had towns for centuries, but they have never been real towns, only clusters of village streets. Never the real *urbs.* The English character has failed to develop the real *urban* side of a man, the civic side. Siena is a bit of a place, but it is a real city, with citizens intimately connected with the city, Nottingham is a vast place sprawling towards a million, and it is nothing more than an amorphous agglomeration. There *is* no Nottingham, in the sense that there is Siena. The Englishman is stupidly undeveloped as a citizen. And it is partly due to his "little home" stunt, and partly to his acceptance of hopeless paltriness in his surrounding. The new cities of America are much more genuine cities, in the Roman sense, than is London or Manchester. Even Edinburgh used to be more of a true city than any town England ever produced.

That silly little individualism of "the Englishman's home is his castle"— and "my own little home" is out of date. It would work almost to 1800, when every Englishman was still a villager and a cottager. But the industrial system has brought a great change. The Englishman still likes to think of himself as a "cottager"—"my home, my garden." But it is puerile. Even the farm-labourer today is psychologically a town-bird. The English are town-birds through and through, today, as the inevitable result of their complete industrialisation. Yet they don't know how to build a city, how to think of one, or how to live in one. They are all suburban, pseudo-cottagey, and not one of them knows how to be truly urban—the citizen as the Romans were citizens—or the Athenians—or even the Parisians, till the war came.

And this is because we have frustrated that instinct of community which would make us unite in pride and dignity in the bigger gesture of the citizen, not the cottager. The great city means beauty, dignity, and a certain splendour. This is the side of the Englishman that has been thwarted and shockingly betrayed: England is a mean and petty scrabble of paltry dwellings called "homes." I believe in their heart of hearts all Englishmen loathe their little homes—but not the women. What we want is a bigger gesture, a greater scope, a certain splendour, a certain grandeur, and beauty, big beauty. The American does far better than we, in this.

And the promoter of industry, a hundred years ago, dared to perpetrate the ugliness of my native village. And still more monstrous, promoters of industry today are scrabbling over the face of England with miles and square miles of red-brick "homes," like horrible scabs. And the men inside these little red rat-traps get more and more helpless, being more and more humiliated, more and more dissatisfied, like trapped rats. Only the meaner sort of women go on loving the little home which is no more than a rat-trap to her man.

Do away with it all, then. At no matter what cost, start in to alter it. Never mind about wages and industrial squabbling. Turn the attention elsewhere. Pull down my native village to the last brick. Plan a nucleus. Fix the focus. Make a handsome gesture of radiation from the focus. And then put up big buildings, handsome, that sweep to a civic centre. And furnish them with beauty. And make an absolute clean start. Do it place by place. Make a new England. Away with little homes! Away with scrabbling pettiness and paltriness. Look at the contours of the land, and build up from these, with a sufficient nobility, The English may be mentally or spiritually developed. But as citizens of splendid cities they are more ignominious than rabbits. And they nag, nag, nag all the time about politics and wages and all that, like mean narrow housewives.

WE NEED ONE ANOTHER

We may as well admit it: men and women need one another. We may as well, after all our kicking against the pricks, our revolting and our sulking, give in and be graceful about it. We are all individualists: we are all egoists: we all believe intensely in freedom, our own at all events. We all want to be absolute, and sufficient unto ourselves. And it is a great blow to our self-esteem that we simply *need* another human being. We don't mind airily picking and choosing among women—or among men, if we are a woman. But to have to come down to the nasty, sharp-pointed brass tacks of admitting: My God, I can't live without that obstreperous woman of mine!—this is terribly humiliating to our isolated conceit.

And when I say: "without that woman of mine!", I do not mean a mistress, the sexual relation in the French sense. I mean the woman: my relationship to the woman herself. There is hardly a man living who can exist at all cheerfully without a relationship to some particular woman: unless, of course, he makes another man play the role of woman. And the same of woman. There is hardly a woman on earth who can live cheerfully without some intimate relationship to a man; unless she substitutes some other woman for the man.

So there it is!—Now for three thousand years men, and women, have been struggling against this fact. In Buddhism, particularly; a man could never possibly attain the supreme Nirvana if he so much as saw a woman out of the corner of his eye. "Alone I did it!" is the proud assertion of the gentleman who attains Nirvana. And "Alone I did it!" says the Christian whose soul is saved. They are the religions of overweening individualism, resulting, of course, in our disastrous modern egoism of the individual. Marriage, which on earth is a sacrament, is dissolved by the decree absolute of death. In heaven there is no giving and taking in marriage. The soul in heaven is supremely individual, absolved from every relationship except that with the Most High. In heaven there is neither marriage nor love, nor friendship nor fatherhood nor motherhood, nor sister nor brother nor cousin: there is just me, in my perfected isolation, placed in perfect relation to the Supreme, the Most High.

When we talk of Heaven, we talk, really of that which we would most like to attain, and most like to be here on earth. The condition of heaven is the condition to be longed for, striven for, now.

Now if I say to a woman, or to a man: "Would you like to be purely free of all human relationships, free from father and mother, brother and sister, husband, lover, friend, or child? free from all these human entanglements, and reduced purely to your own pure self, connected only with the Supreme Power, the Most High?"—then what would the answer be? What is the answer, I ask you? What is your own sincere answer?

I expect, in almost all cases, it is an emphatic "yes." In the past, most men would have said "yes," and most women "no." But today, I think, many men might hesitate, and nearly all women would unhesitatingly say "Yes."

Modern men, however, have so nearly achieved this Nirvana-like condition of having no real human relationships at all, that they are beginning to wonder what and where they are. What are you, when you've asserted your grand independence, broken all the ties, or "bonds," and reduced yourself to a "pure" individuality? What are you?

You may imagine you are something very grand, since few individuals even approximate to this independence without falling into deadly egoism and conceit: and emptiness. The real danger is, reduced to your own single merits and cut off from the most vital human contacts, the danger is that you are left just simply next to nothing. Reduce any individual, man or woman, to his elements, or her elements, and what is she? what is he? Extremely little! Take Napoleon, and stick him alone on a miserable island, and what is he? a peevish, puerile little fellow. Put Mary Stuart in a nasty stone castle of a prison, and she becomes merely a catty little person. Now Napoleon was not a peevish, puerile little fellow, even if he became such when isolated on St. Helena. And Mary Queen of Scots was only a catty little person when she was isolated in Fotheringay or some such hole. This grand isolation, this reducing of ourselves to our very elemental selves, is the greatest fraud of all. It is like plucking the peacock naked of all his feathers, to try to get at the real bird. When you've plucked the peacock bare, what have you got? Not the peacock, but the naked corpse of a bird.

551

And so it is with us and our grand individualism. Reduce any of us to the *mere* individual that we are, and what do we become? Napoleon becomes a peevish, puerile little fellow, Mary Queen of Scots becomes a catty little person, St. Simeon Stylites, stuck up on his pillar, becomes a conceited lunatic, and we, wonderful creatures as we are, become trashy conceited little modern egoists. The world today is full of silly impertinent egoists who have broken all the finer human ties, and base their claims to superiority on their own emptiness and nullity. But the empty ones are being found out. Emptiness, which makes a fine noise, deceives for a short time only.

The fact remains, that when you cut off a man and isolate him in his own pure and wonderful individuality, you haven't got the man at all, you've only got the dreary fag end of him. Isolate Napoleon, and he is nothing. Isolate Immanuel Kant, and his grand ideas will still go on tick-tick-ticking inside his head, but unless he could write them down and communicate them, they might as well be the ticking of the death-watch beetle. Take even Buddha himself, if he'd been whisked off to some lonely place and planted cross-legged under a bhô-tree and nobody had ever seen him or heard any of his Nirvana talk, then I doubt he wouldn't have got much fun out of Nirvana, and he'd have been just a crank. In absolute isolation, I doubt if any individual amounts to much: or if any soul is worth saving; or even having. "And I, if I be lifted up, will draw all men unto me." But if there were no other men to be lifted, the whole show would be a fiasco.

So that everything, even individuality itself, depends on relationship. "God cannot do without me," said an eighteenth century Frenchman. What he meant was, that if there were no human beings, if Man did not exist, then God, the God of Man, would have no meaning. And it is true. If there were no men and women, Jesus would be meaningless. In the same way, Napoleon on St. Helena became meaningless, and the French nation lost a great part of its meaning without him. In connection with his army and the nation, a great power streamed out of Napoleon, and from the French people there streamed back to him a great responsive power, and therein lay his greatness, and theirs. That is, in the relationship. The light shines only when the circuit is completed. The light does not shine with one half of the current. Every light is some sort of completed circuit. And so is every life, if it is going to be a life.

We have our very individuality in relationship. Let us swallow this important and prickly fact. Apart from our connections with other people we are barely individuals, we amount, all of us, to next to nothing. It is in the living touch between us and other people, other lives, other phenomena that we move and have our being. Strip us of our human contacts and of our contact with the living earth and the sun, and we are almost bladders of emptiness. Our individuality means nothing. A skylark that was alone on an island would be songless and meaningless, his individuality gone, running about like a mouse in the grass. But if there were one female with him, it would lift him singing into the air, and restore him his real individuality.

And so with men and women. It is in relationship to one another that they have their true individuality and their distinct being: in contact, not out of contact. This is sex, if you like. But it is no more sex than sunshine on the grass is sex. It is a living contact, give and take: the great and subtle relationship of men and women,

552

man and woman. In this and through this we *become* real individuals, without it, without the real contact, we remain more or less nonentities.

But of course, it is necessary to have the contact alive and unfixed. It is not a question of: Marry the woman and have done with it.— That is only one of the stupid recipes for avoiding contact and killing contact. There are many popular dodges for killing every possibility of true contact: like sticking a woman on a pedestal, or the reverse, sticking her beneath notice; or making a "model" housewife of her, or a "model" mother, or a "model" help-meet. All mere devices for avoiding any contact with her. A woman is not a "model" anything. She is not even a distinct and definite personality. It is time we got rid of these fixed notions. A woman is a living fountain whose spray falls delicately around her, on all that come near. A woman is a strange soft vibration on the air, going forth unknown and unconscious, and seeking a vibration of response—Or else she is a discordant, jarring, painful vibration, going forth and hurting everyone within range. And a man the same. A man as he lives and moves and has being, is a fountain of life-vibration, quivering and flowing towards some-one, something that will receive his outflow and send back an inflow, so that a circuit is completed, and there is a sort of peace. Or else he is a source of irritation, discord, and pain, harming everyone near him.

But while we remain healthy and positive, we seek all the time to come into true human relationship with other human beings. Yet it has to happen, the relationship, almost unconsciously—we can't *deliberately* do much with a human connection, except smash it: and that is usually not difficult. On the positive side, we can only most carefully let it take place, without interfering or forcing.

We are labouring under a false conception of ourselves. For centuries, man has been the conquering hero, and woman has been merely the string to his bow, part of his accoutrement. Then woman was allowed to have a soul of her own, a separate soul. So the separating business started, with all the clamour of freedom and independence. Now the freedom and independence have been rather overdone, they lead to an empty nowhere, the rubbish heap of all our dead feelings and waste illusions.

The conquering hero business is as obsolete as Marshal Hindenburg, and about as effective. The world sees attempts at revival of this stunt, but they are usually silly, in the end. Man is no longer a conquering hero. Neither is he a supreme soul isolated and alone in the universe, facing the Unknown in the eternity of death. That stunt is also played out, though the pathetic boys of today keep on insisting on it: especially the pathetic boys who wrap themselves in the egoistic pathos of their sufferings during the late war.

But both stunts are played out, both the conquering hero and the pathetic hero clothed in suffering and facing Eternity in the soul's last isolation. The second stunt is, of course, more popular today, and still dangerous to the self-pitying, played-out specimens of the younger generation. But for all that, it is a dud stunt, finished.

What a man has to do today is to admit, at last, that all these fixed ideas are no good. As a fixed object, even as an individuality or a personality, no human being, man or woman, amounts to much. The great I AM does not apply to human beings, so they may as well leave it alone. As soon as anybody, man or woman, becomes a great I AM, he becomes nothing. Man or woman, each is a flow, a flowing life. And without one another, we can't flow, just as a river cannot flow without banks. A woman is one bank of the river of my life, and the world is the other. Without the two shores, my life would be a marsh. It is the relationship to woman, and to my fellow-men, which makes me myself, a river of life.

And it is this, even, that gives me my soul. A man who has never had a vital relationship to any other human being doesn't really have a soul. We cannot feel that Immanuel Kant ever had a soul. A soul is something that forms and fulfils itself in my contacts, my living touch with people I have loved or hated or truly known. I am born with the clue to my soul. The wholeness of my soul I must achieve.—And by my soul I mean my wholeness. What we suffer from today is the lack of a sense of our own wholeness, or completeness, which is peace. What we lack, what the young lack, is a sense of being whole in themselves. They feel so scrappy, they have no peace. And by peace I don't mean inertia, but the full flowing of life, like a river.

We lack peace because we are not whole. And we are not whole because we have known only a tithe of the vital relationships we might have had. We live in an age which believes in stripping away the relationships. Strip them away, like an onion, till you come to pure, or blank nothingness. Emptiness. That is where most men have come now: to a knowledge of their own complete emptiness. They wanted so badly to be "themselves" that they became nothing at all: or next to nothing.

It is not much fun, being next to nothing. And life ought to be fun, the greatest fun. Not merely "having a good time" in order to "get away from yourself." But real fun in being yourself. Now there are two great relationships possible to human beings: the relationship of man to woman, and the relationship of man to man. As regards both, we are in a hopeless mess.

But the relationship of man to woman is the central fact in actual human life. Next comes the relationship of man to man. And a long way after, all the other relationships, fatherhood, motherhood, sister, brother, friend.

A young man said to me the other day, rather sneeringly: "I'm afraid I can't believe in the regeneration of England by sex."—I said to him: "I'm sure you can't."—He was trying to inform me that he was above such trash as sex, and such commonplace as women. He was the usual vitally below par, a hollow and egoistic young man, infinitely wrapped up in himself, like a sort of mummy that will crumble if unwrapped.

But what is sex, after all, but the symbol of the relation of man to woman, woman to man? And the relation of man to woman is wide as all life. It consists in infinite different flows between the two beings, different, even apparently contrary, Chastity is part of the flow between man and woman, so is physical passion. And beyond these, an infinite range of subtle communication which we know nothing about. I should say that the relation between any two decently married people changes profoundly every few years, often without their knowing anything about it; though every change causes pain, even if it brings a certain joy. The long course of marriage is a long event of perpetual change, in which a man and a woman mutually build up their souls and make themselves whole. It is like rivers flowing on, through new country, always unknown.

But we are so foolish, and fixed by our limited ideas. A man says: "I don't love my wife any more, I no longer want to sleep with her."—But why should he always want to sleep with her? How does he know what other subtle and vital interchange is going on between him and her, making them both whole, in this period when he doesn't want to sleep with her? And she, instead of jibbing and saying that all is over and she must find another man and get a divorce, why doesn't she pause, and listen for a new rhythm in her soul, and look for the new movement in the man. With every change, a new being emerges, a new rhythm establishes itself, we renew our life as we grow older, and there is real peace. Why oh why do we want one another to be always the same, fixed, like a menu-card that is never changed.

If only we had more sense. But we are held by a few fixed ideas, like sex, money, what a person "ought" to be, and so forth, and we miss the whole of life. Sex is a changing thing, now alive, now quiescent, now fiery, now apparently quite gone, quite gone. But the ordinary man and woman haven't the gumption to take it in all its changes. They demand crass, crude sex-desire, they demand it always, and when it isn't forthcoming then—smash-bash! smash up the whole show. Divorce! Divorce!

I am so tired of being told that I want mankind to go back to the condition of savages. As if modern city people weren't about the crudest, rawest, most crassly savage monkeys that ever existed, when it comes to the relation of man and woman. All I see in our vaunted civilisation is men and women smashing each other emotionally and psychically to bits, and all I ask is that they should pause and consider.

For sex, to me, means the whole of the relationship between man and woman. Now this relationship is far greater than we know. We only know a few crude forms, mistress, wife, mother, sweet-heart. The woman is like an idol, or a marionette, always forced to play one rôle or another: sweet-heart, mistress, wife, mother. If only we could break up this fixity, and realise the unseizable quality of real womanhood: that a woman is a flow, a river of life quite different from a man's river of life: and that each river must flow in its own way, though without breaking its bounds: and that the relation of man to woman is the flowing of two rivers side by side, sometimes even mingling, then separating again, and travelling on. The relationship is a life-long change and a life-long travelling. And that is sex. At periods, sex-desire itself departs completely. Yet the great flow of the relationship goes on all the same, undying, and this is the flow of living sex, the relation between man and woman, that lasts a life-time, and of which sex-desire is only one vivid, most-vivid manifestation.

THE REAL THING

Most revolutions are explosions: and most explosions blow up a great deal more than was intended. It is obvious, from later history, that the French didn't really want to blow up the whole monarchic and aristocratic system, in the 1790's. Yet they did it, and try as they might, they could never really put anything together again. The same with the Russians: they want to blow a gateway in a wall, and they blow the whole house down.

All fights for freedom, that succeed, go too far, and become in turn the infliction of a tyranny Like Napoleon or a soviet. And like the freedom of women. Perhaps the greatest revolution of modern times is the emancipation of women: and perhaps the deepest fight for two thousand years and more has been the fight for woman's independence, or freedom, call it what you will. The fight was deeply bitter: and, it seems to me, it is won. It is even going beyond, and becoming a tyranny of woman, of the individual woman in the house, and of the feminine ideas and ideals in the world. Say what we will, the world is swayed by feminine emotion today and the triumph of the productive and domestic activities of man over all his previous military or adventurous or flaunting activities is a triumph of the woman in the home. The male is subservient to the female need, and outwardly man is submissive to the demands of woman.

But inwardly, what has happened? It cannot be denied that there has been a fight. Woman has not won her freedom without fighting for it: and she still fights, fights hard, even when there is no longer any need. For man has fallen. It would be difficult to point to a man in the world today who is not subservient to the great woman-spirit that sways modern mankind. But still not peacefully. Still the sway of a struggle, the sway of conflict.

Woman in the mass has fought her fight politically But woman the individual has fought her fight with individual man, with father, brother, and particularly with husband. All through the past, except for brief periods of revolt, woman has played a part of submission to man. Perhaps the inevitable nature of man and woman demands such submission. But it must be an instinctive, unconscious submission, made in unconscious faith. At certain periods this blind faith of woman in man seems to weaken, then break. It always happens at the end of some great phase, before another phase sets in. It always seems to start, in man, an over-whelming worship of woman, and a glorification of queens. It always seems to bring a brief spell of glory, and a long spell of misery after. Man yields in glorifying the woman, the glory dies, the fight goes on.

It is not necessarily a sex struggle. The sexes are not by nature pitted against one another in hostility. It only happens so, in certain periods: when man loses his unconscious faith in himself, and woman loses her faith in him, unconsciously and then consciously. It is not biological sex struggle. Not at all. Sex is the great uniter, the great unifier. Only in periods of the collapse of instinctive life-assurance in men does sex become a great weapon and divider.

Man loses his faith in himself, and woman begins to fight him. Cleopatra really fought Anthony—that's why he killed himself. But he had first lost faith in himself, and leaned on love, which is a sure sign of weakness and failure. And when woman once begins to fight her man, she fights and fights, as if for freedom. But it is not even freedom she wants. Freedom is a man's word: its meaning, to a woman, is really rather trivial. She fights to escape from a man who doesn't really believe in himself, she fights and fights, and there is no freedom from the fight. Woman is truly less free today than ever she has been since time began: in the womanly sense of freedom. Which means, she has less peace, less of that lovely womanly peace that flows like a river, less of the lovely, flower-like repose of a happy woman, less of the nameless joy in life, purely unconscious, which is the very breath of a woman's being, than ever she has had since she and man first set eyes on one another. Today, woman is always tense and strung up, alert, and bare-armed, not for love but for battle. In her shred of a dress and her little helmet of a hat, her cropped hair and her stark bearing she is a sort of soldier, and look at her as one may, one can see nothing else. It is not her fault. It is her doom. It happens when man loses his primary faith in himself and in very life.

Now through the ages thousands of ties have formed between men and women. In the ages of discredit, these ties are felt as bonds, and must be fought loose. It is a great tearing and snapping of sympathies and of unconscious sympathetic connections. It is a great rupture of unconscious tenderness and unconscious flow of strength between man and woman. Man and woman are not two separate and complete entities. In spite of all protestation, we must continue to assert it. Man and woman are not even two separate persons: not even two separate consciousnesses, or minds. In spite of vehement cries to the contrary, it is so. Man is connected with woman forever, in connections visible and invisible, in a complicated life-flow that can never be analysed. It is not only man and wife: the woman facing me in the train, the girl I buy cigarettes from, all send forth to me a stream, a spray, a vapour of female life that enters my blood and my soul, and makes me me. And back again, I send the stream of male life which soothes and satisfies and builds up the woman. So it still is, very often, in public contacts. The more general stream of life-flow between men and women is not so much broken and reversed as the private flow. Hence we all tend more and more to live in public. In public men and women are still kind to one another, very often.

But in private, the fight goes on. It had started in our great-grandmothers: it was going strong in our grandmothers: and in our mothers it was the dominant factor in life. The women *thought* it was a fight for righteousness. They *thought* they were fighting the man to make him "better," and to make life "better" for the children. We know now, the ethical excuse was only an excuse. We know now that our fathers were fought and beaten by our mothers, not because our mothers really knew what was "better," but because our fathers had lost their instinctive hold on the life-flow and the life-reality, and therefore the female had to fight them at any cost, blind, and doomed.

We saw it going on as tiny children: the battle. We believed the moral excuse. But we lived to be men, and to be fought in turn. And now we know there is no excuse, moral or immoral. It is just phenomenal. And our mothers, who asserted such a belief in "goodness," were tired of that self-same goodness even before their death.

No, the fight was, and is, for itself. And it is pitiless—except in spasms and pauses. A woman does not fight a man for his love—though she may say so a thousand times over. She fights him because she knows, instinctively he *cannot* love. He has lost his peculiar belief in himself, his instinctive faith in his own life-flow, and so he cannot love. He *cannot.* The more he protests, the more he asserts, the more he kneels, the more he worships, the less he loves. A woman who is worshipped, or even adored, knows perfectly well, in her instinctive depths, that she is not loved, that she is being swindled. She encourages the swindle, oh enormously, it flatters her vanity. But in the end comes Nemesis and the Furies, pursuing the unfortunate pair. Love between man and woman is neither worship nor adoration, but something much deeper, much less showy and gaudy, part of the very breath, and as ordinary, if we may say so, as breathing. Almost as necessary. In fact, love between man and woman is really just a kind of breathing.

No woman ever got a man's love by fighting for it: at least, by fighting *him.* No man ever loved a woman until she left off fighting him. And when will she leave off fighting him? When he has, apparently, submitted to her? (for the submission is always, at least partly, false and a fraud) No, then least of all—When a man has submitted to a woman, she usually fights him worse than ever, more ruthlessly. Why doesn't she leave him? Often she does. But what then? She merely takes up with another man in order to resume the fight. The need to fight with man is upon her, inexorable. Why can't she live alone? She can't. Sometimes she can join with other women, and keep up the fight in a group. Sometimes she *must* live alone, for no man will come forward to fight with her. Yet, sooner or later, the need for contact with a man comes over a woman again. It is imperative. If she is rich, she hires a dancing partner, a gigolo, and humiliates him to the last dregs. The fight is not ended. When the great Hector is dead, it is not enough. He must be trailed naked and defiled; tied by the heels to the tail of a contemptuous chariot.

When is the fight over? Ah when! Modern life seems to give no answer. Perhaps when a man finds his strength and his rooted belief in himself again. Perhaps when the man has died, and been painfully born again with a different breath, a different courage, and a different kind of care, or carelessness. But most men can't and daren't die in their old, fearful selves. They cling to their women in desperation, and come to hate them with cold and merciless hate, the hate of a child that is persistently ill-treated. Then even the hate dies, the man escapes into the final state of egoism, when he has no true feelings any more, and cannot be made to suffer.

That is where the young are now The fight is more or less fizzling out, because both parties have become hollow There is a perfect cynicism. The young men know that most of the "benevolence" and "motherly love" of their adoring mothers was simply egoism again, and an extension of self, and a love of having absolute power over another creature. Oh these women who secretly lust to have absolute power over their own children—for their own good!—do they think the children are deceived? Not for a moment! You can read in the eyes of the small modern child: "My mother is trying to bully me with every breath she draws, but though I am only six, I can really resist her."—It is the fight, the fight. It has degenerated into the mere fight to impose the will over some other creature: mostly, now, mother over her children. She fails again, abjectly. But she goes on.

For the great fight with the man has come almost to an end. Why? is it because man has found a new strength, has died the death in his old body and been born with a new strength and a new sureness? Alas, apparently not so at all. Man has dodged, side-tracked. Tortured and cynical and unbelieving, he has let all his feelings go out of him, and remains a shell of a man, very nice, very pleasant, in fact the best of modern men. Because nothing really moves him except one thing, a threat against his own safety. He is terrified of not feeling "safe." So he keeps his woman there, between him and the world of dangerous feelings and demands.

But he feels nothing. It is the great *counterfeit* liberation, the counterfeit of Nirvana and the peace that passeth all understanding. It *is* a sort of Nirvana, and a sort of peace: in sheer nullity. At first, the woman cannot realise it. She rages, she goes mad. Woman after woman you can see smashing herself against the figure of a man who has achieved the state of false peace, false strength, false power: the egoist. The egoist, he who has no more spontaneous feelings, and can be made to suffer humanly no more. He who derives all his life henceforth at second-hand, and is animated by self-will and some sort of secret ambition to *impose* himself, either on the world or on other individuals. See a man, or a woman trying to impose herself, himself, and you have an egoist in natural action. But the true pose of the modern egoist is that of perfect suaveness and kindness and humility: oh, always—delicately humble!

When a man achieves this triumph of egoism: and many men have achieved it today, practically all the successful ones, certainly all the charming ones, and all the "artistic" ones: then the woman concerned is apt to go really a little mad. She gets no more responses. The fight has suddenly given out. She throws herself against a man, and he is not there, only the sort of glassy image of him receives her shocks and feels nothing. She becomes wild, outrageous. The explanation of the impossible behaviour of some women in their thirties lies here. Suddenly nothing comes back at them in the fight, and they go crazy, demented, as if they were on the brink of a fearful abyss. Which they are.

And then they either go to pieces: or else, with one of those sudden turns typical of women, they suddenly realise. And then, almost instantly, their whole behaviour changes. It is over. The fight is finished. The man has side-tracked. He becomes, in a sense, negligible, though the basic animosity is only rarified, made more subtle. And so you have the smart young woman in her twenties. She no longer fights her man—or men. She leaves him to his devices, and as far as possible invents her own. She may have a child to bully. But as a rule she pushes the child away as far as she can. No, she is now quite alone. If the man has no real feelings, she has none either. No matter how she feels about her husband, unless she is in a state of nervous rage she calls him angel of light, and winged messenger, and loveliest man, and my beautiful pet boy. She flips it all over him, like eau de Cologne. And he takes it quite for granted, and suggests the next amusement. And their life is "one round of pleasure," to use the old banality: until the nerves collapse. Everything is counterfeit: counterfeit complexion, counterfeit jewels, counterfeit elegance, counterfeit charm, counterfeit endearment, counterfeit passion, counterfeit culture, counterfeit love of Blake, or of The Bridge of San Luis Rey, or Picasso, or the latest film star. Counterfeit sorrows and counterfeit delights, counterfeit woes and moans, counterfeit ecstasies, and under all, a hard, hard realisation that we live by money, and money alone: and a terrible lurking fear of nervous collapse, collapse.

These are, of course, the extreme cases of the modern young. They are those who have got way beyond tragedy or real seriousness, that old-fashioned stuff. They are—they don't know where they are. And they don't care. But they are at the far end of the great fight between men and women.

Judging them as a result, the fight hardly seems to have been worth it. But we are looking on them still as fighters. Perhaps there is something else, positive, as a result.

In their own way, many of these young ones who have gone through everything and reached a stage of emptiness and disillusion unparalleled since the decadent Romans of Ravenna, in the Fifth century, they are now, in very fear and forlornness beginning to put out feelers towards some new way of trust. They begin to realise that, if they are not careful, they will have missed life altogether. Missed the bus! They, the smart young who are so swift at hopping on to a thing, to have missed life itself, not to have hopped on to it! Missed the bus! to use London slang! Let the great chance slip by, while they were fooling round! The young are just beginning uneasily to realise that this may be the case. They are just beginning

559

uneasily to realise that all that "life" which they lead, rushing around and being so smart, perhaps isn't life after all, and they are missing the real thing.

What then? 'What is the real thing? Ah, there's the rub. There are millions of ways of living, and it's all life. But what is the real thing in life? What is it that makes you feel right, makes life really feel good?

It is the great question. And the answers are old answers. But every generation must frame the answer in its own way, What makes life good to me is the sense that, even if I am sick and ill, I am alive, alive to the depths of my soul, and in touch, somewhere in touch with the vivid life of the cosmos. Somehow my life draws strength from the depths of the universe, from the depths among the stars, from the great "World." Out of the great World comes my strength, and my reassurance. One could say "God," but the word "God" is somehow tainted. But there *is* a flame or a Life Everlasting wreathing through the cosmos forever, and giving us our renewal, once we can get in touch with it.

It is when men lose their contact with this eternal life-flame, and become merely personal, things in themselves, instead of things kindled in the flame, that the fight between man and woman begins. It cannot be avoided, any more than nightfall or rain. The more conventional and correct a woman may be, the more inwardly devastating she is once she feels the loss of the greater control and the greater sustenance. She becomes emotionally destructive, she can no more help it than she can help being a woman, when the great connection is lost.

And then there is nothing for men to do but to turn back to life itself Turn back to the life that flows invisibly in the cosmos, and will flow for ever, sustaining and renewing all living things. It is not a question of sins or morality, of being good or being bad. It is a question of renewal, of being renewed, vivified, made new and vividly alive and aware, instead of being exhausted and stale, as men are today. How to be renewed, re-born, re-vivified: that is the question men must ask themselves, and women too.

And the answer will be difficult. Some trick with glands or secretions, or raw food, or drugs won't do it. Neither will some wonderful revelation or message. It is not a question of knowing something, but of doing something. It is a question of getting into contact again with the *living* centre of the cosmos. And how are we to do it?

NOBODY LOVES ME

Last year we had a little house up in the Swiss mountains, for the summer. A friend came to tea: a woman of fifty or so, with her daughter: old friends.—"And how are you all?" I asked, as she sat, flushed and rather exasperated after the climb up to the chalet, on a hot afternoon, wiping her face with a too-small handkerchief.—"Well!" she replied, glancing almost viciously out of the window at the immutable slopes and peaks opposite.—"I don't know how you feel about it—but—these mountains!—well!—I've lost *all* my *cosmic consciousness,* and *all* my *love* of *humanity*—"

She is, of course, New England of the old school—and usually transcendentalist calm. So that her exasperated frenzy of the moment—it was really a frenzy—coupled with the New England language and slight accent, seemed to me really funny. I laughed in her face, poor dear, and said: "Never mind! Perhaps you can do with a rest from your cosmic consciousness and your love of humanity."

I have often thought of it since: of what she really meant. And every time, I have had a little pang, realising that I was a bit spiteful to her. I admit, her New England transcendental habit of loving the cosmos *en bloc* and humanity *en masse* did rather get on my nerves, always. But then she had been brought up that way. And the fact of loving the cosmos didn't prevent her from being fond of her own garden—though it did, a bit; and her love of humanity didn't prevent her from having a real affection for her friends: except that she felt she *ought* to love them in a selfless and general way, which was rather annoying. Nevertheless, that, to me, rather silly language about cosmic consciousness and love of humanity did stand for something that was not merely cerebral. It stood, and I realised it afterwards, for her peace, her inward peace with the universe and with man. And this she could *not* do without. One may be at war with society and still keep one's deep peace with mankind. It is not pleasant to be at war with society, but sometimes it is the only way of preserving one's peace of soul, which is peace with the living, struggling, *real* mankind. And this latter one cannot afford to lose. So I had no right to tell my friend she could do with a rest from her love of humanity. She couldn't, and none of us can: *if* we interpret *love of humanity* as that feeling of being at one with the struggling soul, or spirit or whatever it is, of our fellow men.

Now the wonder to me is that the young do seem to manage to get on without any "cosmic consciousness" or "love of humanity." They have, on the whole, shed the cerebral husk of generalisation from their emotional state: the cosmic and humanity touch. But it seems to me they have also shed the flower that was inside the husk. Of course you can hear a girl exclaim: *"Really,* you know, the colliers are darlings, and it's a shame the way they're treated." She will even rush off and register a vote for her darlings. But she doesn't really care—and one can sympathise with her. This caring about the wrongs of unseen people has been rather overdone. Nevertheless, though the colliers or cotton-workers or whatever they be are a long way off and we can't do anything about it, still, away in some depth of us, we know that we are connected vitally, if remotely, with these colliers or cotton workers, we dimly realise that mankind is one, almost one flesh. It is an abstraction, but it is also a physical fact. In some way or other, the cotton workers of Carolina, or the rice-growers of China are connected with me and, to a faint yet real degree, part of me. The vibration of life which they give off reaches me, touches me, and affects me all unknown to me. For we are all more or less connected, all more or less in touch: all humanity. That is, until we have killed the sensitive responses in ourselves, which happens today only too often.

Dimly, this is what my transcendentalist meant by her "love of humanity;" though she tended to kill the real thing by labelling it so philanthropically and bossily. Dimly, she meant her sense of participating in the life of all humanity which is a sense we all have, delicately and deeply, when we are at peace in ourselves. But let us lose our inward peace, and at once we are likely to substitute for this delicate inward sense of participating in the life of all mankind, another thing, a nasty pronounced benevolence, which wants to do good to all mankind, and is only a form of self-assertion and of bullying. From this sort of love of humanity; good Lord deliver us! and deliver poor humanity. My friend was a tiny bit tainted with this form of self-importance, as all transcendentalists were. So if the mountains, in their brutality, took away the tainted love, good for them. But my dear Ruth—I shall call her Ruth— had more than this. She had, woman of fifty as she was, an almost girlish naïve sense of living at peace, real peace, with her fellow-men. And this she could not afford to lose. And save for that taint of generalisation and *will,* she would never have lost it, even for that half-hour in the Swiss mountains. But she meant the "cosmos" and "humanity" to fit her will and her feelings, and the mountains made her realise that the cosmos *wouldn't.* When you come up against the cosmos, your consciousness is likely to suffer a jolt. And humanity, when you come down to it, is likely to give your "love" a nasty jar. But there you are.

When we come to the younger generation, however, we realise that "cosmic consciousness" and "love of humanity" have really been left out of their composition. They are like a lot of brightly coloured bits of glass, and they only feel just what they bump against, when they're shaken. They make an accidental pattern with other people, and for the rest they know nothing and care nothing.

So that cosmic consciousness and love of humanity; to use the absurd New England terms, are really dead. They were tainted. Both the cosmos and humanity were too much manufactured in New England. They weren't the real thing. They were, very often, just noble phrases to cover up self-assertion, self-importance, and benevolent bullying. They were just activities of the ugly; self-willed ego, determined that humanity and the cosmos should exist as New England allowed them to exist, or not at all. They were tainted with bullying egoism, and the young, having fine noses for this sort of smell, would have none of them.

The way to kill any feeling is to insist on it, harp on it, exaggerate it. Insist on loving humanity, and sure as fate you'll come to hate everybody. Because of course, if you insist on loving humanity; then you insist that it shall be lovable: which half the time, it isn't. In the same way, insist on loving your husband, and you won't be able to help hating him secretly. Because of course nobody is *always* lovable. If you insist they shall be, this imposes a tyranny over them, and they become less lovable. And if you force yourself to love them—or pretend to—when they are not lovable, you falsify everything, and fall into hate. The result of forcing any feeling is the death of that feeling, and the substitution of some sort of opposite. Whitman insisted on sympathising with everything and everybody: so much so, that he came to believe in death only, not just his own death, but the death of all people. In the same way the slogan *Keep smiling!* produces at last a sort of savage rage in the breast of the smilers, and the famous "cheery morning greeting" makes the gall accumulate in all the cheery ones.

It is no good. Every time you force your feelings, you damage yourself and produce the opposite effect to the one you want. Try to force yourself to love somebody and you are bound to end by detesting that same somebody. The only thing to do is to have the feelings you've really got, and not make up any of them. And that is the only way to leave the other person free. If you feel like murdering your husband, then don't say: "Oh, but I love him dearly I'm *devoted* to him." That is not only bullying yourself, but bullying him. He doesn't want to be *forced,* even by love. Just say to yourself: "I could murder him, and that's a fact. But I suppose I'd better not."—And then your feelings will get their own balance.

The same is true of love of humanity. The last generation, and the one before that *insisted* on loving humanity. They cared terribly for the poor suffering Irish and Armenians and Congo Rubber negroes and all that. And it was a great deal

562

of it fake, self-conceit, self-importance. The bottom of it was the egoistic thought: "I'm so good, I'm so superior, I'm so benevolent, I care intensely about the poor suffering Irish and the martyred Armenians and the oppressed negroes, and I'm going to save them, even if I have to upset the English and the Turks and the Belgians severely —" This love of mankind was half self-importance and half a desire to interfere and put a spoke in other people's wheels. The younger generation, smelling the rat under the lamb's-wool of Christian Charity said to themselves: No love of humanity for me!

They have, if the truth be told, a secret detestation of all oppressed or unhappy people who need "relief." They rather hate "the poor colliers," "the poor cotton workers," "the poor starving Russians," and all that. If there came another war, how they would loathe "the stricken Belgians"!—And so it is: the father eats the pear, and the son's teeth are set on edge.

Having overdone the sympathy touch, especially the love of humanity we have now got the recoil away from sympathy. The young don't sympathise, and they don't want to. They are egoists, and frankly so. They say quite honestly: "I don't give a hoot in hell for the poor oppressed this-that-and-the-other." And who can blame them? Their loving forbears brought on the Great War. If love of humanity brought on the Great War, let us see what frank and honest egoism will do. Nothing so horrible, we can bet.

The trouble about frank and accepted egoism is its unpleasant effect on the egoist himself. Honesty is very good, and it is good to cast off all the spurious sympathies and false emotions of the pre-war world. But casting off spurious sympathy and false emotion need not entail the death of all sympathy and all deep emotion, as it seems to do in the young. The young quite deliberately *play* at sympathy and emotion. "Darling child, how lovely you look tonight! I *adore* to look at you!"— and in the next breath, a little arrow of spite. Or the young wife to her husband: "My beautiful love, I feel so precious when you hold me like that, my perfect dear!—But shake me a cocktail, angel, would you? I need a good kick—you *angel* of light!"—

The young, at the moment, have a perfectly good time strumming on the keyboard of emotion and sympathy tinkling away at all the exaggerated phrases of rapture and tenderness, adoration and delight, while they feel—nothing, except a certain amusement at the childish game. It is so *chic* and charming to use all the most precious phrases of love and endearment amusingly, just amusingly, like the tinkling in a music box.

And they would be very indignant if told they had no love of humanity The English ones profess the most amusing and histrionic love of England, for example. "There is only one thing I care about, except my beloved Philip, and that is England, our precious England. Philip and I are both prepared to die for England, at any moment."—At the moment, England does not seem to be in any danger of asking them, so they are quite safe. And if you gently enquire: "But what, in your imagination, is England?"—they reply fervently: "The great tradition of the English, the great idea of England."—Which seems comfortably elastic and non-committal.

And they cry: "I would give anything for the cause of freedom. Hope and I have wept tears, and saddened our precious marriage bed, thinking of the trespass on English liberty. But we are calmer now; and determined to fight calmly to the utmost." Which calm fight consists in taking another cocktail and sending out a wildly emotional letter to somebody perfectly irresponsible. Then all is over, and freedom is forgotten, and perhaps religion gets a turn, or a wild outburst over some phrase in the burial service.

This is the advanced young of today. I confess it is amusing, while the coruscation lasts. The trying part is when the fireworks have finished— and they don't last very long, even with cocktails—and the grey stretches intervene. For with the advanced young, there is no warm daytime and silent night. It is all fireworks of excitement and stretches of grey emptiness, then more fireworks. And, let the grisly truth be owned, it is rather exhausting.

Now in the grey intervals in the life of the modern young one fact emerges in all its dreariness, and makes itself plain to the young themselves, as well as to the onlooker. The fact that they are empty: that they care about nothing and nobody: not even the amusement they seek so strenuously. Of course this skeleton is not to be taken out of the cupboard. "Darling angel man, don't start being a nasty white ant. Play the game, angel face, play the game, don't start saying unpleasant things and rattling a lot of dead man's bones! Tell us something nice, something amusing. Or let's be *really* serious, you know, and talk about bolshevism or *la haute finance*. Do be an angel of light, and cheer us up, you nicest precious pet! —"

As a matter of fact, the young are becoming afraid of their own emptiness. It's awful fun throwing things out of the window. But when you've thrown everything out, and you've spent two or three days sitting on the bare floor and sleeping on the bare floor and eating off the bare floor, your bones begin to ache, and you begin to wish for some of the old furniture back, even if it was the ugliest Victorian horse hair.

At least, that's how it seems to me the young women begin to feel. They are frightened at the emptiness of their house of life, now they've thrown everything out of the window. Their young Philips and Peters and so on don't seem to make the slightest move to put any new furniture in the house of the young generation. The only new piece they introduce is a cocktail-shaker and perhaps a wireless set. For the rest, it can stay blank.

And the young women begin to feel a little uneasy. Women don't like to feel empty. A woman hates to feel that she believes in nothing and   stands   for nothing. Let her be the silliest woman on earth, she will take something seriously: her appearance, her clothes, her house, something. And let her be not so very silly and she wants more than that. She wants to feel, instinctively that she amounts to something and that her life stands for something. Women, who so often are angry with men because   men cannot "just live," but must always be wanting some purpose in life, are themselves, perhaps, the very root of the male necessity for a purpose in life. It seems to me that in a woman the need to feel that her life *means* something, stands for something, and amounts to something is much more imperative than in a man. The woman herself may deny it emphatically: because, of course, it is the man's business to supply her life with this "purpose." But a man can be a tramp, purposeless, and be happy Not so a woman. It is a very very rare woman who can be happy if she feels herself "outside" the great purpose of life. Whereas, I verily believe, vast numbers of men would gladly drift away as wasters, if there were anywhere to drift to.

A woman cannot bear to feel empty and purposeless. But a man may take a real pleasure in that feeling. A man can take real pride and satisfaction in pure negation: "I am quite empty of feeling, I don't care the slightest bit in the world for anybody or anything except myself. But I do care for myself, and I'm going to survive in spite of them all, and I'm going to have my own success without caring the least in the :world how I get it. Because I'm cleverer than they are, I'm cunninger than they are, even if I'm weak. I must build myself proper protections, and entrench myself, and then I'm safe. I can sit inside my glass tower and feel nothing and be touched by nothing, and yet exert my power, my will, through the glass walls of my ego."

That, roughly is the condition of a man who accepts the condition of true egoism, and emptiness, in himself He has a certain pride in the condition, since in pure emptiness of real feeling he can still carry out his ambition, his will to egoistic success.

Now I doubt if any woman can feel like this. The most egoistic woman is always in a tangle of hate, if not of love. But the true male egoist neither hates nor loves. He is quite empty at the middle of him. Only on the surface he has feelings: and these he is always trying to get away from. Inwardly he feels nothing. And when he feels nothing, he exults in his ego and knows he is safe. Safe, within his fortifications, inside his glass tower.

But I doubt if women can even understand this condition in a man. They mistake the emptiness for depth. They think the false calm of the egoist who really feels nothing, is strength. And they imagine that all the defences which the confirmed egoist throws up, the glass tower of imperviousness, are screens to a real man, a positive being. And they throw themselves madly on the defences, to tear them down and come at the real man, little knowing that there *is* no real man, the defences are only there to protect a hollow emptiness, an egoism, not a human man.

But the young are beginning to suspect. The young women are beginning to respect the defences, for they are more afraid of coming upon the ultimate nothingness of the egoist, than of leaving him undiscovered. Hollowness, nothingness—it frightens the women. They cannot be *real* nihilists. But men can. Men can have a savage satisfaction in the annihilation of all feeling and all connection, in a resultant state of sheer negative emptiness, when there is nothing left to throw out of the window, and the window is sealed.

Women wanted freedom. The result is a hollowness, an emptiness which frightens the stoutest heart. Women then turn to women for love. But that doesn't last. It can't. Whereas the emptiness persists and persists.

The love of humanity is gone, leaving a great gap. The cosmic consciousness has collapsed upon a great void. The egoist sits grinning furtively in the triumph of his own emptiness. And now what is woman going to do? Now that the house of life is empty now that she's thrown all the emotional furnishing out of the window, and the house of life, which is her eternal home, is empty as a tomb, now what is dear forlorn woman going to do?

Also available from the Blackthorn Press

D H Lawrence *The Complete Short Stories*

All 67 of Lawrence's Short Stories in one volume

£24-95

D H Lawrence *The Complete Plays*

All of Lawrence's six plays and two fragments.

£19-95

D H Lawrence *The Complete Travel Writing*

All of Lawrence's travel writing including the novel

Kangaroo

£24-95

Available from all good bookshops and on Amazon

Printed in Great Britain
by Amazon

82435396R00328